The
marx brothers
Encyclopedia

BLONDES

WARDROBE

GAGS

The
marx brothers
Encyclopedia

GLENN MITCHELL

B.T. Batsford Ltd • London

Acknowledgements

The illustrations in this book include many from stills issued to publicize films made for and/or distributed by (primarily) Paramount Pictures, Metro-Goldwyn-Mayer, RKO and United Artists. Others, where known, are credited within the photo captions themselves. Although effort has been made to trace present copyright owners, apologies are made in advance for any unintentional omission or neglect; we will be happy to insert appropriate acknowledgement to companies or individuals in subsequent editions of the book.

Details of stage and screen plays are quoted here as a matter of historical record and for purposes of constructive criticism.

Printed by Butler & Tanner, Frome

for the Publishers
B.T. Batsford Ltd
4 Fitzhardinge Street
London W1H 0AH

ISBN 0 7134 7838 1

For the siblings

Introduction

While embarking on my previous work, *The Laurel & Hardy Encyclopedia,* I was acutely aware of a large number of existing books on the subject. The rationale for an A-Z compendium was to convey, in an easily accessible arrangement, the varied data that might be sought by an admirer or student. The format lends itself further to anecdotal material plus that ever-popular category, trivia. Existing works had tended to specialize somewhat either in biography, filmography, criticism or other specific topics. No single volume offered immediate access to all facets of their history.

Much the same applies to the Marx Brothers, about whom numerous books have been written (at this point I can hear Groucho saying 'and you're not helping matters'). Compiling a reasonably comprehensive study of two comedians proved to be rather a shoehorned effort; the difficulty was magnified when dealing with an entire family, emphasizing all the more a need for selectivity. The criteria have to be (a) is it useful? and (b) is it amusing? I hope much of the text falls into one or both categories. No solitary work can hope to replace the many, excellent, individual studies that have gone before. The present volume is designed for convenient reference, although Marx admirers may find much that is new to them.

Another key difference between this and the first book is simply the number of films represented. Laurel & Hardy took to cinema early in their careers and were teamed specifically in that medium. The Marxes left far fewer movies and were, in any case, a stage act that happened to be drawn into films. For this reason their stage work is treated on a par with their film projects (with which it was intertwined), in a way which I hope may reconstruct something of these lost entertainments.

As before, I am deeply indebted to many kind friends and organisations. Particular gratitude goes to Michael Pointon, for vast acreages of material and constructive ideas; Robert G. Dickson, for valued archival diggings and much more; Paul G. Wesolowski, Marxman *par excellence* and editor of the invaluable *Freedonia Gazette*; Adrian Rigelsford, who contributed mightily to the picture research in addition to supplying valued information; Mark Newell, who seems able to find almost *anything*; Brian Seaton, who provided much rare audio material; Dick and Beryl Vosburgh; Frank Lazarus; Mark Brisenden; Andrew Simons; Jonathan Cecil; Dirk Maggs; Derek T. Mannering; Graham Agar; David Barker; John Furneaux; Alex Gleason; Irv Hyatt; Derek Mitchell (relation); Robert S. Lewis;

The British Film Institute; the Study Room of the Theatre Museum, Covent Garden; the British Library; Westminster Libraries; the Jackson County Historical Society Archives & Research Library; Carolyn Whitaker, intrepid literary agent; Martina Stansbie and Joshua Dubin, Batsford editors who have kept me in line; and the usual coy (but sincere) thanks to Lionel Q. Devereux, Faker Englund, Emanuel Ravelli, Frank Wagstaff and Harold Schneider, to say nothing of Mrs Emily Upjohn. May their soup never duck.

Glenn Mitchell
London 1996

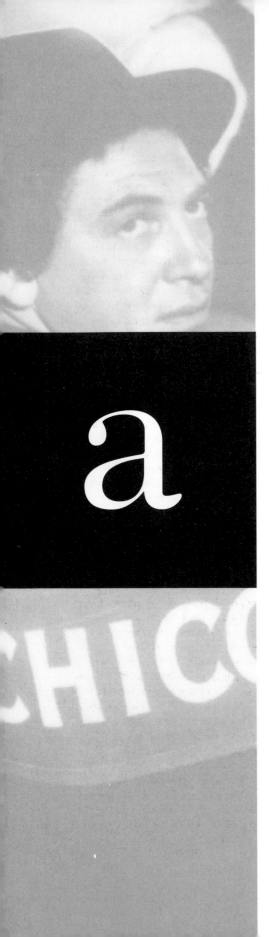

ABANDONED PROJECTS

Although the Marx Brothers made numerous appearances, together and separately, there were several occasions when plans did not reach fruition. Their first, silent, film *Humorisk* (*qv*), was never released; nothing came of a second proposed silent in 1926, to be written by Will B. Johnstone (*qv*) for First National; nor did United Artists (*qv*) carry through their plans to film *Cocoanuts* (*qv*) two years later. Detailed under **Paintings** is an unfilmable Marx Brothers script by Salvador Dali. *The Groucho Phile* mentions a script by director Ernst Lubitsch, in which a man would climb some stairs, enter a room where his wife was sleeping and open a closet door to find Groucho within. 'Believe it or not, I'm waiting for a streetcar,' says Groucho, whereupon a streetcar would arrive, allowing Groucho to board and depart, leaving behind an astonished husband. 'The streetcar went downhill after that; so did the script,' commented Groucho. Lubitsch biographer Scott Eyman concludes that Groucho's disapproval of the script led to its abandonment, citing this routine as an intended segment of Paramount's *portmanteau* film *If I Had a Million* (1932). The film overlaps with the Marxes in terms of personnel (see **W.C. Fields**; **Norman McLeod**; **William A. Seiter**) but was released without any contribution from the brothers themselves. Eyman notes that Lubitsch had appeared as Clown Meyer in German films *circa* 1919, in a style comparable to Groucho's in its sexual aggressiveness and insulting one-liners; indication, perhaps, of the degree to which Groucho may have been influenced by his German background. During their radio series of 1932-3, *Flywheel, Shyster and Flywheel* (*qv*), the Marxes were in conference with Arthur Sheekman (*qv*) over what would eventually become *Duck Soup* (*qv*). Before this idea took shape, initial discussions were over a story entitled first *Oo La La*, then *Cracked Ice*, to be written by

Sheekman and Nat Perrin (*qv*). Once more, Lubitsch was announced as the director of *Oo La La* but was dropped. Precise details of *Cracked Ice*'s first draft are elusive but the second draft resembles *Duck Soup*. Joe Mankiewicz's biographer, Kenneth L. Geist, has mentioned that Mankiewicz was offered a contract with RKO (*qv*), for which Paramount would not release him until satisfied that his script for the rival studio, *In the Red*, did not bear resemblance to the unproduced *Cracked Ice*. The film eventually became Wheeler and Woolsey's best vehicle, *Diplomaniacs* (directed by William A. Seiter [*qv*]) and did not infringe upon the Marx script. It was at this time that relations between the Marxes and Paramount were at their most strained. The comedians formed their own company, Marx Bros. Inc. (*qv*), planning a film of Kaufman and Ryskind's *Of Thee I Sing*, to be directed by Norman McLeod (*qv*). There had been word of Sam Harris and Max Gordon (both *qv*) starring the Marxes in a stage revival of the show and talk continued of stage and film versions even after the Marxes' temporary return to Paramount; they were approached again by Gordon to star in a Broadway musical before signing with M-G-M. Groucho's collaborative film script, *The King and the Chorus Girl* (*qv*), reached fruition in 1937. In the same year he collaborated with Ken Englund on another, unproduced, screenplay, *Madcap Mary Mooney*. The Marx film of 1937, *A Day at the Races*, had started as a somewhat different and similarly unproduced work, *Peace and Quiet*. George S. Kaufman (*qv*) considered several ideas in which Groucho might appear on the Broadway stage; during 1942 he conceived the idea of a stage adaptation of *Franklin Street*, the memoirs of producer Philip Goodman, in which Groucho might play a part. Max Gordon was to produce. Groucho expressed interest and Arthur Sheekman (*qv*) was engaged to adapt the text. The script was complete but Groucho backed out of the project. It is believed that Rodgers and Hammerstein deliberately jettisoned the idea of casting Groucho as the amorous pedlar in their 1943 stage original of *Oklahoma!*, having no wish for this supporting character to steal the show. Groucho later engaged the show's creators in comic banter for a special edition of *You Bet Your Life* (*qv*). Among Groucho's attempts to conquer radio in the 1940s were *The Life of Riley*, which became instead a vehicle for William Bendix (*qv*) and a failed pilot, *The Beverly-Groucho Hotel*. One of the most persistent aborted Marx projects was a biographical film, *The Life of the Marx Brothers*. This was being discussed from the time of *Love Happy*'s conception with that film's producer, Lester Cowan (*qv*). Incorporated into the film would be re-enactments of the team's vaudeville sketches, though it is unclear whether Zeppo or Gummo planned to participate or if Harpo was willing to speak lines. This idea would be discussed periodically into the 1950s but was never filmed. In June 1949 Harpo told the British press of still another Cowan project, to commence after the Palladium engagement. He was to visit France to make a film called *The Clown* playing opposite British actress Glynis Johns. Again, nothing happened. Harpo was supposed to play the lead - presumably a speaking part - in Howard Hughes' version of *Androcles and the Lion* (1952). Work had commenced before Harpo was replaced by Alan Young. It is said that Orson Welles met with Groucho in London during the mid-1950s, to discuss a Marx comedy with a supernatural slant, tentatively called *When You Wish Upon a Star*; once more, nothing materialized. By then *You Bet Your Life* (*qv*) had long since established itself but not everything worked for Groucho on TV. In March 1958 he collaborated with Robert Dwan and Hal Kanter on an unproduced TV script, *Groucho On*

Laughter. The following year Groucho, Harpo and Chico shot footage for an aborted TV show called *Deputy Seraph* (*qv*). Shortly before Chico's death, Billy Wilder wanted to star the team in an updated *Duck Soup*, entitled *A Day at the United Nations* (or *A Day at the UN*). It was really too late and Chico's death finished all talk of a reunion. Woody Allen, of whom Groucho thought highly both personally and professionally, is reported to have wanted Groucho as the psychiatrist in *What's New, Pussycat?* (1965). In 1968 Federico Fellini wanted Groucho to play, in the words of Fellini biographer John Baxter, 'a philosophical pimp' in *Satyricon*. Groucho declined the offer but, probably inadvisedly, accepted a role in Preminger's *Skidoo* (*qv*).

(See also: Animation; Brecher, Irving; Mankiewicz, Herman; Radio; Television)

ACADEMY AWARDS
See: Awards

ACE, GOODMAN
See: *I'll Say She Is!*; Letters

ADRIAN, IRIS (1912-94)
Actress often specializing in floozies, as in 'Mary Lou', her saloon-girl character from *Go West* (*qv*). On stage from age 13, in films from the late 1920s, mixed with stage work for Ziegfeld and elsewhere. Many sound films include *Our Relations* (1936) with Laurel & Hardy (*qv*), Crosby and Hope's *Road to Zanzibar* (1941), Bob Hope's solo vehicle *The Paleface* (1948) and a 1961 Jerry Lewis film, *The Errand Boy*. Later worked often with Jack Benny (*qv*). Of *Go West* she recalled that the Marxes each had a habit of being late on different days, expressing the opinion that there was at that time some disharmony between them. While the team's declining film work probably induced some tensions, it might be added that the Marxes were *always* difficult to track down.

(See also: Blore, Eric; Dumbrille, Douglass; Feld, Fritz; Rumann, Siegfried; Tashlin, Frank)

ADVERTISING
(Marx Brothers films and shows *qv*) 'Where did you ever learn to write such beautiful poetry?' asks Margaret Dumont (*qv*) in *The Big Store*. 'I worked five years for Burma Shave,' replies Groucho, referring to a famous rhyming ad campaign. As with many celebrities, the Marx Brothers were often requested to lend their names to product endorsements. Indeed *Love Happy* would not have been completed but for the sale of advertising space within its climactic scene. This practice, known later as 'product placement', caused protest at the time and has been again the subject of controversy in more recent films. One of *Love Happy*'s sponsors, Bulova Watches, paid the four Marxes for use of their images in printed advertisements as early as the stage run of *Cocoanuts*. The same period brought a campaign using Groucho's image to sell Old Gold cigarettes, despite his famed preference for cigars. More than once Groucho told how he loftily rejected offers of $1,500, $2,500 and $5,000 before accepting an increase to $7,500. The contract was signed and Groucho was given a pre-prepared cheque for the agreed figure. Groucho could not understand how the company had anticipated the precise amount until the representative, when taking his leave, produced a further cheque, this time for $10,000. Groucho watched the cheque being torn up while being told he could have held out for the ten. Old Gold later co-sponsored *You Bet Your Life* (*qv*) during the 1960-61 season, along with Toni Home Permanents and Block Drug, a chain of pharmaceutical outlets. (Groucho betrayed his smoking preferences once more in the 1960s, when he filmed a British commercial for Player's cigarettes.) *You Bet Your Life* had several sponsors during its long run and his slogan for DeSoto-

Plymouth, 'Tell 'em Groucho sent you', became something of a catchphrase during the 1957-58 season. The 1959-60 season was sponsored by Lever Brothers and Pharmaceuticals, Inc. The intervening 1958-59 season was sponsored by Lever Brothers and Toni, the latter of whom manufactured a home permanent called Creamy Prom. Chico and Harpo promoted Creamy Prom in two filmed advertisements, inserted into Groucho's programme. One of these continues to circulate today, containing a short sequence based upon the Marxes' supposed family album. When Groucho and Chico made appearances on radio, they were called upon to endorse the sponsor's products; *Flywheel, Shyster and Flywheel* (*qv*), for example, was sponsored by Standard Oil's 'Essolube' and the show's successor, *The Marx of Time*, by American Oil. The degree of seriousness behind these messages is typified by Groucho's sign-off from an appearance made around 1936, naming a probably fictional sponsor in a pilot that seems never to have been aired: 'Remember, the Hotchkiss Packing Company will not be responsible for any comedians left after thirty days.' In 1958 Groucho and Chico appeared with innovative TV comedian Ernie Kovacs (1919-62) in a commercial short for *The Saturday Evening Post* (to which Groucho had contributed on occasion). Titled *Showdown at Ulcer Gulch*, the film was produced by Chico's son-in-law Shamus Culhane, better known as a top animator. The item was designed to attract potential advertisers and not intended for public screening. In 1961 Harpo made a filmed advertisement for Ford called *Got it Made*, which in the end was not shown. He also made a series of rather surreal TV commercials for Labatt's beer, using abstract settings and bizarre props. Groucho's solo film *Copacabana* (*qv*) was tied into campaigns for Parker Quink and, using pictures of co-star Carmen Miranda (*qv*), Arrow Bras. In *Groucho Marx and Other Short Stories and Tall Tales*, editor Robert S. Bader

notes further Groucho product endorsements, among them Personna razor blades (for a magazine campaign coinciding with *A Night in Casablanca*), General Electric light bulbs and TV tubes, Kellogg's Frosted Flakes and, in the (for him) unaccustomed world of alcohol (*qv*), beers by Blatz and Rheingold plus Smirnoff's Vodka and Teacher's Scotch whisky. Bader's anthology reprints Groucho's text for the Teacher's campaign, entitled *When I Think of Scotch, I Recall the Immortal Words of My Brother Harpo*. The gist of the essay was that Harpo had raided all his brothers' liquor cabinets but found Groucho's stock of Teacher's to be the most worthwhile. The two-page advertisement ran in *Esquire* and *Playboy* during autumn 1973. During one of Harpo's periodic attempts at retirement, he applied for social security payments. Out of costume, this 'Arthur Marx' went unrecognized; asked to declare any recent occupation, he admitted to one day's work and surprised the clerk when disclosing a fee running into thousands. The job had been a TV commercial for Proctor & Gamble. Groucho mentioned this in a letter to Norman Krasna (*qv*) in December 1960; according to a later reminiscence, in 1962 Groucho followed Harpo's advice and applied for it himself, seven years after passing the retirement age of 65. That the two wealthiest brothers should have bothered is somewhat surprising, except perhaps as a joke; were it not for the recommendation to Groucho, one would suspect Harpo's application to have been no more than a prank. Chico, always in need of money, was a far likelier candidate; in the spring of 1957 word had reached Britain of Chico drawing social security. Nora Laing, representing the *Daily Sketch*, met with him and was treated to 'a most un-dole-like lunch' as Chico explained the system: of his brothers, all kept busy except Harpo, who had money 'salted away'. 'Now I spend money as fast as I get it,' continued

Chico, 'I live it up. People in England who read about my getting social security think I'm broke ... but social security isn't charity. It's insurance. Everyone pays into it when they're earning money. When you get to 65 you draw out monthly sums, according to what you've earned. Any month I don't work I draw out 80 dollars. Next month maybe I make 5,000 dollars, so I draw nothing. But the following one, if I'm not working I take 80 dollars again.' Odd though this seems, it was not unheard of in Britain, where at least one top-flight (and very well-heeled) comic did exactly the same.

(See also: Animation; Cars; Children; Documentaries; Gambling; Impersonators; Letters; Radio; Television; Trailers)

AGENTS

(Marx Brothers films and shows *qv*) Showbiz joke: a hospital patient, in need of a heart transplant, is offered the choice of two donors. One is a young athlete, the other an octogenarian theatrical agent. 'I'll take the agent's,' says the patient, 'it hasn't been used.' Theatrical agents are the frequent butt of such jokes, and one suspects heavy irony in the theatrical agent of *I'll Say She Is!* being labelled 'Rich Man'. The team's mother, Minnie Marx (*qv*), handled their earliest deals, for a while borrowing the name 'Minnie Palmer' from an altogether more illustrious personality. Not all of her decisions were in her sons' interest (see **Home Again**) and Chico became their chief negotiator, making token consultations with Minnie. For several years they were represented by United Booking but the task was taken over by the William Morris Agency in the early 1920s. The Marxes remained with them for many years, but Chico was spokesman when selling *Cocoanuts* to Paramount Pictures (*qv*) and it was Max Gordon (*qv*) who arranged their contract for the first West Coast productions. Similarly, Chico was responsible for the team's M-G-M deal with Irving Thalberg (*qv*). Mentioned under **Radio** is a skit in which Groucho and Chico portray unscrupulous, indolent Hollywood agents, possibly as a joke aimed at their brother Zeppo. He had left the act to set up an agency of his own; one of Zeppo's early clients, Norman Krasna (*qv*), was persuaded to switch representation when Zeppo performed the decidedly extra-curricular duty of flattening a drunk who was annoying Krasna in a night club. Zeppo's decision to quit the act was announced on 30 March 1934, but had been a probability for several years. He had never been a full member of the team in a financial sense, being on a fixed - if generous - salary from the Broadway shows while his brothers received a percentage of the profits. Quoted by Sylvia B. Golden in the *Theatre Magazine* for January 1929, Zeppo described himself as 'The fifth wheel ... The Spare'. 'My career on the stage is practically ruined,' he continued, 'because I am afraid of my brothers. I'm the youngest, and from the moment I first went on I would look over at them, who had already been established as comedians, and if I caught them smiling, even good-naturedly, over what I was saying or doing, I would become self-conscious to the point of unhappiness.' Zeppo went on to describe his then-current dealings in real estate but it was the agency idea that provided his escape route. Zeppo entered the business in partnership with Frank Orsatti, initially working eighteen-hour days. Among his more illustrious clients over the years were Barbara Stanwyck, Robert Taylor and Fred MacMurray. The last-named brought with him a $250,000 lawsuit from his former agent, Arthur Lyons, who in 1934 claimed that Zeppo had lured away his client. In January 1936 a Federal Court decided the matter in Zeppo's favour. Later that year Al Boasberg (*qv*) sued the agency, claiming attempts were being made to collect commission on an M-G-M contract which the agency had not negotiated. To say the least, Zeppo's

agency saw turbulent times in its first few years. Gummo had wound up his dress business in 1933 (a move anticipated by Groucho in a magazine article of the period) and came out to help in his brothers' business affairs. He spotted a discrepancy in the profits due to the team from Paramount, a matter attended to with considerable difficulty (see *Duck Soup* and **Marx Bros., Inc.**). Zeppo's flourishing business encouraged Gummo to start a similar operation in New York. Zeppo encouraged Gummo to join him in California but Gummo found himself in the position of an employee under Zeppo and his brother-in-law. Gummo complained and was given a partnership, which lasted until the agency was acquired by MCA in the late 1940s. Gummo had been representing the Marx Brothers and continued in that capacity after the agency had been sold. Zeppo made only one deal for the Marx Brothers, that for *Room Service* in 1938.

(See also: Businesses; Chaplin, Charlie; Fighting; M-G-M; Ryskind, Morrie)

AIRCRAFT
Air travel was not an automatic mode of travel in the Marxes' day. In

vaudeville (*qv*), journeys would be by rail, as would be their trips between New York and Los Angeles in the early 1930s. Things were changing by the middle of that decade; a letter from Alexander Woollcott (*qv*) dated August 1935 refers to Harpo being called back from an air journey for the purpose of retakes. Wartime - as, sadly, is often the case - served to hasten technology and by the 1940s air travel began to dominate. The Marxes had to fly when entertaining the services and, shortly after the war's end, used a runaway aircraft in the climactic scene of *A Night in Casablanca* (*qv*). In *Groucho and Me*, Groucho recalled a movie actor whose stock-in-trade was aviation epics. On boarding a *genuine* plane with Groucho, this bogus Blériot was reduced to quivering cowardice. Although the late 1940s UK visits of Harpo and Chico were made by sea, Groucho - who took to sea travel with immediate nausea - was happy to make his transatlantic hops by air, as when flying to England during 1954, 1964, 1965 and 1971 or when visiting a European film festival in 1966.

Aircraft: *Groucho bids farewell to an air stewardess on arriving in London for a 1964 TV show*

(See also: Boats, ships; London Palladium, the; Monroe, Marilyn; *A Night at the Opera*; Stage appearances [post-1930]; Television; Trains; Wartime)

ALBERTSON, FRANK (1909-64)

Minnesota-born leading man, later in character parts. In films from 1922; with Fox from 1928, who provided an important early rôle in *Prep and Pep*. Among many appearances are *The Farmer's Daughter*, *So This is London*, *A Connecticut Yankee* (UK: *A Yankee at King Arthur's Court*), *Fury* and *Bachelor Mother*, this last written by Norman Krasna (*qv*). In the Marxes' *Room Service* (*qv*) he is Leo Davis, the young playwright who endures the best-intentioned of indignities.

THE ALL-STAR BOND RALLY

See: Guest appearances

ALLEN, IRWIN (b. 1916) (d. 1991)

American producer and writer who came to Hollywood via journalism and broadcasting. Initially concerned with documentaries (notably *The Sea Around Us*), Allen is best-known for his film and TV projects dealing in extravagant tales of adventure and/or disaster, of which *Voyage to the Bottom of the Sea*, *Lost in Space*, *Land of the Giants*, *The Poseidon Adventure* and *The Towering Inferno* are prime examples. Allen receives co-producer credit (with Irving Cummings Jr [*qv*]) on Groucho's *A Girl in Every Port* (*qv*); in 1957 he signed the main three Marx Brothers for his rather off-beat history film, *The Story of Mankind* (*qv*). A witty *communiqué* from Allen to Groucho, seemingly unconnected with mutual film projects, appears in *The Groucho Letters*.

(See also: Guest appearances; Letters; RKO)

ANDROCLES AND THE LION

See: Abandoned projects; Shaw, George Bernard

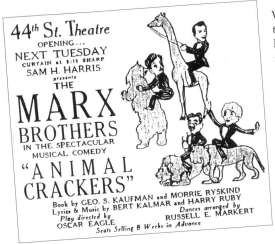

By courtesy of Robert G. Dickson

ANIMAL CRACKERS

(Marx Brothers play; Marx Brothers films and plays *qv*)

As *The Cocoanuts* concluded its phenomenal run, both on Broadway and on tour, playwrights George S. Kaufman and Morrie Ryskind (both *qv*) found themselves with the task of creating a comparable successor. The brothers themselves were at a distance; after *Cocoanuts* had closed, they returned briefly to vaudeville (*qv*) in a sketch based on *Cocoanuts'* final scene and incorporating Margaret Dumont (*qv*), before disappearing for the summer break. Music and lyrics were this time provided by Groucho's friends Bert Kalmar and Harry Ruby (*qv*). Direction was again by Oscar Eagle, with dance numbers arranged by Russell E. Markert. The new play anticipated many later Marx efforts by placing them within an austere setting, in this instance a society gathering in a New York mansion. Margaret Dumont was cast as the hostess, Mrs Rittenhouse (named after a grand but ageing Philadelphia hotel), whose guest of honour, the African explorer Captain Jeffrey T. Spalding (later amended to 'Spaulding'), was played by Groucho. Chico and Harpo were, respectively, the hired musicians Emanuel Ravelli and the Professor. Zeppo was Horatio

W. Jamison, secretary to the Captain; his lot was little improved over that in *The Cocoanuts*, even to the point of retaining the same surname. As before, he has the task of introducing Groucho, who made his entrance in a sedan chair made of bamboo, borne in by a team of Africans. Groucho would sometimes puzzle the audience by entering with one or both of his children on his lap. There is little point here in detailing the plot, which may be found in the entry for Paramount's 1930 film version; it is, however, worth examining how it differs from the film. In general terms, a number of Harpo's visual gags were lost, such as his exit from the first act dragging a heavily-laden trunk in Volga boatman fashion (a still suggests this to have been shot but deleted from the movie). Better known is a Groucho monologue, delivered directly to the audience, combining elements of *On the Road to Mandalay*, *Casey at the Bat* and others. This nonsensical verse, written by Groucho, is sometimes said to have functioned as an *entr'acte* piece but was instead placed mid-way through Act One's third scene. Groucho recalled due laughter on opening night but discovered subsequent audiences often took it seriously. He delivered it again publicly on two occasions during 1972, at the Carnegie Hall concert (*qv*) and when interviewed for BBC Television's *Omnibus*. The text was eventually reprinted in Robert S. Bader's 1993 anthology of Groucho's writings. As with *Cocoanuts'* adaptation, Morrie Ryskind rearranged certain sequences, probably to offset a stage-bound image; for example, a scene in which the Captain proposes marriage to Mrs Rittenhouse *and* Mrs Whitehead is moved to a section far earlier in the story. *Animal Crackers* was further simplified in terms of plotting, in that art expert Chandler becomes owner of the stolen painting, thus eliminating the character of Monsieur Doucet (played on stage by Arthur Lipson). Two major characters, the journalists Wally Winston (Bert Mathews) and Mary Stewart (Bernice Ackerman), have similarly been eradicated, their respective activities being transferred in part to the daughter of the house, Arabella Rittenhouse (played by Alice Wood in the stage production), and artist John Parker (played originally by Milton Watson). In the film Arabella and John are romantically involved; in the play, Mrs Rittenhouse favours Arabella's interest in Winston, while John is paired off with Mary. The original Arabella is a rather more spoiled, immature character than her film counterpart, in whom petulance is replaced by a more endearing youthful irreverence. The presence of journalist Winston allows for additional intrigue, as he is unaware of Chandler's ownership of his paper. When Harpo and Chico reveal Chandler's true background, Winston has a 'scoop' that sees him temporarily fired. One might add in passing that Winston was very clearly modelled on columnist Walter Winchell, which serves to contradict a later account of Ryskind being dissuaded from creating such a character specifically for the film (though it may be true that Winchell's comparatively localized fame meant his *Animal Crackers* equivalent could not serve as romantic lead). Winchell himself was barred from attending the show by the theatre's owners, the frequently-volatile Shuberts; the Marxes, respecting Winchell's right to an opinion (and with their own money invested in the production), made him up as Harpo's understudy so that Winchell could review the play from the wings. The precise details of Chandler's origins were tempered somewhere between *Animal Crackers'* first night and its transference to the screen: his emigration from Czechoslovakia remains unaltered but

in the movie he is exposed as 'Abe Kabibble', a one-time fish peddler, instead of the original's 'Rabbi Cantor'. This more specific ethnic identification is one of several Jewish references deleted from both the Kaufman/ Ryskind plays, suggesting how sensitive such matters had become even by the late 1920s (see also **Race** and **Religion**). It should be explained that the authors, in creating Chandler, were satirizing financier and art connoisseur Otto Kahn, who inspired resentment among his peers by regularly attempting to play down or otherwise deny his Jewish heritage. This is in keeping with the rest of the play, for *Animal Crackers* is designed essentially to attack Long Island's then-current social set, implicit in the film but emphasized all the more in the stage production. The opening number, in which Hives, as major domo, briefs the staff, extends further as butlers and maids describe the mutual contempt between servants and those on whom they wait. The butlers deride the 'trash' spoken by society people, while the maids imply multiple infidelities among the guests; it is in search of such upmarket scandal that journalist Winston is present, prompting a duet with Grace Carpenter called *The Long Island Low-Down*. Mrs Carpenter was played by Bobby Perkins in the stage production, and again had more to do than her counterpart in the film. She leads a number entitled *Cool Off*, while rather more is made of her having painted one of the fake Beaugards; the film retains what seems irrelevant mention of one fake having been painted by a left-handed artist, something which acquires substance when, in the play, Mrs Carpenter is noticed applying lipstick with her left hand. Mrs Carpenter's sister, Mrs Whitehead, was played by Margaret Irving (*qv*) on both stage and screen. The character lost an interesting dimension in the film version, owing to the deletion of a costume party in which the guests are required to portray figures from the court of 'Louis

Groucho as Captain Spalding (later 'Spaulding') in the stage version of **Animal Crackers**. Note the shiny greasepaint moustache, later matted down for film work
Paul G. Wesolowski Collection

57th'. The Captain, as guest of honour, is King; Mrs Rittenhouse is his Queen but this does not prevent him arranging a liaison with 'DuBarry', alias Mrs Whitehead. This revamp of the Napoleon sketch from *I'll Say She Is!* (*qv*) occupies the third scene of act two, which was almost entirely removed from the film save for the wrap-up of plot. It is believed that director Victor Heerman (*qv*) suggested this and the various character excisions, mostly for the sake of brevity. Its absence also removes what was originally Harpo's musical spot which, as in the film of *Cocoanuts*, has been clumsily inserted elsewhere. Several *Animal Crackers* songs disappeared from the film adaptation. *Cool Off* and *The Long Island Low-Down* are detailed above but others include most of the opening 'butlers' and 'maids' scene (trimmed to a briefing by Hives in the film), *News*, sung by Wally Winston, *When Things Are Bright and Rosy* (a duet by Winston and Arabella), two duets between Mary and John (*Who's Been Listening to My Heart?* and *Watching the Clouds Roll By*), an ensemble piece called *Go Places and Do Things* plus a further casualty from the DuBarry scene, *We're Four of the Three Musketeers*. This last was a speciality for the Marxes, among whom was divided its chorus of 'Eenie-Meenie-Minee-(Honk)'. As the play's run continued, they are said to have abandoned the lyric itself ('all for one and two for five'), leaving the chorus - and, presumably, the audience -

hanging in mid-air. As with *Cocoanuts*, *Animal Crackers* was subject to considerable revision as it progressed. It opened at the Forty-Fourth Street Theatre on Tuesday 23 October 1928, and during its 171 performances acquired several gags absent from the original draft. For example, Dumont's speech when unveiling the painting was originally punctuated only by Groucho's remark 'on track twenty-five', but the railroad imagery was later extended into 'no trains will be sold once the magazines have left the depot'. The team found itself on parallel tracks during Spring 1929, when they were required to perform *Animal Crackers* on stage during the evening while re-enacting *Cocoanuts* at

Paramount's Long Island studio during the day. The customary summer break permitted a further month's return to vaudeville, excerpting 'The DuBarry Scene' for a week at the Madison Theatre, Brooklyn, then a further three weeks in New York. In September *Animal Crackers* went on tour. Having recently endured the loss of their mother, Minnie Marx (*qv*), the Marxes managed to open in Boston before sustaining an altogether different blow: the Stock Market crashed in October and all but the perpetually broke Chico had their savings wiped out. On opening night in Baltimore, a disillusioned Groucho sat in his dressing room, unwilling to go on. He missed several cues before Morrie Ryskind went to investigate. It was only when Ryskind threatened to play the part himself that Groucho relented, saying 'nobody deserves to have to look at you for two hours'. The subsequent performance was peppered with ad libs on the stock market, several of which were retained: Groucho's soliloquy, parodying *Strange Interlude* (the original of which was playing at a theatre nearby), thus acquired reference to 'strange figures, weird figures ... Steel 186, Anaconda 74, American Can 138'. The tour concluded in April 1930, at Cleveland, Ohio. It is often said that Zeppo took over as Captain Spaulding in the Fall of 1930, after Groucho had developed appendicitis while playing Chicago; by that time the Marxes were performing in a vaudeville tour of *Napoleon's Return*, based on the main sketch of *I'll Say She Is!*. Groucho is said to have hastened his return as a result of Zeppo's favourable notices, but in truth his absence had meant a reduction in the team's salary. There is also a story of Harpo and Chico switching roles at some point in the run of *Animal Crackers*, merely to see if anyone

*Margaret Dumont and Groucho in costume for the DuBarry scene, omitted from the film version of **Animal Crackers** Paul G. Wesolowski Collection*

would notice (nobody did). The film of *Animal Crackers* was begun shortly after the tour had finished at Cleveland and was released in September 1930. It was evidently a retyped stage script that served as template for this version; when interviewed by Barry Norman, Zeppo spoke of the way the script would periodically be re-typed to incorporate their amendments. Pages reprinted in *The Marx Brothers Scrapbook* bear closer resemblance to the film than those in the opening night text, while *The Freedonia Gazette* (*qv*) has presented original and revised pages in direct juxtaposition. The two stage scripts and the film adaptation provide no less than three different gags when Hives is instructed to 'take the Professor's hat and coat': Groucho's original response was 'and give him a brisk rub-down'; by the second script it was 'and ring for the wagon'; while in the film he says 'and send for the fumigators'. A fourth, lesser alternative, 'and have him shown to the table' appears in a published script for *Animal Crackers* dating from 1984. This edition derives from a stage revival at the Arena, Washington, two years earlier. It was based chiefly on the 1928 text but pepped up with revised dialogue and several additional songs. One of these, *Why Am I So Romantic?*, was written by Kalmar and Ruby for the film version but others are taken from elsewhere in the songwriters' catalogue, among them *Ev'ryone Says 'I Love You'* (from *Horse Feathers*) and the Groucho-Ruby ditty *Show Me a Rose*. There is also a non-Kalmar and Ruby song, Von Tilzer and Brown's *Oh, By Jingo*. Stephen Mellor, Charles Janasz and Donald Corren took the respective parts of the Captain, Professor and Ravelli; in 1988 the show reappeared at the Huntingdon Theatre, Boston, then the Alliance Theatre, Atlanta, with Frank Ferrante, Peter Slutsker and Les Marsden in the roles. In December 1995 a British revival opened at the Royal Exchange Theatre, Manchester. Ben Keaton took the Groucho rôle and

*An advertising card for **Animal Crackers** using portraits from* Cocoanuts!

Joseph Alessi played Chico. Toby Sedgwick, formerly of *Adventures in Motion Pictures* and *Théâtre de Complicité*, played Harpo. Britta Smith took the rôle of Mrs Rittenhouse. Directors were Gregory Hersov and Emil Wolk. The new production incorporated several new party 'acts', spread among a small but versatile troupe of supporting players.

(See also: Cochran, C.B.; Documentaries; Female impersonation; *Flywheel, Shyster and Flywheel*; Gambling; Hotels; Impersonators; Insomnia; Perelman, S.J.; Sheekman, Arthur; Songs; Stage appearances [post-1930]; Television)

ANIMAL CRACKERS

(Marx Brothers film)
Released by Paramount, 6 September 1930 (premièred in New York 29 August). Copyrighted 6 September 1930, LP 1546.
US sources quote 8,897ft; original UK prints listed as 8,764 or 8,674 ft. 98 minutes.
No on-screen producer credit.

Directed by Victor Heerman. Camera: George Folsey. Sound: Ernest F. Zatorsky. Continuity: Pierre Collings. Credited as 'Based on the musical play by George S. Kaufman, Morrie Ryskind, Bert Kalmar and Harry Ruby' (though in fact Kaufman and Ryskind wrote the book, with music and lyrics by Kalmar and Ruby). Screenplay by Morrie Ryskind.

With Groucho Marx (*Captain Jeffrey T. Spaulding*), Harpo Marx (*The Professor*), Chico Marx (*Signor Emanuel Ravelli*), Zeppo Marx (*Horatio W. Jamison*), Lillian Roth (*Arabella Rittenhouse*), Margaret Dumont (*Mrs Rittenhouse*), Louis Sorin (*Roscoe W. Chandler*), Hal Thompson (*John Parker*), Margaret Irving (*Mrs Whitehead*), Kathryn Reece (*Grace Carpenter*), Robert Greig (*Hives*), Edward Metcalfe (billed erroneously as 'Metcalf') (*Hennessey*), The Music Masters (*six footmen*).

'At last, the Captain has arrived'; from the film
version of **Animal Crackers**
BFI Stills, Posters and Designs

A famous painting, Beaugard's 'After the Hunt', is to be exhibited at the fashionable Long Island residence of Mrs Rittenhouse. Guest of honour at this, the social event of the season, is to be noted explorer, Captain Jeffrey T. Spaulding, arriving directly from Africa. The painting's owner, art patron Roscoe W. Chandler, is in attendance as Hives, the butler, instructs the footmen. Chandler is making advances to Mrs Rittenhouse when her daughter, Arabella, breaks up the affair. Mother tries to convince daughter to abandon her interest in penniless artist John Parker when there is a distraction: Captain Spaulding has arrived. He is preceded by his Field Secretary, Horatio W. Jamison, who announces in song the conditions under which the Captain is prepared to stay (warm women and cold champagne amongst others). Spaulding makes his entrance in a kind of bamboo sedan chair, borne by a team of Africans. He is charged as per a taxi fare but refuses to pay the excessive sum of $1.85 from Africa to New York. Mrs Rittenhouse greets him but Spaulding sings that he must be

going. He is persuaded to stay as Jamison sings of his employer's strong moral character. The guests respond with the anthem *Hooray For Captain Spaulding*, which continues even after he attempts a speech. The Captain is welcomed but is more interested in reorganizing the Rittenhouse home and selling his hostess an insurance policy. Mrs Rittenhouse pays tribute to her guest's bravery, immediately prior to his collapse on seeing a caterpillar. Hives announces Signor Emanuel Ravelli, a musician engaged for the party. His first interest is in locating the dining room. He has arrived a day early, but explains both this and an inflated fee in a timetable that includes money for *not* rehearsing. He settles for a million dollars himself, but more will be required for his partner. The partner in question, the Professor, arrives dressed for the opera. He blows smoke bubbles and can produce them in chocolate if requested. Hives takes the Professor's coat and all are shocked when his entire outfit falls away, leaving the Professor in a swimsuit. The shocked guests escape when he starts to set off firearms, though he is defeated when a statue shoots back. He departs in pursuit of a pretty girl.

Later, Hives supervises the painting's display as Mrs Whitehead approaches. She is both former employer of Hives and social rival to Mrs Rittenhouse. Mrs Whitehead engages Hives to switch the Beaugard for a poor copy painted by her sister, Mrs Carpenter. Arabella walks in with John Parker. On being told that John is one of the 'Central Parkers', Mrs Whitehead makes a haughty exit. Arabella and John discuss their future, which in John's view should not depend on Arabella's wealth. Spaulding's plans include marriage to Mrs Rittenhouse, for whom he descends to one knee before asking if she'd wash a pair of his socks ('it's been on my mind for weeks'). Mrs Whitehead disturbs the tender moment and is introduced to the Captain. He suggests marriage to them both but departs amid a group of pretty girls, in the interests of 'wild oats'. John tells Arabella of the copy he once made of the Beaugard. Unaware of Mrs Whitehead's scheme, she devises a similar switch as a means of publicizing John's talents. Elsewhere in the house, Chandler is recognized by Ravelli. He is difficult to place, never having spent time in any prisons, but a birthmark on his forearm pinpoints him as Abe Kabibble, a former fish-pedlar from Czechoslovakia. Chandler offers Ravelli and the Professor $500 to secure their discretion, an offer they refuse (even though the cash is stolen from his pocket) along with a cheque he has been given. Ravelli and partner start to unmask 'Ab-ie the Fish Man' to all and sundry but are content when Chandler succumbs to the Professor's pilfering, which includes his tie, handkerchief, garters and the very birthmark by which he was identified. Chandler barely has time to recover his equilibrium before encountering Spaulding, who attempts to persuade Chandler to sponsor his retirement. He also moots the idea of placing an opera house in Central Park (overnight, when nobody's looking) and the introduction of a seven-cent nickel. John and Arabella attempt to switch paintings as the Professor rushes through, pursuing a girl. Ravelli arrives in search of his partner and receives a request from Arabella to exchange the painting on her behalf. It seems he couldn't do it if it *wasn't* stealing. Ravelli and the Professor lament the absence of anyone willing to give them a card game. The reasons become apparent when Mrs Rittenhouse and Mrs Whitehead agree to play bridge with them (once the Professor has finished wrestling with Mrs Rittenhouse): obliged to cut for partners, Ravelli and the Professor have an ace of spades apiece. When the game concludes, the Professor is wearing Mrs Whitehead's shoes. Nightfall, and amid a terrible storm Ravelli and the Professor sneak in to steal the painting. Ravelli asks his accomplice for a flashlight but receives instead flesh, a flute, Flit and almost anything that sounds vaguely like a flash before the item is produced. The lights go out and they use the flashlight to search, believe it or not, for the flashlight. Mrs Rittenhouse and Captain Spaulding are seated in the darkened room as the would-be art thieves go about their noisy task. The Captain and his hostess depart before the lights return; Ravelli and the Professor have the painting but will not leave via the storm-battered French windows; they prefer those on the opposing side of the room, leading to clear sunshine. Mrs Rittenhouse commences her soirée by introducing Captain Spaulding, with tales of derring-do in Africa. He details shooting an elephant in his pyjamas ('How he got in my pyjamas, I don't know') and has reached the topic of native girls before Mrs Rittenhouse tactfully intervenes. Ravelli entertains at the piano, getting into a version of *Sugar in the Morning* that goes around and around because he can't think of the finish (Spaulding: 'I can't think of anything *else*'). The number is abandoned in favour of *Silver Threads Among the Gold*. The Professor takes a turn at the keyboard but the scene quickly becomes an impromptu

football game and a fight. Ravelli has another try at *Sugar* which the Professor, horseshoes in hand, converts into the 'Anvil Chorus', with Spaulding as makeshift blacksmith. Spaulding presents his gift to Mrs Rittenhouse (at a very low price), a chestful of trophies; it is then time to unveil Beaugard's masterpiece. Hives has concealed the genuine item and Chandler is shocked to see an obvious imitation in its place. The lights are doused momentarily, during which the fake also disappears. Mrs Whitehead and her sister chuckle over their trick, but Hives is nervous; there is talk of summoning the police, and the valet has a prison record. He is doubly horrified on discovering the original to have vanished from its hiding place. They suspect the Professor. Arabella and John discuss the theft, permitting time for the song *Why Am I So Romantic?*, itself taken up by the Professor as a harp solo. Next day, Arabella tells Ravelli to return the painting they took, but it too has vanished. Ravelli suspects Chandler. Spaulding returns from a ride in the grounds and concocts a grievance over the summoning of the police. He dictates a pointless letter to Jamison but is content to introduce himself as a

Scotland Yard man to Inspector Hennessy. The Professor is traced to the garden, where he has spent the night draped in Beaugard's canvas. Mrs Whitehead uses her charms on him before rendering him unconscious with chloroform. When she departs with the picture, he regains consciousness immediately and sets off after a pretty girl. John has found his painting, which is promptly stolen by the Professor. Arabella seeks Spaulding's advice in solving the mystery; John tells him of the recovery and theft of his copy. Spaulding finds a red hair and Hennessy is alerted to the Professor. The officers march off in search of the suspect, unaware that he is right behind them, in police uniform. He drops a painting, the poor imitation painted by Mrs Carpenter. It is left in John's room as bait. Spaulding and Ravelli ponder the crime, deciding to search the house next door and, in the absence of such a building, constructing one for the purpose. Chandler is inconsolable until the police return with a painting; it's the forgery from John's room. The

Animal Crackers: *The Professor and Ravelli blackmail Roscoe W. Chandler*

Professor fills his Flit can from the chloroform as John is called upon to explain the discovery. Arabella, John, Spaulding, Ravelli and Jamison attempt to take the blame until the Professor owns up. He hands over John's painting, which Chandler believes genuine until the Professor also produces the original. John receives his first commission. It is decided that the Professor, having returned the picture, will not be arrested; as the kindly officer pumps his hand, silverware descends from the other sleeve. The decision not to prosecute is overturned but the Professor renders everyone unconscious with the Flit spray. After selecting a cosy spot next to the pretty girl, he anaesthetizes himself.

In reviewing the first Marx Brothers film, *The Cocoanuts* (*qv*), the *Film Spectator* noted how all their best things were reputed to have gone into that picture and wondered what the team might do for an encore. The swift answer was another Broadway show, *Animal Crackers*, which they had been performing during production of the first film. This second screen vehicle is in every way superior to the first. As before, Morrie Ryskind (*qv*) provided the script, from the final version of the show written by himself and George S. Kaufman (*qv*). Certain characters were concertinaed, a few scenes were rearranged and a costume party - known as 'The DuBarry scene' - was jettisoned altogether. One source - presumably quoting Heerman, though he is not specifically identified - describes initial disagreements between Heerman and Ryskind, due in part to Ryskind's alleged intention to replace the artist character with a new creation, a Walter Winchell-type journalist. As noted during evaluation of the stage play, this is contradicted by examination of the original script, in

which *both* characters are present. What is more likely is that Ryskind, in combining these figures into one (as he did with several others), had opted for the journalist, which Heerman probably considered unrecognizable outside of New York. Ryskind later recalled the Marxes suggesting he fight a boxing match with Heerman, when the director favoured uninterrupted

Captain Spaulding decides to sow a couple of wild oats in **Animal Crackers**

comedy scenes. According to Hector Arce, Heerman proved his point by audience-testing four reels comprising comedy alone. That Heerman was determined to make an effective film of his own is evidenced by the famous story, recounted by Lillian Roth (*qv*), of the Marxes being kept in purpose-built prison cells to prevent their disappearance between takes. Harpo recalled this as happening during *Cocoanuts*, but all other accounts disagree. Heerman had been sent from Hollywood to Paramount's East Coast facility; so had Lillian Roth, as a consequence of having gained a reputation for being 'difficult'. Roth and Hal Thompson were assigned the obligatory love story, though in fairness neither is terribly intrusive. As Arabella, Roth eschews the swooning *ingénue* approach in favour of a

convincingly sassy, Kaufmanesque wiseacre. Hal Thompson is at least preferable to the varnished Oscar Shaw (*qv*) of *Cocoanuts*. Another advance over *Cocoanuts* is the set, certainly stagy but constructed with a depth comparing favourably with its predecessor. *Animal Crackers* is not a precise record of the stage show as is often implied, but it's a more than reasonable approximation. Above all, it brought to a worldwide audience that most durable of Groucho's identities, Captain Jeffrey T. Spaulding (the 'T.', according the Captain, stands for 'Edgar'). His entrance is in the best Gilbert and Sullivan manner, with a choral rendition of *Hooray For Captain Spaulding*, blended with his own attempted bowing-out, *Hello, I Must Be Going* and a less-quoted ditty, *The Captain is a Very Moral Man* (in which the lyric belies the title). Chico, alias Ravelli, cloaks supreme craftiness in seemingly impenetrable stupidity and favours necessities over society trappings (he asks, almost immediately, 'Where is the dining-room?'); Harpo, as the Professor, greets the assembled throng as if he were foreign royalty, but is soon clad in a bathing suit and letting off firearms. Zeppo introduces Groucho and, as 'Field Secretary', takes down the Captain's irate letter to 'Hungerdunger, Hungerdunger, Hungerdunger and McCormack'. In the end he is requested to throw away the original and its carbon copies ('Just send a stamp, air mail'). The film loses pace after the dictation scene, petering out somewhat as the story reaches conclusion. The costume ball's deletion kept *Animal Crackers* within manageable length but simultaneously robbed it of a climactic scene. Margaret Dumont (*qv*), repeating her stage rôle as Mrs Rittenhouse (or

Animal Crackers: *Mrs Rittenhouse watches her soirée become a free-for-all*

'Rittenrotten' at one point), expresses polite amusement at her guest of honour and extreme shock when wrestled by Harpo. Also from the stage cast are Louis Sorin (*qv*) as art expert Chandler, Edward Metcalfe (*qv*) as the detective, Robert Greig (*qv*) as Hives and Margaret Irving (*qv*) as Mrs Whitehead. Again in common with *Cocoanuts*, the new film was premièred in New York at the Rialto. *Variety* gave Paramount 'extreme credit for reproducing *Animal Crackers* intact from the stage, without too much of the songs and musical numbers'; this is almost accurate, though it's surprising they didn't miss the DuBarry scene. The main three brothers were praised to the highest but Zeppo was considered lucky 'if in on a split'. It was speculated, humorously but astutely, that Lillian Roth was there to 'work out a contract'; Hal Thompson received short shrift as juvenile lead; while their shared song, *Why Am I So Romantic?* (written for the film version), was dismissed as 'useless'. Mordaunt Hall of the *New York Times*, who had enjoyed their first screen effort, welcomed this 'further example of amusing nonsense' but confined its appeal solely 'to those who revel in the work of these four brothers'. Much of Hall's review is devoted to the famous

routine in which Groucho and Chico debate the notion of searching the house next door, and, should there not be such a house, building one. Hall dwells somewhat on the bridge game, the infinite capacity of Harpo's pockets and Groucho's heckling during the piano speciality. Zeppo and the supporting players are at best acknowledged but Margaret Dumont was credited with 'capital work'. *Picture-Play* for December 1930 repeated *Variety*'s crack about Lillian Roth and, apart from calling Zeppo 'Beppo' (a common error), was mostly encouraging. '*Animal Crackers* comes as a verdant oasis in a month comprised principally of pretty dull films.' Possibly the only disapproving American voice was the *Film Spectator* of 27th September. Having lauded *Cocoanuts*, the *Film Spectator* predicted that unless the Marxes were given better material, 'they will have to follow Clark and McCullough and Moran and Mack back to the stage'. The reviewer enjoyed the harp and piano items but obtained no laughs from the film. 'It is possible that you will like *Animal Crackers*,' he concluded. 'As for me, I am sorry that I saw it. It makes me wonder what under the sun I saw to laugh at in *The Cocoanuts*.' This complete about-face is remarkable, given the identical pedigree of *Animal Crackers* as a stage play and its vast superiority as a movie. Perhaps the

critic had previously been caught at a weak moment and had decided to recant his approval of such rough stuff; in claiming 'they had nothing new to offer' he invites the theory that he was upholding a prediction made in his appraisal of *Cocoanuts*, namely that the Marxes might have trouble finding material for a sequel. The majority of reviewers, if becoming prematurely complacent, disagreed with this reaction; so did British commentators, though an extant 'confidential' report suggests the censor to have been uneasy over certain *risqué* moments (the film was granted a 'U' certificate solely because it was thought children would not understand the dubious references). The *Bioscope* of 26th November 1930 did Zeppo something of a favour by speaking of the 'innumerable comicalities by four

'*Yours not to reason why, Jamison!*'; Captain Spaulding chastises his secretary for leaving out 'the body of the letter' in **Animal Crackers**
BFI Stills, Posters and Designs

exceptionally gifted artists'. Groucho played Captain Spaulding 'on boisterous, aggressive lines'; Harpo's Professor was considered 'a real funniosity'; Chico and Zeppo 'also distinguish themselves'; while Margaret Dumont was 'excellent as the long-suffering hostess'. The presence of Lillian Roth and Hal Thompson was merely acknowledged, along with the

Lucas pondered the idea of him being 'perhaps the cement that binds the brotherhood together, the power behind the throne ... if not, how more than fraternal of Groucho, Chico and Harpo to let him in on an equality'. The *Theatre World* for December 1930 hedged its bets in customary fashion: 'Still, those who enjoyed *The Cocoanuts* will certainly enjoy *Animal Crackers*, and those who did not will know exactly what to expect'. After a lengthy pre-release London run at the Carlton, *Animal Crackers* was unleashed upon the rest of Britain. *Picturegoer*'s Lionel Collier, in the issue of 19 September 1931, compared the Marxes' world to one where '"Alice in Wonderland" is a serious book of

refuge to a clown of the grand school'. *Animal Crackers* resurfaced in London at the Everyman cinema's revival season in 1950 and remained part of the Classic cinema chain's repertory into the late 1970s. From 1956 it entered a legal stalemate in the US, based on the respective film and stage play rights passing into different, non-communicating hands (a fate which, curiously, did not befall *Cocoanuts*). BBC 2 screened the film in 1965 (see **Television**). Untypically for the BBC, their print was missing a three-minute section from Dumont's *soirée*, comprising Chico's rendering of *Silver Threads Among the Gold*, Harpo's turn on the piano, the mock football game and Chico's return to *Sugar in the*

The harp solo was removed to the patio in **Animal Crackers**' *film version*

supporting players. The next day's *Kinematograph Weekly* described 'a scintillating absurdity, similar in character, but even better than *The Cocoanuts*'; the only dull moments occurred 'when breaks are made to introduce the inevitable and sugary love interest'. There was the usual qualification, namely that 'an appreciation of the co-stars' original and rich humour' was necessary, which translates roughly to 'you have to be a fan'. E.V. Lucas in *Punch* joined those who had praised *Cocoanuts* but found the new film even better. At first relieved on discovering it not to be yet another 'all-singing musical comedy', Lucas followed Mordaunt Hall's precedent by lingering over the 'house-next-door' duologue. He further echoed the play's original Broadway reviews by commenting on the spontaneity of performance, felt to belie the attribution to four writers (see credits above). He compared the Marxes' inconsequentialities to those of British music-hall legend Dan Leno, but was at a definite loss when it came to Zeppo. Noting that without the dictation scene Zeppo 'would not exist',

A chorus of My Old Kentucky Home *leads into the finale of* **Animal Crackers**
BFI Stills, Posters and Designs

Animal Crackers *premièred in the UK at London's Carlton theatre ...*

reference'. Two days later, C.A. Lejeune of the *Observer* fell in line by admitting a personal enthusiasm for the team but also an inability to 'guarantee results'. More illuminatingly, Lejeune suggested that 'in the mute Harpo the talkies have paradoxically given

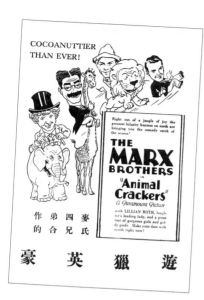

... and **Animal Crackers** *reached Hong Kong in March 1931 (Mark Newell collection)*

Morning. There is a visible splice where this has been removed, yet it should be noted that the difference in footage tallies almost exactly with the varying lengths quoted between American and UK prints in 1930. This BBC copy continued to be used until the 1980s. A slightly abridged *Animal Crackers* was better than nothing, which is precisely what American audiences saw of it - in legal showings, that is - for eighteen years. The legal problem had kept the film out of circulation until Steve Stoliar, a student at UCLA, led a successful campaign to have the film reissued. Groucho attended a trial screening in California before travelling to New York for the re-première in June 1974. *Animal Crackers* was afforded a high profile, prime-time American television debut on CBS in July 1979. A new master - as supplied to the UK for Channel Four and video release - retains the section missing from the BBC print and is of superior quality to most copies. (The author recalls the National Film Theatre once apologizing for a poor print.) As with recent screenings of *Cocoanuts*, the opening credits are slightly reduced to avoid cropping in height. There are other signs of

tidying-up: for example, there is a brief edit to eliminate a small lapse in continuity, when Groucho appears to emerge *twice* from his bamboo carriage. The soundtrack has been re-balanced in some way, most noticeably during the *Hooray For Captain Spaulding* medley, which for some reason was badly recorded in 1930. (*Bioscope* made mention of an occasional harshness in Groucho's voice.) The whole is marred somewhat by occasional damage in the material, taking the form of seemingly printed-in splices that sometimes clip the dialogue. This is particularly annoying during the house-next-door routine and in Groucho's memorable song introduction, 'Somewhere My Love Lies Sleeping - with a male chorus'. These faults are not present in the BBC copy and it is to be hoped that a flawless print may one day be constructed.

(See also: Censorship; Cochran, C.B.; Continuity errors; Fighting; Folsey, George; Gambling; *I'll Say She Is!*; Names; *On the Mezzanine*; Opera; Paintings; Paramount Pictures; Perelman, S.J.; Perrin, Nat; Records; *Risqué* humour; Royalty; Songs; Stage appearances [post-1930]; Television; Vaudeville; Video releases)

ANIMALS

(Marx Brothers films and shows *qv*)
'Are you a man or a mouse?' asks Allan Jones (*qv*) in *A Day at the Races*. 'You put a piece of cheese down there,' Groucho tells him, 'and you'll find out.' When outraged orchestra conductor Jardinet finds a big top instead of a concert platform, his cry of 'animals' is taken as a comment on the society guests; in parallel, the Marxes seemed to encourage sub-human comparisons when choosing titles for their adventures. *Animal Crackers*, *Monkey Business*, *Horse Feathers* and *Duck Soup* fall into this category as does, to a lesser extent, the performing-animal implication of *At the Circus*. *Cocoanuts* has a production number called 'The Monkey-Doodle-Doo' and the Marxes themselves were sometimes depicted

Animals: *Zeppo and a borrowed horse on the set of* Duck Soup

as apes in publicity for the stage show. (It might be added that Captain Spaulding is a veteran of the jungle, 'where all the monkeys throw nuts'!) Animals make occasional contributions to the Marx epics: for example, Harpo's tattoo in *Duck Soup* contains a dog who barks at a cat; another cat, in *Love Happy*, is thought to have swallowed some missing jewels. Harpo, as the most elemental character, has a certain one-to-one relationship with the animal kingdom, hence his fondness for horses in *Animal Crackers* and *Duck Soup*; he drives a horse-drawn garbage wagon in *Horse Feathers*; horses are a natural part of the background to *Go West*; while *A Day at the Races*, of course, centres around 'Hi-Hat'. An exception to Harpo's benevolence to animals is his ruthless dogcatcher in *Horse Feathers*, though among the hounds was his real-life pet, Kayo. For years Groucho owned a dog named Duke; when the team visited London in 1931, Zeppo acquired two Afghan hounds with the idea of breeding them. Feathered creatures appear less frequently, though one should not forget the Groucho duck in *You Bet Your Life* (*qv*). *Duck Soup*'s credits show its titular creatures swimming in a cooking pot, a runaway turkey brings some life to *Room Service* and Harpo gets to ride an ostrich in *At the Circus*. (It has been said that Harpo developed bursitis in the shoulder after falling from the ostrich, but a likelier version, reported in the *New York Evening Journal* of 18 January 1937, describes instead a fall from a Shetland pony while filming *A Day at the Races*.) More recently there has been a real-life American racehorse named 'Rufus T. Firefly', Groucho's alias in *Duck Soup*; in the UK there has been a horse named after that film, plus two others named 'Groucho' and 'Dr Hackenbush', the latter of course commemorating history's best-known equine physician.

(See also: Names; Newsreels; Tattoos; Vaudeville)

ANIMATION

(Marx Brothers films *qv*)
The technique of combining live-action with animation has often been employed in film comedy, though the essentially stage-rooted Marxes had little use for it. Perhaps the nearest to an example is Harpo's tattoo in *Duck Soup* (see **Animals**). Groucho's TV show, *You Bet Your Life* (*qv*), used animation in its title sequences, invariably creating a Groucho caricature with moving cigar and eyebrows. During the 1930s and 1940s, cartoon makers were fond of incorporating film star caricatures into their work, and the Marxes seemed particular favourites. Examples are discovered with considerable frequency, rendering inadvisable any claim to a complete list. At least two of the Fleischer Studio's *Popeye* cartoons make room for a Marx Brother: in *Sock-a-Bye, Baby* (1934), the sailor is in charge of a baby whose sleep is disturbed by Harpo's street-corner musicianship. A later entry, *Puttin' On the Act* (1940), sees Popeye impersonating Groucho. Another cartoon segment, depicting the Marxes on a four-man bicycle which crashes into the *reflection* of a rock, has been identified as a Fleischer cartoon called *Strolling Through the Park*, but this title does not appear in available Fleischer filmographies. Paramount (*qv*) subsequently reorganized the Fleischer unit as Famous Studios. A 1948 Famous cartoon, *The Golden State*, shows Harpo's footprints, outside Grauman's Chinese Theatre, setting off in pursuit of a pretty girl (!); another Famous Studios entry, *Toys Will Be Toys* (1949), caricatures Harpo as a jack-in-the-box. Walt Disney sometimes used cartoons of the Marxes, and it is said that Harpo was the model for Dopey in *Snow White and the Seven Dwarfs* (1937). Further down in the fairy-tale market, Terrytoons' version of the Cinderella story, *The Glass Slipper* (1938), includes a curly-headed, non-speaking Prince who communicates by means of a taxi horn in his belt (and who, for the finale, goes off with Fairy

Godmother Mae West!). Another Terrytoon, *Out Again, In Again* (1948) has magpies Heckle & Jeckle as Groucho and Harpo. Disney Marx caricatures may be found in *Mickey's Gala Première* (1933), *Mickey's Polo Team* (1936), *Mother Goose Goes Hollywood* (1938) and *The Autograph Hound* (1939). A Disney renegade, animator Ubbe ('Ub') Iwerks, spent a decade away as independent producer and made a large number of interesting if undistinguished cartoons. His major character, 'Flip the Frog', met the Marx Bros in 1931's *Soda Squirt*. Another Iwerks film, a two-strip Cinecolor item called *The Brave Tin Soldier* (1934), introduces Groucho as a merciless judge, who says (in an appalling impression of his voice) 'Give him a fair trial - and then we'll shoot him!' As in the much later Famous cartoon, Harpo is represented briefly as à jack-in-the-box, as is Eddie Cantor (*qv*). Among the peripheral Marx caricatures is a Columbia cartoon, *Merry Mutineers* (1936), which does not use them to great advantage but nonetheless provides an amusing scene centred around Chico's piano-playing. Even less mainstream is M-G-M's *Abdul the Bulbul Ameer* (1941), featuring a news commentator who strongly resembles Groucho, though not in voice and minus spectacles (though he sports an authentically Spaulding-like sun helmet). Some of the best film-star caricatures appear in the Warner Brothers cartoons. *Coo-Coo Nut Grove* (1936) has Harpo (caricatured as some sort of canary) in pursuit of a beautiful girl; when captured, she turns out to be Groucho. A later Warner entry, *Hollywood Steps Out* (1941), repeats the gag but with Clark Gable instead of Harpo, who is seen instead placing a lighted match under Greta Garbo's sizeable foot. One might add in passing that Warner character Bugs Bunny has much in common with Groucho, not merely in the type of consciously androgynous pose related above but in stance, attitude to opponents, accent and cigar-like use of a carrot as prop.

(In a radio sketch, 'The Spiwit of Spwing', Groucho adopts a pseudo-adolescent tone that sounds disconcertingly like Bugs.) Bugs also has a tendency to say 'This means war!' rather in the manner of Groucho in *Duck Soup* and *A Night at the Opera* (both *qv*). In *Slick Hare* (1946) Bugs is momentarily disguised as Groucho (sharing a restaurant table with Harpo and Chico) but nothing is made of it. A bizarre sidelight: *Porky's Road Race* (1937) is one of many black-and-white Looney Tunes to have resurfaced in crudely re-traced colour versions. One figure, originally intended to be Charlie Chaplin (*qv*), has had his curly hair coloured blond to resemble Harpo Marx. Sometimes the Marxes make brief appearances in cartoons solely to provide a momentary laugh: fairly typical is the Groucho caricature in Bob Godfrey's *Great - Isambard Kingdom Brunel* (1975). Harpo is conjured up by Merlin in an episode of TV's *The Twisted Tales of Felix the Cat*, called 'Middle Aged Felix'. Among the various planned latter-day Marx revivals was a series of animated cartoons for TV. When Chico died in 1961, *Variety* reported this project as being in preparation by Columbia's TV division, Screen Gems (presumably to be made for them by Hanna-Barbera). Similar things were done with Laurel & Hardy (*qv*), Abbott & Costello and the Three Stooges but the Marx series did not reach fruition, despite continued reports into the mid-1960s. Early in 1980 it was announced that Filmation had acquired the rights to make a cartoon version of the Marx Brothers, but this also seems to have been abandoned.

(See also: Abandoned projects; Deaths; Garbo, Greta; Hats; Kane, Helen; *On the Mezzanine*; Radio; *Risqué* humour; Songs; Woollcott, Alexander)

ARDEN, EVE (b. 1912) (d. 1990)

Former Ziegfeld girl, often in second female leads. Her 'Peerless Pauline', intrepid upside-down walker of *At the Circus* (*qv*), is fairly typical of her

Eve Arden *plays the scheming 'Peerless Pauline' in* At the Circus
BFI Stills, Posters and Designs

tough-but-humorous image. Among other films are *Dancing Lady* (1933), *Stage Door* (1937), *Ziegfeld Girl* (1941), *Cover Girl* (1944), *Mildred Pierce* (1945; Oscar nomination, Best Supporting Actress), the Cole Porter biopic *Night and Day* (1946) and *One Touch of Venus* (1948). Also on TV, as in the series *Mothers in Law* and a 1985 episode of *Steven Spielberg's Amazing Stories* entitled 'Secret Cinema'. Latter-day film roles include that of Principal McGee in *Grease* (1978), a parallel to her teacher role on *Our Miss Brooks* (radio and TV).

(See also: Awards; Children; Seiter, William A.; Perelman, S.J.; Tashlin, Frank)

ARMETTA, HENRY (1888-1945)

Italian actor, born in Palermo but long resident in America; specialized in excitable 'foreigner' roles. Initially on stage, but entered films in 1915 at the invitation of actor William Farnum. Armetta made many silent films but his talkies include Keaton's *The Passionate Plumber* (1932), *Speak Easily* (1932) and *What! No Beer?* (1933); also Wheeler & Woolsey's *So This is Africa* (1933) and *Fra Diavolo* with Laurel &

Hardy (*qv*). Among later films are *Colonel Effingham's Raid* (1945) and *Stage Door Canteen* (see **Guest appearances**). Armetta seems to have been something of a draw in his own right with, one suspects, an ability to stand up for himself; on 18 March 1936 *Variety* reported him as having been released from a Universal contract 'by mutual consent' in order to make 16 personal appearances (which had in turn been 'reticketed at upped figure'). Henry Armetta appears with the Marx Brothers in *The Big Store* (*qv*) as Giuseppi, an old friend of Chico and Harpo whose immense brood goes partly astray. Despite his comparatively brief contribution, Armetta receives specific billing in the theatrical trailer.

(See also: *A Day at the Races* [illus.]; Keaton, Buster; Trailers)

THE ARMY

See: Could Harpo Speak?, Stage appearances (post-1930); Wartime

ASHLEY, HERBERT

See: *At the Circus*

AT THE CIRCUS

(Marx Brothers film)
Released by M-G-M, 20 October 1939.
Copyrighted 10 October (LP 9173).
7,812ft. 87 minutes. (A contemporary
UK source quotes 8,100ft and 90
minutes.)
Produced by Mervyn LeRoy. Directed
by Edward Buzzell. Camera: Leonard
M. Smith. Screenplay by Irving
Brecher. Songs: *Lydia, the Tattooed
Lady*, *Two Blind Loves*, *Step Up and
Take a Bow*, *Swingali*, by E.Y. 'Yip'
Harburg and Harold Arlen. Working
title: *A Day at the Circus*.

With Groucho Marx (*J. Cheever
Loophole*), Chico Marx (*Tony/Antonio*),
Harpo Marx (*Punchy*), Kenny Baker
(*Jeff Wilson*), Florence Rice (*Julie
Randall*), Margaret Dumont (*Mrs
Susanna Dukesbury*), Eve Arden
(*Peerless Pauline*), James Burke (*John
Carter*), Nat Pendleton (*Goliath*), Jerry
Marenghi (*Professor Atom*), Fritz Feld
(*Jardinet*), Barnett Parker (*Whitcomb,
the butler*), Charles Gemora
(*Gibraltar, the gorilla*).

At the Wilson Wonder Circus,
proprietor Jeff Wilson feeds Gibraltar
the gorilla. Jeff has left his wealthy
family in Newport to pursue his love of
the circus. Jeff's fiancée, Julie Randall,
begins her trick riding act, which
commences with the song *Step Up and
Take a Bow*. Peerless Pauline, an
acrobat, expresses her disdain.
Next is Goliath, the strong man,
whose act is ruined by 'Punchy',
his nominal assistant. Jeff owes
$10,000 to John Carter, who
needs the money that night and
will take the circus if necessary.
Jeff promises to repay the full
amount from that day's
receipts. Tony, a circus hand,
hears the conversation and suggests a
lawyer; he contacts 'legal eagle' J.
Cheever Loophole. As the show is
about to move on, Julie reads a
newspaper item about Jeff's family.
Jeff's aunt, Mrs Susanna Dukesbury,
has disinherited him. Julie and Jeff
meet in the railroad station café; there
is a song, *Two Blind Loves*, before they
board the train. Loophole arrives by
taxi. Jeff has instructed Tony to let
nobody board the train without a
badge. Despite Tony's invitation and
the heavy rain, Loophole is not allowed
aboard. Jeff could give Loophole a
badge, but he is aboard the train, and
cannot be reached without a badge.
Another cab brings Punchy and a sea-
lion. When challenged, Punchy has a
coatful of badges; even the sea-lion has
a badge. Eventually Tony relents and
gives his own badge to Loophole.
When Loophole tries to board, he is
told the badge is last year's and is
pushed into a puddle. During the train
journey, Tony entertains colleagues
with his piano playing. Punchy plays
checkers, assisted by the sea-lion.
Pauline and Carter watch Julie and
Jeff. Pauline reminds Carter that he

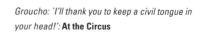

*Groucho: 'I'll thank you to keep a civil tongue in
your head!':* **At the Circus**

will be 'through' if Jeff pays off the
loan. Carter sends Professor Atom (a
midget) and strongman Goliath after
Jeff. Tony and Punchy visit Loophole,
who somehow has boarded the train.
Tony thinks Loophole may find a way
to have Goliath dismissed, allowing
Punchy to become the strongman.
Punchy inflates his chest accordingly.
Loophole is promised a large fee then
introduced to the other passengers. He
sings of an old flame, *Lydia the
Tattooed Lady*. Jeff takes his money
from the cage holding Gibraltar.
Goliath and the Professor sneak up
behind; Jeff is knocked cold and

robbed. He is discovered by Tony and Loophole, revived and introduced to the lawyer. Jeff realizes the $10,000 takings have been stolen (Loophole: '$10,000? That man's hurt bad!'). Loophole takes Jeff away to recover from the attack. Tony and Punchy 're-destruct' the crime. Punchy, fortunately, has experience of the police: he carries a wanted poster of himself, promising a reward of '50 cents for jaywalking'. The re-enactment goes slightly awry, Tony receiving a blow to the head regardless of who takes the role of Jeff. The victim put safely to bed, Loophole asks Tony of any suspicious-looking characters, other than Tony of course. Tony suspects Carter to be responsible, using Goliath to do the job for him. Loophole confronts Goliath but, intimidated, withdraws his services. Julie asks Loophole for any news, explaining how important it is to Jeff and herself. Loophole is back on the case and, returning to Tony and Punchy, finds they have a clue: a cigar butt found at the scene. Suspecting the midget, they visit his miniature berth in the hope of matching it to one of his cigars. Loophole requests a cigar but Tony, failing to grasp the idea, supplies one of his own. This continues and the cigars have to be disposed of quickly. The

attempt concludes as Punchy has a sneezing fit, sending the furniture flying. At the next performance, Pauline does her upside-down act, aided by shoes fitted with suction pads. Tony tells Loophole of her involvement with Carter, suggesting she might know something about the robbery. Carter has placed the money in Pauline's suitcase, with instructions to determine how much Loophole knows of the crime. Pauline is trying out new shoes for the act and is therefore treading the ceiling when Loophole walks in. Loophole asks directly about the money, searches the premises *and* attempts to make a pass. Pauline returns to earth; Loophole retrieves the loot but Pauline turns on the charm and swipes it back again. Loophole sees her place the money in the front of her costume. To retrieve it (while maintaining decency) he asks her to resume her walk on the ceiling. She will oblige if Loophole will do the same. The money duly descends but Pauline is able to drop to the floor after it. She leaves Loophole stuck to the ceiling, where he remains until Punchy comes along to untie the boots. Loophole reaches *terra firma* abruptly. Jeff brings Julie a telegram, offering her a job with a rival circus. She refuses to leave but Jeff is insistent. It is decided that Loophole should pay a visit to Jeff's wealthy aunt, and he departs for Dukesbury Manor. A black sweeper-up takes fright when a caged lion becomes restless. Punchy charms the roaring animal with a trombone lullaby. The black community take him for Svengali and he leads them in a musical number, followed by a harp solo. At Mrs Dukesbury's home, the lady herself is busy on the telephone, informing a friend of the coming *soirée*. She has engaged French conductor Jardinet and his orchestra, with only the '400' of Newport invited. Loophole arrives at the mansion, gaining admission by claiming to be *Mister*

Dukesbury. He makes directly for Mrs Dukesbury, posing as a former sweetheart. The butler has a message from Monsieur Fontaine of the Concert Bureau; Loophole intercepts it and passes himself off as Fontaine. He obtains the Maestro's name from Mrs Dukesbury, suggesting there may be alternate entertainment should Jardinet not appear. He also boosts the fee from $7,500 to $10,000, owing to the 'rate of exchange'. On the train to Chicago, Jeff still wants Julie to join the rival circus. Jeff will lose the show after the following night and will have to find a job. There is a reprise of *Two Blind Loves*. Tony and Punchy go to Goliath's berth in search of the money. Goliath is asleep but needs a periodic lullaby to remain so amid the noise. To ensure his slumber, a glass of water is prepared laced with sleeping pills; Punchy drinks it instead, giving Tony the difficult task of waking Punchy while keeping Goliath asleep. Punchy is revived and Goliath's mattress slit open; Punchy climbs inside and the groggy strongman inspects his now lumpy bed. He puts the mattress on the top bunk, where Tony is hiding. The bed is even lumpier. Goliath flees in panic on hearing a motor horn and 'Rock-a-bye-baby' seemingly from nowhere. When the intruders emerge, Tony quite literally has to knock the stuffing out of Punchy. In Chicago, Jeff receives a phone call from Loophole at Dukesbury Manor. Loophole explains that the circus can be set up in the garden to replace the absent Jardinet. Loophole's next call is to the steamship *Normandie*, on which Jardinet is travelling. Loophole names him as the leader of a dope ring and the conductor is arrested. On the night of the performance, Loophole delays the proceedings as the circus is set up. Outside, Carter has his henchmen sabotage the show. Punchy, riding an ostrich, knocks them out with his taxi horn, which also proves useful in extinguishing burning straw. Loophole finally tells Mrs Dukesbury of Jardinet's indisposition just as the

At the Circus: *Loophole prepares to join Pauline on the ceiling*

enraged Frenchman storms in. Loophole rushes him out, at the same time directing him to a bandstand tethered in the water. At the Manor, curtains part to reveal the circus; at the bandstand, the orchestra starts to play as Tony and Punchy set the platform adrift. Mrs Dukesbury, horrified, assumes the unexpected show

After all seems lost ...

to be her nephew's revenge; Loophole claims instead that he asked Jeff to supply a backup in the event of Jardinet's non-appearance. The circus is well received but Mrs Dukesbury is concerned about Jardinet; Loophole dismisses him as 'probably on his way back to Paris'. This is quite plausible, as the drifting orchestra has reached the ocean. As Mrs Dukesbury is acclaimed by her guests, Carter tries to break up the show by releasing Gibraltar, the gorilla. In the confusion, Mrs Dukesbury is wedged in the cannon; Gibraltar chases Carter up into the trapeze. Punchy joins them, as does Mrs Dukesbury when Tony fires the cannon. Soon Carter, Stuffy, Mrs Dukesbury, Tony and Loophole form an airborne chain, which breaks as Gibraltar walks across. They land safely but Gibraltar keeps Carter aloft, held by his jacket. Carter slips out of the jacket and Gibraltar recovers the stolen money. Jardinet and his orchestra drift away into the distance.

The enormous success of *A Day at the Races* (qv) guaranteed the Marxes a future, at least of sorts, at M-G-M (qv). Their next film, *Room Service* (also qv), was made at another studio but M-G-M lured them back with a three-picture contract. *At the Circus*, the first of these, was however denied two important luxuries: first, there was to be no pre-filming tour, which had become a key factor in the team's methods; second, they were to have only one credited scriptwriter, a comparative novice named Irving Brecher (qv), rather than the two- or three-man operation that encouraged ideas to build. Another newcomer was director Edward Buzzell (qv), a former stage comedian and Broadway contemporary of

the Marxes, whose tenets should ideally have meshed with theirs. This was not always the case, while a secondary clash of styles characterized their relationship with gagman Buster Keaton (qv). Production began with a certain trepidation, at least on Groucho's part, but this was characteristic of his insecurity. Although convinced that the death of Irving Thalberg (qv) marked the end of the Marxes' film career, Groucho had to some degree overcome his pessimism, expressed in a letter to Arthur Sheekman (qv) of 24 June 1939. Groucho described the film as 'progressing rather rapidly', believing also it would be 'much better than I thought. This isn't saying a hell of a lot.' Having established that he hadn't seen the rushes, Groucho betrayed a further lack of enthusiasm by admitting that he

... our heroes prepare a show under the big top ...

... and Punchy fires the cannon

probably wouldn't get around to seeing the film until it played at the Marquis (and then only if the Ritz theatre dispensed with plans to raffle a Buick). Groucho had made the effort by the end of October, as recorded in a letter to Sheekman of 27 October. He was by then 'sick of the whole thing' and vowed never again to see *At the Circus*. Perhaps he had examined the reviews: Frank S. Nugent of the *New York Times* typifies the mixed reaction, noting with seemingly genuine regret this 'rather dispirited imitation of former Marx successes'; *Variety* made a similar comparison but in a more positive fashion, describing a reversion to 'the rousing physical comedy and staccato gag dialog of their earlier pictures'. Perhaps *Variety*, like a few other commentators, had ceased to be impressed by lavish production and preferred to look back on the less tidy, gag-packed Paramount films. *At the Circus* is a rougher diamond than the previous M-G-Ms but has nothing like the pace or humour associated with the Paramounts. Nugent's opinion is altogether more justified, especially when breaking down (as he did) the key elements. Chico's barring of

Groucho from the train bears striking similarities to the password idea of *Horse Feathers* (qv) and, to a lesser extent, his codebook scam from *A Day at the Races*. Similarly revamped from *Races* is Harpo's scene with the black community, today an embarrassment in both films although the original was much lauded in its time. The sequence in the midget's cramped accomodation suggests an attempt to emulate the stateroom scene of *A Night at the Opera* (qv), but does not build and conveys little more than claustrophobia. Tedium sets in when Chico is unable to grasp the difference between *his* cigars and those of the midget; the occasional fleecing of Groucho by Chico and Harpo is one thing, but one expects some co-operation between them when faced with bad guys. In lieu of a proper conclusion, the scene fades out on Harpo sneezing. That this was little more than a gimmick is suggested by the British *Picturegoer* of 22 July 1939:

At last! After almost twenty years of silence on stage and screen, the great mystery of whether Harpo Marx's voice is bass, alto or tenor is to be solved in "A Day at the Circus" [the film's working title]. In the picture, his voice

will be heard for the very first time. Harpo has wanted a speaking voice in the Marx Brothers triumvirate since he first stepped upon the stage, but the odds have always been against him. In "A Day at the Circus" he has finally won his victory. His voice will be heard in one sonorous sneeze - Ka-choo!

As it turned out, Harpo was permitted more than one 'Ka-choo' but the entire piece suggests a publicist's whim. Leaving aside such petty details as Harpo having a speaking part in their earlier acts, and that his professional silence dated back rather more than twenty years, there is nothing to suggest Harpo's ambition to take a speaking rôle. Indeed, he took great pains *not* to speak, at any rate when it might be recognizable, and with rare exceptions adhered to this principle until his farewell performance. This attempted betrayal of their characters has an equivalent in the film itself. An overall emasculation, the inevitable by-product of Thalberg's format, starts to gain momentum in *At the Circus*; for example, all three are intimidated by strongman Nat Pendleton (qv), who met at least token resistance from Harpo in *Horse Feathers* (qv). Not surprisingly, Groucho is at his best with Margaret Dumont (qv), particularly when intruding into her home, posing as a former sweetheart. He deals with the butler in the way he should everyone else, at one point handing the servant a coin with the instruction to get himself a clean shirt. Dumont's 'Mrs Dukesbury', whom Groucho addresses with a cry of 'Snookums!', is at first her most rigid creation since *Cocoanuts* (qv). 'You must leave my room,' she insists, 'we must have regard for certain conventions.' 'One guy isn't enough,' says Groucho to camera, 'she's gotta have a convention.' Mrs Dukesbury quickly succumbs to Groucho's silver tongue; at her *soirée*, a quite different tongue - that of a giraffe - passes along her back, a titillation she attributes to Groucho! For the climactic sequence, M-G-M recruited

'Valerie!'; Loophole recognizes his client in the
deleted courtroom scene of **At the Circus**
BFI Stills, Posters and Designs

performers from the real-life
Hagenbeck-Wallace Circus. This takes
time to set up, both within the plot (as
Groucho stalls by ordering more and
more coffee) and in terms of the film's
construction, but delivers some fair
slapstick despite its uninspired trick
work. The finale, a magnificent shot of
an orchestra playing its way to the high
seas, compensates for much of the
lesser material that has gone before.
This obviously *Night at the Opera*-
inspired motif also goes some way to
remedy an inherent lack of contrast
between characters and setting; as Joe
Adamson has observed, the Marxes
should be placed in a context where
they have no business - such as a
society gathering - instead of the (for
them) natural habitat of a circus.
Nugent, who commented wryly on how
it all must have sounded in story
conference, summed up both
contemporary opinion and that of
subsequent critics in his belief that *At
the Circus* would probably seem
funnier to an audience unfamiliar with
the team's greatest films. *At the Circus*
was received warmly on arriving in
Britain in December 1939. The Second

World War was three months old,
cinemas were just starting to re-open
and Britons were eager for comedy; the
Royal Family were in attendance when
the film premièred at the Empire on 8
December. The BFI's *Monthly Film
Bulletin* of 31 December considered it
a 'vintage film for those who like their
type of humour' (the usual critics'
disclaimer for the Marxes). Taken in
isolation, *At the Circus* works well
enough but is an enormous comedown
after its predecessors at M-G-M.
Nugent thought it indicative that he
could recall only one line, namely when
Eve Arden (*qv*) places a wallet in her
bosom (see **Censorship**). This remains
the film's most-quoted gag, probably
with good reason. The other highlight
(apart from the author's favourite line,
in which Groucho bids farewell to a
chimpanzee with 'Goodbye, Mr.
Chimps') is Groucho's comic vocal,
Lydia, the Tattooed Lady. This and the
film's other songs were provided by
E.Y. 'Yip' Harburg and Harold Arlen,
who in the same year performed an
identical task for an altogether
different production, *The Wizard of
Oz*. *Lydia* remained in Groucho's
repertoire for the rest of his career and
is a favourite among impersonators
(*qv*). War had not yet broken out when
At the Circus was being prepared,
hence the deletion of a verse to the
effect that the Tattooed Lady 'sits on
Hitler'. This was also omitted on at
least the UK sheet music edition (from
Francis, Day and Hunter) but was
reinstated by Groucho for a wartime
radio broadcast. The obligatory love
story, handled by Florence Rice and
Kenny Baker (both *qv*), need be noted
only as being more intrusive than any
since *Cocoanuts* (*qv*). Worse was to
come, but for the moment one can only
lament the presence of things like *Two
Blind Loves* when room could not be
found for a full-scale Groucho routine.
Since he was cast as a shady lawyer, it
made perfect sense to write a sequence
in which his dubious skills were
displayed in court. Such a scene was
written and shot but deleted before

release, and survives only in stills.
Fortunately, these stills and a script of
the sequence were published in the
Winter 1984 *Freedonia Gazette* (*qv*).
The action begins with the judge
(Granville Bates) complaining over
delays in the trial and calling for the
plaintiff's attorney. The missing brief, J.
Cheever Loophole, is snoozing in the
jury box. He is awakened and slips
automatically into a plea to the jury.
When asked why he is sitting among
the jurors, Loophole explains 'I'd
rather have the State owe me three
bucks a day than the plaintiff.'
Loophole cross-examines a timid-
looking man (Byron Foulger) in what is
evidently a breach of promise case. The
defendant has broken his word to
Loophole's client, a 'little child' who,
incidentally, looks big enough to take
care of herself. 'Gentlemen,' continues
Loophole, 'to me a woman has always
been something to revere ... my mother
was a woman ... grand-daughter to Paul
Revere. But that's a horse of another
story!' The opposing lawyer complains,
on the grounds that the plaintiff has
supplied no more than an affidavit with
half the pages missing; 'Well,' replies
Loophole, 'affa-davit is better than
none.' Counsel for the defence
requests a dismissal through lack of
evidence; Loophole, enraged by the
threat to his first case in nine years,
plays his 'trump card' by calling as
witness one Nicholas Bludge (Herbert
Ashley), a detective. Bludge is asked if,
on the night of 27 November, he saw
the plaintiff with 'a certain despicable
playboy'. He is evasive but coaxed into
a reply, eventually naming Loophole as
the culprit. The lawyer approaches his
veiled client (Irene Colman), exposing
her face with a cry of 'Valerie!'
Loophole, calling for an adjournment,
heads for the door. He is met by a
group of telegraph boys, whom he
mistakes for the National Guard.
Instead of a bullet he is treated to an
even more painful experience, namely
Chico's telegram delivered in the
manner of a singing birthday greeting.
Summoned to the circus, Loophole

tells the boys 'Don't wait for an answer. I'll sing it to him myself!' The scene fades out as Loophole exits.

(See also: Animals; Burke, James; Carnegie Hall concert, the; Cars; Censorship; Children; Could Harpo Speak?; Deleted scenes; Gangsters; Gemora, Charles; Lawyers; Le Roy, Mervyn; Letters; Names; Paramount Pictures; Puns; Race; Radio; Records; *Risqué* humour; Royalty; Smoking; Songs; Tattoos; Television; Trailers; Trains; Wartime; Wigs)

AWARDS

Although Groucho was more than once recognized for his quiz show, *You Bet Your Life* (*qv*), it seems incredible (at least in retrospect) that none of the Marx Brothers' films were ever considered for an Academy Award. This may in part reflect the commonly-held belief that they were rather better than their films, but one might at least expect the polished *A Night at the Opera* (*qv*) to have been in the running. Instead, Groucho was among those to receive a special Oscar in recognition of a lifetime's achievement, on the recommendation of Nunnally Johnson (*qv*). When Jack Lemmon presented the statue at the 1974 awards ceremony, Groucho made a point of acknowledging Harpo and Chico, as he had at the Carnegie Hall concert (*qv*). Groucho was clearly aware how much of this latter-day attention was in recognition of the work he had done with his brothers rather than as a solo artist. Two years before, the French government had made Groucho a *Commandeur des Arts et Lettres*, an honour rarely bestowed upon a foreigner. Another unusual honour, if less specifically an award, came about in October 1975, when the Mayor of Los Angeles declared a 'Groucho Marx Day' in commemoration of the comedian's 85th birthday. The following year Groucho received the Sunair Humanitarian Award, presented at the Beverly Hilton with George Jessel (*qv*)

as toastmaster. Previous recipients had included Jack Benny and Lucille Ball (both *qv*). On 16 January 1977 the Marxes were inducted into the Motion Picture Hall of Fame at a convention in Los Angeles. Groucho was present but Zeppo could not attend owing to illness. Harpo's award was collected by his widow, Susan, while Chico's was accepted by his grandson, Kevin Marx Culhane. Also in attendance were Morrie Ryskind, George Seaton, Victor Heerman, Virginia O'Brien, Fritz Feld and Dan Seymour (all *qv*); *You Bet*

1933 as an alternative to the Academy. Groucho was the first Treasurer. In 1937 the Guild honoured Margaret Dumont (*qv*), nominally for her work in *A Day at the Races* (*qv*) but in effect for her many eventful years with the Marx Brothers.

(See also: Arden, Eve; Ball, Lucille; Bendix, William; Calhern, Louis; Coslow, Sam; Cowan, Lester; Krasna, Norman; Seymour, Dan; Sinatra, Frank; *Will Success Spoil Rock Hunter?*

Your Life (*qv*) was represented by George Fenneman and Jose Gonzales Gonzales. The Marxes were among the founding members of the Screen Actors' Guild, incorporated in July

Awards: *Groucho receives his Oscar in 1974*

Kenny Baker *(far right)* as the troubled circus owner in At the Circus; also with James Burke *(m.l.)* and Chico *(left)*

"IS HE MAKING TROUBLE FOR YOU?"

BACK HOME
See: *Home Again*

BAKER, KENNY (1912-85)
Popular singer who adopted Gilbert & Sullivan's *A Wandr'ing Minstrel, I* as his theme tune after playing 'Nanki-Poo' in the 1939 British film version of *The Mikado* (*qv*). Kenny Baker plays the romantic lead in *At the Circus* (*qv*). On radio (*qv*), Baker would later take over from Groucho in the *Pabst Blue Ribbon Town*. Originally a music student, Baker won a singing contest and was soon spotted by Jack Benny (*qv*), with whom he subsequently worked on radio. Broadway work includes *One Touch of Venus* (see **S.J. Perelman**); among film credits are *King of Burlesque* (début), *The King and the Chorus Girl* (*qv*) and *Stage Door Canteen* (see **Guest appearances**).

BALL, LUCILLE (1910-89)
Comedienne, originally a Goldwyn Girl (in which capacity she may be spotted in Cantor's *Roman Scandals*). She drew greater attention as the 1930s progressed and appeared with the Marx Brothers in *Room Service* (*qv*). The film offers no opportunities for her comic talent, which was only permitted to blossom comparatively late on, as in the Bob Hope vehicle *Fancy Pants* (1950), *The Fuller Brush Girl* (also 1950) and *The Long, Long, Trailer* (1954). She attained due prominence on TV in *I Love Lucy*, co-starring her first husband, bandleader Desi Arnaz. Ironically, they acquired the old RKO lot (where *Room Service* was made) as studios for their production company, Desilu. Harpo made a guest appearance on the show in 1955. Groucho was present when, in 1974, Lucille Ball was given the Sunair Humanitarian Award (which Groucho would receive two years later). The occasion was marred when a joke of Groucho's was misinterpreted. A year later they co-presented the Emmy for

Lucille Ball *was a comparative unknown when appearing in* Room Service

best comedy-variety series, though Miss Ball seemed to ignore her co-host, reportedly through being overwrought after learning of a motor accident involving one of her children. Groucho's anger seems to have diminished somewhat by the following year's *Groucho Phile*, in which the comedian spoke fondly of them working together during wartime. At this late date, the comedian seemed anxious to dispel any notions of ill feeling between himself and certain others, notably S.J. Perelman (*qv*).

(See also: Awards; Books; Cantor, Eddie; Buzzell, Edward; Mirrors; O'Brien, Virginia; Radio; Riesner, Charles F.; RKO; Television; Video releases; *You Bet Your Life*)

BANKHEAD, TALLULAH
See: Radio; Television

BARKER, JACK
See: *The Cocoanuts* (play)

BARLOW, REGINALD (1866-1943)
Actor who mixed occasional silent-screen roles with stage work until the 1930s. Earlier talkie appearances include *If I Had a Million* (1932) and the Marxes' *Horse Feathers* (*qv*), in which he is the outgoing college president (making way for Groucho, an even *more* outgoing president). More often in drama, such as Victor Fleming's *The Wet Parade* or Garbo's *Mata Hari* (both 1932); also in such tongue-in-cheek things as *Bride of Frankenstein* (1935).

(See also: Garbo, Greta)

BARNETT, VINCE (1902 or 1903-77)
(Marx Brothers films *qv*)
Pittsburgh-born supporting comic, sometimes with star billing in shorts (as in *Two Lame Ducks*, a 1934 Educational short with Billy Gilbert [*qv*]). Also often in demand for small-time criminal types, as in *Scarface* (1932). In *Monkey Business* the man squashed under Harpo in a deckchair

looks very much like Vince Barnett; in *Horse Feathers* he appears as an extra in the speakeasy. Barnett's entry in *The World Film Encyclopaedia*, evidently prepared during 1932, reveals a surprising background (an education at Duquesne University and Carnegie Technical College before being claimed briefly by vaudeville [*qv*]) and an even more intriguing sideline: as 'Hollywood's only professional insulter', he would be engaged by party hosts to target an unsuspecting guest throughout the evening. A speciality, it seems, was for Barnett to pose as a waiter, dropping soup down his victims' necks. 'Has now abandoned this job entirely for the screen', assured the entry; this may have been mere camouflage, for in the same year, Barnett brought his offscreen expertise to the set of *Horse Feathers*. Joe Adamson quotes Harry Ruby and Arthur Sheekman (both *qv*) to the effect that the Marxes engaged Barnett in his capacity as professional heckler during the film's production. In Ruby's version, Barnett made scathing remarks (in a German dialect) while he and Kalmar were reading out their work; Sheekman offered a variant, in which he had been forewarned of Barnett's contrived, periodic insults but became increasingly annoyed when, at intervals, *everyone* took Sheekman aside to let him in on the gag.

(See also: Practical jokes)

BARRAT, ROBERT (1891-1970)
Burly, New York-born actor of stage and screen, noted for mastery of foreign accents but often in westerns (such as the *Cisco Kid* films); hence his appearance as 'Red Baxter', ruthless saloon-keeper in the Marx Brothers' *Go West* (*qv*). Many other films include Cagney's *The Picture Snatcher* (1933), *Dames* (1934), *Devil Dogs of the Air* (1935), Joe E. Brown's *Sons O'Guns* (1936), and the Crosby-Hope *Road to Utopia* (1945) and *Road to Rio* (1947), the latter directed by Norman Z. McLeod (*qv*).

BARTON, CHARLES (1902-81)
Assistant director on the Marxes' first three Hollywood films, *Monkey Business*, *Horse Feathers* and *Duck Soup* (all *qv*). On the *Monkey Business* set, each of the Marxes had a canvas-backed chair marked with his name; director Norman McLeod (*qv*) had a chair designated 'Macko', while assistant Barton's was marked 'Echo'. Born in San Francisco, Charles Barton gained early experience in vaudeville and repertory work before trying the film business, starting as a prop boy. Among his numerous full director credits are many Abbott & Costello comedies (*Abbott & Costello Meet Frankenstein*, *Africa Screams* and so on) and a prolific career in television.

(See also: Names)

BARTY, BILLY
See: Deleted scenes; Television

BEAGLE, SHYSTER AND BEAGLE
See: Flywheel, Shyster and Flywheel; Radio

BELASCO, LEON (1902-88)
Russian-born character actor, known from films, television and the Broadway stage; played Mr Lyons in *Love Happy* (*qv*). According to an obituary in the *Freedonia Gazette* (*qv*), Belasco latterly owned a Palm Springs home that made him a summertime neighbour of Groucho lookalike Frank Ferrante. Educated in North Manchuria and Japan; originally a musician, Belasco was first violin in the Tokyo Symphony orchestra (in *Love Happy* he plays violin to Chico's piano) before coming to America. Based in Los Angeles, he worked in several bands and made his film debut in *Best People* (1926). Numerous films include *Topper Takes a Trip* (1939) directed by Norman Z. McLeod (*qv*), *Nothing But the Truth* (1941) and *Call Me Madam* (1953).

(See also: Impersonators)

William Bendix *teamed up with Groucho for* A Girl in Every Port ; *also with Dee Hartford, sister to Groucho's third wife, Eden.*

BELL, MONTA (1891-1958)

(Marx Brothers films *qv*) Washington-born producer-director with stage experience, an assistant to Charlie Chaplin (*qv*) and director of several noteworthy silents, among them Garbo's first American film *The Torrent* (1926). Bell was put in charge of Paramount's Long Island studio and thus receives producer credit on *The Cocoanuts* (a task he shared with the uncredited Walter Wanger; no producer is named for *Animal Crackers*). It was Bell to whom fell the unenviable task of querying Groucho's painted moustache (see **Moustaches, beards**); Bell also brought in as director Robert Florey (*qv*), whom he had known for several years. Bell's subsequent productions include *Men in White* (1934), Crosby's *The Birth of the Blues* (1941) and *Beyond the Blue Horizon* (1942); in 1945 directed *China's Little Devils*.

(See also: Folsey, George; Paramount Pictures)

BENDIX, WILLIAM (1906-64)

New York-born, comic 'rough diamond' type who inherited radio's *The Life of Riley* from Groucho, taking it also to TV and a successful film version. In 1952 he and Groucho co-starred in *A Girl in Every Port* (*qv*). In films from 1942 and was nominated by the Academy for *Wake Island* that same year. Lengthy list of film credits includes *The Glass Key* (1942), *The Blue Dahlia* (1942), *A Connecticut Yankee in King Arthur's Court* (1949; UK title *A Yankee in King arthur's Court*) and *The Big Steal* (1949).

(See also: Awards; Guitar, the; Radio)

BENNY, JACK (1894-1974)

Comedian who became something of an American institution, Jack Benny (born Benjamin Kubelsky) built a comic image on parsimony and a degree of prissiness. Benny's biggest laughs came from his reactions to individuals or the world at large, based on a solid characterization. It might be noted that British comedian Benny Hill adopted that forename in conscious homage to Jack Benny. One of Benny's most famous gags involves being given the choice of 'your money or your life', followed by silence as Benny ponders the alternatives. The miserly image (encapsulated in the title of a 1943 film, *The Meanest Man in the World*) was, of course, part of the act; he was in life the most generous of men and highly regarded both in and out of the profession. Another Benny trademark was the violin, learned in youth (he would in time own a Stradivarius); it was as a young violinist, then known professionally as Ben K. Benny, that he found work in the pit band of the Barrison Theatre, in his home town of Waukegan, Illinois. At that time, late 1912, Chico had been out on his own and deliberately placed himself in the theatre pit when Groucho, Harpo and Gummo played there in *Fun in Hi Skule* (*qv*). There followed some impromptu horseplay with Chico (see **Vaudeville**), who from then on was a part of the act. Not content with adding a fourth brother, Minnie Marx (*qv*) also wanted Jack Benny to join them. She had seen him during the Monday rehearsal, picking up their music very quickly. Benny later recalled her inviting him to travel with the boys' act, play fiddle for them in the pit, and do a few comical musical cadenzas, further offering to double his Barrison salary (at that time $7.50 per week). Benny was keen to accept, if a little unnerved by the brothers' wild behaviour, but his parents refused to discuss the idea. For this reason, Benny's vaudeville career developed independently of the Marxes, first as straightforward violinist then, after joining the navy in the First World War, as comedian. Benny is known to have appeared on the same bill with the Marx Brothers at least as early as the spring of 1920, when the brothers presented a sketch called '*N*' *Everything* (see **Home Again**). Benny became close friends with Zeppo, with whom he shared accommodation while on tour in Canada. When interviewed for *The Marx Brothers Scrapbook*, Benny spoke of having been aghast when his quiet act was moved to a spot after the Marxes, who were then performing *On the Balcony* (formerly *On the Mezzanine* [*qv*]); like W.C. Fields (*qv*) before him, he had learnt that 'nobody could follow the Marx Brothers'. He protested to the management but was encouraged to go on and do his act irrespective of what had gone before. Benny soon realized how much the experience had polished and improved his work. He recalled also the practice in which a preceding act would be asked to participate to a greater or lesser degree in the following act, leading the Marxes to charge into Benny's routine, reducing it to fragments and Benny to helpless laughter. It was Zeppo who first introduced Benny to his future wife, Sadie Marks, later known in show business as Mary Livingstone. Her collaborative work, *Jack Benny: a Biography* (with her brother, Hilliard Marks and Marcia Borie) refutes a story of their having first met in 1926, at the Los Angeles store where she

Jack Benny was still 'Ben K. Benny' when supporting the Marxes in 1920
Advertisement courtesy of Robert G. Dickson

was working; instead, she recalls meeting him at her parents' home in Vancouver. It was 1922 and she was not yet thirteen. Her parents were prominent citizens with a fondness for asking vaudeville folk to their home; when the Marx Brothers appeared at the local Orpheum, they were invited to the house for Passover, but Zeppo was the only one to accept. He had brought along Jack Benny, who was also on the bill. Benny had been persuaded by the prospect of the meal and Zeppo's mention of the Marks' young daughters. When he saw *how* young they were, he suggested they make a hasty exit. Young Sadie got her

revenge by arranging a claque to heckle Benny at the Orpheum. This was not, she later admitted, an auspicious beginning to their relationship, which picked up somewhat after their next, 'official' meeting four years later. They were married in 1927 and would become one of the best-known, enduring showbusiness couples. Groucho and Jack Benny would continue to meet over the years, particularly at Hillcrest but also at events such as at

the Gillmore Stadium in 1947, when each played in a comedians' team for a charity baseball match. Three years later Harpo, Jack Benny and Danny Kaye officiated at the opening of Houston's Shamrock Hotel. In 1955 Groucho was a guest on Jack Benny's TV show, partly in front-of-cloth patter but essentially in a sketch with Benny disguised as a contestant on *You Bet Your Life* (*qv*); Benny, who for decades had a running gag in which he claimed to be 39 years old, stood to win the jackpot by giving Jack Benny's real age. Given the choice between this and his supposed financial greed, he decided to forego the money! Benny later spoke of the difficult time Groucho had given his writers; Hector Arce mentions Groucho's reluctance to have Benny on his *real* quiz show, suggesting Groucho to have been very aware of his friend's skill with *ad libs*.

(See also: Awards; Baker, Kenny; Boasberg, Al; Burke, James; Cantor, Eddie; Clubs; Francis, Kay; Hotels; Mayo, Archie L.; Radio; Riesner, Charles F.; Rumann, Siegfried; Ryskind, Morrie; Seaton, George; Sport; Stage appearances [post-1930]; Television)

BENOFF, MAC

Received co-screenplay credit, with Frank Tashlin (*qv*), on *Love Happy* (*qv*). A *Variety* obituary describes him as having originally been a radio gag writer based in New York, who travelled to Hollywood to work as screenwriter. Broadcast credits include Ed Wynn's Texaco programme (see **Flywheel, Shyster and Flywheel**) and work with Fanny Brice playing Fanny Brice's 'Baby Snooks' character (see also **Radio**); also devised the *Duffy's Tavern* series and was brought in to work on the screen adaptation. Other film work includes *Hollywood Canteen* (see **Guest appearances**). In 1950 Benoff was blacklisted for his alleged political sympathies, a not uncommon experience in the McCarthy era; his career picked up in

1953 when devising the *Make Room For Daddy* TV series for Danny Thomas (whom Benoff had developed from a stand-up comedian on the Brice shows), winning the Emmy for two consecutive years. The *Variety* obituary credits him with writing TV's first colour variety special, *Washington Square*, also with having written TV shows for Eddie Fisher and George Gobel plus the script for Stanley Kramer's *Bless the Beasts and Children* (1970). He is described also as former president of the Music Guild of Los Angeles and as an authority on Mark Twain, owning one of the largest collections of manuscripts and memorabilia. Historian Paul G. Wesolowski states that in January 1972, Benoff appeared on a panel with Groucho at a Writers' Guild of America West Workshop, chaired by Mel Shavelson. The panel, which consisted of writers who had worked with Groucho, also included Nat Perrin, Robert Pirosh, Harry Ruby, Morrie Ryskind and George Seaton (all *qv*). According to *The Hollywood Reporter* of 14 January, 'Loud applause greeted Benoff's observation that Marx, who has written numerous books without a ghostwriter is probably "the most literate comedian of our times", yet was the first to acknowledge his debt to the writers of his films.' Benoff is also quoted to the effect that he had been signed to 'doctor' *Love Happy*, most of which had been shot but with 'little continuity and much mish-mash' (implying his contribution to have been the framing device introduced by Groucho). He claimed further to have tried, unsuccessfully, to persuade the producer to expand the role given to an unknown actress because of her considerable beauty; the actress was Marilyn Monroe (*qv*). This function would have been one of Benoff's final public appearances, for he died on 16 November 1972, aged 57.

BERLIN, IRVING (1888-1989)

Russian-born composer (real name Israel Baline), in America from childhood and responsible for many of his adopted country's most famous songs. One of the first biographies of Berlin was written by Alexander Woollcott (*qv*). From the days of *Alexander's Ragtime Band* (not a reference to Woollcott!) via *White Christmas* and beyond, Irving Berlin's illustrious career is legend except, curiously, in connection with the Marx Brothers. They knew Berlin from quite early on and Gummo sang his ragtime-era tune, *Yiddle On Your Fiddle*, in their vaudeville act. This was of the 'ethnic' type that Berlin would soon abandon, and is seldom revived today except in reissues of old recordings. It is believed that *Home Again* (*qv*) later incorporated still another early Berlin composition, *Somebody's Coming to My House*. Also from the 'Teens comes an item that Groucho would never allow Berlin to forget, entitled *Stay Down Here Where You Belong*. Although Berlin would soon become one of the more vociferous campaigners for American involvement in the Great War, in its first months he produced this isolationist ditty, firmly in the spirit of *I Didn't Raise My Boy to be a Soldier* (itself parodied by Groucho who, either at the time or in the later *On the Mezzanine* (*qv*), compared it to a poker game with 'I Didn't Raise My Boy, He Had the Joker'). The lyric is set Down Below, where the devil persuades his son not to visit the earth, there being considerably more hell aloft than he would ever find in his native domicile. Groucho alone had total recall of this noble composition and would sing it at any opportunity, particularly if Berlin was present. It finally came about that Berlin good-humouredly offered Groucho a fee *not* to sing it. Groucho believed, quite reasonably, that Berlin's otherwise impeccable track record could easily survive this occasional embarrassment. More positively, *The Groucho Letters* reprints a 1956 communiqué in which the composer thanks Groucho for prompting a revival of his song, *Simple Melody*, after singing it on TV with Bing Crosby.

Groucho was at that time seeking items for TV work and requested older titles from the Berlin catalogue. It might be added parenthetically that a fragment of Berlin's *All Alone* was sung by Chico in episode 8 of *Flywheel, Shyster and Flywheel* (*qv*); this is believed lost, but extant today is a much later broadcast, *The All Star Cowboy Hour*, in which Groucho sings a fairly horrible cowboy song to the tune of Berlin's *White Christmas*. Berlin was long associated with Sam Harris (*qv*), with whom he built the Music Box theatre in New York. Amid press speculation about his likely marriage in 1925, Berlin told reporters 'I am not engaged to anyone except Sam Harris and I'm engaged to write two shows for him - a new show for the Marx Brothers and the new *Music Box Revue*.' The Marx Brothers show turned out to be *The Cocoanuts* (*qv*), which in time would provide Groucho with another running gag. He would consistently kid Berlin over his score being among the very few for which the composer failed to supply a hit song. Berlin's defence was solid: *Cocoanuts*' author, George S. Kaufman (*qv*), had no time whatever for a number called *Always*. It was duly jettisoned and became a worldwide hit without the aid of either the Marx Brothers or *Cocoanuts*. Conflicting stories circulate regarding its deletion. One is that it succumbed to last-minute pruning when the show was overlong, this 'worthless' item being easiest to remove ('You waive the songs, and I'll waive the story,' said Kaufman); another describes composer and playwright working on the show in adjoining hotel rooms, with Berlin choosing to present *Always* to Kaufman at five o'clock in the morning. Kaufman, skeptical of the infinite devotion promised in the lyric, wearily suggested an amendment to 'I'll be loving you Thursday'. This might be considered greater tribute to Kaufman's beleaguered wit than to his appreciation of popular song.

(See also: Calhern, Louis; Carnegie Hall Concert, the; Krasna, Norman;

At the Gotham Conservatory of Music, Ravelli is filling in for its ailing professor. He is instructing children in his unique piano style when a man calls

Mark Newell Collection

THE BIG STORE

(Marx Brothers film)
Released by M-G-M, 20 June 1941.
7,492ft. (83 minutes).
Produced by Louis K. Sidney. Directed by Charles F. Riesner. Camera: Charles Lawton. Screenplay by Sid Kuller, Hal Fimberg and Ray Golden, from a story by Nat Perrin. Songs: *Tenement Symphony*, music by Hal Borne, lyric by Sid Kuller and Ray Golden; *Sing While You Sell*, music by Hal Borne, lyric by Sid Kuller and Hal Fimberg; and *If It's You*, music and lyric by Ben Oakland, Artie Shaw and Milton Drake. Working titles: *Bargain Basement* and *Step This Way*.

With Groucho Marx (*Wolf J. Flywheel*), Chico Marx (*Ravelli*), Harpo Marx (*Wacky*), Tony Martin (*Tommy Rogers*), Virginia Grey (*Joan Sutton*), Margaret Dumont (*Martha Phelps*), Douglass Dumbrille (*Grover*), William Tannen (*Fred Sutton*), Marion Martin (*Peggy*), Virginia O'Brien (*Kitty*), Henry Armetta (*Giuseppi*), Anna Demetrio (*Maria*), Paul Stanton (*George Hastings*), Russell Hicks (*Arthur Hastings*), Bradley Page (*Duke*).

to take away the instrument. Ravelli explains that his friend, a singer named Tommy Rogers, will soon be there to settle matters. Tommy is an ex-pupil and protégé of the late Hiram Phelps, from whom Tommy has just inherited half of a big store. Tommy does indeed arrive in time, announcing plans to sell his share in the store to finance the building of a new conservatory. Tommy and Ravelli relay the news to the professor as the youngsters resume their unorthodox piano practice. The other half of the store has been left to Martha Phelps; Grover, the store manager, knows of Tommy's intentions and is reluctant to have a potential buyer examine his books. In the event of Tommy's demise, his share passes to Martha; Grover plans an 'accident' for Tommy and a wedding to Martha. He warns his subordinate, Fred Sutton, to watch out for the girl in the record department; she is Fred's sister Joan, who attracts much of Tommy's attention. Tommy and Ravelli step into the store's lift, where the lights are extinguished. When they return, Tommy has sustained a blow to the

head. In Grover's office, Tommy disregards any thought of danger. Grover, seemingly anxious to avoid publicity, discourages summoning the police, but Martha has different ideas. She visits Wolf J. Flywheel, a down-at-heel detective whose office serves also as bedroom and kitchen. Flywheel's assistant, Wacky, is a similarly multi-purpose individual combining the duties of cook, typist and chauffeur. Domestic trappings are hastily concealed as Miss Phelps outlines her story. Flywheel is engaged but must pose as a floorwalker. The stove containing breakfast boils over beneath Flywheel's desk and is passed off as his 'private smokescreen'. Miss Phelps is escorted to Flywheel's car, an ancient specimen threatening disintegration. Once at the store, Wacky is left to deal with the car. He finds Martha's purse on the back seat. Grover briefs his henchmen on the plot; the books are enough to fool Tommy but not the Hastings Brothers, who are potential buyers of Tommy's share. Tommy is in the music department with Joan. A lady customer requests Tommy's new record but is told it is out of stock. Using a home recording machine, Tommy cuts a unique copy of *If It's You* and presents it to her. Joan reflects on Tommy's transformation from 'the toughest kid in the neighbourhood' but warns him not to ignore the potential danger he faces. Martha introduces the new floorwalker to Grover. When asked for his qualifications, Flywheel claims to have been a shoplifter for three years. Their rivalry for Martha's attentions becomes apparent and Flywheel sets out to discredit Grover. Tommy arrives with Ravelli, who describes himself as Tommy's bodyguard. The indiscreet Flywheel replies that he has been hired for that purpose and Martha has to explain herself to Grover. Martha scolds Flywheel but is softened by his poetic love talk. Tommy accepts Flywheel, who tells the furious Grover to 'scram'. Wacky has created a parking space by planting a dummy fire hydrant. He

The Big Store: *Wolf J. Flywheel has a client ...*

answer from Tommy at his hotel. Fred tells her he was with them at the store until five in the morning, examining the books. There is to be a meeting at ten. Grover wants Tommy's bodyguards out of the bed department, where they are catching up on sleep. A sale is organized of their 'in-a-wall' beds. The first customers are astonished to see Flywheel occupying one bed; next is a huge Italian family who, on pressing a button, summon forth the bed containing Ravelli. The Italian man thinks Ravelli is mocking his accent until he is recognized as an old friend from Naples; Wacky is similarly greeted. Wacky pushes a button and

counter and alerts Flywheel to look out for two men in grey topcoats. Fred goes to fetch the police. Ravelli is sent to look for the killers, and decides to draw a crowd by playing the piano. Wacky joins him in a duet. Fred returns with two plain clothes officers, from whom he will separate before meeting again on the second floor. Grover sees them together and kidnaps Fred. The Hastings brothers arrive, wearing grey coats; Flywheel mistakes them for the killers and handcuffs them to a stairway. Tommy has them released but Ravelli and Wacky capture the genuine criminals, who are arrested. As it is half-day closing,

goes to return the purse but is taken for a thief and apprehended. Word reaches Grover's office and Flywheel takes the credit; when the 'thief' is brought in, he is identified instead as both Flywheel's assistant and Ravelli's brother. Flywheel claims to have set it all up to demonstrate how Grover could accuse an innocent man of theft. Wacky returns the purse and, on further request, its contents. Flywheel expresses his contempt for Grover and his ideas on sales technique in a musical item, *Sing While You Sell*. Grover gives the seductive Maggie instructions to lure Tommy to a road house where 'the boys' await. Grover promises they will be together in six months, once Martha, too, has met with an 'accident'. Tommy takes Joan to lunch, leaving Ravelli watching the music counter, Flywheel watching Ravelli and Wacky watching Flywheel. Maggie visits the counter, posing as a reporter wishing to interview Tommy. Demanding to be informed of his return, she goes to another counter for some fabric to match the dress she is wearing. When told it is out of stock, she makes considerable fuss until Wacky supplies a sample, cut from the back of her dress. Next day, Joan clocks in and sees her brother. She is concerned because there has been no

... and his assistant takes down the details

half the family disappears into the wall. There is a panic, not eased at all when Wacky replaces them with children from a different family. Next are children from a Chinese family, then still more from a party of Red Indians. As chaos ensues amid mobile beds and children, Flywheel returns to sleep. Joan has found Tommy, and tells Fred of their engagement. Fred seems awkward, the more so because two gangsters have been hired to kill his prospective brother-in-law. He overhears their plans at the music

Grover suggests the store should be handed over in a formal gathering involving both staff and the press. Ravelli does not believe Wacky could attend such an occasion in his shabby clothing; Wacky strays into a display of eighteenth-century costume and dissolves into one of the outfits. There is a harp, placed between two mirrors. As he begins to play, each reflection takes on a distinct identity, then an entirely different instrument, forming a trio. As Wacky dissolves back to his original clothing, Ravelli informs him that he is to play at the party. Grover learns that the press photographers plan to take only one picture, that of Tommy signing over the store. He plants a revolver in one of the cameras. Flywheel takes Martha aside with talk of matrimony. The show begins with Tommy singing his masterpiece, *The Tenement Symphony*. Flywheel and Ravelli approach the reporters but are ignored. They borrow a camera in order to take their own picture. Grover learns that Fred has escaped and has been seen with Joan; she must be caught. Joan tries to inform Flywheel of the situation but is made to pose with him for a photograph. As the picture is taken, the lights are momentarily doused and Flywheel is left posing with Wacky. Tommy finds Joan, bound and gagged; Flywheel, Ravelli and Wacky develop and print the photograph, which shows Grover kidnapping Joan. Grover enters the darkroom, carrying a gun. He confiscates the negative, burns it then demands the print. The trio escape with the picture and are pursued through the store by Grover and the police. Eventually they trap Grover in a stockroom but the police apprehend them at gunpoint. Tommy tells Grover to come out, which he does but with the photograph aflame. The pressmen want a picture of Grover, who panics and tells them of the concealed gun. Wacky knocks him out. Martha decides to sell her share of the store to the Hastings brothers and departs with Flywheel. Wacky prepares to drive them away but is saved the task by a tow truck.

The Marx Brothers' final film for M-G-M (*qv*) was intended also to be their farewell as a team. They were growing increasingly unhappy with a studio which, if not openly hostile, was certainly indifferent to their needs. Although the road-tour system had been reinstated for *Go West*, *The Big Store* was made to do without such a luxury. The screenplay started with a reasonable pedigree, having derived from an episode of the Groucho-Chico radio series, *Flywheel, Shyster and*

Flywheel (*qv*), even to the point of Groucho and Chico retaining the surnames 'Flywheel' and 'Ravelli'. In consequence, one of the series' writers, Nat Perrin (*qv*), receives credit on *The Big Store* but engaged for the screenplay were three newcomers to the Marxes, Hal Fimberg, Sid Kuller (*qv*) and his partner Ray Golden. As songsmiths-cum-scriptwriters, Kuller and Golden had been closely identified with the Ritz Brothers and this may go some way towards explaining the film's often unsuitable material. A production number, based around the song 'Sing While You Sell', has Groucho joining a group of fashion models with his hair pulled into a quasi-perm and his trousers rolled up; later he joins Harpo in snake-charmer mode and the sequence concludes with the store's entire staff marching in the direction of a lift. The climactic chase, with its reliance on such things as roller skates, undercranking and obvious doubles, is far from the intelligent mayhem associated with the Marx Brothers. As with the gags crafted by Buster Keaton (*qv*) for *At the Circus*, this might have been admirable material for other comedians but simply was not right for the Marxes; one can easily see Harry Ritz mincing along the catwalk with the fashion models, or the club-orientated Ritz trio playing at snake-charming, but when the Marxes engaged in old-fashioned hokum, it was usual for them to do so consciously and satirically, as in Groucho's dance at the beginning of *Horse Feathers* (*qv*). Not that *The Big Store* is without merit; Groucho's wooing of Margaret Dumont (*qv*) is a delight as always, and provides the film's most-quoted gag:

Dumont: I'm afraid after we're married a while, a beautiful young girl will come along, and you'll forget all about me.
Groucho: Don't be silly. I'll write you twice a week.

They first meet when Dumont visits his detective agency, at which Harpo

The Big Store: *A weary Wacky accidentally sets the mechanical beds moving*

works as cook, housekeeper and secretary. Groucho and Harpo seldom worked directly in tandem and this scene works briskly enough: the mechanical contrivances, so inappropriate to the chase sequence, are more effectively channelled when applied to the speedy conversion of kitchen into office. The harp solo is perhaps the most imaginative of its kind, with Harpo's sometimes princely demeanour incarnated within an eighteenth-century costume and drawing-room. Clever matte work enables his mirror reflections on either side to assume individual identities. As Allen Eyles has noted, Harpo's gift for the impossible renders the dream explanation both unnecessary and undesirable. This aside, there is a preponderance of largely dispensable music; a paucity of comedy material is implicit in the presence of no less than two piano items from Chico, though one of them serves posterity by preserving something of the piano switch from *Home Again* (*qv*). That M-G-M considered the music at least as important as the Marxes is suggested by the equal billing of Tony Martin (*qv*). The harp and piano resurface as part of his big number, *Tenement Symphony*. This orchestrated hymn to a melting-pot neighbourhood, reputedly created as a tongue-in-cheek item, is played here with unnerving sincerity and has little to do with Marxian irreverence. The song had its fans at the time (and *still* has them) but both it and the film would have fared better in different company. *The Big Store*'s severest critic (apart from Groucho) is Joe Adamson, who has recoiled at Grover's casual inclination to homicide and the lengthy list of old gags, perhaps the oldest being that in which people assume comic positions after a momentary dousing of the lights. He mentions also a barely-discernible Chico pun, to the effect that it's cheaper to use 'nitrate' ('night rate') when developing a photograph. The age of this joke may be gauged from its use in a magazine cartoon drawn by S.J. Perelman (*qv*) about a decade before, one of a series in which truly ancient or otherwise horrible jokes would be perpetrated with total awareness of their status. Groucho had announced there would be only one more Marx Brothers picture at the time of *Go West*'s release, and his lack of enthusiasm for the project in general - let alone specific gags - permeates a letter written on-set to Arthur Sheekman (*qv*) late in production. Apparently Groucho's dialogue in the fashion-parade scene had fared poorly at a preview, so 'they brought in a little man to write some jokes to replace it - the result will be that these jokes will be six times as unfunny when they reach the screen'. In *The Groucho Letters* this communiqué is dated 23 June 1941, three days after the release date quoted by the contemporary press. A mistake may have occurred in preparing the letter for publication but there is a remote possibility that M-G-M pulled back the film at the last minute, delaying release past the published date. A review in the *Motion Picture Herald* of 21 June was based on

a preview at the Academy Theatre, Inglewood, in which Groucho's lack of enthusiasm was echoed not at all. *The Big Store* was considered 'one of the funniest ever made by the Marx Brothers', its musical elements receiving comparison with those in *A Night at the Opera* (*qv*). The *New York Times* of 27 June, conceding the absence of *Opera*'s invention and the presence of dull stretches, seemed content with the mere presence of the Marxes, 'still the most erratic maniacs this side of bars'. 'In short,' it summed up, '*The Big Store* is of an old Marx Brothers design. But as the last remnant on the counter it's a bargain.' Both reviews displayed total awareness of this as the team's intended farewell, explaining perhaps a willingness to respond with enthusiasm (though it should be noted that, despite its poor reputation, modern audiences still find much amusement in the film). In the UK, the BFI's *Monthly Film Bulletin* ignored this and was altogether more harsh with this 'disappointing' entry. 'Few of the scenes are as funny as they ought to have been,' it was said, 'and some fall down very badly.' Oddly, approval was reserved only for the untypical chase sequence, which for much of the time dispenses with the Marxes altogether.

(See also: Advertising; Armetta, Henry; Cars; Children; Colour; Dumbrille, Douglass; Dumont, Margaret; Gangsters; Grey, Virginia; Harp, the; Letters; Mirrors; Names; *A Night in Casablanca*; O'Brien, Virginia; Piano, the; Puns; Records; Songs; Stage appearances [post-1930]; Stand-ins; Trailers; 'White magic'; Working titles)

BIRTHS

Often overlooked in Marx chronicles is that Chico was not the Marx family's first child. That distinction fell to Manfred Marx, born in 1885 but deceased in infancy. Kyle Crichton makes passing reference to him in his 1951 biography of the team but little further mention was made until late in

the 1970s. Both Hector Arce's *Groucho* and Maxine Marx's *Growing Up With Chico* attribute Manfred's early death to tuberculosis, though Charlotte Chandler quotes Groucho as claiming it was 'a stupid accident'. The former is by far the most likely. Historian Paul G. Wesolowski feels that Groucho was joking when he claimed that Manfred died 'at the ripe old age of three', believing 'three' more effective than 'one' when delivered in anecdotal form. Wesolowski believes also that Manfred lived to be less than a year old, otherwise Harpo would have been next in line and Minnie's favouritism of Chico (as eldest survivor) would not have occurred. This eldest child was commemorated in the youngest, for Zeppo was named Herbert Manfred. Much later, the next three brothers deliberately concealed their true ages, a move dating probably from the commencement of their film work. Chico was born on the 21 March 1887 (neither August nor 1886 as sometimes stated) but claimed 1891; Harpo on 23 November 1888, claiming 1893; and Groucho on 2 October 1890 but admitting to 1895. Gummo was born on 23 October 1892 (some sources quote 1893 or even 1897) and Zeppo on 25 February 1901 (a subject he had become reticent on by the 1950s). All were born in New York and only Groucho was provided with a birth certificate; apparently children born at home were seldom registered unless a doctor assisted with the birth, and the legal requirement to register was not enforced. Acceptance of the middle brothers' bogus dates continued into a 1991 news programme, shown in the London ITV area, commemorating Chico's 'centenary'. Simple arithmetic suggests that, if the 1887 date is accurate (Wesolowski has confirmed it, using the census of 1900), Chico deducted only *four* years from his age instead of the five chosen by his brothers; one might add that when interviewed for *The Marx Brothers Scrapbook* early in 1973, Groucho said that Chico would then have been 87 years old. Groucho had by then owned up to the deception, but many sources perpetuate the myth: Harpo's autobiography quotes 1893 as his birthdate, referring also to Alexander Woollcott (*qv*) as having been six years Harpo's senior; they were in fact separated by less than two years.

(See also: Books; Marx, Minnie; Marx, Sam 'Frenchie'; Names)

BLORE, ERIC (1887-1959)

British actor, recalled in his native country as writer of a Tommy Handley sketch called *The Dis-Orderly Room* (which was performed by Handley and company on the same bill as the Marxes at the London Coliseum in 1922). In American films Blore was best-known for portraying valets, as in some of the Astaire-Rogers musicals or *Swiss Miss* with Laurel & Hardy (*qv*). He plays an English expatriate in the Crosby-Hope *Road to Zanzibar* (1941). Among the more unusual tasks in his long career was voice work in Disney's *Ichabod and Mr Toad*. In the Marxes' *Love Happy* (*qv*) he may be seen as 'Mackinaw', sidekick to detective Groucho.

(See also: Adrian, Iris; Dumbrille, Douglass; Greig, Robert; *On the Mezzanine*)

BOASBERG, AL (1892-1937)

Large, bespectacled comedy writer, often as gagman or script doctor; one of his most renowned sketches is the Burns & Allen classic, *Lambchops*. Like many others, Boasberg started out by selling individual gags to vaudeville comics; his reputation spread rapidly and in time he would write regularly for the top names, including silent and sound films with Buster Keaton (*qv*). Boasberg regularly supplied material for Jack Benny (*qv*) and Bob Hope. He would in addition write for dramatic films, perhaps most notably Tod Browning's bizarre classic *Freaks* (1932). Boasberg acted as gag writer on *A Night at the Opera* and *A Day at the Races* (both *qv*) and was sometimes a

guest at Groucho's home. Boasberg was something of a legendary wit and in his own way as assertive as the Marx Brothers; a now-famous story, told by Arthur Marx in his 1954 *Groucho* biography, has Boasberg prodded for a section of *Opera*'s script, informing Irving Thalberg (*qv*) that he was about to go home, but that the producer could pick it up at his office. Thalberg and the Marxes called at Boasberg's deserted office, where there was no sign of the script; Groucho, aware of the writer's methods, located the script, cut into individual lines and pasted to the ceiling. Once retrieved and reassembled (which took some five hours!), it turned out to be the first draft of the stateroom scene. His experience on *Races* proved turbulent: after insisting on separate credit for the comedy scenes, Boasberg's name was omitted from the film and relegated to an also-ran mention in the *Academy Bulletin*. He then refused to allow even this to be published and finished up placing an ironic trade ad., thanking Sam Wood (*qv*) for his 'clever direction' of Boasberg's 'comedy scenes and dialogue'. Boasberg died suddenly, from a heart attack, on 18 June 1937, only days after the release of *A Day at the Races*. His early death robbed the industry of a major talent; more immediately Groucho and Chico were left without a key witness in a then-current court case, concerning an allegedly pirated radio sketch (see **Radio**). An extensive profile of Boasberg, by Dana A. Snow, was published in the Summer 1987 *Freedonia Gazette* (*qv*).

(See also: Burns, George and Allen, Gracie; Riesner, Charles F. 'Chuck'; Vaudeville)

BOATS, SHIPS

(All films and shows *qv*)
'After fifteen days on the water and six on the boat ...'; thus Groucho's tale of alcoholic seafaring in *Animal Crackers*. The stage sketch *Home Again* is known to have used a prop boat as a special

effect, inherited from its predecessor *Mr Green's Reception*. Both *Monkey Business* and *A Night at the Opera* share the element of placing the Marxes on board ship. The earlier film casts the four brothers as stowaways; the second, made after Zeppo's departure, allows Groucho a ticket but Chico and Harpo remain strictly unpaying guests. At that time the steamship had yet to be supplanted by aircraft as the usual means of crossing the Atlantic, the Marxes' visits of 1922, 1931 and (minus Groucho) 1949 all being made by sea. Groucho, a notoriously poor mariner, was perpetually martyred to seasickness yet still indulged in pleasure trips on boats. In *Horse Feathers* he risks a leisurely trip in a punt but makes sure Thelma Todd (*qv*) does the paddling. There are comparable Venetian-style gondolas in *A Day at the Races*. In *At the Circus* Jardinet is arrested while on a trans-Atlantic liner, and on his release is set adrift on a seaborne bandstand. Two of Groucho's solo films have a nautical tinge: *A Girl in Every Port* places him in the US Navy while *Skidoo* provides him with an aquatic hideout.

(See also: Aircraft; London Palladium, the; Russia; Stage appearances [post-1930])

BOOKS

First of the Marx clan into print was, not surprisingly, Groucho. His first book, *Beds*, was published by Farrar and Rinehart in 1930 and serialized that year in *College Humor*. *Beds* passed into history until revived by Bobbs-Merrill in 1976. For the new edition, Groucho posed for new photos, sharing a bed with various celebrities; in some additional text, he claimed the first edition to be so valuable even *he* couldn't afford it. This was an exaggeration but 1930 copies are indeed scarce. Prior to *Beds*, Groucho had submitted humorous squibs to Franklin P. Adams' *Conning Tower* column and by the mid-1920s was contributing to the infant *New*

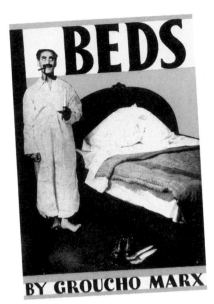

The original 1930 edition of Groucho's first
book, Beds
Michael Pointon Collection

Yorker and other publications. An
invaluable collection of Groucho's
magazine work, from the 1920s to the
1970s, was assembled by Robert S.
Bader in 1993 under the title *Groucho
Marx and Other Short Stories and Tall
Tales* (Faber and Faber). Groucho
tried the book world again in *Many
Happy Returns* (Simon and Schuster
1942), a satire on the tax system. It was
not a success. In 1946 there was a book
of the film *A Night in Casablanca*,
adapted by D.L. Ames. Despite being
published by 'Hollywood Publications
Ltd', it was available only in the UK.
Three years later Groucho's play *Time
For Elizabeth* (*qv*) was published by
Dramatists Play Service, Inc. It seems
surprising that a Marx Brothers
biography did not arrive until their
career as a team was practically over.
Kyle Crichton's *The Marx Brothers*,
published by Doubleday in 1950, was
designed for serialization and
sometimes parts drastic company with
the truth, as when transplanting the
death of Minnie Marx (*qv*) to the early
1930s, at which point the book
concludes without exploring most of
their film work. Although the brothers

were involved in the project, Chico is
said to have contemplated legal action,
not having approved the final text. On
the plus side, Crichton's book records
interesting stories of their upbringing
and early stage material. Heinemann
published a British edition in 1951. A
book by Groucho's son, Arthur,
appeared in 1954. Called *Life With
Groucho*, it contains footnotes
ostensibly by its subject but
subsequently revealed as Arthur's own
work. It was published in the USA by
Simon and Schuster and in Britain
(simply as *Groucho*) by Victor
Gollancz. There have been subsequent
paperback editions. Groucho returned
to the field in 1959 with his own
memoir, *Groucho and Me*. Groucho
had an interest in its US publishers,
Bernard Geis Associates; again, its
British counterpart was published by
Gollancz. There have been translations
into German and French. Latter-day
copies - in Columbus' 'Lively Arts'
series and most recently from Virgin -
include a foreword taken from a
contemporary review by James
Thurber. Harpo's 1961 'autobiography'
was put down for him by Rowland
Barber; *Harpo Speaks!* had the same
US and UK publishers as *Groucho and
Me* and in Britain was trailed by
extracts in the *Sunday Telegraph*.
Harpo Speaks! became a rarity until
reprinted by Robson Books in 1976 and
as a Coronet paperback two years later.
Sadly, the paperback omits the original
drawings by Susan Marx. There have
been at least two French editions. In
America, Limelight reprinted the book
in 1985 and a new UK edition has since
appeared from Virgin. Groucho's next,
Memoirs of a Mangy Lover, was
published in America by Bernard Geis
in 1963. There was no UK edition until
the Futura paperback of 1975, but
copies of an American softback (from
Mayflower) were obtainable during the
1960s. Several English-language
paperbacks have surfaced over the
years; the book has also been rendered
into Spanish, French and German. In
1966 the Osterreichisches

Filmmuseum published Raymond
Durgnat's *The Marx Brothers*, to
coincide with a Vienna film festival
attended by Groucho. The same year
brought a British work, Allen Eyles'
*The Marx Brothers: Their World of
Comedy*, still one of the more
important studies. The original was
published by Zwemmer/A.S. Barnes
and has been much reprinted since. In
1967 Arthur Sheekman (*qv*) edited
Groucho's correspondence into *The
Groucho Letters* (Simon and Schuster).
The Library of Congress had requested
Groucho's papers for preservation in
1964 and this collection was a direct
result. Michael Joseph produced a UK
edition in 1968 and there have again
been several paperbacks plus
translations into French and German.
Again from 1968 is *The Marx Brothers
at the Movies* by Paul D. Zimmerman
and Burt Goldblatt, a detailed
examination of all the Marx films. The
original US edition was by Putnam and
the many reprints include a Japanese
edition. In 1971 Darien House
published *Why a Duck?*, edited by
Richard J. Anobile, consisting of frame
enlargements, stills and dialogue
extracts from all the Paramount films
except *Animal Crackers* and each of
their M-G-M releases. Groucho
supplied an introduction. Studio Vista
published the 1972 UK edition. Pre-
and post-filming scripts for *A Night at
the Opera* and *A Day at the Races* were
published by Viking (US) and Lorrimer
(UK) during 1972. From the same year
is a script/transcript volume of *Monkey
Business* and *Duck Soup* (both *qv*),
again from Lorrimer in Britain and
Simon and Schuster in the USA. (A
subsequent Faber and Faber
paperback combines these with *Races*.)
Still another 1972 book is Arthur
Marx's *Son of Groucho* (pub. David
McKay). This was published in Britain
the following year by Peter Owen. 1973
also brought a very important Marx
Brothers history, Joe Adamson's
*Groucho, Harpo, Chico and Sometimes
Zeppo*. The title conveys something of
its tongue-in-cheek style (it is subtitled

'A History of the Marx Brothers and a Satire On the Rest of the World'). As stated in the Winter 1989 *Freedonia Gazette* (*qv*), this book broke new ground with its extensive consultation of contemporary sources and surviving colleagues, in which respect it differs significantly from earlier memoirs dependent on individual recollection. One of its strengths is a detailed production history of each film, aided by access to scripts in their various draft forms. It was first published by Simon and Schuster in the US and W.H. Allen in the UK. The most commonplace British edition is a Coronet paperback of 1974. Adamson's work underwent slight revision for a UK reprint around 1989 and remains one of the key references. Later in 1973 saw another Anobile work, credited as by 'Groucho Marx and Richard J. Anobile'. This was *The Marx Brothers Scrapbook*, based upon interviews mostly with Groucho but also including Gummo, Zeppo, Susan Marx, Morrie Ryskind (*qv*), Nat Perrin (*qv*), and others. Many illustrations derive from Groucho's collection and are mostly archival treasures; however, Groucho was upset by the transcription method applied to his interviews (containing the strongest of language) and tried, unsuccessfully, to prevent publication. The *Freedonia Gazette* has commented on mis-transcriptions in the interviews. The first American copies, from Darien House, were followed by a large-format US paperback from Grosset and Dunlap and a UK edition from W.H. Allen. Other softbacks, of varying sizes, have appeared since. Another Anobile book was published by Darien House in 1974, *Hooray For Captain Spaulding!* presenting *Animal Crackers* (*qv*) by the same method as *Why a Duck?* The film had been unobtainable for the earlier book, owing to its legal stalemate. In 1975 William Wolf's examination of the films, *The Marx Brothers*, was published in New York by Pyramid Communications. An Italian translation saw print three years later. Groucho's

last books, compiled with the assistance of Hector Arce, appeared in 1976. As its title implies, *The Secret Word is Groucho* leans heavily towards *You Bet Your Life* (*qv*); it was first published by G.P. Putnam's Sons and, in paperback, Berkley Medallion. *The Groucho Phile* is the comedian's own equivalent to the *Scrapbook* and is one of the best sources of rare illustrations and information. The book was published in the USA by Bobbs-Merrill (1976) and Wallaby Books (1977); there followed UK editions from W.H. Allen in 1978 and Galahad Books a year later. Doubleday published Charlotte Chandler's *Hello, I Must Be Going: Groucho and His Friends* in 1978. A UK edition, from Robson, dates from 1979. There have been a number of softback editions. Important though *The Groucho Phile* was, his assistant, Hector Arce, wrote perhaps the most notable Groucho biography to date. *Groucho* is a truly thorough work, thanks to Arce's persistence and that of his research assistant, Paul G. Wesolowski of the *Freedonia Gazette*. G.P. Putnam's Sons published the original hardback of late 1978, many copies of which were destroyed in a flood. Sadly, Arce died soon after Perigree's softcover edition appeared in 1980. Difficult to find (at least in Britain), Arce's exemplary work deserves a wider audience. In the *Scrapbook*, Gummo was quoted as lamenting the absence of a Chico biography. The gap was filled in 1980 by Maxine Marx's *Growing Up With Chico*, a loving but objective account of her father's life. Prentice-Hall published the original; a 1986 Limelight paperback followed. Arthur Marx's *My Life with Groucho: a Son's Eye View* was published in the UK by Robson in 1988. The same year brought the scripts of *Flywheel, Shyster and Flywheel* (*qv*), edited by Michael Barson. This volume was published by Pantheon in the USA and by Chatto and Windus in Britain. 1992 saw Allen Eyles' new work on the team, *The Complete Films of the Marx*

Brothers (Citadel) and another British study, Ronald Bergan's *The Life and Times of the Marx Brothers* (Green Wood). Also from 1992 is *Love, Groucho* (Faber and Faber), a collection of his correspondence to his daughter, Miriam Marx Allen, who also edited the book. Since then there has been Wes Gehring's *The Marx Brothers: a Bio-Bibliography* (Greenwood Press). The recollections of Groucho's chef (!) appeared in a second book bearing the title *The Secret Word is Groucho*. The Marx Brothers have been profiled within many other works, such as Leonard Maltin's *Movie Comedy Teams*. Among the more peripheral items is a novel published in 1989, Ellen Conford's *Genie with the Light Blue Hair*. The story presents a Groucho-like genie, whose resemblance becomes all the more apparent in the cover illustration.

(See also: Appendix 1; Children; Letters; Marriages)

BOXING
See: Fighting; *On the Mezzanine*

BRECHER, IRVING (b. 1914)
Screenwriter for two Marx Brothers films, *At the Circus* and *Go West* (both *qv*). Groucho thought rather less of these films than he did Brecher, who became a good friend. Originally a journalist, Brecher had written for radio before moving into the film world in 1937; his more notable credits include *Meet Me in St. Louis* (1944) and *Bye-Bye Birdie* (1963). Among many projects in between were *The Life of Riley*, a proposed radio series for Groucho which became instead a hit for William Bendix (*qv*) on radio, TV and film. One of Brecher's oddest duties was deputizing for Groucho when the comedian was absent from a stills session. There was considerable resemblance between the two and the age gap was less apparent beneath the greasepaint. This is said to have happened during *Go West*, but none of the stills betray such an imposter; the

Irving Brecher *is said to have deputized for Groucho at a* Go West *stills session. This shot from* At the Circus *seems a likelier candidate*

author's guess is that the alleged switch took place instead on *At the Circus*, and that a much-reprinted Marx portrait *(illustrated)* is actually Chico, Harpo and Irvo.

(See also: Clubs; Documentaries; Home movies; Impersonators; Letters)

BREESE, EDMUND (1871-1936)

Gruff-looking character actor, as in *Duck Soup* (*qv*), in which he plays 'Zander'. Many others, such as *All Quiet On the Western Front* (1930), Capra's *Platinum Blonde* (1931) and *Broadway Bill* (1934), the 1934 *Treasure Island* and *International House* (1933) with W.C. Fields and Burns and Allen.

(See also: Burke, James; Burns, George and Allen, Gracie; Fields, W.C.)

BRICE, FANNY

See: Radio; Vaudeville

BURKE, JAMES (1886-1968)

New York-born of Irish parentage, and frequently cast as a policeman, James Burke was another of the many ex-vaudevillians to work with the Marxes. Long after touring in a double-act with his wife, Burke was cast as John Carter, villain of *At the Circus* (*qv*). Among his many film appearances from the early 1930s on are *Treasure Island* (1934), Fields' *The Man On the Flying Trapeze* (1935), the 1938 *Dawn Patrol*, Jack Benny's *Buck Benny Rides Again* (1940) and *The Horn Blows at Midnight* (1945), and many others into the 1960s.

(See also: Benny, Jack; Breese, Edmund; Dumont, Margaret; Fields, W.C.; Gangsters)

BURNS, GEORGE (1896-1996) and ALLEN, GRACIE (1904 or 1906-64)

A top double-act, from vaudeville (*qv*), and one of show business' great married couples. George - initially the comic - switched to working as feed on discovering the scatterbrained Gracie character was getting bigger laughs from the straight lines. Their *Burns and Allen* radio show was that which prompted the BBC to try its first sitcom (*Band Waggon*) in 1938; they later found equal success in TV until poor health forced Gracie Allen's retirement. From the early 1960s, George Burns worked effectively as a single, achieving near-legendary status, and not merely for longevity. Groucho met Gracie before her marriage to George, but put aside his romantic interest owing to her Roman Catholicism (though none of Groucho's three wives were of the Jewish faith). Burns had no such qualms and frequently joked about her being his 'greatest talent'. As a couple, George and Gracie socialized frequently with Harpo and Susan Marx, would visit for holidays and had unofficial Uncle and Aunt status with the children. *Harpo Speaks!* sometimes seems to borrow from Burns' extensive knowledge of vaudeville history. In *Honolulu*, a 1939 film directed by Edward Buzzell (*qv*), Gracie was surrounded by a quartet of bogus Marxes in the form of a vocal group called 'The King's Men'.

(See also: Children; Impersonators; Marriages; Religion)

George Burns and Gracie Allen *were friends of the Marx Brothers from vaudeville days. Say goodnight, Gracie!*

BURR, RAYMOND (1917-93)

Heavyweight Canadian actor, from the stage and radio, who had played in a few minor films before landing a rôle in *another* minor film, *Love Happy* (*qv*). He is one of the Zoto brothers, henchmen who, at the request of Madame Egilichi, rough up Harpo; quite out of keeping with Burr's subsequent TV eminence as *Perry Mason* and *Ironside*.

(See also: Gordon, Bruce)

BUSINESSES

Prior to joining the army, Gummo had already prepared to leave the Marx Brothers by exploring the world of cardboard box manufacturing. After World War One, he continued in this line but settled instead in the dress business. During the 1930s he quit and joined Zeppo as an agent. Zeppo had made real estate dealings from the 1920s onwards, continuing in this, the agency business and other concerns for years after. Zeppo's company, Marman Products, manufactured the clamping devices for the first atomic raids over Japan in 1945; perhaps more positively, he was involved in the development of a wristwatch from which an alarm would sound if the wearer's heartbeat should fluctuate. Another of Zeppo's involvements was in the growing of fruit crops, in which Harpo also had an interest. For much of the team's Hollywood career they maintained an office run for them by one Rachel Linden, a secretary poached from Herman Mankiewicz (*qv*).

(See also: Agents; Marx Brothers, Inc.)

BUZZELL, EDWARD (1897-1985)

Originally in vaudeville (*qv*) with Gus Edwards (as were variously Groucho, George Jessel and Eddie Cantor [*qv*]), Edward Buzzell shared bills with the Marxes during the 'Teens and, like them, became a comedy star in 1920s Broadway shows (*Sweetheart Time*, *The Gingham Girl*); Buzzell thus knew the Marx Brothers as an exact contemporary. His career switch to the movies (the first of them silent, as in *Midnight Life*, *Little Johnny Jones*) saw him as actor, then actor-director (notably in a series of Vitaphone shorts) then full-time director, starting with Columbia's *The Big Time* (1932). Buzzell was directing for M-G-M (*qv*) from 1938, in which capacity he was reunited with the Marxes for *At the Circus* and *Go West* (both *qv*). Both Joe Adamson and Hector Arce have chronicled the erratic rapport between director and stars, suggesting their contemporaneous status to be incidental. Chiefly, Buzzell wanted them to 'act', for which function Groucho recommended the team's stand-ins. (In a subsequent letter to his daughter, Miriam, Groucho wrote that 'Buzzell tried to graft his own personality on us and it just didn't work'.) Buzzell tried to discipline the comedians by refusing to laugh at any on-set jokes they would make, as when Chico, instructed to look at Harpo rather than the camera, retorted that he'd sooner look at the camera. This was one way to get the picture completed but probably muted any spontaneity in the performances. At the end of *At the Circus* Buzzell took a break in Europe, though not before receiving a handsome send-off from the Marxes. He was treated to a spectacular evening, beginning at the Trocadero (from which, according to Buzzell, the Marxes 'stormed out in a huff'), stopping for soup at tables on the sidewalk before departing for a café, thence to a wrestling ring where, surrounded by ferocious grapplers, they attempted to eat dessert. Final stop was a mortuary, where coffee and cakes were served. Had this been organized by anyone else, the victim would have taken the hint and exited from their company forever; with the Marxes, however, such effort suggests at least a measure of respect and probably even affection (albeit for someone considered worthy of taking down a peg), if only in recognition of his background. Buzzell was later among the interviewees for the BBC *Hollywood Greats* profile of Groucho. Perhaps it was in remembrance of such terse observations that Buzzell told the programme 'Groucho was a vitriolic son-of-a-gun... oh, I liked him, you couldn't help liking him, but you feared him, you know; he had a vitriolic tongue and you stayed away from him if you could'. Buzzell's long list of directing credits includes *Virtue* (1932), *Cross Country Cruise* (1934), *Honolulu* (1939), *Best Foot Forward* (a 1943 film starring Lucille Ball [*qv*] and co-scripted by Irving Brecher [*qv*]), 1943's *The Youngest Profession* (see also **John Carroll** and **George Oppenheimer**), *Keep Your Powder Dry* (1945), *Three Wise Fools* (1946), *Easy to Wed* (1946, again with Lucille Ball in the cast), *Song of the Thin Man* (1947), the 1949 Esther Williams vehicle *Neptune's Daughter*, *Confidentially Connie* (1953) and 1955's *Ain't Misbehavin'*, which he also co-scripted. Buzzell also received director and co-writer credits on his final film, *Mary Had a Little* (1961), produced in England.

(See also: Burns, George and Allen, Gracie; Children; Cummings, Jack; Documentaries; Impersonators; Letters; Practical jokes; Rumann, Siegfried)

*Groucho manoeuvres **Louis Calhern** into an international incident: Duck Soup*

C

CALHERN, LOUIS (1895-1956)

Suave New York-born actor, equally famous in theatre as on screen; his best-known role is as Judge Oliver Wendell Holmes in both the stage production and 1950 film version of *The Magnificent Yankee*, the latter of which brought him an Oscar nomination for Best Actor. Calhern (real name Carl Vogt) is recalled by Marx *aficionados* as 'Trentino', villain of *Duck Soup* (*qv*). His film career dates back to silents of the early 1920s; among numerous talkies are 1932's *Night After Night* (Mae West's film debut), *20,000 Years in Sing Sing* (1932), Wheeler & Woolsey's *Diplomaniacs* (1933), *The Life of Emile Zola* (1936), Danny Kaye's first feature *Up in Arms* (1944), Irving Berlin's *Annie Get Your Gun* (1950), *The Asphalt Jungle* (1950), *Executive Suite* (1954) and *High Society* (1956).

(See also: Awards; Berlin, Irving)

CANTOR, EDDIE (1892-1964)

Large-eyed, frequently *risqué* singing comedian and contemporary of the Marx Brothers. Eddie Cantor was, like Groucho and so many others, a former member of Gus Edwards' juvenile acts; he made the transition from vaudeville (*qv*) to 'legitimate' musical comedy before the Marx Brothers, becoming a headliner in the *Ziegfeld Follies* from 1917. Aside from being a long-time friend, Cantor worked in parallel with the Marxes, often employing the same writers and directors. An early talkie appearance, Ziegfeld's *Glorifying the American Girl* (1929), actually glorifies Mary Eaton (*qv*) in particular but also includes Cantor's sketch with Louis Sorin (*qv*). When *Palmy Days* (1931) opened in New York, Groucho joined Cantor on stage but was chased off after repeatedly interrupting his host. Cantor was married to Ida Tobias in 1914 and stayed that way. A Cantor motif was ostensibly to quote his wife in order to convey an opinion; hence the publicity drawing for *A Night at the Opera* (*qv*) in which he is supposed to say 'The Marx Bros. are three of our foremost comedians ... my wife can tell you the name of the fourth.' (Among the other caricatures are Jack Benny (*qv*) and Stan Laurel, the latter of whom, speech balloon notwithstanding, was *not* a fan of the Marxes.) Later on, Groucho and Eddie Cantor expressed mutual compliments for their respective memoirs, though Cantor genially contradicted a claim in *Groucho and Me*, to the effect that he had given Groucho a disastrous Stock Market tip immediately prior to the Crash of '29.

(See also: Books; Hall, Ruth; *I'll Say She Is!*; Insomnia; Kaufman, George S.;

Laurel & Hardy; McCarey, Leo; Paintings; Perrin, Nat; Ruby, Harry; Ryskind, Morrie; Sheekman, Arthur)

CARICATURES

(Marx Brothers films and shows *qv*)
The Marx Brothers' stylized images have long proved irresistible to caricaturists. Even in vaudeville (*qv*) they were a pet subject of newspaper cartoonists, who lovingly portrayed Groucho's eccentric stance, Harpo's wild grin or Chico's work at the piano. Promotional drawings for their stage shows would sometimes eschew caricature for comparative realism, but press kits for their films worldwide are often rich in imaginative graphics. Among promotional material for

Caricatures: *from the Danish pressbook for*
A Day at the Races
The Freedonia Gazette

A Day at the Races was a strip-cartoon sequence presenting selected gags, with 'links' provided by Metro's own 'Leo the Lion'. It is perhaps indicative of their surreal approach that among their writers was newspaper cartoonist Will B. Johnstone (*qv*). It is said that another cartoonist, one J. Carver Pusey, was hired to create sight-gags for Harpo in *Monkey Business*. Frank Tashlin (*qv*), himself an experienced cartoonist, contributed to both *A Night*

in Casablanca and *Love Happy*. Outside of material linked directly to their work, the Marxes have frequently been depicted by the world's top-flight cartoonists. Al Hirshfeld, possibly *the* name among American caricaturists, represented them on occasion, as when depicting them amid the Comedians' Round Table at Hillcrest or in giving Harpo pride of place within a group portrait of Alexander Woollcott's crowd of friends. Also from New York's literati was James Thurber, who in March 1937 provided caricatures of the Marxes (and some humorous text) to accompany Teet Carle's *Stage* article, 'Laughing Stock: Common or Preferred'. Referring as it did to *A Day at the Races*, the piece also required a drawing of a broken-down horse. Oddly, by the time of *The Marx Brothers Scrapbook* in 1973, Thurber's Groucho seemed to have been transferred to the horse's rear end, from which (it was claimed) Groucho had mostly erased it. The two drawings are absolutely separate in the 1989 Thurber anthology *Collecting Himself* and one can only assume that Thurber had produced a further, combined, copy for Groucho in a moment of mischief. Thurber's comments on *Groucho and Me* (from the *New York Herald Book Review* of 13 September 1959) serve as foreword to modern-day editions of the book itself. Not that the Groucho-Thurber relationship was necessarily smooth: although some of their correspondence appears in *The Groucho Letters*, the later *Groucho Phile* mentions Thurber once getting drunk at a party and trying to hit Groucho with a beer bottle. The incident took place at the home of a quite different cartoonist, Rube Goldberg, another of Groucho's long-time friends. Caricatures of the Marxes can appear in unlikely contexts, as in a tongue-in-cheek 'suicide attack' by the Marxes in one of *2000 AD*'s 'Judge Dredd' stories. When *Mad* published a parody of the 1950s TV cop show *Dragnet* (retitled 'Dragged Net'), Harpo was seen among the musicians

who were on hand to provide the frequently-heard dramatic chords. One of *Mad*'s paperback anthologies of the 1950s, *The Brothers Mad*, was a nod towards a then-current movie, *The Brothers Karamazov*, bearing a cover illustration to match; once its topicality had eroded, later editions substituted a new painting in which Alfred E. Neuman impersonates Groucho, Harpo and Chico. A 1967 experiment from DC Comics, *The Maniaks*, based a story around real-life comedian Woody Allen and incorporated a Hackenbush-like 'play doctor', complete with greasepaint moustache. A pastiche Marx Brothers comedy, entitled 'A Night at Motel 6', appeared in a 1970s underground comic called *Middle Class Fantasies*. Again from the world of underground comics is Gilbert Shelton's *Furry Freak Brothers*, one episode of which saw 'Freewheelin' Franklin' masquerading as 'Groucho Marx, Jr'. Newspaper cartoonists continue to employ caricatures of the team as appropriate; in 1976 some of America's better-known strips inserted Groucho references to coincide with the comedian's birthday, a move prompted by Marx *aficionado* Paul G. Wesolowski. In 1984 London's Victoria & Albert Museum commissioned writer-actor-cartoonist William Rushton to produce a series of drawings. The Marxes were not within Rushton's study of various film stars but found themselves, appropriately, among numerous gatecrashers at the opening of the Great Exhibition of 1851; others included Mae West, Harold Wilson, Charles de Gaulle and a teddy bear-carrying Winston Churchill. The entire set of colour illustrations saw publication as *Great Moments of History*. More recently, a comedy troupe, The Reduced Shakespeare Company, has used a Grouchoesque version of the Bard as its logo.

(See also: Animation; Books; Characters; Clubs; Letters; M-G-M; Names; Paintings; Piano, the; Temple, Shirley; Woollcott, Alexander)

CARLISLE, KITTY (b. 1915)
Actress and singer who married playwright Moss Hart, a frequent collaborator of George S. Kaufman (*qv*). Kitty Carlisle plays Rosa, female romantic lead in *A Night at the Opera* (*qv*). Allan Jones (*qv*), when interviewed in later years, recalled the two of them being hired as singers but becoming justly outraged when the studio wanted them to mime to Metropolitan opera singers for their duet from *Il Trovatore*. It was decided instead to let them record it, allowing producer Irving Thalberg (*qv*) to choose his favourite; Thalberg chose the Carlisle-Jones recording. In the Discovery Channel's 1993 *Biography* programme about Groucho, she recalled having been promised a chance to sing opera seriously in the film, and therefore decided to 'go slumming'. 'Little did I know I was making a classic,' she said. On the same occasion she admitted having been nervous of meeting the Marxes, being an insecure newcomer with foreknowledge of the team's wild reputation; she was instead surprised by their considerable charm. Among

Kitty Carlisle, leading lady of A Night at the Opera

Miss Carlisle's other, comparatively infrequent films are *Murder at the Vanities*, *Here Is My Heart* (both 1934) and *Hollywood Canteen* (1943).

(See also: Documentaries; Guest appearances; *Man Who Came To Dinner, the*; Practical jokes)

THE CARNEGIE HALL CONCERT
In speaking of Groucho's 1972 stage show, known officially as *An Evening with Groucho*, Marx admirers generally refer to 'The Carnegie Hall Concert'. This is a slight misnomer, as he actually performed *three* such concerts, the first of which took place at New York's Carnegie Hall in May 1972, the others following in San Francisco (August) and Los Angeles (December). The double album of 'Evening with Groucho' was compiled from the first two shows. Accompanying Groucho was pianist Marvin Hamlisch, shortly before his worldwide success with *The Sting*'s movie score. Also participating (briefly) was Erin Fleming (*qv*). Groucho's repertoire encompassed

Groucho packs 'em in at **The Carnegie Hall Concert**

most of his familiar songs, plus a selection of forgotten ditties from vaudeville days. Reminiscences varied between his extreme youth and movie heyday, offering in short a capsule history of the man, before a live audience.

(See also: Records; Religion; Songs; Video releases)

CARROLL, JOHN (1907-79)
Actor, singer and producer, usually in leading man roles, as per his Terry Turner in *Go West* (*qv*). Among other films are *Susan and God* (1940), the Abbott & Costello remake of *Rio Rita* (1942), *Flying Tigers* (1943), *The Youngest Profession* (1943), *The Flame* (1948) and *The Plunderers of Painted Flats* (1959).

(See also: Buzzell, Edward; Miller, David; Oppenheimer, George; Trailers)

CAVETT, DICK
See: Documentaries; Television

CEELEY, LEONARD
See: *A Day at the Races*

CARS
(Marx Brothers films and shows *qv*)
It was natural for the Marxes to acquire

cars once they had a reasonable income. Zeppo, a skilled mechanic (he had worked at Ford's prior to joining the act) would tune up and similarly maintain the family's cars. On one occasion he took part in a 6 a.m. motor race with Phil Berg at Muroc Dry Lake. The brothers had originally ridden motorcycles (shades of 'His Excellency's Car' in *Duck Soup*!) but Groucho and Gummo finally pooled their resources in an ageing Chalmers, with a top speed of 25 m.p.h. and non-functional brakes. The Marxes were then living in Chicago and the Chalmers provided a means of dating two girls from across town. Coincidentally, the car would break down every time Zeppo had a date, and it became obvious he was sabotaging it for his own use. He finally bought the car from his brothers and rented it to them as required. Groucho subsequently invested in an unsteady Scripps-Booth, another of the long-forgotten luminaries of the motoring world. When his female guest tried to steady herself on the passenger door, it flew open and permitted the unfortunate woman to land in a mud puddle. Even during its pre-Broadway run, the Marxes' revue *I'll Say She Is!* brought a sufficient boost in income for Groucho to invest in a brand new car. A pristine Studebaker was delivered during a performance at the Walnut Street Theatre in Philadelphia and Groucho was unable to resist a spin during intermission. The journey took Groucho into some of Philadelphia's narrow, eighteenth-century streets, where he became caught in a traffic jam. Forced to abandon the vehicle and return to the theatre, he was in full costume and thus presented an interesting spectacle when intercepted by a cop. Groucho explained who he was and received a police escort - running - just in time to make his entrance. Returning to the scene, he found the car had gone; it was recovered four weeks later. Groucho claimed to have been in his Napoleon costume when out driving, but

historian Paul Wesolowski points out that there would have been no intermission prior to that sketch, and Groucho was more likely to have been in Fairy Godmother garb for the 'Cinderella Backwards' routine, which opened Act Two. In telling the act he did on chat shows (and in *Groucho and Me*) Groucho probably had the Napoleon outfit more suited to the accepted view of a public lunacy - a tutu and tiara, albeit more difficult to describe, would run it a close second. Once established on Broadway, each of the comedians bought new cars, though Chico's Cadillac was paid for by instalments (Groucho paid cash for one later on). Cars sometimes contribute to their on-screen humour. In *Horse Feathers* Groucho explains how he usually goes out with two women at once: 'Particularly in an automobile; I hate to see a girl walk home alone'. Both *Monkey Business* and *At the Circus* feature cab drivers with no hope of obtaining the fare: 'Eighteen-seventy-five' demands a cabbie in the latter film. 'That's what I thought,' replies Groucho, 'the 1940 models run much smoother'. Chico runs the

'Yellow Camel Company' in *A Night in Casablanca*, a flesh and blood alternative to the truck commandeered towards the film's conclusion. Harpo is Groucho's chauffeur in *The Big Store*, ferrying him in a ramshackle vehicle bearing a notice on the back, commemorating Admiral Dewey's triumph in Manila. Detailed elsewhere is surviving footage of Groucho and Harpo in a miniature car race (see **Newsreels**). By the time of *You Bet Your Life* (*qv*), Groucho would receive a complimentary auto from his sponsor - though he was once chided by a member of the public for driving a rival company's car!

(See also: Advertising; Laurel & Hardy; Policemen; Women)

CENSORSHIP
(Marx Brothers films *qv*)
'There must be some way I can get that money back without getting in trouble with the Hays Office'; Groucho's straight-to-camera line in *At the Circus*, after Eve Arden (*qv*) has concealed a stolen wallet in her bosom. The Hays Office was American films'

in-house censorship body, which after 1934 acquired even greater power following the introduction of its infamous Production Code which, by the way, took more than thirty years to overthrow. One of the things that may not have endeared the Marxes to Louis B. Mayer may have been Harpo's decision to chase a scantily-clad stripper around his office, just as the movie mogul was entertaining Hays in person. (There is another joky reference to the Hays Office in Groucho's legendary correspondence with Warners over *A Night in Casablanca*.) As noted in the play entry for *Cocoanuts*, the less tolerant moral standards of film required a toning-down of material, even if a degree of laxity prevailed in the earlier 1930s. *Animal Crackers* has some decidedly *risqué* gags but viewers will notice a severe jump-cut during the song *Hooray For Captain Spaulding*, deleting a line in which Spaulding, referring to Mrs Rittenhouse, says he thinks he'll 'try to make her'. A 1988 book, *The Censorship Papers* by Gerald Gardner, details which cuts were requested (and which were actually made) from *Monkey Business*, *A Night at the Opera* and *A Day at the Races*. The AFI Catalog entry for *Races* cites material from the Producer's Corporation of America (housed at the AMPAS library), to the effect that certain cuts were requested from the script: among them were scenes of underwear hanging on a line; Groucho in effeminate pose; shots of hypodermic needles and a disrobed nurse (the latter of which seems to have been retained); and a choking scene. Groucho recalled a line from *Opera* that got through but was systematically removed in most States, when Margaret Dumont (*qv*) asked 'Are you sure you have everything, Otis?' to which he replied 'I've never had any complaints yet'. One of Harpo's tattoos in *Duck Soup* shows a live dog inside a drawing of a kennel, but Joe Adamson records this as substitution for a censored idea,

showing an outhouse from which an arm would appear to close the door. There is an out-takes reel from Groucho's TV show *You Bet Your Life* (*qv*), preserving some moments that American TV would not permit at that time *(requiring network censorship in editing).*

(see also: Horse Feathers; Deleted Scenes; Tattoos)

CARTOONS / COMIC STRIPS
See: Caricatures

CHAPLIN, CHARLIE (1889-1977)

Eventually the best-known individual in film, Charlie Chaplin was still a comparative unknown when he first met Groucho. The occasion was recalled by Groucho in his various books and, earlier, in a November 1935 interview with journalist Edward Lawrence. Chaplin was touring North America on the Sullivan-Considine circuit with the Fred Karno troupe, whose engagement at Winnipeg coincided with a three-hour stopover for the Marxes, then playing the Pantages time *en route* to the West Coast. According to Chaplin biographer David Robinson, the Karno troupe played Winnipeg for the week of 4 August 1913. Groucho called at the theatre to watch a friend's act, but was impressed above all by Chaplin. Groucho recalled him in a sketch called *A Night at the Club* (a.k.a. *A Night in a London Club*), a seeming hybrid of two other Karno skits, *The Wow-Wows* and *Mumming Birds*, the latter known to American audiences as *A Night in an English Music-Hall*. Groucho recalled Chaplin playing a drunken heckler, spitting crackers at a female vocalist. After the crackers, the unfortunate woman was pelted with oranges, one of which knocked the pianist from his chair. Visiting Chaplin backstage, Groucho noted both the dingy dressing-room (reeking of make-up) and that Chaplin had only one shirt, which would be washed and immediately re-worn, with any interim dirt concealed by a wide, flowing tie. (One might add that Chaplin's Karno salary was actually quite good, but the

man's eccentricity and intermittent frugality were by then well established). Groucho returned to the freezing railroad depot and attempted to convey his enthusiasm for 'the greatest fellow I've ever seen on the stage' with an impromptu impersonation; his chilled contemporaries took no notice. This account, from the 1935 interview, is somewhat at odds with that in the much later *Groucho and Me*. This version suggests the presence of all four brothers during the backstage visit, after Groucho had persuaded them to see Chaplin at a subsequent engagement in Vancouver. Harpo's memoirs, by his own admission fragmented, make no mention of this early meeting and detail only a profound admiration for Chaplin's short film comedies of the mid-'Teens; Chico's daughter Maxine has told a childhood story of being placed on Chaplin's lap during a train journey, but this must date from a much later meeting (Maxine was born after Chaplin's success in films). Maxine relates a tale of Chaplin attending the Marxes' show and baiting his friends by reading a newspaper throughout; their revenge was taken by sending a quartet of stern-looking rabbis to see Chaplin, who took them to be the Marxes in disguise (the serious-minded clergymen did not wait for the act to finish). Whatever the precise details, it is known that Groucho and Chaplin socialized whenever their vaudeville itineraries coincided. One night in Salt Lake City they visited a brothel, a not uncommon activity for young vaudevillians. Chaplin, a shy youth, partook of the evening's social aspect but not its inevitable conclusion, preferring to play with the madam's dog. On leaving the premises, he and Groucho lined up a trio of dustbins, competing for small change in a game of leapfrog. By the time of his acquaintance with Groucho, Chaplin had received an offer to appear in Mack Sennett's Keystone comedies. He had accepted but at one point called Groucho to express misgivings. Groucho assured him of the wisdom in taking the job. By the time of their next meeting, some five years later, Chaplin had become the biggest star in films. Groucho noticed a marked increase in Chaplin's activities with women and an altogether less spartan lifestyle; when visiting the Chaplin home he was greeted by an English butler and served food on gold plates. Groucho later contrasted this with the days when they would play dice for penny stakes, 'and the fellow who won fifty cents was considered a financier'. The two comedians would continue to associate in various ways over the years, as when Chaplin allowed his name on a personal endorsement of *I'll Say She Is!* (*qv*). News film exists of an early 1930s tennis match intended as a Britain v. America challenge, with Chaplin partnered by Fred Perry and Groucho by Ellesworth Vines. Serious attempts to pursue the game vanished as Groucho spread out a picnic on the court, in addition to taking to his sleeping bag. At least two sources claim Chaplin to have been unamused by this spectacle, but if so his anger was carefully circumvented in the newsreel coverage. Cordiality is suggested further by an interview for TV's *Hy Gardner Show* in 1961, in which Groucho recalled this as the occasion when Chaplin had told him 'I wish I could speak on the screen as well as you'; a tribute from the screen's most celebrated mime to perhaps its most accomplished talker. On another occasion they discovered themselves sitting back-to-back in a top Hollywood restaurant, comparing the paranoia that consistently plagued them both: 'There we were,' said Groucho, 'two neurotics sitting and talking, completely terrified about life and their careers! You would think that by now Chaplin would be convinced that he had talent. But he was just as scared as he had been in the old days, when he came to me and asked my advice.' Groucho was among those to imply public support for Chaplin when he needed it. Chaplin's

Monsieur Verdoux (1947) alienated many critics and some of his audience (in the US), partly because of some recent bad press and, above all, for his change of image. A press release for Groucho's contemporary film, *Copacabana* (*qv*), compares his own amended persona to that of Chaplin: 'There's definite excitement in changing your role, and I know that's why Charlie Chaplin changed his routine into the stylish boulevardier stuff [in *Monsieur Verdoux*] ... I can just feel for Chaplin. How he must have wearied of those turned up shoes, that derby hat, that cane, that shuffle. It finally irritated him so much that he just had to switch roles in self defence.' There may well have been a secondary motive to these comments, given that both films were released by United Artists (*qv*). Contact became sparse after Chaplin's exile from the United States, though Groucho sent him an inscribed copy of *The Groucho Letters*. The octogenarian friends were able to compare notes when Chaplin returned to America to collect his Oscar in 1972. Chaplin's advice was to 'keep warm', which Groucho took both as sound sense and measure of Chaplin's slightly greater experience, being eighteen months his senior (!). A photo of the occasion appears on the original album sleeve of Groucho's Carnegie Hall concert (*qv*). A footnote: the *Kinematograph Weekly* of 15 August 1929 reports Chaplin's music-hall mentor, Fred Karno, as having been invited by the William Morris Agency (then representatives of the Marxes) to direct and 'supply and produce the comedy scenes' for the second Marx Brothers talkie. At this time Karno's fortunes had taken a nosedive and he did indeed set off for America, but he is not known to have had any association with the team. It is tempting to regard this story as a typical piece of Karno showmanship.

(See also: Agents; Animation; Awards; Books; Documentaries; *Duck Soup*; Female impersonation; Florey, Robert;

Gilbert, Billy; *Humorisk*; Kennedy, Edgar; Laurel & Hardy; Letters; Mineau, Charlotte; Newsreels; *A Night in Casablanca*; *On the Mezzanine*; Prostitutes; Records; Riesner, Charles F. 'Chuck'; Sport; Television; United Artists; Vaudeville)

CHANNING, CAROL

See: Dumont, Margaret; *Skidoo*

CHARACTERS

(Marx Brothers films and shows *qv*) The characters portrayed by the Marx Brothers overlap significantly with their real-life equivalents. As the eldest surviving son, Chico was indulged somewhat by their mother, Minnie Marx (*qv*). His renegade nature, manifested in his phenomenal pursuit of women and addiction to gambling, was thus unchecked. Chico was able to get away with almost anything, through an engagingly roguish manner that endeared him to people even if he'd just hocked something that belonged to them. A book by his daughter, Maxine, records Groucho's disquiet at an earlier volume in which his apparent condemnation of Chico's ways seemed untempered by accompanying affection. Chico barged through life confidently following his instincts, which, coupled with an extraordinary gift for mathematics, made him a good negotiator for the team even though Chico himself blew his money on gambling. He learned the art of hustling as a youth and this trait permeates the Chico we know from the screen. He is capable of extorting money from anyone, be it art expert Chandler in *Animal Crackers* or, more commonly, Groucho (as in *A Day at the Races* or *Go West*). The Marx Brothers differ from the outside world in that each is a match for the other; yet Chico's skill in manoeuvring cash out of Groucho is entirely at odds with those moments where he seems to exercise the most impenetrable stupidity, notably when he fails to grasp the idea of raising the bidding in *Cocoanuts*. It makes sense, or course, for a Marx to be inherently contradictory but one suspects Chico's idiocy is brought into play only when it facilitates a pun based on misunderstanding ('Why a duck?') or to provide a means of being obstructive for its own sake. Some of his uncomprehending ways seem based on his Italian *emigré* status (the accent was borrowed from a barber *circa* 1912) but this is doubtless a front, as suggested by a further moment in *Animal Crackers* when he is asked how he acquired that nationality. Closest in age and appearance to Chico was Harpo, as untroubled a spirit as his elder brother and blessed with an additional serenity born of an absence of drive. Chico was constantly looking to the future but Harpo was content simply to exist, drifting happily through life and captivating innumerable people along the way. Norman Krasna (*qv*) contained the general view of Harpo in describing him as a 'saint', remarking on the way children or animals would go to Harpo whenever he entered a room. Harpo would see the best in people and those same people would see the best in Harpo, largely because there was little *but* the best in him. It was probably for this reason that Harpo, more than compulsive bookworm Groucho, was accepted by the notably cynical crowd that made up New York's literary set in the 1920s. Harpo modestly attributed this acceptance to his being a much-needed listener, but they had plenty of spectators and a more than passive contribution would have been required. His comic talent was an important qualification but Harpo displayed above all a capacity for uncomplicated fun, a taste for children's games serving as partial demonstration of the essentially child-like (though not childish) simplicity guiding his existence. He became the perfect family man (even though he postponed such a move until middle age), providing a well-adjusted if necessarily fun-motivated environment. The prime difference between Harpo's

private and professional characters is that the latter didn't talk; this is generalization but his sprite-like manner was only somewhat exaggerated from reality. The element of silence - reputedly imposed after he was written a wordless rôle by Al Shean (*qv*) - completes Harpo's detachment from ordinary people, enabling him to convince in outlandish behaviour and impossible feats, gathered elsewhere under the admittedly debatable term **'white magic'**. In his examination of Harpo's artistry for *The Independent Magazine* in February 1989, British actor Jonathan Cecil makes this point while comparing Harpo's hyperactivity (and attention span) to that of a puppy. This feral quality finds frequent outlet in Harpo's habit of handing people his leg, either in lieu of a handshake or merely to provide somewhere to rest. Cecil notes also a hyperactivity of face as well as body, contrasting Harpo's customary look of 'astounded ecstasy' with the 'lip-protruding gravity' that is its opposite; he compares Harpo's 'blank' expression - as when caught with the stolen silverware - to that known in military circles as 'dumb insolence'. In this regard Harpo is united solidly with Chico, both as a partner in crime and as a more kindred spirit than Groucho; in the context of their stories, it is usual for Groucho to meet them as an existing pair, often claiming to be brothers. Harpo and Chico are street children grown up, educated in crime (note Harpo's 'wanted' poster in *At the Circus*) and trained in the reflexes; Chico will respond with an over-hasty 'We no steal-a nothing' before anyone can blink. As a subversive influence, the Groucho character is more capable of working alone. It is he who crashes society or offers some kind of dubious service, such as his horse doctor in *A Day at the Races* or a monumentally decrepit sleuth in *The Big Store*. His glib tongue and plain audacity are enough to insinuate himself where he does not belong, and this despite frequent, direct references to his own

fraudulence (either spoken or implied, as in his evidently fake moustache, eyebrows and spectacles). Groucho is, like Chico, an opportunist but slightly less hamstrung by an obstructive nature. He genuinely wants to marry whichever wealthy *grande dame* Margaret Dumont (*qv*) is portraying and it is often the arrival of Chico and Harpo that places him in jeopardy. As comparable outlaws, they can see through him and take suitable advantage. Not that Groucho is any more prey to civilization than the others; the feral quality noted also in Harpo is never too far from the surface, revealed in part by his equally enthusiastic pursuit of women but sometimes more subtly, as in the piercingly unfazed look in his eye when facing a gunman in *Monkey Business*. Again we see an inherent contradiction in character, for elsewhere in the same film he is sufficiently unnerved to dispose of a revolver he has been given, while the alleged bravery of Captain Spaulding in *Animal Crackers* is severely undermined by his collapse at the sight of a caterpillar. Groucho's gift for words offers the most tangible link between stage character and man. Frustrated by his lack of education, he took up the task himself and if anything overcompensated. TV host Dick Cavett has commented on Groucho's erudition, considering him to have been better-read than many college graduates. Groucho, who did not share his elder siblings' untroubled view of life, worried constantly about money and poverty and was permanently affected when the Crash of 1929 forced him to rebuild his hard-won fortune. Insecurities over money and his lack of education contributed to a life that could never be entirely stable. His cynical humour and talent for insult can easily be interpreted as self-defence. Groucho's real-life wit, comparable to that provided by his writers (whom he would always acknowledge), would sometimes bring difficulties; not merely when guying the outside world but domestically, when his wives would find themselves targeted by his compulsive put-downs. Groucho deeply lamented the failure of his marriages, doubless aware of his ironic position as the Marx Brother most drawn to a conventional home life. Of the younger brothers, Gummo approached Harpo in placidity and reportedly shared with him a tendency towards hypochondria. His place in the family act, essentially a Jewish stereotype, was somewhat usurped when Groucho adopted a similar style in 1915. Gummo made no claim to a strong comic talent and was pleased to make way for Zeppo in 1918. Both Gummo and Zeppo were considered amusing in private life - it is said that Zeppo's forte was essentially anecdotal humour - but it is generally accepted that Zeppo arrived too late for an additional, distinctive style to develop within the Marx Brothers. Very little can be said of his stage character except to say that it seems to have dwindled from what began as a modest contribution. Despite a brief renaissance as leading man in *Monkey Business* and *Horse Feathers*, he was content to follow Gummo's lead in applying his talents away from theatre audiences.

(See also: Books; Children; Cochran, C.B.; Costume; Could Harpo Speak?; Documentaries; Education; Eliot T.S.; Fighting; Gambling; Guitar, the; Harp, the; *Home Again*; Insomnia; Insults; Marriages; Marx, Sam 'Frenchie'; *Monkey Business* [promo]; Moustaches, beards; Piano, the; Puns; Religion; Spectacles; Vaudeville; Wartime; Women; Woollcott, Alexander)

CHICO MARX AND HIS BAND/ORCHESTRA/RAVELLIS

See: Radio; Records; Stage appearances (post-1930)

CHILDREN

(Marx Brothers films and shows *qv*) 'Why, a four-year-old child could understand this report,' says Groucho in *Duck Soup*; 'Run out and find me a

four-year-old child,' he then asks Zeppo, 'I can't make head or tail out of it.' Children are occasionally permitted space in the Marx Brothers' world, as in Harpo's Punch-and-Judy audience in *Monkey Business*, the youngsters who are taught Chico's eccentric piano style in *The Big Store* or, in the same film, the varied offspring brought in by Italian, Chinese and Red Indian couples. The music solos in *A Night at the Opera* have many child onlookers, as do the black communities of *A Day at the Races* and *At the Circus*. A deleted scene from *Races* brought Harpo in contact with a bratty youngster; in *Room Service* he borrows the child-like voice of a 'mama'-doll. In *Go West* there is a screaming infant. In *Horse Feathers* Groucho is supposed to be Zeppo's father. Groucho's pride in his real-life offspring extended to occasions when he would be carried onstage in *Animal Crackers* with one or both of his children perched on his lap.

The Marxes' children are as follows: Maxine Marx, born to Chico and his first wife, Betty, in January 1918; Arthur Marx, born in July 1921 and Miriam Marx, born in May 1927 to Groucho and his first wife, Ruth. When Gummo married Helen Von Tilzer in 1929, he adopted her two-year-old daughter from a previous marriage, Kay; in 1930 they had a son, Robert. Zeppo and his first wife, Marion, adopted two sons, the first, Timothy, in 1944 and another, Thomas, later on; Harpo and Susan Marx adopted four children, starting with William Woollcott ('Billy', later Bill) in 1938;

Children: *Groucho's son, Arthur, visits the set of* Horse Feathers *with his mother, Ruth; his father entertains with a* danse macabre. *(Left) Publicity shot of Chico with his daughter, Maxine Main photo: BFI Stills, Posters and Designs*

there followed Alex, Jimmy and Minnie. Groucho's younger daughter, Melinda, was born in 1946 from his marriage to Kay Gorcey. When Zeppo married Barbara Blakely, he adopted Robert, her son by a previous marriage. All of the daughters have names beginning with 'M' after their grandmother, Minnie Marx (*qv*). In Maxine's case this may have been happy coincidence, for she is said to have been named after actress Maxine Elliott. Maxine embarked on an acting career in youth and has more recently produced a biography of her father. According to the *Film Weekly* of July 8 1939, Maxine very nearly appeared in *At the Circus* (*qv*). Noting her then-recent contribution to the film *Dramatic School*, the magazine informed an enquiring reader that Maxine was the daughter of Chico rather than Groucho. She had been taking acting lessons from her father and, subsequently, 'the professional trainers at M-G-M'. Maxine had declined the *Circus* offer because 'It was the rôle of Peerless Pauline, the upside-down girl. I'm going to make my name by standing on my feet, not my head'. Peerless Pauline's adhesive shoes were filled instead by Eve Arden (*qv*). Arthur Marx, perhaps the most high-profile of the Marxes' second generation, tried pro tennis in the 1940s but became instead a writer, his work ranging from such apprenticeship material as the Pete Smith shorts to a successful play called *The Impossible Years*. He is the author of several showbiz biographies, three of them about his father. He has collaborated on the musical shows *Minnie's Boys* and *Groucho - a Life in Revue* (both *qv*). Miriam, too, set out to be a writer and eventually compiled a volume of her father's correspondence. Bill Marx is a respected composer and musician who worked with Harpo on records in the 1950s. Groucho had show business ambitions for Melinda but she did not pursue such a career, despite appearances on *You Bet Your Life* (*qv*), *The Hollywood Palace*, and other shows. There is a pleasant and revealing story of Gummo's son, Robert, telling his schoolfriends he was Harpo's son; when his parents asked why, he replied, with a child's directness, 'Who's ever heard of Gummo Marx?' As Gummo pointed out, it was not completely true at that time but became so in later years. Although Gummo was the first Marx Brother to quit the stage, it is his grandson, Gregg, who currently acts in TV drama.

(See also: Books; Deleted scenes; Documentaries; *Home Again*; Insults; London Palladium, the; Marriages; Moustaches, beards; Piano, the; Race; Records; *Risqué* humour; Television; Woollcott, Alexander)

CHRISTY, DOROTHY
Stage actress who appeared in occasional comedy films. Her link to the Marxes is, oddly, in the stage version of a film comedy, *A Night at the Opera* (*qv*). Reports of the pre-filming tour reveal her in the eventual Dumont role when playing Salt Lake; this is rather surprising, for she was more typically a leading lady and would have been too young to play socialite Mrs Claypool. The published pre-filming script describes Mrs Claypool as a 'young and handsome widow', a quite suitable role for Dorothy Christy but quite at odds with Groucho's frequent jokes about her age and appearance. Dorothy Christy had planned to be an opera singer, as had Dumont; a background in this and comedy may have been her qualification for the Marx show. Her first film was the 1930 Will Rogers vehicle *So This Is London*. Other appearances include *Playboy of Paris*, *Parlor, Bedroom and Bath* with Buster Keaton (*qv*) and *Sons of the Desert* with Laurel & Hardy (*qv*). The surname, acquired on marrying a Hal Christy, is sometimes mis-spelled 'Christie'.

(See also: Dumont, Margaret)

CIRCUSES
See: *At the Circus*

THE CINDERELLA GIRL
See: *Street Cinderella, the*

THE CIRCLE
See: Radio

CLUBS
'Please accept my resignation. I don't care to belong to any club that would accept me as a member'; Groucho's much-quoted farewell (with variants) to one of Hollywood's clubs. In London's West End there is a Groucho Club, frequented by media and literary types; not surprisingly, its opening was greeted by a rash of jokes based on Groucho's famous missive, though one suspects its name may have been chosen with this very joke in mind. With Jack Benny (*qv*), George Burns, George Jessel and other contemporaries, the Marxes were regulars at the Hillcrest Country Club, though there were occasions when Groucho and Harpo had to re-acquire Chico's membership on his behalf. Groucho and Harpo were among those who headed a successful campaign for Hillcrest to accept non-Jewish people. One of the club's most celebrated institutions was the Comedians' Round Table, at which a comic's off-duty skills would be tested among an intimidating collection of peers. It was an earlier and not officially regulated Round Table to which Harpo had belonged, at the Algonquin Hotel in New York. Though its membership varied depending on whoever dropped in, at its core were prominent wits such as George S. Kaufman (*qv*), Alexander Woollcott (*qv*), Robert Sherwood, James Thurber, Robert Benchley and Dorothy Parker. This informal association manifested itself publicly on occasion, as in a special edition of *Life* in August 1925, parodying other magazines and newspapers. One photograph shows Harpo and Sherwood as Dorothy Parker's 'men', perusing the *Saturday Evening Post* in accord with her dictum to read 'good books'. Chico was a member of the Friar's Club in New York, in the company of comedians like Milton Berle and Phil Silvers; when Chico supplied the sleeve note for an album by Mickey Katz, he made a point of describing Katz as a 'brother Friar'. In the company of friends such as Nat Perrin, Arthur Sheekman and Nunnally Johnson (all *qv*), Groucho was part of two similarly informal societies, the West Side Writing and Asthma Club and the Geezer Club. In 1990 a new comedy club was opened in Boston, named 'Duck Soup' in honour of the Marxes. Chico's daughter was present as a plaque dedicated to the comedians was unveiled.

(See also: Burns, George and Allen, Gracie; Caricatures; *Freedonia Gazette, the*; Records; Ryskind, Morrie)

COCHRAN, CHARLES B.
(1873-1951)

(Marx Brothers films and shows *qv*) British stage impresario, whose reputation for elegant gentility is encapsulated in the phrase describing his show girls as 'Mr Cochran's Young Ladies'. Late in 1930 Cochran conceived the idea to reinstate variety shows at the Palace Theatre, situated at the Cambridge Circus end of Shaftesbury Avenue; he needed an international attraction around which to construct a bill and was offered the Marx Brothers. *Animal Crackers* had finished both as a stage and screen production and their first West Coast picture was in preparation. Three of the four brothers sailed aboard the *Paris* on 24 December 1930, to open *Cochran's 1931 Varieties* on 5 January 1931; Harpo took a different ship, arriving shortly thereafter. Accompanying them were colleagues Ed Metcalfe and Margaret Dumont (both *qv*); also present were Groucho's wife Ruth and their two children, as were Chico's wife Betty and Zeppo's wife Marion. Before embarking, a party was held in Groucho's suite; among the guests were Sam Harris (*qv*), Harry Ruby (*qv*) and a local football team. Arthur Marx has recalled his father's characteristic reaction to the sea; when Harris called for Groucho to sing a chorus of *Hooray For Captain Spaulding*, the Explorer himself was in the bathroom, martyred to seasickness even prior to sailing. Groucho's upset stomach might also have been the result of anxiety; the Marxes had by then earned something of a British following, thanks to the film versions of *Cocoanuts* and *Animal Crackers*, but their painful UK debut at the London Coliseum nine years earlier (see **On the Mezzanine**) had left sour memories. Cochran, aware of the Coliseum débâcle, was therefore sympathetic when the nervous brothers requested an out-of-town try-out at a suburban cinema. He later recalled the team's unbilled performance as 'most encouraging', but 'nothing, however, to

---

PALACE THEATRE
Shaftesbury Avenue, W.1
Managing Director · · · Charles B. Cochran

Charles B.
COCHRAN'S
1931 VARIETIES

4 MARX BROS.
In the Flesh
and a Company of International Artists

Monday, January 5th, 1931, at 8.15
and subsequently Daily, 2.30 and 8.15

Applications for seats should be made to Mr. A. J. Driscoll, Box
Office Manager, Palace Theatre, Shaftesbury Avenue, W.1
Telephone: Gerrard 6834

Prices including Tax:
Orchestra Stalls - - 12s. 0d. & 8s. 6d.
Royal Circle - - - - 8s. 6d.
First Circle - - - 5s. 9d. & 3s. 6d.
Boxes - - - £2 6s. 0d. & £1 3s. 0d.

A handbill announces the Marx Brothers' engagement for British impresario **C.B. Cochran**

---

the laughter and applause with which the first-night audience greeted them at the Palace'. A review signed 'H.H.' says 'each of their entrances was greeted with the sort of roar usually reserved for royal personages or film stars travelling incognito'. Cochran claimed he had 'never heard louder and more sustained laughter over a longer period', and that the team took numerous curtain calls (during which Groucho reminded his audience of the Coliseum audience's hostility). Their forty-minute turn comprised material from *Cocoanuts* and *Animal Crackers* within the customary party setting: the *Stage* of 8 January described it as 'a house party on the eve of a wedding', while the previous day's *Era* sets the action at a party given by Margaret Dumont 'in honour of her daughter's engagement to Zeppo'. Precise content of the sketch is difficult to determine, for there is no traceable submission of the script to the Lord Chamberlain for censorship. This legal obligation seems to have been overlooked until the *Revue* had reached Manchester in February, by which time the Marxes

A contemporary British cartoonist's impression of Chico and Harpo in January, 1931

---

had been replaced with Clark and McCullough. Though by implication a probably illegal presentation, the sketch was critically very well received. The *Times* had praise for the entire programme (featuring a dozen acts) but considered the Marx Brothers to have been 'the substance of the evening's entertainment'. The review reserved particular attention for Harpo, whose brand of zaniness may then have been more accessible to British audiences than that of Groucho, particularly when performing his knife-dropping act. Groucho's contribution, evaluated as 'taking life quite literally, except when he gets a chance of indulging a craving for oratory', was considered best 'while the pianist of the party is playing his tricks'. (Another critic records a moment where, during a gentle passage in the harp solo, Groucho called out 'Softer, I can still hear you!') The *Daily Mail* described a

Three of the Marx Brothers at the Savoy Hotel, January 1931; Harpo arrived later

'Marx Brothers' triumph', again favouring Harpo and his 'amazingly absurd medley of antics' but marvelling when Groucho 'hurls more fun and puns at you in two minutes than most comedians would dare deliver in an hour'; there was praise also for Chico's 'delightful burlesque Italian accent, his air of complete innocence, and his really comical piano-playing'. Zeppo, referred to as 'the good-looking one', was noted only as 'an effective foil to the others'. S.R. Littlewood of the *Morning Post* declared them 'just as funny on the stage as they are on the film' though believed the comic rhythm faltered after the 'really beautiful' harp solo. Littlewood records a further curtain remark from Groucho, 'we never expected to get so far', suggesting once more the comedian's anxiety at returning to London. One might also note Littlewood's mis-spelling of 'Graucho', precursor of a renowned *faux pas* by T.S. Eliot (*qv*) some three decades later. E.A. Baughan, critic for the *Daily News and Westminster Gazette*, noted an enthusiastic response but attributed

this more to their film success than to any especial merit. One might query this review, given that he identifies Chico as 'Beppo' and mistakenly assumes the Marxes to have starred in the failed production of *Cocoanuts* at the Garrick, claiming they 'made no sensation at all'. Otherwise, virtually alone in dissent was a columnist who had been tipped off regarding the Coliseum disaster and expressed only qualified approval of the Marxes. Despite mostly excellent reviews, Cochran noted a decline in business, amid reports of many patrons leaving

Zeppo and his wife Marion in Hyde Park, with one of the Afghans acquired in London. Zeppo had ambitions to breed them

during the Marxes' sketch. He believed, and probably rightly, that the American style of rapid wise-cracking had only a limited appeal among London's theatregoers of the period. The Cochran engagement required two shows a day for four weeks but permitted time for sight-seeing, from their base at the Savoy Hotel. Groucho, Ruth, Zeppo and Marion Marx were accompanied by Margaret Dumont and Ed Metcalfe to the Cheshire Cheese, a Fleet Street pub of considerable history, where they signed the visitors' book. In *Memoirs of a Mangy Lover* Groucho recalls Harpo and Chico finding diversions of their own, as when playing cards with an American comedian based in London. The comedian - unnamed by Groucho - had made a considerable fortune both from acting and marked cards, in which latter capacity he had profited massively from Harpo and Chico. Two weeks into this consistent fleecing, they returned to his Soho flat armed with a deck of their own. This time their host lost heavily and all concerned were suffering from a particularly freezing January night. The victim, anxious to keep the game in progress, heated his flat as far as possible, even to the point of burning his own furniture once the firewood was exhausted. The game concluded once all the furniture had gone. Chico and Harpo eventually made their way into the night, hailing a cab with instructions to 'take us where it's warm'. Harpo's account was somewhat different, making no mention of a third party but recalling only a freezing apartment he and Chico had taken near to the Palace. Instead of succumbing to pneumonia on their last night in London, they wrapped up in all the clothing they had, playing pinochle until dawn with the room's furniture going up in the grate. They left behind a note plus sufficient cash to refurnish. (This version of the tale is less likely, as Chico and his wife seem to have been registered with the others at the Savoy; this additional *pied-à-terre* may have been Harpo's, who had travelled separately, but there would have been no point in staying to freeze if Chico had alternate accomodation.) Altogether more upmarket were Groucho's socializing with London's *literati* and an invitation to visit a Duke. Groucho insisted on taking his children, protocol notwithstanding; such niceties took a further beating when Chico introduced himself with a jovial 'Hiya, Dook', before winning the man's lasting friendship through a mutual love of bridge. Groucho noted the Duke's evident difficulty in maintaining his estate and actually gave him some firewood (shades of the London cardsharp!). He also escorted his brood to such places as the Tower of London, taking time for a game of football with Arthur in Hyde Park. A policeman informed them of the regulations against such things, directing them to a playground instead. Groucho contrasted the constable's methods to those from his native soil, conceding that it was actually a pleasure to be thrown off the grass. An anonymous cutting of the period reports the brothers hosting a cocktail party, speaking also of their reputation for off-screen wit. 'These American "wise-cracks" however are not always easy to understand' says the report, offering 'no prizes' for 'explaining the jokes - if any'. It seems Cochran was correct in assuming that Londoners often failed to understand when the Marxes were joking or not. S.J. Perelman (*qv*) later wrote of Zeppo having bought two Afghan hounds while in England, which by the time of Perelman's acquaintance with them had 'eaten the upholstery of a Packard convertible'. Groucho and family moved on to Paris, staying at the George V hotel before embarking at Le Havre on the *Europa*. One postscript: on travelling through United States customs, Groucho invited trouble by listing his occupation as 'smuggler'.

This might have been taken as the joke it was, had he not registered as 'Julius H.' instead of 'Groucho'. When questioned over items purchased outside of the US, he replied 'Wouldn't you like to know?' and set in motion a thorough search of his family's luggage and persons. He succeeded in getting one item past the officials, a combined lighter and watch set with jewels, by concealing it in his mouth. His triumph lasted until several months later, when customs men arrived at his door demanding the appropriate duty plus a fine. The shop had kept a record of his purchase and reported it. It is no coincidence that the Marxes' next film, *Monkey Business* (*qv*), made much of the team's effort to get through customs.

(See also: Children; Gambling; Hotels; Marriages; Names; Royalty; Stage appearances [post-1930]; Weddings)

THE COCOANUTS

(Marx Brothers play)
(Marx Brothers shows and films *qv*)
The enormous success of *I'll Say She Is!* guaranteed the Marxes a second Broadway show. Not surprisingly, they were approached by several producers but targeted instead an impresario who showed no interest, Sam H. Harris (*qv*). His track record included great success with George M. Cohan and Irving Berlin (*qv*), and had lately added what was to be a lengthy association with George S. Kaufman (*qv*). Harris engaged Kaufman to write the book, in which he received uncredited assistance from Morrie Ryskind (*qv*). Ryskind later received full collaborative credit on *Animal Crackers* and was to adapt both plays for the screen. Music and lyrics were by Irving Berlin, who shared with Kaufman the problem of creating suitable material for a show liable to be appreciated only for its stars. Berlin's considerable talent was at that time somewhat in the doldrums, and his one memorable song for the show, *Always*, did not survive into the

final score (see **Irving Berlin**). The play was directed by Oscar Eagle, with musical numbers staged by Sammy Lee. Kaufman constructed his story around a then-current land boom in Florida, or more specifically the early stages of its decline. Groucho is cast as Henry W. Schlemmer (subsequently renamed 'Hammer', after his character in *On the Mezzanine*), a Florida hotelier whose money is tied up in unsaleable plots of land. His hotel is far from busy and financial salvation lies only in marrying a well-heeled guest, Mrs Potter. She was played by Margaret Dumont (*qv*), in her first association with the Marxes. Mabel Withee (1897-1955)

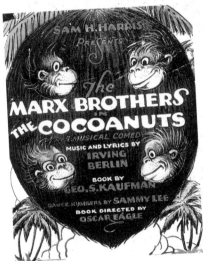

Front cover of the original programme;
the monkey heads lift to reveal those of the
Marx Brothers
Paul G. Wesolowski Collection

took the role of Mrs Potter's daughter, Polly, who is in love with the hotel's chief clerk, Bob Adams, played by Jack Barker (1895-1950). Bob is a would-be architect with big plans for the area; a crooked rival, Harvey Yates (Henry Whittemore), engineers Adams' arrest with the aid of an accomplice, Penelope Martyn (Janet Velie). Chico and Harpo are wandering guests who become embroiled in the various intrigues, while Zeppo's only big moment is in leading the chorus of the song *Florida By the Sea*. It might fairly be said that *Cocoanuts* marks the beginning of Zeppo's decline: he contributed to the comedy scenes of *I'll Say She Is!* but Kaufman and Ryskind, for all their undeniable brilliance, seem to have been at a loss as to how to employ this fourth brother (see also **Monkey Business [promo]**). Relegated to the role of 'Jamison', the desk clerk (and not even chief clerk, as noted above), Zeppo serves mostly as

Sam Harris announces his newest attraction, **The Cocoanuts**, in December 1925
By courtesy of Robert G. Dickson

sounding board for Groucho in the lobby scenes and as note-taker when dealing with detective Hennessy, played by Basil Ruysdael (*qv*). The script (or, to be specific, a transcript of the opening performance, as reprinted in the Kaufman anthology *By George*) makes it plain that *Cocoanuts* was a far better play than the film version would suggest. As with the adaptation of *Animal Crackers*, Ryskind chose to rearrange the action somewhat, presumably to introduce a sense of mobility. Scenes which were originally played consecutively before the same set are later split up, to some degree destroying continuity between Penelope's ingratiating comparisons of

Harpo and Chico to the Prince of Wales and its reversal when Groucho repeats the idea to Mrs Potter. The film, or at least its surviving version, makes scant effort to clarify Bob Adams' position as hotel employee; nor does it retain specific mention of his approach to a Mr Berryman, a potential financier of Bob's architectural plans (and whose reported, but unseen, arrival at the end of the film is thus made even less plausible). The play details far greater indolence on the part of Groucho, particularly when Zeppo tells the protesting, unpaid bellboys that Groucho has yet to arise at four in the afternoon. His comforting postscript, that Groucho always gets up on Wednesday, precedes the manager's arrival. This was evidently shot but deleted from the film, for Groucho makes his entrance descending the stairs, still putting on his coat, allowing time to fend off his staff before meeting a train at 4.15. Again common to both adaptations is the elimination of an entire sequence, in this case an interrogation by Hennessy that degenerates into a minstrel show. It is in this scene that Hennessy's shirt makes its initial disappearance, making it all the funnier when he attends the costume ball *still* minus his shirt. Harpo's musical spot, originally integrated within the party sequence, is moved to an isolated segment in the film version. In the play his harp speciality follows Chico's piano number, which in the stage script incorporates a lost *risqué* moment when Chico is introduced as Signor 'Bordello'. Another dubious line concerns whether Chico and Harpo are truly brothers; Chico explains to Hennessy 'Papa say one thing, another man say something else'. Several others survive into the film, but with qualifying statements to clean them up: for example, Groucho explains that a passkey is Russian for 'pass', but in the film adds 'You know, they passkey down the streetsky' before inviting Mrs Potter to lie down. There is also some

cute business as Harpo, though blindfolded, is able to pursue a pretty girl by scent alone ('That guy must be a police dog,' muses Groucho). Harpo is also involved in an elaborate scam, designed to extract various sums of reward money from Mrs Potter; the money is used to bail Bob Adams out of custody. In the film, this is replaced with Chico and Harpo staging an inept jailbreak. The loss of the minstrel scene deprives us of some splendidly ancient gags plus one of Penelope's songs, in this case *Minstrel Days* (she also opens the second act with *Tango Melody*, which becomes an instrumental in the film). Another loss is the contribution of one Frances Williams (*qv*) who, according to a review by Alexander Woollcott (*qv*), 'shuddered a devastating Charleston'. This was displayed in a set-piece, *They're Blaming the Charleston*, and in a number retained for the film, *The Monkey-Doodle-Doo*. The latter item was reportedly an unused composition dating back to 1913, explaining its stylistic resemblance to songs of the Ragtime era. Another song lost to the film version, *Lucky Boy*, was sung by the assembled cast whenever Bob Adams or Harvey Yates seemed to have won Polly's hand. Mrs Potter's pressure on Polly to marry someone from a more prestigious family is reflected in still another song absent from the film, *Family Reputation*. Perhaps the most serious casualty of all is Groucho's song *Why Am I a Hit with the Ladies?*, sung for a group of girls whom he reminds: 'No, no girls, you're wrong. And besides, Valentino is much taller than I.' (This line survives in *Monkey Business* as a reference to Gary Cooper.) Reportedly cut from the film's preview print was a Groucho-Dumont duet, *A Little Bungalow*, reprised from a scene where the young lovers plan domestic bliss in Cocoanut Manor. The song is set up through the dialogue (Groucho: 'Ah, if we could find a little bungalow, huh ... oh, of course I know we could find one, but maybe the people wouldn't get out')

At the hotel desk in the stage version
of **Cocoanuts**
Paul G. Wesolowski Collection

but the film fails to deliver. The song, recurring at intervals, provides also a finale when Bob is to wed Polly and Groucho seems set to marry Mrs Potter; this pleasant *tête-à-tête* was obviously intended as the focal number (in lieu of *Always*) but failed to catch on. It was replaced in the film by the even less memorable *When My Dreams Come True*. Some of the topical references are worth noting: Kaufman's habit of pleasing regular theatregoers with in-jokes surfaces when, during a frenzied dash between bedrooms, Groucho compares the experience to working for A.H. Woods (a producer known for such farces as *Up in Mabel's Room* and *Getting Gertie's Garter*); when Zeppo asks Groucho why he doesn't sell the hotel, he is told 'I can't find Frank Munsey', an unpopular man described in Howard Teichmann's Woollcott biography as 'a grocery store king who had a fondness for buying and selling newspapers ... in much the same way that he bought and sold fruit and vegetables' (Munsey, who died the

same year *Cocoanuts* was produced, had earlier fired Kaufman from the *Washington Times* for the seemingly heinous crime of being Jewish); Harpo, draped in a shawl, is referred to as Minnie Maddern Fiske, a childhood favourite of Minnie Marx (*qv*) and by that time a veteran actress; while King Alfonso, whose influence over Spanish affairs was under threat, is described as 'looking for a job'. Not in this category - or the script - is a reference to famed cartographer Rand McNally, in a scene where Groucho and Chico peruse a map of Cocoanut Manor. Groucho has engaged Chico to bump up the bidding

at his forthcoming land auction; the scene as written cries out for elaboration over the map itself, which was supplied by the comedians *ad lib* during the play's run (though, oddly, Ryskind later recalled his first contribution being an embryonic version of the routine). Chico interprets a 'viaduct' to the mainland as 'why a duck?' to which Groucho's answer is that it's deep water. When asked 'why-a-no chicken', Groucho explains 'You try to cross over there on a chicken and you'll find out why a duck.' This concludes with Chico none the wiser and Groucho prepared to let him stay that way. They return to the script with Groucho's offer to show Chico the cemetery. Kaufman wrote of its waiting list, but Groucho's *ad lib* tells how they were 'dying to get in there'. Kaufman includes Chico's misinterpretation of 'levees' as 'the Jewish neighbourhood', but it was up to Groucho to add 'Well, we'll Passover that' (these lines were retained for the film, but the stage scripts for *Cocoanuts* and *Animal Crackers* have several ethnic references that were jettisoned prior to filming; see also **Race** and **Religion**). The legend that such interpolations made each performance of *Cocoanuts* unique is probably true (see also **Gangsters** for a Harpo *ad lib*); just as legendary is

Cocoanuts: *a hit with the ladies ...*
Paul G. Wesolowski Collection

The final scene of **Cocoanuts** *was excerpted as* Spanish Knights *for a month's vaudeville in 1928 By courtesy of Robert G. Dickson*

Kaufman interrupting a backstage conversation in order to say 'I think I just heard one of the original lines.' The Brox Sisters, Loraine, Patricia and Bobbe, toured with the show as dancers. In Charlotte Chandler's book *Hello, I Must Be Going* they recalled how their exit would often get an unexpected laugh when Groucho joined the end of the line. *The Cocoanuts* played three weeks in Boston and a further two weeks in Philadelphia before opening at the Lyric Theatre, 42nd Street, on 8 December 1925. There is a tendency to regard the Philadelphia run as somewhat disastrous, but according to the *Freedonia Gazette* (*qv*) of Summer 1981, it grossed $31,000 on its first week and $30,000 during the second (it averaged $24,000 for each week in Boston). It is known that *Cocoanuts* required extensive trimming before its Broadway opening; Laurence Bergreen, in his biography of Irving Berlin, speaks of an overlong production whose patrons would often leave before the curtain fell. This was still a problem on its Broadway

opening, for Woollcott departed to write his review at 11.25 p.m., just as the piano solo was beginning, while Percy Hammond left five minutes later. Wrote Hammond: 'it seemed that the show was just getting under way. As it is now 12.05, I may be able to get back and see how it ends'. There was a formal revision of the show during summer 1926, with, apparently, some insistence on returning to the book but incorporating additional dialogue and songs. One of these, *Ting-a-Ling, the Bells'll Ring*, seems to have been a duet speculating on the romantic leads' happy parenthood. After 377 performances, *Cocoanuts* took to the road in what Groucho later admitted was a lesser version, featuring inferior chorus girls (termed 'road apples') but doing excellent business around America into 1928; a panoramic photo of the cast (reproduced in some editions of *The Marx Brothers Scrapbook*) was taken outside the Broadway Theatre in Denver, Colorado on 30 November 1927; it is of particular interest through the presence of Al Shean (*qv*) and the characteristic absence of Chico, whom Groucho believed had business either with a woman or at a poolroom. The final stop of the tour, at the Biltmore Theatre in Los Angeles, demonstrated how much the Marxes' reputation had preceded them; according to Groucho, Douglas Fairbanks Sr., Mary Pickford and Greta Garbo (*qv*) occupied the first row, sporting Groucho-like moustaches and cigars. Charlotte Chandler quotes King Vidor as claiming instead that it was he, Garbo, John Gilbert and Eleanor Boardman, clad in beards and funny hats. Instead of being fazed, Groucho made cracks in their direction, whereupon the beards were thrown onstage. The Marxes responded by hurling back costumes and props. Aside from a brief revival at New York's Century Theatre in mid-1928, the Marxes' direct involvement with the stage version of *Cocoanuts* officially ends here, though they played in an adaptation of its concluding party

scene, retitled *Spanish Knights*, for a vaudeville engagement while in Los Angeles. They had played *Cocoanuts* there for five weeks before being offered $10,000 a week (plus a percentage of the profits) to appear in vaudeville. *Spanish Knights* opened at the Metropolitan Theater on 9 February 1928 (a month after *Cocoanuts* closed) and was reviewed in the following day's *Los Angeles Times* by Marquis Busby. The reviewer had enjoyed *Cocoanuts* on its recent engagement and had similar regard for *Spanish Knights*, but noted how some of their shared gags had not brought as much laughter the second time around. 'It may be that "Cocoanuts" was here too recently,' he surmised, 'but it is hardly logical to assume that the bulk of the audience had already seen the original version.' Busby conveys some individual details of the performance: '"Groucho" Marx performs as master of ceremonies and gets all mixed up in the stories about the Scotchman (*sic*) and the Irishman, the colored woman, and the country farmhouse', suggesting a conscious satirical mangling of several rather clichéd jokes. Busby also supplies some indication of musical content, often unrecorded in contemporary accounts: '"Harpo" Marx, other than being one of the best clowns on the stage [to]day, is an excellent harpist. He plays "Charmaine" beautifully to the accompaniment of a Filipino stringed orchestra. I was disappointed that he failed to play "Rhapsody in Blue", his best number in "Cocoanuts"'. Despite Busby's only qualified praise, *Spanish Knights* was a success and toured until April 1928. A British production of *The Cocoanuts* had opened at the Garrick Theatre on 20 March of that year. The London cast was headed by Detroit-born comedian Fred Duprez, who took the Groucho role, renamed 'Julius Slimmer' (Kaufman had used Groucho's real name, Julius, in the original script). A contemporary review describes the spontaneity he brought to the part, in a sense tribute to

Kaufman's skill and an exact parallel to the common assumption that Groucho improvised the entire show. Leonard Henry and Max Nesbitt took the Chico and Harpo roles, even to the point of being billed under those names. Max Nesbitt, when not recreating Harpo's pocket-picking, played the ukelele, sharing the musical fooling with his brother Harry. In *Cocoanuts* they had three songs, *Everybody Loves My Girl*, *Bless Her Little Heart* and *Basutoland*, none of which date from the 1925 original. Two further additions were duets between Jamison (Terry Kendall) and Penelope (Pat Kendall), *Cocktail Kid* and *A Million to One You're in Love*. These items, along with several deletions from the original score, suggest this production to have been modelled on the summer 1926 revision. Mrs Potter was played by Madeline Seymour; the role of Polly was taken by Enid Stamp-Taylor. It is difficult to imagine how such a tailored show could be performed by anyone but the Marxes, but despite a brave effort the UK production did poor business. When the Marx Brothers played a London engagement for C.B. Cochran (*qv*) in 1931, the *Observer* mentioned this unhappy production along with plans for the Marxes themselves to appear in either *Cocoanuts* or *Animal Crackers* for British theatre audiences; nothing more was heard. (There were plans for a London revival, using lookalikes, of either *Cocoanuts* or *Animal Crackers* at the beginning of the 1980s, which again came to nothing.) Altogether more worthwhile, and critically very well received, was a much later revival, in 1988, at the Arena Stage, Washington (where *Animal Crackers* had been revived six years earlier). Director Douglas Wager secured permission to stage the production, but with a stipulation from Berlin (then nearing his hundredth birthday) that it should be as per the 1925 original. This was happily agreed to, though an additional hiccup occurred with the discovery that no complete copy of the score was

available, even from the composer. This was duly assembled, but not without difficulty: the lyric for *The Bellhops*, which forms part of the opening number, had survived but not its music; this was transcribed from the film version, where it provides instrumental accompaniment to the bellhops' dance. In the end, this revival proved more than a precise re-enactment of the 1925 version, incorporating as it did all the best gags introduced during the play's run (especially 'why a duck') plus appropriate material from elsewhere in the Marx repertoire, such as the hotel-dominated *A Night in Casablanca* (they

also took the forgivable liberty of inserting *Always*). Certain of the more dated musical items were omitted (as was the harp solo), while Chico's character name was amended to 'Willie the Shill' from the original's more inflammatory 'Willie the Wop'. Harpo retained the name 'Silent Sam'. Groucho was portrayed by Stephen Mellor, Harpo by Charles Janasz, and Chico by Mitchell Greenberg. The thankless Zeppo role was taken by Ralph Cosham. Halo Wines played Mrs Potter.

(See also: Advertising; Characters; *Flywheel, Shyster and Flywheel*; Hotels; Impersonators; Names; Prostitutes; Records; Russia; Stage appearances [post-1930]; Women)

THE COCOANUTS

(Marx Brothers film)
Released by Paramount, 3 August 1929 (New York première 3 May). Copyrighted 2 August 1929, LP 576. Modern sources quote 8,613 ft; original UK prints listed as 8,629 ft. 96 minutes (available copies run approximately 92 minutes at 24 fps). Produced by Monta Bell, Long Island Studios. Associate producer: James R.

Cowan. Directed by Joseph Santley and Robert Florey. Musical director: Frank Tours. Camera: George Folsey.

From the musical play originally presented by Sam H. Harris. Book by George S. Kaufman, adapted by Morrie Ryskind. Music and lyrics: Irving Berlin.

With Groucho Marx (*Mr Hammer*), Harpo Marx (*Harpo*), Chico Marx (*Chico*), Zeppo Marx (*Jamison*), Mary Eaton (*Polly Potter*), Oscar Shaw (*Bob*

Adams), Margaret Dumont (*Mrs Potter*), Kay Francis (*Penelope*), Cyril Ring (*Harvey Yates*), Basil Ruysdael (*Hennessy*), Sylvan Lee (*head bellhop*), Alan K. Foster Girls (*ballet dancers*), Gamby-Hall Girls (*bellhops*).

Cocoanut Beach, in 'the lovely land of Florida' (or so the beach types sing) is busy except for the Hotel de Cocoanut. Its proprietor, Mr Hammer, has to ward off his bellboys - or girls - when they demand to be paid. Hammer convinces them that wages only make wage slaves, and he wants them to be free. Jamison, the desk clerk, brings a telegram requesting rooms for a party of people, who may be interested in buying the land Hammer has for sale. A second telegram cancels the reservation in the event of there being *another* hotel in the vicinity. Strangely pacified, the 'bellboys' go into a dance; Hammer, who 'keeps them dancing for their money', makes for the railroad station in hopes of intercepting the party. Penelope, a shady-looking guest, approaches Harvey Yates, an even shadier-looking guest. They are evidently old partners-in-crime. Yates is annoyed because a clerk at the hotel, Bob Adams, has attracted the interest of Polly Potter - and, by implication, the Potter millions. Yates sees Polly as the sort of bride who could clear his debts. Penelope tells him of a diamond

necklace owned by Polly's mother who, coincidentally, is in the adjoining room to hers. The rooms have connecting doors, which are unlocked. The jewels are kept in a case, locked in a dresser. Yates will invite Mrs Potter and Polly to supper, with the aim of stealing the key from Mrs Potter's bag. Penelope will keep Bob Adams occupied.

Polly and Bob are on the beach, perusing would-be architect Bob's plans for Cocoanut Manor. Bob hopes to interest Hammer in his ideas for developing the area. They sing *When My Dreams Come True* before Penelope and Harvey arrive. They tell Polly that her mother is looking for her; Yates and Bob engage in a verbal joust. In the foyer, Mrs Potter informs her daughter that a 'Boston Yates' is far preferable to Adams. As they exit into the lift, Hammer returns from the railroad station, as Jamison sleeps at the desk. Hammer has had no luck

with the train but the returning Mrs Potter provides another option. He attempts to interest her in the new housing development at Cocoanut Manor. She's rather more interested in Palm Beach, and is even less impressed when left holding a sample of sewer pipe. Two more guests arrive, Harpo and Chico, who are greeted by Hammer and Jamison. They encircle the foyer with hands extended before settling down to fight and register, in that order. Harpo eats the buttons from a bellhop's uniform. Chico asks for a room but no bath; Hammer deduces they're only staying for the winter. Hammer notices their suitcase is empty. 'We fill it before we leave,' he is told. Harpo occupies himself by playing darts with the pens, tearing up letters and eating whatever is available - the potato in which a pen is kept, and some flowers unwisely left nearby. He washes down the repast with ink. With Hammer out of the way, Harpo is able to empty the cash register and, with Chico, use it to play an impromptu 'Anvil Chorus'. On discovering that ringing a bell can summon a female bellhop, they ring for several and give

Cocoanuts: *cordiality becomes confrontation*

*Still in the **Cocoanuts** lobby. A posed shot depicts Harpo in uncharacteristic awe of the female guests*

chase. Next they overhear Penelope and Yates plotting and intrude upon their company. Yates takes Penelope away, calling Harpo a 'bum'. Harpo mouths the word as Chico repeats it with him, transforming it into a drumbeat. Hammer joins them as they exit in true 'Spirit of '76' manner. Penelope considers the new arrivals likely scapegoats for the theft of Mrs Potter's necklace, and decides to invite Harpo to her room. Harpo is busy eating the telephone and drinking still more ink when Chico tells him they need money. Harpo has already stolen a pocket watch, enough to arouse the suspicion of detective Hennessy. The sleuth duly investigates but leaves minus his badge. After more pilfering, Harpo exits via the lift. Chico is approached by Penelope and invited to her room at eleven that night. Later she approaches Harpo with the same invitation. Hammer is busy with his own wooing, aimed at Mrs Potter. 'I don't think you'd love me if I were poor,' she says. 'I might,' replies Hammer, 'but I'd keep my mouth shut.' Harpo wanders to the deserted orchestra room, finds a harp, and plays.

Later he makes for Penelope's room and sneaks under the bed. Penelope is looking into Mrs Potter's room, larceny in mind. Harvey arrives with Mrs Potter's keyring, facilitating the theft. They decide to conceal the stolen necklace for a few days, in a hollow tree stump out in Cocoanut Manor. Harvey draws a map of the spot then returns to Mrs Potter, unaware that Harpo has collected the discarded map in his hat. Chico walks in just as Penelope tries to sneak into Mrs. Potter's room; he departs when Hammer, having entered Mrs Potter's room, walks through the connecting door. From here the three men manage to avoid each other with reasonable efficiency, though complications set in with the arrival of Mrs Potter and Hennessy. Penelope is able to steal the necklace without Hennessy's knowledge; he is also unaware of the steady parade of men through the bedrooms. When everyone

*Mr Hammer woos his one well-heeled resident in **The Cocoanuts***

seems to have gone, Penelope relaxes until Harpo appears from her bed. There is a discreet fade. Hammer prepares for the auction of land. Chico is too broke to be interested and is instead engaged to bump up the bidding. Hammer shows him a map of Cocoanut Manor and tries to explain such things as viaducts. 'Why a duck?' he is asked. Chico's comprehension of the matter goes no further and he is led to the appropriate spot. Before the auction there is a little entertainment (in Groucho's words 'very little'), as Polly and a line of mostly simian-clad chorines treat us to *The Monkey-Doodle-Doo*. The bidding starts, but Chico has failed to understand his purpose in the crowd: he not only builds up the bidding, but outbids everyone with money he doesn't have. Hammer eventually has to accept bids that are literally under-the-counter. Bidding starts for the plot where the auction is taking place - the location, not incidentally, of the hollow tree stump. Yates and Bob bid against each other but Yates is foiled when Harpo drops a coconut on his head. The auction breaks up when Mrs Potter announces the theft of her necklace. Hennessy takes charge. Harpo, knowing the necklace's whereabouts, returns the item but is accused of taking it in order to claim the reward. Yates suggests Bob to be the culprit, which would explain his interest in the plot of land. Penelope concocts a tale of Bob stealing the necklace as a gift for her. Mrs Potter believes the story, insisting that Bob should have no future contact with her daughter. Bob is taken into custody. Mrs Potter decides that Polly should become engaged to Yates, the announcement to be made formally at a dinner that evening. On Hammer's suggestion, Chico and Harpo spring Bob from jail, where he is told of the engagement. Back at the hotel, Bob thanks Hammer while Harpo practises his pocket-picking skills on them. The map is produced and Bob realizes that whoever wrote it out would know something about the robbery. The party, a Spanish-themed affair, commences with dancing. Hennessy arrives, still eyeing Chico and Harpo suspiciously. He is given greater reason when Harpo steals his shirt. He sings 'I want my shirt' and is eventually reunited with the pilfered garment. After the speeches (during which the bored Harpo makes frequent trips to the punch bowl) 'Signor Pastrami, the Lithuanian pianist' is to entertain. 'What is the first number?' asks Mrs Potter. 'Number one,' replies Chico. Harpo directs Polly away from the room. After the music, Polly returns to make her speech. She has the map, written in the same hand as that on her engagement gift from Yates. The erstwhile groom has already departed when Bob arrives with news of a wealthy sponsor for his architectural

plans; the same visitor has brought 400 customers for the hotel, solving Hammer's problems into the bargain. Mrs Potter announces her daughter's new fiancé while Hennessy has both Yates and Penelope in handcuffs. Hammer, Jamison, Harpo and Chico wave us goodbye as the happy couple grab the fade-out.

As the Marx Brothers' biggest stage success, *The Cocoanuts* was a prime candidate for screen adaptation. Their stage tour had concluded near the movie capital early in 1928 and before the year was out, United Artists (*qv*) expressed interest in filming the show. The deal did not go through, perhaps fortunately; a 1928 film of *Cocoanuts* would almost certainly have been silent or at most a part-talkie, something less than desirable for a Marx Brothers show. (However odd it seems today, silent films based on Broadway musicals were commonplace.) After UA withdrew, the show and its stars were offered to Paramount (*qv*) by the William Morris Agency, who wanted $75,000. Walter Wanger (*qv*), a New York representative of the studio, took the offer to Paramount chief Adolph Zukor, who considered the fee excessive. Wanger, clearly anxious to secure the property, arranged a meeting between Zukor, Chico and himself, during which Chico explained how Paramount would be getting the team's priceless backlog of material for the tiny sum of $100,000. The astonished Wanger looked on as Chico persuaded Zukor to buy the rights for $25,000 more than the original figure. That settled, shooting was arranged at Paramount's Astoria studio, Long Island. This New York facility had been of considerable use to artists whose stage commitments forbade travelling to California; W.C. Fields (*qv*) was one of many to have made silent films in and around its locality. There had been plans to close the studio and encourage the various players to migrate west (as Fields was soon to do) but the reprieve came with sound, when Paramount

recognized its suitability for filming Broadway musicals. They had yet to enter the studio when, in January 1929, the Marxes *et al* re-rehearsed *Cocoanuts* for a week at the 44th Street Theatre, where *Animal Crackers* (*qv*) was first presented. This done, it was committed to film on those days not requiring a matinée of the current show. Direction was shared between a Frenchman, Robert Florey (who supervised rehearsals) and ex-Broadway star Joseph Santley (both *qv*); producer Monta Bell (*qv*) had promised Florey dramatic films but had so far failed to deliver, while Santley, despite being billed above Florey, was delegated the secondary tasks of setting up the production numbers and keeping track of the absentee Marxes. As noted elsewhere, Florey wanted to make location shots in Florida, but had to content himself with painted backdrops and simulated grass (i.e. coloured woodshavings). Morrie Ryskind (*qv*), Kaufman's uncredited collaborator on the stage play, adapted *Cocoanuts* for the screen. This consisted primarily of slightly rearranging formerly consecutive scenes and pruning several production numbers. The essential differences between scripts are detailed under the stage version of *Cocoanuts*. In the event, the shooting script underwent further revision as time progressed: Florey, who developed a particular rapport with Harpo (the only brother to express genuine fascination with film-making), added Harpo's ink-drinking and telephone eating, while Groucho was still improvising dialogue as and when the mood took him. This proved unfortunate, since each scene had already been run through, both to verify angles and stop the technicians laughing during a take. Another difficulty was Groucho's inability to keep within the chalk marks indicating camera range; panning was virtually impossible, as early talkie technology required each camera to be sealed in a soundproof box, complete with oxygen-starved operator. For subsequent films, cameras were silenced by the fitting of 'blimps'. In *The Marx Brothers Scrapbook* Groucho speaks of them staying within the chalk boundaries, because 'we did want to be in the movie'; but if later press releases are to be believed, Groucho retained the problem of staying in shot for years thereafter. To allow intercutting, Florey ran five cameras simultaneously and in some cases inserted silent footage, a solution that itself created a problem in lighting. Even when this was surmounted, there remained the handicap of non-selective microphones. In order to pick up dialogue of sufficient volume, the recording level would need to be turned up to the point where any piece of paper would rustle its way deafeningly on to the soundtrack. For this reason, all on-screen paperwork had to be soaked prior to use (something especially apparent in the drooping map of the 'Why-a-duck' routine). Inexperience was not confined to technical matters: of the players, only non-speaking Harpo is exempt from disrupted pacing. Early talkies - meaning essentially those made prior to mid-1930 - are notoriously slow affairs and *Cocoanuts* has such *longueurs* as Groucho and Margaret Dumont (*qv*) entering the lobby at funereal pace before settling down to the dialogue. Once started, there are moments when each speaks over the other's lines, as though they hadn't performed the scene on stage for hundreds of audiences. More forgivable is Chico's obvious (if characteristic) memory lapse in the scene where he and Harpo arrange a jail break for Oscar Shaw (*qv*), a sequence replacing the ingenious scam by which the hero's bail is raised. Shaw, like Mary Eaton (*qv*), had been freshly recruited for the film version and had to learn it from scratch; Chico, used to the stage production, was suddenly faced with a totally new sequence. Shaw has to prompt Chico but the real culprit is Florey, who should have insisted on a retake. When Groucho

wasn't ad-libbing or missing his cue marks, Chico wasn't elsewhere playing cards or forgetting his lines and Harpo wasn't asleep, the film was completed. Preview length was somewhat in excess of the original play's running time, despite the removal of several production numbers; Florey and Santley had interpolated much new material, necessitating further deletions prior to release. One casualty was a duet, *A Little Bungalow*, sung at intervals during the play but believed to have been a Groucho-Dumont item in the film. In its stead the romantic leads warble a Berlin song created for the movie, *When My Dreams Come True*, an obvious attempt to insert a hit tune. Although the song had reasonable success in its day, posterity has awarded it the most resounding of raspberries. *The Cocoanuts* premièred at the Rialto, in New York's Times Square, on 3 May 1929. The comedians were performing *Animal Crackers* that evening and were unable to attend, but Minnie Marx (*qv*) was present. At a later screening, the Marx Brothers feared it would ruin their reputation and requested its destruction; Paramount, encouraged by initial reaction, had more confidence and released their film to considerable acclaim. At the time, *Cocoanuts* was considered something of a breakthrough. Talking pictures themselves were a novelty, full-scale musicals even more so. *Variety*, who knew the team of old, had little to say beyond acknowledging the stage show: of the chorus, mention was made of 'some undressing but no s.a. [sex appeal]'; Groucho's consistent chat was deemed comparable to the original; Harpo's work was done with 'craftsmanship'; and Chico was considered to have more comedy than usual. Zeppo, it was said, 'has to be straight here all of the time', sad confirmation of a role depleted even from his meagre contribution to the play. The only musical number picked out was *When My Dreams Come True*, 'good enough musically but as trite in

idea as the title suggests'. Mordaunt Hall in the *New York Times* correctly appraised the comedy/music ratio in an opening remark, 'Fun puts melody in the shade'. In handing out the honours, Hall believed Groucho monopolized the show, aided by Kaufman's 'crisp lines'. Harpo, in the reviewer's opinion, was 'content with a silence that has proved golden'. Hall regarded Groucho, Chico and Zeppo as all suited to the microphone but noted uneven sound quality, at least during the songs. 'There are quite a few moments when Brobdingnagian heads seem to be served with Lilliputian lung-power' claimed Hall, before describing a bass (Basil Ruysdael?) whose voice faded almost 'into a whisper' for a close-up. It was thought Mary Eaton's singing voice was not done justice, while 'amateurish' Cyril Ring (*qv*) played the villain 'as though everybody but his determined female partner were both sightless and deaf'. The direction was praised only for the few genuinely imaginative shots, especially the pre-Busby Berkeley overhead view of a group of dancers. This was more a mixed review than an outright pasting, though *The Film Spectator* implied a unanimous thumbs-down in New York. 'I had read the New York reviews,' said the *Spectator* scribe, 'and was prepared for something rather terrible. But instead ... I found something highly amusing and diverting, adequately mounted and containing quite a bit of clever photography'. The view was that films beloved of New York critics fared poorly on 'Main Street' (America's encapsulation of the average town), and vice versa, guaranteeing *Cocoanuts* a bright future around the US. This was the critic's first exposure to the Marxes, whom he found a 'refreshing novelty'. Being unfamiliar with the play, he automatically side-stepped a frequent complaint from New York correspondents, to the effect that it merely replicated what they had seen on stage. Particular praise went to the scene involving adjoining bedrooms and its economic use of sound, though

Mordaunt Hall's condemnation of Cyril Ring resurfaces when we are reminded that 'two thieves plot a theft in a hotel room in voices loud enough to be heard from one end of the corridor to the other'. As suggested above, the film earned the team many new admirers around the USA but, perhaps more importantly, *Cocoanuts* made them international stars. The Marxes were virtually unknown in Great Britain, comparatively few audiences having seen them during a visit seven years before. *Cocoanuts* opened at the Carlton, in London's Haymarket, early in July 1929. A trade show was arranged for the morning of Tuesday 16 July, but the reviews were in long before. The *Bioscope* of 3 July considered the plot 'a mere thread on which to hang a series of musical items and the business of some most original and amusing comedians', precise evaluation though the supporting cast also received plaudits. The following day's *Kinematograph Weekly* raved over the Marx Brothers, particularly Groucho, whose patter was 'exceptionally clever and amusing'. 'Harpo Marx,' it continued, 'plays the silent clown's part wonderfully well and also, incidentally, plays the harp and flute excellently.' 'Chico Marx,' we are told, 'varies his role of bonehead Italian with a brilliant show on the piano'. The remaining cast members were dismissed as 'really makeweight'. Once again the erratic sound was criticized: 'Dialogue is well recorded and comes over well. The singing is not so good.' 'Points of appeal' were the 'rollicking knockabout and humour of the stars'. A further *Kinematograph Weekly* reference, from a week later, noted good business and a 'continual round of laughter'. In *Punch* of 10 July, E.V. Lucas said the film had left him with 'but one wish in life and that is to see the **Marx Brothers** on the real stage'. Again hitherto unacquainted with the team, Lucas misattributed their nicknames to an Italian heritage (a common assumption at the time) but was on target in recognizing the

singularity not merely of Harpo tearing up the guests' correspondence but of the hotel manager's offer to assist, the while apologizing for the absence of a second delivery. The plot and songs were, for Lucas, a boring intrusion, 'because such inspired fools as the **Marxes** are rare'. Chief complaint was of the jokes coming at too swift a pace, the result being obliteration of the next line by continued laughter; Lucas anticipated the methods of Irving Thalberg (*qv*) in wondering why nobody in the production 'foresaw such a contingency'. The reviews convey something of the impact the Marxes had on British audiences, at any rate in metropolitan areas. The film went on general release in Britain on 17 March 1930. Nearly two decades later, in *Delight,* J.B. Priestley looked back on his first sight of them with a degree of awe. He had taken shelter in a cinema on a wet day in Golders Green, sat through the newsreel and was totally unprepared for the 'fantastic character' who caused havoc at the hotel desk. Priestley subsequently made the Marxes' acquaintance and watched them 'on the job', as he put it. For all its faults, *Cocoanuts* allows the Marxes to be very funny, though it is seen at an even greater disadvantage today. For years it was the 'lost' Marx Brothers film, absent, for example, from an otherwise complete retrospective of the team's Paramount releases at the Everyman Cinema, London, in 1950. The 1960s saw the assembly of a TV print by MCA, who had acquired the old Paramount library. The result, in Allen Eyles' words 'obviously put together with considerable difficulty', is evidently compiled from incomplete picture and sound negatives plus one or more release prints. The survival of camera negative rather than a contemporary dupe is suggested by some clumsy dissolves in the opening scene, the result of overlapped ends instead of an optically-printed mix (a common practice in those days). Some sections have good picture and sound, though others endure either muddy

picture, poor sound, or both, as though the alternating elements were assembled checkerboard-fashion. The duped picture sections are dismal even by the usual standards of such work, even though superior dupe negative stock was available by the 1960s. Where the sound has been lifted from elsewhere, the quality could sometimes pass for AM radio, complete with background whistle. Recent TV material has optically reduced the opening title sequence, presenting the full silent-frame height. The available print has lost approximately four minutes, though content of the missing segments remains uncertain. Mordaunt Hall's review mentions Harpo playing both harp *and* piano, but until a complete print surfaces - if it ever does - this may perhaps be ascribed to a flawed recollection.

(See also: Abandoned projects; Agents; Berlin, Irving; Characters; Continuity errors; *Duck Soup*; Fighting; *Flywheel, Shyster and Flywheel*; Folsey, George; Francis, Kay; Hotels; Names; *On the Mezzanine*; Opera; Radio; Records; Ring, Cyril; *Risqué* humour; Ruysdael, Basil; Songs; Telephones; Television; Vaudeville; Video releases)

COLLIER, LOIS (b. 1919)
Leading lady of *A Night in Casablanca* (*qv*), usually in 'B' features or serials. Also in *A Desperate Adventure* (1938), *Cobra Woman* (1944), Abbott & Costello's *The Naughty Nineties* (1945) and *Slave Girl* (1947). Retired after *Missile Monsters* (1958).

COLMAN, IRENE
See: *At the Circus*

COLOUR
(Marx Brothers films qv)
The Marx Brothers worked in an era when colour films were few; as Groucho remarked in *The Big Store*, 'Technicolor is s-o-o-o expensive!' Many of Groucho's TV appearances postdate the introduction of colour broadcasting and survive in that form.

There is a rare glimpse of a Technicolor Harpo in *La Fiesta de Santa Barbara* (see **Guest appearances**) but none of the key Marx films were anything but monochrome. Original prints of *A Day at the Races* are said to have used either tinting and/or toning in the water carnival and ballet sequences. Toning differs from tinting in that colour is applied to the emulsion rather than the film base, thus colouring only the opaque sections of the image. It is believed the ballet was in sepiatone and the water carnival tinted blue. Some latter-day appearances were photographed in colour: *The Story of Mankind*, *Will Success Spoil Rock Hunter?* and *Skidoo* (all *qv*). In a letter to his daughter, Miriam, Groucho spoke of his forthcoming film *Copacabana* (*qv*) as being in Technicolor, though it was not to be. Computer-colour versions of this and *A Girl in Every Port* (*qv*) have been released in the USA. In 1986 there were reports of Turner Entertainment looking into the computer colouring of some Marx films. At least two, *A Night at the Opera* and *Room Service*, have since been treated thus. In the latter, Chico's coat is reported to have been tinted maroon instead of its customary green.

(See also: Children; Costume; Letters; M-G-M; Television; Video releases; Wigs)

CONTINUITY ERRORS

(Marx Brothers films *qv*)
Errors in continuity have plagued film-makers since the industry began. It is usual to employ someone to ensure that details of action, costume and so on will match between scenes, but mistakes still happen. In *Cocoanuts*, Groucho refers to an incoming train as being due at both 4.15 and 4.30. When Zeppo arrives to introduce Groucho in *Animal Crackers*, some of the same guests appear to be standing at both the top and foot of the staircase. When Groucho emerges from his bamboo

sedan chair, the film cuts from long shot to close-up, leaving an overlap that shows him climbing from the chair twice (this has been trimmed from copies most recently supplied to TV and video). In *At the Circus* Groucho is drenched prior to boarding the train, but perfectly dry immediately afterwards; there is also no explanation for his having obtained entry to the carriage, after Chico has spent a considerable time keeping him out. According to Joe Adamson, the script details Harpo scooping Groucho on board by means of a mail hook, but this was omitted from the film. The fragmented assembly of *Love Happy* seems to have brought at least one slip, where the name of the theatre changes to and fro. Pre-release deletions from *A Day at the Races* have left several loose ends, not least Groucho's reference to Chico and Harpo staying 'down in that room with those pigeons', when none have ever been seen (nor is there mention of them in the published pre-release script). In the scene where Chico and Harpo disrupt Groucho's supper with Esther Muir (*qv*), we see Groucho send for Scotch, but nothing follows on, owing to the deletion of a gag with Harpo and Chico masquerading as bellboys. When Chico first appears as the house detective, the dialogue suggests this to be instead a return visit. Quite early in the film, Margaret Dumont (*qv*) expresses a possible willingness to help Maureen O'Sullivan (*qv*) financially, even though no approach has been made. The finale sees Groucho reprising a song, *A Message From the Man in the Moon*, which is used only as incidental music in the final cut. *A Day at the Races* is in all other respects perhaps their most polished-looking comedy, despite its inconsistencies; more typically, the most notorious continuity error in the Marx films belongs instead to one of the Paramount releases, *Monkey Business*, in which their real-life father, Frenchie, is reported as both on board ship *and* at the quayside on their arrival.

(See also: Deleted scenes; Marx, Sam 'Frenchie'; Paramount Pictures; Rain; Television; Trains)

COPACABANA (United Artists 1947)

(Groucho solo film)
By 1947, Groucho's attempts to work independently of his brothers had taken him to the ultimately successful *You Bet Your Life* (*qv*) and to this film, co-starring him with 'Brazilian Bombshell' Carmen Miranda (*qv*). Also among the cast are Steve Cochran, Andy Russell, Gloria Jean, Abel Green of *Variety* and Kay Gorcey, Groucho's second wife. The action takes place at New York's famous Copacabana Club, where double-act Lionel Q. Devereux (Groucho) and Carmen Navarro (Miranda) try to attract the attention of an agent (Ralph Sanford). They fail to make an impression and Devereux is given the bum's rush. He and Carmen have been engaged for ten years; she suggests that marriage would enable them to owe money for one hotel room instead of two, but her fiancé proves evasive. Back at the hotel, Devereux is faced with paying their bills or being locked out; he stalls the manager with a bad cheque but is advised to let Carmen become a star in her own right. Devereux decides to retire from the stage to become Carmen's agent. He approaches Steve Hunt (Steve Cochran), boss of the Copacabana, for whom Carmen passes an audition, but Hunt also requires a *chanteuse*. Reluctant to admit to having only one client, Devereux bluffs through a list of names culled from a racing form. Of these, Hunt wants to see 'Mademoiselle Fifi', under which identity Carmen auditions once more, disguised under a veil. This French *alter ego* is booked to appear alternately on the bill with her genuine identity, necessitating a series of quick-change acts every night. Fifi becomes the new sensation, attracting the interest of the club owner and a Hollywood producer. The agent who rejected their old double-act buys Fifi from Devereux for $5,000; Devereux is

A Spanish handbill for **Copacabana**

affections. A one-woman fight is staged in Carmen's dressing room, following which Fifi disappears, her veil and costume dumped into the East River. Devereux is overheard bragging about having 'killed off' Fifi and is prime suspect when her disappearance makes headlines. Devereux stands up to interrogation well but Carmen decides to reappear as Fifi in order to clear up suspicion. The film producer wants the girl *and* the dual-identity tale. The resultant film has Devereux's name all over the credits, allowing him also the chance to join in as Carmen closes the proceedings with a song. *Copacabana* is generally amusing, though Groucho's material is decidedly mixed. Some lines are quite creditable ('Why are you always chasing women?' 'I'll tell you as soon as I catch one'), though others are

familiar persona amid a ranch setting liberally populated by attractive cowgirls. The sequence is in fact rather strange, since the greasepaint-moustached Groucho and the civilian-clothed equivalent (wearing an artificial-looking waxed moustache) are clearly not meant to be one and the same, the one cheering on the other; in fanciful mood, one might interpret this as the old Groucho rescuing the new in his time of need. *Copacabana* was produced by Sam Coslow (*qv*), who also supplied songs, and directed by Alfred E. Green (*qv*). Trivia note: at one point Carmen Miranda's stage act is introduced by twin girls, speaking in unison; to this writer they resemble the Crane Twins, who in extreme youth (17 years earlier, to be precise) performed the same function at the beginning of several Hal Roach comedies. The Cranes are believed to have retired some years before *Copacabana* was produced, but may have been temporarily lured back. Second trivia note: one or two Groucho filmographies misleadingly name a 1976 entry called *Salsa*, a film which incorporates footage from *Copacabana* but has no new Groucho material.

(See also: Agents; Chaplin, Charlie; Colour films; Guest appearances; Home movies; Marriages; Moustaches, beards; Names; Records; Ruby, Harry; Songs; Trailers; United Artists)

COSBY, BILL
See: Television; *You Bet Your Life*

COSLOW, SAM (1905-82)
Producer/songwriter, in which capacities he was associated with Groucho's solo film *Copacabana* (*qv*). Among his more famous achievements as songwriter are *Cocktails For Two*, *My Old Flame* and *Just One More Chance*; with Jerry Bresler he received an Oscar for the Best Short Subject of 1943, *Heavenly Music*. Sam Coslow was at one time married to Esther Muir (*qv*).

(See also: Awards)

Carmen Miranda and Groucho in a backstage flurry from **Copacabana**

delighted to make such a profit from a non-existent girl until discovering that Hollywood is prepared to offer $100,000. The enraged Devereux confronts the agent, who has since begun to suspect the ruse. It becomes clear that Fifi will have to go, the more so when Hunt's secretary, Anne (Gloria Jean) confides to Carmen that the French star is her rival for Hunt's

not; it's particularly discouraging when one of his lines is topped by a cigarette girl, leaving him no response other than an arbitrary eyebrow-wiggle. The sometimes erratic pace suffers all the more when stopping for musical set-pieces, though ironically it is one of these that steals the entire movie. When agent Devereaux recommends a replacement act for Fifi, on bounds the movie Groucho in a Kalmar and Ruby song, *Go West, Young Man*. For a few precious minutes, he reverts to his

COSTUME

(Marx Brothers films and shows *qv*)
The Marx Brothers' costumes are as distinctive as their characterizations. According to plot and other requirements, clothing would vary in minor details but Groucho is identified by pinstriped trousers, red tie and a tapering, swallowtail coat (not a 'tail' coat as is often thought, which is cut laterally at the waist). Allen Eyles has accurately compared the effect of this coat to that of a bird of prey, completing the line initiated at Groucho's nose and continuing along his curiously swooping gait. Present-day comedian Woody Allen has spoken of Groucho's effectiveness as both verbal and visual performer. Chico's Italian image is conveyed by a tight, wide-lapelled corduroy jacket (actually dark green in colour) and checked trousers. This outfit seems to have been adopted as late as the stage version of *Animal Crackers*; photographs from the Broadway production of *Cocoanuts* show him wearing an outlandishly-striped suit. Harpo appeared in sundry pairs of baggy trousers combined with loud shirts and ties (his tie in *The Big Store* is turned inside-out), the whole enclosed within a decrepit raincoat fastened by a tight belt. The belt served also to carry his means of communication, a taxi horn. In *Horse Feathers* Harpo's tattier-than-usual ensemble is removed in one piece. Though threatening imminent disintegration, his raincoat would contain anything from a flashlight to a live dog. Harpo's original raincoat was obtained, second-hand, for offstage use, but soon disassembled itself and became a comedy prop; a December 1921 photo session, reproduced under **On the Mezzanine**, reveals the raincoat as still a thing of the future; in its stead was a quite respectable overcoat. Groucho seems to have his usual swallowtail equivalent, Chico looks much as he did four years later in *Cocoanuts* and Zeppo, ever the straight man, sports a tuxedo.

(See also: Cars; Characters; Hats; *Home Again*; Prisons; Shoes; Smoking; Spectacles; 'White magic'; Wigs)

COULD HARPO SPEAK?

(Marx Brothers films and shows *qv*)
This seemingly absurd question has been put with sufficient frequency to warrant a definite statement. The answer is *yes*, and from all accounts quite eloquently, though with an unusually strong New York accent. Chico's description of him as 'dem and-a duff' in *Monkey Business* can be taken purely as an in-character joke, ditto Groucho's purely mischievous perpetuation of the myth in Charlotte Chandler's book. In *Memoirs of a Mangy Lover* Groucho concocts a wholly fictitious - and comic - reason for Harpo's silence, namely a conversation in which Groucho told him 'If that is all you have to say, you ought never to bother to speak again'. Elsewhere (notably in 'Why Harpo Doesn't Talk', written in 1948 for a Sunday supplement called *This Week*), Groucho tied it to an oft-told vaudeville anecdote concerning a time when he was fined for smoking backstage. His facetious response doubled the fine, which by then totalled $10. The Marxes banded together and the entire company refused to go on unless the fine was cancelled. Despite having a house filled with impatient spectators, the manager refused. It was Christmas, and Harpo suggested donating the fine to the Salvation Army, with the Marxes adding a further ten. The manager at first baulked, then reluctantly agreed, and the show proceeded as planned. Afterwards, the Marxes had to pack up quickly in order to catch the train to their next engagement. The manager took his revenge by having the act's salary delivered in large sacks of pennies, which could not be counted in the time available. On the train, Harpo shouted back expressing the hope that the theatre would burn to the ground, only to learn the following day that it had done exactly that. Consequentially, it was decided that Harpo was safer if

he didn't talk. In truth, Harpo adopted a purely visual style of comedy quite early in his career (see **Home Again** and **Vaudeville**), after Al Shean (*qv*) had, perhaps unconsciously, recognized Harpo's limited capacity for delivering jokes. On those infrequent occasions when he was required to address a public gathering, Harpo would amuse and startle his audience by opening with 'Unaccustomed as I am to speaking ...'. When entertaining servicemen whose wounds had kept them in hospital long after the Second World War, Harpo engaged in his first crosstalk act since *Fun in Hi Skule*, which, judging from a contemporary account, may well have been source for many of the gags (one motif, used again in the touring version of *Go West*, had the apparently idiotic Harpo startling everyone with a stream of polysyllabic words). The *News Chronicle* of 24 February 1947 reported him with a 'song-writer stooge' who quizzed Harpo on 'what he remembers after being mum so long'. The first question concerned his recollection of numeracy; Harpo counted to five, omitting the number three. When asked what had become of the missing figure, Harpo replied 'Oh, three, well, I'm coming to that'. Audiences were particularly fond of Harpo's view of Shakespeare: 'I read everything of his as it comes out'. 'And Marcel Proust?' asked the stooge, earning a conspiratorial 'No! You don't say! So Marcel Prousted again, did she!' 'Don't ask me why it's funny,' concluded the reporter, 'Proust is the same in American as in English - it means nothing, but it does make a colourful verb somehow.' Outside of this and a brief provincial run of *The Man Who Came to Dinner* (*qv*), Harpo remained a non-speaking performer until finally retiring in January 1963, when he closed a farewell concert at the Pasadena Civic Center with a speech to his fans. Britain's *Daily Express* of 22 January quoted the conclusion of his speech as 'the only thing left to say expresses everything I've always felt

Irving Cummings, Sr, *director of* Double
Dynamite

and left unsaid. Thank you.' There is
the strong possibility that Harpo may
be heard singing in *Monkey Business*:
when the Marxes, concealed in barrels,
sing *Sweet Adeline*, there are most
definitely *four* voices to be heard. The
last to finish, a strangulated tenor, does
not resemble the three familiar voices
and may have been a deliberate joke,
permitting audiences to hear Harpo's
voice without betraying its source.

(See also: *At the Circus*; Books;
Characters; London Palladium, the; *A
Night in Casablanca*; Stage
appearances [post-1930]; Television)

COWAN, LESTER (1905-90)

Producer of *Love Happy* (*qv*) and of
various abortive Marx efforts (see
Abandoned projects). Ohio-born
Cowan worked for the Academy of
Motion Picture Arts and Sciences from
its earliest days, turning producer in
1934. Two of his better-known
productions are *You Can't Cheat an
Honest Man* (1939) and *My Little
Chickadee* (1940), both with W.C.
Fields (*qv*). Cowan also produced *One
Touch of Venus* (1948; see also **Eve
Arden**, **Frank Tashlin**, **S.J.
Perelman** and **William A. Seiter**).

(See also: Awards)

CUMMINGS, IRVING (1888-1959)

Directed Groucho in *Double Dynamite*
(*qv*), a film produced by Cummings'
son, Irving Jr. (*qv*). Cummings Sr, born
and educated in New York, made his
Broadway debut in 1908, appeared
alongside such notables as Lillian
Russell and Ethel Barrymore (see also
Television) and entered films as an
actor during either 1909 or 1910. His
sister, Jessie Cummings, also appeared
in silent pictures. Irving Cummings
moved to directing in the mid-1920s; in
1929 he took over the direction of
Fox's *In Old Arizona*; he also directed
a 1931 sequel *The Cisco Kid*.
Cummings' other credits include the
Shirley Temple films *Curly Top* (1935)
and *Little Miss Broadway* (1938), *The
Story of Alexander Graham Bell*
(1938), Fox's *Hollywood Cavalcade*
(1939), the Betty Grable vehicles
Down Argentine Way (1940),
Springtime in the Rockies (1942),
Sweet Rosie O'Grady (1943) and *The
Dolly Sisters* (1945). A *Variety* obituary
credits Cummings as having been

instrumental in launching Tyrone
Power's film career (Cummings directed
one of Power's earliest appearances, the
1936 film *Girls' Dormitory*); *Variety*
also noted Cummings' three-year tenure
as host of the Lux Radio Theater, a
series presenting audio adaptations of
motion picture successes, usually with
the original stars and in the presence of
a live audience.

(See also: Heerman, Victor; Radio;
Seaton, George; Vaudeville)

CUMMINGS, IRVING JR

Producer of *Double Dynamite* and co-
producer, with Irwin Allen (*qv*), of *A
Girl in Every Port* (also *qv*); son of
director Irving Cummings (*qv*). Known
initially as screenwriter at Fox, as in
Yesterday's Heroes (1940), *Lone Star
Ranger* (1943) and *He Hired the Boss*
(1948). First embarked on production
1948; *Double Dynamite* (shelved until
1951) would have been among his
earliest endeavours. Later also in TV.

CUMMINGS, JACK (1900-89)

Canadian-born producer of the Marxes'
Go West (*qv*); started at M-G-M (*qv*) as
an office boy, ascending first to
assistant director, then director. By the
mid-1930s he had attained producer
status, initially in short subjects. His
many feature productions include *Born
to Dance* (1936), *Honolulu* (1939), *I
Dood It* (1943), the Kalmar-Ruby
biopic *Three Little Words* (1950),
Lovely to Look At (1952), *Kiss Me Kate*
(1953) and *Seven Brides For Seven
Brothers* (1954).

(See also: Burns, George and Allen,
Gracie; Buzzell, Edward; Impersonators;
Miller, David; Ruby, Harry)

DOCTORS
(Marx Bros. films qv)

Doctors appear in A Day at the
Races with Groucho (as Dr. Hugo
Z. Hackenbush, a horse doctor mistaken for a patient/people doctor)
and Sig Rumann as another doctor (this time, a people's doctor)

DRAKE, CHARLES (1924-1994)
Actor associated in serious or drama-
tic roles in It Came from Outer
Space (1953), Air Force (1943), and Toba,
The Great (1954), as well as among mo.

Other 1940's and 1950's films. Appeared as the romantic lead, Pierre in *A Night in Casablanca* (1946) with the Marxes. Not to be confused with Charlie Drake, a comic.

DALI, SALVADOR

See: Paintings

DANDRIDGE, DOROTHY

See: *A Day at the Races*

DARLING, HATTIE

See: *On the Mezzanine*

A DAY AT THE RACES

(Marx Brothers film)
Released by M-G-M, 11 June 1937.
Copyrighted 10 June (LP 7207).
9,824 ft (109 minutes).
Produced by Irving Thalberg and
Lawrence Weingarten (though

Hackenbush, was written by Bert Kalmar and Harry Ruby, but not used. An early working title: *Peace and Quiet*.

With Groucho Marx (*Dr Hugo Z. Hackenbush*), Chico Marx (*Antonio/Tony*), Harpo Marx (*Stuffy*), Allan Jones (*Gil Stewart*), Maureen O'Sullivan (*Judy Standish*), Margaret Dumont (*Mrs Emily Upjohn*), Douglas(s) Dumbrille (*Morgan*), Leonard Ceeley (*Whitmore*), Esther Muir (*Flo Marlowe*), Sig Rumann (*Dr Leopold X. Steinberg*), Robert Middlemass (*Sheriff*), Vivian Fay, Ivy Anderson and the Crinoline Choir.

Mark Newell Collection

onscreen credit reads 'A Sam Wood Production'). Directed by Sam Wood. Camera: Joseph Ruttenberg. Screenplay by Robert Pirosh, George Seaton and George Oppenheimer; also (uncredited) George S. Kaufman, Al Boasberg and Leon Gordon. Songs: *Blue Venetian Waters*, *Tomorrow Is Another Day*, *All God's Chillun Got Rhythm* and *A Message From the Man in the Moon*, lyrics by Gus Kahn, music by Bronislau Kaper and Walter Jurmann (the last-named song appears in the final print only as incidental music and in a brief 'reprise' by Groucho). Another song, *Dr*

Dorothy Dandridge has been reported among the black dancers.

A train pulls in at Sparkling Springs Lake. A bus is ready to convey visitors to the Standish sanitarium, but everyone is headed for Morgan's hotel and the nearby racetrack. The sanitarium's owner, Judy Standish, will have to do without Tony, the bus driver, if business does not improve. Tony is willing to work unpaid but suggests Judy should obtain a loan from her one wealthy resident, Mrs Upjohn. This idea is rejected but Judy feels able to offer her a partnership. Judy returns to the sanitarium just as Mrs Upjohn is moving out. The resident doctor has

Tony gives Dr Hackenbush a fine Tootsie-Frootsie-ing in **A Day at the Races**

assured Mrs Upjohn she is in perfect health, whereas she believes herself on the point of a nervous collapse. Judy's anguish is scarcely helped on discovering that her fiancé, Gil Stewart, has spent $1,500 on a racehorse, Hi-Hat. Gil plans to win at the races and give the money to Judy; as this means abandoning his music studies, Judy is against it. She will have nothing to do with Gil until the horse is returned. Mrs Upjohn is leaving for Florida to see Dr Hackenbush, who first diagnosed her condition. Tony persuades Mrs Upjohn to stay by telling her of Hackenbush's imminent arrival. She might be willing to help Judy if Hackenbush joins the staff, being convinced that Hackenbush owns the biggest sanitarium in Florida. Tony wires Hackenbush, who is actually a horse doctor, in his run-down surgery. He needs no further persuasion to leave for the sanitarium. Judy receives a visit from Morgan. She is heavily in debt to him and is offered $5,000 for the place. The debt will be soon be due and if she refuses the offer, she will be left with nothing.

Whitmore, an associate, advises her to accept; Judy prefers to wait one month, to see what Hackenbush can achieve. Mrs Upjohn announces the great medic's arrival. Whitmore, who is obviously on Morgan's side, has instructions to 'go to work' on Hackenbush. Whitmore questions his background, not least his having attended Vassar (which Hackenbush only discovered was a girls' school during the third year). Hackenbush hears a fanfare and departs for the racetrack. Stuffy, Morgan's jockey, has just won a race despite being ordered

to lose. He escapes a beating by hiding in Hi-Hat's stall, where Gil is tending his new purchase. Hi-Hat's former owner, Morgan, can send the animal wild just by speaking. Stuffy greets Tony, who has an ice cream cart. Tony learns that Stuffy has been fired for not throwing a race ('He's honest, but you gotta watch him a little') and recommends him to Gil. The Sheriff arrives to collect Hi-Hat's feed bill. Tony gives him $5, which is retrieved by Stuffy; in this way $5 becomes $15 until the note is placed in an inaccessible pocket. Stuffy reaches into the Sheriff's trouser pocket and pulls out a sock, tied in the middle. He is chased away. Hi-Hat is locked in his stall. They need money to place on a hot tip, a horse named Sun-Up. Hackenbush arrives at the track, ready to bet on the same animal until dissuaded by Tony, whose ice cream business serves to mask his activities as racing tout. For $1 Hackenbush receives a slip of paper marked ZVBXRPL. The necessary code book is free, aside from a dollar printing charge. From here Hackenbush is sold a master code book, breeder's guide and four more books after that. Tony wagers six of Hackenbush's dollars on Sun-Up. Hackenbush discovers the jockey's name, but not the horse. Ten

A Day at the Races: *Mrs Upjohn undergoes rigorous examination*

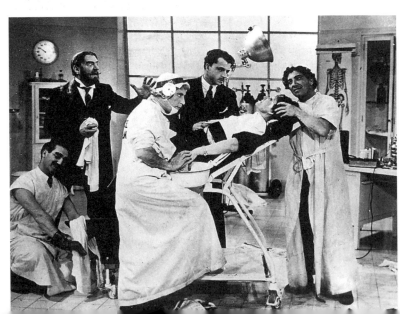

books later, he tries to place a bet on Rosie, but the race has finished. Sun-Up has won, and Tony exits with his winnings plus ten more dollars. Hackenbush takes over the ice cream cart. At the sanitarium, Judy remains 'out' to Gil. Morgan wants to convert the sanitarium to a casino before the season ends; it will go nicely with his racetrack and nightclub. Whitmore is briefed to check Hackenbush's credentials. Judy asks Hackenbush for a photograph, to publicize his association with the sanitarium. On realizing how much depends on him, he nearly confesses his fraudulent status but promises instead to keep Mrs Upjohn content. Whitmore attempts to call Florida but Hackenbush intercepts the call, posing as switchboard operator and Southern colonel. As Whitmore raises his voice in an attempt to be understood, Hackenbush complains via an intercom. Whitmore abandons the call and leaves his office. Stuffy and Tony have been listening at the window. Tony concludes that Whitmore is conspiring with Morgan to get the sanitarium and decides Stuffy should register as a patient in order to spy on him. Mrs Upjohn requests the presence of Dr. Hackenbush. He contradicts evidence of her robust health ('Who are you gonna believe, me or those crooked X-rays?') before seeing Tony and Stuffy. He recognises Tony from the racetrack but proceeds to examine Stuffy. He takes the patient's pulse: 'Either this man's dead, or my watch has stopped'. Tony finds a letter thanking Hackenbush 'for saving my horse'. He is aghast but they realize the deception must continue. Stuffy has found a hypodermic syringe and they exit, each with an anaesthetized leg. Gil is training Hi-Hat when Tony informs him of Hackenbush's true vocation. The secret cannot be kept for long and he resolves to win enough money to save Judy's livelihood. The horse needs food, to be financed by Gil singing and Tony playing piano at that evening's water carnival. The Sheriff

reappears to take Hi-Hat but finds himself leading Stuffy. The carnival opens with a ballet, followed by Gil singing *Blue Venetian Waters*. Judy tries not to be impressed. Tony and Stuffy, in ill-fitting waiters' outfits, look on approvingly. Hackenbush shares a gondola with Judy and Mrs Upjohn but is lured away by the slinky Flo. Gil tells Judy not to rely on Hackenbush but she explains that Mrs Upjohn is happy with him. Gil admits that Hi-Hat is not 'in the pink'; Judy in turn agrees to a reconciliation. Hackenbush takes to the dance floor with Mrs Upjohn but dumps her in favour of Flo. The Sheriff

A Day at the Races: *a posed shot in the stables, with Maureen O'Sullivan and Allan Jones. A corresponding scene in the film shows them looking more dejected, before turning the tables on villainous Douglass Dumbrille*

chases Tony and Stuffy but lands in the water. He is still in pursuit as they make for the podium. Tony plays his piano solo and makes a break, the Sheriff behind him. Stuffy tries a piano piece but hits a clinker: as he strikes the keys harder, the instrument disintegrates, leaving its harp-like interior. He plays *Blue Venetian Waters*. Stuffy escapes arrest by spinning the piano stool - and himself - into the water. Flo reports to Whitmore: she will entertain Hackenbush in her room, so that Whitmore can break in with Mrs

Upjohn, who will insist upon Hackenbush's dismissal. Stuffy overhears and mimes the story to Tony. They interrupt Hackenbush's tryst with Flo but he will not listen. They return posing first as house detectives, then as decorators; by the time Whitmore arrives with Mrs Upjohn, Flo has disappeared beneath the wallpaper and Hackenbush is safe. Next day, Mrs Upjohn begs his forgiveness, which is granted provided she takes on Judy's debts. Gil brings the necessary papers for her to sign but Whitmore arrives with a Dr Steinberg of Vienna, who would like to know more of Mrs

Upjohn's 'ailment'. She is, it seems, the only known case of 'double blood pressure', i.e. low on one side, high on the other. When Whitmore suggests an examination, Hackenbush is ready to flee but is dissuaded. Stuffy feeds Hi-Hat on the contents of Hackenbush's mattress. The examination proceeds, amid much washing of hands. Tony and

Stuffy participate, in white overalls borrowed from a service station. Stuffy takes the patient's purse instead of pulse, and relieves a nurse of her uniform. Mrs Upjohn is nearly upside-down on the adjustable table. She tries to leave with Whitmore and Steinberg when Stuffy turns on the fire sprinklers. They head in the opposite direction when Stuffy leads Hi-Hat into the room. Exit Stuffy, Tony and Hackenbush, on horseback. In the stable, Gil and his three friends blame each other for ruining Judy's business. Judy arrives and bravely accepts that Morgan will own the sanitarium after tomorrow. She and Gil watch some children as Gil sings *Tomorrow Is Another Day*. Stuffy takes a flute and is taken to be Gabriel by a black community. There follows a spirited version of *All God's Chillun Got Rhythm*. Morgan, Whitmore and the Sheriff arrive with proof of Hackenbush's imposture. Hackenbush *et al* escape and Hi-Hat has Morgan cornered, the horse growing increasingly wild on hearing the man's voice. Stuffy exits on the animal, who proves to be an ideal steeplechaser. At the next day's race, Morgan and Whitmore see Hi-Hat among the 'added starters'. Morgan knows that if Hi-Hat wins, Judy will keep the sanitarium, so is determined that his own 'Skee Ball' will be the victor. Morgan has placed guards on all the entrances. Judy and Gil bring Hi-Hat to the track in an ambulance as Hackenbush and Tony keep watch from above an awning as Stuffy goes to join them. Hi-Hat is given away by his angry reaction to Morgan's voice. The Sheriff takes the ambulance away. As the others employ delaying tactics (such as switching on a fan to blow the spectators' hats over the track), Judy fakes a road accident in order to gain control of the ambulance. Gil brings Hi-Hat as one of two horses fixed to a wagon. Stuffy rides the entire ensemble to the starting line. Suitably detached, Hi-Hat joins the race and is encouraged to jump when shown

The pre-filming tour of **A Day at the Races** *in Oregon*
By courtesy of Robert G. Dickson

Morgan's picture. The picture is lost but proves unnecessary when the public address system is rigged up to relay his voice. Morgan's jockey employs foul tactics and both he and Stuffy fall at a water jump. They remount but Morgan's rider narrowly beats Stuffy to the tape. Hackenbush is arrested but when Morgan tries to congratulate his jockey, the horse goes wild. The mud is cleared away to reveals Hi-Hat's number. The decision is reversed and the good guys (including the black community, who have mysteriously reappeared) walk towards the camera in song.

A Night at the Opera (*qv*), the first Marx film with producer Irving Thalberg (*qv*), demanded an instant follow-up. On 8 April 1936 *Variety* quoted Thalberg as believing a lengthy break for the Marxes to be 'unnecessary', the result being that two new scripts were in preparation. First to be produced was that written by George S. Kaufman, George Seaton and Robert Pirosh (all *qv*); the second would be the responsibility of Bert Kalmar and Harry Ruby (*qv*). The rather ambitious plan was to produce both in the summer, leaving the Marxes free for a possible winter show in New York. Curiously, later that month Kaufman was reported as planning to spend the summer in Hollywood, 'not under studio commitment' but with the idea of working on a play with Moss Hart; on 6

May *Variety* stated that the next Marx film would be their first Western, currently being written by Kalmar, Ruby and William Slavens McNutt. The issue of 3 June returns to the Kaufman-Hart play, to be commenced after Kaufman had spent 'two weeks on a picture script for the Marx brothers'. According to Joe Adamson, the original version of *A Day at the Races* was a story called *Peace and Quiet*, set in a sanitarium but not involving racing; it was more recognizable by the time it was ready to go on tour. The road-testing idea, which had paid such dividends with *Opera*, was a foregone conclusion. On 16 June it was announced to the press and was under way in a month. As with *Opera*'s tour, the supporting cast comprised players not used in the film; this time, even Allan Jones (*qv*) was not present. On 24 June *Variety* had published the intinerary as planned, a four-week tour to commence on 17 July in Pittsburgh, each week playing a different circuit. Pittsburgh would be for Warner Brothers, Cleveland for Loew, Chicago for RKO and Minneapolis for Paramount. Each show was designed to run 65 minutes, the Marxes being paid a guaranteed $13,500 per week plus a percentage of the take. Before setting off, the schedule was revised as follows: Lyceum Theatre, Duluth, for 14-16 July; Paramount's Minnesota Theatre, Minneapolis, for the week commencing 17 July; Palace Theatre, Chicago, week commencing 24 July; State Theatre, Cleveland, week commencing 31 July; and the Golden Gate Theatre, San Francisco, week commencing 12 August. The final venue was initially unconfirmed, suggested in part by a report from Les Rees in *Variety* of 22 July naming Detroit as the final stop. At Minneapolis on 18 July, Rees noted a running time of 67 minutes, 18 fewer than the previous day's version. Each performance was preceded by a trailer in which the purpose of the show was explained to the audience, who incidentally laughed loudly despite the necessarily ragged presentation. Rees suspected the Marxes were quite confident of the material and merely touring for the extra salary, but the varying running time suggests this to have been untrue. They finished in San Francisco on 18 August and commenced filming on 3 September. Eleven days later, Irving Thalberg died from pneumonia. Production was shut down until late December, by which time Thalberg's brother-in-law, Lawrence Weingarten, had been put in charge. Sam Wood (qv) was again directing, though under trying circumstances; it is during this film that he seems to have developed his fondness for countless takes of each scene. Lost during filming was a comic song written for Groucho by Kalmar and Ruby, *Dr Hackenbush*. It was intended to accompany Groucho's arrival and it is believed that the comedian himself preferred not to shoot such an elaborate number. He obviously regretted the move, for he later sang it in different shows and on record. Shooting finally ended early in April 1937, with release following in June. Reviews were not as consistently favourable as for *A Night at the Opera* - the *New York Times* said 'somebody must have stolen the gags, for they aren't in the picture' - but it grossed more than its predecessor, in which respect public opinion outweighed that of the critics. The film's protracted

creation was noted by the transparently pseudonymous 'Beverly Hills' of *Liberty* magazine. The review gave it a top rating (three stars) on the strength of its 'many hilarious moments', despite an excessive running time and 'too many dull patches'. Graham Greene, who reviewed *A Day at the Races* for the brilliant (but short-lived) British magazine *Night and Day*, preferred it to *A Night at the Opera* but, feeling 'the capitalists have recognized the Marx Brothers', expressed obvious discomfort over the lavish settings, the ballet and further evidence of a gigantic budget. Though conceding *Races* to be 'easily the best film to be seen in London', Greene confessed a nostalgia for the Paramount films, with their 'cheap rickety sets, those titles as meaningless and undifferentiated as Kipling's: *Duck Soup* and *Horsefeathers*'. Despite 'a kind of perverse passion' for Maureen O'Sullivan (qv) (who, in Greene's words, satisfied 'a primeval instinct for a really nice girl'), it was felt that 'real people do more than retard, they smash the Marx fantasy'. Greene was particularly aghast when the actress reacted to one piece of business with the word 'silly', and in a Marxian setting one cannot help but agree. Context aside, Greene was impressed as ever by the Marxes, particularly Harpo. The charade sequence was

described as 'oddly young and Shakespearian in its lunacy', though posterity may disagree with his view of Harpo's scene with the black community as 'an emotional effect he has never previously secured'. Harpo most certainly has more to do here than in *Opera*, as per Greene's description but perhaps especially in his larcenous displays around the track, the visual gags during the examinations of himself and Margaret Dumont (qv) and in the climactic race itself. As the Marxes' longest starring vehicle, *A Day at the Races* underwent severe trimming in order to bring it down to a manageable duration. Unfortunately, contemporary opinion dictated that most deletions would be in the comedy rather than the 'straight' content, which is why it retains a seemingly interminable and frankly rather pretentious ballet sequence at the Water Carnival. Allan Jones later admitted the musical content to be inferior to that in *Opera*, though contemporary reaction was more sympathetic. The only major casualty from the music department was Jones' love song from the very beginning of the film, *A Message From the Man in the Moon*, which was relegated to incidental music during the water carnival and 'reprised' by Groucho in the finale; this is one of several loose ends to be found in the final version (see **Continuity errors**). Thalberg's early death may have contributed to the flawed result but, whatever the reason, *Races* lost some interesting material in the process of editing. A published script, which like *A Night at the Opera*'s equivalent offers pre- and post-release versions, records some of these lost moments. One of these takes place at the sanitarium, immediately prior to Harpo's examination. Among the patients is a little girl who throws a tantrum when presented with food. Harpo tries to coax her into eating by

In a scene deleted from the final print of **A Day at the Races***, Chico and Harpo prepare fish at the water carnival*

taking a spoonful of ice cream but, according to the script, 'the kid squawks'. The child hits Harpo with a balloon attached to a stick, but the balloon becomes detached and deflates. When the child starts bawling, Harpo attempts to pacify her by re-inflating the balloon, but inhales too deeply and swallows it. On the arrival of a nurse, Harpo hides beneath the bed; the bed is wheeled away but Harpo has vanished. Chico, outside in the corridor, looks for Harpo and is alerted to his presence by the sound of a taxi horn as the bed is wheeled past; Harpo is clinging to the underside of the bedsprings, hitching a free ride as the puzzled staff question the source of the noise. From here Chico wanders into a steam room, emerging to confront Groucho, as per the release version, with news of a 'patient'. There is an extant photograph of the moment where Harpo takes a spoonful of ice cream; other stills preserve deleted material from the Water Carnival, as when Chico and Harpo intrude themselves upon Groucho and party. They examine the contents of a chafing dish and replace it with a fish from Harpo's pocket. 'Hugo!' cries Dumont, 'Look what they're doing!', but Groucho tries to ignore them in favour of a spoon-jumping trick he is attempting. Harpo de-scales the fish with Dumont's lorgnette; Chico builds the fire under the dish, dumping in various items, all the while dropping loud hints about horse doctors. Harpo's mayhem includes filling a pipe with food in lieu of tobacco, and swallowing a *demitasse* complete with cup. 'I think they're cooking my goose' observes Groucho, whose guests depart before the intruders join him at the table. The approaching Sheriff is their cue to leave: 'I don't think we wait for dessert!' says Chico. Harpo catches the spoon that Groucho has been trying to launch into a glass, sending it down the back of Dumont's dress. At the conclusion of the Water Carnival, Harpo mimes Groucho's imminent danger to Chico; once again, stills and

the script reveal a lost moment, as Harpo arrives to discover Chico playing Blind Man's Buff with a group of pretty girls. The message is that Flo Marlowe (Esther Muir [*qv*]) plans to trap Hackenbush in order to get him fired; although they interrupt his *soirée* several times in the film, stills survive of a further, deleted attempt in which Harpo and Chico are disguised as bellhops. The moment is set up in the film, when Groucho calls for 'the bellhop to hop up with some hop Scotch', but nothing follows. As scripted, Harpo opens the door with an oversized master key, entering with Chico, who bears a tray with Scotch, glasses and soda syphon. As Groucho pours a drink, Harpo sprays soda not just towards the glass but all over the tray, from which it rebounds over Chico, Groucho and his companion. 'Hey,' says Groucho, 'just fill the glass, not the room!' Groucho and Chico take refuge behind the sofa as Harpo attempts to stem the now uncontrollable syphon. They make for the table as Chico insists the woman is 'no good'; Groucho, caught sideways when the soda is placed on the table, claims 'If this keeps up she'll float out.' Groucho pretends to have been persuaded to leave ('This is no place for a man who hasn't been in the Navy'), and cons the others into doing the same - but not before Harpo has thrown the syphon back in the girl's direction.

(See also: Animals; Colour films; Continuity errors; Deleted scenes; Doctors; Dumbrille, Douglass; Gambling; Gangsters; M-G-M; Names; Race; Records; Songs; Telephones; Television; Thalberg, Irving; Trailers; Wood, Sam)

A DAY AT THE UNITED NATIONS
See: Abandoned projects

DAY, DORIS (b. 1924)
Actress and singer whose image in films tended towards the virtuous, prompting one of Groucho's most

widely-quoted jokes, as much at the expense of his advancing age as anything else: 'I knew Doris Day before she was a virgin.'

(See also: Insults; Women)

A DAY IN HOLLYWOOD, A NIGHT IN THE UKRAINE
Perhaps the most acclaimed Marx Brothers pastiche, *A Day in Hollywood, A Night in the Ukraine* was the brainchild of Dick Vosburgh, an American-born writer long based in England. Vosburgh had long nurtured a wish to write for the Marxes, frustrated by the knowledge that he was starting out just at a time when the brothers as a team were calling it quits. In a BBC Radio interview, Vosburgh described having taken the project to Richard Jackson, 'who steered it to the right place ... a tiny, 95-seat theatre called the New End in Hampstead'. The show, directed by Ian Davidson, opened there on 10 January 1979 billed as 'a Thirties double feature'. Vosburgh's book and lyrics were complemented by music composed by Frank Lazarus. The first half, *A Day in Hollywood*, presents a context for the Marxes with a revue representing 1930s movies in general, portraying the styles, clichés and stars of Hollywood's golden era; original songs of the period were chosen to illustrate the full spectrum, from the best (*Two Sleepy People, Over the Rainbow*) to the worst (*The Girl Friend of the Whirling Dervish* who, it seems, 'gives him the runaround'). Similarly enshrined was the Hollywood trailer, in a scene announcing the Marx Brothers in *A Night in the Ukraine*. For his Marx Brothers story, Vosburgh went to *The Bear*, a one-act farce by Anton Chekhov ('Russia's top gag writer'), placing the Marxes into a pre-Soviet Ukraine. Groucho is cast as Serge B. Samovar, a lawyer in the tradition of Waldorf T. Flywheel and J. Cheever Loophole. The lawyer, born 'beneath a lucky Tsar', introduces himself with a song, *Samovar the Lawyer*, akin to the

The UK cast of **A Day in Hollywood, A Night in the Ukraine**. *Left to right: Frank Lazarus, Sheila Steafel and John Bay*
Photo: Beryl Vosburgh

Kalmar-Ruby *Hooray For Captain Spaulding* and, especially, *Doctor Hackenbush*. 'They freed the crook and hanged the judge' sings Samovar, establishing his credentials beyond question. Margaret Dumont (*qv*) finds a parallel in Mrs Natasha Pavlenko, a wealthy widow for whom Samovar, arriving to collect a debt, makes an unerring beeline. Chico works as footman to Mrs Pavlenko, sporting a lengthy, perplexing name beginning with 'Carlo', finishing in 'Mozzarella' and containing numerous syllables in between; when asked how he spells it, he replies 'wrong every time'. His exchanges with the lawyer display familial likeness to the best lines from the Marxes' vaudeville acts; when Chico asks 'Have a rough trip?', Groucho replies 'No thanks, I just had one', leading one to suspect Uncle Al and the garbage man to be observing from above. Harpo becomes Gino, the gardener, among whose duties are chasing Masha, the maid and playing a bicycle wheel like a harp (after feeding

the machine a carrot, then giving it a medical examination). Present also are Harpo's Gookie expression (*qv*), the business of producing countless articles from his raincoat and the ink-drinking from the film version of *Cocoanuts* (*qv*). Further in keeping with the Marxes' epics, Vosburgh incorporated a romantic sub-plot (borrowed from another Chekhov work, *The Sea Gull*), involving Samovar's coachman Constantine (an aspiring playwright) and Nina, Mrs Pavlenko's daughter. Samovar the Lawyer was played by John Bay, an American actor who had impersonated Groucho in a one-man show; Chico/Carlo was portrayed by Frank Lazarus, *Hollywood/Ukraine*'s composer; Harpo/Gino was played by Sheila Steafel, one of several women to have made an effective Harpo facsimile; Paddie O'Neil was Mrs Pavlenko; Maureen Scott was Nina; Jon Glover, who had auditioned for the Harpo role, was Constantine; and Alexandra Sebastian was kept on her toes as Masha. Reviews for the New End production were enthusiastic: the *Observer* compared many of the jokes to those written by S.J. Perelman (*qv*); from the *Sunday Express*, Clive Hirschhorn evaluated it as 'for the

sheer fun of it, not to be missed', having high praise for the impersonations; and Larry Adler, writing for *What's On in London*, seemed genuinely surprised by the accuracy of John Bay's performance, describing also a 'very original' Harpo while applauding Paddie O'Neil's work. Miss O'Neil's impersonations of Bette Davis and Katharine Hepburn (in the *Day in Hollywood* section) won unconditional praise from Sheridan Morley of *Punch*, though he seemed less fond of the 'shaky pastiche' that was the second half. Despite a mixed review, Morley said he would 'not be inclined to miss it'. The review appeared on 24 January and it seems fair to speculate that *Hollywood/Ukraine* subsequently grew upon the critic, for by March the *Punch* theatre guide described it as 'Dick Vosburgh's superb Marx brothers' (*sic*) evening'. It was in this month that the show transferred to the Mayfair Theatre, in London's West End. The *Financial Times* of 31 March applauded the change of venue, declaring it 'just about the right size for this kind of intimate cabaret'. 'Slightly more confident playing', it continued, 'would transform *A Night in the*

Ukraine into a joy for non-Marx fanatics: for that strangely large band it will probably make the year'. It is equally probable that the *Guardian's* Nicholas de Jongh was among that large band, for his review of 30 March bucks the trend by favouring *Night in the Ukraine* over its preamble. 'I have to admit', wrote de Jongh, 'that the quick-fire absurd patter and wise-cracking has an appeal to aficionados'. It was during the Mayfair run that American impresario Alexander H. Cohen saw the show and promptly bought the US rights. Cohen had previously taken the Flanders and Swann revues to America, also *Beyond the Fringe* and its Peter Cook/Dudley Moore descendant *Behind the Fridge* (see **Smoking**). *Hollywood/Ukraine* made it to the States by Spring 1980, having been intended for a Broadway opening the preceding Christmas. A revised version, directed by Tommy Tune, tried out in Baltimore on 18 April before commencing at New York's Golden Theater on 1 May. Frank Lazarus, repeating his original role, was sole representative of the London cast. David Garrison took over as Groucho and Priscilla Lopez as Harpo, Sheila Steafel's success having led to an insistence on a woman playing the part. Investors included Neil Simon, Jane Fonda, Carol Channing (who saw the show in London) and the Shubert and Nederlander organisations. Reception in the USA was positive despite a legal argument over use of the team's characters; heirs of Groucho and Harpo, having failed in pursuing an injunction to halt the show's opening, sued for infringement of rights of publicity in the comedians' personas. Although an initial Federal Court decision was in favour of the heirs, a panel of three Appeal Court judges subsequently found against them, though reserving judgment on a technical point (concerning essentially the difference between parody and an unauthorized imitation). It was decided that Californian law should apply in this case rather than that of New York,

because the Marxes had been Californian residents at the time of death. According to *Variety's* report of the proceedings, there had been precedents in California law, notably an unsuccessful suit brought by the heirs of Bela Lugosi, to suggest inherited rights of publicity to be either non-existent or else limited to merchandising (e.g. T-shirts) originated by a celebrity during his or her lifetime. The heirs requested settlement, under which they would drop their suit if paid a token sum of $9,000 (i.e. $3,000 per Marx Brother) and were permitted to act as agents in moving the show to television or film adaptation within a prescribed period. The period elapsed without any such adaptation and full control reverted to the show's creators (at the time of writing, there has still to be a television or film version of *Hollywood/Ukraine*). Priscilla Lopez received a Tony award, as did Tommy Tune and Thommie Walsh for choreography. David Garrison was nominated, as was Dick Vosburgh for the book and Frank Lazarus and Vosburgh for the score. Peggy Hewitt, as Mrs Pavlenko, was nominated for a Drama Desk award, and the entire cast received Drama-Logue awards. Another favourable view was taken by Chico's daughter Maxine, who greeted Lazarus with outstretched arms and a cry of 'Daddy'! Similarly, Harpo's widow, Susan, and son, Bill, had much praise for Priscilla Lopez. The Original Cast Album (on DRG Records) was nominated for a Grammy award. The show has been revived on two occasions at the Edinburgh Festival, the first of which presented *Ukraine* alone, with Michael Roberts as Groucho, the second the entire show with Roberts as Groucho and Frank Lazarus once again as Chico. Revivals have proliferated throughout the USA, including those in Fort Worth (June 1989, this time with a male Harpo), San José (December 1989-January 1990), Oregon (June-September 1990), Ohio (September 1990) and St Louis (December 1990).

(See also: *At the Circus*; Children; *Flywheel, Shyster and Flywheel*; *Groucho - a Life in Revue*; Impersonators; *Minnie's Boys*; Records; Russia)

DEATHS

The Marx family's first-born, Manfred, died in infancy. Chico died on 11 October 1961, the result of arteriosclerosis; he had been experiencing heart problems since 1947 (and, ironically, had faked a heart attack several years before, as a means of escaping a club booking). Similarly, Harpo had suffered a series of heart attacks over a period of several years prior to undergoing bypass surgery. At that time such procedure was comparatively new and Harpo did not survive; he died on 28 September 1964. Gummo died on 21 April 1977. The news was withheld from the ailing Groucho, who followed Gummo soon after, on 19 August. Groucho's death was officially from pneumonia, though he had been progressively incapacitated by strokes since 1971. Zeppo, last of the brothers, succumbed to lung cancer on 29 November 1979. Chico, Gummo and Zeppo are buried in Palm Springs, where they had all lived towards the end. Harpo is popularly supposed to be at Forest Lawn, but the precise location of his gravesite cannot be revealed at the present time. A plaque denotes the site of Groucho's ashes at the Eden Memorial Park, in the San Fernando Valley. He did not receive his preferred epitaph, which was: 'Here lies Groucho Marx - and lies, and lies, and lies. P.S. He never kissed an ugly girl.' (When *Vanity Fair* sought epitaphs from the famous in 1925, the Marxes opted for an old gag with 'Here lie the Four Marx Brothers. The first time they ever went out together.') A bizarre footnote to Groucho's interment followed in 1982, when on May 19 the *Guardian* reported the brief disappearance of the urn containing his ashes from its sealed vault. It was found later that day, some twenty miles away in Glendale, where it had been left on the steps of the Mount Sinai Memorial Park administration building. This strange tale offers still another parallel between Groucho and his old friend Charlie Chaplin (*qv*), whose remains had similarly been removed from their intended site shortly after burial. 'When they put your picture on the front page when you die,' Groucho once said, 'then you know you're important.' He might have been pleased, then, to know that the London *Evening News* did exactly that with the banner headline 'GROUCHO THE ZANY KING DIES'. The news broke on a Saturday, at a time when London still had an evening paper six days a week. Groucho might have been even more entertained by an alleged TV news broadcast in Philadelphia, which ran something like: 'Comedian Groucho Marx took a turn for the worse today ... in fact, he died.' An inept but strangely fitting tribute to the master of *non sequitur*.

(See also: Births; Carnegie Hall Concert, the; *Deputy Seraph*; Doctors; Monroe, Marilyn; Names; Religion; Sheekman, Arthur; Shoes)

DELETED SCENES

(Marx Brothers films *qv*)
It is quite usual for scenes to be shot but discarded from a film prior to release. Nat Perrin (*qv*) has detailed an alternate version of the barber shop sequence of *Monkey Business*, while there exist from the same film at least two stills of Harpo disguised as a nurse, in one of several attempts to elude ship's officer Tom Kennedy (*qv*). One of these stills shows Harpo with a 'child', actually midget actor Billy Barty, with whom Groucho appeared

Deleted scenes: *an alternative interruption to Groucho's evening from* A Day at the Races

on a 1976 TV special (see **Television**). Another still suggests a rejected ending for *Horse Feathers* in which the Marxes play cards as the college burns around them. (*Horse Feathers* has undergone at least partial mutilation since initial release, but these cuts are in an altogether different category.) The radio trailer for *Duck Soup* provides some moments absent from the final print, and there are stills for an alternate version of the radio broadcast sequence in *A Night at the Opera* (itself the subject of probable mutilation in reissue). The slightly ragged final cut of *A Day at the Races* is the result of several cut scenes, detailed in the main entry, to bring it down to playable length. *At the Circus* would probably have been a much better film with the inclusion of Groucho's courtroom scene. The percentage of identifiable deletions in the Marx canon is comparatively low, aside from the considerable number of rejected one-line gags, but it is difficult

to stifle a pang when discovering their later films to have jettisoned comedy routines in favour of dull musical numbers and uninspired romantic sub-plotting.

(See also: Children; Continuity errors; Dumont, Margaret; Female impersonation; Romance; Sport; Trailers)

DEPUTY SERAPH

(TV pilot show)
Various attempts were made to reunite the Marxes after their decision to pursue separate careers. Some of these actually became reality, though one could hardly describe *The Story of Mankind* (*qv*) as a reunion. A TV segment of 1959, *The Incredible Jewel Robbery* (*qv*), sneaked Groucho into an otherwise Chico-Harpo endeavour but a further television project, from that same year, nearly produced an authentic revival. For years, rumour persisted of a Marx Brothers pilot show called *Deputy Seraph*, accompanied by vague talk of a format involving trainee angels. One source asserted this pilot to have been completed; opinions elsewhere were divided. It was therefore a considerable surprise when the July 1981 issue of *Classic Images* had as its cover story an account of the film's rediscovery, in the form of director's rushes totalling sixteen minutes. The footage had been recovered by Dave Riback of a company called Gaines 'Sixteen' Films, which offered the material in 16mm and Super-8. The programme's history was documented for the magazine by Ted Newsom, who identified the producer as Phil Rapp, a British-born comedy writer with experience in vaudeville, radio and television. Rapp had written for George Burns (*qv*), Eddie Cantor (also *qv*) and, among others, Fanny Brice, for whom he created the persona of 'Baby Snooks' (against whom Groucho had pitted wits on radio). Rapp was acquainted with

the Marxes through his membership of the Hillcrest Country Club; he and his co-writer, Richard Powell, devised a format suited to their teamwork while at the same time sparing the ageing comedians any excess physical effort. As suspected, Chico and Harpo were intended as novice angels whose task it was to intercede in earthly problems. Their 'Chief', Groucho, was the titular Deputy Seraph (a pun, of course, on 'seraph' and 'sheriff'). According to Newsom, each would descend to earth as required, taking over the body of an unwitting host: in extant footage, Groucho tells Chico 'You manipulate the uncle, and I'll ... ha, ha ... I'll distract the girl', a plan punctuated by his distinctive wiggle of the eyebrows. In this way other actors would, in effect, portray the team's usual characters by proxy, thus reducing the comedians' workload (particularly Groucho, who was to appear in only a third of the 39 episodes). In seeking financial backing, Rapp drew the attention of Sy Weintraub, President of Sol Lesser Productions and Harvey Shayutin in the United States; from Britain, Sydney Box and the Rank Organisation expressed interest. Under this international deal, the Marxes would be filmed in America with the balance shot at Pinewood Studios in England. The *Classic Images* piece describes this arrangement as post-dating the first script, dated 30 April 1959; yet a British paper, the *Daily Mirror*, reported the $2,000,000 deal - involving only Harpo and Chico - as early as 20 November 1958. In this account, the two brothers themselves were to film in Britain, where 'glamorous actresses' were being sought to appear with them. The Marx project was one of four 39-episode series under negotiation, the others being a science-fiction tale, an adventure series and the exploits of an insurance investigator for Lloyd's of London. 'Negotiations with Harpo and Chico Marx about their series are almost complete', Weintraub told the press, adding an expectation for

production to start 'within three months of the contract being signed with Harpo and Chico'. Given the details of this report and the timescale involved, it seems likely that Groucho was persuaded to contribute only after initial plans had been made, as with *Love Happy* (qv). Whatever the chronology, all three were present when the cameras began to turn. An appropriately celestial set was constructed, providing a background of stars and a cloud-filled floor. Harpo and Chico were clad as angels (though with their usual wigs and hats) but their boss, Groucho, wore a light sports jacket with dark trousers. His moustache and glasses were of the genuine type. Extant footage includes long-shots purporting to be Harpo and Chico, leaping among the clouds with the obvious assistance of a concealed trampoline. In close-up, Chico tells Harpo to disguise himself, and Harpo obliges with a Gookie (qv). Chico tries to tell him to put on his halo, only to receive a handshake. 'Hey,' replies Chico, 'not-a-hello; *halo*! Watch.' Chico's halo appears from nowhere. Harpo does at some stage summon a halo of his own, but starts to eat it. Groucho, the 'Chief', enters on a motorcycle. Differing versions seem to have been taken of this scene, one showing Groucho astride the machine as normal, plus another in which he grips the handlebars but with his body suspended in the air. Surveying his charges, Groucho looks to the camera and asks 'Did you ever see a worse-looking pair of angels? Say the secret word and you can have either one of them.' Chico and Harpo are delighted with his evaluation; Chico extends a hand to Harpo, but receives a leg in return. Retakes are known to have been made necessary by Chico's inability to remember lines; others offer alternate camera angles, with the director's voice sometimes audible. He may be heard also when guiding Harpo through his reaction, in a scene where Chico suddenly vanishes in the direction of earth. Sudden

appearances and disappearances were handled by the usual method of having the actors 'freeze' and the surplus footage trimmed accordingly. A recurrent gag shows Groucho, having taken charge, calling 'phone, please' whereupon a receiver appears in his hand. On two occasions he reacts with variants on 'I wonder how they do that', but on a third contents himself with a quasi-English 'Extraordinary!' Another method of communication is a kind of CB radio fitted to the motorcycle; in one shot, he signs off with 'Roger', allowing one angel to add 'Chico' and the last to mouth 'Harpo', voiced by two blasts on a taxi horn. There is room also for a harp and piano duet, in the inevitable 'Sugar in the Morning'. All the brothers seem reasonably fit for work, Chico looking in rather better shape than in *The Incredible Jewel Robbery*; yet it was Chico's declining health that forced the project's abandonment. He was discovered to be suffering from arteriosclerosis - hardening of the arteries - thus rendering impossible the insurance coverage necessary for production of a weekly series. Chico died two years later. *Deputy Seraph*, in its fragmented form, does not promise great things but at least shows genuine Marxian *cameraderie*; however, it is unlikely to have become classic television.

(See also: Abandoned projects; Clubs; Costume; Characters; Deaths; Documentaries; Food; Harp, the; Home movies; Moustaches, beards; Pianos; Radio; Religion; Songs; Television; Vaudeville; Wigs; *You Bet Your Life*)

DIAMOND, SELMA
See: Radio

DIX, RICHARD
See: *Too Many Kisses*

DUCK SOUP (Marx Bros. Film) with Groucho Marx (Rufus T. Firefly), Harpo Marx (Pinky), Chico Marx (Chicolini), Zeppo Marx (Bob Roland), Margaret Dumont (Mrs. Teasdale), Louis Calhern (Trentino), Raquel Torres (Vera Marcal), Leonid Kinsky

DUCK SOUP (Marx Bros. Film)
Released by Paramount 17 Nov. 1933
Directed by Leo McCarey. Screenplay:
Bert Kalmar, Harry Ruby with additional
dialogue by Arthur Sheekman, Nat Perrin

In the land of Freedonia lies Rufus T. Firefly for an entire day ('Shadowday') while Pinky is occupied cutting Ambassador Trentino's coattails. Trentino asks for Firefly's record, but Chicolini gives a musical kind which is shot down. Chicolini & Pinky have nothing to report but are sent once more to trap Firefly. In the Chamber of Deputies, Firefly attends to important business, such as providing shorter hours by cutting the workers' lunch hour to twenty minutes. Chicolini is outside, tending a peanut stand. He asks Pinky if he has any information, to no avail. A fight breaks out, involving the neighbouring lemonade vendor. The neighbour's hat finishes up on the peanut stand's burner. Chicolini's cry of 'Peanuts' attracts Firefly's attention, and he is offered a government job. In Firefly's office, he accepts the position of Secretary of War. Pinky appears and continues his policy of clipping things, in this case Firefly's quill pen. He identifies himself by a tattoo in his likeness before exiting. He passes Bob Roland in the doorway and bisects his hat. Bob has a letter in which Trentino criticizes Firefly; he believes an insult to the Ambassador would be met by a slap to the face, offering Firefly the excuse to order Trentino from Freedonia. Firefly sets off to insult Trentino at Mrs Teasdale's garden

party. Pinky brings His Excellency's 'car' and once more leaves Firefly sitting in the detached sidecar. At the garden party, Trentino tells Vera of the way Firefly intervenes whenever he tries to get close to Mrs Teasdale. He is assured that Firefly will not be present, just as the man himself is announced. Firefly usurps Trentino's proposal to Mrs Teasdale ('All I can offer is a Rufus over your head') while taking time to insult Trentino. He is met by comparable insults but chooses to take exception to 'upstart'. Firefly slaps Trentino and war seems inevitable. He calls once more for 'His Excellency's car': this time Firefly takes the bike, relegating Pinky to the sidecar. Pinky and the sidecar drive away, leaving the bike standing. We next see Pinky back at the peanut stand. The lemonade vendor, wearing a new hat, takes some peanuts without paying. His new hat is placed on the burner. He overturns the peanut stand but Pinky gains revenge by paddling his feet in the man's lemonade. Trentino is at Mrs Teasdale's residence, explaining that war can be averted if he and Firefly choose to forget their incident. Firefly is persuaded to agree but rekindles the argument when asking Trentino what the insult had been. War is on and Trentino sends Chicolini and Pinky to

obtain Freedonia's battle plans. Vera, Mrs Teasdale's house guest, is to help them. Chicolini and Pinky make inefficient burglars but Vera lets them in. Firefly is also staying: Chicolini and Pinky disguise themselves as the nightshirted Firefly, resulting in three identical figures prowling around. Pinky tries to open a safe but sets a radio blaring: Firefly summons the guards and Pinky, panicking, rushes into a large mirror. When Firefly confronts him, Pinky has to masquerade as Firefly's reflection. Despite Firefly's constant attempts to fool him, Pinky makes a perfect reflection until Chicolini arrives. Pinky escapes, but Chicolini is put on trial for treason. It's obviously a fair trial: Firefly offers him 8-1 on being found guilty; Chicolini demurs, being able to get 10-1 at the barber shop. The trial is interrupted by news of advancing Sylvanian troops. Trentino is on his way for a last-minute peace settlement, which Firefly is willing to accept. He ponders what might happen should Trentino *not* accept his friendship and by the time Trentino has arrived, he is in face-slapping mood again. Exit Trentino, fuming. *Freedonia's Going to War!* is sung *en masse*, in a spirit somewhere between patriotism and a revivalist meeting, especially when leading into *All God's Chillun Got Guns*. Pinky leads the guards and snips the plumes from their headgear. The crowd rushes to a tableau of the Revolutionary War, culminating in Pinky re-creating Paul Revere's famous ride through town. He pauses on seeing a pretty girl, partly undressed, running a bath. He makes his way to her room but disappears when told her husband is approaching. He is the lemonade vendor, and ignores the call to arms in favour of a hot bath. He is startled to find Pinky in the tub beneath him. Pinky receives an invitation to a different girl's home, but shares a bed with his horse instead.

Groucho gets out of bed just in time for his inauguration in **Duck Soup**

Duck Soup: *'His excellency's car!'*

The war progresses amid shot and shell. Firefly is at his headquarters, dressed as a Northern soldier of the Civil War. Pinky is in no-man's-land, recruiting by means of a sandwich board. Chicolini, nominally Freedonian Secretary of War, has deserted to Trentino's side but returns because the food is better. Firefly is now attired as a Confederate officer. Mrs Teasdale, trapped in a bombarded cottage, telephones; Firefly (in Scout uniform) takes the call and arrives there in Hussar's uniform. They try to hold off the enemy with rifle fire but someone has to go for help. Firefly, incidentally, now sports a Davy Crockett outfit. Pinky is chosen but is inadvertently thrust into a cupboard filled with ammunition. A stray cigarette end turns the place into a firework display. Thinking it to be the enemy, the others barricade the door. Firefly's radio messages pay off, and 'help is on the way': there follows library film of fire engines, motorcycle cops, marathon runners, rowing teams, swimmers, monkeys, elephants and dolphins. Pinky has escaped the cupboard by the time Sylvanian troops break down the door. Chicolini and Pinky systematically knock them out as Firefly runs up the score on a curtain rail. Trentino is last to appear, and is held is place as they pelt him with apples. He surrenders, but will have to wait until the fruit runs out. Mrs Teasdale sings *Hail, Hail Freedonia* and the pelting is turned upon *her*.

It is ironic that the Marx Brothers were only ready to make a war film after making peace with Paramount Pictures (*qv*). *Duck Soup* post-dated both an abortive script and a bitter contractual dispute, culminating in the team threatening to go it alone as 'Marx Bros., Inc.' (*qv*). The trouble did not finish there: Richard Meryman describes producer Herman Mankiewicz (*qv*) spending the early weeks of production playing darts with

Duck Soup: *Sylvanian spies report to Trentino*

director Leo McCarey (*qv*); the crunch came when Mankiewicz, always fond of a drink, was taken off the project after blaming his excessive intake (perhaps jokingly) on Harry Ruby (*qv*). It seems reasonable to connect the fall of Mankiewicz to the departure of his boss and fellow card-player, B.P. Schulberg. As on *Horse Feathers* (*qv*), Kalmar and Ruby contributed jokes in addition to the songs. Other material was supplied by Nat Perrin and Arthur Sheekman (both *qv*); much of it originated in the radio series they had written for Groucho and Chico, *Flywheel, Shyster and Flywheel* (*qv*). There was at one time talk of casting them in their radio characters for the new film. The idea of putting the Marxes into a mythical kingdom had been announced as early as August

Duck Soup: *Mrs Teasdale urges Firefly to make friends with Trentino*

1932, in a story provisionally entitled *Oo La La* with Ernst Lubitsch directing. This decision was made shortly after a wildly successful preview of *Horse Feathers* (ultimately the studio's biggest hit of 1932), which did convinced Paramount to hasten production of the next Marx endeavour, despite a contractual implication that each production would be at more or less yearly intervals. There was at that time a vogue for stories in this *milieu*, both serious and otherwise, of which the Mankiewicz film *Million Dollar Legs* is partially representative. Coupled to this fondness for Ruritanian-style settings was a fascination with Europe's increasing number of dictators, topics which were lampooned even in the comic strips. Elzie Segar's 'Thimble

*Pinky finds one of **Duck Soup**'s titular heroes in this posed shot*

Theatre' took Popeye first to the fictional land of Nazilia (so named before the Nazis took control in Germany), then established him as dictator of a would-be paradise called 'Spinachova'. By December 1932 *Oo La La* had become *Cracked Ice*, to be written by Kalmar and Ruby (it has been claimed that another writer, Grover Jones, also contributed to this first draft). As noted under **Abandoned projects**, the first script's content is difficult to determine. According to the Winter 1988 *Freedonia Gazette* (*qv*), the second draft of *Cracked Ice* is a recognizable *Duck Soup* prototype. By March the title had become *Grasshoppers* but the Marxes were already set to quit Paramount. The dispute was settled by May, when the Marxes returned to California. *Duck Soup*'s script was completed on 11 July but underwent considerable revision during shooting. This was due in no small measure to Leo McCarey, who had taken with him much of the Hal Roach style on leaving that studio three years before. McCarey was assigned to *Duck Soup* after his successful vehicle for Eddie Cantor (*qv*), *The Kid From Spain*, on which Kalmar and Ruby had also worked. To McCarey may be attributed several ingredients of *Duck Soup*, including the title: it had been used for an embryonic Laurel & Hardy two-reeler released early in 1927 and would see additional service as a 1942 short starring Edgar Kennedy (*qv*). Kennedy's presence in the Marx film was probably at McCarey's instigation, especially as he engages Harpo and Chico in the type of leisurely, exchanged violence McCarey had pioneered at Roach. Another legacy is the very Laurel & Hardy-like sequence in which Harpo and Chico stage a break-in. Their unsuitability to the task, locking themselves out after gaining admission, bears strong similarity to a Laurel & Hardy short of 1930, *Night*

Owls. McCarey adapted such motifs to suit the Marxes, however, for as Joe Adamson has noted, the Marxes differ from L&H in that they bungle the task deliberately. Another McCarey contribution, the mirror routine, predates his tenure at Roach, having been essayed by Chaplin (*qv*) in 1916's *The Floorwalker* and reprised by Max Linder in *Seven Years' Bad Luck* (1921) (*Variety* credited an old stage act, the Schwartz Brothers, as originators). For the two or three people still unacquainted with this gag, it involves lookalike characters simulating the presence of a mirror by matching each other's every move. In this case it is a nightshirted Groucho who confronts the disguised Harpo, who has crashed into a wall-sized mirror. As with the other adapted routines, the Marxes give it an extra edge by displaying full awareness of the imposture rather than any genuine attempt to convince; Groucho, for example, allows his 'reflection' a three-dimensional presence by momentarily changing places with him. The game is up only when a third 'Groucho', an

identically-attired Chico, arrives on the scene. Harpo revived the routine for his 1955 guest appearance on *I Love Lucy* (see **Television**). Aside from McCarey's interpolations, changes during production were many. *The American Film Institute Catalog*'s entry for *Duck Soup* quotes a *Hollywood Reporter* item in which Norman Krasna (*qv*) was borrowed from M-G-M to write an opening sequence, suggesting his acquaintance with Groucho to have begun here. Lost along the way was a scripted romance between Zeppo and Raquel Torres (*qv*) and with it a Kalmar-Ruby love song called *Keep On Doin' What You're Doin'* (used instead for the following year's Wheeler & Woolsey comedy *Hips, Hips Hooray*). After worthwhile rôles in the first two West Coast pictures, Zeppo was relegated to being Groucho's secretary, as in *Animal Crackers* (*qv*), something which may have prompted his decision to leave the act soon after. Surviving radio commercials (see **Trailers**) suggest Zeppo's intended rôle to have been that of Groucho's son, approximating that in *Horse Feathers*.

retiring somewhat into the background, a trend that would continue into *A Night at the Opera* (*qv*). 'The gags are vulgar, adroit, infectious, and wholly irresponsible,' added the reviewer, 'and the film travels with the throttle wide open. If you don't find the Marx fooling funny, for heaven's sake keep away'. Allowing for the obligatory warning to non-admirers, Lejeune's comments may be taken as fairly representative; *Duck Soup* was taken with with greater seriousness by *The Times*, who saw within it confirmation of a long-suspected satirical intent within the Marx Brothers. The satire was regarded as 'by no means obtrusive, and it is never allowed to oppress the pure chaos of their comedy', but served to provide 'direction and a little order to their fantasy'. *Duck Soup*'s reception was sufficiently good for one to query its reputation as a commercial failure. In fact, it did respectable business, albeit not to the extent of *Horse Feathers*, and this in a year when the Depression was at its worst. It has been suggested that an anti-war comedy was mistimed for 1933, given the mood of despondency and comparatively fresh memories of a World War only fifteen years earlier; yet times of economic depression frequently encourage dark humour and comedies set in the Great War had proliferated almost since the Armistice. The break with Paramount had less to do with any financial disappointment than the breakdown of relations before production. Posterity's view of *Duck Soup* is as the best-paced vehicle of the team's career, its disregard for logic equalling that of *Horse Feathers* but with none of the stop-and-start structure. When Groucho can change uniforms between shots and 'help' is

Conversely, Harpo's character name, 'Brownie' (cited in the pressbook), reverted to 'Pinky' as per *Horse Feathers*. The harp and piano solos, often candidates for deletion over the years, succumbed to a general streamlining; rumours notwithstanding, these interludes were not included even in original prints of the film. (At a 1976 theatrical revival of *Duck Soup* the author, aware of the absent solos, noted a collective audience murmur when Harpo plucked some piano strings in the manner of a harp; the mass disappointment was almost tangible.) The film was finished during October 1933 and released a month later. Mordaunt Hall's *New York Times* review of 23 November described it as 'extremely noisy without being nearly as mirthful as their other films', though he reported considerable laughter during the mirror scene (while admitting uncertainty as to which was the real Groucho), enjoyed Harpo's bogus Paul Revere ride and found amusement in Harpo's scissoring of coat-tails, hats and any other vulnerable clothing. Margaret Dumont (*qv*), in her first Marx appearance since *Animal Crackers*, was rated as 'satisfactory'. Joe Bigelow (alias 'Bige') in *Variety* of 28 November noted the rapid pace but

expressed approval at the way fewer laughs ran into each other than in previous films. In a remark similar to the 'four-year-old child' gag in the film (see **Children**), Bige thought the story 'could easily have been written by a six-year-old' but recognized any scenario as being incidental to the comedy. While aware of the mirror routine's age, it was thought sufficiently well done for it to gather 'a new and hilarious comedy momentum all over again'. There was comment on Groucho's increase in physical as opposed to verbal humour as well as the deleted musical solos. Dumont's reappearance was acknowledged as 'making it perfect for Groucho'. *Duck Soup* premièred in the UK (again at the Carlton) in February 1934. *Variety*'s favourable view was echoed, to a point, by C.A. Lejeune of the *Observer*: '*Duck Soup* is like every other Marx picture ever made, only it's made considerably better than some'. In detailing a slight shift in character emphasis, Lejeune spoke of Harpo

Sinatra & Jane Russell in comedy initially titled
It's Only Money (filmed in 1948), as a confidant.

despatched via stock film of everything from swimmers to stampeding elephants, it becomes clear that Marxian anarchy has for once been channelled by a sympathetic comedy director instead of someone content for them to stay on the chalk marks. As early as 1950 (when it was revived at two London venues, the Curzon and the Everyman), Dilys Powell of the *Sunday Times* regarded the film as the best entertainment in a 'saddish week'; it was lauded at a 1960s festival with Groucho in attendance, by which time he was prepared to admit the comedic superiority of the Paramounts, and *Duck Soup* in particular, to the more profitable M-G-M films that were to follow. Original US prints of *Duck Soup* bore the NRA symbol, part of the government's campaign for economic recovery. This would not have appeared on British copies but is present in the BBC and Channel Four prints, suggesting origins in American master material rather than a dupe negative for overseas. The aptly-named *Freedonia Gazette* (*qv*) investigated a report dating back to *Time* magazine in November 1933, concerning a complaint about *Duck Soup*. The disgruntled party was Harry B. Hickey, Mayor of Fredonia, New York, who queried use of the town's name. The

Marxes' response was that they should change the name of their town, suggesting further that if Mayor Hickey did not sport a black moustache, play the harp, chase girls or speak with an Italian accent, then the Marxes, not he, were Mayor of Fredonia. 'The old gray Mayor ain't what he used to be,' it was decided. The magazine's research disclosed several photos of the Mayor, all of them taken by Paramount's publicity department; one of them shows a calendar dated two months before the supposed complaint. Freedonians everywhere may draw their own conclusions. The title *Duck Soup* was used twice when attempting to launch a humour magazine in Britain during 1978 and 1985; it is the movie itself that restores the hero's will to live in Woody Allen's *Hannah and Her Sisters* (1988).

(See also: Animals; Animation; Books; Breese, Edmund; Calhern, Louis; Cars; Censorship; Dumont, Margaret; Fighting; Harp, the; Home movies; Impersonators; Laurel & Hardy; Marx, Sam 'Frenchie'; M-G-M; Opera; Paramount Pictures; Piano, the; Politicians; Prison; Radio; Records; *Risqué* humour; Songs; Tattoos; Television; Video releases; Wartime; Wigs)

DOUBLE DYNAMITE (RKO 1951)
Groucho Marx appeared opposite Frank

DUMBRILLE, DOUGLAS (or DOUGLASS) (1890-1974)
(Marx Brothers films *qv*)
Canadian-born actor, in films from 1931. Dumbrille is best recalled as a suave, pencil-moustached villain in comedy films, including several with Abbott & Costello (*Ride 'Em Cowboy* [1942], *Lost in a Harem* [1944], *The Foreign Legion* [1950]). He is the manipulative racetrack owner, Morgan, in the Marxes' *A Day at the Races* and murderous store manager Grover in *The Big Store*. He has also been reported among the cast of *Monkey Business*. Elsewhere in Dumbrille's impressive filmography are *I Am a Fugitive From a Chain Gang* (1932), Joe E. Brown's *Elmer the Great* (1933), Frank Capra's *Broadway Bill* (1934), *The Lives of a Bengal Lancer* (1935), Capra's Oscar-winning *Mr Deeds Goes to Town* (1936), Eddie Cantor's *Ali Baba Goes to Town* (1937), *Firefly* (1937; see **Allan Jones**), *Mr Moto in Danger Island* (1939) and the Crosby-Hope *Road to Zanzibar* (1941). Later active in TV in addition to film work, one of his latter-day cinema appearances being the 1956 remake of *The Ten Commandments*.

(See also: Adrian, Iris; Blore, Eric; Cantor, Eddie; Criminals; Gangsters; Gilbert, Billy)

DUMONT, MARGARET (1889-1965)
(Marx Brothers films and shows *qv*)
Margaret Dumont was, in Groucho's words, 'practically the fifth Marx Brother', to the extent that many people assumed she and Groucho to be married in real life. Born Marguerite Baker in New York, she was opera-trained and had appeared extensively in Britain and Europe before reaching the Broadway stage. She retired on marrying one John Moller Jr, but on his death returned to the stage, his fortune having been less than imagined. Her

Chico has no piano solo in Duck Soup,
but Groucho joined him at the keyboard
between takes

first encounter with the Marx Brothers was as the first of a succession of *grandes dames* in 1925's *The Cocoanuts*. She had not been sufficiently warned and her experiences in this and the follow-up, *Animal Crackers*, were of being manhandled and affectionately humiliated, as when being stripped off in trains while on tour, or an occasion when Harpo pulled out her petticoat while on stage in *Animal Crackers*. She never carried through her regular threats to leave, and was genuinely fond of the Marx Brothers. She would spend Christmases with Groucho, whom she insisted on calling 'Julie', an abbreviation of his real name. Miss Dumont repeated her stage roles when the shows were filmed, and accompanied the team to England when engaged by C.B. Cochran (*qv*). She was omitted from the Marxes' first West Coast productions but returned for *Duck Soup*, *A Night at the Opera*, *A Day at the Races*, *At the Circus* and *The Big Store*. Such a close identification with the Marxes destroyed any chance she stood of a dramatic career, for although she worked sometimes in comparatively straight films, most of her non-Marx work was with other comedians. Detailed elsewhere is her appearance

in Wheeler and Woolsey's *Kentucky Kernels* (1935). With W.C. Fields (*qv*) she was in *Never Give a Sucker an Even Break* (1941) and the deleted segment of *Tales of Manhattan* (1942). A set from the latter was re-used in her 1943 film with Laurel & Hardy (*qv*), *The Dancing Masters* (1943). In *Up in Arms* (1944) she supported Danny Kaye. She worked with Jack Benny (*qv*) in *The Horn Blows at Midnight* (1945) and with Abbott & Costello in *Little Giant* (1945). Among her last films were *Zotz!* (1962) and *What a Way to Go!* (1964). Throughout all this, she was recognized above all as a foil for the Marxes, particularly when the Screen Actors' Guild voted her best Supporting Actress for *A Day at the Races*. Groucho regularly described her as never understanding any of the jokes, asking him 'Julie, what are they laughing at?' Such total naïvety is possible but somewhat implausible, and contradicted totally by at least one close friend, Carol Channing. Miss Channing's father was a prominent Christian Science lecturer; Margaret Dumont, also a Christian Scientist, regularly attended his lectures and thus knew Carol from childhood. Dick Vosburgh, who has written material for Carol Channing, asked her about Margaret Dumont's supposed lack of

humour; the reply was that she had a fine sense of humour and understood the jokes perfectly well. Some indication of this is evident in the films, where she permits herself an occasional smile at the goings-on; it is even more apparent in a TV show, *The Hollywood Palace*, recorded shortly before Dumont's death in 1965. She and Groucho engage in a re-enacted scene from *Animal Crackers*, during which the actress makes little attempt at seriousness, and indeed breaks up more than once. It is quite possible that Margaret Dumont succeeded in putting one over on Groucho, who genuinely believed her to be without humour. In evaluating the scene in *Animal Crackers* where Zeppo chooses to omit the bulk of Groucho's dictated letter, Joe Adamson says 'it takes a Marx Brother to pull something like that on a Marx Brother and get away with it'; it might also be said that it would take an unofficial Marx Brother to pull a scam on Groucho lasting some forty years.

(See also: Awards; Burke, James; Marriages; Practical jokes; Ruby, Harry; Television; Women)

DOCUMENTARIES (Marx Bros. *qv*) Extracts of Marx Bros. films are seen in M-G-M's Big Parade of Comedy (M-G-M, 1964), and That's Entertainment II (M-G-M, 1976). In 1982, PBS-TV introduced viewers to The Marx Bros. in a Natshell (1982), narrated by Gene

EATON, JAY (1900-70)

Supporting actor, one of the three
aviators replaced by Harpo, Chico and
Allan Jones (*qv*) in *A Night at the
Opera* (*qv*). Various roles in silents
(among them Colleen Moore's last
non-talking subject, *Synthetic Sin*) and
many talkies, among them *Libeled
Lady* (1936) and Danny Kaye's *The Kid
From Brooklyn* (1946).

(See also: McLeod, Norman Z.;
Oppenheimer, George; Sedan, Rolfe;
White, Leo)

Eaton's other theatre work includes
Kid Boots with Eddie Cantor (*qv*) and
Kalmar & Ruby's *The Five O'Clock
Girl* opposite Oscar Shaw (*qv*). The
two were reunited for the film version
of *Cocoanuts* (*qv*).

(See also: Francis, Kay; Ruby, Harry;
Shean, Al; Sorin, Louis)

EDUCATION

The Marx Brothers' schooling was
sparse; like his brothers, Harpo
attended New York's PS 86 ('PS'
meaning 'Public School' in the
American sense) between the ages of

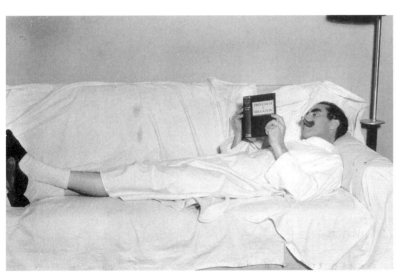

EATON, MARY (1901-48)

Singer and dancer born in Norfolk,
Virginia; occasionally in silent films but
recalled chiefly as a stage star. Her
theatrical debut was in *Over the Top*
(1917); later in *The Royal Vagabond*
(1919) for George M. Cohan and Sam
Harris (*qv*). Other important stage
work includes *The Ziegfeld Follies* for
1920-22 (she is enshrined in Ziegfeld's
1929 film *Glorifying the American
Girl*). Once deputized for Marilyn
Miller in *Sally* after only one rehearsal;
is remembered also for having
successfully defied Ziegfeld's ban on
his female stars marrying (her husband
was Millard Webb, director of
Glorifying the American Girl). Mary

*Education: a nightshirted Groucho between
takes of* Duck Soup, *improving his mind with
'Principles of Education'*

five and eight, by which time he had
wearied of being thrown out of the
window by larger boys and never
returned. Harpo later became very
well-read, thanks mostly to the
influence of Alexander Woollcott (*qv*).
Chico was alone in finishing high
school, possibly through his genius for
mathematics; if required, he could
memorize the numbers on a bank note
and repeat them in all permutations
months later (if *not* required, he would
forget them immediately).
Unfortunately, he devoted most of

these skills to working out odds. Groucho was pulled out of school before his thirteenth birthday, a not-uncommon thing when children were required to contribute to the family income. To an even greater extent than Harpo, Groucho was mostly self-educated, a constant reader and reasonably successful as an author in his own right. It is perhaps ironic that a family with scarcely any formal education should make its name with a sketch called *Fun in Hi Skule* (*qv*), itself a vague ancestor of the schoolroom scene in *Horse Feathers* (*qv*).

(See also: Books; Doctors; Fighting; Gambling; Wigs)

EDWARDS, GUS

See: *Fun in Hi Skule*; Vaudeville

ELIOT, T.S. (THOMAS STEARNS) (1888-1965)

American-born poet, dramatist and critic, long a naturalized Briton. Groucho and Eliot exchanged correspondence - and portraits - from 1961. Despite a momentary gaffe in addressing 'Graucho' Marx, the Eliot-Marx friendship flourished and Groucho, with his wife Eden, the Eliots for dinner while in England for TV's *The Celebrity Game* in 1964. Prior to the trip, Groucho told Barry Heenan (of the listings magazine *TV Times*) that he thought it would be a good time to meet Eliot, after years of correspondence, given that ITV were financing the visit. 'I could hardly expect T.S. Eliot to pay my way. All he offered was a dinner and I don't even know if he can cook'. Groucho had made a point of absorbing the poet's

work, such as *The Waste Land*, only to find Eliot more interested in discussing the Marx Brothers. After Eliot's death, Groucho contributed to a commemorative record album in his memory.

(See also: Impersonators; Letters; Marriages; Records; Television)

ERSKINE, CHESTER (1905-86)

Producer, director and writer, active in theatre, films and television; wrote and directed Groucho's solo film *A Girl in Every Port* (*qv*). Among many film credits are *The Egg and I* (1947), *All My Sons* (1948) and the 1952 adaptation of Shaw's *Androcles and the Lion*, for which Harpo was initially considered as lead.

(See also: Abandoned projects)

FELD, FRITZ (1900-93)

German-born character actor and comedian, originally on stage; in American films from the mid-1920s, sometimes as director; plays Jardinet, outraged orchestra conductor of *At the Circus* (*qv*). In July 1938 the *Hollywood Reporter* mentioned his departure from the cast of *Room Service* (also *qv*) in favour of a role in *Campus Confessions*. Among other comedy appearances are Howard Hawks' *Bringing Up Baby* (1938), Danny Kaye's *The Secret Life of Walter Mitty* (1947), the Abbott & Costello films *Mexican Hayride* and *The Noose Hangs High* (both 1948), Eddie Cantor's *If You Knew Susie* (1948), the 1954 Bob Hope vehicle *Casanova's Big Night* and 1967's *Barefoot in the Park*, with Feld in the not unaccustomed role of restaurant proprietor. Other latter-day work includes films with Jerry Lewis (*The Errand Boy*) and Mel Brooks. One of Feld's last roles was in a 1989 TV movie, *Get Smart Again*, itself a revival of the 1960s *Get Smart* series co-devised by Brooks. Feld was quite prolific in television, both in series episodes and the BBC's film history chronicle, *Talking Pictures*. Feld was also coordinator of a community theatre bearing his name. In January 1977, Feld was among the guests at a convention in Los Angeles, when the Marxes were accepted into the Hollywood Hall of Fame (Groucho was also in attendance). Feld is profiled in a 1986 book, Jordan R. Young's *Reel Characters*, to which he also contributed a foreword.

(See also: Adrian, Iris; Awards; Cantor, Eddie; McLeod, Norman; Rumann, Siegfried)

FELLINI, FEDERICO
See: Abandoned projects

FELLOWES, ROCKCLIFFE
(1885-1950)

Ottawa-born actor, from the stage; early theatrical experience included work with Minnie Maddern Fiske (*passim* for cross-references). In films from 1917's *The Easiest Way*, working for virtually every major Hollywood studio; among many silent credits are *The Price of Possession* (1921), *The Spoilers* (1923), *Trifling With Honor* (1923), *The Road to Glory* (1926), *The Understanding Heart* (1927) and *The Third Degree* (1927). A gangsterish trend in Fellowes' roles was all the more apparent in his talkies (the last being in 1934), including *20,000 Years in Sing Sing* (1932) and the Marx Brothers' *Monkey Business* (*qv*) as Joe Helton, a gang leader wishing to retire into high society.

(See also: Gangsters)

FEMALE IMPERSONATION
(Marx Brothers films *qv*)

Although a staple of comic tradition, female impersonation plays little part in Marx Brothers humour, though Groucho's theatrical début in The LeRoy Trio (*qv*) leaned heavily on the device (he offers a vague hint of this style in the catwalk scene of *The Big Store*). What few examples there are mostly concern Harpo, whose elfin traits perhaps bear stronger resemblance to feminine characteristics than those of his more down-to-earth brothers. It may be significant that, like Chaplin (whose early films include some creditable female impersonations), Harpo has often been impersonated by women. Stills exist from *Monkey Business* showing a deleted sequence in which Harpo, as a stowaway pursued by ship's officer Tom Kennedy (*qv*), disguises himself (unconvincingly) in a nurse's uniform. Less elaborate but partially representative is the business in *A Night at the Opera* where Harpo uses food in the manner of make-up, less an attempt at female impersonation than, as historian Donald W. McCaffrey has said, a child playing the game of being a woman (as he does after stealing Mrs Whitehead's shoes in *Animal Crackers*). Later in the film, Harpo and Chico momentarily don female gypsy

costumes when infiltrating the opera's chorus. As a youth, Harpo's voice took longer than usual to break, something which, combined with his slight build, permitted him to engage in a practical joke. Harpo would have been sixteen when Groucho, an ambitious fourteen-year-old, was employed at a theatrical wigmaker's. For a lark, Groucho brought home some of the ladies' wigs, and after wearing them for a joke it was decided that Harpo, with Groucho's assistance, should borrow their mother's clothes and make up as what may politely be termed a 'good-time girl'. Thus disguised, Harpo terrified a hypochondriac friend of Al Shean (*qv*), while charming the man's elderly father and outraging the women of the household. In relating this incident in his memoirs, Harpo recalled it as having made him 'the family character'. In the same work, he described a woman named Metcalfe who, in clear anticipation of *Viktor/Viktoria*, worked in vaudeville (*qv*) as a female impersonator while posing as a man in everyday life; also Groucho's ejection from a vaudeville bill when, deputizing for the master of ceremonies, he introduced a female impersonator billed as 'the Creole Fashion Plate' as 'the Queer Old Fashion Plate'. Though blunt with regard to this topic (as about

most things), and despite occasional jokes on the subject, Groucho shared with his brothers a lack of prejudice against homosexuals, unusual for the day (Groucho is said to have greeted a New Year by dancing on a table with Noël Coward). Among the less mainstream Marx-related books is the memoir of a gay chef employed by Groucho in the 1970s. Groucho once mentioned a party given by six gay cast members of *Animal Crackers* (*qv*), whose hosts were dressed and made up convincingly as women. That the Marxes were invited to attend was taken by Groucho as a token of high regard and, one imagines, implied trust.

(See also: Chaplin, Charlie; *A Day in Hollywood, A Night in the Ukraine*; Deleted scenes; Impersonators; Marx, Minnie; Prostitutes; *Risqué* humour; Shoes; Wigs)

FIELDS, W.C. (1880-1946)

William Claude Dukenfield, better known as W.C. Fields, is recalled with affection as a comedian who built a positive approach on the most negative of attitudes. Often compared to Falstaff, his fondness for drink and rejection of conformity have made him an idol for several generations of

mavericks, actual or aspiring. In this rebellious aspect (tempered in his case by the eloquent tongue and grandiose manners of an old-school rogue), he forms a near-equivalent to the Marx Brothers, with whom his career draws several parallels. Like them, Fields made his name in vaudeville (*qv*) and would sometimes appear on the same bill. On one celebrated occasion Fields absented himself when required to go on after them, citing a bizarre-sounding, incapacitating ailment. Groucho recalled questioning Fields about this years later, to be told he had invented the complaint solely to avoid having to follow the Marx Brothers. Another account, from Fields himself, was written for *Coronet* magazine in 1943 (and subsequently reprinted in *W.C. Fields By Himself*): 'The Marx Brothers began with an act called "Fun in Hi Skule" ... the only act I could never follow. In Columbus I told the manager I broke my wrist and quit.' The joint Marx-Fields billing at Keith's, in Columbus, Ohio, has been confirmed and, by implication, this version of the tale. Just as the Marxes introduced comedy into a 'straight' singing act, Fields was not initially a

Female impersonation: *Harpo 'plays the game of being a woman' in* A Night at the Opera

*'Take that Groucho Marx outta here, please!'; a protest from **W.C. Fields** in his 1941 film,* Never Give a Sucker an Even Break

comedian in the accepted sense. While Harpo switched from speaking roles to pure mime, Fields started out as mute juggler and would not introduce dialogue until much later. Both the Marxes and Fields graduated to musical comedy (as in Fields' famous show *Poppy*) in addition to making films for Paramount (*qv*) on the East Coast. Similarly, each relocated to California with the same studio and were in turn more or less finished in films after 1941. In that year Fields made his last starring vehicle, *Never Give a Sucker An Even Break*, employing the services of none other than Margaret Dumont (*qv*). They worked together again a year later in a segment shot for, but deleted from, *Tales of Manhattan*. Separate from the Dumont scenes of *Sucker* is a moment where a cleaner (Minerva Urecal) pushes a broom under Fields' impressive nose: 'Take that Groucho Marx outta here, please,' he insists. *Sucker* is an eccentric Fields exploit much beloved by *aficionados*; more widely acclaimed in the Fields canon are *It's a Gift* (1934), *The Old Fashioned Way* (1934), *The Man On the Flying Trapeze* (1935) and *The*

Bank Dick (1940). Similarly famous are his contributions to the 1935 version of *David Copperfield* and the multi-part *If I Had a Million* (1932). Less often revived is the 1933 version of *Alice in Wonderland*, with a heavily-disguised Fields as Humpty Dumpty. Both this and *It's a Gift* were directed by Norman Z. McLeod (*qv*), who also directed a non-Fields segment of *If I Had a Million*. One of the best-known anecdotes concerning Fields and alcohol was told by Groucho. He recalled a visit to the Fields residence, where he was shown a vast supply of drink. 'Don't you know Prohibition is over?' asked Groucho. 'It may come back,' replied his cautious host. W.C. Fields may be seen with Chico in one of the *Hollywood on Parade* series (see **Guest appearances**).

(See also: Alcohol; Benny, Jack; Burke, James; Burns, George and Allen, Gracie; Carnegie Hall concert, the; Cowan, Lester; Documentaries; *Fun in Hi Skule*; Marriages; Moustaches, beards; Seiter, William A.; Taggart, Ben)

FIGHTING
(Marx Brothers films and shows *qv*)

Fighting: a typical Harpo-Chico scrap, from the auction scene of Cocoanuts
BFI Stills, Posters and Designs

'Remember, you're fighting for this woman's honour, which is probably more than she ever did!'; Groucho's favourite line from *Duck Soup* and one of his more devastating put-downs of Margaret Dumont (*qv*). It was athletic Zeppo, of all the Marx Brothers, who earned the reputation of 'scrapper'. At school, he had a tendency to beat up the other pupils, verified in a show of hands when a class was asked which of them had been hit by Herbert Marx. His pugilistic tendencies are recorded variously (see **Agents**, **Herman Mankiewicz**) but were most prominently on display in *On the Mezzanine*. It is therefore quite in keeping for Zeppo to handle the climactic fist fight of *Monkey Business*. When in the same film Chico and Harpo are engaged as bodyguards, they demonstrate how 'tough' they are by having Harpo sock Chico on the jaw. This isn't enough to satisfy Chico, who insists on being knocked down and then, as final proof, sent clear across the room. In building up momentum, Harpo, his teeth clenched, goes cross-eyed, breathing more and more heavily in the manner of a locomotive gathering steam (an expression referred to generally as his 'get tough' face). He is capable of flattening an ally but less effective against genuine adversaries: in *Horse Feathers* Chico and Harpo are cornered by two bullying football players, and as Chico instructs Harpo to get tough, he repeats the piston-like breathing but,

when ready to strike, delivers no more than a limp-wristed slap to each opponent. Harpo is promptly floored. He is at least able to deck the villain of *The Big Store* with a single punch, albeit one placed after misdirecting his victim's attention. Other Chico-Harpo skirmishes reflect something of their street-urchin background: illustrated is an example from *Cocoanuts*; in *Duck Soup* they square up in Queensberry fashion, only for Harpo to hook around a kick to Chico's rear end ('Hey, upstairs this time, no downstairs'). This routine probably dates back to *Home Again* or, at the latest, *On the Mezzanine*, in which policeman Edward Metcalfe (*qv*) would attempt to intercede. Publicity for *A Day at the Races* - which may or may not be taken as reliable - informs us that Chico once tried to be a boxer, but 'gave it up after slugging for one hour to a draw'. Generally speaking, the Marxes reserve genuine violence for each other, as in a scrap between the foursome in *Cocoanuts* or Harpo knocking over Groucho with a feather - containing a sash weight - in *Monkey Business*. There are exceptions for truly deserving cases, as in the climactic fight from *Monkey Business* noted above or the final capture of the Nazis in *A Night in Casablanca*. In *Animal Crackers* Harpo engages Margaret Dumont in a mock wrestling match, imitating the real thing with 'punches' ostensibly on the referee's blind side; but it should be noted that the punches are completely pulled and the worst that befalls Dumont is being lifted into the air. Groucho, too, in *The Cocoanuts*, mocks an assertive Dumont by adopting a wrestling stance with the challenge 'I'll play you one more game. Come on, the three of you!' Further measure of this token violence lies in their real-life sponsorship of a fairly hopeless boxer known as 'Canvasback' Cohen during 1933; several references exist to this foray into boxing management, one of them in Oscar Levant's *A Smattering of Ignorance* (1940). Levant describes one occasion

when Canvasback 'exceeded his ordinary quota by being knocked down five times in the first round'. The boxer made his unsteady way to the corner, where Groucho and Harpo made ready to patch up their battered *protégé*; on reaching the stool, he was pushed to the floor by Harpo, who took his place and was fanned by Groucho. A contemporary press release for *Duck Soup* records the Marxes withdrawing their support after Canvasback finally managed to win a fight. The Winter 1988 *Freedonia Gazette* published details of an unfortunate postscript, when Groucho reminisced about Cohen in a 1949 edition of *You Bet Your Life* (*qv*); Cohen, by then an anonymous postal clerk, tried to sue for invasion of privacy but was unsuccessful. The judge thought there might be grounds for slander or libel, but Cohen declined, with the admission of a 'sad' boxing career.

(See also: Education; Insults; *Risqué* humour; Television; Trailers)

LA FIESTA DE SANTA BARBARA
See: Colour; Guest appearances

FISHER, ART
See: Names

FLEMING, ERIN (b. circa 1942)
Secretary and companion to Groucho during his latter years, an actress who may be seen in Woody Allen's 1972 film *Everything You Always Wanted to Know About Sex (But Were Afraid to Ask)*. Accounts vary greatly as to the nature of their relationship, claiming either that she gave him an incentive to live or that it was all rather negative; it is not the purpose of the present work to speculate. Shortly before Groucho's death, legal battles began and Nat Perrin (*qv*), a trained lawyer, became Groucho's conservator until the comedian's grandson, Andy Marx, took up the position. A subsequent court case, concerning Fleming and the estate, went on for some years thereafter.

(See also: Carnegie Hall Concert, the; Documentaries)

FLOREY, ROBERT (1900-79)
(Marx Brothers films and shows *qv*) Co-director, with Joseph Santley (*qv*), of the film version of *Cocoanuts*, Robert Florey is remembered rather more for *Murders in the Rue Morgue* (1932), *The Beast With Five Fingers* (1946) and a rather strange wartime tale combining aviation with theology, *God Is My Co-Pilot* (1945). Parisian-born Florey arrived in America in 1921 and became part of Chaplin's circle later in the decade; Florey wrote a Chaplin biography (published in Paris) as early as 1927 and, two decades later, was an associate director on Chaplin's *Monsieur Verdoux*. It was Chaplin who drew attention to Florey by screening the latter's experimental, low-budget ($93!) film *The Life and Death of 9413 - a Hollywood Extra*, made in collaboration with montage specialist Slavko Vorkapich. One of those present was Monta Bell (*qv*), another Chaplin associate who had known Florey for some time. Bell was also in charge of Paramount's facility at Long Island, and when directors were sought for the new talking pictures, Florey was offered a job. The speed and economy with which *Hollywood Extra* had been made proved a deciding factor with Bell and co-producer Walter Wanger. One source claims that Florey had enjoyed the stage production of *Cocoanuts* and when assigned to the film version, renewed his acquaintance with the Marxes by attending a performance of *Animal Crackers*; Florey himself, interviewed for *The Marx Brothers Scrapbook*, states that Bell had asked him if he had seen *Cocoanuts* and, on being told he had not, suggested they should both see *Animal Crackers*. It was only after attending the show that Bell broached the topic of filming *Cocoanuts*. Florey later admitted a lack of enthusiasm for the project. He had been promised dramatic subjects and had so far been given everything but. Whether or not

he appreciated the Marxes on stage, Florey is often said to have displayed a different opinion on set. He is generally quoted as finding them unfunny and concentrated his efforts on getting the picture made, incorporating cinematic effects where possible; he had wanted to do location work in Florida, where the story is set, only for Bell to query the point of such realism in a picture where a man sports an obviously fake moustache. For all his seeming lack of enthusiasm, Florey did at least devise Harpo's gags of eating the telephone and drinking ink ('After all,' he said, 'as long as the thing was crazy anyway, one might as well add to it'). Otherwise he realized there was little point in trying to direct comedy routines that had already been performed hundreds of times on stage, contenting himself with what he termed 'directing traffic'. Florey said he enjoyed working with the team, particularly Harpo, with whom he would have liked to work on a solo vehicle; yet in the 1970s, Groucho was scathing about Florey, insisting he had at that time a poor command of English and had no business directing them. Florey's lack of English is undocumented elsewhere (he was certainly quite fluent later on) and it is tempting to believe Groucho's view of Florey was marred by subsequent events, as seems to have happened with Herman Mankiewicz and S.J.Perelman (both *qv*); one possible reason may be Florey's latter-day comments on the film itself, most of them unfavourable.

(See also: Chaplin, Charlie; Moustaches, beards; Paramount Pictures)

FLYWHEEL, SHYSTER AND FLYWHEEL
(radio series)

(Marx Brothers films and shows *qv*) Although the team's radio work has been reasonably well preserved, their first important series, *Flywheel, Shyster and Flywheel*, disappeared into almost immediate obscurity. Though broadcast live, the shows were

recorded (contrary to myth) but the discs were not kept. Little was known save for its situation, Groucho and Chico operating a shady law firm, and the overall impression (conveyed in *Groucho and Me*) of the show having expired after the withdrawal of its sponsor, Standard Oil. It was known also to have started life as *Beagle, Shyster and Beagle* until legal problems interceded. In the absence of any recordings or scripts, *Flywheel's* importance remained unappreciated until 1988, when the texts of 25 episodes - all but number 21 of the series - were discovered at the Library of Congress in Washington. They had been registered there for copyright purposes and remained undisturbed until located by author Michael Barson. The scripts required slight editing, primarily to ensure uniformity of character identification but also to remove unnecessary preambles, links and commercials from all but the first episode. The publication of the scripts in book form was greeted by Marx *aficionados* as an important event, and with good reason; the shows were not only funny, but shared plot and dialogue elements with Marx Brothers films made before *and after* the radio series. In his introduction to the scripts, Barson details many such parallels: episodes 17 and 19 are, respectively, reworkings of *Animal Crackers* and *Cocoanuts*; more of *Animal Crackers* resurfaces in episode 23; while *Monkey Business* is drawn upon for two sequences in episode 25. Most significantly, numerous *Duck Soup* gags were written initially for *Flywheel*, while a much later film, *The Big Store*, was based upon episode 15. Possibly the most famous (or notorious) Marx Brothers pun, the 'Sanity Clause' joke of *A Night at the Opera*, appears in embryo form in episode 3. Barson's introductory essay provides a detailed account of the show's history, as does Paul Wesolowski's chronicle of the Marxes' activities at this time (in the Winter 1988 *Freedonia Gazette* [*qv*]). The latter makes clear the intertwined

nature of *Flywheel* with *Duck Soup's* creation, explaining the high proportion of *Flywheel* gags used in the film. The Marx series was intended as part of a 'strip' called the *Five Star Theatre*, broadcast from Monday to Friday. The Marxes occupied the Monday evening slot; others were filled by Charlie Chan mysteries, drama and presentations of opera and orchestral music. Joint sponsors were Standard Oil and Colonial Beacon Oil Company, the idea being to compete with Texaco's programme starring comedian Ed Wynn. Because of this collaboration and the likelihood of violating the US anti-Trust laws (designed to curb monopolies), early episodes of the *Five Star Theatre* were broadcast only to the East Coast. The Marxes were paid a sum variously reported as $6,500 or $7,500 per week, $1,000 of which was for writers' fees. The main writers were Arthur Sheekman and Nat Perrin (both *qv*); in an interview with Barson, Perrin recalled Tom McKnight and George Oppenheimer (*qv*) being brought in to ease the strain of writing a weekly series. Wesolowski mentions them within a list of alleged contributors (among them Herman Timberg, who wrote the Marxes' *On the Mezzanine* back in 1921), noting also that Groucho denied hiring the majority of them. The first show aired on 28 November 1932, over NBC's Blue network. This and the next five broadcasts were relayed live from NBC's New York station, WJZ (to which there is punning reference in the film version of *Cocoanuts*). Originally, Groucho portrayed 'Waldorf T. Beagle, attorney at law', with Chico retaining the name 'Ravelli' from *Animal Crackers*. The switch to 'Flywheel' came after three episodes, following threats of legal action by a real-life attorney named Morris Beegel (Groucho later wrote of people calling the man's office, asking for him, then enquiring as to his partner Shyster before hanging up!). The surnames 'Flywheel' and 'Ravelli' reappeared in *The Big Store*. What might have been a jarring change was

FLYWHEEL, SHYSTER AND FLYWHEEL

The BBC revival of **Flywheel, Shyster and Flywheel** had a superb regular cast and guest stars to match. Left to right: Lorelei King, Frank Lazarus, guest Dick Vosburgh, Michael Roberts, guest Spike Milligan and Graham Hoadley. Photo: Les Otter/BBC

covered in a gag where Groucho's secretary, Miss Dimple, answered a telephone query with 'I know that used to be the name of the firm, but the boss got a divorce and changed his name back to Flywheel'. Wesolowski identifies the actress playing Miss Dimple as Mary McCoy, citing also Broderick Crawford - decades before his TV fame in *Highway Patrol* - among the supporting players. Mary McCoy was replaced, temporarily, by Marjorie Fields when Groucho and Chico returned west after programme six. Subsequent episodes were relayed from a vacant sound stage at RKO (*qv*). Again according to Wesolowski, the intention had been for Harpo, Zeppo, Bert Kalmar and Harry Ruby (*qv*) to join the others in New York to work on their next film; these plans were reversed when the Marxes' father, Frenchie, suffered a slight heart attack (he died five months later). *Flywheel* concluded its initial 13-week booking and was renewed for a further 13. The writing maintained a high standard, albeit increasingly reliant on the brothers' earlier work. The final episode was broadcast on 22 May 1933. *Flywheel* had obtained respectable ratings, but not enough for the sponsors to continue. It is generally held that its 7.30 p.m. slot worked to the show's detriment, given that a much wider audience would have tuned in at 9.00 or 9.30. Thus *Flywheel* was put into suspended animation until its scripts were uncovered 55 years later. By this time, the large number of Marx impersonators, many of them very good, made a revival of the shows inevitable. Attempts included a session in New York during May 1989, to benefit New York's Museum of Broadcasting, with Dick Cavett taking the Groucho part. The performance

was sponsored by McCann-Erickson, the advertising agency responsible for the show's first airing in 1932. Another production, in April 1990, was at the Stackner Cabaret in Milwaukee, presented as an hour-long show in the manner of a radio broadcast. Four months later the material was adapted into a variety format by the Bloomsburg Theatre Ensemble in Philadelphia. Still another version derived from Germany, reportedly without any duplication of the original characterizations. The most successful was from BBC Radio, whose first series of *Flywheel, Shyster and Flywheel* was preceded by much publicity. Even before the pilot had been recorded, BBC Radio 2's *Gloria Hunniford Show* interviewed scriptwriter Mark Brisenden about the new project. Also present were Michael Roberts and Frank Lazarus, veterans of *A Day in Hollywood, A Night in the Ukraine* (*qv*), who were offered the respective Groucho and Chico roles on the recommendation of Dick Vosburgh. While in the studio, they performed extracts from the *Hollywood/Ukraine* show and, by way of a 'trailer', a sample of dialogue unique to the original *Flywheel*. Good though the scripts were, Brisenden realized considerable work was necessary. Certain episodes worked more effectively than others, while a further difficulty lay in the fact that each episode, minus its commercials and other superfluities,

ran considerably less than the required thirty minutes. In consequence, the decision was taken to combine elements from different episodes, sometimes transferring the stronger scenes of weaker scripts to those that worked well in their original form. Initially, each new show drew upon an average of two-and-a-quarter original scripts. Brisenden added some of his own material to the result, the percentage of which grew as time progressed. There was, in addition, a weekly song, usually alternating between Groucho and Chico numbers but sometimes offering a duet. New lyrics were supplied by Lazarus and Vosburgh, the latter of whom also appeared in a couple of episodes. Choice of material covered the expected items: *Lydia, the Tattooed Lady, Show Me A Rose* and so on for Groucho; *Ev'ryone Says 'I Love You'* and other songs for Chico. From *Cocoanuts* came *The Monkey Doodle-Doo*, a speciality for Frances Williams (*qv*) in the stage version and a chorus number, led by Mary Eaton (*qv*) in the film. *Flywheel* converted it into a Chico item, sung by Lazarus to his own Chico-style piano accompaniment. George S. Kaufman's daughter, Anne Kaufman Schneider, was present at the recording with her husband Irving; she said 'That's usually a clumping chorus number and a bit of a dead spot. From now on I'm going to insist that Chico does *The Monkey Doodle-Doo* in every revival of *Cocoanuts!*' Other titles were sought as the original catalogue became exhausted. One of these, a Groucho-Chico duet called *Life is So Peculiar*, was sung originally by Groucho and Bing Crosby in *Mr Music* (*qv*). Another duet, *Sing Me a Sensible Song*, was a Lazarus-Vosburgh composition recycled (in the tradition of the original *Flywheel*) from *A Day in Hollywood, A Night in the Ukraine*. The song was present in *Hollywood/Ukraine*'s London production but left the score during its pre-Broadway run. Perhaps the most inspired choice was a popular song from the early 1930s, *My Brother Makes the Noises For the Talkies* (laced with sound effects), converted into a Chico song with implied reference to Harpo. The reconstructed show was fairly seamless and the new *Flywheel* scored an instant success on its début in June 1990. Producer was Dirk Maggs, whose experience in radio has blended mainstream projects with offbeat work such as this and adaptations of super-hero comic strips. In addition to Londoner Mike Roberts and South African-born Frank Lazarus, the regular cast included two Americans, Lorelei King (as *every* female character) and Vincent Marzello. Graham Hoadly played various roles in addition to functioning as announcer. Among the occasional guest artists were William Hootkins and, in the third series, Spike Milligan. In developing his legendary *Goon Show* of the 1950s, Milligan had been heavily influenced by the Marxes and *Flywheel* was his way of fulfilling a lifelong ambition to work with them. Those fortunate enough to obtain tickets were treated to a show with full orchestra and, very convincingly, Roberts and Lazarus in full costume and make-up. The first series of six programmes was broadcast on BBC Radio 4, with a subsequent repeat; the shows were later re-broadcast on Radio 2. A second series followed in 1991 and a third was broadcast during July and August 1992. All have been repeated, while an

episode set at Christmas has seen additional service over the festive season. The shows were also taken by the BBC Transcription Service for distribution to overseas radio stations. International recognition was confirmed in 1992, when the second BBC series received the Gold Medal at New York's International Radio Festival. During 1991 the show had been runner-up at Barcelona's Premios Ondas Awards, in addition to being nominated at both the British Comedy Awards and the Sony Awards. After all that, a fragment of the original *Flywheel* was recovered on disc. The extract, from the final episode, combines new material with elements of *Monkey Business* and *Animal Crackers*; above all, it displays how authentic was the BBC's re-creation. Music links, unidentified in the scripts, turned out to be an inversion of *Hooray For Captain Spaulding*, the 'official' version of which was used in the revival. There is at least one rather cute departure from the script: Chico has to deliver a consciously awful pun about a Red Indian sleeping with his head towards the fire, 'to keep his wigwam' ('wig warm'); 'Some joke, eh, boss?' asks Chico, to which Groucho replies with an unscripted 'In a word, no!' Part of this recording may be heard in a documentary, *Unknown Marx Brothers*. In October 1992 the BBC staged a concert, before a live audience, commemorating the Light Entertainment Department's 70th anniversary. The programme, broadcast in November, presented *Flywheel* among the newly-produced extracts from classic BBC Light Entertainment shows. The occasion brought forth a new Lazarus-Vosburgh duet for Groucho and Chico, entitled *Tootsie Frootsie Ice-a-Cream* (clearly inspired by Chico's fraudulent sales pitch in *A Day at the Races*). The first BBC series eventually found its way into cassette release, with a sleeve note by Nat Perrin. He believed this incarnation of *Flywheel* to be rather better than the original; a great tribute to a great show.

(See also: Advertising; Berlin, Irving; Books; Documentaries; Eliot, T.S.; Garbo, Greta; Impersonators; Lawyers; Marx, Sam; Names; Puns; Radio; Songs; Stamps)

FOLSEY, GEORGE (1898-1988)

Cinematographer, from silent days to the 1960s; photographed *Animal Crackers* (*qv*) and was interviewed for the 1982 documentary *The Marx Brothers in a Nutshell*. Nominated for an Oscar no less than thirteen times; notable work includes Rouben Mamoulian's *Applause* (1929), *Men in White* (1934), *The Great Ziegfeld* (1936), *Meet Me in St Louis* (1944), *Adam's Rib* (1949) and *Seven Brides For Seven Brothers* (1954).

(See also: Bell, Monta; Cummings, Jack; Documentaries)

FOOD

(Marx Brothers films and shows *qv*) Part of the Marxes' elemental quality is an interest in food. Their essentially street-urchin heritage dictates the pursuit of life's basics and it is not surprising that Chico's first query in *Animal Crackers* concerns the location of the dining room. Food must be obtained even when circumstances preclude a consistent supply: much of *Room Service* is concerned with the principals being starved out of a hotel room, and their various means of obtaining sustenance; similarly, stowaways Groucho and Chico steal the Captain's lunch in *Monkey Business*; a parallel situation in *A Night at the Opera* finds Groucho ordering a sizeable meal for uninvited guests Harpo, Chico and Allan Jones (*qv*); later in the same film, they obtain more food at a party with the steerage passengers; while still later Harpo uses breakfast as a form of make-up. Described elsewhere is a deleted scene from *Opera*'s sequel, *A Day at the Races*, in which Chico and Harpo become impromptu chefs at the water carnival. It is usually Harpo, the brother most guided by instinct, who is hungry. When deprived of food in *Love Happy*, he takes a bite from an apple placed on his head in William Tell fashion. Suitably famished in *A Night in Casablanca*, he pretends to bite off Chico's thumb; hunger is duly relieved when they appoint themselves Groucho's food-tasters (Groucho: 'This food doesn't look any more poisoned than any other hotel food'). As each munches the opposite end of a stick of celery, Groucho wonders 'Wouldn't it be great if they ate each other?'. (In the same film, Harpo mimes 'soup' and 'rice' to convey the word 'surprise'!) Sometimes food provides a living in itself, as in Chico's peanut stand from *Duck Soup* (which concludes with Louis Calhern and Margaret Dumont [both *qv*] being pelted with apples!). It can also be good (or bad) pun material, hence Groucho's *Cocoanuts* line about 'a cup of coffee, a sandwich and you ... from the opera "I eat-a"' (Aïda!). Their occasional culinary desperation on-screen has its roots in real life. Harpo's autobiography describes a vaudeville diet dictated by economy, much of it 'boardinghouse spaghetti, chili and beans'. In his famous 1931 article, 'Bad Days are Good Memories', Groucho recalls spending a week as one of the 'Nightingales' (*qv*) in lodgings at Atlantic City, where fish was plentiful but not meat. They received nothing but fish all week, until Groucho 'began to feel something like a cannibal'. Retelling the story later in *Groucho and Me*, he remembered swapping his *Bar Mitzvah* pen for some roast beef sandwiches to feed himself and his brothers. He had been given the pen only four years earlier, at the age of thirteen. 'The next time I ate fish', said Groucho, 'I was forty'. Also in *Groucho and Me* is a story Groucho had originally written up for *Variety* on January 1 1936, under the title 'Mackerel for Xmas'. This is an account of a boardinghouse in which actors were considered second-rate guests, so much so that the five resident vaudeville acts were served mackerel instead of the turkey reserved for more

respectable folk at Christmas. They refused it and the Marxes, empty of stomach, filled that evening's performance with baffling *ad-libs* about mackerel. On returning to their digs, the actors broke into the icebox. They discovered not just the fish but turkey and cranberry sauce, which were duly demolished. The Marxes left a note saying 'Guess who?' prior to departing for alternative accomodation.

(See also: Deleted scenes; Female impersonation; Hotels; Puns; Religion; Vaudeville; Women)

FOULGER, BYRON
See: *At the Circus*

THE FOUR NIGHTINGALES
See: Nightingales, the

FRANCIS, KAY (1903 or 1905-68)
Leading lady, originally from Oklahoma, she was educated in New York and divided her time between modelling and secretarial work. Her theatrical career began after two disastrous marriages, the first of which brought her the surname 'Francis' (she had been born Katherine Gibbs). She worked first as an understudy, then in touring plays. Her screen début was in *Gentlemen of the Press* (1929), directed by Millard Webb; in her next film she was second female lead after Millard Webb's wife, Mary Eaton (*qv*); this was the Marx Brothers' *Cocoanuts* (*qv*), taking over Janet Velie's stage role as scheming villainess Penelope. Miss Francis' work in the film earned her a $500-per-week Paramount contract. Subsequent work at the studio included the revue film *Paramount on Parade*, Leo McCarey's *Let's Go Native* (both 1930) and Ernst Lubitsch's *Trouble in Paradise* (1932). She was

Kay Francis *plays 'Penelope' in the film version of* Cocoanuts

long associated with Warner Brothers after marriage (her fifth) to director Kenneth MacKenna; among many titles are *One Way Passage* (1932), *Mary Stevens M.D.* (1933), Jolson's *Wonder Bar* (1934) and *I Found Stella Parish* (1935). Personal difficulties - not least an alcohol problem after splitting from MacKenna - harmed her career and, despite worthwhile contributions to the Cary Grant-Carole Lombard *In Name Only* (1939) and Jack Benny's version of *Charley's Aunt* (1941), it was a downhill slide into Monogram cheapies and a return to the stage. Latterly based in New York, in a retirement enforced by poor health.

(See also: Benny, Jack; Heerman, Victor; Mayo, Archie L.)

THE FREEDONIA GAZETTE

Established in 1978 as journal of the Marx Brothers Study Group or 'Marx Brotherhood', *The Freedonia Gazette* is the type of enthusiasts' publication that tends to appear at irregular intervals. (There had been an earlier Marx journal, *Re: Marx*.) The magazine, edited by historian Paul G. Wesolowski, takes its name from the mythical country in which *Duck Soup* (*qv*) is set. This high-quality, well-produced chronicle of Marx Brothers lore delves into the team's lives and careers in addition to keeping track of such things as revival shows, video releases and news of related people. Very importantly, there have been examinations of work often overlooked in Marx histories, e.g. stage shows, broadcasting, out-takes *et al*. Interviews have appeared with Allan Jones, Kitty Carlisle, Nat Perrin (all *qv*) and others; there have also been interviews with Groucho's son, Arthur Marx and, by courtesy of British film critic Barry Norman, Zeppo Marx.

(See also: Appendix 1; Children; Documentaries; and *passim*)

FRIES, OTTO H. (1890-?)

Character comedian, born in St Louis, who entered films in 1914. Comedy experience includes work at Sennett, Educational, Fox and Roach; at the latter studio, proved useful in both mainstream product and when taking over roles in German-language versions, at a time before multiple-language productions had made way for dubbing and sub-titling (his name suggests German origins and, as with the Marxes, probable bilingual status). Otto Fries may be seen as supporting player in many feature films: one such is *Monkey Business* (*qv*), in which he plays the Second Mate, whose sizeable moustache is 'snooped' into oblivion by Harpo and Chico; another is *A Night at the Opera* (*qv*), in which he is the lift operator (referred to by his real forename) who is at first courteous, then kicks Groucho downstairs.

(See also: Moustaches, beards; Perrin, Nat)

FUN IN HI SKULE

(Marx brothers play; Marx brothers films and plays *qv*)
The Marxes' initial act, as singing 'Nightingales' (*qv*), became redundant in 1910 after their future as comedians was confirmed by a legendary performance in Nacogdoches, Texas. At this time vaudeville (*qv*) was practically awash with schoolroom acts, inspired by those created by Groucho's old employer, Gus Edwards. It was natural for a fledgling comedy team to follow a popular trend and the team thus re-entered the scholarly life. Originally called 'School Days' (another direct lift from Edwards), *Fun in Hi Skule* became the first Marx Brothers act in which comedy was the key ingredient rather than music. In keeping with contemporary tastes, the Marxes were broken up into ethnic stereotypes. Groucho, as the stick-carrying teacher, worked as a 'Dutch' or German-accented comic, in frock coat and a 'scratch' wig simulating baldness; the accent was borrowed from his maternal grandfather, the coat from his uncle Julius who, in a possibly elaborated account by Kyle Crichton, surrendered it reluctantly and anxiously awaited its return after each performance. A little of Groucho's 'Dutch' accent crops up in the *Monkey Business* promo (*qv*). Groucho sat at a desk towards the rear of the stage. Either side were doors marked 'Boiz' and 'Goils'. Gummo, one of the pupils, was a 'Hebrew Boy'; his classmate Harpo, or 'Patsy Brannigan', was an Irish-cum-rural type, sporting a red wig and several blacked-out teeth. Chico, not in the original cast, contributed his newly-acquired Italian character after meeting his brothers in Waukegan late in 1912 (see **Jack Benny**). One character in the act, a stereotyped sissy, was played by Paul Yale. According to Groucho in *The Marx Brothers Scrapbook*, Yale had prissy - not to say barely comprehensible - lines such as 'Strawberry shortcake, huckleberry pie. Are we in it. Ra, Ra, Ra!' Paul Yale's stage partner and future wife, Dot Davidson, was also in the Marx troupe; they toured in vaudeville and stock companies as 'Yale and Davidson'. Paul Yale died in January 1967, aged 75. Elsewhere among the 'pupils' were several girls, one of them a Lucille or Lillian Textrude, another (according to a contemporary photo) the Marxes' Aunt Hannah. There were also two of the tap-dancing Harris Brothers, originally a quartet who had been in Gus Edwards' school act; a *Variety* obituary for George, the youngest (who died in 1954, aged 63) describes the team being broken up when conscripted in the First World War. George later spent twenty years as a stagehand at the Warner Theatre in Youngstown, Ohio. A trade-paper cartoon from a performance at the Lyda Theater, Chicago, in January 1911 (reproduced in *The Groucho Phile*) gives us some of the gags: Groucho says 'This is a fine bunch of smart dunces' and 'Don't think because I am a fool I am a Dutchman'; Gummo, clutching his abdomen, claims 'Someone stuck me in the back of the stomach'; Harpo, sitting at a desk, is told to remove 'that

thing' from his head. The 'thing' was a bucket-shaped hat, providing a running gag in which Groucho would repeatedly tell him to take it off, only for Harpo to offer a token gesture of tipping it from behind, allowing the hat to fall back in place. Harpo had yet to abandon dialogue and could thus explain why he was late for school: 'My mother lost the lid off the stove, and I had to sit on it to keep the smoke in.' Aunt Hannah, as a schoolgirl with as thick an accent as Groucho's, offered the teacher an apple. He placed the apple in a desk drawer, where it exploded. Having vented his wrath, teacher tried to sit at his desk, only for Harpo to pull away the chair. Groucho picked himself up and finally took his seat at the desk, ready to pursue the incidental matter of education. This question-and-answer session, though lost in performance, has a kind of disreputable immortality through being preserved variously by Kyle Crichton and the memoirs of Groucho and Harpo. Gummo would take centre stage, looking to the audience:

Groucho: What are the principal parts of a cat?
Gummo: Eyes, ears, nose, cheeks, feet and tail.
Groucho: You've forgotten the most important. *(stroking his upper lip)* What does a cat have that I don't have?
Gummo: Kittens.

Harpo's turn would require him to go through the alphabet. 'Give me a start,' he would ask, and Groucho would, with difficulty, coach him as far as 'A'. 'Ah,' said Harpo. 'Not *ah*,' chided Groucho, 'A.' 'That's the alphabet, "A",' said Harpo, starting to return to his seat. Groucho brought him back. 'There's more?' asked Harpo. There was indeed but Harpo required *another* start with 'B'. When 'buh' sounds proved futile, Groucho offered a clue: 'What buzzes all around and gets all the honey?' Harpo responded with the name of whichever local *roué* seemed appropriate. When Groucho illustrated the clue with a buzzing sound, Harpo made swatting gestures. 'Bee!' cried the exasperated tutor. Accepting *this* as the complete alphabet, Harpo once more tried to resume his seat. Determined to reach 'C', Groucho asked Harpo about the first thing he did each morning, leading him with 'Sssssss - '. Receiving a blank look, Teacher, his patience severely tested, shouted 'C! The first thing you do in the morning when you wake up is "see".' 'That's not the first thing I *do* in the morning,' replied Harpo. Teacher returned to the subject of general knowledge:

Groucho: What is the shape of the earth?
Harpo: I don't know.
Groucho: What's the shape of my cuff-links?
Harpo: Square.
Groucho: Not these. The ones I wear on Sundays.
Harpo: Oh. Round.
Groucho: That's it. Now what is the shape of the earth?
Harpo: Square on weekdays, round on Sundays.

Kyle Crichton attributes the above Harpo lines to Chico, who possibly took them over on joining the act. It is believed that Harpo obtained a further laugh when belying his idiocy with a long, erudite speech; audiences were just as stunned when he proved able to play serious music on the harp. Another gag saw him using a trap in order to disappear under the carpet, seemingly flat. *Fun in Hi Skule*'s second half took the form of rehearsing for the school concert; this was the cue for various cast members to do their respective turns. Specially purchased was a song called *Peasie Weasie*, a series of punning anecdotes in which they could take turns *ad infinitum*. Groucho revived the song for a 1959 TV appearance (still extant) with Dinah Shore. The latter sequence developed into a second act of its own, *Mr Green's Reception* (qv), taking place ten years later. Initially they played as a double bill, until *Fun in Hi Skule* was dropped.

(See also: Could Harpo Speak?; Education; Fields, W.C.; the Gookie; *Horse Feathers*; Religion; *Risqué* humour; Television; Wigs)

GALLAGHER AND SHEAN

See: Documentaries; *I'll Say She Is!*;
On the Mezzanine; Shean, Al

GAMBLING

(Marx Brothers films and plays *qv*)
'Chico was the gambler of the Marx
Brothers,' wrote Groucho in 1963. It's
fair to say that each of them gambled to
a reasonable degree, the ever-cautious
Groucho being least enthusiastic. To
Chico, however, and to a lesser extent
Zeppo, gambling was a way of life, long
before the term 'compulsive gambler'
had entered the language or become
recognized as similar to alcoholism.
Even allowing for the team's habit of
vanishing from a film set at every
opportunity, Chico was the most
difficult to find; when not in pursuit of
a pretty girl, he would find a telephone
to contact his bookie or disappear
altogether, to be traced hours later at a
poker game. On several occasions
Morrie Ryskind (*qv*) described one of
Chico's disappearances during the
filming of *Cocoanuts*, ostensibly to
nurse a headache; after a while,
assistant director Joseph Santley (*qv*)
grew frantic and sought Ryskind's
assistance. Ryskind, familiar with
Chico's activities, very quickly traced
him by phone to a game at the New
York Bridge Club. Chico had inherited
a fondness for pinochle from his father,
Sam 'Frenchie' Marx (*qv*). Frenchie,
Chico and Harpo were experts and
Groucho later expressed the opinion
that his father was probably closer to
them as a consequence. Frenchie could
not be called a serious gambler, though
Kyle Crichton relates the tale of
Frenchie winning a bet from a theatre
patron who insisted Harpo to be a
genuine mute. The dispute was settled
with a backstage visit to Harpo. On
discovering Sam's identity, the victim
took it in good part - providing he
received Harpo's autograph. Marx
Brothers lore is filled with tales of
poolrooms, dubious card games, crap
games and indeed any suspect wager
by which cash might change hands, but
Chico started early: as a youth, he

would pick up some short-lived
employment but never reach home
with his salary. At the Carnegie Hall
concert (*qv*), Groucho related an
incident when his brother worked for
the Klauber Horn company, which
manufactured toilet paper; Chico's
weekly pay had made its customary
disappearance so the resourceful lad
took home some of his employers'
merchandise, claiming he had been
unable to resist a sale. Earlier accounts
substitute 'blotters' for the more
prosaic goods, but Marx anecdotes, like
the brothers themselves, tend to
reverse tradition in becoming more
reliable *after* the passage of time.
Chico's adolescent gambling habit was
financed largely, and reluctantly, by his
immediate family; Frenchie was an
inefficient tailor even without his son
consistently pawning either his shears
or the trousers of a newly-made suit
(he finally took to making two pairs for
each customer). Harpo's watch made
frequent trips to the pawnshop until he
hit upon the idea of removing one of
the hands. Chico was once found
knowingly playing cards with crooked
opponents, merely to see if he could
beat them despite. This dogged
optimism did much to further the
brothers' careers but proved virtual
suicide at the card table or racetrack.
In this respect Chico's mother, Minnie

Gambling: *Chico professed not to know how
much he'd lost over the years*

g

Marx (*qv*), may have followed *his* example, for Alexander Woollcott (*qv*) once described a bored Minnie, after her sons' success, taking up poker and regularly having to pawn her jewellery owing to a 'weakness for inside straights'. It is understood that Harpo and Zeppo were more conservative and therefore better gamblers than their elder sibling, though Groucho attributed the failure of Zeppo's second marriage to a preoccupation with cards. Harpo in turn once dropped a sizeable sum while visiting France with Woollcott and friends in 1928, but generally adopted a lighter approach; he secured a loan after the 1929 Stock Market crash by reducing a boat-load of hardened gamblers to hysterics, using a children's game called 'Pinchie Winchie'. The idea was to pinch or similarly jab the next person in line, varying the action as it progressed; Harpo added an extra dimension by palming some burnt cork, leaving a smudge on the face of his unsuspecting victim. Harpo as on-screen gambler is visible when Chico organizes an impromptu sideshow game of knocking out villains in the climactic scene of *Monkey Business*; in *Horse Feathers* Harpo scoops the contents of a fruit machine and, in similar fashion, a payphone. Chico and Harpo could be formidable when working in tandem, as demonstrated by the card sequence in *Animal Crackers*. In real life, Harpo once tipped off his brother to an opponent's hand by observing the game, making a discreet exit and relaying the information to Chico by telephone; another account, described in the **C.B. Cochran** entry, tells of their revenge on a card sharp in London. As solo gambler, Chico's success was such that by the mid-1920s he was consistently borrowing against his salary by many months, and continued to work through the 1940s and 1950s despite declining health. It is known that the later Marx films, particularly *A Night in Casablanca*, owe their existence in part to Chico's continuing gambling debts (see also

Gangsters); it was through a similar fear of retribution that Chico once absented himself, unannounced, from the cast of *Cocoanuts* when it played Detroit. Until Chico's blithe reappearance, his nearest and dearest had no idea whether or not he had been murdered. One might add in passing that a highlight of *A Night in Casablanca* shows Chico and Harpo breaking the bank at a casino. Chico's brothers would deliberately withhold part of his money in order to finance him when necessary, usually with Gummo as custodian; even then, Chico remained broke. A famous tale has Chico evaluating his gambling losses over the years with the advice 'find out how much Harpo has; that's how much I've lost'. This vague calculation was alien to Chico's mathematical brain and probably served to project a sanguine attitude; Groucho noted that Chico 'sleeps better than I do'. Nat Perrin (*qv*) has said that Chico actually *bragged* about the huge sums he had lost. Both this carefree appearance and the financial imprecision were dispelled only once, at least publicly, at a press conference when in Britain for a TV show in 1959. According to the *Daily Mirror* of 1 October, he admitted losing $2,000,000 over thirty years, before going on to warn young people of the dangers of gambling. Chico mentioned how his brothers had saved their money and had done very well, before returning to his usual persona with a parting jest: 'I might be down to my last million but I still got plenty of laughs left.' Peripherally, one might repeat a story from the May 1982 *Freedonia Gazette* (*qv*) about a visitor to M-G-M's Grand Hotel in Las Vegas, who won Nevada's second-largest jackpot - $773,102 - on one of a number of slot machines named after M-G-M stars. His first choice was a machine named after Groucho, on which he lost a total of $400, but his luck altered when switching to that named after Judy Garland. Perhaps Groucho's machine thought it was Chico playing.

(See also: Characters; Clubs; Education; Insomnia; Marriages; M-G-M; Names; Politicians; Stage appearances [post-1930]; Television; Women)

GANGSTERS
(Marx Brothers films and shows *qv*) The movie industry fell in love with the idea of gangsters at much the same time as it did the Marx Brothers. *Monkey Business* concerns the rivalry between gangster factions, each side enlisting the aid of the Marxes; Jennings of *Horse Feathers* is of the type, if not so stated; Morgan in *A Day at the Races* is very obviously a racketeer; the same might be said of Carter in *At the Circus*; *The Big Store*'s Grover is not really in the category, for he has to hire a pair of hit-men to do his dirty work; but Madame Egilichi of *Love Happy* has a team of thugs all her own. In Groucho's last film, *Skidoo* (*qv*), it is *he* who is the gang boss. Concerning real-life encounters, it was naturally Chico the gambler who most frequently brushed with the underworld. Zeppo, when a strong-armed teenager, had started to hang around with such people until dragooned into the act as Gummo's replacement; one could therefore speculate on Minnie having twin motives for bringing her youngest son into the team. Groucho once recalled being shot at on a golf course by an irate Dutch Schultz and his gang. This was in New York during Prohibition, when such things were not too unusual. Around the same time Harpo introduced an ad lib during the stage run of *Cocoanuts* that could have cost him his life: he interrupted Groucho's scene with Margaret Dumont (*qv*) by chasing a chorus girl across the stage, unaware that she was the girlfriend of Legs Diamond. Fortunately Diamond did not witness the event and Harpo promptly found a different chorine. Zeppo and his first wife, Marion, fell victim to a gang of thieves in June 1933. They were hosting a dinner party and both the couple and their

assembled friends were tied up while the place was ransacked. A modern-day footnote: in Winter 1985 the *Freedonia Gazette* (*qv*) mentioned two wanted men who wore 'old suits', one sporting a Harpo-style wig, the other a Grouchoesque moustache. At that time they had robbed six banks in the Los Angeles area and were referred to by FBI agents as 'the Marx Brothers'.

(See also: Alcohol; Burke, James; Burr, Raymond; Dumbrille, Douglass; Fellowes, Rockcliffe; Gambling; Landau, David; Marriages; Marx, Minnie; Massey, Ilona; *A Night in Casablanca*; Sport; Woods, Harry)

GARBO, GRETA (1905-90)

Swedish-born actress Greta Garbo has intrigued generations through her classical features and enigmatic personality. It is known that, in her younger days at least, she was capable of belying her austere image with a degree of frivolity, as when joining several other stars in comic disguise at a Los Angeles performance of *The Cocoanuts* (*qv*). The script for episode 4 of *Flywheel, Shyster and Flywheel* has Groucho asking his secretary what's playing at the movies: '*Grand Hotel* with John Barrymore,' he is told. 'I'd rather have a small boarding house with Greta Garbo' comes the reply. Groucho offers a quick imitation of her in *A Night at the Opera* (*qv*), when he requests the departure of detective Henderson with that immortal line, 'I vant to be alone'. There is also mention of her in Groucho's song *Lydia, the Tattooed Lady*; otherwise, her legend was such that even Groucho could be slightly fazed: one of his pet anecdotes concerned the time he entered a lift at M-G-M, to find himself standing behind a woman clad in mannish-styled suit and wide-brimmed slouch hat. In mischievous mood, he tilted the hat over her eyes, only to be astonished when she turned and revealed herself to be Garbo. The startled Groucho excused himself with 'I thought you were a fellow I knew from Kansas City'.

(See also: Animation; *At the Circus*; Barlow, Reginald; Bell, Monta; Marshall, Tully; Oppenheimer, George; Songs)

GEMORA, CHARLES (1903-61)

Phillippines-born actor, whose Hollywood career was as make-up specialist and professional ape impersonator. Gemora, enclosed within the appropriate skin contributes to the Marxes' *At the Circus* (*qv*) as 'Gibraltar', the gorilla. Exactly *which* ape was Gemora is open to question: Groucho spoke of a gorilla skin which had a manager, and an actor to fill that skin who *also* had a manager; thus two managers for one gorilla. The occupant insisted on making ventilation holes, so the skin's owner took it back. Another ape costume had to be located, but all they could obtain was an orangutan skin, a much smaller item requiring occupancy by a midget. The result was a sudden switch in height between apes and, according to Groucho's version on Dick Cavett's show, the comedians received hundreds of letters from puzzled fans. Although there is no obvious discrepancy in ape dimensions when viewing the film, there is of course the possibility of a huge Marx following among picky anthropologists.

(See also: Television)

GILBERT & SULLIVAN

See: Metcalfe, Edward; *Mikado, the*; Records; Television

GILBERT, BILLY

(William Gilbert Baron) (1893-1971) Former stage actor, known for Hal Roach comedies with Laurel & Hardy (*qv*) and others; full-length films include *Firefly* (see **Allan Jones** and **Douglass Dumbrille**), the Alice Faye musical *Tin Pan Alley*, Chaplin's *The Great Dictator* and Disney's *Snow White and the Seven Dwarfs* for which he provided the voice of Sneezy. Later often on TV. He turns up on ship during *A Night at the Opera* (*qv*) as the musician who, after persuasion, allows

Chico, Harpo and Allan Jones (*qv*) to entertain the passengers. Billy Gilbert, Kenny Baker (*qv*) and Harpo Marx were among the many to appear *gratis* in the 1943 film *Stage Door Canteen* (see **Guest appearances**).

(See also: Animation; Chaplin, Charlie)

A GIRL IN EVERY PORT (RKO 1952)

(Groucho solo film)
Groucho's second solo outing for RKO (*qv*) pairs him with character comedian William Bendix (*qv*). They are cast as sailors who spend much of their time in the brig, usually for one disreputable scheme or another. When the Bendix character is persuaded to blow an inheritance on a worthless horse, they are given leave from custody to put the matter to rights. They discover the horse to be the twin of an altogether more successful animal and are thus provided with a perfect 'ringer'. The other horse belongs to a waitress, played by comedienne Marie Wilson (*qv*). The film has several amusing sequences, as when the sailors hide no less than *two* horses aboard ship, but somehow the laughs seem strained. In *The Groucho Phile* there is an admission that the principals may have been too old for such a film, and it's true to say that Groucho, though belying his 61 years, makes a decidedly

ancient mariner. As a result, he and Bendix come over more effectively as bogus colonels from the Deep South, allowing Groucho to indulge in his best Dixie dialect. A bonus: in one scene, Groucho takes to his beloved guitar (sadly under-used in his film work) as the pair vie for Marie Wilson's attentions (Bendix plays the mandolin). Produced by Irwin Allen and Irving Cummings, Jr (both *qv*); directed by Chester Erskine (*qv*). Screenplay by Chester Erskine, based on the story *They Sell Sailors Elephants* by Frederick Hazlitt Brennan.

(See also: Guitar, the; Names)

THE GOOKIE

A Harpo trademark from *Fun in Hi Skule* (*qv*) and possibly earlier, the 'Gookie' describes a disgusting facial expression in which Harpo would inflate his cheeks, keeping his mouth open with tongue tucked between lower lip and teeth, while simultaneously crossing his eyes. Allen Eyles' word for it is 'ghastly'; Alexander Woollcott (*qv*), in his 1928 *New Yorker* essay on Harpo, 'Portrait of a Man with Red Hair', wrote of people 'screaming in their sleep' for weeks after a sudden confrontation with the face. Harpo recalled using the Gookie to scare a woman in the audience during *On the Mezzanine* (*qv*). 'Gookie' started life as

the corrupted nickname of a Mr Gehrke, a New York tobacconist whose duties included the delicate art of cigar-rolling. He was seemingly unable to accomplish this task without contorting his features into the expression detailed above, and was enraged when young Harpo would duplicate it, looking through the window with a cry of 'Gookie, Gookie!' Harpo used the face at some point within every Marx Brothers film, perpetuating what might be called the nearest to authentic horror in the team's repertoire.

(See also: Race; Smoking; Television)

GORDON, ARTHUR
See: Vaudeville

GORDON, BRUCE (b. 1919)

Appears in *Love Happy* (*qv*) as one of the thuggish Zoto brothers, along with

Raymond Burr (*qv*). He should not be confused with three other actors of the same name, two of them (one British, one American) active in silent pictures, the other a British contemporary. Other appearances include *The Buccaneer* (1958), *Curse of the Undead* (1959), the *Untouchables* TV show (and its 1958 cinema prototype, *The Scarface Mob*), *Rider On a Dead Horse* (1962), *Tower of London* (1962), *Slow Run* (1968) and *Hello Down There* (1968).

GORDON, KITTY
See: *I'll Say She Is!*

GORDON, MAX (1892-1978)

(Marx Brothers films *qv*) Theatrical producer and sometime agent, born Mechel Salpeter in New York; a friend of Groucho's in the late 1920s, it was he who called Groucho on the morning of the Stock Market crash with the immortal words 'Marx! The jig is up!' Shortly after meeting Arthur Sheekman (*qv*) in 1930, Groucho collaborated with him on material for Gordon's revue *Three's a Crowd*. Gordon assisted in negotiating the three-picture Paramount contract commencing with *Monkey Business*. According to his memoirs, *Max Gordon Presents*, Paramount chief Jesse Lasky paid him $250 a week plus a share of the profits; in what was then a revolutionary deal, the Marxes were to receive 50 per cent of the net profits over $400,000 on each picture, the first $10,000 going to Gordon. He recalled having forgotten the arrangement until eighteen years later, when Gummo called with the news that '*Horse Feathers* was just one thousand dollars short and that it would not be long before I began collecting the money owed me.' Suspecting a practical joke, Gordon had his lawyer verify the contractual terms. 'I mention this,' said Gordon, 'partly because I wish to pay tribute to such honesty and partly because it provides a clue to one of the

*A full-blooded **Gookie** from* A Day at the Races

many reasons for my deep regard and affection for those beloved Marx brothers.' (It might be added that when Gordon suffered a breakdown after losing all his money on a failed show in New York, Harpo visited him with comforting words and a gift of $4,000; half was from Groucho who, on a subsequent visit, assured Gordon of a further supply if necessary.) The startling delay in Gordon's percentage may indicate why relations started to break down between Paramount and the Marxes during 1933. Before commencing *Duck Soup* that year, the comedians were involved in a bitter contractual dispute with the studio. Despite having taken a job with Paramount as consultant, Gordon was interested in forming a new company with Sam Harris (*qv*) and others, with the Marxes as potential stars; with the Paramount dispute raging, the comedians were willing to listen (see **Marx Bros, Inc.**). After the team's eventual break with Paramount, Gordon tried unsuccessfully to lure them back to the stage; he later produced *Everybody Loves Me*, a play written by Groucho's son, Arthur.

(See also: Abandoned projects; Agents; Children; Insomnia; Paramount Pictures)

GO WEST

(Marx Brothers film)
Released by M-G-M, 6 December 1940. Copyrighted 11 December (LP 10112).
7,227 ft (79 minutes).
Produced by Jack Cummings. Directed by Edward Buzzell. Camera: Leonard Smith. Screenplay by Irving Brecher. Songs: *Ridin' the Range*, music by Roger Edens, lyrics by Gus Kahn; *As If I Didn't Know*, *You Can't Argue With Love*, music by Bronislau Kaper, lyrics by Gus Kahn; *From the Land of Sky Blue Water* by Charles Wakefield Cadman.

With Groucho Marx (*S. Quentin Quale*), Chico Marx (*Joseph Panello*),

Mark Newell Collection

Harpo Marx (*Rusty Panello*), John Carroll (*Terry Turner*), Diana Lewis (*Eve Wilson*), Walter Woolf King (*John Beecher*), Robert Barrat (*Red Baxter*), June MacCloy (*Lulubelle, the saloon girl*), Tully Marshall (*Dan Wilson*), George Lessey (*railroad President*), Mitchell Lewis (*Pete*), Iris Adrian (*saloon girl Mary Lou*), Joan Woodbury (*third saloon girl*), Arthur Housman (*drunk*).

S. Quentin Quale is at the railroad station, headed west. Also at the station are Joe Panello and his brother Rusty. It is intended that Rusty will travel west, pick up plenty of gold and send it to finance Joe's trip. Rusty has spent all

but $10 of the $70 required for the fare; Quale is short precisely $10 for his own ticket. Quale, seeing his opportunity, tries to sell Rusty some authentic Western clothing. Each item is supposedly priced at a dollar but Joe demands $9 change each time, having given Quale a $10 bill. It is actually the same note each time, retrieved from Quale's pocket by a thread. In time the thread becomes detached, but Quale does not notice Rusty cutting open his trouser leg. Quale accepts a fleecing, but has made other financial arrangements, in other words a wad of money in his hat; Rusty swaps hats with him before they go their respective ways. There is a meeting at the office of the President and General Manager of the New York and Western Railroad. Terry Turner, visiting from the West, enquires of the railroad's plans to run track north from Cripple Creek around the mountains. He requests an alternate route, linking Cripple Creek to the Pacific via Dead Man's Gulch. The otherwise worthless land was once owned by his dishonest grandfather, who sold it to one Dan Wilson; Terry hopes the deal will reconcile the two families so that he may wed Wilson's granddaughter, Eve. Out in Dead Man's Gulch, Joe and Rusty are digging for gold. They have had as much success as Dan Wilson, who has wasted

S. Quentin Quale equips Rusty for frontier life in **Go West**
BFI Stills, Posters and Designs

Go West: *a long-distance view of the saloon set, as Quale travels downstairs the hard way*
BFI Stills, Posters and Designs

forty years mining the area. He plans to move on, explaining that he cannot retire because of a need to support his granddaughter. Dan will find work to raise the necessary $10 to buy a grubstake. Joe offers to lend him the $10; Dan insists on leaving them the deed to his land as security. When Joe and Rusty reach Birch City, they are to call on Dan's granddaughter, Eve, with the message that Dan will be back soon. Eve is at home when Terry rides in. He has sold Dead Man's Gulch to the railroad for $50,000 and wants to find Dan. In town, Joe and Rusty are caught by the pangs of thirst and enter a rough saloon. Its owner, Red Baxter, receives a letter from John Beecher in New York. Beecher is from the railroad but is also joint owner of some land with Baxter. He tells Baxter to obtain the deed to Dead Man's Gulch in order for them to sell their own land to the railroad - at their price. Red sends Indian Pete and his men to find Dan Wilson, but they have been trying to locate him for weeks. Joe and Rusty have no money but intercept a beer as it slides, Western-style, along the bar. When caught, Joe writes Baxter an IOU for 10 cents on the back of the deed. It is placed in the cash register. Outside, Joe and Rusty ask at the telegraph office for directions to

Wilson's cabin. They are given a telegram for Wilson, which asks him to meet Beecher concerning the sale of his land. Joe and Rusty read the telegram and go to the station in Wilson's place. Beecher disembarks from the train as Joe calls his name. Beecher identifies himself, but Joe and Rusty refuse to recognize him without a carnation. They provide one, walk away, then greet him enthusiastically. Joe explains that they hold the deed to Wilson's land, but has to stall when asked to produce it. Joe tells Beecher that the deed is being kept at home in Birch City, where they will travel by stagecoach. Also on board are Baxter's girlfriend Lulubelle, plus a woman with a baby; *en route* they pick up Quale, who has been pacing in the desert. Quale tries to sell Lulubelle a necklace, but when Joe offers him $1 (and '$9 change, please') he throws it out of the

window. During the bumpy journey, Beecher offers Joe $500 for the land. Quale offers $1,000, claiming to represent an oil company. Beecher raises his bid to $1,500 but Quale eventually beats him with an offer of $6,000. At Birch City, Quale enters the saloon, guns blazing. He meets Lulubelle and the other girls and demands to see Baxter when told Lulubelle is his girlfriend. Baxter is ready to shoot until Beecher intercedes, telling him that Quale will be selling them the deed. Red has Lulubelle look after Quayle, who asks Joe for the deed. Joe requests 10 cents in order to get it back. Lulubelle goes on stage to sing *You Can't Argue With Love*. Between verses, Lulubelle sits on Quale's knee, as he speculates on what his 'people' will say of their liaison. He is interrupted by a belching drunk. Joe and Rusty go to the cash register, exchange a dime for the deed and present it to Quale. Joe demands the money but Quale promises to return after an appointment. Joe and Rusty celebrate, with Joe at the piano. Upstairs, Baxter and Beecher put the deed in their safe and refuse to pay Quale the $10,000 promised him. He refuses their offer of $500 and threatens them with the law. This idea is forgotten after a display of Red's sharp-shooting. Quale is tripped downstairs. Rusty takes on Red in

Publicity pose with Diana Lewis, early in production of **Go West**. *The train is a mock-up*

The climactic train ride of **Go West**. In the film, John Carroll and Diana Lewis pursue the train by means of a buckboard

classic gunfighter tradition, but draws a clothes brush in lieu of a revolver. Mirth turns to panic when the brush actually fires. Rusty, Joe and Quale make their escape. They visit Eve Wilson as promised. Expecting to see a child, they have brought a huge rag doll. They are reluctant to tell Eve what has happened, but she can tell something is wrong. The full story is related and Eve, though philosophical, asks them not to tell her grandfather. Resolving to help, they return to the saloon, breaking into the room housing Baxter's safe. Lulubelle and the other girls, overhearing the intrusion, fetch drinks and plan to keep them busy while Baxter is sent for. Joe and Quale drink with the girls while Rusty blows the safe. Rusty obtains the deed but Baxter and Beecher have the others at gunpoint. Rusty escapes detection by hiding in a roll-top bureau, then sneaks up behind Baxter with a model cannon. Beecher in turn holds up Rusty; Eve arrives and holds up Beecher; Indian Pete holds up Eve; finally, Terry arrives and holds up Pete. Rusty hands the deed to Terry, who will deliver it to the New York officials personally. Though temporarily defeated, Baxter and Beecher plan to make Terry miss the next day's train, forcing a seven-day wait during which they can sell their land to the railroad. Eve, Terry, Quale and the Panellos ride through the

night, singing *Ridin' the Range*. They stop at an Indian reservation where, curiously, Quale's image appears on a totem pole. Quale and Joe antagonize the tribe but they warm somewhat to Rusty, especially after he plays a loom in the manner of a harp. Morning, and Baxter's men are guarding the train. Terry and Eve ride off to the next station, but Quale, Joe and Rusty tie up the engineers and commandeer the locomotive. Their guide is an instruction book which, sadly, provides no details on how to stop. Quale asks one of the engineers what to do, and is told 'Brake! The brake!' Rusty breaks the brake and the train roars past the next station. Terry and Eve continue to give chase. Baxter and Beecher spot them and, unaware of the change in drivers, head for the locomotive with instructions to ignore all stops prior to New York; Quale, Joe and Rusty move back into the first coach just as the villains arrive to untie the engineers. Baxter and Beecher corner the trio in the rear car, but Baxter's gun has been replaced by Rusty's clothes brush. The chase continues along the carriage roof, heading toward the front of the train; Quale and the Panellos lose ground when caught in a signal, but are able to jump across when their car is detached from the train. They try the same with the villains' coach but remain on the wrong side, forcing Rusty to act as human bridge. Baxter and Beecher are knocked out and locked in a cupboard. The train must be stopped, so Joe tells Rusty to pour water on the engine.

Rusty negotiates the outside of the train, carrying only a mugful of water; he is picked up by a mail hook and dumped back into the rear car. Lulubelle releases Baxter and Beecher, who make for the locomotive. Joe and Quale are dumping the tender's supply of wood as the engineers fight back with oil cans. The oil catches Baxter, who accidentally operates a pedal that releases both the wood supply and the engineers. Quale returns to the coach, acting as bait so that Rusty can once again knock out the villains. They are returned to the cupboard. Quale and Joe reach the footplate just as Rusty seems to be pouring water in the firebox. The train slows down, but Rusty has used kerosene by mistake and the locomotive returns to speed. Terry and Eve resume the chase. Rusty kicks what remains of the brake and the train finally stops. Terry and Eve climb aboard, but the villains have been released and Terry is knocked cold. Baxter and Beecher set off for New York in Terry's wagon. There being no fuel, the train must be powered by anything to hand, including luggage and a supply of popcorn ('Pop goes the diesel!'). Baxter and Beecher dislodge part of the track, sending the train in a wide circle. After picking up and dislodging a farmhouse, the train is restored to its intended course. By now most of the coaches have been chopped up for fuel, leaving barely a skeleton. The villains are disposed of when their wagon crosses a bridge in the train's path. Baxter and Beecher are dumped in the river while the fragmented train speeds to New York. The day arrives to drive the Golden Spike. Terry, Eve and Dan Wilson are reconciled, and the railroad President acknowleges his debt to all concerned. Quale and Joe hold the historic spike as Rusty wields the hammer; his backswing drives the railroad President into the earth and the boys shake hands all round.

Though separated by three films, *Go West* was conceived only months after the release of *A Night at the Opera* (*qv*). In May 1936 it was announced that two new stories were being written for the Marx Brothers, one of which became *A Day at the Races* (*qv*); scheduled for production immediately thereafter was a Western, to be written by Bert Kalmar, Harry Ruby (*qv*) and one William Slavens McNutt. Producer was to have been Irving Thalberg (*qv*), whose premature death later in the year probably accounts not only for the Western's postponement but also the rejection of Kalmar and Ruby's completed draft. In its stead was a script by Irving Brecher (*qv*), who had written *At the Circus* (*qv*) in 1939. Similarly re-engaged was the director of *Circus*, Edward Buzzell (*qv*). Neither had contributed memorably to the first collaboration. Groucho's correspondence with Arthur Sheekman (*qv*) betrays a jaded spirit from the outset. A letter of October 1939 refers to *Go West* as 'another turkey', mentioning an intended production date of only three to four weeks hence. This did not happen but, after another five months, the Marxes were at least permitted a try-out tour. This had been denied them for *At the Circus* but temporarily reinstated. The stage version of *Go West* played from late April to early May 1940, with stops including Detroit and Chicago. Nat Perrin (*qv*) was on hand as a gag writer. From Detroit, Groucho wrote to his daughter Miriam, explaining he had plenty of time on his hands 'except for a few rehearsals and four or five performances'. In a letter dated 12 June, Groucho told Sheekman of a planned start on 1 July, 'by which time, I'm sure, we will have forgotten all the dialogue so carefully rehearsed on the road.' The first day of July arrived and cameras did not turn. On that day, Groucho wrote again to Sheekman, noting the continued postponement; 'I read the script and I don't blame them,' he added. Delays continued until (according to a letter to Arthur

Marx) the dye in Groucho's hair needed replenishing. He was greying and the dye was to ensure a match between hair, moustache and, one suspects, a hairpiece. Production was finally underway in mid-July and continued into October. Release was in December 1940 but widespread reviews date from early the following year. *Variety* liked the film as a whole, lauded the script and direction, and attributed much of its effectiveness to

Go West goes East. Programme for a screening to RAF personnel in India
Mark Newell Collection

the stage tour. The Marxes were said to 'handle their assignments with zestful enthusiasm', a remark speaking volumes for their acting ability. In February 1941 *The New York Times*, disappointed, thought the Marxes less funny than before and, apart from a few 'snappy lines', remarked on the corniness of the material. The train sequence was the only one considered of genuine merit and it is this scene that conquered the British press. When *Go West* was trade-shown at the Cambridge, *The Cinema* of 18 February found room on its front page

to declare the manic train ride 'one of the maddest and merriest climaxes ever devised for the screen'. A full review was published two days later, applauding the 'characteristic adventures' supplied by Brecher and expressing the opinion that Buzzell had 'outdone all his previous efforts' in 'one of the best and definitely the most exciting of all the Marx Brothers films'. The same day's *Kinematograph Weekly* was of like mind, noting a gradual but effective build-up to the climactic sequence, noting along the way various highlights such as Groucho's fleecing at the beginning, the musical breaks and the business of robbing a safe. Even the *Monthly Film Bulletin*, fussier than most in terms of film structure, complained only about a degree of abruptness between scenes. 'The Marxes are in their element in a plot which affords excellent opportunities for their special brand of fooling', said *MFB*, 'and their antics on that final wild train journey must be seen to be believed'. There is no denying the excellence of *Go West*'s finale, one of the few occasions on which a Marx film does not tail off before the end title. There is something irresistible about a train powered eventually by its own dwindling carcass and the sight gags within are pulled with all the finesse one expects from the best silent comedies. The film also begins extremely well, in one of those routines where we are reminded that Groucho can outwit anyone on earth except his brothers. Unfortunately this is not consistent through the film, there being too many sequences in which the Marxes are intimidated by gun-slinging Westerners or outwitted by saloon girls. None would have stood a chance in earlier exploits and it is especially disconcerting to see Groucho and Chico lose control of themselves through alcohol. During a stagecoach journey, the mother of a screaming child scores off the Marx Brothers by blaming 'the jerks in the coach', a designation better applied to the Three

Stooges. As noted elsewhere, Buzzell attributed *Go West*'s flaws to the Marxes being 'old men trying to be pixies', but this is to disregard their established characters. The *New York Times*' accusation of corniness might have been unjustified but for *Go West*'s reliance on Western cliché for its own sake, as in Harpo's showdown with Robert Barrat (*qv*). Although the Marx version was planned earlier, Laurel & Hardy's *Way Out West* (1937) handles the time-honoured plot, that of a stolen deed, with effective satire whereas *Go West* merely uses it as a framework. It would be interesting to know how effective *Go West* might have been under Thalberg's supervision, with Kalmar and Ruby supplying the script.

(See also: Adrian, Iris; Barrat, Robert; Carroll, John; Cummings, Jack; Documentaries; Guitar, the; Harp, the; Hats; Housman, Arthur; King, Walter Woolf; Laurel & Hardy; Lewis, Diana; M-G-M; MacCloy, June; Marshall, Tully; Names; Race; Shoes; Songs; Stage appearances [post-1930]; Telephones; Trailers; Trains; the Wild West)

GRAVES
See: Deaths

GREAT BRITAIN
See: Cochran, C.B.; *Home Again*; London Palladium, the; *On the Mezzanine*; Radio; Royalty; Sport; Stage appearances (post-1930); Television

GREEN, ALFRED E. (1889-1960)
Director of Groucho's solo film *Copacabana* (*qv*). In silents from 1912; directed high-profile efforts such as two 1921 Mary Pickford vehicles (in collaboration with Jack Pickford), *Through the Back Door* and *Little Lord Fauntleroy*; also directed several Colleen Moore films, *Sally* (1925), *Irene* (1926), *Ella Cinders* (1926) and *It Must Be Love* (1926). Talkie career generally undistinguished, but *Disraeli* (1931) and *The Jolson Story* (1946) are fair recommendations. It was

presumably the success of the Jolson biopic that led him to direct *The Eddie Cantor Story* in 1953.

(See also: Cantor, Eddie)

GREIG, ROBERT (1880-1958)
(Marx Brothers films *qv*)
Australian-born, British-accented actor of portly frame who, like Eric Blore (*qv*), was America's idea of a perfect English butler. He took precisely that rôle in the stage and screen versions of the Marx Brothers' *Animal Crackers* as Hives, major-domo *chez* Rittenhouse. He appears again with the Marxes as a bearded professor in *Horse Feathers*. Among other notable films are Lubitsch's *Trouble in Paradise* (1932), the Chevalier-MacDonald *Love Me Tonight* (1932), Wheeler & Woolsey's *Cockeyed Cavaliers* (1934), *Clive of India* (1935) and the 1941 Preston Sturges classic *Sullivan's Travels* (in which Blore also appears).

(See also: Kinsky, Leonid; Moustaches, beards; Todd, Thelma)

GREY, VIRGINIA (b. 1917)
Leading lady of *The Big Store* (*qv*); often in 'B' pictures. Within a long list of other films are *Who Killed Doc Robbin?* (1948), *The Bullfighter and the Lady* (1950), *The Last Command* (1955) and *Madame X* (1965).

(See also: Television)

GROUCHO - A LIFE IN REVUE
The 'official' stage presentation of Groucho's life story was born from the meeting of actor Frank Ferrante and Groucho's son, Arthur. Ferrante was studying at the University of Southern California, where he performed his one-man show, *An Evening with Groucho*, as his senior project. Towards the end of his life, Morrie Ryskind (*qv*) expressed the view that Ferrante was 'the only actor aside from Groucho who delivered my lines as they were intended to be'. Arthur Marx also saw Ferrante and decided he was ideal to

An intimidated **Robert Greig** *in* Animal Crackers

star in a proposed biographical presentation of his own. *Groucho - a Life in Revue* opened off-Broadway in October 1986 at the Lucille Lortel theatre, New York City. The show was directed by Richard Carrothers and Arthur Marx, the latter of whom wrote the script in collaboration with Robert Fisher. Among previous Marx-Fisher efforts were *The Impossible Years* and an earlier Marx-based musical, *Minnie's Boys* (*qv*). By a clever production trick, Chico and Harpo were portrayed by one actor, Les Marsden (already known for his one-man show, *A Night at Harpo's*), who impressed those unfamiliar with his earlier show by considerable skill on both piano and harp. Marguerite Lowell played all the women in the story, ranging between showgirls, floozies, wives and the magnificent Margaret Dumont (*qv*). The play takes Groucho all the way from boyhood to old age, incorporating much straight-to-audience rapport from Marsden and Ferrante, for whom the production was a *tour de force*. This applied not merely to his replication of the standard Groucho character but, most unusually, in a striking moment where he turned from the audience, applied grey to his hair and, suitably bereted, became the octogenarain Groucho both physically and vocally. The new play earned instant acclaim, Ferrante receiving the 1987 Theatre World Award (he was also nominated for the Outer Critics Circle Award for the 'Most Striking Debut of the Season'). The play transferred to London in the late summer of 1987, playing provincial dates at the Yvonne Arnaud Theatre, Guildford and the Ashcroft Theatre, Croydon, before opening at the Comedy Theatre on September 16. Arthur Marx alone directed the London production. Irving Wardle of the *Times*, regarding Ferrante as 'the closest replica we are ever likely to see of the man himself', welcomed a closer view of a vaudeville team 'whom we know only through their films'; Charles Osborne of the *Daily Telegraph* was justly awed by the 24-year-old Ferrante's ease in conveying a Groucho aged anywhere between middle age and near-death; this same transformation was lauded by Milton Shulman of London's *Evening Standard*; while even the comparatively few dissenters felt obliged to praise the impersonations. The show's stay in England was high-profile in the extreme, Arthur Marx and Frank Ferrante being interviewed on BBC TV's peak-time talk show *Wogan* and the cast performing extracts from the play in a variety programme, *The Ronnie Corbett Show*.

(See also: Children; *A Day in Hollywood, a Night in the Ukraine*, Gordon, Max; Impersonators; Letters)

GUEST APPEARANCES

Like most other stars, the Marxes were sometimes called upon to make appearances in films other than their own. Chico and W.C. Fields (*qv*) are seen with female autograph hunters (actually the Earl Carroll Girls) in one of Paramount's *Hollywood On Parade* series. The reel is in effect a commercial for a concurrent Paramount feature, *Murder at the Vanities* (1934). Several Earl Carroll girls, returning to New York by train, peruse a photo album given to them by Jack Oakie. The album, supposedly commemorating some of their activities while in Hollywood, leads into the Chico-Fields sequence. Chico, in an ordinary suit and a beret, is seen with Fields as they sprint away from the girls, hurdling a succession of low

hedges: 'Gee, I hope they catch us,' says Chico, to which Fields replies 'I'm afraid they won't!' Once apprehended, Fields announces their refusal to sign any autograph books, but invites the girls to sign his and Chico's, requesting also the girls' telephone numbers. 'Hey, Bill,' says Chico, 'it's last year's book - maybe it's last year's girls, though. We can bring *them* up to date, too!' Groucho appears in a separate segment of this one-reeler, speaking over the local KHJ radio station from a screening of *Murder at the Vanities*. He is out of make-up, sporting top hat and evening dress. 'Good evening, everybody,' he says. 'There's really nothing I can do because Harpo is in Russia, Chico is in the theatre and Zeppo heard that I was going to make a speech here tonight, so he didn't show up at all.' Another in the series, number A-9 (1932), shows Groucho, Chico and Harpo dozing on sun-loungers, apparently swatting the flies that have landed on each other, but engaging instead in a small-scale battle armed with rolled-up newspapers. They return to full consciousness (of a sort) when approached by Groucho's daughter Miriam. Harpo gathers the child in his arms and pretends to eat her foot. The Marxes are then distracted by some pretty starlets, one of whom is chased into a pool by Harpo. A more fleeting Harpo appearance takes place in a two-reel curiosity from M-G-M (*qv*), *La Fiesta de Santa Barbara*, released in December 1935 (sometimes dated

1936). Unavailable for years, this 'Musical Revue' was known to have been shot in Technicolor, causing much speculation on the colour of Harpo's wig. This subject was eventually revived and revealed Harpo not in costume but in his favoured civilian garb of sports jacket and open-necked shirt. The wig is absent and much of his natural brown hair obscured by a Red Indian head-dress. Harpo's contribution, lasting but seconds, consists of him taking gleeful gulps of wine from a brace of Mexican gourds. Says narrator Pete Smith: 'Harpo Marx enters into the spirit of the fiesta - and the spirits of the fiesta enter into Harpo. Time Marxes on!' Harpo is one of many Hollywood names seen at a banquet celebrating the fiesta of the title; the film is actually of greater value to fans of Buster Keaton (*qv*), who is seen extensively. Trivia note: later in the film, Ted Healy (then recently estranged from the Three Stooges) makes passing reference to 'the Four Marx Brothers', who had by then become three. An 'M-G-M Miniature', *Hollywood - the Second Step* (1936), features Chico and Maureen O'Sullivan (*qv*); a studio press release, dating from the preparation of *A Day at the Races* (*qv*), details its history:

Chico, who always wanted to play a serious part, got his chance at last. But

Guest appearances: *Harpo in 1943's* Stage Door Canteen
BFI Stills, Posters and Designs

it was all in fun. The Mad Marxian volunteered to help his friend, director Felix Feist, by portraying a movie star in the Metro-Goldwyn-Mayer short subject, "**THE SECOND STEP**", Carey Wilson's story of a girl extra's experiences in Hollywood.

An out-of-make-up Groucho has been spotted as an extra in a full-length Paramount film starring George Raft, *Yours For the Asking* (1936). According to the November 1979 *Freedonia Gazette* (*qv*), Groucho and Charlie Ruggles happened to have been sunbathing at Coronado Island Beach when a Paramount crew arrived for location filming; Groucho and Ruggles, insisting it was a public beach, refused to budge and thus remain visible in the final film (mention was made of these famous 'extras' in the film's pressbook). Groucho and his first wife, Ruth, are also reported in a 1937 M-G-M two-reeler, *Sunday Night at the Trocadero*. The war years brought greater reason for extra-curricular appearances, hence the two 1943 Columbia *Screen Snapshots* entries, directed by Ralph Staub, one of which (number 2 in the series) shows Groucho performing a radio sketch plus a duet with Carole Landis in *The Pabst Blue Ribbon Town*. Columbia reissued the duet segment in a later 'Snapshot', *Hollywood's Greatest Comedians* (1953). The second entry (number 8) includes Groucho, Chico and Harpo. The same year brought Harpo into *Stage Door Canteen*, directed by Frank Borzage and released by United Artists (*qv*). All involved contributed their services *gratis* to this wartime fund-raiser, based on the real-life Canteen in New York. In one scene, a woman attempts to make a telephone call, only to find

she is sharing the booth with Harpo. He chases a blonde through the club, only to be intercepted by a GI, who insists Harpo should remove his hat when there are ladies present. Harpo obliges, but also leers at the woman, who screams and runs off. Harpo then settles down to play Hoagy Carmichael's *Stardust*. (Some filmographies confuse this production with 1944's *Hollywood Canteen*, in which Harpo does not appear.) In the final months of the war, Harpo contributed to a two-reel War Bond promotion made by 20th Century-Fox, *The All-Star Bond Rally* (1945). During this show-within-a-show, MC Bob Hope follows a song by Frank Sinatra (*qv*) by announcing 'a brief interlude with the classics'. The stage curtains part to reveal a harp; a commotion is heard at the back of the theatre, which turns out to be Harpo, honking his taxi horn and chasing a screaming girl. They reach the stage and Harpo forsakes his quarry for the instrument. He plays a solo and rests his head against the harp as the curtains close once more. Another scream, and the girl reappears, this time followed by Bob Hope, who pauses to deliver a sales pitch for War Bonds. Harpo looks quite old in this film, due mostly to less extensive hair covering; instead of his usual wig, it resembles more his own curled, dyed hair in *A Night in Casablanca* (*qv*), which entered production later that year. During the 1950s such appearances tended to be more on television (*qv*) than in the cinema, though Chico is seen participating in a professional roller derby in a 1950s short entitled *Sports Antics*, discovered by historian Robert Bader. Groucho's contributions to the 1950s features *Mr Music* and *Will*

Success Spoil Rock Hunter? and *Double Dynamite* are examined in greater detail (under those titles) elsewhere, as is his role in Preminger's 1968 disastrous *Skidoo* (*qv*); he also appears solo in *Copacabana* & *A Girl in Every Port*. (See also: Advertising; Animation; Armetta, Henry; Baker, Kenny; Children; Colour; *Copacabana*; *Double Dynamite*; Gilbert, Billy; *Girl in Every Port, A*; Home movies; Marriages; *Monkey Business* [promo]; Newsreels; Paramount Pictures; Radio; Records; Russia; Television; *Too Many Kisses*; Wartime; Wigs)

THE GUITAR

(Marx Brothers films *qv*)
Just as Harpo and Chico had their musical specialities, so Groucho was a skilled guitarist. The Marxes shared an aptitude for music - Zeppo played saxophone, for example - but these talents were not always incorporated into the act. Groucho tended to keep his guitar out of the Marx films, except when serenading or otherwise trying to impress Thelma Todd (*qv*) in *Monkey Business* and *Horse Feathers*; the only other instance is when providing unobtrusive guitar accompaniment to a song in *Go West*. Groucho dusted off the instrument when singing *My Bonnie* with William Bendix (*qv*) in *A Girl in Every Port* (*qv*) and for another duet - on TV - with his daughter, Melinda. One of Groucho's many celebrated visitors was the guitar virtuoso, Segovia. The maestro declined to play at Groucho's home because the comedian's guitar was strung with steel instead of gut.

(See also: Children; Documentaries; Harp, the; Piano, the; Television)

HAIR
See: Moustaches, beards; Wigs

HALL, RUTH
(b. 1912)
Florida-born actress who takes the *ingénue* role of Mary Helton in *Monkey Business* (*qv*). Ruth Hall's acting career began on the amateur stage while still at school; her film debut came about when director Henry King put her into *Hell Harbor* (1930), starring Lupe Velez. She was a 'Wampas Baby' of 1932. Her full name, Ruth Hall Ibañez, is of interest; her uncle, Vicente Blasco Ibañez, was the original author of *Blood and Sand* and *The Four Horsemen of the Apocalypse*. Ruth Hall is also known to fans of early 1930s comedy through *Her Majesty, Love* (1931) with W.C. Fields (*qv*), Joe E. Brown's *Local Boy Makes Good* (1931) and, especially, as leading lady of *The Kid From Spain* (1932) with Eddie Cantor (*qv*). Other films include *Miss Pinkerton*, a 1932 vehicle for Joan Blondell.

(See also: McCarey, Leo; *Monkey Business* [promo]; Ruby, Harry)

HANNAH AND HER SISTERS
See: *Duck Soup*

THE HARP
The instrument from which, of course, derives Harpo's nickname. The family's original harpist had been Minnie's mother, whose worn-out harp had fascinated Adolph/Arthur/Harpo in boyhood. Around the time of *Fun in Hi Skule* (*qv*) Harpo expressed a wish to learn the instrument and Minnie, always searching for 'class', obtained one through Al Shean (*qv*). The harp cost $40 and was an ancient model without pedals. Harpo taught himself to play - learning which shoulder to rest it on from a picture in Woolworth's window - and tuned it within his own context, or in other words unlike any other harp in the world. The original harp was unscathed when they were involved in a train wreck, but Harpo still obtained sufficient compensation from the railroad company to obtain a new harp. In his memoirs, Harpo recalls deliberately wrecking the instrument to claim the money; this is not mentioned in a different account, a Chico-Harpo photo-strip called 'Harpo's First Harp' in the *Graphic* of 27 May 1949. It does add, however, that he reassembled the pieces and sold it for $250, only to learn it was subsequently re-sold to an antiques dealer for $750. According to this version, the original $40 model had been financed by a collection taken around the family, to which Chico

contributed the gold filling from a back tooth. Harpo played the harp daily, a labour of love, and used a small, silent, practice version to keep his fingers toughened. He employed tutors over the years but wearied of paying them when all they wanted to do was hear *him* play. An exception was Mildred Dilling, a harpist who became the comedian's lifelong friend. She died in December 1982, aged 88. According to Kipp Wessel in the November 1980 *Freedonia Gazette* (*qv*), Harpo visited a woman reputed to be the world's greatest harp virtuoso while in France during 1928. She was a recluse who refused to leave the attic in which she lived; after waiting three days for an appointment, Harpo paid $15 an hour for a recital in her cramped abode. The harp remained through all the Marx shows and films except *Duck Soup* and *Room Service* (both *qv*). His concentration during these solos is apparent and all trace of his wild comedy disappears; as he said himself, this was when the man took over from the stage character. Variants on the harp include the use of a disembowelled piano in *A Day at the Races* (*qv*) and a weaving loom in *Go West* (*qv*).

(See also: *Big Store, The*; *Cocoanuts, The* [play]; *Horse Feathers*; London Palladium, the; Marx, Minnie; Religion; Russia; Trains; Vaudeville)

HARRIS, SAM H. (1872-1941)

Theatrical producer who worked closely with George M. Cohan until they took opposing views in the theatrical strike of 1919. It was because Harris had taken the actors' side that Groucho, in particular, wanted Harris to produce the Marxes' Broadway shows. Harris was not among those to approach the team after the success of *I'll Say She Is!* (*qv*) but was instead contacted by his then associate, Irving Berlin (*qv*), at Harpo's request. Harris had already begun his long tenure as producer for George S. Kaufman (*qv*) and the three combined to create the second Marx Brothers musical, *The Cocoanuts* (*qv*). Harris went on to produce their third Broadway hit, *Animal Crackers* (also *qv*), and probably would have continued with them had Paramount (*qv*) not lured the team to Hollywood. They were briefly connected once more, when a rift with the studio led to the formation of Marx Bros., Inc. (*qv*); a subsequent career hiatus, between the Marxes' contracts with Paramount and M-G-M (*qv*), led to discussions with Harris over a new stage musical (see **Abandoned projects**).

(See also: Ruby, Harry; Ryskind, Morrie; Shaw, Oscar)

HART, MOSS

See: Carlisle, Kitty; In-jokes; Kaufman, George S.; *Man Who Came to Dinner, the*; Stage appearances (post-1930)

HATS

(Marx Brothers films and shows *qv*) Hats were a significant adjunct to the team's costumes and personalities. Chico's Italian *emigré* character usually favoured a hat that came to a point, prompting a remark that his *head* was shaped that way. Harpo's top hat - which was still intact in *Cocoanuts* but grew increasingly battered thereafter - is perfect for his peculiar brand of anarchic elegance, suggesting gentility within this wild creature. Groucho sports a topper on occasion (as in *Duck Soup* and *Room Service)* but is often depicted with the explorer's pith helmet of his most famous role, in *Animal Crackers*. Usually the hat fits the profession; hence the academic mortar board in *Horse Feathers*, a sleuth's deerstalker in *Love Happy*, the North African hotel manager's fez in *A Night in Casablanca* or Harpo in a jockey's cap for *A Day at the Races*. The squashed headgear of Groucho's lawyer character in *At the Circus* suggests little more than poverty and an awkward journey, but an air of

Hats: *Groucho wearing the beret he favoured in latter years, in a 1971 publicity photo for ATV's Marty Feldman Comedy Machine*

middle-class management is implicit within his wide-brimmed derby of *A Night at the Opera* (he wore a similar hat years earlier in *On the Mezzanine*). The straw boater, still somewhat in vogue in the 1930s, enables each brother to impersonate Maurice Chevalier in *Monkey Business* itself and its promo (*qv*); another straw hat is one of two pieces of Edgar Kennedy headgear destroyed in *Duck Soup*. Groucho's numerous costume changes in the same film bring an assortment of hats ranging from a Busby to a Davy Crockett special. Groucho - again in a top hat - swaps Harpo's derby for another in the Crockett style in *Go West*. More multiple hats are worn as part of a ruse to sneak out luggage in *Room Service*. Sometime around the late 1960s, Groucho began to favour a beret in everyday life. The reason for this, it has been said, is that he could keep the beret in his pocket and thus avoid paying for a hat-check!

(See also: Costume; Kennedy, Edgar; the Wild West)

HECHT, BEN (1894-1964)

New York-born writer whose acquaintance Harpo made during the pre-Broadway tour of *I'll Say She Is!* (*qv*). Best recalled for his plays, in collaboration with Charles MacArthur, notably *The Front Page*. Hecht wrote the original story for what would become the final Marx Brothers film, *Love Happy* (*qv*).

(See also: Woollcott, Alexander)

Victor Heerman *laid down the law as director of* Animal Crackers

HEERMAN, VICTOR (1893-1977)

British-born Victor Heerman (pronounced 'Herman') directed the Marx Brothers in their film version of *Animal Crackers* (*qv*). Born of theatrical parents (Anliss Bell and Victor Heerman, Sr), Heerman spent the greater part of his life in America, starting as a child actor and progressing to Broadway shows. His first connection with cinema was with the Kinemacolor company, which developed a colour film system based on filters. Heerman worked in silent

comedies for L-KO, Sennett and others, as writer and director; later with Selznick, De Mille, First National and Paramount (*qv*). Feature credits as director include *Dangerous Maid* (1923) with Constance Talmadge, *Rupert of Hentzau* (1923) with Irving Cummings (*qv*), *The Confidence Man* (1924), *Irish Luck* (1925) and *Old Home Week* (also 1925). Among late 1920s films are *Rubber Heels* (1927) with Ed Wynn, *Ladies Must Dress* (1927) and *Love Hungry* (1928). Heerman's activities as screenwriter continued in parallel, perhaps the best-known example being his screenplay for the 1921 Jackie Coogan vehicle *My Boy*. *Animal Crackers* aside, Heerman's talkies as director are few: principally the 1930 films *Personality*, *Sea Legs* and co-directorship of the revue-format *Paramount On Parade* (see **Kay Francis**, **Helen Kane** and **Lillian Roth**). Latterly concentrated on writing rather than directing, as in the 1933 *Little Women*, which he scripted in collaboration with his wife, writer Sarah Y. Mason. Heerman's date of birth is given sometimes as 1892; place of birth reported as either London or Surrey.

(See also: Prisons)

HEIGHT

Various sources describe Groucho as having been 5' 8" tall. Harpo and Chico were both somewhat shorter, seeming closer to 5' 4". They were of indistinguishable height but had a long-standing wager as to who was taller. Chico claimed an edge of one-sixteenth of an inch and would consistently win; one day Harpo proved him wrong, but only after having himself temporarily stretched for the occasion.

HOLLYWOOD ON PARADE

See: Guest appearances

HOME AGAIN

(Marx Brothers sketch)
(Marx Brothers shows and films *qv*)
The Marxes had been playing

successfully in *Mr Green's Reception* until reviewers began to suggest the comedians themselves were rather better than their show (an opinion still current about many of their films). Around the late summer of 1914 the Marxes' uncle, Al Shean (*qv*), wrote and staged a new act for them. Prior vaudeville endeavours would have been compiled variously from the brothers' own contributions, those of their Uncle Al and, not to put too fine a point on it, stolen from other acts (which were not copyrighted), something fairly widespread in the world of vaudeville at that time. Shean had recently split as half of 'Gallagher and Shean' and doubtless welcomed the alternative activity. *Home Again* has a place in history as the occasion when Harpo became a professional mute. Legend, as with most Marx anecdotes, varies in the telling but it is understood that Shean gave Harpo somewhere between one and three lines in his new opus. When Harpo protested, Shean removed what little there was, advising his nephew to try visual comedy. Harpo later claimed to have introduced the taxi horn - stolen from an actual cab - when first adjusting to this non-speaking role. Some of Shean's dialogue may have been best avoided, at least outside of New York. Harpo related a specimen of local humour that perplexed audiences by the time they had reached the Midwest: 'This must be the Far Rockaway boat,' said Groucho. 'How do you know?' came the query. 'I can smell the herring' was the response. After a probable adaptation to the outside world, the act played effectively on tour (débuting at Chicago's Windsor Theatre, on 7 September 1914), though Minnie shocked her brood by placing a somewhat rash advertisement in *Variety*: she promised that *Home Again*, with its cast of seventeen and '38 minutes of laughs', would bring at least enough business to cover the entire company's salary for the week; if not, theatre managers could ask them to work for free. This brave gesture, advertising 'the Greatest Comedy Act in Show Business, Bar None', was greeted by the Marxes with horror, but proved enough to encourage bookings into New York. *Home Again* was based on the premise of *Mr Green's Reception* (itself an outgrowth of *Fun In Hi Skule*), in which a seemingly old Groucho played party host. The guests would consist essentially of his brothers, a few male singers and a generous selection of pretty girls; one girl, Betty Karp, was married to Chico. Paul Yale, from *Fun in Hi Skule*, was in the original cast as 'policeman' and 'master of ceremonies'; the policeman role was taken by Ed Metcalfe (*qv*) following Yale's departure. The total ensemble seems to have varied anywhere between sixteen and twenty people, prompting a remark in a British paper, the *Stage*, to the effect that 'they carry too many passengers in the remainder of their company'. The Marxes had revived *Home Again* in preference to *On the Balcony* after their first week in Britain during 1922. The *Stage* described *Home Again* as 'without plot', but its basic situation is outlined in the *Era* of 28 June 1922: 'The first scene depicts the docks and piers of the Cunard Line, where the whole party land and have some quiet fun with an American policeman. The second scene, which is supposed to transpire two weeks later [three weeks in other accounts], takes place in Henry Hammer's villa on the Hudson. Hammer, as before, is amusingly interpreted by Julius Marx. Two of the brothers are accomplished musicians, and get enthusiastic receptions for their brilliant work on the piano and the harp.' For this appearance, Groucho retained the character name 'Hammer' from *On the Balcony* (see **Names**). It is sometimes claimed that in *Home Again* he was still the 'Mr Green' of their earlier sketch, but Sime Silverman of *Variety* cites the name 'Schneider' in his review of the show at New York's Palace,

Home Again at its prestigious Palace booking in February 1915 …
By courtesy of Robert G. Dickson

… and still on the road, in San Francisco, for two weeks opening on 27 January 1918. Groucho played golf with Frank Crumit during this visit, scoring a hole in one
By courtesy of Robert G. Dickson

where the Marxes opened on 22 February 1915. His German persona was dropped after the *Lusitania* was sunk; a subsequent billing amends the family name to a more innocuous 'Jones'. (A review of *Home Again's* British revival claims that Groucho repeated his 'Mr Hammer' role from *On the Mezzanine*, but this may have been an error.) In passing, it should be noted that the Palace booking was the pinnacle of success in vaudeville terms; topping the bill was an opera star, Emma Calve, who failed to appear. According to historian Robert G.

Dickson, she developed laryngitis and was forced to postpone for a week (she was replaced by May Irwin and Josie Collins). America's entry into the Great War was still in the future when a twelve-year-old S.J. Perelman (*qv*) saw *Home Again* at Keith's Theater in Providence, Rhode Island, during the week of 15-20 January 1917. Perelman's account, in his essay *I'll Always Call You Schnorrer, My African Explorer*, was not written until 1952 (and slightly misdates the appearance to 1916) but is vivid and ties in reliably to contemporary descriptions. According to Perelman, New York's Cunard Docks were suggested by 'four battered satchels and a sleazy backdrop', this last representing also the gangway of the *Britannic*. Perelman describes Groucho with the swallowtail coat, spectacles and unlit cigar of his mature years, though he is known to have worn a plaid-trimmed smoking jacket in at least the second part of the show (his brothers and the other male guests wore tuxedos). Groucho was accompanied by a wife who sported a feather boa; he remembered her as a large woman, forming a prototype for Margaret Dumont (*qv*) if not quite in the same league. He was encumbered also with a dapper but notably sassy offspring, Harold, played at that time by Gummo. Harpo, a 'nondescript', and Chico (alias 'Toni Saroni') were two of his less reputable fellow-passengers. Groucho's opening monologue blended *non sequitur* with his real-life aversion to the sea: 'Next time I cross the ocean, I'll take a train … now I know that when I eat something, I won't see it again.' Gummo, though playing 'straight', heckled him with sufficient frequency for Groucho to remark 'Nowadays you don't know how much you know until your children grow up and tell you how much you don't know.' Zeppo took over the role of Groucho's son when Gummo enlisted in 1918; he had joined the act briefly during September 1915,

HOME AGAIN

A piano switch from **Home Again** *was revived in* The Big Store

"Go on
let me hear
you play
something"

making this the only sketch ever to have employed five Marx Brothers. Sime had praise for the rough-house comedy provided by Harpo and Chico, prophetically marking out the 'comedian who doesn't talk' for a future on the Broadway stage. He did, however, suggest the deletion of Harpo's 'expectoration'. Harpo set about the surreptitious theft of the female passengers' lingerie; Chico offered Groucho the hand of friendship, adding 'I'd-a like to say goombye to your wife.' 'Who wouldn't?' concurred Groucho. In January 1964, Groucho quoted this line to Eddie Cantor (*qv*), who had asked him for two lines that had generated the biggest laughs for him; he mentioned also a further *Home Again* joke, in which Gummo/Zeppo would say 'Dad, the garbage man is here,' to which Groucho's reply was 'Tell him we don't want any!'; this gag would recur in Groucho's repartee, both public and private, for the rest of his life (see **On the Mezzanine**). The opening scene, 'in two', ran for ten minutes before the backdrop was lifted to reveal the full stage, ostensibly the lawn at Groucho's villa, overlooking the Hudson River. In chronicling the next scene, Perelman echoes the *Stage* reviewer in describing the plot as 'sheerest gossamer'; an apparent theft provided Harpo with an excuse to search two of the girls. The culprit became obvious when Harpo introduced what was then a new routine, in which a detective shook his hand while silverware descended from Harpo's other sleeve. (Some sources place this gag in the opening dockside scene, with Harpo confronted by a cop; Harpo himself attributed its introduction to *On the Mezzanine*). According to Perelman, Harpo then played *The World is Waiting For the Sunrise*, Chico offered *Chopsticks* and the pair escaped aboard a papier-mâché boat, mounted on wheels. The

description here is still from Perelman's sometimes facetious text; others claim the entire cast sailed off on a genuinely impressive mock-up vessel, though Groucho's recollection, to Charlotte Chandler, matches Perelman's. Groucho also told Chandler of a gag where Harpo would tug on a rope, sending the passengers tumbling. Harpo later added some business of missing the boat, pretending to swim after it while spewing water. Those who remained onstage sang *Over the Alpine Mountains E'er So Far Away*. Curtain. The musical content evidently varied over the years. A billing for the Orpheum theatre in Oakland, California, for October 1915 (reprinted in *The Marx Brothers Scrapbook*) details *Sweet Kentucky Lady* as the finale. This song was published at the time along with *Walking Thru Lovers' Lane* (absent from the 1915 bill), the latter crediting Chico as lyricist and part-composer. Another published song from the show, *Sailin' Away On the Henry Clay*, also seems to have been introduced later on. The lyric was by Gus Kahn, whose daughter would later marry Groucho's son, Arthur (his second marriage, incidentally, was to Kahn's former daughter-in-law). Gummo had a number clearly designed to set the scene for act two, titled *Villa on the Hudson*; another song, *Don't Say Good-Bye*, was sung by an unrelated male vocalist. Some female

vocals were handled by a girl named Mary Orth. Despite the comedy content, the Marxes were convinced initially that *Home Again*'s success would rely upon music, partly the Chico-Harpo numbers but more especially the type of featured vocalist used in *Mr Green's Reception*. One of these, Chico's former partner George Lee (often referred to as 'Moe', a probable nickname), punctuated the vocals with business using his prominent chin. Lee considered himself worthy of a higher salary than the Marxes and departed, probably when *Home Again* was written; no contemporary sources indicate his presence after *Mr Green's Reception*. Chico, ever-confident, reminded his brothers precisely whose act it was; as a result, Groucho took over Lee's contribution, singing three popular songs of the period, *Get Out and Get Under*, *Won't You Be My Little Bumblebee* and *Somebody's Coming to My House*. Lee had invariably stopped the show by delivering the last item in full-blooded Al Jolson manner, which Groucho tried to emulate; Chico, who accompanied Groucho on piano, took to waltzing him around the stage after the first verse and chorus; Harpo, hitherto concealed behind the piano, leapt to the keyboard and continued playing until pushed away by Chico (who was shoved back to the instrument - or kicked in the rear - by Groucho). Chico accompanied

Groucho until the song's conclusion, with Harpo feigning unconsciousness. A similar Chico-Harpo switch at the piano may be seen today in *The Big Store*. In the version of this story related in *Groucho and Me*, Lee is given the fictional name 'Manny Linden'; less in dispute is that the success of this routine gave the Marxes true confidence in their abilities to please an audience, even without the dubious augmentation of a popular vocalist (a trend that would be reversed later in their career). This type of knockabout confirmed *Home Again*'s place as a variety bill-topper, one that would serve the Marxes well for several years. The *San Francisco Chronicle* of 28 January 1918, in reviewing that week's Orpheum attractions, claimed that *Home Again* 'caught the audience on the instant and enthusiasm never waned. Although the act is long, it never drags, and something is happening every minute. While it is funny, it is also marked by dances requiring unusual skill, has many pretty girls and pleasing music. Even the comedy playing on harp and piano is done in a manner to show the ability of the trained performer. Arthur Marks (*sic*), the "Nondescript", was all of that. The audience could not look at him without laughing, and a grimace or a motion from him was the signal for an outburst. Indeed there was no player in any number who did not seem to be appreciated to the limit of merit.' A performance at this venue was described by Peter George, one of the *Home Again* company, in an interview with a New Jersey paper, *The Courier News*, of 28 December 1974 (reprinted in the May 1980 *Freedonia Gazette* [*qv*]). George said that 'the house really went crazy. The applause was so great that they wouldn't let the boys off the stage - they were so damn good - one played piano, one the harp, and the other wisecracked while one danced'. It was during 1918 that Zeppo assumed the role of dancer after Gummo's departure; Zeppo's dancing partner, Ruth Johnson, became Groucho's first

wife. After the interruptions imposed by war conditions and the disastrous *Street Cinderella* (*qv*), *Home Again* became first *Back Home* then *N' Everything*. The latter was a *Home Again* variant, again by Al Shean, described by Allen Eyles as 'the ludicrous attempts of a *nouveau riche* family to break into society'. Once more the *San Francisco Chronicle* provides comment, in a review by Marjorie C. Driscoll published on 29 March 1920. The title '*N Everything* was considered apt description, the whole being evaluated in 'There has not been anything like it before, and there probably will not be anything like it again, at least until the Marx four are around once more'. Harpo was praised for his mime, harp solos 'both serious and comic' and 'comedy falls that would make a slapstick picture-producer pale with envy'. 'He is quite the funniest comedian that has stirred the mirth [of] Orpheum audiences for some time', added the report. Of the others, Groucho was 'a clever eccentric dancer, comedian, and general utility man. Herbert Marx is a dapper society dancer, and Leonard Marx is a piano-teasing character comedian with gifted fingers. Mary Orth, Ruth Tyrrell, Clarence Sterling and Bertine Carpenter form an accompaniment for the Marx antics.' A closing remark provides early explanation of the international acceptance that greeted the Marxes' first films, while simultaneously differentiating them from much of vaudeville's standard output: 'The act has a finish and care for detail that suggests some of the French clown acts'. *Home Again* reverted to its original title and format for the London revival. Its scale influenced each of their subsequent vaudeville sketches, which from this point began increasingly to resemble the musical-comedy

format of the team's peak years on Broadway and in films.

(See also: Berlin, Irving; Characters; Children; Fighting; In-jokes; Marriages; Marx, Minnie; Names; *Night in Casablanca, A*; Songs; Vaudeville; Wartime; Wigs)

HOME MOVIES

(Marx Brothers films *qv*)
Most film stars have left 'peripheral' footage in the form of newsreels (*qv*) and other extracurricular items. An often neglected area is that of home movies, showing them in private life or in off-duty moments between takes. Quite a few exist of the Marxes, perhaps the earliest being one of Chico and family at the beach. Another shows Groucho outside his home in California during the early 1930s, with Ruth, his first wife, and their two children, Arthur and Miriam. Groucho imitates a child-like way of tripping down the front path before he and the youngsters wave to Ruth at the doorway. He meets his children and they wave to Ruth.

Home movies: *UK package versions of* A Night in Casablanca *were probably the first Marx items in 8 mm release. Note the pre-decimal price, a week's wages for some people in the late 1960s. This was enough to buy only a two-reel extract*

The family are also in a home movie made by a lake, which has a pleasant shot of Miriam, Arthur, Ruth and Groucho lined up. These are very much in the style of conventional home movies (though perhaps better photographed), as are much later colour items of Groucho and Harpo at poolside, the latter doing his smoke-bubble routine (see **Smoking**). Extant in private hands is a 16 mm Kodachrome colour reel taken of Groucho in the 'Hollywood Victory Caravan' during the Second World War. Although the reel is silent, Groucho is very obviously singing *Doctor Hackenbush*. Yet another colour reel dates from a trip Groucho took with Irving Brecher (*qv*). Harpo was filmed alongside a painting of himself as Gainsborough's 'Blue Boy' (see **Paintings**) but perhaps the most interesting privately-shot Harpo footage shows him as a guest at William Randolph Hearst's castle, San Simeon. He is shown sitting within a line of female guests, one of whom has her skirt hitched up by Harpo. The smaller gauges have done more than preserve these privately-shot items; they have also supplied editions of the Marxes' professional films to the home market. For years, only *A Night in Casablanca* and *Love Happy* were available for purchase; British feature and extract versions were widely circulated on 8 mm, and it is known that a French company had at least one clip from *Love Happy* in release. A full-length *Room Service* later joined the 8 mm lists and a single-reel version was issued for 16 mm sale in the UK. Some of the team's work for Paramount (*qv*) made its way to 8 mm and 16 mm purchase when Castle Films (a branch of Universal) released a trio of single-reel Marx titles. One, retitled *Pigskin Capers*, was drawn from the finale of *Horse Feathers*; another, *This is War?*, derived from *Duck Soup*; while the remaining item consisted of an abridged *Incredible Jewel Robbery* (*qv*). There followed two extracts from *Monkey Business*, one retaining the

original title with its companion redubbed *The Stowaways*. Castle was eventually superseded by Universal 8/16 mm, who paired the *Monkey Business* extracts into a two-reel edition, at the same time replacing the *Horse Feathers/Duck Soup* issues with two-reel 'highlights' versions. There are also reports of a full-length Super-8 edition of *Duck Soup*. It is apparent that at least some of Castle's one-reel editions survived under the Universal 8 banner. M-G-M (*qv*) remained out of the 8 mm market for many years but finally relented with a pair of two-reel extracts from *A Night at the Opera*. Other Super-8 Marx Brothers releases include the *Monkey Business* promo (*qv*), several trailers (*qv*), TV commercials, the *All-Star Bond Rally* (*qv*) and the *Go West Young Man* segment from Groucho's solo film *Copacabana* (also *qv*). In 1981 the team's long-lost TV pilot, *Deputy Seraph* (*qv*), was released on Super-8 and 16 mm. Today the market for such editions has been largely overtaken by video releases (*qv*).

(See also: Advertising; Children; Documentaries; Marriages; Prisons)

HORSE FEATHERS

(Marx Brothers film)
Released by Paramount, 19 August 1932 (premièred in New York 10 August). Copyrighted 18 August 1932 (LP 3209).
6,367 ft (68 minutes) (available copies are somewhat abridged; see below).
Produced by Herman Mankiewicz

(uncredited). Directed by Norman Z. McLeod. Camera: Ray June. Screenplay by Bert Kalmar, Harry Ruby, S.J. Perelman and Will B. Johnstone. Additional material (uncredited) by Arthur Sheekman. Sound: Eugene Merritt. Songs *I'm Against It, I Always Get My Man* and *Ev'ryone Says 'I Love You'* by Bert Kalmar and Harry Ruby.

With Groucho Marx (*Professor Quincy Adams Wagstaff*), Harpo Marx (*Pinky*), Chico Marx (*Baravelli*), Zeppo Marx (*Frank Wagstaff*), Thelma Todd (*Connie Bailey*), David Landau (*Jennings*), Reginald Barlow (*retiring President*), James Pierce (*Mullen*), Nat Pendleton (*McCarthy*), Robert Greig (*Professor*), Edward J. LeSaint (*Professor*), Edgar Dearing (*bartender*), Vince Barnett (*customer*), Florine McKinney (*Peggy*), Ben Taggart (*policeman*).

Huxley College inaugurates its new President, Professor Quincy Adams Wagstaff. He takes the podium as soon as he has finished shaving. Professor Wagstaff has come to the college to get his son, Frank, out of it. Frank is the type for whom studies take a definite second best to girls. Frank greets his father from behind the girl perched on his lap. Wagstaff Sr conveys his philosophies in song, a medley proclaiming *I'm Against It* and *I Always Get My Man*. His bearded colleagues join in the whoop-de-doo. After the ceremony, Frank congratulates his father but is rebuked for spending too much time with 'College Widow' Connie Bailey.
Frank explains that what Huxley needs is a good football team, and good players. He recommends two such players, who may be found at a local speakeasy. The footballers, Mullen and McCarthy, are paid to join Darwin, Huxley's rival college, by the disreputable-looking Jennings. They will be Darwin's secret weapon in the forthcoming Thanksgiving Day game. Elsewhere in the speakeasy is Baravelli

A contemporary collage from **Horse Feathers** *commemorates talents from both sides of the camera*

the iceman, supplying orders for different types of booze from one huge bottle. He is put on the door with orders to demand the password 'swordfish'. Wagstaff arrives and is given a clue: it's the name of a fish. Wagstaff suggests 'Mary', on the grounds that she drinks like one. Baravelli gives away the password and allows Wagstaff inside. Baravelli steps outside, but Wagstaff won't let him return, having changed the password. Since he can't remember the new password, he joins Baravelli outside. They knock for admission and gain entry along with Pinky, the dogcatcher, who presents a fish with a sword through it. Pinky nonchalantly wins a pile of cash from a fruit machine, orders a 'Scotch' by means of a Caledonian jig and pours the whole bottle through a dummy glass into a bottle of his own. Wagstaff tells Baravelli that he's looking for the two football players that always hang around in the bar; Baravelli explains

that he and Pinky always hang around there, and the pair are duly invited to join Huxley's team. Pinky obtains more money from a streetcar conductor's belt and, denied use of the fruit machine, wins the jackpot on a payphone. Wagstaff settles his tab by asking to cash a cheque for $15.22; he accepts the change and promises to send such a cheque if he ever receives one. Frank visits Connie Bailey, telling her that his father wants him to give her up. He sings *Ev'ryone Says 'I Love You'*. Out on the street, Pinky is whistling the same tune as he feeds flowers to his horse. His wagon is blocking traffic but a cop makes no impression when issuing a ticket or showing his badge (Pinky has plenty of his own). Pinky chases a dog, with the cop in pursuit; the cop finishes up caged in Pinky's dog wagon, which bears the sign POLICE DOG FOR SALE. Wagstaff discusses policy with a brace of yes-man professors, who mention Frank's involvement with

Connie. He calls her to arrange a visit. Baravelli and Pinky arrive, bearing ice which they place in the safe. Pinky warms his hands by throwing books on the fire. Wagstaff persuades them to forsake their task for a place at Huxley - and the football team. They sign the form but require a seal; Pinky fetches one of the fish-eating variety. In class, a professor is teaching anatomy. Wagstaff queries his methods but the professor is sure his students will bear him out. Baravelli and Pinky do so, literally. Wagstaff takes up the lecture as Pinky and Baravelli return, Pinky atop Baravelli's shoulders, wearing the displaced lecturer's cap, gown *and* beard. Pinky replaces the anatomy chart, first with a picture of a horse then an Edwardian-style pin-up stolen from the speakeasy. Pinky owns up and Wagstaff decides to keep a pretty girl after school ('there's no fun in keeping *him* after school!'). The lecture ends in a pea-shooter battle. Connie Bailey receives a call from Frank, who is about to visit. Jennings is with her. He has a sizeable bet on Darwin and instructs Connie to obtain Huxley's football signals from Frank. He takes his coat and leaves, unaware that Pinky is in the coat-rack. Frank arrives and goes to fix them a drink. Wagstaff is the next visitor, putting up an umbrella and removing his rubber overshoes. He tells Connie to give up his son, before making a pass at her himself. He exits when there is a knock at the door. Pinky enters, carrying ice. Connie does not need ice and it is dumped out of the window. Wagstaff returns and is on Connie's lap when Frank brings in the drinks. Son is disposed of by outraged father. Another knock on the door, and Wagstaff disappears while Baravelli delivers more ice (again disposed of via the window). Baravelli tries his luck with Connie and is little dissuaded when Wagstaff joins them on the sofa. Pinky brings in more ice, but has

Horse Feathers: *Wagstaff has changed the speakeasy's password; now doorman Baravelli can't get in*
BFI Stills, Posters and Designs

learned to pitch it straight through the window. Jennings walks in, demanding to know who the visitors are: Wagstaff claims to be the plumber; Baravelli, it seems, is giving Connie singing lessons. They repair to the piano, where Baravelli delivers another version of *Ev'ryone Says 'I Love You'*. There follows a piano solo. Wagstaff and Baravelli depart, amid Jennings' threats. Football practice comes around and Wagstaff finally discovers he has engaged the wrong players. Wagstaff instead engages Baravelli to kidnap Darwin's two stars; Jennings approaches Baravelli with a proposition, but is turned down because Baravelli will be too busy kidnapping Darwin's players. Jennings tells him where they may be found and gives him $500 for Huxley's signals. He is given Darwin's signals instead ('they cost me $200 ... I gotta make a little profit'). Pinky is beneath Connie's window, where he serenades her on the harp (once more, *Ev'ryone Says 'I Love You'*). Jennings instructs Connie to obtain the football signals from Wagstaff. She and Wagstaff spend a quiet trip on the lake, Connie paddling the boat as Wagstaff sings (wait for it) *Ev'ryone Sings 'I Love You'* to his own guitar accompaniment. She is after the football signals and topples overboard in the struggle. She calls for a 'life-saver' and is thrown a circular sweet of that name. Baravelli and Pinky arrive at the home of their intended kidnap victims, Mullen and McCarthy; they are comparative giants and the erstwhile kidnappers become captives themselves, stripped to their underwear. The football players set off for the game but Baravelli and Pinky escape by sawing through the floor. They land amid a gathering of ladies, from whom they borrow a few flimsy garments. Baravelli commandeers a bicycle but Pinky travels in style,

driving a horse-drawn garbage wagon in the manner of a chariot. They reach the game and don uniforms. Wagstaff is busy coaching the wrong team as Baravelli hitches a ride on a stretcher. The game progresses strangely, the more so after Wagstaff replaces an injured player. Pinky has the ball on elastic but his moment of triumph comes when taking to his makeshift chariot, travelling the length of the field and dumping a seemingly endless supply of footballs on the line. Huxley wins. Fade out, fade up on a wedding. Connie says 'I do'; Wagstaff, Pinky and Baravelli also agree and proceed to climb all over her.

The idea of putting the Marxes into a college story was conceived even before their previous film, *Monkey Business* (qv), had been released. In the *New Yorker* of 4 July 1931, journalist Marguerite Tazelaar quoted Harpo to the effect that a new picture would be started the following January, entitled *The Marx Brothers at Vassar*. Although obviously a fabricated title (Vassar being America's pre-eminent girls' college), the academic setting had sufficient substance for Harpo to add, with comparative seriousness, 'anyway, it will be a college picture'. It is difficult to determine who first suggested such a setting though, as noted elsewhere, both this and the

ocean liner background of *Monkey Business* have been attributed to ideas submitted by Bert Granet. Dorothy Herrmann makes a fair case in attributing its plot to S.J. Perelman (qv), the only ex-collegiate on the writing team. Herrmann compares the story, concerning a college sacrificing education for the sake of sport, to Perelman's own student diatribes in the college magazine *Brown Jug*. 'Only a man who was forced to endure four years in a place where he didn't fit in and that refused to graduate him could have made such devastating fun of it,' she concludes. Not that *Horse Feathers* should be confused with real colleges, or at least one hopes not. American colleges have long been somewhat abstracted in the cinema, and although the films have been popular in their native land, they tend not to export

Harpo becomes a pin-up in this posed shot from **Horse Feathers**

well to Great Britain. Not surprisingly, those that are shown in the UK tend to be vehicles for star comedians, whose appeal makes up for the baffling institutions and terminology. *Horse Feathers* works in the UK solely because of the Marx Brothers, for whom the setting takes at best second place. The film was created in much the same way as *Monkey Business*. As before, Norman McLeod (*qv*) directed and Herman Mankiewicz (*qv*) was producer. Mankiewicz biographer Richard Meryman describes him bringing in a gagman called Henry Myers, who attempted to follow the producer's dictum of doing things 'sensibly' by reading out some prepared notes. As he did so, the Marxes occupied themselves by trying to spit into a cup placed on the floor, with the stakes at a dollar each. Meryman also describes Mankiewicz having to withhold the best material until late in production, owing to Groucho's habit of repeating *Horse Feathers* dialogue while at the Hillcrest club and demanding replacement lines. Main script credit goes to Bert Kalmar, Harry Ruby (*qv*), S.J. Perelman and Will B. Johnstone (*qv*); as noted elsewhere, Johnstone contributed variously but received onscreen mention on the strength of revamped material from *I'll Say She Is!* (*qv*) Kalmar and Ruby, who had provided music and lyrics for *Animal Crackers*, made their official gag-writing debut in addition to supplying the new film's songs. The uncredited Arthur Sheekman (*qv*) is believed to have added material late in scripting. Filming of *Horse Feathers* commenced in either late March or early April 1932 but was subject to a ten-week delay when Chico was slightly injured in a road accident (see **Stand-ins**). In the intervening period, director Norman McLeod visited Britain, where he told journalists of the Marxes having 'debagged' him when first arriving to make the film. When shooting resumed, Chico was barely able to participate in the football sequence

(filmed at Occidental College) and had to use a double. Chico was not alone in risking life and limb during *Horse Feathers*. Thelma Todd (*qv*), required to topple from a boat shared with Groucho, was in quite genuine difficulties and had to be rescued. Production wrapped after shooting the wedding finale, to replace an intended conclusion (extant in stills) in which the Marxes play cards as the college burns down around them. *Horse Feathers* was released in September; *Variety*, though believing the college football plot 'promises much and delivers more', suggested a tendency towards formula: Thelma Todd was considered 'a luscious eyeful and swell foil for the Marxian boudoir manhandling, which is getting to be a trademarked comedy routine'. The business of them trooping in and out of her apartment goes straight back to the Napoleon sketch from *I'll Say She Is!*, via *Cocoanuts* (*qv*) and the DuBarry scene from *Animal Crackers'* stage version. When *Horse Feathers* was released, the Marxes were featured on the cover of *Time* magazine, showing them in Harpo's garbage-wagon chariot with the caption 'Beyond the Alps lies more Alps, and the Lord Alps those that Alp themselves'. This, one of the most famous lines from the Napoleon sketch, recurs in *Horse Feathers* when it is Groucho's turn as schoolteacher. In an even further look back, this routine is often cited as representing the spirit, if not the actual dialogue, of their early vaudeville act *Fun In Hi Skule* (*qv*). An example:

Groucho: Now then, baboons. What is a corpuscle?
Chico: That's easy. First is-a Captain, then is-a Lieutenant, then is a Corpuscle.

In commenting upon increasingly formula methods, *Variety* turned its attention to the piano and harp solos. It was claimed that the Marxes themselves, aware of the interruption to the comedy, wanted to dispense with

these interludes but were dissuaded at the insistence of exhibitors. This is hardly likely, for such deletions were mooted not just when making the films but even during the Broadway shows, but Harpo and Chico would somehow manoeuvre their reinstatement. Groucho was prime mover away from these specialities, as evidenced by his much-quoted comment, to camera, on the piano solo in *Horse Feathers*: 'I've got to stay here, but there's no reason why you folks shouldn't go out into the

'I could stay here all day if you didn't get up';
Wagstaff to Connie Bailey in **Horse Feathers**

lobby until this thing blows over.' Perhaps this is why he permits himself a guitar piece in this film, something he rarely essayed professionally. In *Monkey Business* he fools around somewhat with the instrument, and in the much later *A Girl in Every Port* (*qv*) he provides accompaniment for a duet with William Bendix (*qv*), but on this occasion he serenades Thelma Todd with a Kalmar-Ruby song, *Ev'ryone Says 'I Love You'* (which ev'ryone has a crack at during this

Pinky, bold charioteer of **Horse Feathers**

movie). Mordaunt Hall of the *New York Times* had no complaints over the music or indeed anything resembling a tendency towards repetition. 'Some of the fun is even more reprehensible than the doings of these clowns in previous films,' said Hall, 'but there is no denying that their antics and their patter are helped along by originality and ready wit'. As in earlier Marx reviews, Hall devotes much of his text to the enthusiastic quoting of gags but reserves space to compliment the supporting cast. Across the Atlantic, opinion was mostly favourable but with slightly greater qualification. C.A. Lejeune, in the *Observer* of 18 September 1932, spoke first of the diverse sentiments the comedians inspire, comparing them to measles ('You either take them, or you are immune from their particular germ of infection'). Lejeune distinguished the Marxes from their contemporaries through their total uninterest in eliciting empathy: 'They coolly turn their backs on the audience and get on with their own business'. Revealingly, Lejeune expressed the belief, to some degree still current, that Britons had still fully to appreciate the Marxes' specifically American methods, in which respect they were compared to cartoonist George Herriman (of *Krazy Kat* fame) and columnist Ring Lardner.

British audiences, it was held, favoured a more personal approach and the Marxes had actually withdrawn even further into their own company when appearing on the London stage for C.B. Cochran (*qv*). Lejeune preferred Harpo's cutlery-dropping to anything in *Horse Feathers*, especially in live performance. 'We know that anything can happen in the movies,' it was added, 'even live seals. On the stage the laughter comes from the contrast between the object and its strait surroundings'. (One of the film's least plausible gags sees Harpo producing a candle that burns at both ends.) Such direct comparison of the Marxes on stage and screen is rare, but Lejeune goes on to mention their stage habit of expressing boredom with each other, rarely manifested on film but evident in Groucho's attack on the piano item. Lejeune's overall opinion was of *Horse Feathers* not being their best but possessing 'grand moments'; an intriguing final point concerned Harpo as musician, mainly that he was too good a harpist and undertook his performance with a seriousness alien to the Marxian philosophy. In similar vein, London's *Times* of 19 September 1932 evaluated *Horse Feathers* in terms of the team's characters, believing it 'quite impossible to mistake the Marx Brothers for human beings. They are half human and half wild creatures, not unlike ourselves in their desires, but

with few of the repressions which hold society together'. The review goes on to cite as examples some of the gags, with the dubious claim that 'their humour, however elusive to an earnest critic, goes straight to its mark with the average audience. Incongruity is its most obvious ingredient.' One might say that average audiences did not necessarily respond to the Marx Brothers, always a somewhat specialized taste in the UK, especially in this, perhaps the team's quirkiest vehicle. The implication here seems to be of a vastly amused audience but of a critic on whom it was partially lost. According to Herbert Thompson's editorial in *Film Weekly* of 23 September, 'Everyone seems to agree that the latest Marx Brothers' comedy, *Horse Feathers*, does not come up to the standard of *Animal Crackers* or even that of *Monkey Business*', as though the latter film had been a disappointment. Thompson went on to note how the new film had set 'pro-Marxians and anti-Marxians at one another's throats again', while himself adopting a position of detachment. He expressed dissatisfaction at the degree

Horse Feathers: *Between takes of the football game, Professor Wagstaff pauses for a choc-ice*

Harpo's pursuits have been heavily curtailed in modern prints of **Horse Feathers**. *This scene is among the casualties*
BFI Stills, Posters and Designs

dogcatcher's net, but neglects his task in favour of a nearby hound. Groucho descends with a sickening thud. It is believed that some of the cuts were made deliberately, possibly for television or for a theatrical reissue conforming to the restrictive Hays Code; there is in addition reason to suspect partial loss of the original negative, for much of the abridged section is obviously duped from a battered old print. Aside from the sudden drop in image quality, most of this scene is badly scratched and interrupted by several obtrusive splices, clipping out sections of

of vulgarity in the film, while speculating on whether a particularly 'Rabelaisian' Groucho line had been comprehended by the censor. There is some foundation for this viewpoint, at least by the standards of 1932: Groucho's meaning is clear when he says 'I think the faculty knows what it can do with its suggestions'; while in a parallel moment, when asked what he's doing with a cigar in his mouth, he replies 'Do you know another way to smoke it?' The likeliest candidate for disapproval is Groucho's remark to Thelma Todd while out boating: 'I wanted to get a flat bottom, but the girl at the boat house didn't have one.' No attention was drawn to the questionably symbolic presence of Groucho's umbrella and rubbers while visiting the College Widow, but some of Harpo's business was considered 'unnecessarily vulgar'. The gist of *Film Weekly*'s full-scale review was that it was their most shapeless vehicle to date and would delight *aficionados* but nobody else. Again there was criticism of at least one (unidentified) joke as being 'in very bad taste', though it was allowed that 'most of them just succeed in evading nastiness, though not vulgarity'. Such raised eyebrows may seem surprising to anyone familiar with *Horse Feathers* in its present version, which has undergone considerable mutilation - not to say outright censorship - since initial release. Both the *Observer* and *Film Weekly* reviews

mention a lost Harpo gag, in which he makes dogcatching easy by planting fake lamp-posts - a large one for big dogs, a smaller one for Pekes, Pomeranians and the like - before waiting nearby with a net. (It might be added that *Kinematograph Weekly*, in a mostly enthusiastic review, considered the dogcatcher scenes 'rather too blatantly vulgar'.) Another cut gag has him switching the 'dogcatcher' sign on his hat to 'kidnapper' when pursuing a girl. This might have been excised prior to release but, whatever the reason, his altered badge remains unexplained in the film.

In present copies, he is also the only Marx Brother not to get his turn on the couch with the College Widow, owing to the deletion of a scene in which he is said to perform a headstand on her lap. Similarity to the Napoleon sketch is heightened when learning that, on Groucho's return, Harpo hides behind Thelma Todd, doing both the multiple-arms routine and the gag in which Groucho's rubber overshoes are on Harpo's feet, remaining there despite Groucho's efforts. When the Marxes have to exit via the window, Harpo is ready to catch Groucho with his

dialogue. This applies to all revivals since the 1960s, including TV and home movie material. An extensive search has taken place for an unmutilated *Horse Feathers*, so far without success. An at least reasonably complete print was still circulating in the UK during the 1950s on the Classic cinema chain. It was at such a screening that British writer David Parlett took extensive notes, providing a vivid account of what has since been lost. Despite *Film Weekly*'s partial condemnation, the magazine found space to quote extensively from the film's dialogue, under the heading

'Some Bright ReMarx'. As a matter of fact, the shapeless, vulgar *Horse Feathers* is today one of the team's most-quoted works, even by those who cannot remember which film supplied the lines (it was nonetheless surprising to find reference to the 'swordfish'

Hotels: *a pose from* Room Service

routine in an episode of the 1990s *Superman* TV series). *Horse Feathers* was Paramount's most profitable release of 1932, as a result of which they were eager to rush the team's next picture into production; the chronicle of that next picture, *Duck Soup* (*qv*), explains why this did not quite happen.

(See also: *Animal Crackers* [play]; Animals; Barnett, Vince; Boats, ships; Censorship; Clubs; Deleted scenes; Doctors; Education; Fighting; Gambling; Greig, Robert; Harp, the; Home movies; Johnstone, Will B.; Paramount Pictures; Pendleton, Nat; Piano, the; Radio; Records; *Risqué* humour; Ryskind, Morrie; Sheekman, Arthur; Songs; Sport; Stage appearances [post-1930]; Taggart, Ben; Telephones; Television; Temple, Shirley; Todd, Thelma; Video releases; Weddings)

HOTELS

(Marx Brothers films and shows *qv*)
The Marx Brothers' background as much-travelled, urban types may serve to explain the importance of hotels in their life and work. The transient, informal nature of hotels offers

considerable scope for complex business between varying characters, and not only on stage; Joe Adamson records a real-life incident when Harpo, for a prank, dragged an unsuspecting woman into a hotel lobby with the cry 'Register us both!'. At the Carnegie Hall concert (*qv*) Groucho told the strange tale of Uncle Julius - after whom he had been named - finding work as an arsonist, whose task it was to burn down hotels in the Catskills. The Marxes would probably have liked to do as much for some of their awful lodgings in vaudeville (*qv*) but graduated to more prestigious venues when touring in musical comedy. Their sketch *On the Mezzanine* took place in a hotel; coincidentally, when they played the routine in London, they shared a bill with Cissie Loftus, whose dog Harpo had walked - and lost! - during a boyhood stint as hotel bellhop. The team's first fully-fledged play, *The Cocoanuts*, was set in a Florida hotel, a locale retained for the film version; their next, *Animal Crackers*, gave Margaret Dumont (*qv*) the name of 'Rittenhouse', after a hotel in Philadelphia. Of their later work, both *Room Service* and *A Night in Casablanca* are centred around hotels. Noted under **Radio** is a failed Groucho pilot of 1946, *The Beverly-Groucho Hotel*. As detailed elsewhere, Groucho was furious when in 1965 his London hotel was not equipped to receive the new BBC 2 service, which was then screening *Animal Crackers*.

(See also: Benny, Jack; Cochran, C.B.; Food; Leacock, Stephen; London Palladium, the; Names; Religion)

THE HOUSE THAT SHADOWS BUILT
See: *Monkey Business* (promo)

HOUSMAN, ARTHUR (or HOUSEMAN)
(1890-1942)
Famed comic drunk of the screen, as in the saloon sequence of *Go West* (*qv*). Housman (real name Hauseman) was a familiar face in Hal Roach comedies,

particularly those with Laurel & Hardy (*qv*). Stan Laurel recalled him as breaking tradition with most 'drunk' acts by being a genuine alcoholic, never completely sober; the on-screen intoxication was, however, Housman's comedy style and not the result of his real-life problem. He had earlier been a star of silents, in which he started with the Edison company; it is possible that his career suffered as the drinking progressed. Housman can be spotted in numerous sound films, such as the 1932 Harold Lloyd comedy *Movie Crazy* and Lubitsch's 1934 version of *The Merry Widow*.

HUMORISK
(also known as **HUMOR RISK** and **HUMORESQUE**)
Few Marx Brothers projects have attracted as much speculation as this silent, one-reel film, popularly supposed to have been made around 1920 though at least one source (Kyle Crichton's *The Marx Brothers*) places it during the stage run of *Cocoanuts* (*qv*). Part of the confusion may perhaps to be attributed to the announcement, in 1926, of a proposed silent Marx film for

Hotels: *Harpo rests at his London hotel in 1949; a 'do not disturb' sign speaks on his behalf*

First National. Groucho himself (in
The Groucho Phile) dates *Humorisk* as
either 1920 or 1921. No information
seems available save for the brothers'
own recollections, chiefly those of
Groucho in his 1931 article *Bad Days
Are Good Memories* (from the
Saturday Evening Post) and as related
to Crichton some twenty years later.
According to the earlier account, the
four Marxes each contributed $1,000 to
the project, as did Jo Swerling (*qv*),
Max Lippman and Al Posen. Swerling's
involvement suggests the earlier date to
be correct. Crichton's version credits
Posen as producer, claiming that an
associate named Nathan 'Nucky' Sachs
raised a capital of $6,000, enough to
acquire both script and use of a studio
(actually a converted warehouse) in
New York. Other scenes were taken at
Fort Lee, New Jersey, an area that had
been America's film capital until the
industry migrated West. The short-
lived production company is believed
to have adopted the name 'Caravel
Comedies' and the film itself directed
by Dick Smith. Details of the film's
action are, to say the least, sparse:
Groucho told Crichton it was an
attempt at a Chaplinesque 'humor with
pathos', allowing Groucho the chance
to become famous without his 'dopey
brothers'; he was obviously joking but
the remark goes some way towards
explaining the abandonment of their
usual stage characters. In this evident
parody of movie melodrama, Harpo
played 'Watson', the romantic lead,
whose entrance (wearing a high hat)
was made via a coal chute into a
basement. The final scene had
Groucho, a villain of the old school,
walking slowly away, his progress
impeded by a ball and chain. Hector
Arce's *Groucho* cites a supporting cast
that included a married couple named
Ralston along with a chorus line from
one of the Shubert theatres. *The
Groucho Phile* names the leading lady
as none other than Mildred Davis, who
performed the same task in Harold
Lloyd's films until marrying him in
1923. Arce provides a further clue to

the action by describing a scene taking
place in a cabaret. In 1931, Groucho
recalled the completed reel being
shown to an audience of youngsters at a
matinée in the Bronx, whose lack of
interest ensured the film's immediate
withdrawal. Crichton claims the film
was never shown publicly and quite
deliberately destroyed but for one
rogue print; he implies further that the
Marxes' friends sometimes used this
print, actual or imagined, to engage in
some jovial blackmail. Arce in turn
claims that the only print was burned
and the negative consigned to Posen's
closet. Whether a copy escaped or not,
it is unlikely to surface at this late date.
In 1970, Leonard Maltin (in *Movie
Comedy Teams*) quoted Groucho as
saying 'It was never finished and it
wasn't very good. Fortunately there are
no copies available'; later, in *The Marx
Brothers Scrapbook*, Groucho again
claims the film was unfinished, an
unlikelihood given other extant
accounts. At this point he dismisses the
subject with no apparent interest, yet
later in the text expresses some
desperation to obtain the film;
Charlotte Chandler quotes Groucho
further as offering $50,000 for a copy.

Marion Hutton *tries the sultry look for a* Love
Happy *portrait*

Humorisk was by all accounts a terrible
film but it is likely that Groucho's
shuddering recall had eventually been
tempered, either through nostalgia or a
belated archival sense.

(See also: Abandoned projects; *Too
Many Kisses*)

HUTTON, MARION (1920–86)
Known primarily as a band singer with
Glenn Miller and as sister of energetic
1940s star Betty Hutton, Marion Hutton
(born Marion Thornburg) played Bunny
Dolan, wisecracking friend to the
female lead of *Love Happy* (*qv*). Among
her few other films were Olsen &
Johnson's *Crazy House* and Abbott &
Costello's *In Society* (both 1944).
Latterly fought successfully against an
addiction both to alcohol and
prescription drugs (an unfortunate
parallel to her sister's well-publicized
difficulties) and established a
rehabilitation programme for alcoholics
in California's women's prisons.

I'LL SAY SHE IS!
(Marx Brothers play)
(Marx Brothers films and shows *qv*)
The Marxes made the all-important switch from vaudeville (*qv*) to 'legitimate' musical comedy more through necessity than anything else. The powerful Keith-Albee circuit objected to the team appearing in Britain without their permission (see **On the Mezzanine**) and relegated them to lesser venues. The Marxes rebelled, taking up instead with the Shubert brothers in a brief, calamitous tour of *The Twentieth Century Revue*. As the tour neared conclusion, Chico started to talk to Charles Dillingham, an impresario willing to give them a Broadway show. By the time the Marxes were at liberty, Dillingham's promises had undergone some amendment. He offered them a touring version of an existing show based originally around another ex-vaudeville team, Montgomery and Stone. The salary was good but not the prestige, and Minnie Marx (*qv*) advised against making such a retrograde career move. The time had come to try Broadway. That this was a desperate, make-or-break move cannot be overstated: the Marxes were blacklisted, broke and very close to abandoning show business altogether. It was Chico who first met their new show's eventual backer, a coal millionaire named James P. Beury. It is generally accepted that Chico, characteristically, made his acquaintance in a card game; just as plausible is Kyle Crichton's version, in which Chico's talent for pleasant coincidence led to a chance meeting with one Tom Johnstone in New York. They were outside the Palace Theatre and when Johnstone enquired what Chico was doing, he was told 'Nothing, and I don't even think I'm allowed to stand here.' Johnstone had recently been engaged by a producer, Pittsburgh-born Joseph M. Gaites (1873-1940), to write the music for a show built around British actress Kitty Gordon (1878-1974). Miss Gordon, who had recently married into the aristocracy, built a considerable American following both in theatre and the silent cinema (she had been among the other headliners when the Marxes presented *On the Mezzanine* at New York's Palace in 1921). The composer's brother, newspaper cartoonist Will B. Johnstone (*qv*), supplied the book for this show, called *Love For Sale*. Both this and a hastily-revamped successor, *Give Me a Thrill*, had expired quickly and the scenery (itself recycled from other failed productions) was currently residing in the Walnut Theatre, Philadelphia. It had made its way there after Gaites had met Beury, who wanted to dabble in show business. Crichton states that Beury had bought the theatre and was looking for a production to occupy it; Tom Johnstone took Chico to meet Gaites and *I'll Say She Is!* started to become reality. Groucho used to claim he could interpret each of their titles with this one exception, but later (as verified by a fragment of script) explained it as the second half of a popular expression that began 'Isn't she a beauty?' The basic idea of *Give Me a Thrill* was retained for the new show, which had a vague plot centred around 'Beauty', a bored heiress, and her promise to marry the man who could provide the greatest thrill. Muriel Hudson took the role of Beauty in the original production, but was replaced by Lotta Miles (*qv*) for the New York opening. Some sources mention a discouraging try-out in a notably rough area of Brooklyn, but historian Paul G. Wesolowski has noted the absence of any contemporary evidence of such a performance. Instead, local press references to the first authenticated presentation, in Beury's home town of Allentown, Pennsylvania, make rather a lot of such an 'auspicious' show making its début in their locality. *I'll Say She Is!* played at Allentown's Lyric theatre at the end of the week preceding their intended opening in Philadelphia. Performances were on

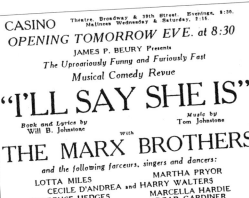

Advance publicity for the Marxes' début on Broadway
By courtesy of Robert G. Dickson

the evenings of Thursday, Friday and Saturday, with matinées on the second and third days. This was enough for them to adapt, if necessary, to a 'legit' audience and to correct any flaws, without drawing the attention of out-of-town critics. It was therefore the Marxes' caution, rather than Beury's desire to enhance his local reputation, that took the show to Allentown. The comedians knew this was their last chance in the theatre and were not prepared to take risks. The show survived and opened as planned in Philadelphia, on 4 June 1923. Business on the first night was slow but Beury was pleased and word spread quickly regarding the show's comedy; some of it was furnished unwittingly by one particularly inept chorus girl, whose inclusion was a condition of Beury's patronage. Groucho later claimed she was dividing her attentions between Beury and Harpo. She was something of an embarrassment and Groucho later wrote that she was kept out of the opening night by means of a 'Mickey Finn'. It proved impossible to exclude her on a permanent basis, and she could not be fired because the show needed more money. It was a relief to the Marxes when she made a voluntary exit from both the show and Beury's

life, accompanied by a chorus boy and dreams of a great theatrical future; Beury's subsequent assistance depended on her *not* being in the cast. The fate of the chorine's romance is unknown but her theatrical dreams were evidently thwarted; Groucho recalled seeing her shortly thereafter, when she waited upon him in a restaurant. He left a generous tip. *I'll Say She Is!* played through a hot Philadelphia summer until September, when it was taken to Boston for a week, followed by a week in Detroit, before settling into a ten-week stay in Chicago, where Harpo first met Ben Hecht (*qv*). It was during the show's next stop, a three-week tenure in Kansas City, that Groucho began his friendship with Goodman Ace (see **Letters**). From Kansas City the show played single weeks in St Louis, Cincinatti, Buffalo, Cleveland, Washington DC, Baltimore (for two weeks) and Brooklyn. The show was in its eleventh month by the time they returned to Philadelphia for a further three-week engagement, and the Marxes threatened to quit unless Gaites brought them into New York. A home was duly found in a minor Broadway theatre, the Casino, where the show was expected to last a few weeks before going back on tour. The usual account of opening night, on 19 May 1924, makes mention of Minnie attending despite a broken leg (sustained while being measured for a dress) but above all conveys the impression that New York's first-string critics would have ignored the Marxes but for the chance postponement of another show due to open that evening. Hector Arce, in his exhaustive *Groucho* biography, insists there to have been no coincidence, as both productions (the other being Mistinguette in *Innocent Eyes* at the Winter Gardens) were in

Shubert-owned theatres, and the astute proprietors saw no reason for them to clash. Whatever the reason, New York's most influential scribes *did* cover the first night and thus cemented the Marxes' Broadway reputations, in a show lasting 304 performances at the Casino. Most vociferous among the critics was Alexander Woollcott (*qv*), who thereafter formed a close friendship with Harpo. *I'll Say She Is!* has a place in legend not merely as having permanently established them in the upper echelons but also through being their only Broadway show not preserved on film. The climactic sketch, with Groucho as Napoleon, was widely quoted at the time and has been the subject of considerable reminiscence, but the rest of the show was known to posterity only through isolated gags and a few photographs. Gerald Boardman, in his book *American Musical Theatre: a Chronicle*, suggests the survival of at least some of the comedy sketches in typescript form; in turn, the rediscovered *Monkey Business* promo provides an in-performance glimpse of the first such scene (revived from *On the Mezzanine*), taking place in a theatrical agency. It started with a song-and-dance item called *Do It*, performed by the 'agent' and a group of chorus girls. The agent was played by Jack Sheehan in the original production and by Ed Metcalfe (*qv*) after transferring to New York. Zeppo was first to enter, commencing the scene's rhyming dialogue with 'My name is Sammy Brown, and I just came into town'. He would then audition for the agent with an imitation, which in New York was of dancer Joe Frisco (Philadelphia audiences were treated instead to a perhaps incestuous facsimile of Gallagher and Shean, as per the original sketch in *On the Mezzanine*). The agent, unimpressed, would have to endure a similar impression by the next hopeful, Chico; next to arrive would be Groucho, introducing himself as a 'dramatic actor' but turning out to be yet another

Napoleon and his 'advisors' compete for Josephine (Lotta Miles) in **I'll Say She Is!** *Paul G. Wesolowski Collection*

difficult to identify today, but probably would have alternated between songs and comic blackouts. Before an 'art curtain', decorated with what seems to have been a line-drawn landscape, the Social Secretary again led the male cast (plus a group of maids) in *Give Me a Thrill* before the next scene took them into 'Beauty's Reception Room'. In this scene, Beauty sang *The Thrill of Love*, assisted by two pages played by the Melvin Sisters. Scene four returned to front-of-cloth for 'descriptive' business with the heiress and her erstwhile suitors. Scene five saw the 'Thief' escorting Beauty to a 'thrill' in Chinatown, first in a street scene with the songs *When the Shadows Fall* and *Break Into Your Heart*, then to an opium den for scene six. It was here that Cecile D'Andrea and Harry Walters performed a Chinese variant on the Apache dance, in which Walters, as the 'Hop Merchant', tore most of the clothes from the 'White Girl', Miss D'Andrea. After this unsocial spectacle, the Social Secretary took over with the song *San Toy*. This was reprised as Beauty's 'dream' in scene seven, an elaborately-staged number called *The Dream Ship*. While in Chinatown, Beauty was accused of murder: scene eight was therefore a courtroom sketch with, if contemporary accounts are to be believed, Harpo as judge. Groucho was an attorney to whom the outcome seemed assured: 'You are charged with murder, and if you are convicted you will be charged with electricity.' His loyalties, however, seemed divided between prosecution and somewhat pessimistic defence. When Beauty asked why Groucho was so convinced of a guilty verdict, he replied 'I'm going to be your lawyer' (*Flywheel* in embryo!). The sketch included two classic Harpo routines, one of them when lured into a poker game by Chico; Harpo demonstrated his

would-be Frisco; finally Harpo completed the brotherhood, handing the agent a card containing his section of the rhyme (the agent would read it and go into an involuntary 'Frisco' of his own). In a spoof of the popular rhyme, Zeppo was identified as 'Doctor', Groucho as 'Lawyer', Chico as 'Poorman' and Harpo as 'Beggarman'. Other visitors to the office were the 'Chief' (Lloyd Garrett), 'Merchant' (Philip Darby) and 'Thief' (Edgar Gardiner). The agent, in perhaps a jaundiced theatrical joke, was the 'Rich Man'. These roles are again as allocated during the New York run; in the Philadelphia production, Zeppo was 'Merchant' while a double-act, Willie Baggot and Bigson Herbert,

took the respective roles of 'Thief' and 'Doctor'. Messrs Baggot and Herbert also had an acrobatic scene, titled *In a Sheik's Tent*, that seems to have departed with them prior to New York. It was in the agent's office that they began to compete for Beauty's attention; the cry would go up, 'Isn't she a beauty?', to which they would chorus 'I'll say she is!' Her 'Social Secretary' (Gertrude O'Connor in Philadelphia, Florence Hedges in NY) led them in comic business with the song *Give Me a Thrill*, an obvious survivor from the Kitty Gordon show of that title. There followed another song, *Pretty Girl*. Scene two took place front-of-cloth, as the stage set was changed. Much of this 'in one' business is eccentric method of dealing cards, licking the thumb of one hand before using the other, then dealing from the bottom of the deck (later reprised in *Animal Crackers*). Harpo also incorporated his vaudeville trademark, in which policeman Edward Metcalfe praised Harpo's honesty, shook his hand and thereby caused silverware to plummet from Harpo's other sleeve (which also resurfaced in at least the film version of *Animal Crackers* and in live shows *ad infinitum*). The defendant was acquitted. Another 'art curtain' interlude (scene nine) preceded the song *Rainy Day* (scene ten). Scene eleven brought back the curtain as another song, *Wall Street Blues*, set the mood for scene twelve, a futuristic Wall Street set designed in austere monochrome. Centre stage was a giant tickertape machine, with players costumed as abstract 'bull' and 'bear' figures at opposite ends of the stage. The tableau itself, entitled *The Tragedy of Gambling*, was the first to use the entire stage area; populating it were players costumed as 'The Gambler', 'the Fairy', 'Cards', 'Penny', 'Dice', 'Dime', 'Racing', 'Dollar', 'Roulette', 'Gold Coin' (represented as a discus player in gold) and 'The Greed of Gold'. Each was summoned by Mary Melvin (one-half of the Melvin Sisters) who, costumed as the fairy, appeared from within the tickertape machine. This type of scene had clearly become overworked in shows of the period, prompting a reference in Woollcott's review to 'the regular allotment of statues coming to life'. The next item, the 'Silver Ballet', was followed by a second D'Andrea and Walters speciality, 'The Lure of Gambling'; scene thirteen, 'Industry - the Plaything of Wall Street' took the show up to intermission. One of the show's more renowned gags had the Marxes following a D'Andrea and Walters routine with a direct parody, performing a ballet in tramp costume. Groucho recalled it as being after their dance in the Wall Street sequence, though the programme suggests it may

instead have been punctuation to the final D'Andrea and Walters number (see below). Act Two opened with the Melvin Sisters, front-of-cloth, while the second scene was a pageant depicting 'The Inception of Drapery', wherein the 'Rich Man' provided Beauty with an international wardrobe. The heiress herself wore a 'Beauty Dress' until other examples were brought from Japan, the South Seas, the 'Zulus', 'Timbuctoo', Brittany, Russia and Hindustan (Harpo later recalled a dance team who complained regularly over 'the goddam beads on the floor left over from the Hinderstan bit'). Beauty was bedecked in feathers, jewels, lace and the like but the general purpose seems to have been to display her in as many transparent costumes as possible. Following this revealing travelogue was scene three, a sketch titled *Cinderella Backwards*. This item, in a sense a capsule description of the show's plot, acquired greater relevance with the appearance of Groucho as a pipe-smoking Fairy Godmother, replete in the appropriate costume above longjohns and, in at least some performances, socks and garters. Despite occasional suggestions to the contrary, it is evident that Beauty took the role of Cinderella rather than Groucho. Next was scene four, the Hawaiian tableau, then a front-of-cloth reprise of *Only You*, a duet between Beauty and the 'Chief'. It was probably during this sequence that Harpo interpolated some business in which he pulled a rope across the rear of the stage and, at the song's conclusion, was seen also to be tugging fiercely at the rope's opposite end. The illusion was, naturally, achieved by means of a double. Scene six took Beauty to the Marble Fountain, where D'Andrea and Walters offered a version of the Pygmalion and Galatea legend, entitled 'The Awakening of Love'. Next was 'The Death of Love', in which Zeppo, Harpo and Groucho participated (suggesting this to have been the Tramp Ballet). Scene seven, more business before the 'art curtains',

separated this segment from the next, a sketch with Chico and Ed Metcalfe called 'The Hypnotist' (another probable repeat from *On the Mezzanine*). The routine culminated in Beauty's latest 'thrill', a hypnotic regression into the court of Napoleon. A pierrot dance linked this moment into the show's most famous sketch, 'Napoleon's First Waterloo', written by Groucho and Will B. Johnstone. It presented Groucho as the French emperor, taking reluctant leave of Josephine, alias the heiress. This never-filmed routine was known only through a number of scattered photos and quotes until Groucho resurrected the original script (for *The Groucho Phile*) in 1976. The script itself does not play nearly as well as contemporary reactions would indicate; much of the action is either not described or referred to only as 'business', while it is evident that some of the clumsier phrasing would have been revised in performance. A footman announces Josephine and her Emperor. Groucho contemplates whether he should depart for battle in Egypt and calls for his advisors, the gentlemen-in-waiting François (Chico), Alphonse (Zeppo) and Gaston (Harpo). Zeppo approaches Groucho, arms outstretched, but embraces Josephine instead; Chico, following on, does the same; Harpo, when his turn comes, drops all pretence and heads straight for the Empress. Groucho is advised to leave for the North Pole, Africa, Russia or indeed anywhere, leaving Josephine with the Court. Groucho's doubts concerning her fidelity have something to do with the other three smothering her with kisses. He departs for the Alps, reminding us that 'beyond the Alps lies more Alps, and the Lord 'Alps those that 'Alp themselves' (a much-quoted line that resurfaced in *Horse Feathers*). Groucho has scarcely left before Zeppo and Josephine meet, intent on romance. A knock on the door sends Zeppo into hiding; Groucho returns, via the back door, for his sword. He departs once again, but a second knock on the door means that Zeppo must go back into hiding. This time the visitor is Chico, passionate and unconcerned when reminded Josephine is an Empress ('Well, you don't Empress me very much'). Chico agrees to entertain at the piano. He has time for his customary musical item before Groucho returns to fetch another sword, having lost the first in battle. Another reason is a growing suspicion of his beloved's faithlessness: 'Jo, you're as true as a three-dollar cornet'. Chico is still in hiding when Harpo arrives for his own tryst with Josephine. He plays piano for her but must be concealed when Groucho reappears. Harpo sits on the couch with Josephine on his lap, leading into the time-honoured routine of using his arms as hers. Groucho asks for his 'rubbers', which are provided when Harpo's feet are thrust forward. Groucho is suitably unnerved ('they must have crossed you with an elephant'), but takes the footwear and returns to duty. Harpo plays the harp as accompaniment to the Empress, who sings *Glimpses of the Moon*. This leads into a harp solo, concluding just as there is a knock at the door. Groucho reappears, from behind the couch. By this time he is convinced that Josephine has not been alone. He takes some snuff and scatters it around, bringing the various lovers, sneezing, out into the open. Harpo is wearing a gas mask. The culprits are taken out to be shot, and offstage gunfire suggests the demise of Zeppo and Chico. A third shot implies Harpo to have joined them, until he reappears firing shots at the guards, who are in their underwear. Curtain. Contemporary and subsequent accounts bear testimony to Groucho's use of an ancient gag, referring to the French national anthem as the 'Mayonnaise'; this joke, absent from the script, earned conspiratorial groans even in 1923 but the comparison between Josephine and a three-dollar cornet earned due applause. Anecdotal references place one of the best lines toward the end of

the sketch (where it should rightly have been), but the script incorporates it near the beginning: again the scripted version is clumsy but in performance Josephine seems to have declared 'I am true to the French army', to which Groucho would reply 'Thank God we have no navy!' The script also details several topical gags which were presumably replaced as the run continued. One evident addition was Groucho putting on a specific brand of sock suspender before entering battle, based on the manufacturer's claim that metal would never touch the wearer. Groucho portrayed the French emperor with a misplaced *élan*, complete with a tunic fitted with epaulettes that would rise when a string was pulled. One can get a little idea of the performance (plus some of the lines) from equivalent scenes in *Cocoanuts* and, especially, *Horse Feathers*. The Marxes revived the sketch, retitled 'Napoleon's Revenge', for personal appearances in New York (October 1930) and on tour (October 1931-January 1932). An alternate title for this presentation was 'Schweinerei', defined by Groucho at the time as a Yiddish colloquialism meaning 'a lot of hooey' or, in more cogent terms, a miscellany of leftovers. The Napoleon scene would have been impossible to follow in comedic terms, so there was instead an up-tempo musical break, from 'Yerkes' Happy Six' in Philadelphia and, in New York, 'a bit of Tango Jazz' from Nat Martin's orchestra. The final scene was still another exotic tableau, 'Beauty's Russian Garden'. *I'll Say She Is!*, dissected thus, seems intermittently turgid and probably would be to a modern audience. It was, however, much in keeping with the period's revue format and it is easy to imagine the Marxes' impact within an often 'straight' context; Brooks Atkinson, in his book *Broadway*, makes an important point when reminding us how 'explosive' the Marxes were 'inside the boxlike structure of Broadway stages' as opposed to within the

limitless vistas of film. Examination of *Cocoanuts'* film version gives some idea of what was expected, as do other contemporary filmings of Broadway musicals (notably Eddie Cantor's *Whoopee*). It has been assumed that Paramount (*qv*) did not film *I'll Say She Is!* owing to the absence of a plot; this seems odd considering the large number of revue-format films produced in this period, including the studio's own *Paramount on Parade*. Whatever the reason, posterity has been denied an important part of Marx Brothers history.

(See also: Agents; Cantor, Eddie; Cars; Chaplin, Charlie; *Home Again*; London Palladium, the; Names; Russia; Shean, Al; Stage appearances [post-1930]; *Too Many Kisses*)

IMPERSONATORS

One of the inevitable by-products of fame, impersonators have frequently turned their talents to replicating the Marx Brothers' characters. They can turn up in unexpected places, as in a 'history-of-the-movies' pageant within the 1964 Cliff Richard film *Wonderful Life*. Peter Sellers was fond of impersonating Groucho, as in a now elusive 1951 short called *Let's Go Crazy* or as punctuation to his gypsy violinist act on TV's *The Muppet Show*. An episode of the *M.A.S.H.* TV series, 'Yankee Doodle Doctor', has Hawkeye (Alan Alda) and Trapper (Wayne Rogers) appearing in an army training film masquerading as Groucho and Harpo. The series was developed for TV by Larry Gelbart, who wrote Groucho's material for his appearance on the *Marty Feldman Comedy Machine*. There are in particular innumerable Groucho lookalikes, professional and amateur, many of them appalling but fortunately counterbalanced by a reasonable percentage of creditable facsimiles. Groucho occasionally met some of them, as when visiting Ron Moody backstage at a 1954 production called *Intimacy at 8.30* at London's Criterion

Impersonators: *Groucho saw Ron Moody's impersonation of him in the 1954 revue* Intimacy at 8.30 *at London's Criterion theatre*

Theatre. (Moody, who appeared with Chico in a 1959 radio show called *London Lights*, has performed as Groucho in several shows.) When Groucho stepped out to do the Carnegie Hall Concert (*qv*), he faced an audience wearing Groucho masks. The trend began during the team's heyday; child star Mitzi Green visited Chico in order to perfect an impression; she didn't quite make it, but photos of her as Groucho and Harpo were published in *Film Weekly* of 5 December 1931. A 1939 film directed by Edward Buzzell (*qv*), *Honolulu*, incorporates a musical

number in which Gracie Allen is surrounded by a quartet of Marx lookalikes portrayed by a vocal group, the King's Men (being 1939, it meant two Grouchos and no Zeppo). From still earlier, Harpo's autobiography reproduces a photograph taken at a New York costume party of the 1920s in which Groucho, Harpo, Chico and Zeppo are impersonated by, respectively, George Gershwin, Justine Johnson, Jules Glaenzer and Richard Rodgers. It was such a party, at Groucho's home in 1947, that saw all the guests masquerading as Groucho. Harpo was among the Groucho lookalikes, though Groucho himself was dressed as Harpo. This gathering later inspired a parallel scene in the 1973 film *The Way We Were*; Groucho was present at the shooting, at the

invitation of its star, Barbra Streisand (who wore a Harpo costume). As noted elsewhere, a surprising number of Harpo lookalikes have been women, as detailed under **Lucille Ball**, **Female impersonation** and **Television**. One of the most effective, Sheila Steafel, appeared in the London cast of *A Day in Hollywood, A Night in the Ukraine* (*qv*), a pastiche Marx show whose history is detailed fully in a separate entry, as is that of *Minnie's Boys*. John Bay, *Hollywood/Ukraine*'s first Groucho, had a dry run in the character through a 1970s TV series devoted to impressionists called *Who Do You Do?* Dick Vosburgh, who wrote material for this programme (ditto the book for *Hollywood/Ukraine*) recalls Bay having been nervous of using his name in such a series, preferring to lift a Groucho identity with the billing 'Jack Driftwood'. John Bay, who died tragically young in 1982, toured in a one-man Groucho show, *An Elephant in My Pajamas*. Another Vosburgh sketch, for the mid-1960s satire show *BBC-3* (shown on BBC 2), was based on Groucho's then-recent donation of his papers to the Library of Congress. Groucho was played by Leonard Rossiter; Chico by Bill Oddie; while Eleanor Bron portrayed Margaret Dumont (*qv*). Rossiter's performance was not forgotten, for in 1977 he repeated it during an ITV tribute to songwriter E.Y. 'Yip' Harburg, singing *Lydia, the Tattooed Lady*. Bill Oddie played Chico again in a brief section of *The Goodies and the Beanstalk* (BBC-TV 1974) with Graeme Garden as Groucho and Tim Brooke-Taylor as Harpo. Late 1979 saw British writer/comedian Barry Cryer, who had presented a Groucho radio profile three years earlier, in two Groucho-style ads for Henri Winterman cigars. Paddie O'Neil (of *Hollywood/Ukraine*) played the Dumont character. Alec Baron's stage show, *Groucho in Toto*, was shown on Britain's Channel Four in December 1982. Specific revivals of Marx Brothers plays require reasonably

Impersonators: *Monty Python's Terry Jones stood in as Harpo for one night during the London run of* Hollywood/Ukraine. *Just as the Marxes influenced the Goons, so the Goons influenced Python. A clear lineage*
Photo: Beryl Vosburgh

convincing lookalikes: *The Cocoanuts* and *Animal Crackers* (both *qv*) have been successfully re-staged using impersonators, similarly the Groucho-Chico radio show *Flywheel, Shyster and Flywheel* (*qv*). Frank Lazarus, from *Hollywood/Ukraine*, played Chico in the BBC's version of *Flywheel*; taking the Groucho role was Michael Roberts, who appeared in two Edinburgh Festival revivals of the same musical. Roberts and Lazarus played the parts again in a comedy for BBC Radio 3, *A Night at the Wasteland*, based on the idea of the Marxes engaging T.S. Eliot (*qv*) to write them a script. The play was broadcast on 26 July 1992. More recently Roberts has demonstrated his impeccable Groucho through a one-off radio programme (in which Roberts supplied *all* the voices)

and in a new series of *Who Do You Do?* Perhaps tying with Roberts as Best Posthumous Groucho is Frank Ferrante, an American comedian who devised a one-man show while still at college. Groucho's son, Arthur, saw his act and the result was the very successful *Groucho - a Life in Revue* (*qv*). Ferrante has since provided a voice for BBC Radio's adaptation of *The Groucho Letters* and *Groucho Was My Father*, the latter based on correspondence between Groucho and his daughter, Miriam. Ferrante also took over John Bay's show. Space does not permit a complete listing of Marx impersonators in the USA, but special mention should go to Les Marderosian (later Marsden) and his Harpo tableau, *Love Me and the World is Mine*, Ron MacCloskey's *Groucho: a Comic in Three Acts* and Lewis J. Stadlen's *Groucho!* Of course, nobody impersonated the Marxes better than each other, as when Chico and Harpo switched roles for fun and, especially, the three Grouchos of *Duck Soup* (*qv*).

(See also: *Animal Crackers* [play]; Animation; Belasco, Leon; Books; Burns, George and Allen, Gracie; Children; *The Incredible Jewel Robbery*; Letters; Names; *A Night at the Opera*; Rumann, Siegfried; Songs; Television)

THE INCREDIBLE JEWEL ROBBERY

The final public appearance of Groucho, Chico and Harpo was in *The Incredible Jewel Robbery*, an episode of CBS TV's *G.E. Theater*. The titular robbery is committed by Harpo and Chico, who (using other stolen goods) camouflage their car as a police vehicle. When delivering the *coup de grâce*, Harpo is wearing a Groucho disguise and is ultimately 'arrested' by accomplice Chico, who is dressed in police uniform. Eventually they are apprehended and put into a police identity parade. The real Groucho turns up and is identified as the robber. Harpo hands Groucho his leg and, as the Groucho 'duck' from *You Bet Your Life* (*qv*) descends, Groucho says 'We don't speak until we see our lawyer!' This is the only line of dialogue in a show otherwise presented in mime. Groucho's appearance would have been a genuine surprise to contemporary viewers, for his contract with NBC required him to be unbilled. An abridged version of the half-hour show, which aired on 8 March 1959, was issued to the 8 mm and 16 mm market in the early 1970s.

(See also: Home movies; Television)

IN-JOKES

(Marx Brothers films and shows *qv*) Humorous inside references are rare within the Marx canon, though George S. Kaufman (*qv*) incorporated a number of sly comments on prominent people in the stage text of *Cocoanuts*. Kaufman and his frequent collaborator, Moss Hart, are combined into 'Moss Kaufman' on a mailbox pulled from Harpo's coat in *Love Happy*. Detecting specific Marx family jokes proves difficult, though Allen Eyles cites the moment in *The Big Store* when Chico, with a camera, says 'Look at me and laugh,' to which Groucho replies 'I've been doing that for years.' Another example concerns the opera singer, identified by some sources (though not all) as 'Madame Frenchie', on board ship in *Monkey Business*. Soon after, in an extra role, may be seen Sam 'Frenchie' Marx (*qv*), in his only screen appearance. At the beginning of the film it seems that *four* voices may be heard singing in the hold, possibly a sly means of getting Harpo's voice on the soundtrack. The *Monkey Business* promo (*qv*) preserves a sketch which, in an earlier version, showed the Marxes imitating Gallagher & Shean (of which their Uncle Al was one half). The highlight of *At the Circus*, Harburg and Arlen's song *Lydia, the Tattooed Lady*, mentions 'Captain Spaulding exploring the Amazon' amid the illustrated woman's myriad delights. This refers to Groucho's character in *Animal Crackers* which, incidentally, was designed to satirize one or two real-life figures of the time. When the Marxes crash an aircraft back into jail in *A Night in Casablanca*, Groucho cries 'home again', probably a wry comment on their natural habitat but nonetheless also the title of a vaudeville sketch that served them for many years. Joe Adamson's *Groucho, Harpo, Chico and Sometimes Zeppo* details a sly reference within *A Day at the Races*, wherein Groucho's medical credentials include 'Dodge Brothers, late '29'. Apparently this refers to the brothers Dodge having drunk themselves to death on the proceeds of selling out to Chrysler, who sent each Marx a new Dodge in gratitude for even this dubious plug.

(See also: Continuity errors; Could Harpo Speak?; *Home Again*; *I'll Say She Is!*; *On the Mezzanine*; Names; Prisons; Shean, Al; Songs; Vaudeville)

INSOMNIA

'He's got insomnia, he's trying to sleep it off.' Chico's explanation, from *A Night at the Opera* (*qv*), of a slumbering Harpo in Groucho's steamer trunk. Naturally the ever-serene Harpo was never troubled by sleeplessness, and would react to troubled times by dozing off; Chico, too, no matter how much money he'd lost or how many hoodlums were consequently in pursuit, would sleep like the proverbial baby. It was, unsurprisingly, Groucho the worrier who was plagued by insomnia. He attributed the condition mostly to having been wiped out in the Market Crash of 1929. Sleeplessness was rife and several 'remedies' were recommended to him, one of them a bath scented with pine needles. His first attempt was successful to the point where he nearly drowned; daunted though he was by this near-Marat status, there is evidence that Groucho continued to use this treatment on occasion. Otherwise it would be a mask for the eyes and one or two sleeping tablets, which he would do his best to ration. Having little inclination to oversleep, it was usual for Groucho to arrive early - if not bright - on the set each morning. His brothers were notoriously tardy and therefore less than receptive when Groucho instigated fines for lateness. They retaliated by paying a surreptitious visit to Groucho's home, where they barricaded the garage, thus ensuring that *Groucho* paid up.

(See also: Practical jokes)

INSULTS

(Marx Brothers films *qv*)
Groucho's talent for consistent, sometimes aggressive speech often manifests itself in the insult. Unlike certain comedians to whom this is virtually a sole activity, with Groucho it was an extension of his character and point of view instead of a technique for its own sake. Some of Groucho's insults are aimed at worthy targets; others are purely for sport, the victim merely a convenient bystander. Margaret Dumont (*qv*) took the brunt of it all, as if erstwhile suitor Groucho was testing their relationship. One of the more renowned occasions is in *Duck Soup*, when he says 'I hear they're going to tear you down and put up an office building where you're standing.' In *Animal Crackers* Groucho tells her 'You're one of the most beautiful women I've ever seen, and that's not saying much for you.' *At the Circus* contains his imagined recollection of shared evenings: 'The night I drank champagne from your slipper ... two quarts. It would've held more, only you were wearing innersoles.' Perhaps fortunately for her morale, Miss Dumont was not the only target. Siegfried Rumann (*qv*), for example, receives a couple of choice put-downs when Dumont is examined in *A Day at the Races*:

Rumann: She looks as healthy as any woman I've ever met.
Groucho: You don't look as though you ever met a healthy woman!

Groucho (to Rumann): In case you've never done it, this is known as washing your hands.

Again in *Duck Soup*, Groucho, as Rufus T. Firefly, deliberately concocts a stream of insults in order to antagonize Ambassador Trentino. One of them:

Groucho: Maybe you can suggest something. As a matter of fact, you do suggest something. To me you suggest a baboon.

Nor are his fellow-siblings exempt. Two related specimens from *Horse Feathers*:

Groucho (to *Zeppo*): I married your mother because I wanted children. Imagine my disappointment when *you* arrived.

Groucho (to *Chico*): Baravelli, you've got the brain of a four-year-old boy, and I'll bet he was glad to get rid of it.

Chico, of course, can defend himself. In *Duck Soup* he asks Groucho a riddle: 'What is it got a big black moustache, smokes a big black cigar, and is a big pain in the neck?' More usually the Marxes attack the outside world, even those who might be worth cultivating. 'You got "it",' says Chico to a pretty manicurist in *Monkey Business*, 'and you can keep it.'

Groucho's reputation for invective was absorbed into his private life. It has been said that his marriages suffered through an inability to stop directing barbed comments towards his wives, for whom, especially in company, the joke wore thin. To the general public, insults were somewhat expected of him and consciously solicited, all the more so after *You Bet Your Life* (*qv*) had become a success. Arthur Marx has described a timid-looking man arriving at Groucho's home, asking if the comedian would insult his wife. 'You ought to be ashamed of yourself,' began Groucho's obliging response.

'With a wife like that, it should be easy to think of your own insults.' If approached in this way by a fan, Groucho's devastating put-downs might not necessarily be funny, but they would be in keeping with his image. Norman Krasna (*qv*) witnessed several of these and recalled Groucho saying that if Krasna had tried it, the remark would be considered rudeness; however, an insult from Groucho would be repeated, with pride, to the recipient's family and friends. For Groucho, the drawback was that he could no longer deliver an effective insult if he really wished to.

(See also: Children; Marriages; Wigs)

IRVING, MARGARET

Kentucky-born actress from vaudeville (*qv*), in which she toured as half of 'Irving and Moore'; New York debut with Sam Harris and Irving Berlin's *Music Box Revue*. Both she and Milton Watson (John Parker in the stage version of *Animal Crackers*) were in

the Broadway production of *The Desert Song*. Played 'Mrs Whitehead' in both stage and screen versions of *Animal Crackers* (*qv*). When engaged by Sam Harris, his advice was to 'dress yourself in tin drawers and have some fun'. Perhaps the advice was taken too literally, for at one performance the Marxes approached the footlights to announce, in a playground-style chant, that Miss Irving had a boil on her rear end. Subsequent biographical and career details for Margaret Irving are elusive but she is known to have signed at least briefly for Hal Roach in the mid-1930s. She is among the interviewees in a documentary programme, *The Marx Brothers in a Nutshell*.

(See also. Berlin, Irving; Documentaries; Harris, Sam)

IT'S ONLY MONEY
See: *Double Dynamite*

JOHNSON, NUNNALLY (1897-1977)
Georgia-born film producer and writer, originally a journalist and author. He collaborated with Arthur Sheekman and Nat Perrin (both *qv*) on the story and screenplay for *Kid Millions*, starring Eddie Cantor (*qv*). Elsewhere among the many famous films bearing his name are *The Grapes of Wrath*, *Tobacco Road*, *How to Marry a Millionaire* and *The Dirty Dozen*. Nunnally Johnson was part of Groucho's circle of literary friends from the late 1920s and remained a lifelong confidant, even during a protracted sojourn in Europe (selections from their correspondence of this period, dated between 1959 and 1963, may be found in *The Groucho Letters*). It was Johnson who proposed Groucho's special Oscar in 1974.

(See also: Awards; Books; Letters; Stage appearances [post-1930]; Writers)

JOHNSTONE, WILL B.
(Marx Brothers films and shows *qv*)
A former cartoonist for the New York *Evening World*, Will B. Johnstone is credited with the famous joke showing an impoverished taxpayer wearing a barrel. He entered the Marx Brothers' story in 1923, when his composer brother, Tom, adapted a failed show into the Marxes' revue *I'll Say She Is!* Will wrote the new show's book and lyrics, thus commencing an intermittent association which, interspersed with his cartooning, would last more than a decade. Johnstone was tipped to write a silent Marx film for First National in 1926 but this was abandoned; his next intended work for them was a radio series to be co-written with S.J. Perelman (*qv*), but their basic premise became instead *Monkey Business*. Johnstone's name appears again on *Horse Feathers*, and although he is known to have been involved throughout production (primarily devising visual gags with Harpo), a *Hollywood Reporter* item of August 1932 speaks of Johnstone having sued to obtain a credit after material was

incorporated from *I'll Say She Is!* Johnstone's final contribution, uncredited this time, was to the initial treatment of what would become *A Day at the Races*. Will B. Johnstone died in 1944, aged 62; Tom Johnstone died in 1970, aged 81.

(See also: Abandoned projects)

JONES, ALLAN (1907-92)
(Marx Brothers films *qv*)
Singer and actor, born in Pennsylvania of Welsh emigrants; father of present-day singer Jack Jones. Allan Jones began his professional career in radio, performing operettas while still studying music. M-G-M (*qv*) first approached him for a role opposite Jeannette MacDonald in *Naughty Marietta*, but a delay in extricating himself from a theatrical contract with the Shuberts meant that he was replaced with Nelson Eddy. Jones' first notable appearance was with the Marx Brothers in *A Night at the Opera*; his work in this and the subsequent *A Day at the Races* earned Groucho's full approval. These were the team's first films made after the departure of Zeppo, and it might be said that Jones' interaction with the Marxes was such that he combined Zeppo's former role with that of the usually more detached romantic lead. Between the two Marx films, Jones was loaned to Universal for the 1936 version of *Show Boat*; among other films of the period are *Rose Marie* (1936), *Firefly* (1937, from which derived Jones' theme tune, *The Donkey Serenade*) and *The Great Victor Herbert* (1939). His 1940 film *One Night in the Tropics* was used to introduce Abbott & Costello. Aside from brief appearances, Jones' film career effectively finished in 1945, but he continued to appear prolifically on stage. He was a frequent visitor to Great Britain. Jones enjoyed working with the Marx Brothers and recalled being made welcome. As he told Jay Rubin of *Classic Film Collector*: 'They were delighted to have someone who could sing and act. God knows Zeppo

couldn't.' Jones became good friends with the team and met up again with Chico when both were appearing in England.

(See also: Carlisle, Kitty; Characters; Dumbrille, Douglas; Dumont, Margaret; Gambling; O'Sullivan, Maureen; Practical jokes; Records; Ring, Cyril; Songs; Stage appearances [post-1930]; Thalberg, Irving; Wood, Sam)

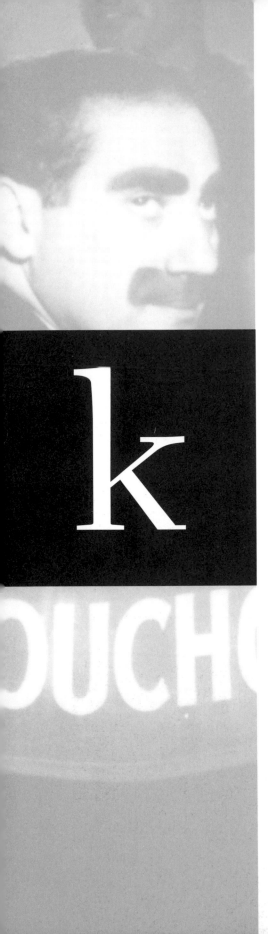

KALMAR, BERT
See: Ruby, Harry

KANE, HELEN (1908-66)
Singer and actress who, as Helen Schroader (or Schroeder), made her theatrical début with the Marx Brothers in *On the Balcony*, known originally as *On the Mezzanine* (*qv*). She travelled to Britain with the team in 1922. Kyle Crichton's Marx biography claims she was booked to appear but missed the boat, a story since disproved. Helen appeared subsequently in revue and on the Broadway stage; she acquired the surname 'Kane' on her first marriage and became identified as the 'boop-oop-a-doop' girl, as enshrined in the Kalmar and Ruby number *I Wanna Be Loved By You*. Coincidentally, this song was brought to a later generation when covered by Marilyn Monroe (*qv*), who herself received an early break with the Marxes in *Love Happy* (*qv*). Again coincidentally (or perhaps not), the Monroe vocal style was described in John Springer's book *All Talking! All Singing! All Dancing!* as 'almost a take-off on Helen Kane'. Miss Kane dubbed her own singing voice (and was around to offer advice) when Debbie Reynolds played her in the Kalmar-Ruby biopic *Three Little Words*. Helen Kane's own film career was mostly confined to a brief early-talkie heyday at Paramount's Long Island studio. Principal titles are *Nothing But the Truth* (1929), *Sweetie* (1929), *Pointed Heels* (1929), *Dangerous Nan McGrew* (1930) and *Paramount On Parade* (1930). In 1931, she and the Marxes were among those to donate their services to a stage show for Heywood Broun (see **Stage appearances [post-1930]**). Helen Kane is not to be confused with actress Marjorie 'Babe' Kane, whose early 1930s shorts for Sennett are sometimes misattributed to Helen; another occasional myth credits her with supplying the voice for the Fleischer studio's cartoon star, Betty Boop; despite a phenomenal resemblance, both physically and vocally, Miss Kane

was not only uninvolved with the series but actually made an unsuccessful attempt at legal action.

(See also: Animation; *I'll Say She Is!*; Paramount Pictures; Roth, Lillian; Ruby, Harry)

KATZ, SAM
See: Marx Bros., Inc.

KAUFMAN, GEORGE S. (1889-1961)
(Marx Brothers films and shows *qv*)
In his day America's leading playwright and one of the key talents in theatre history, George S. Kaufman's first involvement with the Marxes was in 1925's *The Cocoanuts*. Harpo had become a close friend of Kaufman's the preceding year, when introduced to New York's literary set by Alexander Woollcott (*qv*). It has been suggested that Woollcott's acerbic style was a strong influence on Kaufman's work; in turn, Kaufman has sometimes been credited with 'creating the Groucho character' in his script for *Cocoanuts*. The Woollcott-Kaufman link makes sense but Groucho's persona was evidently quite recognizable, if not fully defined, before any professional association with Kaufman. Though acquainted socially, it took producer Sam Harris (*qv*) to unite Kaufman and the Marxes professionally. Kaufman was nervous of any tampering with his work, but in the end was willing to tolerate *ad-libs* from the Marx Brothers. Not that Kaufman accepted it without protest: a much-repeated anecdote has Groucho defending his departure from the text with a conscious cliché, 'Well, they laughed at Edison, didn't they?', to which Kaufman replied 'Not at the Wednesday matinée, they didn't'. The team mutated *Cocoanuts* into something identifiably their own, and although Kaufman insisted on some reversion to the book, he was not averse to incorporating the Marxes' better interpolations. Groucho, whose respect for Kaufman was both uncommon and mutual, took some

pride in being the only actor permitted to *ad-lib* in a Kaufman work (making no mention of any similar amendents by his brothers). Kaufman's uncredited collaborator on *Cocoanuts* was a new writer named Morrie Ryskind (*qv*). For their next Marx show, *Animal Crackers*, Ryskind received full collaborative credit. The Kaufman-Ryskind partnership later earned the Pulitzer Prize for the political satire *Of Thee I Sing*; there were plans for the Marxes to star in a film version but these came to nothing (which Ryskind, at least, considered just as well). Instead, the next Kaufman-Ryskind work for the Marxes was for *A Night at the Opera*, superseding an earlier draft by Kalmar and Ruby. For this, Kaufman, whose initial experiences with the film colony had been less than satisfactory, had to be persuaded away from New York by the combined efforts of his wife, Beatrice, and Morrie Ryskind. Kaufman and producer Irving Thalberg (*qv*) proved the most compatible of colleagues, despite (or because of) an exchange recalled by George Seaton (*qv*) in *The Marx Brothers Scrapbook*, wherein Thalberg had invited Kaufman to address him by his first name. 'I'll call you Irving', responded the playwright, 'if you'll call me Mr Kaufman!'. Kaufman was involved again with the follow-up, *A Day at the Races*, but did not believe his contribution warranted screen credit. The matter of fair billing was always important to Kaufman. He worked best in tandem and, in the event of a partner having conceived the initial idea for a play, would insist on that partner receiving first credit; so while *Dinner at Eight* was by 'George S. Kaufman and Edna Ferber', *The Man Who Came to Dinner* (*qv*) was credited to Moss Hart and George S. Kaufman. Harpo joined Hart and Kaufman in a production of the play in 1941 (see **Stage appearances [post-1930]**).

(See also: Abandoned projects; Berlin, Irving; Carlisle, Kitty; Ruby, Harry; Television)

KEATON, BUSTER (1895-1966)

One of the top handful of silent-film comedians, from a background in vaudeville (*qv*). By the mid-1930s Keaton's career had plummeted into an oblivion caused by studio difficulties, marital breakdown and alcoholic problems. He eventually climbed back to professional respect and personal contentment, but was for some time able to make a living only on the industry's comparative periphery. He was re-engaged by M-G-M (*qv*) as a troubleshooting gag man, unaware that his 1928 film *The Cameraman* was still being used by the studio as a compulsory training film for its contracted comedians (including the Marxes). It was as a gag man that Keaton contributed much to Red Skelton's success. He has been reported as writer on many M-G-M comedies, though later recalled having 'failed to click' with Abbott & Costello. Much the same applied to the Marx Brothers, for whom he attempted to devise visual material for *At the Circus* (*qv*). In his memoir, *My Wonderful World of Slapstick*, he described a gag in which Harpo, selling gas-filled balloons, hands his stock to a midget while finding change for a customer. The midget rises into the air until being grabbed back by Harpo, who makes slapping gestures as if to chastise the midget for his lack of weight. Another gag involved straw being put into the baskets on the back of a camel.

Harpo could see the animal but not a keeper holding its reins. Harpo replaces some straw that has fallen from the baskets and, just as he adds another solitary straw, the keeper bends to find a match. The animal is accidentally pulled to his knees. Harpo suspects this literally to have been the straw that broke the camel's back, removes it and is pleased when the animal returns to its feet, thus proving the old saying. 'When I acted this out for the Marx Brothers,' said Keaton, 'Groucho asked with a sneer, "Do you think that's *funny?*" Harpo and Chico just stared at me in disgust.' Keaton biographer Rudi Blesh quotes Buster's reply to them as 'I'm only doing what Mr Mayer asked me to do,' to which Keaton added '*You* guys don't need help.' Here was the problem. Harpo had always been obliged to find his own visual material and knew what was right for him; the Marxes as a group were capable of selecting their own writers and to enforce such a clash of styles was unfair to all concerned. As Joe Adamson has implied, the straw routine has much more in common with Keaton's approach than with Harpo's. Keaton believed this material to be the equal of anything he had devised for his own silent comedies; this may be true, but it would not have worked in a Marx Brothers setting.

Buster Keaton *was a glum gagman on* At the Circus

Significantly, Keaton explained that he worked better with Skelton because his methods were more reminiscent of Keaton's own. There is, however, the suggestion of enmity between Keaton and Groucho: one source quotes Groucho's view of Keaton as an unfunny has-been (and, one suspects, a worrying presence, given Groucho's perpetual fear of downfall and poverty); Keaton is said in turn to have disliked Groucho because he had taught his grandchild to cheat at cards. It is difficult to believe this to have influenced Keaton's opinion during the making of At the Circus, as Groucho's first grandchild was not born until several years after the film's completion. Whatever the truth, any suggestion of prolonged ill feeling between Keaton and the Marxes is at least tempered by Maxine Marx's account of Chico's funeral, in which she describes a tearful Buster Keaton among the mourners.

(See also: Armetta, Henry; Christy, Dorothy; Guest appearances; MacBride, Donald; McLeod, Norman Z.; M-G-M's Big Parade of Comedy; Seymour, Dan; Todd, Thelma)

KENNEDY, EDGAR (1890-1948)

Burly, balding comedian famous for his 'slow burn', a graduate of vaudeville (qv), boxing, Keystone, Roach and RKO (qv) (where he had his own long-running series). It was presumably Leo McCarey (qv) who hired him for the Marx Brothers' Duck Soup (qv), in which Kennedy is drawn into an exchange of indignities with Harpo and Chico, and later finds Harpo in his bath. Coincidentally, one of Kennedy's own short comedies, from 1942, also uses the title Duck Soup. Other feature work includes the 1937 version of A Star Is Born and Harold Lloyd's 'comeback' film Mad Wednesday.

(See also: Kennedy, Tom)

KENNEDY, TOM (1885-1965)

Brother of Edgar Kennedy (qv) and, like him, a former boxer: was once America's amateur heavyweight champion. Frequent supporting roles include Monkey Business (qv) in which he is the nearsighted ship's officer who spends much of his time chasing the four stowaways.

(See also: M-G-M; Spectacles)

KIBBEE, ROLAND (1914-84)

Writer, producer and director with experience in journalism; with Joseph Fields he scripted the Marxes' 1946 film A Night in Casablanca (qv) after having provided radio material for Groucho. In the same year he co-wrote (with Harry Segall) another film for UA release with the same director, Archie L. Mayo (qv), Angel On My Shoulder. Other screenplays include Ten Tall Men (1951), The Crimson Pirate (1952), The Desert Song (1953), Vera Cruz (1953) and Now You See It, Now You Don't (1967), which he also produced. Among films as producer and/or writer are Brock's Last Case, Moll Flanders and The Midnight Man. Also many TV credits as deviser, writer or producer, such as The Virginian, It Takes a Thief, Columbo and Barney Miller.

(See also: Radio; United Artists)

THE KING AND THE CHORUS GIRL (1937)

Groucho received co-screenplay credit, with Norman Krasna (qv), for this Warner Brothers comedy, produced and directed by Mervyn Le Roy (qv). Some contemporary advertising incorporated a small picture of Groucho, announcing 'he wrote it!' Its plot, about a European king willing to sacrifice his throne for an American girl, bore strong parallels (very strong) to the recent abdication of Britain's King Edward VIII. He had been under attack before, as Prince of Wales, when his playboy image was ridiculed in a Raymond Griffith feature of 1925, He's

a Prince (a.k.a. A Regular Fellow); Cocoanuts (qv), written the same year, also makes several references to him. King and Chorus Girl were played, respectively, by French actor Fernand Gravat and American comedienne Joan Blondell; Edward Everett Horton received third billing. Warners denied any reference to the lately retired King but Picturegoer at least was unconvinced. In the issue of 3 April 1937, the editor published an open letter to 'Warner Bros., Mervyn Le Roy, Max Milder, etc.' (without specific mention of Krasna and Marx) concerning the 'King and Chorus Girl Outrage'. A raw, pro-Royalist nerve had been touched, to the extent where 'it is a painful shock in this year of grace 1937 to find a reputable film organisation indulging in such an outrage on good taste', with a star 'who in appearance, poise and manner in the film bears so striking a resemblance to the Duke of Windsor [the ex-King's new title] that it has been widely commented on by the critics'. The piece takes particular issue with the film's promotion in the United States, noting, among others, a Variety advertisement bearing the slogan 'Reign, Reign, Go Away, H.R.H. Wants to Play'. Picturegoer had done its homework: 'The glib official explanation that the picture was planned long before the recent British Constitutional crisis and was in production before King Edward VIII abdicated ... is by no means good enough for us' it stated, noting Warners' acquisition of the story as late as August 1936 and that production had commenced late in November, 'a bare week or two before the Abdication'. 'The crisis,' it added, 'was already looming large on the horizon, particularly in the United States, where the public was much better informed than we were'. The editor was, of course, quite right and it was not until the 1970s that Groucho was prepared to admit any similarity to be 'intentional'. He quoted also a review in Life calling it 'the season's silliest movie', which today may be seen as a more sensible evaluation. When Edward relinquished his throne, many of his child subjects, noting the time of year, adapted a familiar Christmas carol into 'Hark the herald angels sing, Mrs Simpson's pinched our King'. This wry humour finds its present-day equivalent in everyday jokes concerning Royal matrimonial crises of the 1990s, themselves often taken more seriously in the press than by its readers; for example, when scenes were unveiled from an American TV movie about a well-known Princess, British commentators declared less a lapse in taste than amusement over its apparent stiltedness. For all that, it seems fair to say that Britons consider their Royalty fair game for satire among themselves, but take a poor view of criticism from overseas. It would be interesting to know if Edward himself was offended (if notice he took at all), given his reported enthusiasm both for the Marxes and American comedians in general.

(See also: Baker, Kenny; Royalty; *Time For Elizabeth*)

KING, WALTER WOOLF (1896-1984)

One of many Broadway stars who, like the Marxes, found work in movies, actor and singer Walter Woolf King made his film début in *Golden Dawn* (1930). Functioned occasionally as leading man (notably in *Swiss Miss* with Laurel & Hardy [*qv*]) but was more effective as the suave villain in two Marx Brothers films: *A Night at the Opera* (*qv*) casts him as Lassparri, temperamental operatic tenor; while in *Go West* (*qv*) he is Beecher, a conniving railroad man. *A Night at the Opera* was the first Marx film minus Zeppo, who had become an agent; coincidentally, *Variety* of 29 January 1936 credited his agency with negotiating for Walter Woolf King a new 13-week radio series, sponsored by Socony-Vacuum Oil. King was at that

time starring on Broadway in *May Wine*. Other films include *Call it a Day* (1937), *Balalaika* (1939) and *Today I Hang* (1942). Early billings, as in *A Night at the Opera*, were sometimes as Walter King.

(See also: Agents; Massey, Ilona)

KINSKY, LEONID (or KINSKEY) (b. 1903)

Russian-born actor, from St Petersburg, frequently in American films with a European setting and most effective as a subversive 'agitator', as in *Duck Soup* (*qv*). Among other films: Lubitsch's *Trouble in Paradise* (1932), *The Cat and the Fiddle* (1933), *Les Misérables* (1935), *The Girl From Scotland Yard* (1937), *The Great Waltz* (1938), Astaire and Rogers' *The Story of Vernon and Irene Castle* (1939), *Down Argentine Way* (1940) with Betty Grable and Carmen Miranda (*qv*), *I Married an Angel* (1942), *Can't Help Singing* (1944), Bob Hope's *Monsieur Beaucaire* (1946), *Alimony* (1949) and Sinatra's *The Man with the Golden Arm* (1955). Prolific TV appearances from the 1950s on.

(See also: Greig, Robert; Sinatra, Frank)

KRASNA, NORMAN (1909-84)

New York-born playwright and screenwriter, originally in journalism after having studied law. Plays include *Louder, Please* (his first), *Small Miracle*, *The Man With Blond Hair*, *John Loves Mary*, *Kind Sir* (filmed in 1958 as *Indiscreet*, starring Ingrid Bergman and Cary Grant), *Who Was That Lady I Saw You With?* (of which Krasna subsequently produced a film version), *Sunday in New York*, *We Interrupt This Program* and *Lady Harry*. Another play, *Dear Ruth*, was based upon the family life of Groucho Marx: Groucho becomes Judge Harry Wilkins who, like the prototype, has a wife named Ruth and a daughter named Miriam; the Judge is at one point described as borrowing a

Groucho line. Arthur Sheekman (*qv*) adapted the play for its 1947 screen version. One of its sequels, *Dear Brat* (1951), was directed by William A. Seiter (*qv*). As screenwriter, Krasna received the Best Screenplay Oscar for *Princess O'Rourke* (1943), which he also directed. He was nominated also for *The Richest Girl in the World* (1934), *Fury* (1936) and *The Devil and Miss Jones* (1941). Among numerous further credits are *Bachelor Mother* (1939), *The Flame of New Orleans* (1941) and *White Christmas*, the 1954 revamp of Irving Berlin's *Holiday Inn*. It has been said that Norman Krasna first met Groucho while visiting the set of *A Night at the Opera* (*qv*), though he is reported as a contributor to its predecessor, *Duck Soup* (*qv*); their resultant friendship produced two collaborative works, *The King and the Chorus Girl* and *Time For Elizabeth* (both *qv*). Latterly functioned as producer and relocated to Switzerland with his wife, Erle Galbraith Jolson (widow of Al). From here he maintained a steady correspondence with Groucho (see **Letters**) and was among those who discussed the comedian in BBC-TV's *Hollywood Greats* profile. He may also be seen on film in *The Marx Brothers in a Nutshell*.

(See also: Albertson, Frank; Awards; Berlin, Irving; Children; Documentaries; Insults; Marriages; Rumann, Siegfried; Ryskind, Morrie; Television; Vera-Ellen; Women)

KULLER, SID (1910-93)

New York-born screenwriter, usually in collaboration, as on *The Goldwyn Follies* (1938), the Marxes' final M-G-M film *The Big Store* (*qv*) and *The Slaughter Trail* (1951). Also a songwriter, collaborating on material for *Paris Follies of 1956*. In 1960 he produced and scripted a sequence for *Stop! Look! Laugh!*, an anthology of Three Stooges segments.

LANDAU, DAVID

Played Jennings, the villain in *Horse Feathers* (*qv*). Other notable films include King Vidor's *Street Scene* (1931), the rather odd Marion Davies-Clark Gable film *Polly of the Circus* (1932), *Arrowsmith* (1932) with Ronald Colman and Helen Hayes, and the Paul Muni drama *I Am a Fugitive From a Chain Gang* (1932).

(See also: Gangsters)

LAUREL & HARDY

Stan Laurel (1890-1965) and Oliver Hardy (1892-1957) were contemporaries of the Marxes and in a sense rivals, though not in directly the same format. Stan Laurel did not care for the Marxes but Oliver Hardy enjoyed their work; he also knew Chico quite well from their shared enthusiasm for horse racing. Groucho shared a caravan with them when touring in 1942. He was not a fan, as he told Frank Muir in the 1972 *Omnibus* programme, admitting that, while they did not amuse him much, the same might have applied in reverse (he was in fact half right). Groucho was however polite enough to send a Laurel & Hardy society an autographed picture saying L&H were 'the greatest'. Comparable grace underscores the following peculiar story, as told by Groucho on various occasions: he was once stopped by a speed cop who, on recognizing him, chose to forget about the ticket. Before taking his leave, the policeman felt obliged to ask Groucho why there weren't more Laurel & Hardy films on TV!

(See also: Cantor, Eddie; Documentaries; Gambling; Policemen; Wartime)

LAWYERS

(Marx Brothers films *qv*)
'I didn't know you were a lawyer. You're awfully shy for a lawyer,' says Thelma Todd (*qv*) to Groucho in *Monkey Business*. 'You bet I'm shy,' comes the response, 'I'm a shyster lawyer!' Ever the frustrated academic, Groucho slips into the role of lawyer with consummate ease, making it quite appropriate for his replica in *A Day in Hollywood, a Night in the Ukraine* (*qv*) to do likewise. As early as *I'll Say She Is!* (*qv*), Groucho played a lawyer in one sketch, going on to make a first-class legal adventurer in the radio series *Flywheel, Shyster and Flywheel* (*qv*) and the 1939 film *At the Circus*. He regained the title 'Attorney at Law' for a 1947 sketch on the *Philco Radio Time*. In *Duck Soup* he pleads Chico's case with a request to send him to jail. The prosecution has great difficulty in eliminating Chico's testimony when he responds by asking for 'a nice cold glass eliminate' (see **Puns**). 'I was going to get a writ of habeas corpus,' says Groucho, 'but I should've gotten a writ of you instead.' In the Marxes' preceding film, *Horse Feathers*, Groucho muses over a proposition put by Chico. He promises to discuss it with his lawyer, and 'if he advises me to do it, I'll get a new lawyer'. Much of Captain Spaulding's letter in *Animal Crackers* is peppered with indecipherable legal jargon, conveying the impression that he knows what he's talking about, even if nobody else does. When *A Night in Casablanca* drew complaints from Warner Brothers, Groucho took on their legal department (see **Letters**). As late as 1971, Groucho portrayed a crooked lawyer as guest on British TV's *The Marty Feldman Comedy Machine*. There were occasions when the Marxes had need of *bona fide* legal advice; one such was the court case over an allegedly pirated script (see **Radio**). There were also two actions taken over *A Day at the Races*, concerning material said to have been submitted by other writers before production.

(See also: Prisons; Television)

LEACOCK, STEPHEN (1869-1944)

British-born humorist, in Canada from childhood, Stephen Leacock followed the twin careers of comic scribe and university lecturer, writing quite seriously on the subject of economics.

to establish the Warner Brothers' gangster *genre* with *Little Caesar* (1930); among other 1930s director credits are *I Am a Fugitive From a Chain Gang* (1932), *Tugboat Annie* (1933), *Gold Diggers of 1933* and *They Won't Forget* (1937), which he also produced. In the same year he was producer-director of a Groucho Marx-Norman Krasna collaboration, *The King and the Chorus Girl* (*qv*). Much later films include *Mister Roberts* (1955), on which he shared director credit with John Ford, and *Gypsy* (1962), which Le Roy both produced and directed.

(See also: Krasna, Norman)

THE LEROY TRIO
Groucho obtained his first show business job by answering an advertisement in the New York *World*. It was the summer of 1905, when 14-year-old Groucho was, understandably, quite naïve. The job offered four dollars a week plus room and board; he made his way on foot to an upstairs tenement apartment, located four miles away near Second Avenue and Twenty-eighth street. The youngster was greeted by LeRoy himself, who wore lipstick and a kimono. Auditions were to be held on the roof, where some thirty youngsters had gathered. The roof was made of tin and produced an unearthly racket when danced upon by thirty ambitious hoofers. The LeRoy Trio had signed for a 'distinguished vaudeville tour' and needed a singer and dancer to complete the threesome. Groucho, one of only three vocalists in the group, was asked if he knew any 'ragtime' but, unsure of the genre, responded by singing *The Palms* (an item learned during a recent, unlikely stint with a Protestant church choir). This is how Groucho remembered it in a 1931 magazine article, 'Bad Days Are Good Memories', but a subsequent account (from 1959's *Groucho and Me*) amends the song to the Marx family's perennial *Love Me and the World is Mine*. Whatever the repertoire, Groucho got the job. From

Groucho was devoted to his humour, which equates somewhat to his own in blending absurd fantasy with acutely-observed foible. Leacock's celebrated 'Boarding House Geometry' would have struck a chord with Groucho in its punning juxtaposition of academic loftiness with more basic concerns: 'The landlady can be reduced to her lowest terms by a series of propositions'. Another of Leacock's prime tales concerns a stage magician who, weary of an audience whisperer, invites him up for the usual audience-participation routine. After cutting his tie, smashing his watch and so on, the magician concludes the performance without attempting to restore the items. This reverses a true-life occasion when Groucho, unrecognizable in civilian garb, attended a performance by Harry Houdini. Groucho, responding to Houdini's request for a volunteer from the audience, was asked

Lawyers: *J. Cheever Loophole, legal eagle of* At the Circus

to look into the illusionist's mouth and to tell everyone what he could see. Groucho said 'Pyhorrhea' and returned to his seat.

(See also: Practical jokes)

LEONARD, BENNY
See: Fighting; *On the Mezzanine*

LE ROY, MERVYN (1900-87)
Producer of *At the Circus* (*qv*) during a tenure at M-G-M (*qv*) in which he also produced *The Wizard of Oz* (1939) and directed films including *Waterloo Bridge* (1940), *Random Harvest* (1942) and *Madame Curie* (1943). Born in San Francisco, Mervyn Le Roy's career took him to vaudeville (*qv*) then into silent films as an actor and gagman. He took up directing in 1927 and did much

the dancers, LeRoy selected a 'tough East Side kid' named Johnny Morris; the 'tour' seemed to consist only of two weeks in Colorado but Groucho rehearsed with them for an identical period before setting off for Denver. Groucho recalled the act as opening with an incongruously Chinese-attired black quartet, followed by LeRoy and his young sidekicks in drag, singing *I Wonder What's the Matter with the Mail?* This was evidently designed to be sung by a man living off immoral earnings, but LeRoy's preferred costume had been established. Next was Groucho, in altar-boy costume, with *Jerusalem, Lift Up Your Gates and Sing* (which at one performance led a misplaced zealot to cry 'Hallelujah!'); then the other lad, with a tap-dance; and finally, LeRoy's reappearance in other female guises, first singing Victor Herbert's *Kiss Me Again*, then masquerading as the Statue of Liberty, guarded by the military-clad youths. The engagement was marred when one of Johnny's shoes flew off and struck a member of the audience, for which the act was fined $20, or somewhere between a third or half the act's total salary. (Another account, circulated to newspapers during May 1932, attributes the fine to Groucho's breaking voice.) This was followed by a split week between Victor and Cripple Creek. At Victor, LeRoy and the dancer ran away together, taking with them Groucho's entire personal fortune ($8), which had been concealed under his mattress. Groucho was stranded but able to raise a little cash by selling a bellboy costume, one in which he had publicized the act while off-duty. He took a job in Cripple Creek, making deliveries from a grocer's wagon; the horses got the better of him and raced Groucho through the town, along narrow mountain paths and finally back to the main street. At journey's end, one of the horses dropped dead. Stories vary as to how he returned home; one is that he had earned enough for the ticket home, but lost his 'grouch bag' (a leather money pouch favoured by

vaudevillians) containing food money and subsisted on bananas and peanuts supplied by 'kindly old ladies' on the train; another is that Groucho thought it prudent to hide in his lodgings until Minnie could send him the fare home. Groucho's one compensation was that he could speak of his 'Denver engagement' when seeking further employment. Recalling this calamitous time in 1931, Groucho retained LeRoy's correct name, similarly identifying the third participant as 'Johnny Morris, an actor now in Hollywood'; these names appear also in the newspaper feature. By the time of Kyle Crichton's Marx Brothers biography. In 1950, caution had evidently set in, LeRoy becoming 'Le May' and Morris 'Jimmy Benton'. 'Le May' was repeated in Arthur Marx's first book four years later. *Groucho and Me*, in which the majority of names are altered, refers to 'Larong' and 'Morton', but LeRoy's correct name was revealed once more when Groucho, interviewed for *The Marx Brothers Scrapbook*, was sufficiently confident of his demise and consequent inability to object. Confirmation of this appears in *The Groucho Phile*. Johnny Morris/Morton was amended to 'Kramer' for the *Scrapbook*; again *The Groucho Phile* supersedes, stating clearly 'Johnny Morris (not Morton)'. The 1930s accounts minimize Johnny's role in Groucho's misfortunes, hence the possibility of Groucho being able to use his real name without fear of retribution. Hector Arce's subsequent *Groucho* opts for Morris, which amid the blur may be perhaps the likeliest option.

(See also: Animals; Books; Female impersonation; Marx, Minnie; Names; *Risqué* humour; Vaudeville; Wigs)

LETTERS

In *Animal Crackers* (qv), Groucho has Zeppo take down a nonsensical letter to his lawyers, 'Hungerdunger, Hungerdunger, Hungerdunger and McCormack'. The message consists mostly of gratuitous '*ipso facto*' and 'to

wit' insertions, conveying nothing whatsoever; Zeppo is eventually reduced to sending only the stamp, by air mail. Zeppo has a similar task in *Duck Soup* (qv) when, in the middle of being inaugurated as his country's leader, Groucho chooses to contact his dentist. The letter is supposed to contain a cheque, but Zeppo will be fired if he encloses it. Given these examples, it should be no surprise that literary-minded Groucho was the most prolific letter-writer among the Marxes. He was delighted when in 1964 the Library of Congress requested his correspondence for preservation. Three years later a selection was published as *The Groucho Letters* and revealed the scope of his friends: the expected recipients included Chico, Harpo, Gummo, Arthur Sheekman (qv), S.J. Perelman (qv), Norman Krasna (qv) and Nunnally Johnson (qv); among other friends were Goodman Ace, a friend since the days of *I'll Say She Is!* (qv); Ace and his wife starred in a radio show called *Easy Aces*. Of Groucho's fellow-professionals, perhaps the most distinctive correspondence is that of comedian Fred Allen, whose typescript was exclusively in lower case. The literary world was fairly represented, not least by T.S. Eliot (qv), James Thurber and E.B. White. There is even correspondence

Letters: *a bogus-looking missive to British fans*

142

with President Harry S. Truman, with whom Groucho seems to have enjoyed a surprising rapport. Less diverse, but equally well written, is the series of letters written to his daughter Miriam, collected under the title *Love, Groucho*. By contrast, Harpo could take years to answer a letter; but his self-proclaimed illiteracy is contradicted by extant samples of his letters to Alexander Woollcott (*qv*). During Hollywood's peak years, it was usual for the publicity people to fabricate letters from movie stars to the fans. One example (*illustrated*) was released for the benefit of British audiences around 1940.

(See also: Books; Caricatures; Children; Education; Politicians)

LEVANT, OSCAR
See: Fighting

LEWIS, DIANA (b. 1915)
Leading lady of *Go West* (*qv*). Among other films are Fields' *It's a Gift* (1934), *He Couldn't Say No* (1937), *Gold Diggers in Paris* (1938), *First Offenders* (1939) and her last, *Cry Havoc* (1943). Retired after marriage to actor William Powell, who appeared with Harpo in *Too Many Kisses* (*qv*).

(See also: Fields, W.C.)

THE LIFE OF RILEY
See: Bendix, William; Brecher, Irving; Radio

THE LIFE OF THE MARX BROTHERS
See: Abandoned projects

LOEW, DAVID L. (1897-1965)
Producer-director, a son of M-G-M co-founder Marcus Loew. David Loew produced *A Night in Casablanca* (*qv*), for which he and the Marxes established Loma Vista Films, a short-lived partnership of which Loew was President. David Loew's latter years were spent making TV documentaries for CBS.

(See also: M-G-M; Sidney, Louis K.)

LONDON PALLADIUM, THE
(Marx Brothers films and plays *qv*) London's premier variety theatre, dating back to 1910. Performers the world over see it as perhaps the most prestigious of venues. The immediate post-war years saw a steady parade of Hollywood stars appearing on the London stage, a policy initiated by Bernard Delfont (later Lord Delfont), then finding his way as an impresario. Laurel & Hardy (*qv*) were first to be invited, in 1947; Chico made the trip in the same year; while Danny Kaye was to make the most profound impression, making his London début in 1948. It was Val Parnell who presented Harpo and Chico at the Palladium in 1949, minus Groucho who was by then occupied with *You Bet Your Life* (*qv*).

The three completed filming of *Love Happy* by January 1949, whereupon the press reported a split. The London *Evening News* of 26 January quoted them as saying 'we can make more money if we go our own ways'. Harpo, it seems, was contemplating television work; Groucho had his game show; while on 27 January Chico set sail on the *Queen Mary* for a twelve-week tour of Britain, landing at Southampton on 1 February (see **Stage appearances [post-1930]**). At a press conference from London's Savoy Hotel, Chico

denied rumours of a split, and was quoted in the *Star* of 2 February about the team's forthcoming autobiographical film (see **Abandoned projects**). The subsequent presence of Harpo for the Palladium season made it a more convincing Marx Brothers event. Harpo, who also made the trip on the *Queen Mary*, arrived with his wife, Susan, on 26 May, accompanied by their 12-year-old son, Bill (then still 'Billy'). The London *Evening Standard* concentrated on interviewing Mrs Marx, commenting on their 13-year marriage and noting her youth compared to Harpo. Billy, who was to be taken on tours while his father was working, was photographed for the *Evening News* and *Daily Mirror*, the latter showing him matching a wild

Prior to Harpo's arrival, Chico toured Britain solo in 1949. When playing the Glasgow Empire in March, he was persuaded to attend the Scottish Industries Exhibition

expression with Harpo. The *Star* that evening noted the presence of Harpo's taxi horn plus a lariat he had brought as an additional prop. Harpo explained his method of testing gags by asking himself if they would make a child laugh; he believed children were more critical of humour than adults. It was him thus. (The wig contrasted sharply with a business suit on 14 July, when Harpo attended a function at the Commonwealth Gift Centre in London.) A series of pictures record them working out an item at the piano, either sharing the keyboard or with Chico brandishing a ruler in the manner of a conductor's baton. Their seriousness in preparation, implied in the text, becomes all the more apparent in these backstage shots. In speaking of their earlier film work, Harpo cited *A Night at the Opera* as the best, though Chico placed it second to *Animal Crackers*. Of the unreleased *Love Happy*, Dowdall claimed 'they rate it a very good film, [but] they will not boost it as their "best ever" until it has been seen'. Their four-week engagement opened on 20 June, to what are generally termed 'mixed reviews'. According to the *Sunday Express* 'Harpo and Chico Marx ... will charm you into laughter that hurts'. The *Times* spoke of the Marxes arriving, one by one, 'to captivate London', crediting Harpo and Chico with 'such an evening in the music-hall that we are reluctant to leave'. Various

In July 1949, Harpo visited the Commonwealth Gift Centre at Lowndes Square in London. With him are Brigadier C. Peto, the Member of Parliament for Bideford and Dame Joan Marsham, Head of the Personal Service League. At this time, Harpo and Chico wore their stage wigs for all public appearances

perhaps with this in mind that he expressed an interest in appearing in English pantomime, mentioned again in the *Star* on 18 June (Harpo was uncertain whether or not he would take a speaking role). The *Stage* subsequently reported their appearance at a party given by Val Parnell. On 27 May the *Graphic* published a photo strip of Harpo and Chico apparently acting out the story of 'Harpo's first harp'. There followed three weeks of rehearsal, during which the brothers were visited by journalist James Dowdall and photographer Raymond S. Kleboe, representing *Picture Post*. The article (published in the issue of 25 June) is mostly about their prior history but offers some insight into the occasion, particularly in the photo captioning. Presumably for

reasons of image, the brothers were contractually obliged to wear their stage wigs in the presence of photographers; it is unclear whether the idea was theirs or that of the promoters, but it is significant that most latter-day pictures of Harpo show

Programme—(Continued)

9. DUNCAN'S COLLIES · Canine Actors

10. VAL PARNELL presents

HARPO & CHICO MARX

OF THE SCREEN'S GREATEST COMEDY TEAM THE MARX BROS.

MATINEE on WEDNESDAY of each week at 2.40

PAUL FENOULHET and his ORCHESTRA

routines were listed: Chico's piano; Harpo's blowing of smoke bubbles and 'straightening a young lady's skirt with a pair of scissors', reminiscent of a gag in *The Big Store*; Chico sporting an Ibsen-like beard; and the piano duet. Special praise, as ever, went to Harpo's knife-dropping business, this time in the company of a British policeman. Also present was the card-cheating routine, dating back to *I'll Say She Is!* and probably earlier, incorporating (according to the *Sunday Express*) the gag from *Horse Feathers* where Harpo uses an axe to 'cut the cards'. There was, of course, customary silence for the harp solo; the *Stage* echoed earlier UK film reviewers in preferring their 'musical interludes', evaluating the piano duet as 'one of the best things in the act'. Despite the ingredients, the *Times* reviewer believed 'it is not what they do that counts, but what they are', distinguishing them from other comedians, musicians and 'fantastics' by a 'combination of fun and fantasy with something else, a mixture of worldly wisdom and naivety, of experience but also of an innocence never altogether lost, of dignity and absurdity together, so that for a moment we love and we applaud mankind'. Heady stuff, but as concise

an appreciation of the Marxes as one could wish. The *Manchester Guardian* continued in like vein, comparing their sense of 'lunatic insecurity' to 'watching the March Hare playing tricks on an indulgent Mad Hatter'. Chico's piano style was in turn defined as 'selecting each note, as it were, independently, like a naughty boy ringing other people's doorbells'. It was made plain that Harpo and Chico 'delighted an audience well disposed to admire them', but that the supporting acts, particularly the American impressionist Dave Barry, earned applause in their own right. The *Daily Telegraph*'s critic also favoured Barry plus the wire-walking skills of Harold Barnes, but, as with the *Stage*, seemed happiest with Harpo and Chico only during their musical items. Of the comic routines, it was decided the brothers were better with 'a silly story and a spacious background for their comedy', adding 'Within the limits of the footlights they are only partially amusing'. The review conceded there were 'many funny moments', but decided 'they cannot be regarded as an unqualified success'. The *Sunday Pictorial* of 26 June incorporated brief comment from a fan 'disappointed' in their 'straggly, erratic act', noting that the 'streak of madness is there, but it only shines between yawns'. A little later, on 23 July, *Picturegoer* deemed the show 'a success, but not a riotous success in the Danny Kaye fashion ... to see the remaining two without Groucho is like hearing a symphony orchestra without the first violins'. The Palladium engagement drew respectable business plus its share of backstage visitors; on 5 July, Elspeth Grant of the *Graphic* noted Harpo's kindness in receiving two young students of the harp, Audrey Webster and Aileen McArdle, permitting them to play on his own harp (worth £900) and instructing them in his own musical style. The *Sketch* magazine reported a 'special dispensation' from Val Parnell, enabling them to accept an invitation from Mrs Douglas, wife of

the US Ambassador, to appear at the Allied Circle Ball on 12 June. The item was published on 20 July, by which time Benny Goodman had moved into the Palladium and the Marxes had moved on; Chico played three more weeks before returning to the USA, first at the Hackney Empire, then on to Bristol and Manchester. Some contemporary sources imply that Harpo followed the Palladium stint with a week at the Birmingham Hippodrome, but examination of the trade press reveals an entirely different show for that week. It seems equally likely that he returned home shortly after closing in London.

(See also: Children; Cochran, Charles B.; Could Harpo Speak?; Harp, the; Marriages; Martin, Tony; Moustaches, beards; *On the Mezzanine*; Piano, the; Smoking; Television; Vaudeville; Wigs)

LOVE HAPPY

(Marx Brothers film)
Released by United Artists, 3 March 1950. UK release, by Monarch, delayed (see text).
7,694 ft (85 minutes).
Executive producer Mary Pickford. Produced by Lester Cowan. Directed by David Miller. Screenplay by Frank Tashlin and Mac Benoff, from a story by Harpo Marx and, uncredited, Ben Hecht. Camera: William C. Mellor. Later UK releases (via DUK) as *Love Happy* and, later, *Kleptomaniacs*.

With Harpo Marx (*Harpo*), Chico Marx (*Faustino the Great*), Ilona Massey (*Madame Egilichi*), Vera-Ellen (*Maggie Phillips*), Marion Hutton (*Bunny Dolan*), Raymond Burr (*Alphonse Zoto*), Melville Cooper (*Throckmorton*), Paul Valentine (*Mike Johnson*), Leon Belasco (*Mr Lyons*), Eric Blore (*Mackinaw*), Bruce Gordon (*Hannibal Zoto*), Marilyn Monroe (*Grunion's client*) and Groucho Marx (*detective Sam Grunion, narrator*).

Private eye Sam Grunion addresses the audience, telling them of the missing

After considerable delay, British distributors Monarch were able to release the team's 'newest! funniest! musical'; it was certainly their newest
Michael Pointon Collection

Romanov diamonds. Grunion has spent eleven years investigating the million-dollar theft, a trail that finishes with a group of strolling players. In voice-over, he introduces dancer Mike Johnson; Maggie Phillips, another dancer, in love with Mike; Bunny Dolan, Maggie's best friend, who has invested her last $300 in the show; and Harpo, who is out filching food for the impoverished company. Harpo operates outside a plush delicatessen, which has a sideline in stolen diamonds. Madame Egilichi steps out of a limousine; the manager, Throckmorton, points to a crate while informing her that the 'sardines' have arrived. Madame Egilichi, aware of nearby policemen, would prefer to speak in Throckmorton's office. She swishes in, haughtily. Harpo, seeing a cop, pretends to look in the store window. Beneath him is a delivery platform and he joins the crates in the delicatessen's basement. Harpo fills his coat with food as Throckmorton, unaware of Harpo's presence, searches through the sardine cans. Throckmorton finds a can marked with a Maltese cross; a cutaway view shows it contains a diamond necklace. He places it in his pocket but Harpo, puzzled at Throckmorton's interest in

sardines, switches it for another. Throckmorton reports to Madame Egilichi. Her search for the Romanov diamonds has required eight weddings in three months - eight commissars, two ambassadors and a Grand Duke - and she is aghast when the can carries no mark. Throckmorton insists it to be the correct can, but examination of the contents proves otherwise. Madame Egilichi's henchmen, the Zoto brothers, work Throckmorton over until he remembers seeing a tramp-like figure. The police are alerted and a $1,000 reward offered. Harpo exits via the pavement lift and heads for the theatre, where rehearsals continue. Faustino the Great approaches Mike Johnson for a job. Aware that Mike is hiring unknowns, Faustino claims to be most unknown for mind-reading, juggling and working as usher. Mike, uninterested, goes to see Maggie, Bunny and his erstwhile partner in the show, Mr Lyons. Max Yorkman, a backer, was expected at ten o'clock; that was ninety minutes before, and Mr Lyons wishes to reclaim his scenery and costumes. Lyons demands either Mr Yorkman or the sum of $1,100; Faustino overhears and claims personal friendship with the absent backer, who supposedly sent him over to ask for a job. Lyons is pacified, while Mike offers Faustino a part in the show, explaining there will be no money for salaries until the show opens and is a success. Harpo eludes two policemen seeking a 'fuzzy-haired shoplifter' but is rushed by the actors when bringing them food. Harpo, entranced, watches Maggie dance; Faustino, asking him for food, concludes that Harpo is in love. Harpo offers him the marked sardine can but Faustino prefers ice-cream. Harpo passes the sardine can to Maggie, who decides to save it until the following day. Bunny rehearses an energetic musical number; Harpo is drawn in and he escapes to the front of

the theatre. Harpo retreats on seeing a policeman, and is pursued back into the auditorium. He hides behind the rear stalls but is betrayed when the rows of tip-up seats start to fall forward. The police bring Madame Egilichi a series of itinerants until finally producing Harpo. She says it is not the man sought but dismisses the officers, promising to give Harpo a good meal. She uses her hypnotic charms on Harpo and has the Zoto brothers search him. His coat provides a phenomenal number of items, among them legs from a store dummy, a sled, an umbrella, a welcome mat, a mailbox, a barber's pole, a block of ice and even a live dog. The room starts to fill up and the search is abandoned. The Zoto brothers are sent to the next room as Madame Egilichi questions Harpo. His resolute silence means a return to the Zoto brothers' mercies, but Harpo seems to enjoy the rough treatment. Grunion takes up the story: Maggie has eaten all the food Harpo has brought over three days, except for the 'sardines' which would save the show. Dress rehearsals continue with the 'Sadie Thompson' number. Madame Egilichi paces angrily as Harpo is tortured. He has been made to smoke a pipe for six hours; spent four hours on a revolving rack; and is currently tied out of reach of food while water drips on his head. He has been with them for three days without uttering a word. They try a William Tell-inspired torture but Harpo grabs the apple to eat. As the only person able to locate the diamonds, Harpo must be kept alive and is thrown into a room. He finds a telephone and calls the theatre as Madame Egilichi listens in. Faustino answers, recognizing Harpo by the sound of his taxi horn. Faustino tries to read his mind and instructs Harpo to place the receiver on his head. The message he gets is that a beautiful woman wants to marry Harpo for his sardines. Seeing her as a potential source of money, Faustino suggests she visits the theatre - 'We've got-a lots of sardines here'. Madame Egilichi and the Zotos set off for the theatre. Lyons, unconvinced now of Yorkman's backing or of Harpo's wealthy bride, continues to have his property removed from the stage. Faustino, trying to appeal to him through music, plays the piano. Respite is brief and the stage is soon empty. Without scenery or costumes, Mike announces the show's closure. He refuses to stage the production without them and is rebuked by Maggie and Bunny. When Maggie contemptuously offers him the sardines to eat, the can is at last opened but thrown in the waste basket. Madame Egilichi arrives, searches in vain for the sardine can and offers Mike sufficient funds to open the show. Harpo escapes from Madame Egilichi's suite, high above the city streets. He knots sheets together, forming not a rope but instead a makeshift parachute. Bunny points out how long Mike and Madame Egilichi have been discussing their 'business deal'; Maggie would prefer not to believe the worst. A cat upsets the waste basket when nosing around the sardines. Bunny takes cat and sardine can outside. Mike returns with mixed news: Madame Egilichi will back the show, but further discussions will prevent him taking Maggie to dinner, which was her promised birthday treat. Madame Egilichi is brought every sardine can on the premises, each of which is systematically discarded in the alley. Faustino is sent to obtain more. Harpo returns to find the cat and the now-exposed diamonds. He pockets the jewels and leaves the cat to its meal. Throckmorton finds the marked can, assumes the diamonds are now within the cat and brings the animal to Madame Egilichi. Faustino brings her anchovies instead of sardines. Harpo finds Maggie, disconsolate. She speaks of travelling, with Harpo as her manager, but breaks down in tears. Harpo goes to his home, a shack filled with various strange articles. He brings a harp and plays *Happy Birthday* for Maggie, using one hand for the instrument and the other to hold candles. He gives her the diamonds

before playing *Way Down Upon the Swanee River*. When the piece concludes, he sees Maggie has gone. The show *Love Happy* opens. Grunion brings the narrative up to date: having heard of Madame Egilichi's investment in the show, Grunion is back on the trail. He is about to leave for the theatre with an associate, Mackinaw, when they are confronted by Ivan, a gun-toting representative of the Romanovs. Grunion has so far been paid 100,000 zloties and his employers demand the necklace (Grunion: 'Did you ever try to spend a zloty in this country?'). Grunion is given sixty minutes, to be gauged with an hourglass. Grunion tops it up from the fire bucket but is to die in any case. A beautiful client visits the office and Grunion, not unreasonably, tries to follow her out; Ivan keeps him at gunpoint. The show is about to open. Maggie, dressed in the Sadie Thompson costume, adds the necklace given to her by Harpo and is spotted by Madame Egilichi's thugs. Mike sees the necklace, declares it 'phony' and removes it, promising to buy her the genuine article. The reconciled couple leave the necklace in the piano. The curtain is raised but Maggie is held prisoner in her dressing room. Harpo overhears and goes for help. Mike is also dragged into the room as Harpo conveys the situation to Faustino. By the time they arrive, Bunny has joined the captives, who are forced to provide either diamonds or their lives. Outside, Harpo and Faustino see a chorus girl wearing prop diamonds on her rear end; they are obtained and brought to the dressing room. They allow themselves to be chased to the roof, Harpo keeping them in pursuit as Faustino returns to the auditorium. Harpo eludes the villains by way of mechanical neon signs as Faustino plays piano onstage. From a private box, Madame Egilichi sees the necklace leap up from within the piano. Faustino grabs the necklace, leaves the stage and tells Lyons of the jewels and of his intention to save both Harpo and

the show. Harpo has taken refuge in a gigantic cigarette advertisement, consisting of a smoke-blowing penguin. When cornered, he overpowers the gunmen by producing smoke from his body. Faustino reaches the scene just as Harpo is pursued through a trapdoor. He calls after, offering the diamonds. Harpo returns, squashing Faustino under the door. In the confusion, their respective sets of jewels are exchanged. Harpo resumes his flight and Grunion appears, investigating all hiding places. He meets Madame Egilichi but his greetings are received with a slap. Grunion insists he will find the diamonds, but decides not to follow when learning she has a gun. Madame Egilichi confronts Faustino, who hands over what he believes are fake diamonds. She is told Harpo has the real necklace. Harpo has left his pursuers tied up, maypole-fashion; Grunion takes charge but Madame

Harpo in the jaws of a cigarette ad from **Love Happy**
BFI Stills, Posters and Designs

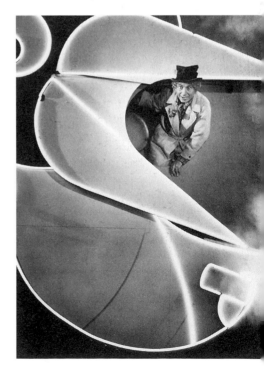

Egilichi says she will kill whoever has the diamonds. She sees Harpo slip them into Grunion's pocket and feigns love for the detective. As they go off together, Harpo slyly reclaims the jewels and, unaware of their true value, dances into the night. Back in his office, Grunion details his latest case. His new secretary, Faustino, plays cards with the dog. Grunion takes a call from his new wife - the former Madame Egilichi.

When Joe Adamson's *Groucho, Harpo, Chico and Sometimes Zeppo* was published in 1973, he remarked upon the way *Love Happy* was omitted from every Marx memoir, as if erased from their minds; 'My swan-song was *A Night in Casablanca* [*qv*]', wrote Groucho in *Groucho and Me*, thereby expunging not merely *Love Happy* but also his subsequent solo film ventures. At the time of Adamson's observation, work was in progress on *The Marx Brothers Scrapbook*, in the course of which Groucho at last commented on the film. Most of his recollections here and in a later volume, *The Secret Word is Groucho*, concern Marilyn Monroe (*qv*) playing a minor role. 'It was a terrible film and I tried to blot it out of my mind,' he wrote in *Secret Word*, explaining its absence from earlier books. Strictly speaking, Groucho had cause to regard *A Night in Casablanca* as his final film with the Marx Brothers, since *Love Happy* began life as a solo project for Harpo. Groucho thought his brother was trying to emulate Chaplin (*qv*), to whom Harpo had sometimes been compared, but such an idea had periodically been mooted since Robert Florey (*qv*) directed the team in *Cocoanuts* (*qv*). The original story, *The Sidewalk* (later amended to *Diamonds in the Sidewalk*), was suggested by Harpo and written as a vehicle for him by Ben Hecht (*qv*). 'It was never designed as a Marx Brothers film' said director David Miller (*qv*) in a later interview for *Classic Images*. Producer Lester Cowan (*qv*) seems to have been at least as preoccupied with

constructing a biographical film, *The Life of the Marx Brothers* (see **Abandoned projects**). In short, none of the principals had intended to make the film that became *Love Happy*. The usual story is that Chico, in need of money, was added to the cast during production, with Groucho contributing at the last minute because it had to be sold as a Marx Brothers film; it is instead evident that such mutation dated back to the script's first treatment. In the *Classic Images* interview, Miller recalled Harpo approaching him about a part for Chico after production had commenced; yet as early as 20 June 1947, Groucho wrote to his daughter, Miriam, mentioning a film Ben Hecht was writing for Harpo *and* Chico. A subsequent letter, of 25 September, immediately post-dates the deal between Harpo, Chico and Lester Cowan and already mentions Groucho's guest role as narrator. His letter of 18 October, when he was setting up *You Bet Your Life* (*qv*), speaks once more of the film, describing it as 'the story [Hecht] wrote for Harpo, and finally Chico got in it, and then I suddenly found myself in it for a brief bit'. David Miller recalled Groucho coming in solely because Chico had been added to the cast, but Groucho's version is that the film could not obtain financing unless all three were involved. Whatever the reason, Groucho did more than a 'bit', as noted below, and it is in this respect that *Love Happy*'s emphasis shifted during filming. Production was due to commence in March 1948 but was postponed, first until late June, then to August, when filming commenced. Miller *et al* had not been able to road-test the material as planned. 'We had writers who didn't know about gag construction' said Miller, though it should be said that screenwriters Mac Benoff and Frank Tashlin (both *qv*) were reasonably experienced in that department and *Love Happy* seems a curious lapse. Though all three Marxes had been signed months before, most

of the film had been shot prior to Groucho's contribution, which he dashed off in about ten days. Looking at the result, Groucho's after-the-event involvement becomes obvious: most of his scenes form a framing device for the story, beginning with a pre-credit monologue extending over shots of the leading characters. Groucho, as detective Sam Grunion, speaks to us from his office, to which we return at intervals as he provides links. It is in this setting that he first takes a real part in the story, when a gun-toting villain arrives, but there is no interaction with the other characters until the final rooftop scene. This sequence offers mute confirmation of the financial difficulties implied earlier, as Harpo escapes from Madame Egilichi's henchmen by means of various illuminated advertisements. Today, accusations of 'product placement' are fairly frequent but in the 1940s such practice was virtually unheard of; despite total lack of precedent, *Love Happy* could be completed only by the sale of onscreen advertising space. In fairness, the gags themselves are quite funny: after concealing himself within a giant, neon-created penguin advertising Kool cigarettes, Harpo is able to subdue his pursuers with smoke blown from everywhere in his anatomy (well, *almost* everywhere); another ad depicts a series of escalating Mobil horses, on which Harpo is seen ascending as the lights flash on and off. Filming was completed in January 1949, whereupon a press statement announced the Marxes' intention to go their separate ways. Chico set off for a British tour, to be joined in the summer by Harpo for an engagement at the London Palladium (*qv*). *Love Happy* lingered somewhat but received a startlingly good review from the *New York Times* on 8 April 1950, in which it was called 'helter-skelter entertainment' with the Marxes 'in fine fettle'. It was allowed that 'some of the gags fall with a flat thud', noting how in this and their last few films the comedians had seemed rather better than their material. However, the critic rhapsodized over most of this 'pot-pourri of mirth', even the heavily-sponsored rooftop chase. *Variety*, only slightly more guarded, considered this last as the type of situation in which 'the Marx Bros. can get away with almost anything', regarding some scenes as 'obviously contrived but plenty laugh-provoking'. *Love Happy* was long in reaching Great Britain. Hecht's involvement, though uncredited, was known and there had been a UK embargo on his work since he had made scathing comments on the British involvement in Palestine. In the intervening period, any Briton anxious to see it had to travel to Paris, as did Elaine Dundy (wife of Kenneth Tynan). *Love Happy* was eventually shown to the British trade press at the end of July 1951. *The Cinema* of 1 August thought it 'very good comedy entertainment' with 'good star attraction', regretting only the comparatively sparse presence of Groucho. 'Groucho makes the most of his limited opportunities,' it was said, 'and Harpo and Chico are as full of lunatic vitality as ever', especially in the 'familiar and preposterous' episode of Chico interpreting a message from Harpo. The work of Ilona Massey, Vera-Ellen and Marion Hutton (all *qv*) was similarly appreciated. Overall tone of this review and its *New York Times*

counterpart is of sheer gratitude in seeing the Marx Brothers in any form, their collaborative output having consisted of only two films since 1941. The BFI's *Monthly Film Bulletin* was less easy to please. In July 1951 it described *Love Happy* as 'disappointing', its plot 'over-detailed but slapdash' and the revue's musical items 'indifferent'. The main flaw was said to have been Groucho's limited rôle, which had upset their style of teamwork. This is a valid point, though Chico was not necessarily 'subdued' to the extent implied. The review is on target when noting an effort to make Harpo a sympathetic figure with both love interest and some sort of home: 'But Harpo has few of the characteristics of the pathetic clown and is at his best in the customary scenes of destructive action'. This, perhaps, underlines a basic error in Harpo 'doing a Chaplin', as Groucho believed. Harpo's uninhibited character provides a positive, vicarious experience for his audience, despite attempts to impose pathos in several films, starting with *A Night at the Opera* (*qv*). He was aware of this, yet could still be persuaded into a role where assertiveness is eroded by an unaccustomed vulnerability. *MFB* recognized Harpo's 'undiminished vigour' but, the rooftop scene aside, regarded him as unable to carry the

essentially familiar material without Groucho's assistance. *Love Happy*'s poor reputation is reflected in its conscious omission from a BBC retrospective in 1972. It is better viewed from its intended status, as a Harpo film in which his brothers appear as guests, though it has never been advertised as such. A US reissue (paired with Abbott & Costello's *Africa Screams*) chose to exploit its dubious place in history by emphasizing the film's brief glimpse of a then-unknown Marilyn Monroe (*qv*). British reissues have been under the original title and, on one occasion, as *Kleptomaniacs*. Trivia fans will doubtless be enthralled to learn that the author once saw a poster for *Love Happy*'s Danish release, bearing a name translating to the descriptive 'Sardine Mystery'.

(See also: Abandoned projects; Advertising; Animals; Blore, Eric; Books; Burr, Raymond; Continuity errors; Costume; Food; Gambling; Names; *Risqué* humour; Smoking; Songs; Television; Trailers; United Artists; 'White magic'; Wigs; Working titles)

LUBITSCH, ERNST
See: Abandoned projects; *Duck Soup*; Francis, Kay

MacBRIDE (or McBRIDE), DONALD (1889-1957)

New York-born actor, on stage and screen; played the harassed hotel inspector in the Broadway original and Marx Brothers film of *Room Service* (*qv*). Leonard Maltin's *Movie Comedy Teams* reports him in the Burns & Allen shorts made at Paramount's Long Island facility; he has also been spotted among the guests in *Animal Crackers* (*qv*), made at the same studio. Further shorts include a 1936 two-reeler with Buster Keaton (*qv*), *The Chemist*. Amid numerous features are *The Story of Vernon and Irene Castle* (1939), *The Gracie Allen Murder Case* (1939), *Here Comes Mr Jordan* (1941) and several Abbott & Costello comedies, such as *Little Giant* (1945).

(See also: Burns, George and Allen, Gracie; Dumont, Margaret; Paramount Pictures; Seiter, William A.)

MacCLOY, JUNE

Michigan-born actress with experience in nightclub cabaret and in *George White's Scandals*. Occasional films include *June Moon* (1931); her cabaret style is suggested in *Go West* (*qv*), when as saloon girl Lulubelle she sings *You Can't Argue with Love*.

MANKIEWICZ, HERMAN (1897-1953)

(Marx Brothers films *qv*)
Producer, screenwriter and renowned Hollywood wit, usually noted for a heavily-disputed contribution to *Citizen Kane* (1941). Comedy *aficionados* have a high regard for his film *Million Dollar Legs* (1932), starring W.C. Fields (*qv*) and also featuring Susan Fleming, Harpo's future wife. Mankiewicz's younger brother, Joseph, later a respected writer/producer/director in his own right, provided the film's story; some say Herman had virtually nothing to do with the script, and that it was the work of Joe Mankiewicz and Henry Myers, but this remains a matter of controversy. Joe's biographer, Kenneth L. Geist, records Joe taking a temporary job as dramatics and baseball counsellor in a summer establishment for boys, Camp Kiwana, which was mostly owned by the Marx Brothers. Geist quotes Groucho (from *The Marx Brothers Scrapbook*) as regarding this as the younger Mankiewicz's start in show business, organizing shows with children; in the full interview, Groucho makes no mention of any financial interest in the camp but mentions his son, Arthur, as having stayed there. Joe Mankiewicz himself is quoted as having had a fist fight with Zeppo (as did many others!) when the latter refused to relinquish the position of first base on the camp's baseball team. Herman Mankiewicz's role in Marx Brothers history is as uncredited producer, or 'supervisor', of their first three screen originals, *Monkey Business*, *Horse Feathers* and, in its earlier stages, *Duck Soup*. Impressions of him are contradictory and not always complimentary, in this respect suggesting an at least partial affinity with the Marxes. On arriving in California to prepare *Monkey Business*, S.J. Perelman (*qv*) recalled being confronted by 'a large, Teutonic individual with an abrasive tongue, who had been a well-known journalist and the *New Yorker*'s first dramatic critic'. Perelman noted the producer's comparative penury, the result of card-playing and a taste for the high life, despite a marriage to one of Hollywood's 'hierarchy' (Mrs Sara Mankiewicz). His initial advice was delivered in an easygoing fashion, warning Perelman and Will B. Johnstone (*qv*) to wear 'asbestos pants' when dealing with the Marxes. This avuncular manner turned to rage on a later encounter, when Mankiewicz returned from his customarily gigantic lunch to sleep it off in his office. The naïve writers disturbed the slumbering producer with a question concerning the brothers' psychologies and how to write for them. Mankiewicz, unaccustomed to such rarified talk, provided an extremely basic comment on each brother before ordering the

nervous scribes to 'get back to your hutch'. Mankiewicz left them to it for six weeks. Groucho's recollections of him are brusque: in *The Groucho Phile* he is skeptical of Mankiewicz's *auteur* status, describing him as 'an irritating drunk who didn't give a hang about the movie project' (there is no mention of him in the book's index); in the *Scrapbook* he makes similar mention of Mankiewicz's drinking, but his views seem altogether less terse, describing him as 'a funny man ... a good writer but he didn't like to work ... an interesting character and a provoking one'. According to this account, alcohol rendered Mankiewicz of little use to the films' creation, but he kept his job because Paramount executive B.P. Schulberg continually owed him money from card games. A typical Mankiewicz day would see him call his wife to catch up on the gossip, pause for a nap, disappear for a boozy lunch and then, as in Perelman's recollection, spend the afternoon asleep. Groucho accused Mankiewicz of hating the writers, corroborating Perelman's remark about the hutch but in considerably stronger terms. He recalled further Mankiewicz's collaboration on plays with both Marc Connelly and George S. Kaufman (*qv*), neither of them successful. The failure of these efforts was commemorated in a wry caption added to a picture in Mankiewicz's office, showing him with the two playwrights. According to Geist, Mankiewicz had been assistant drama editor under Kaufman at the *New York Times*. It is possible that something may have happened to sour the Mankiewicz-Groucho relationship (as with Groucho's rift with Perelman), for Joe Adamson mentions a time when, in the 1920s, Broadway star Groucho would call at the Mankiewicz residence and, on seeing Mrs Mankiewicz, would enquire 'Can Herman come out to play?' Adamson's narrative of the Paramount years - often taken from interviews with the survivors - suggests a producer who contributed to the general banter and, outside of a blunt

nature (which wouldn't normally have bothered the Marxes) seemed agreeable and an accepted part of the *coterie*. Mankiewicz's biographer, Richard Meryman, describes Harpo leading 'the little Mankiewicz boys in Indian war dances through the middle of family Passover Seder ceremonies' and quotes a *Hollywood Reporter* item of 1937 in which Harpo and Susan Marx were among those to have sent gifts on the birth of Mankiewicz's daughter. Nat Perrin (*qv*), interviewed for *The Marx Brothers in a Nutshell*, considered Mankiewicz 'more or less one of the boys', describing how, at their first meeting, the producer took a pack of cards from his desk and challenged all comers to a hand of casino for $10. Geist in turn says that Joe obtained the summer camp job because Herman was a friend of Groucho. Meryman hints at reasons for Groucho's abrupt recollections of Mankiewicz: one is Groucho's view of himself as prime influence on the Marx Brothers films, a debatable point; another is Mankiewicz's belief in the superiority of his own wit over that of the Marxes, manifesting itself in especial disdain for the material submitted by Groucho's close friend, Arthur Sheekman (*qv*); while elsewhere Meryman describes Mankiewicz as having tried, jokingly one suspects, to accuse Harry Ruby (*qv*), Groucho's best friend and *not* a great drinker, of encouraging his alcoholic indulgences.

(See also: Abandoned projects; Documentaries; Fighting; Paramount Pictures; Ryskind, Morrie)

THE MAN WHO CAME TO DINNER

It was to satisfy the dramatic ambitions of Alexander Woollcott (*qv*) that Moss Hart and George S. Kaufman (*qv*) fashioned this play, in which Woollcott and his friends are depicted, in only somewhat exaggerated form, *à clef*. In requesting a tailored stage vehicle, Woollcott stipulated only that the central character should not be based

directly on his real-life persona. The authors found this impossible but Woollcott accepted the result, in which a waspish, manipulative celebrity takes over a family's home after sustaining a minor injury on their doorstep. The plot is reputed to have been conceived when Hart told Kaufman of a recent visit from Woollcott, who had been especially difficult. Hart believed that only a prolonged stay, the result of perhaps a broken leg, could have been worse. For the purposes of the play, Woollcott became 'Sheridan Whiteside', journalist, lecturer and broadcaster (Woollcott's genuine sponsor, Cream of Wheat, was in turn lampooned as 'Cream of Mush'). Of the eminent people in Woollcott's acquaintance, several are mentioned by name (notably Eleanor Roosevelt) but those onstage are given appropriate pseudonyms. One of these, 'Beverly Carlton', is a transparent alias for Noël Coward; just as recognizable is 'Banjo', or in other words Harpo in his offstage, speaking version. When the play was completed, Woollcott decided against playing the lead. His first choice, British actor Robert Morley, was passed over in favour of Monty Woolley, a drama professor with stage ambitions. Morley later took the rôle in London. Woolley starred in the original production, which opened on Broadway in October 1939 following provincial tryouts. Its instant success prompted some regret in Woollcott, who decided he would like to play the lead in a second company, based in Chicago. He lost this opportunity to Clifton Webb (who was to play another Woollcott-like character in the 1944 film *Laura*) but was instead given the third company, based first in California before touring the east (the latter would be postponed when Woollcott suffered a heart attack). Woolley was retained for Warner Brothers' film version, released in 1942. In the original production, David Burns was cast as 'Banjo'; for the film, Jimmy Durante took the part, investing in it an intriguing blend of his own mannerisms with those of Harpo, the latter especially apparent in Durante's frequent use of an open-mouthed stare. Similarly, Durante is costumed very much in the manner of the off-stage Harpo, his open-necked shirt and sports coat approximating those worn by Harpo in *La Fiesta de Santa Barbara* (see **Guest appearances**). The film version omits Whiteside's enquiry about Banjo's brothers, presumably to limit unnecessary parallels to any real-life personages; censorship in turn probably ensured the loss of Whiteside's opening line, 'I may vomit'. When Woollcott's tour took him in the direction of Harpo and family during January 1940, he received a telegram (reprinted in *The Marx Brothers Scrapbook*) reading 'EXPECT YOU TO DINNER FRIDAY NIGHT I MAY VOMIT'. Harpo did not take the part of 'Banjo' with Woollcott but appeared thus, in a rare speaking rôle, when Kaufman and Hart portrayed Whiteside and Carlton at the Bucks County Playhouse, New Hope, Pennsylvania, between 28 July and 2 August 1941 (see also **Stage appearances [post-1930]**). Curiously, a group portrait of the three men shows Harpo in a business suit rather than the informal clothing approximated by Durante. *The Man Who Came to Dinner* was an enormous success in its day and remains popular both as a film and in stage revivals.

(See also: Could Harpo Speak?)

MARRIAGES

Chico was first to marry, to Betty Karp on 22 March 1917. They first met when Betty was introduced to him by a girl with whom Chico had worked for the song publishers Shapiro, Bernstein; the Marxes were then playing in *Home Again* (qv) at the Palace. They arranged a date but Betty stood him up; they did not meet again until the Marxes just happened to be appearing near her home in Brooklyn, and Betty was boasting to a friend how she knew Chico Marx. They visited the theatre

Chico and his first wife, Betty Karp, dine out; their companion at left is Sophie Tucker, the 'Last of the Red-Hot Mamas', a friend since vaudeville days

and Chico recognized her; a second date was arranged and this time it was Chico's turn not to appear. Love flourished despite, and Betty found herself joining the *Home Again* company. Despite his frequent infidelities, and an involvement with Lillian Roth's sister, Ann, the marriage survived into the 1940s. Chico remarried in August 1958, to Mary De Vithas. A Chico obituary in *Screen* magazine of 20 October 1961 said they met 19 years before, when she was an M-G-M actress; they'd actually been living together for many years, Mary accompanying Chico on his post-war visits to Britain. Groucho married Ruth Johnstone on 4 February 1920; they were divorced on 15 July 1942. Their relationship gradually deteriorated as Ruth wanted an active social life while Groucho favoured domesticity. As Ruth spent more time at her tennis club, she developed an alcohol problem that contributed to their estrangement. Groucho's next marriage, to Kay Gorcey, began on 21 July 1945 and ended on 12 May 1950. Last was Eden Hartford, whom he married on 17 July 1954; the divorce was on 4 December 1969. A famous story has Groucho seen with her in public soon after, with Groucho

claiming he wanted to be close to his money. It is said that all of Groucho's wives suffered from some form of alcohol problem; some view it as a result of the pressure induced by Groucho's compulsive put-downs, albeit an essentially humorous instinct, but this must remain conjecture. Zeppo married Marion Benda on 12 April 1927; they divorced on 17 May 1954. He married Barbara Blakeley on 18 September 1959; three years after their divorce in 1973, Barbara married Frank Sinatra (qv). Gummo married

Actress Susan Fleming forsook her movie career on marrying Harpo in 1936. Here she returns to the schoolroom in a Paramount publicity photo

Helen Von Tilzer on 16 March 1929, a match that lasted until her death in January 1976. Harpo had planned to marry an aviatrix named June Fleming, but she was killed in an air accident; he later met another Fleming, Susan, whom he married on 28 September 1936. This enormously successful marriage endured until Harpo's death.

(See also: Children; Deaths; Gambling; Roth, Lillian; Stage appearances [post-1930]; Television; Weddings; Women)

MARSHALL, TULLY (1864-1943)

An important name in silent cinema, Tully Marshall was later in character rôles, such as elderly prospector Dan Wilson in the Marxes' *Go West* (*qv*). Nevada-born Marshall (real name William Phillips) was on stage from youth, appearing in plays such as *Paid in Full* and *City*; also produced *Builders*. He was already a veteran of forty-five years' acting experience when making his film début, as a high priest in D.W. Griffith's *Intolerance* (1916). That same year he took the role of Fagin in a film version of *Oliver Twist*. Other silents include *The Covered Wagon* (1923), Chaney's *The Hunchback of Notre Dame* (1923) and *He Who Gets Slapped* (1924), Von Stroheim's *The Merry Widow* (1925), Garbo's first American film *The Torrent* (1926), *Twinkletoes* (1926) with Colleen Moore, *The Cat and the Canary* (1927) and *The Trail of '98* (1928). Among his talkies are *Mammy* (1930), *Arsène Lupin* (1932), *Scarface* (1932), *Grand Hotel* (1932), *Red Dust* (1932), *Souls at Sea* (1937) and *A Yank at Oxford* (1938).

(See also: Bell, Monta; Garbo, Greta)

MARTIN, TONY (b. 1914)

Singer and actor Tony Martin plays Tommy Rogers, part-owner of *The Big Store* (*qv*). Martin (born Alvin Morris, Jr) originally divided his efforts between music and athletics but opted for the former as a career. Initial experience as band musician and

Tony Martin *charms Virginia Grey in* The Big Store

vocalist led to radio work, then films. His first was the Astaire-Rogers musical *Follow the Fleet* (1936). There followed a Fox contract and, soon, star status; a move to M-G-M (*qv*) was interrupted by distinguished war service but he returned to star in the Jerome Kern biopic, *Till the Clouds Roll By* (1946). Martin continued to make successful films and records, his recordings of *Stranger in Paradise* and *Walk Hand in Hand* making the British charts in April 1955 and July 1956 respectively. Martin has been a frequent visitor to the UK, usually with his wife, dancer Cyd Charisse. They were booked for the London Palladium (*qv*) at the time of Groucho's death in 1977, during which visit Martin recorded a BBC Radio tribute to Groucho.

(See also: Documentaries; Radio; Records; Songs; Vera-Ellen)

THE MARX OF TIME
See: Radio

MARX BROS., INC.

During contractual problems with Paramount (*qv*) prior to the filming of *Duck Soup* (*qv*), the Marxes surprised the studio and the world at large by forming their own company. 'The Marx Brothers, Inc.' was a revolutionary step for film stars at that time, very few of whom attempted to challenge the powerful studio system (the Marxes subsequently became founding members of the Screen Actors' Guild). The London *Evening News* of April 19

1933 carried a story from Reuter's describing the new company: 'Their concern ... is authorised to issue 100 shares of its 1,000-share capitalization, the stock having no par value'. The story provides brief details of the comedians' split with Paramount and their intention to become independent producers. The *Evening News'* own correspondent refers to the Marxes having been placed under a five-year contract with another new concern, Producing Artists, Incorporated, a company designed to 'finance the makers of pictures, relieving them of the burden of studio, overhead and other liabilities'. The story cites a screen version of Kaufman and Ryskind's *Of Thee I Sing* as the Marxes' first new project, adding that their last Paramount picture, *Cracked Ice*, had been 'left unfinished' when a dispute arose over their profit-sharing arrangement with the studio (though in fact it had reached only scripting stage). Fuller details emerged to the press via *Film Daily*, naming the founding head of Producing Artists Pictures as Sam Katz (1892-1961), a Russian-born pioneer of the cinema chain business. When aged only 13, Katz had started as a nickelodeon pianist for Carl Laemmle - the future head of Universal - in his first theatre on Chicago's West Side; with Barney Balaban, Katz went on to create a huge theatre empire before joining Paramount in 1925. He became vice-president of that organization prior to quitting in 1932 to form the new company. The deal took Katz into partnership with Marcus Heiman and two Marx associates of long standing, theatrical producer Sam Harris (*qv*) and Max Gordon (*qv*), the latter of whom had represented them in the Paramount deal. The Marx film was to be the company's first, scheduled for production during summer 1933 for release in the autumn. The director was to be Norman Z. McLeod (*qv*), who had directed their last two pictures; also recruited was Gummo, who took over his brothers' financial affairs after the failure of his dress business. This was brave talk, of the type mostly unheard since the formation of United Artists (*qv*) in 1919; it is difficult to determine how far the Marxes really intended to proceed with the venture, but it seems unreasonable to suggest it to have been simply a lever in their dispute with Paramount. It was more likely a lack of producing capital that forced a return to Paramount and what would become *Duck Soup*; they were reconciled with the studio by May 18, announcing *Duck Soup*, with Leo McCarey (*qv*) directing, as their final Paramount film. Producing Artists' *Of Thee I Sing* was to follow. Plans for *Of Thee I Sing* continued into the next year but finally evaporated when the team was signed by Irving Thalberg (*qv*). Sam Katz later became an executive at M-G-M (*qv*) and was eventually board chairman of the Stanley Kramer Corporation.

(See also: Abandoned projects; Agents; Awards; Kaufman, George S.; Ryskind, Morrie)

THE MARX BROTHERHOOD
See: *Freedonia Gazette, the*

MARX, MINNIE (1864-1929)
The woman who was to become mother to the Marx Brothers was born Minna Schoënberg in Dornum, Germany. She was the child of entertainers Lafe (alias Louis) Schoënberg and his wife Fanny, who travelled as magician and harpist. In a commonplace pattern for the mid- to late-nineteenth century, they produced a total of eleven children, three of whom did not survive. It was therefore ten Shoënbergs who emigrated to the United States in 1880. Minna anglicized her name to Minnie, after child actress Minnie Maddern (later Minnie Maddern Fiske, to whom there is reference in the stage script of *Cocoanuts* [*qv*]). A younger brother, who became famous on the stage, adopted the name Al Shean (*qv*). It was in the USA that Minnie met Sam Marx

(*qv*), whom she married in 1884. Their first child, Manfred, was born about a year later (see **Births**) but died when still an infant. By the turn of the century, the remaining, and still considerable, family occupied a small apartment on East 93rd Street, a Jewish neighbourhood in New York. In addition to Minnie and Sam, there were the surviving Marx sons; Minnie's parents, known to the children as 'Opie' and 'Omie' (or 'grandpa' and 'grandma'); Minnie's sister Hannah and her husband Julius Schickler (whose forename became the young Groucho's); and Hannah's daughter, Polly. Groucho said Polly 'wasn't a bad-looking girl, but her rear end stuck way out. You could play pinochle on her rear end.' It was at Polly's marriage service that Groucho and Harpo made a terrible mess of the plumbing (see **Weddings**). Hannah's son later adopted the name 'Lou Shean' and formed a short-lived act with Chico. It has been said that the Marxes' maternal grandfather lived to be a hundred years of age, but other accounts suggest he had lied about his birthdate and was in fact much younger. As noted elsewhere, Sam ran the household and administered purely nominal discipline to the unruly Marx boys. They were not suited to any particular form of employment and it was the success of brother Al that convinced Minnie to put her sons on the stage. Groucho tried his luck with a few acts before Minnie combined him with Gummo and, shortly afterwards, Harpo, as an ensemble described in the **Nightingales** entry. At one time both Minnie and Hannah participated in this troupe, billed then as 'The Six Mascots'. Some measure of Minnie's supreme confidence - which she passed on to Chico - may be gathered from her creation of a singing act comprised of a family mostly unencumbered by vocal talent. To secure bookings for them, she uprooted the family to Chicago (where vaudeville's second echelon was centred) and set herself up as 'Minnie Palmer, Chicago's only lady

producer'. She had appropriated the name from a popular soubrette of the period, not necessarily to invite confusion between the two but more than probably. The real Minnie Palmer died in May 1936, aged 71. It was a mixture of audacity and bribery (using Sam's cooking) that secured engagements for the act; Chico recognized this as implied admission of inadequacy and started arranging the deals. Even when not appearing herself, Minnie travelled with the act during its formative years, if only to curb any onstage fooling by calling, from the wings, 'Greenbaum!', a salutary reminder of the gentleman who held their mortgage. She was with them for a London engagement in 1922 and was ensured the best seat when their plays opened on Broadway; she refused to miss the New York première of *I'll Say She Is!* (*qv*) despite having broken her leg during a dress fitting. Once the Marx Brothers were successful, Minnie attempted to launch others into the business, but never with the same results. *Vanity Fair* noted how, 'feeling suddenly idle', Minnie 'went into the gingerbread business'. This was when nominating her for the 1925 'Hall of Fame', something probably instigated by Alexander Woollcott (*qv*), who had become as great an admirer of Minnie as he was of her offspring; he recorded Minnie's attempt to put her chauffeur on the stage as late as 1928. Minnie lived long enough to see their talkie début in *Cocoanuts* (qv) but, after attending a family gathering, died of a massive stroke in September 1929. At the funeral, Woollcott had no words to comfort the Marxes save for observing an Irish name in the Jewish cemetery, declaring that deceased a 'spy'. Ample compensation was supplied in his obituary for *The New Yorker* (reprinted in Woollcott's *While Rome Burns*). According to Woollcott, Minnie 'was in this world sixty-five years and *lived* all sixty-five of them'; he wrote also of the way Minnie had not merely borne or raised the Marx Brothers, but had actually 'invented' them. 'They amused no one more,' added the journalist, 'and their reward was her ravishing smile.' Woollcott recalled her nearly forgetting to attend the opening of *Animal Crackers* (qv) but making the occasion just in time, saying 'We have a great success.' The Marxes had reassembled after the summer but had yet to begin touring in *Animal Crackers* at the time of Minnie's death. Recording Minnie's exit in the presence of her entire family, Woollcott believed that Minnie, had she known, would have smiled, winked and said 'How's that for perfect timing?' An outsider's view of Minnie Marx might be that of a pushy, dominant stage mother. This she was, but she was devoted to her boys and it was reciprocated. They were unanimous in believing that, with the possible exception of Groucho, none of the Marx Brothers would otherwise have amounted to anything. They retained loving recollections of her eccentricities, such as arriving at gatherings tightly corsetted and sporting a blonde wig (the latter to combat grey locks), only to discard both shortly thereafter; the entrance was the thing. In Minnie's honour, each of the Marxes' daughters received names starting with 'M'.

(See also: Agents; Books; Children; Education; Female impersonation; Gambling; Harp, the; *Minnie's Boys*; *On the Mezzanine*; Piano, the; *Street Cinderella, the*; Vaudeville; Wartime; Wigs)

MARX, SAM 'FRENCHIE' (1861-1933)
Born Simon Marrix in Alsace-Lorraine, the Marx Brothers' father emigrated to the USA in 1881. He became Sam Marx to fall in line with relatives already in the new country. His marriage to Minnie, *née* Minna, Schoënberg in 1884 produced six sons (see **Births**), five of whom lived to adulthood (it has been suggested there were half-siblings of whom Minnie was unaware!). Sam's English was functional at best. He spoke *Plattdeutsch*, a form of low-country German, in adulthood but as a child was fluent in French. His sons nicknamed him 'Frenchie' because of his essentially Gallic ways, which extended into considerable culinary skills. Unfortunately, he chose to make his living not as a chef but as a tailor, a vocation in which he was hamstrung by his refusal to use a tape measure and by Chico's constant pawning of either his shears or the completed garments. Sam bowed completely to Minnie in running the household, staying home with young Zeppo while his wife and elder sons were out on the road. He was, however, delegated the task of disciplining the brood, albeit in token spankings that scarcely stung; it is said that Harpo's gentle manner was inherited from his father. Once his sons had achieved eminence, Sam became something of a *boulevardier*, a well-dressed man-about-town. This was unimpaired by an incurable unfamiliarity with American life that did not end with the language barrier. On one occasion he entered a cab, believing it to be the chauffeur-driven car he had left earlier. His mistake was revealed only when the cabbie, sitting down to eat, baulked at being instructed to give the car a wash. After Minnie's death in 1929 and his sons'

relocation West, Sam settled in California and was thus on hand for a bit part in *Monkey Business* (qv). A similar cameo role was planned for *Horse Feathers* (qv) but his health did not permit. Frenchie died on May 11 1933. In March of that year Groucho had contributed an affectionate profile, 'Our Father and Us', to *Redbook* magazine. The text appears in Robert S. Bader's anthology, *Groucho Marx and Other Short Stories and Tall Tales*.

(See also: In-jokes; *Duck Soup*; Marx, Minnie; Russia)

MASSEY, ILONA (1910-74)
Hungarian actress in American films, inevitably somewhat exotic as in *Love Happy* (qv), in which she is international temptress Madame Egilichi. According to a syndicated newspaper obituary, she was born in Budapest, working as dressmaker and theatre singer in order to finance a trip to Vienna. It was there that the local opera company gave her the lead in *Tosca*; she took a screen test in London and was signed by M-G-M, who put her in the Nelson Eddy vehicle *Rosalie* (1938) and cast her opposite him in *Balalaika* (1939). Many other screen appearances, such as *Honeymoon in Bali* (1939), *International Lady* (1941), *Frankenstein Meets the Wolf Man* (1943) and *Jet Over the Atlantic* (1958). Although an American citizen from 1947, she was among the more vociferous protestors after the 1956 Hungarian uprising and subsequent Soviet oppression.

(See also: King, Walter Woolf; *Risqué* humour; Television)

MAYER, LOUIS B.
See: M-G-M

MAYO, ARCHIE L. (1891 or 1898-1968)
New York-born director of *A Night in Casablanca* (qv), originally on stage in musicals, touring Europe, Australia and the USA. Appeared as a film extra before working as a gagman,

graduating to director status first in short comedies, then full-length silent features. His talkies include Jolson's *Sonny Boy* (1929), *Doorway to Hell* (1930), the John Barrymore *Svengali* (1931), *Night After Night* (1932), *The Life of Jimmy Dolan* (1933) with Douglas Fairbanks Jr and Loretta Young, *Bordertown* (1934), *The Man with Two Faces* (1934) with Edward G. Robinson, the Jolson-Keeler *Go Into Your Dance* (1935), a 1935 Perry Mason story called *The Case of the Lucky Legs*, an early Bogart, *The Petrified Forest* (1936), the 1940 remake of *Four Sons*, Jack Benny's version of *Charley's Aunt* (1941) and *Crash Dive* (1943) with Tyrone Power.

(See also: Benny, Jack; Francis, Kay; Kibbee, Roland; Seaton, George)

McCAREY, LEO (1898-1969)

(Marx Brothers films *qv*)
Director, writer and sometime producer whose reputation was first made at the Hal Roach studio, where he took over the position of supervising director in 1927. Prior to his departure, McCarey was responsible for teaming Laurel & Hardy (*qv*) in addition to other scripting and directing work.

Leo McCarey *directed the Marxes once - but superbly - in* Duck Soup

McCarey's distinguished career is landmarked by his Oscar-winning *The Awful Truth* (1937), *Love Affair* (1939) and *Going My Way* (1944); among many others are *Indiscreet* (1931) with Gloria Swanson, Eddie Cantor's *The Kid From Spain* (1932), *Six of a Kind* (1934) with W.C. Fields and Burns & Allen, Mae West's *Belle of the Nineties* (1934), *Ruggles of Red Gap* (1935) and Harold Lloyd's *The Milky Way* (1936). Perhaps highest in reputation today is McCarey's only film with the Marx Brothers, *Duck Soup*. For this film (actually titled after the first recognizable Laurel & Hardy short), McCarey provided a successful blend of his silent-comedy heritage with the altogether different Marxian approach; though harmonious in effect, it is understood that McCarey did not care much for the experience, though the reliability of at least one source, from the mid-1960s, has sometimes been queried. The comparative failure of *Duck Soup* at the box-office and the extraordinary acclaim of its immediate successors (*A Night at the Opera* and *A Day at the Races*) led to its long-term disparagement by the Marxes themselves, although Groucho lived long enough to see posterity's viewpoint. At a film festival in the late 1960s he named *Duck Soup* as their best movie, implying the reason for this with a simple 'McCarey directed it.'

(See also: Burns, George and Allen, Gracie; Cantor, Eddie; Fields, W.C.; O'Connor, Robert Emmett; Ruby, Harry; Wood, Sam)

McLEOD, NORMAN Z. (Zenos) (1898-1964)

Director of the Marx Brothers' *Monkey Business* and *Horse Feathers* (both *qv*). Some idea of McLeod's working relationship with the Marxes is conveyed in a *Film Weekly* article of 24 June 1932, written during McLeod's visit to the UK and entitled 'Debagged by the Marx Brothers'. McLeod spoke of their irresponsibility both on and off-set, holding up production by keeping cast and technicians in hysterics, noting also their lack of punctuality and reluctance to appear early in the morning. They responded to a 9 a.m. call in full make-up, but not their own: 'Harpo had put on Groucho's moustache, Chico was running round crazily in Harpo's wig, while Zeppo shot off wise-cracks in Chico's dialect'. On another occasion Zeppo, having ascertained that McLeod had no immediate need for him on-set, decided to absent himself. When McLeod asked where he was heading, Zeppo replied 'Oh, just going up to San Francisco for a couple of weeks.' McLeod describes Harpo and Chico as always chasing girls, and Groucho as never ceasing to make jokes while the cameras turned, to the point where many good laughs had to be cut for the sake of time. According to McLeod, the comedians themselves devised a certain amount of dialogue and business; 'Often they get right out of hand and run away with a scene. They forget the "business" of the scenario and carry on making up the action on the spur of the moment. I always let these scenes run until they dry up, and sometimes the funniest part of a scene has never been in the original plan.' The title of the piece derives from McLeod's recollection of the Marxes arriving to make *Horse Feathers*: 'Suddenly they all came trouping in at the door obviously bent on revelry. As soon as they saw me they shouted "Hello, Mac!" and all four pounced on me, got me on the ground, and tore my pants off ... this episode took place in the outer part of the studio, with a dozen or so amused onlookers watching the Brothers tearing round the studio waving my pants.' It is something of a tribute to this Michigan-born clergyman's son that he was able to survive two Marx Brothers films and continue to make others; Nat Perrin (*qv*) has described McLeod as 'quietly bewildered by this hurricane called the Marx Brothers'. McLeod worked originally in animation before turning screenwriter; perhaps it

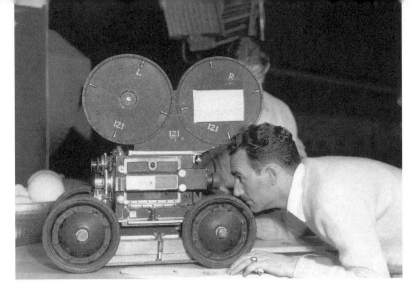

Norman Z. McLeod *was the team's first director after moving to Hollywood*

was this grounding in cartoons and Marx Brothers exploits that led him often to be given fantasy stories, notably *Alice in Wonderland* (1933), *Topper* (1937), *Topper Takes a Trip* (1939) and *Remember?* (1939). McLeod was in semi-retirement when engaged for a 1961 episode of TV's *The Twilight Zone*, subtitled *Once Upon a Time*, starring Buster Keaton (*qv*). Amid his long list of directing credits are *It's a Gift* (1934) with W.C. Fields (*qv*), *Pennies From Heaven* (1936) with Bing Crosby, *Lady Be Good* (1941), *Jackass Mail* (1942) with Wallace Beery, Danny Kaye's *The Kid From Brooklyn* (1946) and *The Secret Life of Walter Mitty* (1947), the Crosby-Hope *Road to Rio* (1947) and the Bob Hope vehicles *The Paleface* (1948), *My Favorite Spy* (1951) and *Casanova's Big Night* (1954). He was also one of the many directors of *If I Had a Million* (1932).

(See also: Abandoned projects; Feld, Fritz; Paramount Pictures; Practical jokes; Seiter, William A.; Vera-Ellen)

METCALFE, EDWARD
Supporting player who joined the company of *Home Again* (*qv*) as replacement for Paul Yale. Metcalfe took over the role of police detective, whose job it was to shake Harpo's hand as cutlery descended from the comedian's other sleeve. Metcalfe, who introduced Groucho to the work of Gilbert & Sullivan, remained with the Marxes through *On the Mezzanine*, in which he accompanied them on their UK visit of 1922; he worked with them again in the Broadway runs of *I'll Say She Is!* and *Animal Crackers*, still shaking Harpo's hand and duplicating his role of policeman in the latter's film version (in which his surname is mis-spelt 'Metcalf'). Edward Metcalfe was present once more when the Marxes revisited London in 1931; he died on 2 April 1951, aged 84.

(See also: Cochran, C.B.; Mikado, the; Policemen)

M-G-M
(Marx Brothers films *qv*)
Hollywood's premier studio was ruled by Louis B. Mayer, with an equal say from Irving Thalberg (*qv*). It was Thalberg who signed the Marx Brothers in 1934, strictly against Mayer's wishes. Under Thalberg's *aegis* the Marxes had their two biggest successes, *A Night at the Opera* and *A Day at the Races*. It was during production of the former that Mayer is believed to have visited the set, asking 'How's the picture going, Groucho?', to be told 'I don't think that's any of your concern.' Recalling this snub to the most powerful man in Hollywood (who was, incidentally, on a higher salary scale than the President), Groucho told Frank Muir of Thalberg's hatred for Mayer, adding 'I always had a capacity for hating someone who my boss also hated'. It was a hostile Mayer who was in charge after Thalberg's early death, explaining the Marx films' steady deterioration. *At the Circus* was denied a road tour, something Mayer considered an unnecessary expense; such a tour was permitted for *Go West*, but Bert Kalmar and Harry Ruby (*qv*) did not supply the final script as

The Marx Brothers were reduced to three on joining **M-G-M**

planned; *The Big Store* was denied both top-flight writers *and* a road tour. By the time of its release, the Marxes had thoroughly wearied of film-making.

(See also: Censorship; Documentaries; Keaton, Buster; Loew, David L.; Wood, Sam)

M-G-M'S BIG PARADE OF COMEDY
See: Documentaries

MIDDLETON, CHARLES
(1884-1949)
Stern-looking Kentuckian, originally from the stage. His gaunt, august appearance was effective in drama (such as *I Am A Fugitive From a Chain Gang* and *The Grapes of Wrath*) or in comedy, notably Harold Lloyd's *Welcome Danger* and four films with Laurel & Hardy (*qv*), *Beau Hunks*, *Pack Up Your Troubles*, *The Fixer-Uppers* and *The Flying Deuces*. There are elements of both styles in his fake mystic of *Palmy Days*, starring Eddie Cantor (*qv*). He is perhaps best recalled as Ming the Merciless in the *Flash Gordon* serials. In the Marxes' *Duck Soup*, he is the similarly merciless prosecutor of Chicolini, on trial for espionage in Freedonia.

(See also: Ryskind, Morrie; Woods, Harry)

MIDGETS
See: *At the Circus*; Deleted scenes; Television

THE MIKADO
Groucho fulfilled a longstanding ambition when, in 1960, he was given a starring part in a Gilbert & Sullivan opera. He had been introduced to their work by an informed vaudeville colleague, Edward Metcalfe (*qv*). In his 1972 *Omnibus* interview, Groucho mentioned how, as a young man, he had been taught much of Gilbert & Sullivan by Metcalfe: 'I'd never heard of Gilbert & Sullivan until he started singing these songs, and I realized what a wonderful treasure this was.'

Metcalfe did Groucho a favour but not necessarily those to whom Groucho's interest seemed less explicable; Arthur Marx has described how bored his mother would be by Groucho's incessant playing of Gilbert & Sullivan records, or by his loving repetition of G&S anecdote. Visitors at this time and for years after would often be required to listen to the operas along with their host. During breaks in *You Bet Your Life* (*qv*) Groucho would fill in by singing excerpts from their work and he was even heard warbling *Take a Pair of Sparkling Eyes* (from *The Gondoliers*) when arriving for a London press conference in 1954. The TV production of *The Mikado* was broadcast by NBC on 29 April 1960, adapted and produced by Martyn Green, directed by Norman Campbell and sponsored by the Bell Telephone Company, as a part of their Bell Telephone Hour. Associate Producer credit went to Robert Dwan, who worked with Groucho on *You Bet Your Life* (*qv*). Groucho starred as Ko-Ko, the Lord High Executioner. Stanley Holloway was Pooh-Bah (Lord High Everything Else), Robert Rounseville played Nanki-Poo, Helen Traubel was Katisha (providing a parallel to Margaret Dumont [*qv*]), the Mikado himself was Dennis King and the 'three little maids from school' were Barbara Meister, Sharon Randall and Groucho's daughter Melinda. The Norman Luboff Choir served as citizens of Japan. Donald Voorhees directed the Bell Telephone Orchestra. The programme occupied an hour slot and was originally a colour videotape; available material seems to be a monochrome kinescope ('telerecording' in UK parlance), or in other words a film transfer from TV. Goddard Lieberson of Columbia Records produced an excellent cast album of the show. A TV postscript to *The Mikado* was Groucho's rendition of *Tit Willow* on Dick Cavett's programme. On reaching the word 'obdurate', Groucho asked if anyone in the audience knew what it meant. Nobody responded, so Groucho

abandoned the song and resumed conversation with the host.

(See also: Children; Marriages; Opera; Records; Television; Vaudeville)

MILES, LOTTA (1899-1937)
Leading lady in the New York production of *I'll Say She Is!* (*qv*), which established the Marx Brothers on Broadway. Though billed as 'Carlotta' in the programme, she had actually adopted the name 'Lotta Miles' as punning contribution to an advertising campaign by the Kelly tyre company. Career details are sparse but David Ragan's *Who's Who in Hollywood, 1900-1976* mentions one film, a 1935 Mascot production called *Waterfront Lady*.

(See also: O'Connor, Robert Emmett; Pratt, Purnell)

MILLER, ANN (1924-)
Actress and dancer who as an up-and-coming talent took the part of Hildy in the Marxes' film adaptation of *Room Service* (*qv*). (She claims to have been 14 when she made the film.) She is better known for her roles in such musicals as Berlin's *Easter Parade* (1948), *On the Town* (1949) and *Kiss Me Kate* (1953). In 1963 she took part in a radio tribute celebrating Groucho's birthday.

(See also: Berlin, Irving; Vera-Ellen)

MILLER, DAVID
(1909-92)
Director of *Love Happy* (*qv*), New Jersey-born David Miller's first experience of film was as a copy boy at National Screen Service, where trailers were made. He formally entered the film industry in 1930 as a second assistant cutter at Columbia Pictures. During the 1930s he edited various M-G-M short subjects before starting to direct them, working for a while under producer Jack Cummings (*qv*). Miller's first opportunity for feature-length work came when he was asked to take

over 1941's *Billy the Kid*. His third feature, *Flying Tigers* (1943), was made on a joint loan-out to Republic with John Carroll (*qv*), who received second billing after its star, John Wayne. Miller spent part of the war in Frank Capra's battle-location unit, making the series *Why We Fight*. Miller had known Capra since helping to cut his film *Ladies of Leisure* in 1930. In one of his rare interviews, conducted by James Bawden for issue 126 of *Classic Images*, Miller recalled that after *Love Happy* 'Groucho became a big booster', recommending Miller to Bing Crosby. As a consequence, Miller directed Crosby and Barry Fitzgerald in *Top o'the Morning* (1949). Among David Miller's best-known films are *Sudden Fear* (1953), *Twist of Fate* (1954, also co-wrote), *The Opposite Sex* (1956), *The Story of Esther Costello* (GB 1957) and *Lonely Are the Brave* (1962); less memorable were *Hail Hero!* (1969) and *Executive Action* (1973)

(See also: M-G-M; Monroe, Marilyn)

MINEAU, CHARLOTTE (1891-?)

Statuesque actress, usually in comedy, often seen in Chaplin shorts of the 'Teens (she is the store detective in 1916's *The Floorwalker*). Work in the 1920s includes a Hal Roach short of 1927, *Love 'Em and Weep*, one of the early pre-teaming appearances of Laurel & Hardy (*qv*). In the Marx Brothers' *Monkey Business* (*qv*) she is the woman caught in an illicit *liaison* by Groucho, who is himself engaged in a not dissimilar activity with Thelma Todd (*qv*).

(See also: Chaplin, Charlie)

MINNIE'S BOYS

A title describing the Marxes in relation to their mother, Minnie Marx (*qv*), the first *Minnie's Boys* was to have been a biographical film produced by Sol Siegel, the man responsible for 1947's fictionalized Pearl White biopic, *The Perils of Pauline*. (Siegel also produced the 1952 comedy *Monkey Business*, which bears no other similarity to the

Marx Brothers film of that name.) Siegel's project reached no further than scripting stage. It was an entirely different *Minnie's Boys* that actually saw production, as a stage musical. Producer Arthur Whitelaw discussed the project with Groucho, who in the end received a consultant's credit. According to Hector Arce, Groucho vetoed Whitelaw's choice for Minnie, Totie Fields, in favour of Shelley Winters (who resembled Groucho's mother to some degree). The book was written by Groucho's son, Arthur, in collaboration with Robert Fisher. The show tried out from late 1969 and finally opened at New York's Imperial Theatre on 26 March 1970. Although ostensibly a chronicle of the Brothers' development as personalities and entertainers, a titular obligation seems to have diverted the play's overall focus towards their mother. Given that most audiences would have been attracted instead by the team's own reputation, this seems an odd decision, except perhaps as the family's tribute to their matriarch. As related in the play, the Marxes' tale is at times almost as interesting as the true story would have been. There is a surface resemblance between the two, mostly in terms of place names, Minnie's corralling of her directionless offspring and the fact that their father was an inept tailor, but otherwise drama has mostly overtaken history. For example, Minnie joins the cast of *Fun in Hi Skule* (*qv*) dressed as a giant rabbit; Zeppo is with the team throughout (at an impossibly early age) and Gummo never enters show business; the Marxes' vaudeville blacklisting is supposed to have resulted from a financially limiting contract with Albee, and consequent insistence on a pay rise; while in a rousing finale, it is implied that their stage characters became permanent only with *I'll Say She Is!* (*qv*). This last, however untrue, works as a dramatic device because the show deliberately (and perhaps wisely) does not burden the actors with a consistent need for close impersonation; such a move is

fine for a pastiche but less suited to a nominal life history. Instead, there are periodic hints at what is to come, as in a song (*Where Was I When They Passed Out Luck?*) in which the various brothers, lamenting their imagined lack of gifts, inadvertently name the talents with which they have been endowed. Easily the best thing in the score (by Larry Grossman and Hal Hackady) is a Tango-like piece, *You Remind Me of You*, obviously inspired by Groucho's 'Everything about you reminds me of you' remark in *A Night at the Opera* (*qv*). Designed to represent a prototype encounter with Margaret Dumont (*qv*), this becomes a duet between Groucho and a theatrical landlady. Groucho, who joined the cast onstage at the opening night's conclusion, later expressed approval of his portrayal by Lewis J. Stadlen; Chico was played by Irwin Pearl; Harpo by Daniel Fortus; Gummo by Gary Raucher; and Zeppo by Alvin Kupperman. Arny Freeman played Sam 'Frenchie' Marx (*qv*). *Minnie's Boys* lasted just over two months. There had been a total of 64 performances after 80 previews, and losses were in excess of $550,000. Apart from an original cast album (on Project 3 TS 6002D), there were a number of amateur productions around the USA and, in 1972, at the Melbourne National Theatre. An intended American revival in 1979, starring Martha Raye, was abandoned only through financial problems. In 1980, the actor who played Groucho in the Australian revival, John Diedrich, was director and star of a production of *Oklahoma!* touring Great Britain; when the company agreed to stage a late-night charity show, Diedrich chose *Minnie's Boys*. It was in this way that, on 9 May 1980, *Minnie's Boys* received its UK première, at the Bristol Hippodrome (where the Marxes themselves appeared in 1922). The show was slightly adapted for this revival, placing less emphasis on Minnie and incorporating more material in the team's familiar style. Diedrich directed but did not repeat the Groucho role, which was taken by Linal Haft. A further charity show was staged at the Grand Theatre, Leeds, on 3 July 1980. There were hopes of bringing it to London in a full-scale professional version, but nothing came of it. A report of the UK presentations, and an interview with John Diedrich, were contributed by Peter Dixon to the November 1980 *Freedonia Gazette* (*qv*).

(See also: Abandoned projects; Characters; Children; Impersonators; *On the Mezzanine*; Records; Television; Vaudeville)

MIRANDA, CARMEN (1913-55)

Known as 'the Brazilian Bombshell' (though actually born in Portugal), Carmen Miranda gave extroversion a new meaning; her loud clothing (with matching voice) complemented vivid make-up and distinctive headwear, the latter of which tended to comprise the weekly stock of a busy fruiterer. She was engaging for all that, and gyrated her happy way through a succession of Fox musicals of the war years (*Down Argentine Way*, *The Gang's All Here*, etc.). There is also rumour of a 'special' film designed to entertain wartime servicemen, in which she performed a high-kicking dance *sans* underwear. Matters had quietened down somewhat by the time she co-starred with Groucho in *Copacabana* (*qv*) in 1947, though she had a hectic time on-screen when trying to portray both her usual character and a veiled *alter ego*. So hectic, in fact, that Groucho had comparatively few opportunities to shine; in *The Secret Word is Groucho* he punningly recalled both the experience and his co-star's distinctive headgear. He had 'a peachy time' on the picture, but was aware of 'playing second banana to the tropical fruit on Carmen Miranda's head'. For all that, Groucho liked Carmen Miranda but did not work with her again; according to letters anthologized in *Love, Groucho*, the studio would have liked further Marx-Miranda efforts but

Groucho's loud suit can't compete with **Carmen Miranda***'s outfit; a publicity pose for their only film together,* Copacabana

Groucho believed her accent tended to obscure the feed lines.

(See also: Advertising; Kinsky, Leonid; Letters)

MIRRORS

(Marx Brothers films *qv*)
As the team's primarily visual comedian, one would expect Harpo to dominate any routines involving mirrors; yet it is Groucho who, in *A Day at the Races*, offers condemning analysis of what turns out to be his own reflection, while Groucho and Harpo have a fifty-fifty share in the celebrated mirror sequence of *Duck Soup*. Harpo repeated the latter sequence with Lucille Ball (*qv*) in 1955 (see **Television**). In *The Big Store*, Harpo has an ingenious mirror sequence to himself, when he appears to play in a trio comprising himself and two quite independent reflections.

(See also: White magic)

MR GREEN'S RECEPTION

(Marx Brothers sketch)
(Marx Brothers films and shows *qv*)
A direct outgrowth of their sketch *Fun in Hi Skule* (with which it played initially), *Mr Green's Reception* was in effect a second act added to the earlier routine, acquiring its own existence as the original schoolroom skit was discarded. The errant pupils, now adults, are invited to the country cottage of their former teacher, Mr Green, to celebrate his decade of retirement. Long after outgrowing hurled oranges and comparing the earth to Sunday cufflinks, each contributes to the party with either jokes or musical specialities, among them of course the harp and piano. The production effect of the cast departing on a prop boat seems to have been retained, but specific details of the

sketch are elusive; cast seems to have been much the same as the school act. *Harpo Speaks* describes Minnie Marx (*qv*), always seeking 'class', investing in a gross of red paper carnations to decorate the teacher's cottage. It was Harpo's job to pin these to the set. (The same source offers a poignant reminder of the show, from when Minnie suffered a fatal stroke in 1929. She did not respond to any words until Harpo said he had come to pin the carnations on Mr Green's cottage, whereupon Minnie smiled and died almost immediately.) Harpo's version is that the 'garbage man' joke originated in this show (see also **Home Again** and **On the Mezzanine**) but Groucho's more reliable memory suggests a later début. They are known to have performed this sketch *circa* 1913-14 to generally good effect, though reviews became less enthusiastic and, presumably, audiences: Groucho's much-quoted 1931 article, *Bad Days Are Good Memories*, speaks of *Mr Green's Reception* playing to four people in Battle Creek, Michigan, in a theatre with seating capacity nearing three thousand. In the late summer of 1914 *Mr Green's Reception* was given a complete overhaul by Al Shean (*qv*) as *Home Again*.

*The **Mr Green's Reception** company on tour. Gummo, centre back; Chico, second from left in middle row; Groucho, fifth from right; Harpo, left of foreground*
Paul G. Wesolowski Collection

(See also: Books; Harp, the; Piano, the; Vaudeville)

MR MUSIC (Paramount 1950)
Groucho made a guest appearance in this Bing Crosby vehicle, probably as a result either of their contemporary radio work together or because the script was by Arthur Sheekman (*qv*). The plot is about a songwriter (Crosby) whose work takes second place to just about everything. The film holds little interest and is overlong; the best sequence is the meeting of Crosby and Groucho backstage and their duet to the Johnny Burke-James Van Heusen song *Life is So Peculiar*.

(See also: *Flywheel, Shyster and Flywheel*; Guest appearances; Paramount Pictures; Radio; Songs)

MONKEY BUSINESS
(Marx Brothers film)
Released by Paramount, 19 September 1931. Copyrighted 17 September 1931, LP 2486.
6,947 ft (contemporary UK footage quoted as 6,298 ft); 77 minutes.
Produced by Herman Mankiewicz (uncredited). Directed by Norman Z. McLeod. Assistant director (uncredited) Charles Barton. Camera: Arthur L. Todd. Screenplay: S.J. Perelman and Will B. Johnstone. Additional dialogue: Arthur Sheekman. With Groucho, Harpo, Chico and Zeppo Marx (*themselves*), Rockcliffe Fellowes (Joe Helton), Harry Woods

Above: Mark Newell collection
*Below: Four stowaways - enough to sing 'Sweet Adeline' - in **Monkey Business***
BFI Stills, Posters and Designs

(*Alky Briggs*), Thelma Todd (*Lucille Briggs*), Ruth Hall (*Mary Helton*), Tom Kennedy (*Gibson*), Otto Fries (*Second Mate*), Ben Taggart (*Captain*), Evelyn Pierce (*manicurist*), Vince Barnett (*man in deckchair*), Maxine Castle (*opera singer*), Leo Willis (*gangster*), Sam 'Frenchie' Marx (*dockside onlooker*).

Aboard an ocean liner, Gibson, a ship's officer, reports to the Captain with news of four stowaways. The number has been determined by their singing *Sweet Adeline*. We see the quartet below, residing in barrels marked 'kippered herring'. They escape detection until the barrels are raised

Monkey Business *echoes Groucho's own recent adventures with Customs. Here they pose in line for the benefit of the stills photographer; in the film, their attempts to pass through are made separately*
BFI Stills, Posters and Designs

aloft, whereupon they are chased through the ship (pausing to entertain the paying passengers with an impromptu musical item). Harpo conceals himself beneath a man sitting in a deckchair while Groucho confronts the Captain about his supposed incompetence. He takes over the Captain's office, joined by Chico, and has the skipper's lunch sent up. Gibson fails to spot them and they sit down to eat. The Captain, permitted to sit at his own dinner table, suspects them of being stowaways, and is locked into a closet. Gibson resumes the chase as Groucho and Chico depart with the food. Harpo leans against a wall, covering the first two letters of a sign that reads 'women'. A gentleman passenger is ejected from the room. Zeppo makes the acquaintance of Mary Helton as Harpo hides out in a children's Punch-and-Judy show. Gibson tries to extricate him but the Captain takes Harpo for a puppet. He changes his mind and grabs Harpo's leg. He and Gibson tug mightily at the

limb, joined in time by Harpo. The stowaway exits on a small trolley. Chico is in the barber shop, making time with a pretty manicurist ('You got 'it'... and you can keep it'). Chico and Harpo masquerade as barbers, and 'snoop' the Second Mate's moustache to oblivion. Among the passengers are gangster Alky Briggs and his wife Lucille, a woman restless through being confined to their cabin. Briggs wants Joe Helton, also a passenger, to 'put the okay' on his gang; he leaves the cabin, unaware that the clothes closet contains a

fugitive Groucho. He makes time with Lucille and adopts an outraged tone when Briggs returns, issuing threats. Briggs is impressed by Groucho's nerve. When Zeppo also takes refuge in the cabin, Briggs realizes they are stowaways and takes them on as henchmen. They are given guns, which are disposed of promptly. Harpo acquires a frog from a lily pond (its presence on an ocean liner unexplained); Chico is pursued by Gibson. They observe a chess game and take over the board. Joe Helton, meanwhile, examines a newspaper describing him as a millionaire racketeer returning to America with his daughter, Mary. She has been to a finishing school and Joe intends to retire into smart society. Briggs arrives for a 'friendly talk' but Helton will not sanction Briggs' take-over of his former territory. Harpo and Chico wander in with the chessboard and send Briggs on his way, using Harpo's taxi horn to simulate a rifle. They are engaged as Helton's bodyguards; Groucho, from the rival faction, looks in ('I'm spying on you!'). Helton feels confident enough to take a walk on deck. His

Harpo pilots a bustle in the party scene of
Monkey Business
BFI Stills, Posters and Designs

erstwhile bodyguards lose track of him and he is trailed by the re-armed Groucho and Zeppo. They lose him and run into Briggs and his wife, engaged in a fearful row. Groucho leaves Briggs the gun, thinking he has greater need of it. He then finds Helton, offering him an insurance-style bodyguard service. Groucho reasons that instead of two men attacking him and two men defending him, it would be more economical to hire Groucho to perform both functions. Between chasing girls, Harpo loses his pet frog. He tries to retrieve it from a hoarse passenger who claims to have a frog in his throat. The ship docks in New York. An opera diva speaks to the press but is interviewed by Groucho instead ('Is it true you're getting a divorce as soon as your husband recovers his eyesight?'). The photographer discovers Harpo under the hood instead of his camera. Zeppo promises he'll never leave Mary Helton, before disappearing with Gibson in pursuit. The stowaways try to disembark but can go nowhere without a passport. Fortunately Zeppo has run into a celebrity, Maurice Chevalier, and stolen his passport. Each of them takes the passport through Customs, trying to justify ownership by singing Chevalier's *You Brought a New Kind of Love To Me*. Harpo attempts the illusion by means of a gramophone strapped to his back. None of them succeed but when a passenger faints, 'Doctor' Groucho has him sent ashore by stretcher. When the stretcher is placed on the quayside, Gibson is furious to see four stowaways emerge. A newspaper informs us of a party at Helton's, intended as Mary's society début. Briggs has placed some of his thugs among the musicians; Harpo and Chico arrive on the running board of a limousine, but cannot get past the bouncers. Mary, dancing with Zeppo,

notices the strange people who are present. Groucho is among them, making nonsense announcements and chasing various women. Helton announces 'the sweetest little thing in the whole wide world' but Harpo, a rose between his teeth, appears in lieu of Mary. He is escorted away. Out on the verandah, Groucho is briefed by Briggs. After Briggs has left, Lucille appears and is wooed by Groucho, who miaows in best tomcat fashion. Amid a Viennese waltz, Groucho suggests they 'lodge with my fleas in the hills' but Lucille vanishes on her husband's

London takes **Monkey Business** to its heart, if not unconditionally
Mark Newell Collection

return. Groucho is ordered to spy on Helton, but makes no effort to do so. Chico disposes of the pianist and takes over. Harpo floats around the dance floor concealed in a detached bustle. Groucho introduces a soprano, accompanied on the harp. Harpo takes the instrumentalist's place, thumbing his nose at the singer while playing *O Sole Mio*. Chico requests the tune that goes 'da-da-da-da-dum-da' and is treated to a harp rendition of *Sugar in the Morning*. Helton learns that Mary has been abducted. Groucho, aware of Briggs' plans, leads them to an old barn. He and Chico arrive by cab,

cheat the driver out of his fare and set up a picnic in a haystack. Mary is in the loft (Chico: 'It's better to have loft and lost ...'); the two rescuers are chased by one of Briggs' henchmen. Harpo arrives, keeping the man at bay with a pitchfork until he grabs it away and snaps it. Zeppo is on hand to knock him cold and heads for the captive girl. Briggs reaches the barn but Harpo and Chico knock out his henchmen. Zeppo engages Briggs in a fist fight as Groucho offers a radio-style commentary. Helton is on cue to congratulate the victorious Zeppo as the others pitch hay. 'What are you doing?' he asks. 'I'm looking a for a needle in a haystack' replies Groucho.

Monkey Business was a departure for the team in two ways: it saw their migration to Hollywood after years based in New York, where their first two pictures had been made; it was also their first vehicle written specifically for the screen, with no opportunity to test the material on live audiences. Paramount (*qv*) wanted them on the West Coast and, with no Broadway commitments, the Marxes acquiesced. They began looking for writers towards the end of 1930, recruiting S.J. Perelman, Will B. Johnstone and Nat Perrin (all *qv*). Of these only Johnstone, who had written for them in the past, knew what to expect. It was up to Perelman and Johnstone to concoct a first draft, while the Marxes disappeared to fulfil a London engagement for C.B. Cochran (*qv*). They had not intended to write a film at all: according to Perelman, they were supposed to devise a radio series, but Groucho deemed the 'misty notion' of placing the Marxes as stowaways on a liner as more suited to their new film. Hector Arce's *Groucho* records both this idea and the college setting of

Horse Feathers (*qv*) to have been submitted to Groucho by a writer named Bert Granet, who was not involved in either film. These submissions may have been coincidental but Granet was compensated by some non-Marx screenwriting with Arthur Sheekman (*qv*). The absence of any acrimony is implicit in Granet and his wife, Charlotte, becoming two of Groucho's closest friends later in life. In the Marxes' absence, Perelman, Johnstone and Perrin were shipped off to California, were they were entrusted to producer Herman Mankiewicz (*qv*). Perelman's account suggests he and Johnstone were fine as long as they left Mankiewicz to an after-lunch snooze. The producer had advised caution when dealing with the Marx Brothers, and was vindicated at one point when Mankiewicz had to intercede on their behalf, albeit by default: a wire from the anxious Marxes suggested these novice scribes should be dismissed, a recommendation Mankiewicz wisely ignored. On returning from England, the comedians (minus Zeppo) contributed two days' work to a benefit show for Heywood Broun before heading west for a meeting with their writers. Perelman described more than the expected number of people in attendance, three of the four brothers having brought wives (Harpo, then unmarried, was accompanied by two girlfriends) plus additional writers (presumably Sheekman and Perrin), various friends and even pets; Zeppo had acquired two Afghan hounds while in Britain and, quarantine notwithstanding, had them in tow. Chico's dog decided to pick a fight with these seemingly illegal immigrants just as the nervous writers prepared for execution. It might as well have been a garrotting, for after Perelman concluded his reading, complete with camera angles, the silence was broken by Groucho's evaluation: 'It stinks.' Work was needed and rewriting commenced. According to Joe Adamson, the second draft was mostly

by Perelman and Arthur Sheekman, while some contributions are evidently those of Nat Perrin. Individual gags were the product of many hands, some of them hired for the occasion such as ex-vaudeville man Solly Violinsky and cartoonist J. Carver Pusey (whose contribution has been disputed), along with Mankiewicz, the Marxes themselves plus such informal visitors as Eddie Cantor (*qv*). Al Shean (*qv*) has been credited with supplying one line. Elements were incorporated from the team's recent UK visit, not least when introducing a British-style Punch-and-Judy show and converting their old agent's office sketch (filmed separately to promote this feature) into an equivalent of Groucho's traumatic experience with Customs (detailed in the **C.B. Cochran** entry). One might add that an on-screen newspaper confirms the voyage as being between London and New York. It was hectic but seemingly appreciated by most of the talents involved, though fledgling director Norman McLeod (*qv*) was unnerved by Zeppo's decision to visit San Francisco in mid-shooting and Nat Perrin mourned his deleted first version of the barbershop scene. Perelman, in keeping with his attitude to California and the movie business it housed, described instead 'five months of drudgery and Homeric quarrels, ambuscades, and intrigues that would have shamed the Borgias'. Although the film loses momentum during the party sequence, and simply stops altogether after filling seven reels, *Monkey Business* includes some of the Marxes' best work and is much quoted. Groucho has some memorable put-downs (several of them noted above), Chico's mental processes are allowed full rein (as when calling Columbus' route to America 'Columbus Circle' or dismissing the Captain's bed as 'That'sa the bunk') and Harpo performs the aforementioned gag with the 'women' sign. Instead of importing an unrelated juvenile, Zeppo becomes the romantic lead, both an economical move and a substantial role sometimes

misattributed to him in earlier shows. Even their father, Sam Marx (*qv*), may be seen as an onlooker as his sons wave to Tom Kennedy (*qv*) from the dockside. He is also supposed to be visible on board ship, either through a continuity error or an inside joke, but is difficult to spot. Margaret Dumont (*qv*) was disposed of for this and the next picture, her place being taken somewhat by comedienne Thelma Todd (*qv*). Perelman justly considered *Monkey Business* 'a muscular hit', but would have been outraged when, in *Life* magazine of 30 October 1931, Harry Evans credited Groucho with 'making the lines seem more original than they are'. (It should be noted that *Life* was a contemporary humour magazine, not the august journal later bearing that name.) A little earlier, on 13 October, *Variety*'s favourable review seemed more conscious of the gags than any supposed story, while commenting subliminally on the team's migration west by comparing the plot to 'one of those California bungalows which miraculously spring up overnight'. On 18 October, Mordaunt Hall of the *New York Times* gave the writers rather more their due: 'S.J. Perelman and William B. Johnstone, who are responsible for the story and some of the comic lines, have given these Marx Brothers plenty of opportunity to air their peculiar brand of humour.' Hall, reporting upon the previous day's early-morning screening, compared the experience to laughing at a midnight presentation of Chaplin's *The Gold Rush* several years before. Though opinion was reserved as to whether it was funnier than their preceding film, *Animal Crackers* (*qv*), 'few persons will be able to go to the Rivoli and keep a straight face'. In dwelling upon some of the gags, Hall noted that 'even the sober Zeppo gets a laugh ... when he declares that there is mighty pretty country around there, as he points to the ocean'. Hall's preoccupation was with Groucho's lines, among them his self-description as someone who has licked his weight in wild caterpillars, plus the immortal 'I've worked myself up from nothing to a state of extreme poverty.' Reaction in the UK was mixed. The team's east coast films had made a considerable impact, though their appeal seems to have been essentially urban. The *Kinematograph Weekly* of 1 October 1931 seemed quite definite about *Monkey Business* 'not coming quite up to the standard of the stars' previous pictures' (a view completely opposed by the *Daily Mail*, incidentally), though allowing it to be an 'excruciating diversion for all who can appreciate their brand of humour'. The review spoke of 'bright gags' and 'brilliant absurdities', repeating its view of Groucho as 'the presiding genius of this happy team' plus the usual difficulty in catching all of the fast-paced jokes. It was decided that the team's methods were already becoming 'a little stale', but the whole review suddenly becomes rather suspect when we are told that Zeppo plays piano while Chico handles the love interest. *Monkey Business* was still enjoying its pre-release London run at the Carlton when Maurice Grossman, of Britain's *Film Weekly*, supplied an 'interview' with the Marxes for the issue of 5 December. 'I entered the studio full of pep and punch,' wrote Grossman; 'I left it a dithering wreck.' Much of the piece resembles a publicist's fabrication, or more specifically a contemporary Englishman's idea of Marxian humour, especially when attributing to Groucho some fairly atrocious grammar. There are occasional flashes of authenticity, one of them a reference to Groucho's first book, *Beds*, then virtually unknown in Britain; it is however unlikely that any interviewer would have found them at Paramount, as was implied, after the completion of *Monkey Business*. More importantly, the article serves as measure of the comedians' growing, if specialized, British following. A later *Film Weekly*, from 17 June 1932, emphasizes the divided British reaction in its description of *Monkey Business* as

'a film which has delighted thousands and annoyed thousands'. This remark was designed to accompany a reader's letter, calling the film 'absolutely terrible. Honestly, how they got on the screen is beyond my comprehension.' This lack of comprehension might also have applied to the gags which, with all the best will in the world, were light years beyond most of the things being done in Britain prior to the Second World War. Today *Monkey Business* is a TV perennial on both sides of the Atlantic, in good prints though with a re-recorded soundtrack given to sibilance and flutter, especially during the closing music. A transcript of the film, published in book form, notes a slightly different sequence of events in the National Film Archive print, in which Zeppo's first scene with Ruth Hall (*qv*) takes place immediately after Groucho and Chico have commandeered the Captain's meal. It is possible, though not probable, that original UK prints of *Monkey Business* were edited in this fashion.

(See also: Barnett, Vince; Barton, Charles; Boats, ships; Books; Chaplin, Charlie; *The Cocoanuts* [play]; Continuity errors; Dancing; Deleted scenes; Doctors; Fellowes, Rockcliffe; Female impersonation; Fighting; Gambling; Gangsters; Gordon, Max; Hall, Ruth; Harp, the; Home movies; Insults; Mineau, Charlotte; *Monkey Business* [promo]; Names; Opera; Paramount Pictures; Piano, the; Radio; Records; Ryskind, Morrie; Sheekman, Arthur; Taggart, Ben; Television; Video releases; White, Leo; Woods, Harry)

MONKEY BUSINESS (promo)

After years of speculation over the long-lost *Humorisk* (*qv*), posterity was instead permitted its earliest slice of Marx Brothers material by means of a re-enactment. When *Monkey Business* (*qv*) was in preparation, Paramount Pictures (*qv*) needed an advance glimpse for its promotional feature, *The House That Shadows Built*. This fifty-minute film incorporates clips

from early silent productions plus details of Paramount's forthcoming releases for the 1931-2 season, some of which seem never to have been completed. Scenes are incorporated from a few of these productions but *Monkey Business* is represented by an unrelated, five-minute sketch from their Broadway show *I'll Say She Is!* (*qv*). The sketch had been adapted into that show from their earlier *On the Mezzanine* (*qv*) thus making it the oldest specific Marx routine preserved on film. The scene opens in the office of theatrical agent, Mr Lee. Zeppo arrives, identifying himself as Sammy Brown, singer and dancer. He offers an impression of Maurice Chevalier and, complete with straw boater, sings 'You Brought a New Kind of Love to Me'. The agent is unimpressed. The next visitor is Chico, also sporting a straw boater. He gives his name as Tomalio,

Monkey Business (promo): *A thirsty foursome in the agent's office set. Note the large portrait of Maurice Chevalier, target of their impersonations both in this item and the feature it was designed to promote*

an acrobat, but auditions with a further Chevalier routine (albeit with an Italian accent). He receives much the same response as did Zeppo. Groucho enters, describing himself as a 'dramatic actor' in a Dutch-comic voice. The accent is discarded as he claims to be 'Caesar's ghost'. Groucho, it seems, once played in *Ben-Hur* ('a girl, she played the part of Ben ... I played Hur'). He offers still another Chevalier turn. Harpo completes the quartet and is greeted enthusiastically by his brothers. Until now most of the dialogue has been in rhyming couplets but this is abandoned after the agent reads Harpo's calling-card: 'My name is what d'ya care/My home is anywhere/People say I'm awful dumb/So I thought to you I'd co-!' The agent breaks off, furious, but Groucho pacifies him by suggesting Harpo might be crazy. He employs a simple test, asking Harpo if he wants to go on the stage. Harpo nods. 'Crazy,' concludes Groucho. Chico tells Mr Lee of Harpo's dancing skills. Harpo borrows the agent's boater for a dance version of the Chevalier song. 'I wouldn't offer him a dollar a week!' says Mr Lee. 'Not so loud,' replies Chico, 'he'll take it!' Zeppo tells Mr Lee how funny the others can be while detailing a play he has written. He continues despite Mr Lee's attempt to speak on the telephone. Harpo plays with the receiver while Chico and Groucho carry on their own loud conversations. Harpo inflates a rubber glove, which he 'milks' into his hat. The soundtrack is filled with four incoherent voices when a girl (Ruth Hall?) walks in. Groucho and Chico make a fuss of her; Harpo walks across the desk, perches on the agent's head and joins their greeting. Zeppo continues to describe his play as the scene fades. The sketch bears little resemblance to anything in the final version of *Monkey Business*, aside from one line of dialogue (Groucho responds to Chico with 'There's my argument; restrict immigration'). Less specific parallels are the Chevalier imitations plus the casting of Ben Taggart (*qv*) as

the agent. This film was discovered in the late 1970s and transcribed in Charlotte Chandler's book, *Hello, I Must Be Going*. When evaluating the sketch, Chandler makes an important point by detailing Zeppo's pivotal role; although he adds to the chaos, Zeppo is sufficiently lucid to form a bridge between his brothers and the outside world, a function eminently more useful than Groucho's customary dismissal of him as 'only the juvenile' might suggest. It is reasonable to assume that Zeppo had more to do onstage until *Cocoanuts* (*qv*) relegated him to a subsidiary position. Chandler credits the Cinémathèque Française for supplying a print of this film, but the survival of further originals is implied by the varying quality of available copies. The American Film Institute's *Catalog of Motion Pictures* notes the absence of any copyright registration despite such a notice on the feature's opening titles. Its apparent Public Domain status has resulted in this item having been widely circulated in home movie and video form.

(See also: Characters; Hall, Ruth; Home movies; Trailers; Video releases)

MONROE, MARILYN (1926-62)

A twentieth-century icon, Marilyn Monroe's life and career need no elaboration in these pages save to record *Love Happy* (*qv*) as one of her first screen appearances. She may be seen for little more than an instant towards the film's conclusion, as a prospective client of detective Sam Grunion (Groucho), who attempts to follow her out of the office despite being cornered by a gun-toting villain. In a *Classic Images* interview, director David Miller (*qv*) recalled there having been room for a foil for Groucho and that Johnny Hyde, Miller's agent, brought along another client, Marilyn Monroe. According to Miller, Hyde was very much in love with Monroe but they were never married. Monroe was one of three actresses who auditioned

for producer Lester Cowan (*qv*), who asked Groucho to attend. Miller said she had dirty fingernails and 'a look of bewilderment', all of this overlooked because 'she fairly oozed sex'. Not surprisingly, it was the latter that commanded Groucho's attention. When asked which girl he favoured, Groucho responded that it would be crazy to hire anyone but Monroe. Each candidate had been required to walk up and down the room; when attending a festival in Vienna during April 1966, Groucho described Monroe as 'the greatest walker I ever saw'. She did the scene in a spectacularly low-cut dress, with the result that Groucho could scarcely remember his dialogue. *Love Happy* did little to advance Monroe's career (or that of the Marxes), though Cowan is said to have found her a few jobs in commercials. In the event, she benefited whatever future *Love Happy* had in reissues, especially when it was billed as 'the picture that discovered Marilyn Monroe'. A postscript: Arthur Marx (in *My Life With Groucho: a Son's Eye View*) recalls that, a few days after his late father's cremation, a letter was found to the effect that Groucho did not wish to be cremated, preferring instead to lie alongside the remains of Marilyn Monroe at the Westwood Cemetery. 'The same old Groucho,' concluded his son. 'Even after he had shuffled off this mortal coil, he wanted to lie throughout eternity alongside the most glamorous sex symbol of the age.'

(See also: Deaths; Kane, Helen)

MOUSTACHES, BEARDS

(Marx Brothers shows and films *qv*) Groucho's moustache is perhaps the team's best-known symbol worldwide. He later admitted it gave him something to hide behind, one of several indications of Groucho's underlying insecurity. The fact that his moustache is painted (as are the eyebrows) is entirely in keeping with his character's fraudulent nature, a transparently artificial adornment openly challenging disbelief from the outside world. As a device, it succeeds to the point where it is often overlooked, as evidenced by the number of would-be impersonators who have used an actual moustache. The illusion is assisted, of course, by the vague acceptability of such a 'flat' decoration, even if composed of greasepaint; by contrast, when Bobby Clark (of the Clark & McCullough team, who were contemporaries of and, in a sense, successors to the Marxes on Broadway) favoured painted spectacles, the absence of any third dimension made for idiocy rather than audacity. The usual explanation of the painted moustache is that Groucho was once late for a performance of *On the Mezzanine* in 1921 and hastily smeared on a makeshift equivalent (the reason for his lateness varies between having rushed back after the birth of his son to a more prosaic dallying in a restaurant). When nobody seemed concerned, he decided it was much less trouble than attaching a crêpe version, despite an initial objection from the theatre manager. The painted eyebrows followed later. Less often quoted today (but widely circulated in the 1930s) is that he abandoned the original

moustache after it caught fire when he lit a cigar. Whatever its genesis, Groucho retained the greasepaint version from vaudeville until the late 1940s, when a more plausible (though still artificial) moustache was adopted for *Copacabana* (*qv*). It is said that Paramount's Monta Bell (*qv*) tried to get Groucho to use a crêpe moustache for the film version of *Cocoanuts*, on the grounds that the greasepaint reflected their studio lights; Groucho's only concession was to mute the effect with talcum powder. Groucho recalled Walter Wanger (*qv*) as having made the request, but the idea was in any case probably that of director Robert Florey (*qv*). Groucho seldom wore a real moustache although a few 1920s photographs exist showing him with a short-lived smudge above the lip. It was around the time of *You Bet Your Life* (*qv*) that a decision was taken to grow a genuine moustache. Groucho had decided on a normal, non-comic image in this new environment but at the same time was anxious to be recognizable; when out of make-up, Groucho could pass incognito, useful in private life but reputedly irksome when he was overlooked amid other stars

Moustaches, beards: *Groucho abandoned his greasepaint moustache for a realistic - but still fake - equivalent in* Copacabana. *He grew a real one soon after*

during wartime tours. The moustache stayed with him for the rest of his life. Other facially hirsute types surface in the Marx films: in *Monkey Business* Harpo and Chico 'snoop' a ship's officer's moustache into oblivion; Groucho systematically yanks the beards of his fellow professors in *Horse Feathers*, one of whom, played by Robert Greig (*qv*), later has his beard stolen by Harpo; similarly, three aviators in *A Night at the Opera* lose their beards (and uniforms) to Harpo, Chico and Allan Jones (*qv*); elsewhere in the film, Groucho adopts a false beard when the brothers attempt to confuse a policeman; Sig Rumann (*qv*) sports a suitably Germanic goatee in each of his films with the team, to which (in *A Day at the Races*) Groucho remarks 'and don't point that beard at me - it may go off!' Again in *Monkey Business*, Chico regrets the absence of his grandfather in the stowaways'

Marilyn Monroe, *then an unknown actress, appears briefly in* Love Happy. *In the film itself, she is seen in Groucho's office; here she joins him on the rooftop set*

barrels, on the grounds of there being insufficient room for his beard. When Groucho suggests bringing the man himself and sending for his beard later, Chico explains that it is coming by 'hair-mail'.

(See also: Colouring; Fries, Otto; London Palladium, the; Paramount Pictures; Smoking; Stage appearances (post-1930); Vaudeville; Wigs)

MUIR, ESTHER (1903 or 1907-95)

Statuesque blonde, somewhat typed as beautiful-but-intimidating; remembered as Flo, the wallpapered girl of *A Day at the Races* (*qv*). She was at one time married to choreographer Busby Berkeley; another of her husbands was Sam Coslow (*qv*), who worked with Groucho as producer/ songwriter for *Copacabana* (*qv*). Comedy fans also recall Miss Muir in Wheeler and Woolsey's *So This is Africa* (1933) and *On Again, Off Again* (1937). One of her last films was *Misbehaving Husbands* (1940), a low-budget PRC vehicle for silent veteran Harry Langdon. According to a profile by Stephen Luminello (in the May-June 1994 *Films in Review*) she was born in Andes, New York, and was forced to abandon a Vassar scholarship on the death of her father. She moved to New York City in search of modelling and acting work, obtaining the latter solely on the strength of having acted in high school productions. Her Broadway career began with a small role in *Greenwich Village Follies of 1922*, culminating in the very successful 1929 show *My Girl Friday*. Again according to Luminello, a Warner Brothers contract intended for Muir went instead to Joan Blondell, who replaced her when *My Girl Friday* went on tour. She migrated west in any case, making her film début in Keaton's *Parlor, Bedroom and Bath* (1931). Her work in *A Day at the Races* included the pre-filming tour, during which she earned sufficient respect for the Marxes to insist on her being retained. She could take the knockabout gags

and was at least once capable of bettering the comedians; she told *Films in Review* of having caught them asleep and bribing the chorus girls to paint their toenails red. The Marxes were left with the problem of explaining it to their wives. According to the *Los Angeles Times*, Esther Muir was living in New York at the time of her death. An exact birthdate for the actress is difficult to determine: American obituaries cite 1903, though 1907 seems to have been more generally accepted hitherto. The *L.A. Times* reports dates varying between 1895 and 1903, the earlier of which has been quoted in at least one UK reference. The chronology of Esther

Muir's early life renders a pre-1900 date extremely unlikely.

(See also: Keaton, Buster; Practical jokes; Torres, Raquel; Women)

Esther Muir *gets wallpapered in* A Day at the Races *(top) and (above) takes centre stage in a contemporary advertisement*
Main picture: BFI Stills, Posters and Designs

NAMES

(Marx Brothers shows and films *qv*)
The Marx Brothers' somewhat
mythological status is reinforced in
their names. Those given at birth are
well known but warrant detailing here;
the same applies to their nicknames
and those by which they were known in
various adventures. Chico started life as
Leonard, and was known usually as Leo
or, sometimes, Lenny. Harpo was
Adolph before anglicizing the name to
Arthur, though in practice he switched
from being called 'Ahdie' to 'Artie'.
Groucho was Julius Henry, after an
uncle wrongly suspected of being rich.
Gummo was Milton, while Zeppo
began as Herbert. Accounts vary as to
the nicknames' origin: when
interviewed by Barry Norman for a
BBC television series, *The Hollywood
Greats*, Zeppo cited a tale not in accord
with the accepted version, in which his
elder brothers shared a dressing room
with a troupe of German acrobats,
whose lack of English caused them to
label the brothers according to their
respective interests. When quoting the
story in his book *The Movie Greats* (it
was not used in the programme),
Norman expressed doubt as to its
authenticity, if only through the
unlikelihood of non-English speakers
constructing descriptive nicknames in
favour of straightforward originals. One
might add that the Marxes' parentage
left them sufficiently fluent in German
for there to have been no language
barrier. The famous and otherwise
universally accepted story is that their
nicknames were bestowed *circa* 1915
by vaudeville monologuist Art Fisher,
during an engagement at Galesburg,
Illinois. One source pinpoints the date
as 15 May 1914, but historian Paul G.
Wesolowski doubts such precision. A
trade paper, *Frank Queen's New York
Clipper*, confirms the Marxes in *Mr
Green's Reception* at Galesburg for 14-
16 May 1914, but does not list Art
Fisher. There is the possibility that
Fisher, an elusive figure in
documentation, was either a local
comic or a last-minute addition.

Wesolowski adds that Galesburg's
papers for that week eschewed theatre
news for a monumental local story,
further hindering verification. It was
Groucho who specified Galesburg as
the venue, his reliability in
documenting other key events lending
credibility; this also makes
chronological sense, for their
nicknames began to receive press
attention within a year of this
appearance. The story itself has Fisher
and the Marxes discussing vaudeville's
recent obsession with names ending in
'o', after a popular newspaper strip.
Fisher was dealing cards and offered
one to 'Harpo'. This brought enough
amusement for him to continue with
'Chicko', after Leo's habit of chasing
'chickens' or 'chicks' (in the feminine
sense). Unsmiling Julius became
'Groucho' and Milton was named
'Gummo', either through wearing
gumshoes (see also **Shoes**) or because
he would sneak up on people as though
wearing them. Zeppo was not present
at the fateful card game (explaining, in
part, his dissenting account) and his
name is less easy to trace. One rather
flimsy version insists that it refers to the
Zeppelins going over at the time of his
birth, substantiated slightly by an
airship motif illustrating his chair on
the *Monkey Business* set. Harpo
recalled that his brother's athleticism
earned him the name 'Zippo' after Mr
Zippo, a trained ape; Herbert justly
favoured a slight amendment.
Elsewhere 'Zippo' is described as
having been a well-publicized freak;
again, the amendment is
understandable. Chico's daughter
Maxine relates an entirely different
story, from the time when most of the
family worked on a farm; in mock-rural
attitude, Chico and the youngest
sibling addressed each other as 'Zeke'
and 'Zep'. This story, by far the most
plausible, is referred to by Zeppo in an
interview with Sylvia B. Golden in the
January 1929 issue of *Theatre
Magazine* (though claiming it was he
who was called 'Zeke', which
subsequently became Zeppo); much of

Names: *the team's nicknames, as explained by canvas chairs on the set of* Monkey Business

the piece is Marxian confusion but Chico's name is again said to derive from chasing 'chickens' and Groucho defines his name, ironically, as 'because I'm always smiling'. Gummo offers an alternative to his usual definition, namely 'because I said I'd never stick to the stage'. Further interest lies in Zeppo's real name being given as 'Herbert Manfred', implying some commemoration of the family's lost first child (see **Births**). The newspaper character referred to in the Art Fisher story is often quoted as 'Knocko the Monk', but this was not a consistent title. The 'monks', or monkey characters, would vary according to episode. *The Groucho Phile* reprints a specimen from December 1910 under the strip's first consistent title, 'Sherlocko the Monk', a Sherlock Holmes type who has a sidekick named Watso. The supporting cast, whose names also finish with 'o', include on this occasion a sour character called 'Groucho', suggesting that Julius may have been first to receive a nickname (the cartoonist, Gus Mager, later had to humanize and variously adapt

'Sherlocko' into 'Hawkshaw the Detective' after complaints from Arthur Conan Doyle's US representatives). In a 1959 BBC-TV programme, *Showtime*, Chico claimed (as have several others) that Groucho's name derived from a 'grouch-bag', a money pouch worn over the chest by vaudevillians (see also **The LeRoy Trio**); Groucho sometimes refuted this theory, insisting that the name referred instead to his dour temperament. Significantly, his *Monkey Business* chair is illustrated with a frowning face. A contemporary cutting from *Variety* (reprinted in *The Marx Brothers Scrapbook*) details the new names, though less than accurately: Gummo appears with a solitary 'm' and 'Chicko' has lost the 'k'. The latter name kept its revised spelling but the brothers themselves adhered to its original pronunciation. The article sanitizes the name's origin, however, describing Leo/Chico as 'an expert on fowl'! A chick (feathered variety) illustrates the back of Chico's canvas chair on the set of *Monkey Business*. The nicknames became known to vaudeville audiences but reverted to strictly private use for *I'll Say She Is!* As a 'legitimate' production, the show was deemed

unsuited to such informality and the original programme describes them by their pre-Fisher titles. Once their nicknames became known to the Broadway world, the programme was suitably amended, reportedly on the insistence of Alexander Woollcott (*qv*). Groucho continued to sign his magazine articles 'Julius H. Marx' into the mid-1920s (and would use the name on official paperwork late in life), but it was Groucho, Chico, Harpo and Zeppo who appeared in the programme when *The Cocoanuts* opened in 1925. Their earlier names had very limited afterlife, surfacing when Groucho's son was named Arthur; of the other Marx children, all the girls had names beginning with 'M', after Minnie (a name given to Harpo's daughter). In contrast, Harpo named his son Bill. One might add that Harpo's own name underwent further amendment in middle age when he adopted the middle name 'Duer', to honour novelist Alice Duer Miller, a close friend. The names given to them in plays and films were invariably quite superfluous, the comedians remaining always identifiably themselves: Groucho's were frequently colourful (if unnecessary), and he would often sign correspondence 'Jeffrey T. Spaulding' or 'Doctor Hackenbush'. His character in vaudeville's *Home Again* started out as 'Schneider' but soon lost the German name; reports of *Home Again*'s latter days, and of its successor, *On the Mezzanine*, refer to him as 'Mr Hammer', a name he would revive in the film version of *Cocoanuts*. Harpo's names tended to make reference either to his silence, temperament or red hair (see **Wigs**); otherwise in vaudeville he was generally billed as a 'nondescript'. Chico was usually given something vaguely Italian-sounding. Their character names are as follows:

The Cocoanuts (stage):
Groucho: Henry W. Schlemmer. Harpo: Silent Sam. Chico: Leo the Wop. Zeppo: Jamison.

Animal Crackers (stage and film):
Groucho: Captain Jeffrey T. Spalding (later 'Spaulding'). Harpo: The Professor. Chico: Emanuel Ravelli. Zeppo: Horatio W. Jamison.

The Cocoanuts (film):
Groucho: Mr Hammer. Zeppo: Jamison. (Harpo and Chico are billed under those names, though a 'wanted' poster describes Harpo as 'Silent Red'.)

Monkey Business:
Billed under their usual nicknames.

Horse Feathers:
Groucho: Professor Quincy Adams Wagstaff. Harpo: Pinky. Chico: Baravelli. Zeppo: Frank Wagstaff.

Duck Soup:
Groucho: Rufus T. Firefly. Harpo: Pinky. Chico: Chicolini. Zeppo: Bob Roland ('Bob Firefly' before rewrites).

A Night at the Opera:
Groucho: Otis B. Driftwood. Harpo: Tomasso. Chico: Fiorello.

A Day at the Races:
Groucho: Dr Hugo Z. Hackenbush. Harpo: Stuffy. Chico: Antonio (Tony).

Room Service:
Groucho: Gordon Miller. Harpo: Faker (Englund). Chico: (Harry) Binelli.

At the Circus:
Groucho: J. Cheever Loophole. Harpo: Punchy. Chico: Antonio (Tony) Pirelli.

Go West:
Groucho: S. Quentin Quale. Harpo: Rusty Panello. Chico: Joe (Joseph) Panello.

The Big Store:
Groucho: Wolf J. Flywheel. Harpo: Wacky. Chico: Ravelli.

A Night in Casablanca:
Groucho: Ronald Kornblow. Harpo: Rusty. Chico: Corbaccio.

Love Happy:
Groucho: Sam Grunion. Chico: Faustino the Great. (Harpo was billed under his usual nickname.)

The revision of their names in *Cocoanuts* seems to have been in keeping with an overall softening of ethnic references in both this and *Animal Crackers*. Those in *Duck Soup* were amended somewhat during the film's preparation (see **Trailers**). An early draft of *A Day at the Races* names Groucho 'Cyrus P. Turntable', but this was jettisoned in favour of 'Dr Quackenbush'; incredibly, this in turn became 'Hackenbush' after the fear of legal action from more than thirty real-life physicians bearing that name (there is, incidentally, mention of a Dr Quackenbush in the 1935 film adaptation of Thackeray's *Vanity Fair*, retitled *Becky Sharp*). According to Allen Eyles, 'S. Quentin Quale' is a vulgar pun that escaped the censor's attention, referring to 'San Quentin quail' or, in other words, the type of under-aged girl known as 'jail bait'. 'Wolf J. Flywheel' commemorates the Marxes' earlier radio series, *Flywheel, Shyster and Flywheel* (*qv*), one episode of which provided the basis for *The Big Store*. Chico's name in both this film

and the radio series, 'Ravelli', was itself recycled from *Animal Crackers*; he used it also in another radio series, *The Circle*. Groucho's solo films (all *qv*) offer a further selection of names: in *Copacabana* he is Lionel Q. Devereux; *Double Dynamite* calls him Emil J. Keck; *A Girl in Every Port* casts him as 'Benny' or, in full, Benjamin Franklin Lynn; while in *Skidoo* he plays a gang boss referred to throughout as 'God'! Harpo's name has resurfaced in latter years. In the 1970s, a singer calling himself 'Harpo' had chart success with a song called *Movie Star*; while talk show hostess Oprah Winfrey's forename is actually a reversal of 'Harpo', after whom she has named her production company.

(See also: Barton, Charles; Censorship; Children; Doctors; Documentaries; Marx, Minnie; Marx, Sam 'Frenchie'; Race; Radio; Records; Songs; Television; Vaudeville; *Will Success Spoil Rock Hunter?*)

NAPOLEON'S RETURN/REVENGE
See: *I'll Say She Is!*; Stage appearances (post-1930)

'N' EVERYTHING
See: *Home Again*

NEWSREELS
Aside from the mainstream releases, there is a percentage of 'sidelight' material contained in newsreels. One item records the team placing their handprints outside Grauman's Chinese Theatre; another the tennis game with Groucho and Charlie Chaplin (*qv*); still another shows Groucho and Chico attending a costume party in September 1933, honouring Walt Disney (Chico is dressed as a witch, while Groucho wears a type of equine boiler suit labelled 'Rex the Wonder Horse'). Also preserved is a motor race - in miniature cars - in which Groucho and Harpo compete against child star Jackie Cooper (Harpo wins by a small margin). A Russian news clip shows Harpo entertaining at a reception

during his visit there in 1933; other clips from the period seem to derive not from news items but editions of Paramount's *Hollywood On Parade* shorts. There are a few brief clips of Groucho and Harpo entertaining troops during the Second World War, usually shot silent; there is a very pleasant sound item from Movietone, in which Chico does a piano singalong with a group of recuperating servicemen. When he arrived in England at the beginning of 1949 he was interviewed at the quayside by a very old-school BBC type. Chico did the interview in character and was asked if he *always* spoke that way. He replied that he spoke like an Italian in their films, 'but I saw what they did to Mussolini, so now I'm-a Greek!'

(See also: Animals; Cars; Documentaries; Home movies; Wartime; Video releases)

A NIGHT AT THE OPERA

(Marx Brothers film)
Released by M-G-M, 15 November 1935 (New York première 8 November). Copyrighted 29 October 1935 (LP 5926).
8,438 ft, 93 minutes; original running time is quoted as 96 minutes. Available copies seem somewhat abridged (see below).
Produced by Irving Thalberg (uncredited). Directed by Sam Wood, assisted by Lesley Selander and Edmund Goulding (both uncredited). Camera: Merritt B. Gerstad.
Screenplay by George S. Kaufman and Morrie Ryskind, from a story by James Kevin McGuinness and an earlier draft (uncredited) by Bert Kalmar and Harry Ruby. Additional dialogue (uncredited) by Al Boasberg. New songs: *Alone*, music by Nacio Herb Brown, lyrics by Arthur Freed; *Cosi-Cosa*, music by Bronislaw Kaper and Walter Jurrman, lyrics by Ned Washington.

With Groucho Marx (*Otis B. Driftwood*), Chico Marx (*Fiorello*), Harpo Marx (*Tomasso*), Kitty Carlisle

The pre-filming tour of **A Night at the Opera** *at Portland, with Dorothy Christy in lieu of Margaret Dumont*
By courtesy of Robert G. Dickson

(*Rosa Castaldi*), Allan Jones (*Ricardo Baroni*), Walter Woolf King (*Rudolfo Lassparri*), Margaret Dumont (*Mrs Claypool*), Siegfried Rumann (*Herman Gottlieb*), Edward Keane (*Ship's Captain*), Robert Emmet(t) O'Connor (*Henderson, plain-clothes officer*), Leo White, Rolfe Sedan, Jay Eaton (*visiting aviators*), Otto Fries (*Otto, lift operator*), Billy Gilbert (*orchestra leader in party for steerage passengers*).

Mrs Claypool has been awaiting her dinner companion, Otis B. Driftwood, for some time. He is paged, and discovered sitting at a different table with a much younger woman. Driftwood leaves her with the bill and joins Mrs Claypool for another meal. Driftwood has been engaged - at a high salary - to get Mrs Claypool into society. Three months have elapsed and he has done nothing. Driftwood

steers the would-be socialite away from the topic by protestations of love, and points out another diner: Herman Gottlieb, Director of the New York Opera Company. Driftwood has arranged for Mrs Claypool to invest $200,000 in the company, guaranteeing social acceptance as a patron of the arts. Gottlieb is introduced to Mrs Claypool and explains how her patronage will enable him to sign Rudolfo Lassparri, the famous tenor. At the Opera House, Lassparri goes backstage to find his dresser, Tomasso, posing in the mirror clad in his employer's Pagliacci costume. Tomasso removes it, but has Lassparri's naval uniform from *Madam Butterfly* underneath. This is also removed, revealing still another costume, that of a peasant girl. Lassparri beats the unfortunate lackey and fires him. Tomasso is thrown out of the dressing room and found by Rosa, the company's diva. She comforts Tomasso as Lassparri makes a pretence of welcoming him. Lassparri's door closes and the sounds of mayhem resume. Rosa has no interest in Lassparri's advances, preferring to dine with Ricardo, who has a minor role in the opera. Fiorello arrives at the theatre to collect his mail; he doesn't work there, but nor does he work anywhere. Fiorello is greeted by Tomasso and they exchange identical gifts, a salami sausage. Tomasso cuts his with an axe. The opera proceeds and Ricardo greets Fiorello in the wings. They studied music together - Ricardo singing and Fiorello piano - but neither has made progress. Fiorello considers his friend to be Lassparri's superior and offers to become his manager. They watch Rosa as she sings; Ricardo wants to marry her but does not think it possible until he is a success. Driftwood joins Mrs Claypool and Gottlieb in their box just as the opera concludes. Gottlieb plans to offer Lassparri $1,000 a night to sing in New York. Driftwood considers how he can get a piece of the money. Tomasso delivers Gottlieb's card to Lassparri, who is surrounded by

A Night at the Opera's stateroom scene: near the beginning ...

admirers. Lassparri invites Rosa to join him for dinner with Gottlieb, implying she could be his leading lady in New York. She leaves instead with Ricardo, while Lassparri takes out his anger on Tomasso. Driftwood intervenes and Tomasso knocks Lassparri cold. Driftwood meets Fiorello, who claims to represent 'the greatest tenor in the world' but is suspiciously vague about the name. Driftwood thinks he means Lassparri and a contract is arranged by which Driftwood receives all but a fraction of the fee. The contract itself is gradually amended to a narrow strip of paper by having sections torn off. When Fiorello queries one section, he is told it is the standard Sanity Clause. 'You can't fool me,' he responds, 'there ain't no Sanity Clause.' Negotiations over, Gottlieb discovers the dazed Lassparri and Driftwood learns whom Fiorello really represents. Lassparri has been signed by Herr Gottlieb. The SS *Americus* sails amid tearful goodbyes. Prior to boarding, Rosa introduces Ricardo to Gottlieb, but the impresario is uninterested. Lassparri makes an

excuse not to sing a farewell to his public (as he is not being paid), but Rosa is happy to oblige. She sings *Alone* at the ship's rail, and is joined in a duet by Ricardo, standing on the quayside. Gottlieb is impressed by Ricardo's singing but will not consider him until he has made a reputation. As the voyage begins, Driftwood delivers a love note from Ricardo to Rosa. Next is a visit to Mrs Claypool's cabin, but she finds his presence improper and is persuaded instead to visit him.

Driftwood reaches the cabin chosen for him by Gottlieb, discovering there is scarcely room both for him and his trunk. On opening his luggage, he finds it consists of Fiorello, Tomasso and Ricardo. As they will leave only after being fed, Driftwood orders them a meal. Before the food is brought, two girls arrive to make up the room; an engineer calls to turn off the heat; a manicurist offers to cut Driftwood's nails ('You'd better make them short, it's getting kinda crowded in here'); next is the engineer's assistant; then a girl looking for her Aunt Minnie, who wants to use the 'phone; she is followed by a cleaner then, at last, the stewards who are bringing food. Mrs Claypool keeps her appointment with Driftwood, opens the door and everyone tumbles outside. At dinner that evening, the Captain pays tribute to his honoured guests, a trio of bearded, uniformed aviators. Among the guests, Gottlieb and Driftwood vie for the affections of wealthy Mrs Claypool. She would prefer Driftwood not to associate with characters such as those she saw around the Opera House; those same characters leave Driftwood's cabin in search of food, which they find at a party among the steerage passengers. Their hunger satisfied, Ricardo sings *Cosi-Cosa* and

... and at its zenith

Gottlieb (Siegfried Rumann) and Otis B. Driftwood compete for Mrs Claypool on board ship in **A Night at the Opera**

Fiorello offers a piano solo. Tomasso takes a turn at the keyboard before switching to the harp for a reprise of *Alone*. Lassparri points out the stowaways to the Captain, who has them placed in the brig. Next day, Driftwood assists the stowaways by throwing them a rope, with which Tomasso can escape via the porthole. He is winched up and down and becomes soaked, but eventually makes his way to the aviators' cabin. When the *Americus* reaches New York, the aviators are bound and gagged, their uniforms stolen and beards clipped off. Wearing them are Fiorello, Tomasso and Ricardo, attending a public reception at City Hall. The Mayor introduces them and Fiorello improvises a speech, detailing their attempts to fly but repeated trips back to get more fuel; Tomasso stalls with endless drinks of water, which loosen his beard. They escape but make headline news. Breakfast in Driftwood's hotel room is interrupted by Henderson, a plain-clothes policeman; his suspicions are aroused by the presence of army cots and of a breakfast table set for four. The contents of the adjoining rooms are systematically rearranged as Henderson tries to give chase; in the end he is convinced he is in the wrong room, as Driftwood, Fiorello and Tomasso pose as an elderly couple plus rocking chair. Ricardo has slipped away to Rosa's room. Lassparri catches Ricardo emerging (innocently) from Rosa's bedroom and makes insinuations. Ricardo strikes him. Lassparri departs, making threats. Driftwood reaches his office, greeting the opera company in high spirits. On finding his name being removed from his office door, Driftwood confronts Gottlieb but finds Lassparri, Mrs Claypool and Henderson also in attendance. Mrs Claypool has fired him, obviously under pressure but ostensibly through his continued association with Fiorello and Tomasso. The lift operator insists on Driftwood departing via the stairs, assisting his journey with a well-placed kick. Driftwood rejoins the stowaways on a park bench. Their despondency escalates on meeting Rosa, whom Lassparri has also had dismissed. A plan is needed. Gottlieb arrives for that evening's performance of *Il Trovatore* to find Driftwood and comrades in his office. They promise to give themselves up if he will permit Rosa to sing, but Gottlieb will not agree. He tries to call Henderson and is knocked cold by Tomasso. Backstage, Tomasso adds *Take Me Out to the Ball Game* to the orchestra's music. Driftwood, wearing Gottlieb's clothes, sits beside Mrs Claypool; Gottlieb, in his underwear, calls the police. Driftwood introduces the evening while Fiorello and Tomasso, batons in hand, engage the conductor in a duel. Gottlieb, now in Driftwood's clothes, reappears and Driftwood, Tarzan-style, makes for the next box. The music switches to *Take Me Out to the Ball Game* and Driftwood sells peanuts. Fiorello and Tomasso disguise themselves among the gypsy chorus. Gottlieb is disposed

Fiorello, Ricardo (Allan Jones) and Tomasso borrow aviators' uniforms - and beards - in **A Night at the Opera**

of briefly but is back in the wings ready to hit Fiorello with a frying pan. Henderson, assuming Gottlieb to be Driftwood, knocks him out instead. Tomasso knocks out Henderson before rejoining the chorus. Gottlieb and Henderson adopt gypsy costume and pursue them across the stage. Tomasso takes to the ropes controlling the backdrops and Lassparri finds himself singing before streetcars, a fruit cart and a battleship. Tomasso descends from high above, ripping through the backdrop. Cornered, he runs up the backdrop again. Aloft, he turns out the lights; when they return, Lassparri has disappeared. He is kept tied up in a crate, suspended high above, as Gottlieb is forced to allow Ricardo and Rosa their chance. They are triumphant and Lassparri, once released, is booed off. Gottlieb agrees to take responsibility for them all, and the company has two new stars. As Driftwood and Fiorello arrange to tear up *another* contract, Tomasso responds by ripping open the back of Gottlieb's coat. Rosa and Ricardo sing their encore.

After five films with Paramount (*qv*), mutual disenchantment had set in and the Marxes were not offered a new contract. Following completion of their last film, *Duck Soup* (*qv*), Harpo accepted an invitation to Russia (*qv*) while his brothers looked around for other deals. Despite continued talk of filming *Of Thee I Sing*, movie offers were not forthcoming and the nearest to any activity was a Groucho-Chico radio series called *The Marx of Time* and a stage role for Groucho in a revival of *Twentieth Century* (see **Stage appearances [post-1930]**). The radio series began in early March 1934, and towards the end of the month Zeppo announced his intention to leave the act in order to become an agent. It was therefore a trio that Chico was trying to sell, initially to Sam Goldwyn, then to Irving Thalberg (*qv*), 'boy wonder' producer of M-G-M (*qv*). Groucho later recalled that Thalberg

had wearied of Louis B. Mayer and was looking for stars to sign personally, in anticipation of forming a separate company; Groucho also remembered that the deciding factor was Goldwyn's unselfish advice for them to go with Thalberg. It is believed that Chico met Thalberg in a bridge game, his customary milieu; Thalberg, for his part, agreed to a meeting in which his plans would be outlined. Just as Minnie Marx (*qv*) had aimed to do, Thalberg wanted to put the team into 'class' productions. These were to have stories that would build, plus enough in the

Allan Jones with Chico and Harpo in
A Night at the Opera

way of romance and production numbers to lure a female audience, hitherto considered unappreciative of the Marx Brothers' efforts. The comedy style would be left untouched, except that each scene would be designed to advance the plot in some way and paced so that each laugh would be permitted to die down before the next line was delivered. Perhaps jokingly, Thalberg suggested the new trio might work for less money than a quartet; 'Without Zeppo,' replied Groucho, 'we're twice as good'. On signing with M-G-M on 19 September 1934, the Marxes were paid generously and, as with the earlier Paramount deal, were entitled to a percentage.

The problem of timing the laughs was resolved by the simple expedient of taking the show on tour; it took a Thalberg to spot what should have been an obvious move for the Marxes, who were in essence a stage act that just happened to make movies. Those laughs could not be obtained without a script: for this purpose a draft was prepared by James Kevin McGuinness who, according to Joe Adamson, concocted an unplayable story in which *Harpo* is 'the greatest tenor in the world' but, by coincidence, fails to utter a sound throughout. This was

abandoned in favour of a second version by Bert Kalmar and Harry Ruby (*qv*), who had been engaged to supply the film's songs (though none of their compositions survived into the final version). Again according to Adamson, they adapted the theatrical anecdote in which a deliberately-staged flop is massively oversold to its backers, only to become an unintentional hit. Thalberg rejected this on the grounds that he wanted a straight story as basis, believing that comedy built on comedy would not hold together. He may have been right: there were two attempts to

Tomasso and Fiorello abduct Lassparri

film the story in the 1960s, one of them Mel Brooks' *The Producers*, detested by the critics but earning cult status from its show-within-a-show, *Springtime For Hitler*. There was at least progress in the new draft: the format suited their characters; Groucho was given the name Otis B. Driftwood; they had created Mrs Claypool, a natural for Margaret Dumont (*qv*); and the idea was conceived of starting the film in Italy before relocating the story back to America. The Kalmar and Ruby draft was turned over to studio writers George Seaton and Robert Pirosh (both *qv*), but Groucho remained dissatisfied. The next logical step was to approach George S. Kaufman and Morrie Ryskind (both *qv*). Kaufman was reluctant to travel west, harbouring unpleasant memories of Hollywood after his involvement with Goldwyn for Cantor's *Roman Scandals*; he relented only after much persuasion from his wife, Beatrice, and Morrie Ryskind. Fortunately, Kaufman took to Thalberg and vice versa; Ryskind was similarly impressed and a new Kaufman-Ryskind draft was presented to Thalberg. Ryskind later recalled a stony-faced Thalberg considering it to be some of the funniest material he'd read. The

script was given independently to the teams of Kalmar and Ruby and Pirosh and Seaton for further embellishment, each writing duo being kept unaware of the other's involvement. By the time they were ready to go on tour, the Marxes had still another gagman, Al Boasberg (*qv*), a prolific script doctor and writer for such talents as Jack Benny (*qv*). Kaufman had returned to New York but Ryskind was on hand to provide amendments. Ryskind later recalled a problem in early performances, where Groucho, his confidence shaken after the break with Paramount, over-compensated with unduly aggressive delivery. This was

quickly remedied. A press release (referring still to a score by 'Ruby and Kalmar') details a tour of the 'larger cities of the coast region over the Fanchon and Marco circuits'. The show was to run fifty minutes, including 'actual scenes and comedy situations from the picture. These scenes are to be laid in an open-air restaurant, a steamer state room, a hotel room and an opera house scene.' Ryskind was mentioned as 'feeling the pulse of the audience from the wings', passing or rejecting material as appropriate. *Variety* of 27 March 1935 mentioned their show (then a 'travesty on *Rigoletto*') as touring with Ryskind in attendance, detailing the stops as Salt Lake (from 18 April) followed by Portland, Oregon, then Seattle, San Francisco and possibly Los Angeles. *Variety* named Hazel Hayes, Olga Dane, Tudor Williams and Roy Russell as the Marxes' fellow-principals; when opening at the Paramount Theatre, Salt Lake, Allan Jones (*qv*) was sole representative of the eventual supporting cast. In Portland, the *Morning Oregonian* published details of Ryskind and director Sam Wood (*qv*) attending the shows. In one story, possibly pre-prepared, the Marxes are reported as making a comedian of opera singer Olga Dane, removing her

Gottlieb insists on Rosa and Ricardo singing an encore ...

skirt - to reveal pink bloomers beneath - as she sings an aria from *Il Trovatore*. Miss Dane does not appear in the finished film and the skirt-stealing joke is relegated to an incidental part of the opera sequence. Individual lines and whole routines underwent drastic revision; Boasberg's original stateroom scene was a modest affair that grew as the tour progressed, gaining tremendously when Chico introduced the 'and two hard-boiled eggs' business. Nonetheless, it was in danger of removal until Thalberg decided otherwise; in turn, Boasberg threw out a fire scene intended as a climactic moment (just as an equivalent had been deleted from *Horse Feathers*). Once satisfied with the content and timing, they returned to the studio and commenced filming in June 1935. This concluded in mid-August but retakes were required; a letter written by Alexander Woollcott (*qv*) on the 16 August refers to Harpo being called back that day, just as he was boarding an aircraft bound for the east. Retakes were then expected to last ten days. The completed film was previewed to a mostly unresponsive audience. Legend has it that it was shown again, unaltered, in a different house to overwhelming acclaim, but Groucho (in his 1972 *Omnibus* interview) insisted there had been perhaps fifteen minutes' worth of cuts by the second preview. The hard work paid off. Andre Sennwald of the *New York Times*, though guardedly calling it 'a trifle below their best', regarded it as 'considerably above the standard of laughter that has been our portion since they quit the screen'. Otis Ferguson of *The New Republic* added to the plaudits, yet implied he shouldn't like the team. This most polished of Marx vehicles was considered 'a leaky ship, and caulked to the guards with hokum ... it seems thrown together, made up just as they went along out of everybody's else's own head', accusing it of stealing from René Clair's *Le Million* and the Keystone comedies, suggesting a

plethora of old jokes and wrapping it up, rather condescendingly, as 'one of the most hilarious collections of bad jokes I've laughed myself nearly sick over'. The misconception of the Marxes as slapstick comedians was and is a common one but the identifiable borrowings in *Opera* are few, while the notion of improvising a meticulously road-tested movie serves only as tribute to the team's illusion of spontaneity. *A Night at the Opera* premièred in the UK at the Empire, Leicester Square, in February 1936. On 1 March, C.A. Lejeune of the *Observer* thought it 'seems to be the best of all the Marx Brothers pictures so far', remarking upon the superior presentation, gags,

a variant of the studio's lion trademark, in which the animal was replaced by Groucho, Chico and Harpo. This sequence was shot but deleted from the final film, to be used instead for the theatrical trailer (see **Trailers**). Clifton Fadiman, in the January 1936 edition of *Stage* (an American magazine, not the British theatrical paper), explains that it produced too big a laugh prior to the 'straight' opening scene, which depicted 'everybody singing' (mentioned also in Otis Ferguson's review). Some idea of the 'everybody singing' introduction may be gleaned from the pre-filming script (not a pre-tour version), published together with a transcript of the film itself in 1972. In

... so another contract is torn up, ditto Gottlieb's jacket

editing and a 'more evenly distributed' emphasis between the team. From the same day's *Sunday Times* is one of the few pessimistic reviews, from Sydney W. Carroll, who preferred the 'fireworks' of *Animal Crackers* and others to the 'incongruity' of interspersing Marx comedy with a large proportion of serious items. Posterity sometimes takes Carroll's side but at the time *Opera* was their biggest success and, as predicted by Thalberg, drew an unprecedented female audience. As the Marxes' first film at M-G-M, it was to have been opened by

this, a Milan street scene shows the chorus of *Pagliacci* spreading from person to person, ultimately reaching the waiter who serves Mrs Claypool. No such sequence is visible in today's prints of the film, in which the opening titles fade to black preceding a straight cut to a shot of the waiter approaching Mrs Claypool. There is an obvious join in the soundtrack, so the first line, delivered by the waiter, comes out as '[CLICK] Gentleman has not arrived

A NIGHT IN CASABLANCA

With director Sam Wood on the set of **A Night at the Opera**

yet?' Similarly, when the scene changes to the opera house and Harpo in Lassparri's dressing room, there is but a momentary glimpse of the auditorium, with an obvious splice at either end of the shot, before we see Harpo in his employer's costume. Corresponding clicks and jumps in the music serve as further evidence of mutilation. The Italian location is not established and only becomes apparent as the film progresses; further, there are at intervals a number of printed-in 'jump-cuts', some of them corresponding to references to Italy in the script. There is but scant possibility of the meticulous Irving Thalberg allowing such a choppy-looking film into release, as confirmed by Fadiman's eye-witness account. Charlotte Chandler's book transcribes a conversation (*circa* 1972) during which Morrie Ryskind discusses with Groucho the likely mutilation of this and other films. 'Even when I see *A Night at the Opera*,' said Ryskind, 'I know there's a scene missing.' (In passing, one might note that the loss of footage from *Horse Feathers* has been much discussed over the years, but the apparent dismemberment of *A Night at the Opera* has received no attention whatever.) These cuts obviously post-date the original release, and must have

been inflicted during one of *Opera*'s several reissues. Exactly which reissue is difficult to determine, though it should be mentioned that *Opera* was re-released in Britain during 1944, prior to the end of the Second World War (an American reissue followed in 1948, to test the Marxes' box-office potential after their 'comeback' in *A Night in Casablanca* [*qv*]; a further reissue was in 1964). It may have been that wartime sentiments encouraged the deletion of all reference to an Axis power, albeit one by then out of the running. This seems the only plausible explanation, even though the film retains numerous Italian names and, of course, Chico's usual characterization. The discovery of a fuller version now seems unlikely: all prints circulated to theatrical reissue, 16 mm libraries,

television, home video and (in the 1970s) Super-8 release derive from this same master. Even an ostensibly pristine Treasures print, supplied to the BFI by Turner Entertainment (the film's present owner), is the chopped-around edition, suggesting no other version to be extant even in studio hands. A footnote: *A Night at the Opera* is said to have been the inspiration for a 1992 comedy starring Mel Smith and John Turturro, called initially *Sitting Ducks* but released eventually as *Brain Donors*. Turturro and Smith played characters based on, respectively, Groucho and Chico.

(See also: Carlisle, Kitty; Characters; Christy, Dorothy; Eaton, Jay; Female impersonation; Fries, Otto; Garbo, Greta; Gilbert, Billy; Home movies; Impersonators; Insomnia; King, Walter Woolf; O'Connor, Robert Emmett; Policemen; Prisons; Records; Sedan, Rolfe; Songs; Stage appearances [post-1930]; Television; Video releases; White, Leo; Wigs)

A NIGHT IN CASABLANCA

(Marx Brothers film)
Released by United Artists, 10 May 1946.
7,655 ft (85 minutes).
Produced by David L. Loew. Directed by Archie L. Mayo. Camera: James van Trees. Screenplay by Joseph Fields,

One of a series of **Opera** *publicity stills with starlet Frances MacInerney*

Roland Kibbee and (uncredited) Frank Tashlin. Song: *Who's Sorry Now?* by Ted Snyder, Bert Kalmar and Harry Ruby. Working title: *Adventure in Casablanca.*

With Groucho Marx (*Ronald Kornblow*), Harpo Marx (*Rusty*), Chico Marx (*Corbaccio*), Charles Drake (*Lt Pierre Delmar*), Lois Collier (*Annette Bernard*), Sig Ruman (*Count Pfferman/Heinrich Stubel*), Lisette Verea (*Beatrice Reiner*),

By courtesy of Robert G. Dickson

Lewis Russell (*Governor*), Dan Seymour (*Captain Brizzard, Prefect of Police*), Frederick Giermann (*Kurt*), Harro Mellor (*Emile*), David Hoffman (*spy*), Paul Harvey (*Mr Smythe*).

A man dies at the Hotel Casablanca. He is the manager, the third within six months to have been murdered. All likely suspects are rounded up, except the sinister-looking Count Pfferman and his entourage, which consists of Beatrice Reiner and two henchmen-cum-valets, Kurt and Emile. Among Casablanca's waifs and strays is Pierre,

a French pilot. He is on reserve but wears his uniform in the absence of any civilian clothes. Pierre tells the authorities of being to forced to fly a group of Nazis and their loot out of Paris during the Occupation. He was supposed to take them to South America but deliberately crashed in Casablanca. When he returned to the aircraft, the loot had disappeared. The hotel was then under Nazi administration but has since passed to the French government. Pierre believes someone is attempting to gain control of the hotel in connection with the missing treasure; finding evidence of this will prove he acted patriotically. The authorities have no time for the story, wishing only to solve the recent murders and appoint a new manager. Count Pfferman is handed a letter by Kurt; he consults a Nazi code book but sends for Beatrice to help decipher the message. Kurt returns with Beatrice, telling her the Count is preparing to accept managership of the hotel from the Governor-General. The Count is dressed by Rusty, a *bona fide* if troublesome valet; he fails to notice that his waistcoat, then jacket, have been put on inside-out. Nor is he immediately aware of the cane placed down his back, with his hat perched at the top. The letter is from a contact in South America: they are warned against further delay, as discovery of the treasure would be disastrous. Rusty vacuums the suite, causing the Count's toupée to disappear into the machine. The Count has a distinctive scar on his head and is thus rendered unable to meet the Governor-General. At the hotel's supper club, Beatrice sings while the Governor-General awaits Pfferman. When he does not appear, it is decided to appoint someone else. The job will be offered to the manager of an out-of-the-way venue, the Desert View Hotel, where news of the murders will not have arrived. The toupée is recovered by a cleaner and handed in. Annette, Pierre's sweetheart, works at the hotel and examines the find. According to a

label, it was made in Berlin for a Heinrich Stubel. She takes the toupée to Pierre. In the marketplace, Corbaccio is fixing the meters on his taxi camels. He greets his friend Rusty, then overhears the Governor-General and Prefect of Police discuss the new manager's arrival. Corbaccio meets the newcomer, Ronald Kornblow, and provides a camel to the hotel. Kornblow meets his new associates, detailing such plans as switching all the room numbers for the sake of fun. He is deemed impossible but retained in the absence of any other candidates. Annette finds Pierre and shows him the toupée. He recognizes the owner as a top Nazi from the Parisian Occupation. Although it is unlikely to be collected, Pierre asks Annette to place it among the lost property. Pfferman is still confined to his room. Beatrice has an idea and exits, as Rusty walks in bearing a mop instead of the toupée. Furious at his valet's mistake, Pfferman slaps Rusty. Kurt joins in, and is challenged to a duel. Swords are used but Rusty prepares himself with protective football clothing. Even without it he is a surprising match for Kurt, who eventually collapses from exhaustion. Beatrice slinks her way towards Kornblow at the hotel desk. She invents a story of a lost diamond clip as an excuse to examine the lost property. Kornblow finds no jewellery but produces a toupée ('Some guy must've blown his top'), which Beatrice secretly takes away. Beatrice departs with an invitation for Kornblow to hear her sing at the supper club that evening. She approaches the lift as Rusty emerges, caricaturing her haughty pose with cigarette holder and lorgnette. Beatrice sings at the cabaret and is congratulated by the Count, now back in circulation. She is briefed to make a rendezvous with Kornblow at the Rue Lafayette, where Kurt will arrange a motor 'accident'. Pierre, also at the supper club, is approached by a shady individual who overheard him discuss the toupée. He can provide information but, having been unlucky at the roulette table, demands money. Corbaccio decides to help Pierre, obtaining tips by providing tables for those queueing to dine. Kornblow, dancing with Beatrice, finds there is increasingly less floor. Kornblow agrees to meet her at Rue Lafayette. Corbaccio is asked to deputize for the house pianist; Rusty takes the money to Pierre while Corbaccio plays for the patrons. Annette tells Pierre of the toupée's disappearance. She has been unable to locate Kornblow but he staggers out of the night, wounded partly by Beatrice's non-appearance but mostly through having been hit by a car. Kornblow is introduced to Pierre and told the entire story. Rusty, outside the Count's room, hears Kurt chastised for bungling the murder attempt. He listens further as Pfferman instructs Beatrice to lure Kornblow into a compromising position, enabling the Count to break in and kill him in 'self-defence'. Rusty goes to Corbaccio, conveying the scheme in mime. Pfferman has Kornblow book him on a flight to Tunisia. Corbaccio and Rusty try to alert Kornblow to the danger but he fails to comprehend Rusty's mime. Corbaccio tells him outright and volunteers as bodyguard. When Kornblow's lunch arrives, the new bodyguards test it enthusiastically. In the foyer, Rusty sweeps up as Kornblow mans the desk. He offers

little help to a guest whose trunks have not arrived ('Put your pants on, nobody'll know any difference') and queries the marital status of a well-to-do couple named Smythe. He receives a call from Beatrice inviting him to her room. Despite his earlier disappointment, he goes. He and Rusty enter the lift but it sticks between floors. Rusty climbs through the top of the car and finds a panel inside the lift shaft. It leads to a chamber filled with jewellery and art treasures. There is also a harp, which he plays. Five hours later he returns to the car with an idea: he takes an axe and severs the lift cables. The car descends rapidly and

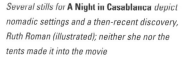

Several stills for **A Night in Casablanca** *depict nomadic settings and a then-recent discovery, Ruth Roman (illustrated); neither she nor the tents made it into the movie*

the two men emerge shaking and shuddering. Kornblow arranges another date with Beatrice, despite Corbaccio's warnings. She tells him the Count is away, but it is arranged for him to break in on their canoodling after fifteen minutes. Kornblow appears bearing flowers, champagne plus an ice-bucket in a stand. Corbaccio knocks on the door: 'You got a woman in there?' Kornblow suggests they meet in his room, taking with him the assorted paraphernalia plus a gramophone. Pfferman, revolver in hand, breaks into an empty room. He finds a note from Beatrice directing him to Kornblow's room in fifteen minutes. The liaison continues until Corbaccio knocks once more. Beatrice suggests a return to her room and the Count is left another note. Kornblow reaches Beatrice's room but Corbaccio has beaten him to it. Corbaccio takes both the champagne and Beatrice, leaving Kornblow outside. By chance, Kornblow meets the Count who, embarrassed, claims to have missed his connections. 'I missed a few myself tonight' is the reply. Back in the supper club, Corbaccio and Rusty find some

A Night in Casablanca: *a reception for the new manager*

money and try their luck at the roulette wheel. They place everything on number five, keeping it there as it continues to win. As they threaten to break the bank, Kornblow is summoned; he allows them to continue and spins the wheel himself, convinced the same number will not recur. The bank is duly broken and Pfferman alerts the authorities, accusing all three of conspiracy. He adds that Kornblow was in fact operator of a roadside motel rather than manager of the Desert View Hotel. Pfferman is appointed manager. Kornblow, Rusty and Corbaccio are jailed; so is Annette, to whom Rusty had given some of the winnings. Pierre will be flown out for trial by the military authorities. In the cell, Rusty produces a Rembrandt from his coat. As he obviously knows the whereabouts of the treasure, they organize an escape. Rusty's mouth is lathered to simulate rabidity; the guard investigates and is overpowered. The Count and his henchmen are packing for a trip to South America. Beatrice summons the police after overhearing Pfferman's intention to abandon her. Kornblow, Rusty, Corbaccio and Annette reach the office of the Prefect of Police. He is absent and a bogus

order is issued for all officers to assemble in the courtyard. Annette goes to the airport as Kornblow *et al* make for the Count's suite. They delay the packing while remaining unseen; Rusty and Corbaccio hide in one trunk, Kornblow and Beatrice in another. Kornblow, Rusty and Corbaccio emerge as the trunks are being transported across the desert. The lorry hits a bump and they are left behind. Annette and Pierre escape the aerodrome guards and take a car into the desert. They pick up the others, pursue the lorry and reach the airstrip just as the Nazis' aeroplane starts to move. Using a truck, they draw

'I'm Beatrice Reiner, I stop at the hotel'; 'I'm Ronald Kornblow, I stop at nothing.' **A Night in Casablanca**

alongside and place a ladder across to the aircraft. As they board, Beatrice, emerging from the trunk, helps them overpower the Nazis. Pfferman and one of the henchmen are pushed out, leaving only the pilot. Rusty knocks him out and, once he is revived, knocks him out again. Pfferman takes the truck from Pierre, picking up the other henchman. Annette brings the police, who follow the plane until it takes off. Rusty seems a competent pilot until he tries 'no hands'. They crash into the jail. The Count arrives and a fight

breaks out, soon joined by Pierre. Next on the scene are the police, who arrest Pfferman. Pierre and Annette kiss. 'If a thing like that could only happen to me,' says Beatrice, wistfully. Kornblow, Rusty and Corbaccio prepare to oblige and chase her off through the marketplace.

Four years after their 'farewell' film, *The Big Store* (*qv*), the Marx Brothers were willing to try again. Producer David Loew (*qv*) persuaded them to consider a parody of *Casablanca* (1942), with elements of other Warner/Bogart movies thrown in. (Coincidentally, Groucho had dinner at the Bogarts' while the film was in rehearsal.) Chico, whose gambling debts necessitated steady work, is said to have been under threat by gangsters at this time; this and the promise of a pre-filming tour were enough to convince Groucho and Harpo. Loew formed with the Marxes a production company called Loma Vista, the type of entity that tends to exist to make one solitary picture. The tour, Harpo's idea, consisted primarily of service audiences but was enough to inspire confidence, get the routines in shape and enable the brothers - particularly Chico - to memorize the material. There was a brief hiatus after Groucho's wedding to

Chico pretends to be aghast for this **Night in Casablanca** *still*

Kay Gorcey on 21 July 1945, but the Marxes were on the road during August. A letter from Groucho to his daughter, Miriam, describes the show as having been 'dreadful' until they threw out most of the original jokes. This may explain why a reported first draft, with character names like 'Humphrey Bogus', has very little in common with the finished film. This original script, by Joseph Fields (*qv*), was largely superseded by the brothers' own interpolations and material from Roland Kibbee (*qv*), Frank Tashlin (*qv*) and others (also jettisoned was the working title, *Adventure in Casablanca*). At the time of this letter, at Oakland on 24 August 1945, Groucho thought they had the makings of a good picture, unless director Archie L. Mayo 'bungles it up'. It is possible that word had travelled about the punning first draft; the only hurdle at this point was in fending off Warner Brothers' legal department, who objected to use of the name 'Casablanca'. Groucho responded by questioning Warners' exclusive right to the city of Casablanca, noting, ironically, a potential confusion between Harpo and Ingrid Bergman. Groucho disputed not only Warners' claim to Casablanca but also their right to call themselves brothers, the Marxes having long been billed that way. He concluded with a mock-serious tirade against the ambitious, 'ferret-faced shyster' out to cause a rift between the brothers Warner and Marx. Curiously, Warners' next letter chose to take him seriously and, in the interests of compromise, requested details of the film's plot. Groucho explained how he was to portray a Doctor of Divinity on the Gold Coast, with Chico 'selling sponges to barflies who are unable to carry their liquor' and Harpo playing 'an Arabian caddy who lives in a small Grecian urn on the outskirts of the city'. Warners either didn't know when they were being kidded, or had started to enjoy the saga (one suspects the former). They wrote again asking for clarification of the plot. This time

Beatrice arranges a trap for Kornblow in **A Night in Casablanca**

Groucho explained there had been revisions, his role having become that of 'Bordello, the sweetheart of Humphrey Bogart'. Harpo and Chico were recast as 'itinerant rug peddlers who are weary of laying rugs and enter a monastery just for a lark.' Other attractions included a waterfront hotel filled with girls and an unexpected plot twist when 'Gladstone makes a speech that sets the House of Commons in an uproar'. This ended all enquiries from Warner Brothers. By 18 September the Marxes were spending long hours at the General Service studio, rehearsing scenes that had not played on tour (actual shooting had been delayed by an industry strike); filming started on 3 October and the comedians were pleased with the rushes they saw three days later; by 12 October they had completed the first of seven weeks' shooting without interference from

pickets; on 23 November they saw an encouraging rough-cut and, in a letter to Miriam six days later, Groucho believed it would be superior to their last three pictures. That all was not quite finished is suggested in a letter of 5 December to Sam Zolotow of the *New York Times* Drama department, lamenting having to arise at seven each day for a nine o'clock call, only to wait until three in the afternoon before acting a scene. Further evidence of Groucho's weariness permeates a recollection, in *Groucho and Me*, of hanging on a ladder between a truck and an aircraft, pondering whether he should be doing such things at his age. He is said to have asked Harpo if he, too, was tired of it all; 'Yes' was the brief response. At the first preview, in

January, the film ran 113 minutes and was received unenthusiastically by audience and Marxes alike. Groucho was furious at Mayo, a 'fat idiot' who, he believed, had ruined their tightly-constructed picture. It was expected that perhaps fifteen minutes should be lost by the second preview, after which Groucho glumly noted the contrast of 'good stuff' with stodgily old-fashioned directing and the suspected need for retakes. There was much hacking and Groucho was pacified - though by no means totally - after a third preview late in January. Groucho thought it would do reasonable business but 'the critics won't throw their hats in the air. If they throw anything, it'll probably be their dinner'. Groucho's prediction was reasonably accurate: *A Night in Casablanca* drew patrons but critics, overall, were more pleased to see the Marxes than the picture itself. James Agee, in *The Nation*, spent much time praising Groucho as a sophisticated talent and his 'use of the brain for fun's sake'. Agee recommended the film, albeit not their best, 'for the worst they might ever make would be better worth seeing than most other things I can think of'. He believed the material had potential but fell flat, a parallel to Groucho's views on the stage sketches and Mayo's subsequent handling of them; he decided also that the Marxes were 'tired', again true but probably not the reason for any inadequacies.

Rusty and Corbaccio's luck at the casino leads to charges of conspiracy in **A Night in Casablanca**

Agee considered this film to contain Harpo's best performance, being more central, 'more acid, more subtle'. *Variety* took a kindly view: 'This isn't the best the Marx Bros. have made but it's a pretty funny farce'. Highlights were given as being Harpo's duelling scene, Groucho's interrupted liaison with Lisette Verea (*qv*), the switch-around with the luggage and the climactic aeroplane chase. These opinions were far from unanimous: 'The world should be noticeably happier this morning considering that the Marx brothers are back on the screen, after a five-year absence,' said the *New York Times*. 'But the sad truth is that this battered old world is not much merrier than it was, say, on Friday, for the spark seems to have gone from the madcap Marxes'. It was claimed that many of the gags sounded 'as wheezy as an old Model T Ford panting uphill on two cylinders', though the duelling scene and Chico-Harpo charade business drew praise. The airborne finale was dismissed as 'silly without being amusing'. In Britain anticipation was considerable, to the point where *Illustrated*, true to its name, trailed this 'long delayed treat' with two pages of stills on 9 March 1946. The brief text informed readers that *A Night in Casablanca* 'will please the vast army of Marx supporters as much as it will fail to thrill those who "just can't see anything in them"'. This echoes almost every British review the team ever received but greater interest lies in the penultimate paragraph:

According to advance publicity, producer David L. Loew offered Harpo an extra fee of £10,000 to utter just the one word, "Murder!" But Harpo refused. He prefers to stay silent, as ever.

The same tale appears in Jim Marshall's piece for *Leader* magazine of 8 June. Quoting the original US price of $55,000, Marshall tells us that Harpo considered the idea before rejecting the offer with a mute shake of

the head. The article itself again concerns itself essentially with the comedians instead of the new picture, though mention is made of both the Warner correspondence and *Night in Casablanca*'s purpose of keeping Chico away from the racetrack. Perhaps the most intriguing UK promotion was a novelized book of the film, unavailable elsewhere, from which an extract was published in the July issue of *Lilliput*. The section chosen was the charade scene, a reprise of similar business in *A Day at the Races* (*qv*). In both films, Harpo's message is of a woman attempting to trap Groucho; similarly duplicated are the attempts of Chico and Harpo to disrupt the *soirée*. Such reworkings are not uncommon but somehow two in a row might be called excessive. The trap is avoided in Groucho's dealings with the hotel management, which could easily have become 'Cocoanuts Revisited'; instead Groucho has some good lines, especially when accusing the well-to-do Mr and Mrs Smythe of being the usual 'Smith' couple with no baggage (all this because Groucho was addressed as 'clerk'). *Kinematograph Weekly*, aware of the liberal borrowings from earlier films, decided that a post-war UK audience 'may turn anywhere for laughs'. They repeated the notion of the team being 'jaded and tired' but much of this seems the fault of contemporary atmosphere. *A Night in Casablanca*, conceived before the war's end, inherits the *noir* look both of its initial target - the Bogart films - and of its period. To say the least, the idea of Nazis and multiple murder requires a skilled hand and even Chaplin could not make the black comedy of *Monsieur Verdoux* palatable to most 1940s audiences. Groucho thought *Night in Casablanca*'s music inappropriate and altogether more suited to Hitchcock's recent film, *Spellbound*. *A Night in Casablanca* is not a bad film, and one can readily accept Groucho's endorsement of it over *The Big Store*. However, it would be interesting to learn if a true parody of *Casablanca* would better have suited the context than a reversion to the team's customary approach. Virtually the only reminders of Bogart are the presence of Dan Seymour (*qv*) and Groucho's line 'You don't have to sing for me - just whistle!'

(See also: Aircraft; Animals; Books; Censorship; Children; *Cocoanuts, the* [play]; Collier, Lois; Dancing; *A Day at the Races*; Drake, Charles; Fighting; Gambling; Guest appearances; *Home Again*; Home movies; Hotels; In-jokes; Kibbee, Roland; Letters; Marriages; Moustaches, beards; Names; Prisons; Prostitutes; Radio; Ruby, Harry; Rumann, Siegfried; Russell, Lewis; Shoes; Smoking; Songs; Spectacles; Stage appearances [post-1930]; *Street Cinderella, the*; Telephones; Tours; Trailers; United Artists; Verea, Lisette; Wartime; Wigs)

NIGHTINGALES, THE

The first identifiable Marx family act was a singing group assembled by Minnie. The initial personnel were Groucho, Gummo and a girl singer, Mabel O'Donnell, who was cursed with either a squint or a glass eye. This affliction, concealed by a pre-Veronica Lake peek-a-boo hairstyle (actually a wig supplied by Minnie), extended also to her sense of key; Groucho later recalled how she would lead the act from G to A flat. Another difficulty was imposed by a terrible crush Mabel had on Groucho, making her rather a nuisance at times. As a means of obtaining prestigious bookings, they started out under the auspices of Ned Wayburn, the producer-director-songwriter whose acquaintance they had made during Groucho's stint with Gus Edwards. Wayburn offered advice and permitted use of his name, no small advantage; a *Variety* obituary lists some of his achievements, such as devising a form of tap-dancing known as 'ensemble prancing'. Wayburn later staged the hugely successful *Hello, Ragtime* in London and worked for many years with Ziegfeld. When

The Four **Nightingales**. Left to right: Gummo, Lou Levy, Groucho and Harpo
BFI Stills, Posters and Designs

Wayburn died in September 1942, *Variety* quoted his given age as 68, but conveyed the general opinion that he was older. *Ned Wayburn's Nightingales* made their bow in September 1907, first in Wilmington and then in New York. Once Minnie had assumed control of the act, Mabel O'Donnell was fired but the Nightingales, now exclusively male, remained 'three' owing to the addition of a lad named Lou Levy ('Leo Levin' in some accounts, suggesting the use of a stage name). This remained so until the summer of 1908, when an engagement at Henderson's, Coney Island, required a quartet. It was at this point that Harpo, hitherto barely-employable, was recruited as a vocalist. Minnie had supplied them with white, nautical-style outfits (from Bloomingdale's department store) and it may be said that Harpo's nerve-wracked début was followed by a hurried laundering of his trousers. Thus the Four Nightingales travelled the north-west and south of

the USA until 1910; a photograph suggests Levy's replacement by another young hopeful, Freddie Hutchins. Exact details of the act are obscure but it had a plot centred on Groucho as a butcher's boy, distracted by Harpo as the others stole the wieners in his delivery basket. One of the songs, a German dialect item called *Ist Dach Nicht Ein Schnitzelbank?* was sung by Groucho. The Nightingales became for a while 'The Six Mascots' with the addition of Minnie and her sister Hannah; this came to an end when the supposedly young girls proved to have sufficient weight for their chairs to collapse.

(See also: Marx, Minnie; Vaudeville)

The **Nightingales** *became* The Six Mascots *with the addition of Minnie (right) and Aunt Hannah. Groucho is to the foreground; Harpo plays piano; Gummo smiles in the background; the expressionless lad is probably Freddie Hutchins*
Paul G. Wesolowski Collection

O'BRIEN, VIRGINIA (b. 1921)

Actress and vocalist, noted in 1940s films for her ability to sing while remaining absolutely expressionless. In *The Big Store* (*qv*) she plays Kitty, a counter assistant; the production number *Sing While You Sell* permits her a deadpan solo, bringing a touch of swing to *Rock-a-bye-baby*. Close observers will notice her smiling at the number's conclusion, as all concerned disappear into a lift. She worked again with Groucho, on radio (*qv*), during the first half of the *Pabst Blue Ribbon Town* series. Miss O'Brien's other films include *Hullabaloo* (1940), *Ship Ahoy* (1942), *DuBarry Was a Lady* (1943, with Lucille Ball [*qv*]), *Till the Clouds Roll By* (1946), *Merton Of the Movies* (1947) and *Francis of the Navy* (1955). Later retired to raise a family. She reappeared in the 1970s for a Disney live-action comedy, *Gus* (1976), and at the Motion Picture Hall of Fame Convention in Los Angeles, when the Marx Brothers were honoured in January 1977.

(See also: Awards)

O'CONNOR, ROBERT EMMETT (or EMMET) (1885-1962)

Milwaukee-born character actor, from vaudeville (*qv*), whose bulldog features dictated a career portraying mostly cops or other tough guys; he is the determined - if not necessarily bright - detective Henderson in *A Night at the Opera* (*qv*). Long experience in silents; early talkie credits include Jolson's *The Singing Fool* (1928) and Colleen Moore's *Smiling Irish Eyes*, directed by William A. Seiter (*qv*). Among many others are *Our Blushing Brides* (1930), *The Public Enemy* (1931), Eddie Cantor's *The Kid From Spain* (1932), *The Picture Snatcher* (1933), *Waterfront Lady* (1935), *Little Lord Fauntleroy* (1936), *Tight Shoes* (1941) and *Meet Me in St Louis* (1944).

(See also: Brecher, Irving; Cantor, Eddie; McCarey, Leo; Miles, Lotta; Pratt, Purnell; Policemen; Ruby, Harry)

ON THE BALCONY

See: *On the Mezzanine*

ON THE MEZZANINE

(Marx Brothers sketch)
(Marx Brothers shows and films *qv*)
The lavish ensemble piece *Home Again* led to a direct follow-up, again employing a sizeable cast and, as also with *The Street Cinderella*, suggesting an air of musical comedy rather than vaudeville. *On the Mezzanine* (known initially as *On the Mezzanine Floor*) was written by Herman Timberg, whose brother, Sammy, later became known as a composer in films. Like Groucho, Harry Ruby, Eddie Cantor (both *qv*) and many others, Herman Timberg was a graduate of Gus Edwards' shows. He died in 1952, aged 60. A *Variety* obituary mentions Timberg's former status as a vaudeville headliner, one of his innovations being the 'crawl-off', in which he would exit on all fours. By the early 1920s Timberg had turned his attentions to writing and management, among his then-recent credits being the music and lyrics for *Tick-Tack-Toe* (1919-20). Timberg has been reported as a contributor to the Marxes' radio series of 1932-3, *Flywheel, Shyster and Flywheel* (*qv*). Timberg's sister, who both managed and appeared in the new show, had been in vaudeville since the age of twelve and worked under the name Hattie Darling; one of her admirers was boxing champion Benny Leonard who, coincidentally, was also a great fan of the Marx Brothers. In common with many sportsmen, Leonard was attracted to show business (as well as to its actresses) and it was this connection that resulted in Leonard contributing both financially and in person to *On the Mezzanine*. Charlotte Chandler's book *Hello, I Must Be Going* records Hattie Darling's comments on working with the Marxes, not least that *On the Mezzanine* brought her the best notices of her career. She recalled having several changes of costume, for which reason she asked the Marxes for the star dressing room. Their response was to give her just that, located high up

On the Mezzanine: *early Marxes frozen in time, from a photo session of December 1921 By kind courtesy of the Jackson County Historical Society Archives & Research Library*

in the building, allowing her scarcely enough time to reach the stage. In retaliation, she said, 'I took Harpo's red wig and I wiped the whole floor with it. But they were so wonderful to me.' The act made its début in February 1921, playing mostly on the Poli circuit until transferring to Keith's for June-July and September-October (having taken a break during August). It was on leaving the Keith time that the act mutated slightly into *On the Balcony*. The remainder of that autumn was filled with engagements at other theatres prior to commencing a tour of the

Orpheum circuit in December. The Winter 1988 *Freedonia Gazette* (*qv*) preserves a brief moment of this tour's history, reprinting two publicity photographs taken of the Marxes while appearing at the Main Street Theatre, Kansas City, Missouri, on 16 December 1921. The print run of 200 photographs (100 of each) is described as having been delivered to the comedians at the Orpheum Theatre in Calgary, Alberta, on 14 January 1922. The pictures survive only in modern-day prints obtained from the slightly damaged glass negatives, held by the Jackson County Historical Society (see **Costumes**). *On the Mezzanine*'s opening scene was set in the office of a theatrical agent, Mr Lee. Each of the Marxes entered, one by one, offering an imitation of Gallagher and Shean. This would have been intended to satirize a popular trend, for in 1921 Gallagher and Shean impressionists had proliferated to the point where Keith's Circuit issued an edict limiting such impersonations to one per night. The dialogue (except, of course, for Harpo) was based on rhyming couplets: Zeppo was first to arrive, claiming 'My name is Sammy Brown, and I just came into town; saw your ad., you're Mr Lee - say, you can make a mint on me.' This sketch was re-used for a subsequent Shubert tour and in the brothers' first Broadway show, *I'll Say She Is!* It was filmed in 1931 as a promotional film; for fuller description see **Monkey Business (promo)**. As the various hopefuls tried out for the agent, Zeppo attempted to sell him a new play he had written. The second half of the show consisted of the play itself, enacted by the aspiring theatricals. Setting was the lobby of a hotel, with a balcony built overhead within the set (hence the act's various titles). This was structured with sufficient informality to permit the harp and piano solos plus whatever comic business could be interpolated. One routine, in which a girl (initially Hattie Darling) would play the violin after being hypnotized, became still another ingredient of *I'll Say She Is!* Despite

Timberg's nominal authorship, Groucho would add material of his own: for example, when Chico sat down to play, he requested songs under parody titles, as in *Slipshod Through the Cowslips* (*Tiptoe Through the Tulips*) or the much-recycled pun (as in *Animal Crackers*) *I'm a Dreamer, Montreal* (which rhymes with the original *Aren't we all* when spoken with an American accent!). The most widely quoted line has Zeppo announcing 'the garbage man is here', to which Groucho would reply 'Tell him we don't want any' (a gag probably repeated from *Home Again*). When interviewed for the Chandler book, Groucho resurrected another gag: 'Did you ever see Lincoln without a beard?' - 'No' - 'Well, I look like George Washington with a mustache.' Harpo claimed to have originated the business of giving someone his leg in lieu of a handshake during this show; he also cited *On the Mezzanine* as the origin of his knife-dropping routine but S.J. Perelman (*qv*) recalled seeing it in *Home Again*; nonetheless, in *Harpo Speaks!* he provides its context within this show. Before the Marxes arrived at the hotel lobby, a pretty girl would make arrangements by telephone; 'How will I know you?' she asked, to be told to expect someone in a brown suit and wearing a white carnation. The Marxes, having eavesdropped, appeared in precisely that guise. The hotel detective, on the trail of some stolen silver, had been told to look for a man with brown suit and white carnation; when out-talked by Groucho and Chico, he turned instead to Harpo, persuading him to keep away from the other two and, consequently, a life of crime. As noted elsewhere (under *Home Again*, *I'll Say She Is!*, *Animal Crackers* and others), when the detective pumped Harpo's hand, the missing silverware would fall from Harpo's other sleeve. The routine was gradually extended to milk the laughs, adding more and more silverware; it was eventually capped with Groucho asking 'I can't understand what's

On the Mezzanine *had become* On the Balcony *before its UK début at the London Coliseum. Lydia Lopokova and friends arranged a memorable welcome for Monday's second house*
Michael Pointon Collection

delaying that coffeepot' before that very item hit the floor. Harpo estimated using twenty items of silverware at initial performances but building up to three hundred; he described also a further sidelight, in which he would stare at a selected woman from the audience in a 'modified Gookie' (*qv*) while all this was going on. One woman fainted at the sight of him. Few, if any, of the female cast escaped his attention; Jack Benny (*qv*), who toured with them on the Orpheum Circuit during 1922 and earlier, remembered that 'Harpo kept running on and off the stage chasing girls'. When Benny Leonard made an appearance, he would discuss the fight game with Groucho, demonstrate some shadow-boxing, then take on the Marxes in a mock bout; the athletic Zeppo was reassigned to the role of referee after catching Leonard with a genuinely forceful punch! The Marxes, though handicapped with oversized prop gloves, put effort into the scene and Leonard is said to have retaliated by inflicting much damage (Groucho received a black eye).

Presumably, a gag in which the Marxes limped through a parody of 'the Spirit of '76' served as punctuation to these onstage battles (Harpo described ruffling a few patriotic feathers as a consequence). They can be seen repeating this gag in *The Cocoanuts* and, in Harpo's solo version, *Animal Crackers*. *On the Mezzanine* survived Benny Leonard's retirement from the act. Also replaced were Hattie Darling and most of the supporting cast. The romance between Leonard and Hattie Darling never blossomed and she found marital bliss with a jeweller named Weinstein. Hattie Darling Weinstein died in Chicago in April 1992, at the age of 95. As noted above, by 1922 the show had mutated slightly into *On the Balcony*, a title in any case more comprehensible when presented to a British audience. Some other minor alterations were made for the UK: according to a *Stage* review, their impersonation offered to the theatrical agent was amended to one of Charlie Chaplin (*qv*). Other sources suggest the famed 'garbage man' joke to have become a diluted 'the dustman is here'/'Tell him we don't want any; who needs dust?' The Marxes took this version of their sketch, billed as a 'musical revuette', to London in 1922, opening at the Coliseum, St Martin's Lane, on 19 June. The trip was made at Chico's suggestion. When interviewed for *The Marx Brothers Scrapbook*, Groucho claimed it was Harry Weber of United Booking who had made the arrangements; Kyle Crichton's book, Harpo's memoirs and Hector Arce's much later *Groucho* biography are instead unanimous in attributing the deal to Abe Lastfogel of the William Morris agency, who had recently taken over representation of the team. A supporting cast of seven included Ed Metcalfe (*qv*) and a young actress billed then as Helen Schroader (or Schroeder), but known later as Helen Kane (*qv*). Also on the bill were comedian Tommy Handley (in a sketch written by Eric Blore [*qv*]), Cecilia 'Cissie' Loftus (whose dog Harpo had

walked years before, when working as a hotel bellhop) and a troupe of Russian dancers, advertised as 'Lydia Lopokova, Leonide Massine, Lydia Sokolova and Leon Wojcikowski in a "Divertissement"'. Notices were enthusiastic: a review in the *Stage* of 22 June (sometimes misattributed to the *Times*) said the Marxes 'kept the audience in one continuous roar of laughter with comic business that was as fresh and original as it was funny'. There was praise also for the music, though the harp solo was considered to have been placed at the wrong point in the proceedings. 'The Marx Brothers are very welcome, for they have something new to offer and something that is really amusing,' added the reviewer, suggesting only a slight adaptation to 'English conditions' as a means of ensuring full comprehension of their material. The previous day's *Era* had similarly approved, considering them 'quite the funniest and cleverest crowd America has sent us, [meriting] the fabulous salary they are credited with receiving' (reportedly £400 per week). A sense of awe is implied in its account of a 'non-stop entertainment', during which 'the audience are not allowed a moment's respite from laughter'. Perhaps significantly, what would later become a frequent criticism of the team was considered here something of a tribute: 'The audience inevitably must have missed as many laughs as they received'. Groucho was lauded most as comedian, while some confusion existed as to whether Chico or Zeppo was the harpist of the group. Alone of the brothers, Harpo was not mentioned by name; this may be explained through simple examination of the theatre programme for that week, from which he was omitted. Such a mistake hints at an ill-starred London début, a notion confirmed in what has become perhaps the most notorious incident in Marx Brothers history. Accounts vary in minor details but relate substantially the same sad tale. The nervous Marxes had been assured by their agent that London audiences would 'eat it up'; they nearly did, but not in the way anticipated. It should be noted that the *Stage* reviewer makes specific reference to a performance on the Monday *afternoon*; by the Monday evening, their act generated no laughs and its title grew increasingly unfortunate as those in the balcony started to whistle. Groucho, disappearing into the wings, was heard to say 'They must know *some* language, but what the hell is it?' Assuming some barrier of accent if not language, Groucho tried to clarify his lines by mouthing them. This brought the ultimate insult to an actor, pennies hurled to the stage. In those days British pennies were substantial in size (and value), and could inflict more than psychological injury. Groucho walked to the footlights, raising a hand for silence. 'Friends,' he announced, 'it's been an expensive trip over. Would you mind throwing a little silver?' This brought the one genuine laugh of the evening and was much quoted around London (one 1930s source attributes the line to Chico, but this is contradicted by all other accounts). An article in *The New Movie Magazine* for January 1932 describes the audience, taking Groucho's request literally, as throwing shillings and thus providing more money than they received for the week's engagement. This is highly unlikely, given the purchasing power of a shilling (now 5 pence) in 1922 and the company's quite generous salary. Monetary details aside, the Marxes were determined to succeed in London ('We'll lick the Redcoats yet!' said Groucho). They had been welcomed by the matinée audience and were baffled by the change of mood. Harpo later recalled the manager's explanation of what had happened, verified in a subsequent letter from Groucho to *Variety*: their success in the first house had led to them being moved to the end of the programme, displacing the Russian dance troupe (then in its final week). The enraged *prima donna* had

arranged a claque to ensure the Marxes' failure in the evening's prime spot. The manager himself was impressed by the Marxes and clearly did not hold them responsible. Harpo mistakenly remembered the team being transferred to the Alhambra for the second week, as a means of pacifying the dance troupe; he and his brothers instead played two full weeks at the Coliseum before moving on. It is untrue to say they were cancelled on the spot, only to be booked by a

From the opening week's programme at the Coliseum; the omission of 'Arthur' Marx did not bode well

rival circuit on the strength of Groucho's ad lib; nor did the Coliseum management attempt to break the contract by suggesting the brothers might prefer to cancel the balance of their engagement. Another myth has Chico insisting on them playing Manchester for the second week, polishing up their earlier *Home Again* prior to returning to London. Each of these accounts bears some similarity to what *did* happen, chiefly a switch to the more sedate *Home Again* from the 26 June. (As with a later London engagement, neither sketch seems to have been submitted to the Lord

Chamberlain for censorship, probably because the contents of a variety bill constituted a grey area; for this reason, texts for these shows do not appear in the Lord Chamberlain's collection at the British Library.) Although the revived piece was less frenetic, the *Era* of 28 June believed it 'closely vies with *On the Balcony* for quick-fire humour'. The following day, the *Stage* astutely recognized the lack of 'dramatic significance', being aware instead of *Home Again*'s prime function as a 'display of the fine comedy work of the three comedian brothers'. The review went on to anticipate Sam Harris and, especially, Irving Thalberg (both *qv*) when speculating that 'if the Marx Brothers could only be seen in a well-written and adequately produced show there indeed would be a hit of the season'. The *Times* had ignored the Marxes' first week (except in its advertising) but ventured an opinion on 27 June. Some awareness of the Monday evening fiasco is implicit in a description of the replacement sketch as 'considerably better than that which they introduced ... a week ago'. Condescension permeates a recommendation of the team's versatility, noting the way all four "brothers" (quotations theirs) seemed able to 'sing, dance and play musical instruments indiscriminately' (though one doubts Harpo ever sang a note). The *Times* also considered Marx humour 'a little too trans-Atlantic for English audiences', even if conceding 'some of their remarks are subtle in the extreme'. This probably fair evaluation (for the time) preceded some evident knife-twisting when declaring '[the Marx Brothers] so obviously enjoy their own performance that it cannot be long before they persuade their audiences to do the same'. *Home Again*'s move to the Alhambra was not until the third week, commencing 3 July; the *Era* of 5 July mentioned how 'their recent appearance at the Coliseum created something of a sensation', assuring those who had missed them of 'another opportunity of seeing this company in a remarkably entertaining act'. *Home Again* impressed with its 'originality', the punchy American-style dialogue (this time lauded rather than merely tolerated) and the mute contribution of Harpo, singled out as 'one of the drollest silent comedians we have seen for many a day'. 'The Marx Brothers ... once more establish themselves as laughter-makers of the front rank', said the next day's *Stage*, reporting 'much that is clever and amusing in the form of instrumental work and comic business, and Alhambra audiences are well pleased'. The Alhambra engagement concluded the team's work in London. On 10 July they opened at the Bristol Hippodrome, and on 17 July commenced their final week, this time at the Hippodrome in Manchester. Among the other attractions was a young Northern comic named Sandy Powell, then some years before his great success in theatre, radio, films, television and a long-running series of comedy records. When quoted in the November 1981 *Freedonia Gazette*, 81-year-old Powell retained vivid memories of the Marx Brothers, chiefly of their style being rather beyond the comprehension of contemporary British audiences but much admired by their fellow professionals. It was usual for the Tuesday matinée audience to consist mostly of off-duty acts from the smaller halls, occupying free seats. As professionals, they greeted the Marxes enthusiastically despite being, in Powell's words, 'too "pro-ey"'. Powell recalled *Home Again*'s party format, in which various performers would be allowed their turn to entertain. The closing line, after the participants had exchanged good-byes, would be Groucho calling 'Minnie, they've gone. Get the supper ready.' This remark was clearly aimed at their mother, Minnie Marx (*qv*), who had accompanied them to England and would almost certainly have attended each performance. Finally, after forty minutes of mayhem, Groucho would get a laugh by stating the painfully obvious: 'Ladies and gentlemen, that concludes our

performance.' It was from Manchester that Groucho wrote to *Variety* concerning the Coliseum incident and its reasons; word had travelled and he was anxious to dispel any false notions. On 29 July, the Marx company sailed from Liverpool aboard the *Cedric*, bound for New York.

(See also: Abandoned projects; Berlin, Irving; Cochran, C.B.; Fighting; *Flywheel, Shyster and Flywheel*; Hotels; London Palladium, the; *Minnie's Boys*; Names; Russia; Vaudeville)

OPERA

(Marx Brothers films and shows *qv*)
It is strange to think of the robust Marx Brothers constantly working in parallel with that highbrow institution, opera. *A Night at the Opera* deliberately uses it to contrast their wild spirits, but impromptu versions of the 'Anvil Chorus' crop up in both *Cocoanuts* and *Animal Crackers*. Elsewhere in *Cocoanuts* Groucho introduces 'a cup of coffee, a sandwich, and you, from the opera I eat-a [*Aïda*]'. The eclecticism of vaudeville (*qv*) led to them being booked to play *Home Again* on the same bill as a major opera star, Emma Calve (who, for unrelated reasons, did not appear). A fictional diva is subjected to Groucho's interviewing technique in *Monkey Business*; another, from the same film, produces sufficient racket for Harpo to cover his head. It may have been Groucho's enthusiasm for Gilbert & Sullivan, culminating in his TV version of *The Mikado* (*qv*), that prompted Kalmar and Ruby's comic-opera receptions in *Animal Crackers* and *Duck Soup*. Whoever conceived the idea, it was not without influence: a 1934 M-G-M extravanganza, *Hollywood Party*, introduces a VIP in almost identical fashion.

(See also: Dumont, Margaret; In-jokes; Insults; Metcalfe, Edward; M-G-M; Puns; Ruby, Harry)

OPPENHEIMER, GEORGE (1900-77)
New York-born playwright, author, screenwriter (often in collaboration) and critic, initially in publishing; has been reported as a contributor to the Marxes' early radio series *Flywheel, Shyster and Flywheel* (*qv*); also worked on *A Day at the Races* (*qv*). Other work includes Eddie Cantor's *Roman Scandals* (1933), in collaboration with William Anthony McGuire, Arthur Sheekman (*qv*) and Nat Perrin (*qv*). Among later assignments are *Libeled Lady* (1936), Garbo's *Two-Faced Woman* (1941), *The Youngest Profession* (1943) and the *Topper* TV series.

(See also: Buzzell, Edward; Carroll, John; Eaton, Jay; Garbo, Greta; Ruby, Harry)

O'NEILL, HENRY
See: Trailers

O'SULLIVAN, MAUREEN (b. 1911) (d.1998)
Irish-born actress, daughter of a Major in the Connaught Rangers. Born in Boyle and raised in Killarney, she was convent-educated in Dublin and London before being sent to a finishing school in Paris. In American films from 1929 when director Frank Borzage, seeing her in a Dublin café, cast her opposite John McCormack in *Song o' My Heart*; best recalled as Jane to Johnny Weissmuller's Tarzan in jungle epics for M-G-M (*qv*) and for being the mother of present-day actress Mia Farrow. In *A Day at the Races* (*qv*) she is Judy Standish, whose sanitarium is saved by the Marxes and Allan Jones (*qv*). She is further reported with Chico in one of the M-G-M Miniatures, *Hollywood - the Second Step* (1936). The February 1937 issue of *Screen and Radio Weekly* includes a feature article attributed to the actress, in which she describes the Marxes as 'cute' despite their wild reputation. Apparently she had been warned to expect practical jokes and rough treatment, but believed that as heroine she had been spared this, unlike

Margaret Dumont and Esther Muir
(both *qv*). Groucho, whose first
marriage was by then in very poor
shape, was actually very taken with her
and wanted to propose marriage; much
later he suggested the attraction to
have been mutual, but stymied by both
having been married at the time.

(See also: Boasberg, Al; Carlisle, Kitty;
Guest appearances; Marriages; Sinatra,
Frank; Wood, Sam)

Maureen O'Sullivan *with Groucho in* A Day at the
Races

PABST BLUE RIBBON TOWN

See: Documentaries; Guest appearances; O'Brien, Virginia; Radio

PAINTINGS

The plot of *Animal Crackers* (*qv*) centres around the theft of no less than three copies of the same painting; when the Marxes (without Zeppo) contributed *gratis* to Heywood Broun's 1931 revue *Shoot the Works!*, each was rewarded with one of Broun's paintings. Away from the stage, the four brothers themselves were captured in oil by John Decker, respected painter and drinking buddy of W.C. Fields (*qv*). The picture hung in Groucho's home and was displayed to television viewers on *Person to Person*. Also by Decker is a revised version of Gainsborough's *Blue Boy* with Harpo's face; there is colour home movie footage of Harpo with Decker, in which Harpo examines the picture and compares the likeness. All the more extraordinary is a photo spread in the July 1950 issue of a British pocket magazine, *Lilliput*: in one of its double-page juxtapositions, the magazine printed a photo of Harpo from his recent UK visit, seemingly playing two recorders simultaneously, in the manner of pan pipes; opposite was a detail from Rubens' *The Triumph of Silenus*, showing a Harpo lookalike in identical pose. Harpo has frequently inspired comparison to mythology's fauns, elves, sprites and other mischief-makers, leading one to suspect Rubens and others as Marxmen ahead of their time. Most definitely of the Marxes' time was surrealist artist Salvador Dali, who in the 1930s produced a series of drawings of the team. They were designed to accompany a bizarre and unplayable script, called *The Marx Brothers On Horseback Salad* (he also constructed a similarly unplayable harp, strung with barbed wire). Dali's drawing of Groucho shows him as 'The Shiva of Big Business', answering a telephone with each of his multiple arms. Harpo is depicted in musical pose, the harp decorated with a tongue

and his head adorned by a lobster plus, presumably as dessert, an apple. Dali's portraits of Groucho and Harpo were displayed as part of the Smithsonian Institution's *Hollywood: Legend and Reality* exhibition during 1986 and 1987, initially at its own National Museum of American History, then at New York's Cooper-Hewitt Museum, Miami's Center of Fine Arts, the Cincinatti Art Museum, the Denver Art Museum and the Natural History Museum of Los Angeles County. The Dali *opus* may perhaps be taken in the tongue-in-cheek (if not tongue-on-harp) spirit that once persuaded Groucho to pose for a photograph dressed as Whistler's Mother. Harpo sometimes tried his hand at painting: on one occasion he engaged a nude model, only for Eddie Cantor (*qv*) to look in and be startled by the sight of a naked woman. It was probably at this time that Robert Benchley caught Harpo's attention with a discourse on painting, to be told that Harpo had recently taken it up himself. Alexander Woollcott (*qv*), convinced that Harpo could produce a masterpiece, promised that he and Benchley would arrange an exhibition and due press coverage. When work had reached an advanced stage, the two men paid Harpo a visit. Posing for him was a nude female model, a rose between her teeth. When Harpo had convinced himself of the work's completion, he showed the result to his visitors; he had painted a huge banana.

(See also: Home movies; Stage appearances [post-1930]; Television)

PARAMOUNT PICTURES

(Marx Brothers films *qv*)
A development from Adolph Zukor's Famous Players and Jesse Lasky's company, Paramount brought Harpo to the screen in 1925's *Too Many Kisses* (*qv*) before capturing the team *en masse* four years later in *The Cocoanuts*. This and *Animal Crackers* were filmed at their Astoria, Long Island studio but the Marxes were

brought to Hollywood for the next three, *Monkey Business*, *Horse Feathers* and *Duck Soup*. A reorganization to the company brought fears that money due the Marxes would never be paid and *Duck Soup* was only made after a considerable battle. The resulting acrimony was one of the reasons for the end of their association; ironically, the Marxes played several Paramount theatres during their stage tours for M-G-M (*qv*). Long after the dispute was settled, Paramount invited Groucho to a screening of DeMille's *Samson and Delilah* (1949), in which the muscular Victor Mature starred opposite willowy Hedy Lamarr. After the show, a studio executive asked Groucho's opinion; in rather more direct words than these, he replied that no film could hold his interest in which the leading man had a bigger bust than the leading lady. Groucho later noted a reluctance to invite him to any subsequent screenings, though within that period he contributed to Paramount's *Mr Music* and *Skidoo* (both *qv*).

(See also: Agents; Gordon, Max; Mankiewicz, Herman; Marx Bros., Inc.; RKO; Ryskind, Morrie)

PEACE AND QUIET
See: *A Day at the Races*

PENDLETON, NAT (1899-1967)
(Marx Brothers films *qv*)
Iowa-born actor whose muscleman image typed him in bovine roles, despite his college graduate status. Much of this may be traced to his background in wrestling, for which, according to David Ragan, he was a silver medallist at the 1920 Olympics. As such he appears as the thuggish McCarthy in *Horse Feathers* and is the aptly-named Goliath, strongman of *At the Circus*. Career started in silents; among many other talkies are De Mille's *The Sign of the Cross* (1932), *The Beast of the City* (1932), Frank Capra's *Lady For a Day* (1933), Mae West's *I'm No Angel* (1933), *The Thin*

Man (1934) and *Another Thin Man* (1937), *The Great Ziegfeld* (1936), the British-made Jessie Matthews vehicle *Gangway* (1937), Abbott & Costello's *Buck Privates* (1941) and *Buck Privates Come Home* (1947) and the *Dr Kildare* series.

PERELMAN, S.J. (1904-79)
(Marx Brothers films and shows *qv*)
American writer, born Simeon Joseph Perelman but known throughout his life as Sidney or, to friends, Sid. Under any name (or initials) Perelman was one of the world's most celebrated humorists. A Marx Brothers fan from childhood, he would later record his memories of their vaudeville sketch *Home Again* for posterity. During 1931-2 he collaborated on the screenplays for the first Marx films produced on the West Coast, *Monkey Business* and *Horse Feathers*. When at Brown University in the 1920s, Perelman edited the college paper,

Brown Jug; subsequently a regular contributor to *Judge*, predominantly but not exclusively as cartoonist, this early work being anthologized five years after his death as *That Old Gang O'Mine*. In his introduction to this collection, Richard Marschall makes the point that Perelman's *Judge* and *College Humor* articles, long pre-dating the *Holiday* and *New Yorker* pieces with which he is more closely identified, would have been those that first impressed the Marx Brothers. According to Marschall, Perelman depicted Groucho in both texts and drawings before any professional association existed; when Perelman's first collection, *Dawn Ginsbergh's Revenge*, appeared in 1928, it carried a

S.J. Perelman (*seated on mudguard*) *is central in this group of* Monkey Business *personnel. Left to right: Groucho, Solly Violinski, Perelman, Will B. Johnstone and Arthur Sheekman*
BFI Stills, Posters and Designs

now famous dust-jacket endorsement by Groucho: 'From the moment I picked up your book until I laid it down, I was convulsed with laughter. Some day I intend reading it.' Perelman's biographer, Dorothy Herrmann, records also Groucho's potentially misleading first attempt, namely 'This book will always be a first edition.' Perelman's widely-quoted account of his first meeting with Groucho, and resultant screenwriting for the team, was penned in 1961 for *Show* magazine under the title 'The Winsome Foursome'; collected after Perelman's death in *The Last Laugh*, it sometimes falls short on specific details but may be relied upon in spirit (albeit couched in Perelman's jaundiced humour) and for its general events. Perelman describes he and his wife Laura attending a stage presentation of *Animal Crackers* in New York; date is given as Fall 1931, an obvious mistake as Perelman's first screen work for the team, *Monkey Business*, was already in release and *Animal Crackers* had finished touring almost a year before. Given the speed of subsequent events, the performance is more likely to have been when the Marxes made a personal appearance tour (in their old Napoleon sketch from *I'll Say She Is!*) to publicize the screen version. While in the audience, Perelman was handed a note, in response to the card he had sent Groucho backstage. Groucho had agreed to see him and was duly present - clad in his underwear - when Mr and Mrs Perelman called at his dressing room. According to Perelman, Groucho's reason for seeing the young (and fairly impoverished) scribe was in response to a need to locate new writers for a proposed radio series. Perelman was to collaborate with Will B. Johnstone (qv), the newspaper cartoonist who had written *I'll Say She Is!* for the Marxes in 1923. Perelman was taken aback, having had no prior experience in scriptwriting. Groucho claimed that Johnstone probably had as little idea of the job as Perelman, adding 'I can't imagine two people

worse equipped for the job, but there's one thing in your favour. You're both such tyros [novices] you might just come up with something fresh.' The two duly met, establishing a rapport but produced little more than the idea of casting the brothers as stowaways on an ocean liner. This was the idea presented to the team on meeting with them for lunch at the Astor Hotel. Once Chico had finished placing bets on the telephone, Groucho had vented his disgust over his stock-market losses and Harpo had chased enough girls, Perelman and Johnstone bravely offered their plot strand. They feared the worst as the Marxes conferred, only to be told that, far from serving a 'fly-by-night radio serial', their idea would instead be the foundation of the team's next film. The dazed writers were hustled off to the Paramount building, given contracts and despatched by train to California. It was a similarly abrupt hiring session that brought Nat Perrin (qv) out for the same project. (The radio series did not come to fruition during 1931, and one can only surmise that other commitments saw its cancellation or that it eventually made the airwaves a year later as *Flywheel, Shyster and Flywheel* [qv]). In the end, Perelman contributed to *Monkey Business* and *Horse Feathers* and was quick to deny frequent claims that he had written virtually their entire repertoire; latterly Perelman would not even discuss his work with the team, feeling his many literary achievements were being overshadowed by a brief hiatus in his career. There are numerous collections of Perelman essays, many of them from *The New Yorker*; a play co-written with Ogden Nash, *One Touch of Venus*, was directed for the screen by William A. Seiter (qv) from a screenplay co-authored by Frank Tashlin (qv). Outside of the Marx films, Perelman as screenwriter (a role he detested) is most closely identified with Mike Todd's 1956 epic, *Around the World in 80 Days*. Groucho was peeved by Perelman's implied rejection of their

association plus any notion of Perelman's dominance in their films (*not* instigated by the writer), the more so after their friendship cooled considerably (to say the least). The reason behind this rift is obscure, though Groucho attributed it to a London interview conducted by Kenneth Tynan, presumably that for the *Observer* in 1964. Examination of the text reveals nothing outwardly hostile but Groucho spoke of competition between the two humorists. It has been suggested that a 1952 Perelman essay (known eventually as *I'll Always Call You Schnorrer, My African Explorer*) may have upset Groucho with an uncomplimentary account of a visit to the set of *A Girl in Every Port* (qv); a more likely culprit than this essentially joky affair is Perelman's rueful 'Winsome Foursome' essay. In 1976 Groucho attempted to dispel notions of a feud, explaining simply that the respective humour of Perelman and the Marxes did not always mesh. Perelman visited Groucho towards the end of the comedian's life but, according to Dorothy Herrmann, the reunion was underscored by continuing grudges, at least on Perelman's part.

PERRIN, NAT (b. 1907) (d. 1998)

(Marx Brothers films qv)
Screenwriter and later producer; originally a law student, Nat Perrin began his show business career just as he was about to take his bar exams. An early scriptwriting ambition manifested itself in a Groucho-Chico sketch written on his own initiative; a contact promised to get it to the Marx Brothers by way of Frieda Fishbein, Moss Hart's agent; when this fell through, Perrin borrowed the agent's stationery in order to approach them directly. This he did when the Marxes made a personal appearance in Brooklyn, promoting the film of *Animal Crackers*. Perrin's sketch and bogus letter were sent backstage and Groucho agreed to meet him. Although there was no place for the sketch, new writers were

required for the team's first West Coast film, *Monkey Business*, and Perrin was invited to join them in California. A meeting was arranged with Chico at Paramount's New York offices, where finances were to be agreed. Once there, Chico asked Perrin how much he required as salary. Perrin was unsure so Chico suggested $100 a week. Perrin had once lost out on a publicist's job at Warner Brothers, because his face betrayed disappointment at an offer of $25 a week; in consequence, he was convinced that Paramount would consider this an excessive sum, and attempted to have the fee reduced. On reaching California, Perrin was dismayed to learn that his co-writers were earning at least ten times that figure. The bad news was compounded on discovering he had passed his law exams and would have been earning far more from his original vocation. Perrin was present at the fateful reading of the script's first draft, when an increasingly forlorn S.J. Perelman (*qv*) strove to impress the Marxes with the material he and Will B. Johnstone (*qv*) had created. It was from here that Perrin and the other new recruits began to contribute. Perrin contributed several scenes and later told Lee Server (for the book *Screenwriter*) of a *Monkey Business* routine he had written, in which stowaways Harpo and Chico hide in the ship's barber shop. As written, Harpo was supposed to use black shoe polish on a customer's white shoes, strictly inadvertently; as played, he used the black polish deliberately. Perrin was disappointed to see the routine's motive altered, though one should note how Harpo's character suits conscious mischief rather than ineptitude. (After all that, the scene didn't even make it to the final version; available prints substitute a gag with Harpo and Chico systematically removing an officer's moustache.) Perrin's next job, Keaton's *The Sidewalks of New York* (1931), was arranged by producer Herman Mankiewicz (*qv*); his second

assignment for the Marx Brothers was the radio show *Flywheel, Shyster and Flywheel* (*qv*). Perrin wrote *Flywheel* with a fellow *Monkey Business* inductee, Arthur Sheekman (*qv*). When interviewed for the *Flywheel* script book, Perrin recalled writing the first episode with Sheekman, Groucho and Chico while on the train east. As noted elsewhere, *Flywheel* overlapped with the scripting of *Duck Soup*, and much of the Sheekman-Perrin material for the radio show was re-used in the new film. Their partnership continued into a brace of Goldwyn films starring Eddie Cantor (*qv*): the first, *Roman Scandals* (1933), was adapted by William Anthony McGuire from a story by George S. Kaufman (*qv*) and Robert Sherwood; George Oppenheimer (*qv*), Sheekman and Perrin were credited for 'additional material'. Cantor's next film, *Kid Millions* (1934), was from an original story and screenplay by Sheekman, Perrin and Nunnally Johnson (*qv*). Further collaborations seem less Marx-like, notably the 1936 Shirley Temple films *Stowaway* and *Dimples*. The Sheekman-Perrin partnership concluded amicably, each pursuing his own projects while continuing to meet socially; they also kept contact with the Marxes, for whom Perrin supplied gags during the pre-filming tour of *Go West*. Perrin receives credit on the Marxes' final M-G-M film, *The Big Store*, itself based on a *Flywheel* episode. Many other films include Olsen & Johnson's *Hellzapoppin'* (1941), *Abbott & Costello in Hollywood* (1945) and *Song of the Thin Man* (1947). Later in television, where he is best-known for developing *The Addams Family* as a sitcom; it might be added that John Astin's Gomez in these shows is often reminiscent of Groucho. Nat Perrin, whom Groucho nicknamed 'the Deacon' through an alleged clerical resemblance, remained a close friend of the comedian throughout his life. During Groucho's last months, Perrin was for a while named his conservator.

(See also: Documentaries; Fleming, Erin; Letters; McLeod, Norman; Puns; Seiter, William A.; Temple, Shirley)

THE PIANO

In childhood, the family could afford only for Chico to have piano lessons, the idea being for him to teach Harpo; he didn't, and Harpo taught himself to a large degree, though with a repertoire consisting only of *Love Me and the World Is Mine* and *Waltz Me Around Again, Willie*. The more accomplished Chico could obtain jobs in nickelodeons, only for his near-lookalike, Harpo, to take them over. Some of Chico's youthful jobs were in brothels; a curious sidelight regards a legal settlement made to him in the late 1940s, after a film was alleged to have represented him as a 'mad pianist' who had at one time played in a bordello. Harpo's worst experience was in a tavern run by a family presided over by a homicidal matriarch. Chico's piano style consisted of rhythm played with the left hand and most of the melody picked out with the right hand's index finger. For all its simplicity, it charmed audiences the world over; Chico would 'practice' each day by soaking his hands in warm water for ten minutes.

(See also: Harp, the; *Home Again*; Prostitutes)

PICKFORD, MARY

See: *Love Happy*; United Artists

PIROSH, ROBERT (1910-89)

Screenwriter and director who acted in the former capacity on *A Night at the Opera* and *A Day at the Races* (both *qv*). Robert Pirosh won the Oscar for his story and screenplay for *Battleground* (1949), of which he was also associate producer. Long list of notable screenplays, among them *I Married a Witch* (1942) and Danny Kaye's first Goldwyn feature, *Up in Arms* (1944). Credits as writer-director include *Go For Broke* (1951), *Washington Story* (1952) and *Valley of*

The piano: *Chico and an attentive audience in* A Night at the Opera

the Kings (1954). Later wrote prolifically for TV series, such as *Hawaii Five-O*, *Ironside* and *The Waltons*. Pirosh was interviewed for a 1982 documentary, *The Marx Brothers in a Nutshell*.

(See also: Documentaries)

POLICEMEN

(Marx Brothers films and shows *qv*) 'I'm Henderson, plain clothes man'; 'You look more like an *old* clothes man to me.' Groucho's instant put-down of Robert Emmet O'Connor in *A Night at the Opera*, prior to bringing him close to a mental breakdown. The Marx Brothers played characters who were the natural opponents of law and order. As early as *Home Again* they employed a policeman as foil, who would be the man to shake Harpo's hand as silverware fell from the other sleeve. The hapless detective of *Cocoanuts* cannot even keep his shirt, let alone arrest Chico and Harpo; in *Animal Crackers* Groucho poses as a Scotland Yard man while Harpo, a suspect, follows the force disguised in one of

their own uniforms; while Harpo entraps a cop in a dog-catcher's wagon in *Horse Feathers*. The officers of the law in *A Night in Casablanca* actually get to throw them in jail, but their captivity is only temporary.

(See also: Cars; Laurel & Hardy; Metcalfe, Edward; O'Connor, Robert Emmet; Prisons; Seymour, Dan)

POLITICIANS

(Marx Brothers films and shows *qv*) Here and there the Marx Brothers are contrasted with political figures in addition to other sacred cows, as when greeted by the Mayor in *A Night at the Opera*. Detailed elsewhere is the story of a complaint from a real-life Mayor over *Duck Soup*. This film has the reputation of a political satire, which in effect it is even if couched in farcical terms. It was probably this film that prompted Billy Wilder's never-realized idea for the Marxes, *A Day at the United Nations*. There is reference to President Roosevelt's 'fireside' broadcasts in *Room Service* (see **Radio**) and in a stage performance of *Animal Crackers* Groucho is said to have obliterated the harp solo with an *ad lib* about a political scandal. As one

can imagine, the unorthodox Marxes were not given to the hidebound in political terms. Nat Perrin (*qv*) put it well by saying 'Groucho was a liberal ... and Harpo was a liberal ... and Chico bet on the Chicago White Sox'. The Marx Brothers supported liberal politics but generally in discreet terms. When Heywood Broun ran as a left-wing candidate in 1931, the team not only voted for him but (minus Zeppo) participated in his benefit revue, *Shoot the Works!* (see **Paintings** and **Stage appearances [post-1930]**). In 1953, attempts were made to persuade Groucho to run for Governor of California, an office subsequently filled by a quite different actor named Reagan. In *Memoirs of a Mangy Lover* (1963) Groucho mentions a then-recent campaign for him to run for *Vice*-President, the idea being for him to experience the unusual sensation of never having to say anything. This is in a section headed 'Marxist Philosophy, According to Groucho', resurrecting a pun on Karl Marx that wore out its welcome in Marx reviews many years before (Groucho, of course, was entitled to use it). Its most-repeated incarnation is in a *graffito* from the Paris student riots of 1968, when an anonymous hand scrawled 'Je suis Marxiste - tendance Groucho' on an unsuspecting wall. To return to the adult world, Groucho once spent a reasonably pleasant visit with President Truman, but also had to apologise for a joke - since lost to posterity - made about Truman on radio. Far less cordial were Groucho's latter-day comments about Richard Nixon, to the effect that America's only hope would be his assassination. Groucho subsequently withdrew the remark, believing in votes rather than violence; just the same, details later emerged of a sizeable FBI file on the comedian, the result of his somewhat blunt statement. A more pleasant postscript: in its edition of 20 October 1990, *The Economist* quoted a senior Brussels diplomat, who compared Italy's presidency of the European Community to a trip with the Marx Brothers as drivers; a follow-up appeared on 17 November, in the form of a letter ostensibly from the Marxes and forwarded by 'a senior Italian official'. The letter made its point amid scattered references to Marx movies and the famous 'four-year-old child' quip.

(See also: Abandoned projects; Children; Gambling; Letters; Pratt, Purnell; Race; Sport)

PRACTICAL JOKES

(Marx Brothers films and shows *qv*)
It is to be expected that the Marxes were fond of practical jokes. A full account might fill a book but it's worth mentioning the time they sent Kitty Carlisle (*qv*) some flowers, giving the name Allan Jones (*qv*); they were sent COD. Sam Wood (*qv*) took rather a lot from them, as when Chico stole some money from him and returned it in the form of bagged-up coins. Another time Chico, disguised, delivered Wood a telegram informing him the Marxes had gone away during shooting. Joe Adamson quotes a story from the making of *Duck Soup* when the Marxes had agreed to an early-morning meeting with Bert Kalmar and Harry Ruby (*qv*). The Marxes arrived more than three hours late, feigning outrage over having waited for the others at RKO. When informed they were making the film at Paramount, the Marx response was 'Don't change the subject'. Elsewhere is documented an elaborate joke when Ruby appeared on-stage in *Animal Crackers* after being cheated out of a birthday present. Detailed under **Female impersonation** is an early Harpo prank, while later he considered the grandiose Alexander Woollcott (*qv*) an ideal target. Noted elsewhere is an account of the Marxes stripping Woollcott of his clothes when he visited their dressing room. The critic was less displeased when the Marxes, invited to one of his gatherings, created a disturbance outside on a merry-go-round borrowed for the occasion.

Margaret Dumont (*qv*), who in some ways took herself even more seriously than did Woollcott, was an especially vulnerable target, particularly on tour. Margaret Irving (*qv*), herself an occasional victim, has spoken of the way Miss Dumont would variously be stripped or otherwise humiliated on each train journey, threatening to depart at each stop but never actually doing so. Sometimes the Marxes would prey on each other, as when Chico and Harpo deliberately made Groucho late for the studio (see **Insomnia**); otherwise it took bravery and imagination to put one over on them, of the type displayed by Al Boasberg or Esther Muir (both *qv*).

(See also: Censorship; Could Harpo Speak?; McLeod, Norman; Paramount Pictures; Prisons; RKO; Spectacles; Thalberg, Irving)

PRATT, PURNELL (1886-1941)

Illinois-born actor with stage experience; plays the Mayor in *A Night at the Opera* (*qv*). In films from silent period; among numerous talkies are Harry Richman's *Puttin' On the Ritz* (1930), *The Public Enemy* (1931), *Grand Hotel* (1932) and *Waterfront Lady* (1935).

(See also: O'Connor, Robert Emmett; Miles, Lotta; Politicians)

PREMINGER, OTTO

See: *Skidoo*

PRISONS

(Marx Brothers films *qv*)
There are occasional references to prisons in the Marx Brothers' saga. The strictly unofficial incarcerations of Chico and Harpo in *Horse Feathers* or that of the heroine of *Monkey Business* are outside the category; however, Chico and Harpo retrieve Oscar Shaw (*qv*) from jail in *Cocoanuts*, even though Harpo is locked in and has to remove a bar in order to follow on. It is often said that director Victor Heerman (*qv*) kept the ever-elusive

Marxes in specially constructed prison cells between takes of *Animal Crackers*; in the film itself, Chico thinks he may recognize Roscoe W. Chandler from either Sing Sing, Joliet or Leavenworth. The latter establishment is mentioned again in *Duck Soup* when Chico is given a choice between 'ten years in Leavenworth, or eleven years in Twelveworth'. *A Night in Casablanca* places all three in a cell, to which they return inside a crashed aircraft. Chico, Harpo and Allan Jones (*qv*) share a ship's brig in *A Night at the Opera*; later in the film, when their arrest as illegal immigrants seems inevitable, Groucho serves them breakfast with a motherly 'C'mon, you'll be late for jail!' In real life, their acquaintance with such environs was mercifully sparse: when *I'll Say She Is!* (*qv*) played Philadelphia, Groucho had fun at a local reporter's expense by fabricating tales of charitable prison visits dating back ten years; the item, from the *Philadelphia Record*, was discovered by and reprinted in the *Freedonia Gazette* (*qv*) for Summer 1981. When a Groucho-Chico radio sketch took them into court over copyright problems, the comedians requested details of the best prisons; Chico asked whether he would be required to have his head shaved. On another occasion Harpo, dressed as Kaiser Wilhelm for a costume party, was forced to hitch-hike home; he was held by the police on suspicion of vagrancy, partly because Chico wouldn't take the matter seriously enough to come along to identify him!

(See also: Boasberg, Al; Gangsters; Policemen; Practical jokes; Radio)

PROSTITUTES

'Those whores, they just loved us ... and usually for free.' So said Zeppo to Barry Norman when interviewed shortly before his death. In an age when travelling actors were not necessarily welcomed in strange towns, the local brothel offered a place not only for sex but also general hospitality in the form of food, drink and music. As implied in Zeppo's recollection, the Marxes were popular in such establishments, partially through their ability to entertain the girls with music and jokes. There were very rare exceptions: in *Memoirs of a Mangy Lover* Groucho spoke of an actor who had made himself objectionable one evening, but was invited to stay despite; he was ushered into a room, asked to undress and subsequently left to the mercies of a horde of rats. He grabbed his clothes and escaped into the night, as the madam and her girls watched, laughingly, from an upstairs window. This account, published in 1963, does not name the actor but at a London press conference, in July 1964, the victim was revealed as none other than Harpo. Normally the most amiable of people, Harpo had that evening displayed an uncharacteristic lapse in grace and was made to face the consequences. It was a Montreal streetwalker who initiated Groucho at the age of 16, when, ironically, he was touring in a play called *The Man of Her Choice*. She approached him after the show, the result being that Groucho exchanged his virginity for something requiring a specialized kind of doctor. Treatment, though primitive at that time, was successful but Groucho never forgot his poor luck. Later, in *Groucho and Me*, he expressed the controversial opinion (for 1959) that legalized brothels were a good idea, rather than attempting to suppress the entire business. There are implied jokes about prostitutes in the Marx films, inevitably few given the censorship of the period. One likely candidate is in *A Night at the Opera* (*qv*) when Groucho, aghast to hear of an opera singer receiving $1,000 a night, retorts 'You can get a phonograph record of Minnie the Moocher for 75 cents. For a buck and a quarter you can get Minnie!' There is an apocryphal story of a very old, frail Groucho being stopped by a woman who said 'Old man, you've had it,' to which his reply was 'In which case, how much do I owe you?'

(See also: Chaplin, Charlie; Piano, the; Vaudeville; Women)

PUNS

(Marx Brothers films *qv*)
'How would you like to have somebody steal one of your heifers?' asks Groucho of a cow in *Monkey Business*. 'I know, heifer cow is better than none,' he continues, 'but this is no time for puns.' The *Cambridge Encyclopedia of Language* conveys a precise definition of an addiction to making puns, as identified by a German scientist in 1939; it is known officially as Förster's Syndrome and it may fairly be said that Groucho and Chico were among its most chronic sufferers. In *Animal Crackers* they have scarcely met before the following is exchanged:

Groucho: How much would you want to run into an open manhole?
Chico: Just the cover charge.
Groucho: Well, drop in sometime.
Chico: Sewer.

Puns have a profoundly mixed reputation; revered by some, they are condemned by others as a lower form of wit than sarcasm. (The author's personal opinion is that they are detested by those with insufficient wit to make them.) There is a double, or triple edge to puns, in that simple onomatopoeia combines with lateral thinking and, as Joe Adamson has observed, a considerable degree of audacity. As explained by Mark Brisenden in a *Daily Telegraph* piece called 'When Puns Were Fun' (a review of Robert Bader's 1993 Groucho anthology), puns are today much less in vogue than in the 1920s. In those heady days they were perpetrated by leading scribes with a mixture of pride and outright defiance, particularly if horribly contrived. Few are more contrived (or more horrible) than Chico's claim (in *Cocoanuts*) to have reached America on the 'Atlantic Auction', or that in *Monkey Business* his grandfather's beard is 'coming by hairmail'. Here are a few of the better ones:

Monkey Business:
Briggs: Didn't I give you two gats?
Groucho: Well, we had to drown the gats, but we saved you a little black gitten.

Horse Feathers:
Chico: You sing high, uh?
Connie: Yes, I have a falsetto voice.
Chico: That's-a funny, my last pupil, she had a falsetto teeth.

Duck Soup:
Chico: We shadow him all day.
Trentino: But what day was that?
Chico: Shadowday!

The above should be sufficient to satisfy punsters without unduly offending the rest of humanity. However, no discourse on Marx Brothers puns can ignore the legendary gag in *A Night at the Opera* where Groucho, explaining a contract, mentions a (wait for it) sanity clause. 'You can't fool me,' replies Chico, 'there ain't no Sanity Clause!'

(See also: Animals; *The Big Store*; Books; *Flywheel, Shyster and Flywheel*; *I'll Say She Is!*; Race)

RACE

(Marx Brothers films *qv*)

'Red man, you're a white man' says Groucho, to what would today be called a Native American, in *Go West*. Race was not as sensitive an issue at that time and Groucho is here ridiculing a then-familiar expression. In *Monkey Business* he parodies directly a racist cliché, 'why don't you go back where you came from', when speaking to a party guest who is dressed as an Indian Chief; this guying of bigotry combines intriguingly with two other points, namely that (a) he's not a real Indian and (b) they were in America before the 'white' people had even heard of the place. Parallel to this is a reference in the song introducing Captain Spaulding in *Animal Crackers*, describing him as 'the only white man' to have covered every part of Africa, the kind of jingoistic talk then associated with exploring. In both *Monkey Business* and its promo (*qv*), Groucho follows a piece of Chico idiocy with 'There's my argument - restrict immigration', but he is clearly referring only to one specific Italian *emigré*. There are three specific moments in the Marx films that cause discomfort to modern viewers. One of these, in *Duck Soup*, is Groucho's 'The Headstrongs married the Armstrongs, and that's why darkies were born'. This refers to an old minstrel song (of the sort parodied later in the film) and the joke is designed solely to convey an archaic reference while simultaneously noting a similarity to the lyric. (The same title formed the basis for a pun in *Flywheel, Shyster and Flywheel* [*qv*].) An identical principle applies when in *Horse Feathers* Groucho resurrects 'For He's A Jolly Good Fellow' with 'He's only a shell of his former self, which nobody can deny'. The other scenes concern Harpo's Pied Piper-like influence upon black communities in *A Day at the Races* and *At the Circus*, embarrassing today but accepted - not to say enjoyed - when first screened. Though undoubtedly patronizing, they are at least not in the category of direct racial gags sometimes found in pre-war comedies. It is said that some American TV screenings omit the relevant section of the earlier film, but all such appearances in the UK have been uncut. For the most part, the Marx films have no need of racial material. The Marxes themselves were occasional victims of prejudice (see **Religion**) and most certainly did not inflict it upon others. Groucho, who at one time supported a campaign against racial discrimination, took great exception when Sam Wood (*qv*) complained about a mixed-race baseball team.

(See also: Puns; Television)

RADIO

(Marx Brothers films *qv*)

Screen actors were frequent radio guests before TV became the mass entertainment. Often they would plug their latest appearances or star in sound adaptations of their screen successes (see **Irving Cummings**). American radio sold commercial space for extended studio-made programmes trailing forthcoming movies, those for the Marxes being described under **Trailers**. Surprisingly, Harpo was the first Marx to speak on radio, in a 1926 broadcast with Admiral Byrd (to whom there is joky reference in *Duck Soup*!). As a mime, Harpo was unsuited to radio but made occasional forays, as in a 1944

Bing Crosby *Command Performance* (made by AFRS, the American Forces Radio Service) in which he communicates by taxi horn before providing harp accompaniment to Crosby singing *My Blue Heaven*. In 1932, Groucho and Chico were approached by the *Lucky Strike* programme; neither this nor a 30-minute CBS pilot, for intended sponsorship by Chevrolet, reached fruition, but the end of the year saw the start of what became *Flywheel, Shyster and Flywheel* (*qv*). Under **Guest appearances** are details of film preserving Groucho on KHJ radio in 1933. 1934 brought *Flywheel*'s successor, *The Marx of Time*, guying current affairs and the recently-launched *March of Time* newsreel. It ran on CBS for 8 weeks from 4 March. Groucho was reporter 'Ulysses H. Drivel' (or Ulysses H. Drivvle), assisted by Chico as 'Penelli'. Sponsor was American Oil. Extant today is what may have been another Groucho-Chico pilot, *The Marx Brothers Show*, recorded in Hollywood. Its pilot status is suggested by a bogus-sounding sponsor, 'the Hotchkiss Packing Company', and Groucho's announcement referring to forthcoming Friday night broadcasts. The main sketch presents Groucho and Chico as shady Hollywood agents, possibly as a joke aimed at Zeppo and Gummo (see **Agents**). There follows a comic monologue about Groucho's supposed war experiences, then a song, 'Pennies From Heaven', with female vocalist Hollis Shaw, an apparent discovery of the Marxes. Also taking part are Bill Goodwin and the Raymond Paige Orchestra. The show, sometimes identified as being from CBS, has been dated from 1938, but a joke about Jean Harlow (who died in 1937), plus use of *A Night at the Opera*'s music, suggest perhaps 1936. It was around this time that Groucho and Chico performed a radio sketch that eventually landed them in court for unauthorized use, The skit was allegedly written by Al Boasberg (*qv*)

Groucho and Chico attend court over a radio sketch

with Garrett and Carroll Graham. Boasberg was said to have granted the Marxes permission but died shortly before the hearing. A decision was reached late in 1937 with Groucho and Chico having to pay a fine (see also **Prisons**). The decision may have served to reverse the comedians' policy, announced in May of that year, to take a two-year break from films in order to concentrate on radio. They were not entirely absent from the air during this period, for historian Michael Barson has reported a 1937 guest appearance on Louella Parsons' *Hollywood Hotel* programme. It has been said that invitations to participate, at Miss Parsons' personal request and strictly unpaid, could be declined only at the risk of subsequent pillorying in her column. When Bob Hope's first series, sponsored by Pepsodent, commenced in October of 1938, the regular guests included Groucho and George Burns (*qv*). Also present was a singing group, 'Six Hits and a Miss', who appeared with the Marxes in *The Big Store*. The final Marx Brothers series, *The Circle*, began its series of 25 hour-long shows on the CBS Red Network in November 1939. Sponsored by Kellogg's, the 'circle' was a supposed club comprised of celebrities, their activities ranging from

songs and jokes to comparatively serious debate. Among its 'members' at various times were Ronald Colman, Carole Lombard, Cary Grant, Lawrence Tibbett, Madeline Carroll and guests such as Noël Coward and Alexander Woollcott (*qv*). The second episode, from 22 November 1939, still exists: Groucho and Chico (playing 'Ravelli' again!) challenge prospective member Jose Iturbi to an erstwhile duel and engage him in a song routine similar to the 'I-want-my-shirt' business from *Cocoanuts*. Much of the programme's latter section is a far from oblique comment on the reasons behind the recently-declared war in Europe. This brave, experimental series contrasts sharply with most of its brash contemporaries and was applauded more by critics than the general public. Once the Marxes had retired from films in 1941, radio became a higher priority. Groucho was a guest both on *Information, Please* (October '41) and in several of Rudy Vallee's shows. Chico tried a series, *Chico's Barber Shop*, and later appeared with his band on the *Fitch Bandwagon* (or, in Chico's parlance, the 'Fish Wagon'). Available recordings are dated from late 1943, but Chico is thought to have discontinued his band during the summer of that year; preserved are Chico's banter with MC Toby Reed, plus various musical items, some with vocalist Mel Torme. Other Chico broadcasts include 'Noodlin' Around' (AFRS *Command Performance*) and an appearance with the 'Quiz Kids'. Groucho performed for 63 consecutive weeks (without a summer break) on the CBS *Pabst Blue Ribbon Town* during 1943-4. Among the regulars was Virginia O'Brien (*qv*), later replaced by Fay McKenzie; others included Donald Dickson, the Robert Armbruster Orchestra and, during 1943, Leo Gorcey of the 'Dead End Kids' and 'Bowery Boys' films (whose ex wife, Kay, married Groucho in 1945). Film of Groucho with guest Carole Landis is detailed under **Guest appearances**. Chico was guest in three shows and Harpo contributed to the final edition. The show resumed with Kenny Baker (*qv*) replacing Groucho. *Blue Ribbon Town* was written, directed and produced by Dick Mack; among other known writers were cartoonist Fred Fox, who died in August 1981, and Selma Diamond, who later provided material for Ed Sullivan, Jimmy Durante, Milton Berle and others. Reportedly the model for Rose Marie's wisecracking character in TV's *The Dick Van Dyke Show* of the early 1960s, Selma Diamond died in 1985, aged 64. Despite this show's success, Groucho's luck in radio remained poor. With Irving Brecher (*qv*), he co-created *The Life of Riley* but was forced to abdicate the starring role to William Bendix (*qv*) in order to attract a sponsor. Another failed pilot was *The Beverly-Groucho Hotel* in 1946. Many of Groucho's 1940s variety appearances survive: 'Groucho's Mother' (with Betty Grable and Bill Goodwin) and *The All Star Cowboy Hour* (with Martha Tilton and Hy Averback), both from the AFRS *Mail Call*; 'Livingstone Marx, African Explorer' (AFRS *G.I. Journal*); a bogus game show from AFRS *Command*

Performance, 'Dr People Are Double and Take It Truth or Ignorance it Pays to Be Information', with Ken Carpenter; 'Dr G. Marx Hackenbush' (*Philco Radio Hall of Fame*, 12 March 1944); 'Groucho in the Marines' (*Chase and Sanborn Program*, 10 June 1945); 'Groucho the Patient', 'Groucho the Hypochondriac' and 'The Spiwit of Spwing' (*Birds Eye Open House*, 1945); 'Groucho Marx, Attorney at Law' (with Bing Crosby in *Philco Radio Time*, 12 February 1947); and 'Groucho in Chicago' (ditto, 30 April 1947). 'The Spiwit of Spwing' is one of Groucho's semi-regular contributions to Dinah Shore's radio programmes of 1945-6, both she and announcer Harry Von Zell participate in the sketch. The title character is played by Arthur Q. Bryan in his 'Elmer Fudd' voice from the Warner cartoons (see also **Animation**). Bryan's colleague at Warner, Mel Blanc, contributes to 'Livingstone Marx', as do Johnny Weissmuller, Verna Felton and Lucille Ball (*qv*). In addition to gags, Groucho was also permitted to sing: the February 1947 show has Groucho singing his song from *Copacabana* (*qv*), 'Go West, Young Man'; that from 30 April presents Groucho, Crosby and Dorothy Shay singing 'Feudin', Fightin' and Fussin'; 'Groucho the Patient' provides a chance to use 'Dr Hackenbush'; the quiz parody detailed above (itself anticipatory of Groucho's future direction) is followed by 'Lydia, the Tattooed Lady'; the *All Star Comedy Hour* includes a strange Western song to the tune of 'White Christmas'; and there is a Groucho-Jolson duet in the *Kraft Music Hall* of 7 April 1949. The key to Groucho in radio proved to be that he fared better in at least semi-extemporized form rather than following a script; his hugely successful game show *You Bet Your Life* (*qv*) was born from an occasion when Bob Hope accidentally dropped his script during a broadcast with Groucho, who deliberately followed suit and joined Hope in ten minutes of brilliant ad libs. Arthur Marx has described this taking

place on *The Walgreen Show*, an annual special sponsored by Walgreen Drugstores. *You Bet Your Life* obviously inspired a Groucho-Jolson sketch called 'A Quiz for Jolson', performed on the *Kraft Music Hall*, 18 November 1948 (similar Groucho/Jolson items exist from the Kraft shows of 13 January, 7 April and 26 May 1949). In turn, NBC's *The Big Show* of 12 November 1950 used Groucho in a sketch called 'Plebo - You Bet Your Life!' with Tallulah Bankhead, Ezio Pinza, Fanny Brice (as 'Baby Snooks'), Hanley Stafford, Jane Powell, Meredith Willson and Jimmy Wallington. Groucho may be heard in a painful rendition of 'Some Enchanted Evening'. When Chico visited England for a TV appearance in *Showtime*, he also topped a radio variety bill in the BBC Light Programme's *London Lights* (7 October 1959), produced by Trafford Whitelock. Introduced by Jack Watson, it featured Anne Shelton, Lyndon Brook, Ian Wallace, Bernard Spear, Ron Moody (see also **Impersonators**), the Terry Sisters and the Adams Singers. Script was by Gene Crowley. When Harpo's memoirs were published in 1961, his wife, Susan, deputized at radio interviews. Groucho's final radio appearance was probably his greeting to the *KFI 50th Anniversary Show* on 16 April 1972. Radio gags in the Marx films are varied: in *Cocoanuts*, Chico mistakes a 'radius' for 'WJZ' (a New York station that later carried *Flywheel!*); when the Marxes sing 'My Old Kentucky Home' near the end of *Animal Crackers*, Groucho tells us 'this programme is coming to you from the House of David'; he adopts a similar announcer's role, using a lamp as microphone during the climactic fight of *Monkey Business*; in *Horse Feathers* Harpo and Chico nearly have to listen to radio coverage of a baseball game that didn't occur; later in the film, their attempted burglary is interrupted by a blaring radio set; and still later, Groucho summons help by means of the airways. In *A Night at the Opera*, Chico, Harpo and Allan Jones (*qv*) are faced with open mikes on arrival in New York, while one of the best lines in *Room Service* comes when Groucho, on learning that the young playwright has no fireside at home, asks 'Then how do you listen to the President's speeches?'

(See also: Berlin, Irving; Characters; Children; Doctors; Documentaries; Fighting; Lawyers; Marriages; Names; Records; Religion; Songs; Television; Wartime)

RAIN

(Marx Brothers films and shows *qv*) Gummo Marx earned that nickname from his gumshoes, or wet weather footwear. There is not a drop of rain in *Horse Feathers* but Groucho still has an umbrella and galoshes, for reasons suggested elsewhere. Chico, in oilskins and sou'wester, is far better prepared than he for the cloudburst in *At the Circus*. Groucho gets a thorough soaking, as Harpo uses an umbrella to shield the one creature equipped to deal with the conditions, a sealion. When Chico and Harpo escape with a stolen painting in *Animal Crackers*, behind one set of French windows is a violent thunderstorm; the opposite set opens upon bright sunshine, prompting Chico's cry of 'California!'

(See also: Continuity errors; Laurel & Hardy; Names; Trains; 'White magic')

RECORDS

(Marx Brothers films and plays *qv*) Much of the Marx history is contained in commercially-issued sound recordings. There were no cast recordings of the Broadway shows, but a discography compiled by Robert S. Bader for the *Freedonia Gazette* (*qv*) cites a Victor Record by the International Novelty Orchestra, the B-side of which, 'Only You', is from *I'll Say She Is!*. The 'Victor Light Opera Company' recorded a medley from the stage score of *Cocoanuts*, issued in the USA on Victor 35769 and in the UK (as simply 'Light Opera Company') on

HMV C-1460. 'Ting-a-Ling, The Bells'll Ring', added on the mid-1926 revision, was recorded by Roger Wolfe Kahn and his Orchestra on Victor 20116 (USA) and HMV B-5424 (UK). A song from the film version, 'When My Dreams Come True', was recorded (among others) by Fred Waring's Pennsylvanians (US: Victor 35769; UK: HMV B-5672). Years later, the soundtrack album appeared on Sountrak STK 108 (reissued, with colour sleeve, on Sandy Hook SH 2059).

From the film of *Animal Crackers*, the 'Captain Spaulding' medley appeared on a British album, *Hollywood Sings* (Living Era AJA 5011), though slightly marred by being transferred too fast. Another Living Era album, *Flappers, Vamps and Sweet Young Things* (AJA 5015) has Lillian Roth (*qv*) plus an uncredited Hal Thompson singing the film's love theme, 'Why Am I So Romantic?' (a contemporary cover, by Van Phillips and his Orchestra, was released in Britain on Columbia CB 161). Both Living Era albums appeared in 1982. The same year brought a British single (MCA 758) 'Ev'ryone Says "I Love You"', from the soundtrack of *Horse Feathers*. The A-side was an edit of Groucho's and Chico's renditions of the song (though not Zeppo's!), while Harpo's solo formed the B-side. Groucho's version crops up again in *Hollywood Party* (Pelican LP130). Extracts from all five Paramount films were collected into a 1970 album, *The Marx Brothers; the Original Voice Tracks From Their Greatest Movies*. This selection, introduced by Gary Owens (then famous for *Rowan and Martin's Laugh-In*) was issued on Decca 79168 in the US and (minus the original gatefold sleeve and poster) MCA 2533 in Britain. Of the M-G-M films, there

was once an LP version of *A Night at the Opera* (RE-Sound RST 7051). A commercial recording of the song 'Alone', by Allan Jones (*qv*), was made fourteen years after the film's release. 'A Message From the Man in the Moon' was omitted from *A Day at the Races* (except as incidental music and in a 'reprise' by Groucho) but was recorded in Paris by Josephine Baker (UK: DB 1743). Also from *Races* is 'All God's Chillun Got Rhythm', covered by Judy Garland on Decca 1732. Groucho's song from *At the Circus*, 'Lydia, the Tattooed Lady', was recorded by Orrin Tucker and his Orchestra (US: Columbia 35249); later versions are on a 1961 Stubby Kaye single (UK: Polydor NH 66827), and, incredibly, by Kermit the Frog on *The Muppet Show* LP (Pye NSPH 19). The film's ballad, 'Two Blind Loves', was recorded by Perry Como on Decca 66718. *The Big Store* provided Tony Martin (*qv*) with 'Tenement Symphony', recorded on RCA Victor 20-3274. The film, incidentally,

Records: *A&M advertise their double-album of Groucho's 1972 concerts*

shows Martin cutting a home-made disc of 'If It's You', recorded commercially by Vaughan Monroe and his Orchestra on RCA's Bluebird label (B-11245). Harpo's solo from *Stage Door Canteen* (see **Guest appearances**) was used on the *Stage Door Canteen/Hollywood Canteen* LP (Curtain Calls 100/11-12). There is a reported soundtrack album of

Groucho's solo film *Double Dynamite* (*qv*), while his dialogue with Marilyn Monroe (*qv*) in *Love Happy* has surfaced on several albums, among them Sandy Hook SH 2013/Legends 1000/1. A recent French release, the triple CD *The Marx Brothers Sing and Play* (Chansons Cinema CIN 004), collects all the musical items from the Marx films for Paramount and M-G-M (both *qv*).

Radiola's *Marx Movie Madness - On the Radio!* (MR 1097), published in 1979, collects the radio trails for their films (see **Trailers**). That for *A Day at the Races* is also among the many delights on *Three Hours ... Fifty-Nine Minutes ... Fifty-One Seconds with the Marx Brothers* (Murray Hill 931680), a four-volume set later reissued on two double albums by the American Album and Tape Corp., as *The Very Best of the Marx Brothers* (AAT 201/2 and 202/2). This set remains the most comprehensive selection of Marx radio material. Others include Radiola's *Groucho on Radio!* (MR-1072), Nostalgia Lane's *Groucho*, Mark 56's similarly entitled *Groucho!* and one of the Memorabilia Records 'When Radio Was King' series. Among general anthologies to contain Marx extracts are *The Golden Age of Comedy* and Warner Brothers' *The Age of Television*. Groucho's appearance in *The Mikado* was released on LP by Columbia (mono OL 5480/stereo OS 2022) and reissued in the CBS Collectors' Series (OAL 5480). Extracts were used on a 1975 British album, *Gilbert & Sullivan's Greatest Hits* (CBS Harmony 30060). Groucho sings 'Father's Day' on *'Here's Johnny' - Magic Moments From the Tonight Show* (Casablanca SPNB 1296); he is also in a Decca release of *Face to Face*, 20th Century-Fox's *My Favorite Story* and a British HMV memorial album dedicated to T.S. Eliot (*qv*). Groucho's one-man show of 1972, *An Evening with Groucho* (see **The Carnegie Hall Concert**), was released as a double-album on A&M SP-3515.

There have been single-LP and cassette reissues.

Chico was the first Marx to make specific commercial discs, recorded with his band for the Hit label and released in June 1942: *We Must Be Vigilant/Johnny Doughboy Found a Rose in Ireland* (7003) and *Eloise/Here You Are* (7004). Other recordings of Chico's band surfaced in 1992 on CD, *Desi Arnaz & Chico Marx: The Great Hollywood Orchestras* (Laserlight 15 767). During 1951, Harpo made three RCA Victor 78s of harp solos, *Stardust/Tea for Two* (47-4186), *Guardian Angels* (written by Harpo)/*Swanee River* (47-4187) and *Bouree/Chanson Dans La Nuit* (47-4188); in 1952 these became a 10" LP, *Harp by Harpo* (LPM 27). There followed two 12" albums, with arrangements by Harpo's son Bill; *Harpo in Hi-Fi* (Mercury MG 20232, released in the UK as *Harpo - That's All* on Philips' Wing Label) from 1957 and *Harpo at Work* (Mercury MG 20363) in 1958. Hoagy Carmichael's *Stardust* from the RCA sessions was reissued in 1957 on RCA International's *Hooray For Hollywood* (itself reissued in Britain in 1980). Harpo also recorded an album of spirituals with gospel singer Mahalia Jackson, with whom he appeared on TV in the *Kraft Music Hall* in 1959 and *The Red Skelton Show* in 1962. One track, Harpo's own 'Guardian Angels' appeared on a compilation of the singer's work (*Let's Pray Together*, CBS BPG 62230).

In 1951 Groucho made a record with Danny Kaye, Jimmy Durante and Jane Wyman, *Black Strap Molasses/How D'Ye Do and Shake Hands* (US: Decca 27748; UK: Brunswick 04794). Later that year he recorded the following tracks, released on American Decca 78s: *Hooray For Captain Spaulding/Omaha Nebraska* (28158)/*Dr Hackenbush, Father's Day* (28159); and *Go West Young Man/Show Me a Rose* (28160). All were

released in the UK on Brunswick; Decca collected them into a 10" LP titled after the first song (DL 5045); a UK subsidiary, Ace of Hearts, used them as one side of a 12" album (AH 103) shared with Jerry Colonna. A recent CD, *Here's Groucho* (MCA Special Projects MCAD-20847) comprises all the Decca 78s plus extracts from the Decca album of soundtrack clips. Perhaps the rarest Marx release is *The Funniest Song in the World*, a 'Young People's Records' collection to which Groucho contributed in 1949. There were issues on 78, 45 and LP. Among peripheral issues are *Mickey Katz: the Borscht Jester* (US/UK Capitol T-1445 [mono], ST-1445 [stereo]), for which Chico wrote the sleeve note; also Harpo's brief comment on the rear sleeve of Allan Sherman's *My Son, the Folk Singer* (Warner Brothers W-1475), to the effect that he was buying six copies. Sherman's disc was gently kidded by Bill Marx's *My Son the Folk Swinger* (Vee Jay VJLP 3035).

All of the Marxes' own records are quite rare today (the author does not recommend following Harpo's example in *Duck Soup*, when he shoots a record out of the air!). Collectors will know of Queen's albums titled after *A Night at the Opera* and *A Day at the Races*, similarly Phil Collins' commemoration of Captain Spaulding, *Hello, I Must Be Going*. Elton John's *Don't Shoot Me - I'm Ony the Piano Player* features a poster for *Go West* in its sleeve design, but this is beyond the scope of a strictly Marx discography.

(See also: Children; Radio; *Risqué* humour; Songs; Stage appearances [post-1930]; Television)

RELIGION

'Beyond the Alps lies more Alps, and the Lord Alps those that Alp themselves'; a line from *I'll Say She Is!* and *Horse Feathers* (both *qv*). The Hays Office probably would have queried this had *Horse Feathers* been made after the 1934 Production Code and it is a wonder that, despite its pre-Code vintage, *Animal Crackers* was allowed to retain Groucho's possibly blasphemous 'Africa is God's country and he can have it' (the same might be said of a *Duck Soup* song, *All God's Chillun Got Guns*). None of the Marxes was religious in a strict sense. Although from a Jewish family, there is no evidence of them observing a kosher diet or, some of their weddings apart, observing any festivals after their own bar mitzvahs; and even that was attended by Groucho solely to collect the gift of a fountain pen. They celebrated Christmas in the same, secular way as do many non-Christians, contradicting one account of an elderly Groucho rejecting (jokingly, if at all) a Christmas tree that had been brought in. The Marxes were proud of their heritage but refused to play on it, though Gummo portrayed a stereotyped 'Hebrew Boy' in vaudeville (*qv*) and Groucho switched from a German to a Jewish character when the *Lusitania* was sunk. Such broadly-painted aspects were quietly abandoned as time progressed, and detailed under the stage productions of *Cocoanuts* and *Animal Crackers* are examples of Jewish references that would be dropped prior to filming. Retained in the screen version of *Cocoanuts* are mild, interpolated Jewish references (during the 'why a

duck' routine) but the opening night script of *Cocoanuts* includes an unfilmed and rather startling moment in which Groucho introduces a group of Spanish musicians, or at least supposedly: 'They are Spaniards like the Marx Brothers. They're Spaniards but the accent is on the last syllable. They're Span-yids.' This is the type of remark presumably intended to ward off prejudice by getting there first, but it is a wonder the team - or playwright George S. Kaufman (*qv*) - felt compelled to use it. Later on, Groucho would become annoyed at certain Jewish comics whose exaggerated ethnic routines he considered belittling; he was conscious of religious and racial prejudice and exerted none himself, in common with his brothers. The published letters to his daughter, Miriam, include his counselling of a boyfriend of his daughter's, who had experienced anti-Semitism in the services. A famous story - which, like many Marx anecdotes, varies enormously in the telling - concerns Groucho with either his son or one of his daughters at a 'restricted' hotel, club, or some such. When told he couldn't use the pool, Groucho asked if the child, being only half-Jewish, could go in up to the knees. Many years earlier, in or around 1927, Harpo and a friend arranged bookings at a hotel, to receive in return a wire saying 'Trust you are Gentile'; the enraged Harpo

entered the building, in quasi-Scottish apparel, signed in as 'Harpo MacMarx' and asked for directions to the nearest synagogue. He departed with a contemptuous Gookie (*qv*). Chico's daughter Maxine has described a similar incident, during the summer of 1929. Chico, his wife Betty and Maxine were staying at Lake George, New York and looked in at a nearby hotel. The assistant manager, embarrassed, explained that the hotel did not admit Jews. Maxine, who had never before experienced such attitudes, was doubly confused owing to her father's otherwise sought-after status. Chico summed up the matter briefly: 'There are some stupid people who don't like Jews. We don't need that hotel.' Harpo seems to have been the most theologically inclined of the brothers, recording in his memoirs disgust at an anti-religious play he had seen in Russia, a non-specific belief in a greater power and, on his death, leaving his harp to Israel. The usual whispering game metamorphosed this story into a quite untrue variant, to the effect that Gummo had been buried there. Later in life, Groucho started to attend a synagogue, probably to please Erin Fleming (*qv*), who had converted to Judaism. Groucho seems to have had no religious belief throughout his life: his son, Arthur, was at one time sent to Sunday school to please the boy's maternal grandmother, and after enquiring as to the day's lesson, Groucho systematically explained why he didn't believe any of it. Arthur was married in a Jewish ceremony, where his father asked the officiating clergyman 'Is it true you fellows breed like rabbis?' When taken to a mystic by, as he put it, 'an early wife', Groucho expressed total disbelief in the concept of a hereafter. The meeting was centred around a woman who, once in a trance, welcomed questions of any sort. 'What's the capital of North Dakota?' asked Groucho, before being thrown out. For Groucho, his lack of faith in life after death was confirmed by an understanding he had made with

Chico and Harpo, in that whoever died first would, in the event of an afterlife, make every effort to contact those remaining on earth. 'So far I have not heard from them' he said later. Groucho's consciousness of his Jewish identity, though presumably a matter of heritage alone, was extremely strong: on hearing of the Israeli massacre at the 1972 Olympics, Groucho was so shocked that he actually suffered a stroke, forcing the postponement of his Los Angeles stage show from September until December. On a brighter note, Groucho claimed a large stock of anecdotes regarding 'cops and priests'; a favourite in the latter category concerns a trip to Rome, where Groucho dropped a cigar. He blasphemed and found himself confronted by a priest. Groucho's embarrassment evaporated on finding the priest to be a fellow-American, who offered a replacement cigar with a cheery 'Groucho, you just said the Secret Word!'

(See also: Carnegie Hall Concert, the; Censorship; Characters; Children; Deaths; Harp, the; Hotels; Letters; Marriages; Policemen; Race; Roth, Lillian; *Skidoo*; Swerling, Jo; Weddings; *You Bet Your Life*)

RICE, FLORENCE (1911-74)

Leading lady of *At the Circus* (*qv*). Among many other films are the Jeanette MacDonald-Nelson Eddy *Sweethearts* (1938), *Broadway Melody of 1940* and *Father Takes a Wife* (1941).

RIESNER, CHARLES F. 'CHUCK' (1887-1962)

Former actor, with experience in vaudeville (*qv*) and musical comedy (for Charles Dillingham) prior to taking up gag writing for Keystone and other studios; also song lyricist. Riesner joined Chaplin's stock company on the latter's move to First National in 1918, graduating to assistant director. Directed Chaplin's half-brother, Syd, as in *The Man On the Box* (1925) and

Gibraltar the gorilla abducts **Florence Rice** *in this* At the Circus *still. That's supposed to be the Marx Brothers' job*

The Better 'Ole (1927); received director credit on Keaton's *Steamboat Bill, Jr* (1928). On the introduction of sound, Riesner directed M-G-M's sometimes oddball *Hollywood Revue of 1929*, in which Jack Benny (*qv*) is co-host. Another early talkie, *Reducing* (1931), stars Marie Dressler and Polly Moran. Riesner's track record suggests a suitable director for the Marx Brothers in *The Big Store* (*qv*), though the results are not memorable. Among Riesner's later films are *Meet the People* (1944) with Lucille Ball (*qv*) and Abbott & Costello's *Lost in a Harem* (1944). His surname is sometimes spelled 'Reisner'.

(See also: Chaplin, Charlie; Keaton, Buster; M-G-M)

RING, CYRIL (1893-1967)

Actor, a leading man of the 'Teens but latterly in supporting roles. Cyril Ring was from a theatrical family; his sisters were actresses Blanche and Frances Ring, the latter of whom married silent-screen star Thomas Meighan. Cyril Ring appeared in a number of Meighan's films, such as *The Conquest of Canaan* (1921), *Back Home and Broke* (1922), *Homeward Bound* (1923), *The Ne'er Do Well* (1923) and *Tongues of Flame* (1924). Played Harvey Yates, crooked contender for the leading lady's hand in the film version of *Cocoanuts* (*qv*). Ring was less prolific in his subsequent talkie career, but kept busy; he can be seen in Fox's silent picture-era comedy

Harpo and Groucho with **Charles F. 'Chuck' Riesner** *on the set of* The Big Store. *Note Groucho's real-life, octagonally-framed glasses*

Hollywood Cavalcade (1939), Irving Berlin's somewhat disastrous *Second Fiddle* (1939), the first Crosby-Hope 'Road' picture, *Road to Singapore* (1940), Abbott & Costello's 'introductory' film *One Night in the Tropics* (1940) and their later *In*

Society (1944), also two of the Fox series starring Laurel & Hardy (*qv*), *Great Guns* (1941) and *The Bullfighters* (1945).

(See also: Berlin, Irving; Jones, Allan)

RISQUÉ HUMOUR

(Marx Brothers films and shows *qv*) The Marxes were essentially a clean act and in vaudeville had to be, the restrictions on - and fines imposed for - improper material being quite severe. At one venue Groucho was fined for uttering, out of context, an only vaguely suggestive line from a song, 'and when I woke up in the morning she was gone.' Broadway shows were far more

liberal; noted under the stage entry for **Cocoanuts** are gags either deleted from or slightly cleaned up for the film version. Present in the film is a telegram informing us that 'Aunt Fanny had an eight-pound boy. Can you come to the wedding?', suitably qualified by interpreting it as an invitation to the wedding of Aunt Fanny's eight-pound boy. *Animal Crackers* retains some decidedly *risqué* gags, one of them when Groucho, with a trunkful of souvenirs, absently indicates Dumont's anatomy when describing 'this magnificent chest'. In the same film, his account of an African expedition concludes with 'We took some pictures of the native girls, but

they weren't developed. But we're going back again in a couple of weeks.' Still another, a song introduction quoted elsewhere, loses impact owing to damage in recent copies of the film. In *Monkey Business* a woman makes the mistake of saying 'you have the advantage of me', allowing Groucho say 'Not yet I haven't, but wait till I get you outside'. Groucho's cavortings with Thelma Todd (*qv*) in this film carry the threat of a 'walloping' from her husband. 'Always thinking of your husband,' muses Groucho. 'Couldn't I wallop you just as well?' Also in *Monkey Business* is the lavatorial gag in which Harpo leans against a sign so that it reads 'Men' instead of 'Women'; in *Duck Soup* Groucho, locked in a bathroom, calls out with a request either to be released or thrown a magazine. Detailed in its own entry are the various *risqué* gags in *Horse Feathers*, several of them missing from available prints. Again from *Duck Soup*, we are led to assume Harpo has gone to bed with a girl, until a bedside array of shoes is seen to include those of his horse. Harpo and horse share the bed, as the girl slumbers elsewhere. Detailed under **Censorship** is a line from *A Night at the Opera* that was cut by most local authorities around the USA. Among the film's other dubious lines is that delivered when Groucho is told Dumont has dispensed with his services: 'Why, she hasn't even had them yet,' he exclaims, which *may* of course refer to his professional idleness. When discovering she has 'twin beds' in her cabin, Groucho slyly calls her a 'little rascal'. One, it seems, is a day bed, on which Groucho takes a rest. Dumont tells him to get up, asking 'What would people say?' 'They'd probably say you're a very lucky woman,' she is told. Such jokes became fewer as the Hays Code started to take real effect, making all the more startling a *Love Happy* joke in which Ilona Massey (*qv*), standing before an illuminated sign, reveals a silhouette that causes Chico's hat to stand erect. *Love Happy* was prepared around the time Groucho commenced his quiz game, *You Bet Your Life* (*qv*). Marx Brothers legend includes an unverified line, possibly from the radio version, which would in any case have been censored prior to broadcast. It concerns a woman contestant who spoke of her many offspring. Asked to explain her large family, she could only suggest 'I love my husband,' to which Groucho replied 'I like my cigar, but I take it out once in a while!'

(See also: Animals; Dumont, Margaret; Female impersonation; Prostitutes; Smoking; Vaudeville)

RKO

RKO stood for Radio-Keith-Orpheum, or in other words 'Radio Pictures' distributed by the very same Keith-Orpheum concern who had earlier blacklisted the Marxes in vaudeville (*qv*). The team's only RKO film was *Room Service* (*qv*) but they had used the studio's sound stages some five years before, when broadcasting *Flywheel, Shyster and Flywheel* (*qv*). They also appeared in some RKO theatres on their pre-filming tours. As a solo artist, Groucho appeared in two RKO films, *Double Dynamite* and *A Girl in Every Port* (both *qv*). After the RKO studio had been sold to Desilu, Harpo returned as a guest in *I Love Lucy*.

(See also: Ball, Lucille; Television)

ROOM SERVICE

(Marx Brothers film)
Released by RKO, 30 September 1938. Copyrighted 23 September (LP 8346). 78 minutes.
Pandro S. Berman in charge of production. Assistant to producer: Philip Loeb. Directed by William A. Seiter. Camera: J. Roy Hunt. Screenplay by Morrie Ryskind, from the play by John Murray and Allan Boretz, as produced by George Abbott.

With Groucho Marx (*Gordon Miller*), Chico Marx (*Harry Binelli*), Harpo Marx (*Faker Englund*), Lucille Ball

(*Christine Marlowe*), Frank Albertson (*Leo Davis*), Ann Miller (*Hilda Manny*), Cliff Dunstan (*Joe Gribble*), Donald MacBride (*Wagner*), Philip Loeb (*Timothy Hogarth*), Philip Woods (*Simon Jenkins*), Alexander Asro (*Sasha Smirnoff*), Charles Halton (*Dr Glass*).

Gordon Miller's theatrical company has been staying at, and rehearsing in, the White Way Hotel. The bill has reached $1,200 and Miller's company is permitted to remain only because the manager, Joe Gribble, is Gordon's brother-in-law. Joe has been promised 10 per cent of the show. Miller is being pestered by Sasha, a Russian waiter, who was once a famous actor in his native land. Miller takes a 'phone call from Christine, who works for a rival producer named Fremont. Christine cannot attend rehearsals until her boss goes to lunch. Miller reminds her of the $250 she has invested in the show - and of his promise to make her a star. Complications set in with the arrival of Wagner, a hotel efficiency expert. Joe is understandably nervous when Wagner checks the books. Miller decides to skip, aided by Binelli. They avoid losing their baggage by donning several layers of clothes; Binelli calls Faker Englund to assist. The entire cast will re-register under their own names instead of Miller's, and the problem will be solved. Faker arrives, prepared for the extra clothing by wearing no shirt. Christine walks in, telling them they cannot leave; she has found a potential

backer, Mr Jenkins, whom she has talked out of doing business with her boss. He has a copy of the play, called *Hail and Farewell*, to read. A knock on the door precedes not Jenkins but Leo Davis, author of the play. Davis has 'burned his bridges' (Faker inspects his britches) and is depending on the play's receipts to pay his hotel bill. Miller would rather Davis returned home but is alarmed at Davis' threat to approach Fremont. Miller invites Davis to stay with him as Christine departs to ask Fremont for an advance in salary. Davis goes to wash up as Faker loots his luggage. Binelli receives word that he's being dispossessed and takes Davis' typewriter away to pawn; Miller goes with him, wanting to do the same. Davis, unaware of the theft, calls the finance company with a request for someone to collect the money still owed on the typewriter. The next visitor is Hilda Manny, in search of Miller. Davis discovers they are from the same town, and that he knew her uncle. Hilda is invited to stay and tells Davis of Sasha, the would-be actor. Wagner has discovered Miller's debt and arrives with Joe to see Binelli moving in. Wagner has been promised a vice-presidency if he 'puts the hotel on its feet' and is horrified to see yet another guest added to Miller's 22-strong entourage. He exits just before Miller's return. He tells Joe of the prospective backer; Joe informs Davis that he will be responsible for half of Miller's bill should he move in. Jenkins is on his way and Joe is persuaded to leave. Davis is rapidly becoming disillusioned. Jenkins is ushered in and explains he is representing a prominent businessman who favours anonymity. Much of the secrecy concerns his employer's wish for a young lady to be given an acting job in the production. Davis protests but Miller suggests a minor role. The cheque is to be presented at 10.30 the following morning, in Miller's hotel room. Joe is told of the money but the cast have already been locked out of their rooms. The keys will be returned, providing

Plundering Leo's meagre belongings in **Room Service**

they keep quiet; Wagner then gives Miller twenty minutes to pay up. Wagner is unmoved to learn that Miller's play would fill the hotel's theatre for the first time in three years. There is no option but to stay in the room, preventing a lock-out. Faker brings in a camp bed and his few belongings, among them a caged bird. Like Binelli, he has been dispossessed. Miller recalls that a sick man cannot be evicted; as Faker and Binelli are not registered, Davis has to feign illness. He is put to bed and painted with spots. Wagner brings in detectives, who flee at the sight of Davis. Exit Wagner, fuming. Hunger sets in and Miller tries to order food. His disguised voice is recognized. Sasha is persuaded to bring food when Miller hints at a part in the play. The man representing the finance company arrives but is told that Davis has gone insane and been taken to a maternity hospital ('because he's crazy'). Davis, it seems, has kept the typewriter because he likes to hear the little bell ring. He leaves for the hospital. Faker brings in a live turkey, acquired from a raffle he was running. The bird takes wing and escapes through the window. Sasha brings food and Miller decides not to displace his original actor in Sasha's favour. Hilda telephones Davis, who assures her he is in good health and promises to meet her. Christine brings more food and a contract in Fremont's forged writing.

In the absence of Davis, Faker masquerades as the patient when Wagner and Joe bring Dr Glass to investigate. Faker manages to simulate an 'ah' by means of a talking doll. The debt collector returns, only to be told that Davis has been moved to the County Hospital. They bid him goodbye with an outstretched salute and cry of 'Hail and Farewell', as in Davis' play. Wagner disappears when told that nineteen of Miller's party have been found in the ballroom. Christine is dispatched with instructions for them to meet in the foyer. Dr Glass pronounces the patient fit but is locked in the bathroom. Faker is at the window and sees Davis outside, kissing Hilda. Next he spots the turkey on a neighbouring ledge. Jenkins returns with the cheque, which will clear in five days. To speed the transaction, Jenkins can arrange for certification to be rushed through; his employer's identity is revealed in confidence, and proves to be a prominent financier named Fiske. Wagner enters the room and reveals the true situation to Jenkins; he

Jenkins decides to leave, his panic escalating on discovering the abducted physician. Taking the wrong door, he finds Faker, baseball bat in hand, chasing a turkey around the room. The bat strikes Jenkins, rendering him unconscious. The doctor is released but blames Wagner for the whole affair. He understands that Miller is trying to negotiate a legitimate deal with a major financier and resigns in disgust. Jenkins is revived and Wagner tries to make amends, claiming to have confused Miller with another guest of that name. Jenkins agrees to sign the contract and makes his way out. Wagner has the cheque placed with the hotel and will guarantee the amount personally. Miller can draw against it immediately. After Wagner has gone, Davis returns. He passed Jenkins and discovered that the cheque is being stopped. Scrutiny of the contract reveals that Jenkins has not signed. Miller realizes they have five days before Wagner discovers the truth, and goes ahead with his plans. The play reaches opening night, but Joe discovers the cheque has bounced;

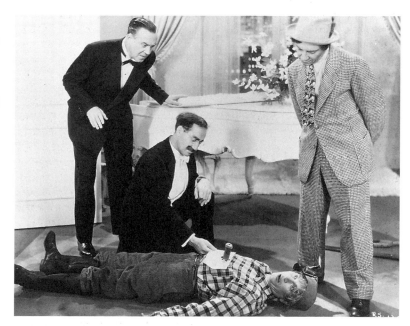

discovers also that Joe is Miller's brother-in-law. Wagner will have everyone arrested, including Joe.

Room Service: *Faker lives up to his name; a faked suicide*

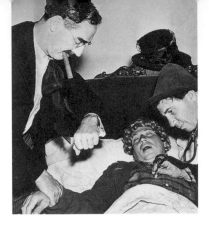

Room Service: *it's Faker's turn as the patient*

so does Wagner when the bank asks him to verify a receipt actually signed by Miller. Binelli is told to stay in the room with Miller while Wagner brings a 'surprise'. Davis joins them. Joe calls Miller with the bad news, by which time there are detectives on the door. Davis is heartbroken, having planned to marry Hilda after the play's opening. Faker is added to the group of captives. They plan for Davis to fake his suicide, so that an ambulance will be summoned and Davis can sneak into the theatre. Wagner returns, informing them that the Sheriff will take away the scenery fifteen minutes into the performance. Enter Davis, claiming that Wagner drove him into taking poison. Wagner, eager to avoid publicity, sends Joe to fetch an antidote and leaves the others to keep working on him. Davis will have to prolong his death scene in order to stop Wagner

dump the body outside, but Wagner will not permit such sacrilege. They play for time instead by saying a few words over the body, adding a tribute in song. The debt collector calls in, having failed to locate Davis at the County Hospital. By this time a further 'Hail and Farewell' is sufficient to send him on his way. Wagner finally goes for the police, but opens the door to find an apparently dead Faker. There is a prop knife in his chest, skewering a note blaming Wagner for both suicides. The 'body' is taken outside to an alleyway, where a cop becomes suspicious. Wagner tells him it is an actor who passed out through over-excitement. He and Miller go to the wings, where the play (with Sasha in the cast) is a great hit. The climactic scene shows a group of miners bearing the remains of a dead comrade; Wagner is horrified to see it is Faker, the knife still in his chest. He is even more shocked when comforted by Davis, back among the living. Wagner collapses.

A crisis in **Room Service**: *the contract has not been signed*

Room Service, a stage play written by John Murray and Allan Boretz, was presented on Broadway by George Abbott. From its opening on 19 May 1937, it was a smash hit without, it should be stressed, the Marx Brothers. They entered the story only when RKO (*qv*) wanted to make a film version. The studio paid $255,000 for the rights - a record sum - and engaged the Marxes for a further $250,000, the only Marx Brothers deal arranged by Zeppo. (Groucho's only comment was that it should have been more.) At this stage both the comedians and M-G-M were agreeable to a loan-out, their attitudes to one another having become ambivalent since the death of Irving Thalberg (*qv*) during preparation of *A Day at the Races* (*qv*). Adaptation was by Morrie Ryskind (*qv*), whose prime task was to introduce some authentic Marx material and rewrite Harpo's 'Faker' role as a mute, allowing Chico (Harpo's usual interpreter) to deliver most of his original lines. As Allen

Room Service: *Under siege*

interrupting the play. Hilda visits the apparently dying man, but is told of the ruse and returns to keep an eye on the play. Davis returns to bed as Wagner and Joe bring medication. Davis is liberally dosed but eventually plays dead. As they mourn the young playwright's passing, the performance has reached its second act. 'He died too soon,' says Miller. 'An hour too soon,' adds Binelli. Wagner, aware now that money is not so important, decides to call the police. The others offer to

Eyles has noted, there was also a need to conform to Hollywood's then-current censorship, renaming the play-within-a-play *Hail and Farewell* instead of *Godspeed*, and toning down Wagner's frequent exclamations (hence his repeated cry of 'Jumping butterballs!'). Wagner is played by Donald MacBride (*qv*), repeating his stage role; others from the original are Clifford Dunstan (Gribble), Philip Woods (Jenkins) and Alexander Asro (Sasha). Philip Loeb, who plays Timothy Hogarth, was the stage version's Harry Binion, a character reworked as Binelli for Chico. There seems to have been an effort to provide new blood for the film: Frank Albertson, Lucille Ball and Ann Miller (all *qv*) were only starting to make their names, and it must be said that *Room Service* did not help greatly. Production began in late June 1938 and wrapped early in August, for release late in September. As the only Marx film not written for them from the outset, one might expect a mixed reaction: *Variety* decided it would 'satisfy on the laugh score' even if some people would miss the harp and piano solos (omitted for the first time since *Duck Soup* [*qv*]) and Groucho's usual quasi-romantic pursuits. The non-original story was considered 'a more staple structure on which to hang their buffoonery'. Frank S. Nugent of the *New York Times* contrasted it more directly with the play, making an interesting point when reminding us how the original characters were motivated by desperation whereas the Marxes do extraordinary things purely for fun. For this reason, Nugent believed some of the supporting figures more effective than the stars. He liked the film, however, the verdict being 'a comedy to be laughed at moderately if you saw the play, immoderately if you missed it'. In the UK, the British Film Institute's *Monthly Film Bulletin* found it all very funny ('there is no falling-off in the power of the Marx Brothers to raise laughs'), despite little attempt being made to disguise its stage origins. Some incredulity was expressed at the humour wrung from a bogus suicide, the treatment being 'so utterly wild that the edge is taken off it'. In an odd, parenthetical, comment there was mention of the runaway turkey sequence: 'Not everybody will care for this' it was stated. Today, *Room Service* is low on the list of Marx favourites but, for a while, was one of the more ubiquitous titles owing to the comparative ease in obtaining RKO material. It has its share of laughs but is claustrophobic in a way unknown even to the primitive talkies made at Astoria. Historian Leonard Maltin has seized, with just glee, upon what he considers an unintentional comic highlight. This occurs late in the film, when Frank Albertson provides Ann Miller with a brief resumé of the film's numerous intrigues; a few well-chosen words and she suddenly comprehends all, when in reality she should be even more baffled than before.

(See also: Agents; Animals; Ball, Lucille; Censorship; Children; Doctors; Feld, Fritz; Home movies; Hotels; M-G-M; Miller, Ann; Radio; RKO; Television; Trailers)

ROTH, LILLIAN
(1910-80)
Actress and singer, leading lady in the film version of *Animal Crackers* (*qv*). Lillian Roth may be said to have endured more than her share of poor luck; an early reputation for being 'difficult' was perhaps more circumstantial than anything else. When Paramount (*qv*) loaned her to Cecil B. DeMille for *Madame Satan* (1930), she expressed a reluctance to perform some hazardous stunts; on another occasion, she refused to appear opposite a comedian who had made a quiet, uncomplimentary reference to her Jewish background. In her autobiography *I'll Cry Tomorrow* she recalls being shipped off to New York 'to be kicked in the rear by the Marx Brothers'. The idea was to teach her a lesson but she rather enjoyed working with them, retaining pleasant memories and later offering singular insight into the film's shooting. She recalled Zeppo being first to arrive each morning, at around 9.30; half an hour later a 'phone call would be made to awaken Chico; Harpo would arrive, find nobody around, and disappear to his dressing-room for a nap; Chico's appearance would generally coincide with the discovery of a sleeping Harpo; finally Groucho, still equipped for an early round of golf, would ask 'Anybody for lunch?' Thus no work was done except from mid-afternoon until 5 p.m., when everyone left for the day. The actress recalled further delays resulting from the constant *ad libs*. She claimed responsibility for several retakes when breaking up over one line, less in anticipation of the line itself than of Groucho's eccentric delivery. *Animal Crackers* was completed behind schedule, but Miss Roth had the consolation of a promised Hollywood role opposite Maurice

Lillian Roth *was cast in the film of* Animal Crackers *by way of punishment*

Chevalier (*qv*). While returning to the West Coast, she discovered the film was underway without her. Lillian Roth's professional and private difficulties would in time lead to a chronic alcohol problem, and much of *I'll Cry Tomorrow* deals with this and her recovery. When published in the 1950s, such confessions were not the commonplace they have since become, making the book rather sensational for its day. It was filmed in 1957 with Susan Hayward as Roth.

(See also: Marriages; Records; Religion)

ROYALTY
(Marx Brothers films and shows *qv*) There is something vaguely appealing about the apparent mismatch between the robust Marxes and royalty. When in France with Alexander Woollcott (*qv*), Harpo met King Alfonso of Spain, a tone-deaf monarch who employed a man for the sole purpose of alerting him whenever the national anthem was played. There is a joke at King Alfonso's expense in the stage script of *Cocoanuts*. Joe Adamson has quoted a rejected song from *Duck Soup* in which Groucho, as prospective founder of a despotic dynasty, asks how he can produce an heir 'if a King can do no wrong'. Among the Marxes' numerous British admirers was the pre-war Prince of Wales, who became Duke of Windsor after abdicating as King Edward VIII (an event lampooned in *The King and the Chorus Girl* [*qv*]). Harpo described travelling to Europe

to promote *A Night at the Opera* during Edward's brief reign of 1936, and being presented to the uncrowned monarch after a stage performance. Not being a British subject, Harpo decided to extend a hand rather than bow; Edward, clearly an *aficionado*, reversed the comedian's usual gag and gave Harpo his leg. Harpo's memoirs are, by his own admission, unreliable and no available evidence confirms a 1936 visit. Harpo also recalled Edward, as Prince of Wales, witnessing the convoluted 'flash-flesh-flask' business of *Animal Crackers* and afterwards sending them a hamper containing each of the items mentioned. Groucho's son, Arthur, in *Son of Groucho*, in turn describes Edward as having visited his father backstage after a performance of the show, inviting the Marxes to 'look him up' should they be in London. The chances of Edward having seen the show are slim: according to the 'Pro & Con' section of the November 1980 *Freedonia Gazette* (*qv*), Edward was in the United States during September 1924, and could well have seen *I'll Say She Is!*. This becomes less likely when considering there is no mention of it in the American press, which at that time took considerable interest in Edward's decidedly un-Royal behaviour; it was this very notoriety that led King George V to prohibit any future American trips by his sons. (Edward's playboy ways are commemorated somewhat in *The Cocoanuts*, with its frequent question 'Did anyone ever tell you that you look like the Prince of Wales?') In consequence, the next time Edward could have seen the Marxes in person would have been during the London engagement for C.B. Cochran (*qv*) in 1931. Arthur Marx writes of a bereavement rendering the Prince unable to attend, but he may have been present despite (which would also tie in with Harpo's story of their meeting). If Edward saw them in person at any time, this would have been the likeliest venue, especially given the team's burgeoning London reputation after

their first two films. A further possibility is that he had earlier seen the film version of *Animal Crackers* and arranged for the gift to be delivered backstage. It is not known if the flashlight routine was among the elements of *Animal Crackers* incorporated into the Cochran show. The same issue of *Freedonia Gazette* contains an intriguing letter from someone masquerading as 'Benjamin Tibbets, Bishop Wallop (England)', a name and location borrowed from British comedian Will Hay. The letter quotes *The Chicago Daily Times* of 28 July 1936, by which time Edward had become King and the Marxes were road-testing *A Day at the Races* at the local Palace Theatre. The report mentions Edward having named the Marxes as his favourite comedians, going on to detail the comedians' intention to visit London for the following year's Coronation. 'London theatre managers, familiar with His Majesty's special liking for the Marx Brothers, are anxious to have them make personal appearances during the festivities. That they will give a command performance before the King himself is highly probable'. This tale smacks somewhat of a press agent's fantasy but the truth will probably never be established; Edward, of course, relinquished the throne and it was his brother who was crowned, as King George VI, in 1937. It was this immediate Royal Family that attended the London première of *At the Circus* in December 1939.

(See also: Prisons; Stage appearances [post-1930])

RUBY, HARRY (1895-1974)

(Marx Brothers films and shows *qv*) Famed songwriter (real name **Rubinstein**), in partnership with **Bert Kalmar** (1884-1947); they were the subjects of a 1950 biopic, *Three Little Words*, with Fred Astaire and Red Skelton. Legend has it that one of their early hits, *Who's Sorry Now?*, was written as a private joke but saw

publication despite. It was revived for the Marxes' *A Night in Casablanca* in 1946 but the Marx-Kalmar-Ruby association dates back much further. Both Kalmar and Ruby had been in vaudeville (*qv*) and, like Groucho, Ruby was among the many graduates of a school act belonging to Gus Edwards. During the Great War, Ruby worked for the Watterson, Berlin and Snyder publishing company, working directly as assistant to Irving Berlin (*qv*) during the creation of his morale-raising show, *Yip, Yip Yaphank*. Kalmar and Ruby's initial contact with the Marxes came when Groucho, still in vaudeville, visited them at their publishers' offices. Groucho admired the songwriting team who, flattered, returned the compliment. Ruby subsequently became one of Groucho's closest friends. Kalmar and Ruby established themselves as Broadway talents during the 1920s, as with Clark & McCullough's *The Ramblers*. Their first professional involvement with the Marxes was in providing the music and lyrics for the stage original of *Animal Crackers* in 1928. They had earlier been associated with its co-author, George S. Kaufman (*qv*), in an ill-starred venture of 1923, *Helen of Troy, New York*. *The Groucho Letters* reproduces a letter dated 16 August 1923, in which Ruby promises to give Groucho the details of *Helen*'s out-of-town run 'as soon as I can stop crying'. *Animal Crackers* proved an altogether happier association and the score provided Groucho with *Hooray For Captain Spaulding*, his lifelong theme tune. An oft-repeated anecdote from the show concerns an arrangement by which the four Marxes, producer Sam Harris (*qv*), George S. Kaufman, his collaborator Morrie Ryskind (*qv*), Bert Kalmar and Harry Ruby contributed $10 apiece toward a bathrobe when each celebrated his birthday. When Ruby's turn neared, he dropped unsubtle hints, unaware that the others had decided to cancel the idea. By way of revenge, Ruby waited until the performance was underway before climbing into a prop trunk that was to be presented to Groucho on stage. During the scene, Ruby appeared from within, baffling audience and cast with the question 'Where's my bathrobe?' Even Groucho was momentarily stuck for a response. Kaufman once described the gaunt Harry Ruby as resembling 'a dishonest Abe Lincoln'. A quirky humour meant that he and Bert Kalmar were capable of providing scripts in addition to the music. They wrote screenplays for the Marxes' *Horse Feathers*, *Duck Soup* and early drafts of both *A Night at the Opera* and *Go West*. In June 1936 *Variety* reported them as engaged by Jack Curtis and Sam Harris for a new musical called *Saratoga Chips* 'upon completion of their current Marx Brothers yarn for Irving Thalberg'. The Marxes' next 'yarn' became *A Day at the Races*, in which no Kalmar-Ruby material seems present. Among other films for which they supplied both songs and screenplays are two Wheeler & Woolsey vehicles, *Hips, Hips Hooray* (1934) (which also has Thelma Todd [*qv*] in the cast) and *Kentucky Kernels*, a 1935 film known in Britain as *Triple Trouble*. Much of the work for other comedians is, by necessity, more conventional but a Marxian ring may sometimes be heard. In their screenplay for *Hips, Hips Hooray* (co-written with Edward Kaufman), Robert Woolsey announces his presence to a businessman's secretary, showing his card for an instant before declaring 'That's long enough. I'll tell him myself.' Having barged into the man's office, business proceeds in true Groucho fashion:

Man: Did you wish to make an investment?
Woolsey: What else would I be doing here? When you want a hot dog, you go to a hot dog stand, don't you?
Man: Oh, why yes.
Woolsey: Well, cut it out. Those hot dogs'll kill you.

Hips, Hips Hooray also has a Kalmar-

Ruby song originally intended for *Duck Soup*, titled *Just Keep On Doin' What You're Doin'*. *Kentucky Kernels*, written with ex-Hal Roach director Fred Guiol, incorporates an exchange curiously reminiscent of Groucho and Chico:

Woolsey: What would take a man's mind off of a woman?
Wheeler: Another woman.

There is even Margaret Dumont (*qv*), in the role of child welfare officer. She is greeted as though in more familiar company:

Woolsey: You look perfectly charming this morning.
Dumont: Oh, do you really think so?
Woolsey: No, but I had to say *something*.

Later in *Kentucky Kernels* is a banqueting scene with a semi-spoken song, *Anything is Possible*, which is somewhere between the *Captain Spaulding* medley from *Animal Crackers* and the inaugural fuss of *Duck Soup*. Something of Groucho's nonchalance toward Alky Briggs in *Monkey Business* can be discerned in Robert Woolsey when, challenged at gunpoint while hiding in a girl's bed, he mutters 'Fine way to treat a guest ... you must come around see me sometime.' The overall effect, however, is much less than the Marxes, if only through Woolsey displaying a less consistent bravado. Kalmar and Ruby's script for Eddie Cantor (*qv*) in *The Kid From Spain* (1932) echoes the customs scene of *Monkey Business* when Cantor gets in line to cross the Mexican border. When an official asks for identification, Eddie produces a photograph:

Cantor: This will show you who I am. You see, I live on a farm in a small town. This is a picture of one of my cows eating corn.
Official (examining a landscape with neither cows nor corn): Where's the

corn?
Cantor: The cow ate it up.
Official: Where's the cow?
Cantor: Well, after she ate up the corn, there's no use in her hanging around.

This is similar territory to Kaufman and Ryskind's 'building-a-house-next-door' idea of *Animal Crackers*, but not quite; in comparing this scene to the Marxes' equivalents, Joe Adamson states that Cantor 'just doesn't convey the feeling of a hallucination', to an extent pinpointing how essential the Marx Brothers were to the material as opposed to any theories suggesting the reverse. Although Kalmar and Ruby wrote no further Marx scripts after the aborted versions of *A Night at the Opera* and *Go West*, they provided a song, *Go West Young Man*, for Groucho's 1947 film *Copacabana* (*qv*). A few years after Bert Kalmar's death, Harry Ruby and Groucho formed an official, if informal, songwriting partnership (see **Songs**). Extant today is an appearance of the two on the *Steve Allen Show* with Ruby accompanying Groucho at the piano. 'This man is allegedly a composer,' says Groucho, 'and can only play in one key ... Beethoven played in *every* key.' 'Yeah,' counters Ruby, 'but he's not in this show.' 'You know why, don't you?' adds Groucho. 'He wouldn't work for this money!' Elsewhere in the show Groucho chides Ruby for his merely functional piano style, asking 'What became of those fancy twirls of yesteryear?' 'Groucho, please don't pick on me,' pleads Ruby. 'I play by ear - the same as you sing!'

(See also: Documentaries; Eaton, Mary; Home movies; Kane, Helen; McCarey, Leo; O'Connor, Robert Emmet; *Story of Mankind, the*; Television; Thalberg, Irving; Vera-Ellen)

RUMANN, SIEGFRIED (later billed as SIG RUMANN or RUMAN) (1885-1967)
(Marx Brothers films *qv*)
Hamburg-born actor, long resident in America and known mostly for comedy

roles. Rumann began his theatrical career as a repertory actor in his native Germany; on travelling to the USA he found work in Broadway shows, among them the stage production of *Grand Hotel*; his first film was *The Royal Box* (1929). Surprisingly, David Ragan's *Who's Who in Hollywood 1900-76* mentions a parallel career during Rumann's first years in the States, as a bacteriologist at the University of Southern California. In the Marx

Sigfried Rumann, known later as 'Sig Ruman', loaned his Teutonic presence to three Marx Brothers films

Brothers' *A Night at the Opera* he plays impresario Herman Gottlieb, a Teutonic blusterer in the classic mould. The film's direct successor, *A Day at the Races*, casts him as Viennese specialist Dr Steinberg who, as in the earlier film, threatens Groucho's influence over Margaret Dumont (*qv*). He was a welcome addition to the team's 'comeback' film, *A Night in Casablanca*, as the villainous Count who is responsible for the premature demise of several hotel managers. A mere sampling of Rumann's other film work: *Maytime* (1937) with Jeanette MacDonald and Nelson Eddy, *This Is My Affair* (1937), *Suez* (1938), *Honolulu* (1939), *Ninotchka* (1939) with Greta Garbo (*qv*), *Tobacco Road* (1941), Jack Benny's *To Be Or Not To*

Be (1942), *Night and Day* (1946), *Give My Regards to Broadway* (1948), *On the Riviera* (1951) with Danny Kaye, *White Christmas* (1954), the 1954 Martin & Lewis vehicles *Living It Up* and *Three Ring Circus*, Jerry Lewis' solo film *The Errand Boy* (1961), *Robin and the Seven Hoods* (1964) and Billy Wilder's *The Fortune Cookie* (1966).

(See also: Adrian, Iris; Benny, Jack; Berlin, Irving; Buzzell, Edward; Feld, Fritz; Impersonators; Krasna, Norman; Seiter, William A.; Vera-Ellen)

RUSSELL, LEWIS (1885-1961)

Played Galoux, one of the French officials in *A Night in Casablanca* (*qv*). A more notable appearance is in Billy Wilder's *The Lost Weekend* (1945); others include the 1945 Betty Hutton film *Cross My Heart* and a 1948 melodrama, *Kiss the Blood Off My Hands*.

RUSSIA

It was at the suggestion of Alexander Woollcott (*qv*) that Harpo decided to visit Soviet Russia. At that time the Communist regime was still regarded as a bold experiment by certain Western commentators, several of whom actually made the trip. Woollcott, a near-compulsive traveller, decided to pay a visit and, in a letter of 3 October 1932, invited Harpo to accompany him. Harpo declined the offer. Woollcott found Russia 'delightful and continuously satisfactory' despite its expected rigours and was of the opinion that Harpo would find an appreciative audience. Although the USA was only starting to formalize diplomatic relations with the USSR, Woollcott knew enough people to have certain strings pulled. These were tugged in the direction of Maxim Litvinoff, the Soviet Foreign Minister whose visit to the USA was to mark the opening of Russo-American communication. Woollcott was very good at organizing his various friends and before anyone could blink, Harpo had received a formal invitation to

appear as guest star at the Moscow Art Theatre, the first time an American had been so honoured. There was a false start: he left Los Angeles on 5 August 1932 (in an aeroplane owned by comedy film producer Hal Roach), intending to sail from New York to France, where he would visit an elderly lady harpist whose acquaintance he had made on a prior trip. From Paris he would fly to Moscow, thence to Leningrad, Budapest and Prague. Harpo reached New York, but was forced to abandon the trip through professional and other commitments (the illness of his father may have precluded any distant travel). After more than a year's hiatus and another film, *Duck Soup* (*qv*), Harpo set off once more. He was in New York long enough to pick up half a dozen collars and some replacement, multi-coloured harp strings before embarking for Hamburg on 14 November 1933. Prior to sailing, Harpo gave an exclusive interview to B.F. Wilson of *Screen Book* magazine. It was revealed that Harpo was an 'unofficial ambassador' *en route* to Russia at the very time that Litvinoff was doing his public-relations job in Washington. Harpo had received word from husband-and-wife acting team Alfred Lunt and Lynn Fontanne, who had preceded him to Russia and were enthusing over the high standard of Soviet theatre. 'I don't work up much enthusiasm about anything any more,' said Harpo, 'but I certainly am looking forward to this'. The evidently naïve interviewer asked how Harpo might surmount the language barrier. 'I won't have to speak,' replied Harpo, 'you ought to know that!' Harpo was to perform in mime and play the harp, as per his stage work in the US. He had at least prepared himself with a smattering of Russian terms, one of which he quoted to the magazine. To those unacquainted with the language, Harpo recommended using the term on a Russian, after which one could 'tell friends who visit you at the hospital just what the word means'. During the Atlantic crossing, Harpo was one of the very few passengers not afflicted by seasickness. His stomach was turned, however, on arriving in Germany. The Nazis had been busy and terrified Jewish shopkeepers were finding their premises disfigured. Harpo promptly left Germany, making his way by rail to the border between Poland and Russia, where he had to change trains. Another American traveller had warned him of likely excess baggage charges on entering the country. As US currency was much sought after, he loaned Harpo the necessary amount in roubles. On being presented with the money, the Soviet customs wanted to know where it had been obtained. Unconvinced by Harpo's explanation, the authorities proceeded to examine his eccentric baggage: on finding Harpo's bizarre stage props they had reason to doubt his sanity. According to Kipp Wessel's account in the November 1980 *Freedonia Gazette* (*qv*), the comedian avoided a padded cell by signing affidavits to the effect that he was 'harmless and of sound mind'. The more prosaic version in his memoir, *Harpo Speaks!*, attributes his release to the timely reappearance of his careless American benefactor. Harpo averted future problems by claiming to be a distant cousin of Karl Marx. On arriving for rehearsals, Harpo was put in the care of a gigantic, female comrade who combined the functions of guide, interpreter and spy. The Soviet theatre officials were at first unenthusiastic and discourteous; Harpo was on the point of leaving Russia but was intercepted by a telephone call from Litvinov's British-born wife, Ivy. She was anxious for him to stay and made known her influence within Soviet affairs; it should be mentioned that her husband was second only to Stalin in the Soviet pecking order. Harpo awaited a second telephone call but received instead some altogether friendlier Russian visitors, an entourage designed to assist and work with him. The next day, diplomatic relations were formally opened between the USSR and the

USA. Harpo recalled having given successful previews before his formal opening in Moscow, followed by engagements in Leningrad before a return to the capital; he is known instead to have made his first 'official' performance at the Leningrad Music Hall on 18 December, following ten days of rehearsal. Woollcott had arranged for Harpo to be looked after by two American writers, Walter Duranty (correspondent for *The New York Times*) and Eugene Lyons; Harpo remembered one of the previews as being a reception for the American press, and although the sequence of events is unclear, such an event was indeed arranged by A.A. Troyanovski, the new Soviet Ambassador to the USA. The occasion is preserved in a Russian newsreel showing Harpo, in formal attire instead of his stage costume, playing the harp. Aside from the harp solo, his sketch occupied six minutes within a twenty-five minute presentation, assisted by a couple (Yona Bey and Helen Ketal) recruited from the Moscow Art Theatre. According to Harpo, he had been supplied with a plot (of which he was kept ignorant) by two writers whom he nicknamed 'George S. Kaufmanski' and 'Morrie Ryskindov'. This was deemed necessary because the rather literal Russian audience needed some motive for his usually impromptu clowning. Although Harpo was onstage throughout the play, he was given a specific cue at which to commence his own routine, comprising bits of business from *I'll Say She Is!* and *The Cocoanuts* (both *qv*). *The New York Times* published a report from the Leningrad opening, describing how Harpo 'brought down the house in the Music Hall as a capacity audience of usually phlegmatic Soviet theatregoers applauded, stamped and cheered for twenty-five minutes during and after his six-minute act'. Soviet reviews were similarly ecstatic. Harpo received a congratulatory telephone call from William C. Bullitt, the newly-appointed United States Ambassador, from whom

he would hear once more while in Russia. After a week in Leningrad, Harpo moved on to the Moscow Art Theatre. He gave the first of two shows on 30 December, introduced as 'one of the world's greatest comedians' by film director V.I. Pudovkin. Present among the many Soviet dignitaries was Maxim Litvinoff, fresh from his successful diplomatic mission to the United States. When the two men shook hands backstage, Litvinoff, evidently prepared, reversed one of Harpo's pet gags by allowing silverware to fall from his own sleeve! There followed a banquet in Harpo's honour. Amid all the official attention, Harpo received a visitor who had come to compliment his performance. To Harpo's surprise, the man wore a familiar-looking American suit; closer examination revealed it to be Harpo's own, stolen backstage during a performance of *Cocoanuts* some years earlier. The suit's disappearance was suddenly explained when the wearer turned out to be one of Chico's distant in-laws. Before returning home, Harpo received a further communication from the US Embassy. William Bullitt asked if Harpo would smuggle out some secret papers, in a package attached to his leg and concealed beneath a sock. Harpo agreed, but grew increasingly nervous about the consequences of being caught, to the point where he started to limp. Once out of Russia, he headed for Berlin, where his Russian fur hat and coat earned cries of 'Eskimo' from the local children. He moved on to Paris and boarded the *Ile de France* for America, arriving in New York on 9 January 1934. He was not permitted to disembark until two government agents had visited his cabin to retrieve the papers. Harpo gave his leg a much-needed scratch and sincerely thanked the agents for ending his constant fear of discovery. Woollcott met him on the quayside as did Gummo and his wife, Helen. At a press conference, Harpo expressed every wish to return to Russia but never did, though Ivy Litvinoff visited him in America nine years later. A few more decades were to pass before the Marxes were transported East by proxy in the pastiche musical, *A Day in Hollywood, A Night in the Ukraine* (*qv*). There has since been a quite different play presenting the Marxes in a Russian locale, entitled *A Night at the Revolution*.

(See also: Harp, the; Impersonators; Kaufman, George S.; Marriages; Marx, Sam 'Frenchie'; Newsreels; Politicians; Race; Religion; Ryskind, Morrie)

RUYSDAEL, BASIL (1888-1960)
Appeared as Hennessy, the detective, in both stage and screen versions of *The Cocoanuts* (*qv*). Prolific on stage and a familiar voice on American radio; his many films include *The File On Thelma Jordan* (1949), *Pinky* (1949) and *The Blackboard Jungle* (1955).

(See also: Policemen)

RYSKIND, MORRIE (MORRIS) (1895-1985)
(Marx Brothers films and shows *qv*) New-York born writer whose long association with the Marxes began on Broadway; later among the founders of the Screen Writers' Guild. As a teenager, Ryskind earned small sums from his poetry and, as did Groucho and George S. Kaufman (*qv*), contributed to Franklin P. Adams' newspaper column 'The Conning Tower'. Ryskind subsequently attended the Columbia School of Journalism, where he became friends with Herman Mankiewicz (*qv*). Six weeks before he was due to graduate, Ryskind was expelled over a radical essay he had written for the campus journal. By this time America had entered the Great War but, having failed a Navy medical, Ryskind instead took a job at the New York *World* under Herbert Bayard Swope; others to establish journalistic

reputations here would be Mankiewicz, Robert Benchley, Alexander Woollcott (*qv*) and Norman Krasna (also *qv*). From 1920 Ryskind functioned as poet and playwright; his anthology of verse, *Unaccustomed As I Am*, was published by Knopf in 1921. The book led to an offer to write for silent pictures in Hollywood, following which Ryskind returned to New York as a film publicist. While many of his contemporaries associated with the Algonquin Round Table (of which Harpo was a member), Ryskind favoured a parallel group, the Cheese Club, through which he gained experience as playwright when they staged a deliberately awful show entitled *One Helluva Night*. Producer Sam Harris (*qv*) expressed interest but it was a different project that brought about Ryskind's career change. In 1925, Ryskind was working at the New York office of Paramount (*qv*) when a chance meeting with George S. Kaufman led to an offer to collaborate on a new play, the Marxes' second Broadway show, *The Cocoanuts*. By his own request, Ryskind was uncredited on the book, on the grounds that he had not been present when the story was conceived. *The Cocoanuts* initiated Ryskind's lifelong friendship with Groucho, who was Best Man at Ryskind's wedding in 1929. After *Cocoanuts*, other musical-comedy projects followed until Ryskind worked again with Kaufman, this time with full credit, on the next Marx show, *Animal Crackers*. Ryskind later adapted both plays to the screen and, while declining an initial offer to join the Marxes in California, later claimed to have performed 'long-distance rewriting' on *Monkey Business* and *Horse Feathers*. During this period he co-scripted Eddie Cantor's film *Palmy Days* (1931) and collaborated with Kaufman on the stage musical *Of Thee I Sing*, which earned them the Pulitzer Prize.

(Ironically, Ryskind was presented with his award by the same man who had thrown him out of college!) According to Ryskind, it was Zeppo who, on behalf of Irving Thalberg (*qv*), approached Ryskind with the idea of he and Kaufman working on *A Night at the Opera* (Zeppo remained Ryskind's agent for many years). Although Kaufman's tenure in Hollywood was brief, Ryskind stayed on and later adapted *Room Service* for the Marx Brothers. Of Ryskind's non-Marx films, perhaps the best-remembered is *My Man Godfrey* (1936); among many for which he was employed for rewrites are Jack Benny's *The Meanest Man in the World* and Fred Allen's *It's in the Bag*. Ryskind's youthful radicalism had by this time made way for extreme conservatism, something that did not affect his relationship with the liberal-minded Groucho. Ryskind, who attributed the change at least in part to the influence of Sam Wood (*qv*), found his Hollywood career effectively terminated in 1948 after he testified against the 'Hollywood Ten'. Latterly, Ryskind wrote for the conservative *National Review* and provided a syndicated column for the Los Angeles *Times*. He was among those to share his reminiscences in the BBC TV *Hollywood Greats* tribute to Groucho and the American-made *Marx Brothers in a Nutshell*. His memoirs, assembled in collaboration with John H.M. Roberts, were published nine years after his death under the title *I Shot an Elephant in My Pajamas* (after a celebrated line in *Animal Crackers*).

(See also: Abandoned projects; Agents; Benny, Jack; Cantor, Eddie; Clubs; Doctors; Documentaries; *Groucho - a Life in Revue*; Impersonators; Letters; Middleton, Charles; Politicians; Sport)

SALSA
See: *Copacabana*

SANTLEY, JOSEPH (1889-1971)
Director and screenwriter, born in Salt Lake City; co-director, with Robert Florey (*qv*), of the film version of *Cocoanuts* (*qv*). From a theatrical family (he also married within the profession, to actress Ivy Sawyer), Santley was an actor from boyhood, achieving particular fame in a play called *Rags to Riches*. A syndicated newspaper item of 1932 describes the young Groucho being hired for a play, presumably *The Man of Her Choice* (see **Vaudeville**), in direct competition with the Santley vehicle. Santley was a full graduate to Broadway productions by the age of 21; he appeared in Irving Berlin's *Stop! Look! Listen!* and the Berlin-Harris *Music Box Revue of 1921* and was thus acquainted with the original composer and producer of *Cocoanuts* in addition to having considerable stage experience of his own. Santley was already directing films (usually shorts) at Paramount (*qv*) when he was called in to assist Florey. Santley's main task seems to have been locating the absentee comedians and setting up the musical items, though Florey's interview in *The Marx Brothers Scrapbook* implies the pre-Busby Berkeley overhead shots to have been his own, ditto the film's equally imaginative through-the-piano view of Chico.

(See also: Berlin, Irving; Gambling; Harris, Sam)

SCHOOL DAYS
See: *Fun in Hi Skule*; Vaudeville

SCREEN ACTORS' GUILD
See: **Awards**; **Marx Bros., Inc.**

SEATON, GEORGE (b. 1911) (d. 1979)
Screenwriter, with M-G-M (*qv*) from 1933 after theatrical experience as actor and producer. Collaborated with Robert Pirosh (*qv*) during scripting of *A Night at the Opera* and *A Day at the Races* (both *qv*); later received an Oscar for *Miracle On 34th Street* (1947). Co-producer of the Oscar-nominated *The Tin Star* (1957). Other credits include *The Doctor Takes a Wife* (1940), *That Night in Rio* (1941) directed by Irving Cummings (*qv*) and the Jack Benny films *Charley's Aunt* (1941) and *The Meanest Man in the World* (1943). Seaton attended the Marxes' induction into the Motion Picture Hall of Fame in 1977.

(See also: Awards; Benny, Jack; Benoff, Mac; Documentaries; Francis, Kay; Mayo, Archie L.)

SEDAN, ROLFE (1896-1982)
Comic actor, known to American television viewers as the mailman in *The Burns and Allen Show*. Rolfe Sedan joined Jay Eaton and Leo White (both *qv*) as the three aviators in *A Night at the Opera* (*qv*). He is reported also in *Monkey Business* (*qv*). He may be seen again with Leo White in *Done in Oil* (1934), a Hal Roach short starring Thelma Todd (*qv*) and Patsy Kelly, also numerous features, ranging up to 1970s comedies such as Mel Brooks' *Young Frankenstein*.

(See also: Burns, George and Allen, Gracie; Keaton, Buster)

SEITER, WILLIAM A. (1892-1964)
New York-born veteran of silent films, originally an artist and writer who had worked also in the importing of glassware and china; directed the Marx Brothers in *Room Service* (*qv*). In private life a keen sportsman who excelled at golf, tennis and yachting, William Seiter made an energetic start in films as a cowboy double, at Selig in 1915. As a director, he was associated early on with Chaplin imitator Ray Hughes and worked prolifically through the 1920s, usually in light comedies (notably the 1925 version of *Skinner's Dress Suit*) that would sometimes star Laura La Plante, whom Seiter married in November 1926. He also directed Colleen Moore in some of

William A. Seiter, *director of* Room Service

her last silents and first talkies. His 1930s credits include a segment of the multi-part *If I Had a Million* (1932), Wheeler & Woolsey's *Peach O'Reno* (1931) and *Diplomaniacs* (1933), Laurel & Hardy's *Sons of the Desert* (1933), and the Astaire-Rogers *Roberta* (1935). Two 1936 films starring Shirley Temple (*qv*), *Stowaway* and *Dimples*, were directed by Seiter from screenplays by Arthur Sheekman and Nat Perrin (both *qv*). Among later films are *This is My Affair* (1937), *You Were Never Lovelier* (1942), with Fred Astaire and Rita Hayworth, also *One Touch of Venus* (1948), adapted from a play by Ogden Nash and S.J. Perelman (*qv*).

(See also: Arden, Eve; Chaplin, Charlie; Fields, W.C.; Krasna, Norman; Laurel & Hardy; McLeod, Norman; O'Connor, Robert Emmett; Rumann, Siegfried; Tashlin, Frank)

SEYMOUR, DAN (1915-93)

Heavyweight supporting actor, born in Chicago; stage experience encompassed burlesque and nightclub work, also the legitimate stage (including *Room Service* [*qv*], later filmed by the Marxes). Dan Seymour is familiar from Bogart's *Casablanca* (1942), *To Have and Have Not* (1944) and *Key Largo* (1948); he is also in the Marx Brothers' tilt at the genre, *A Night in Casablanca* (*qv*), as Captain Brizzard, Chief of Police. He and Groucho were reunited at the Marxes' Motion Picture Hall of Fame presentation in 1977; despite not

Captain Brizzard, alias **Dan Seymour** *(left), in* A Night in Casablanca

having met for a considerable period, Groucho recognized Seymour instantly, greeting him with 'How are you, Captain Brizzard?' Elsewhere in the Seymour filmography are *Cloak and Dagger* (1946), *Rancho Notorious* (1952), *The Buster Keaton Story* (1957), *The Sad Sack* (1957) and Disney's *Escape to Witch Mountain* (1975).

(See also: Awards; Keaton, Buster; Policemen)

SHAW, GEORGE BERNARD (1856-1950)

Famed Irish playwright and philosopher who made Harpo's acquaintance when visiting Alexander Woollcott (*qv*) during a visit to France in 1928. In *Harpo Speaks!*, Harpo recalls being caught sunbathing nude near Woollcott's villa when Shaw arrived in search of his host. Woollcott later prepared some facetiously-designed notepaper for Harpo, incorporating decidedly mixed comments from the eminent; Shaw is quoted as saying 'I was much embarrassed by Harpo Marx'. Playwright and comedian were reunited as guests of William Randolph Hearst and Marion Davies at Hearst's estate, San Simeon. Shaw was long among the Marx Brothers' champions, and has been much quoted to the effect that the Marxes were his four favourite actors, with everyone else following afterwards.

(See also: Abandoned projects; Erskine, Chester)

SHAW, OSCAR (1889-1967)

Philadelphia-born actor and singer (real name Schwartz), onstage in New York as chorus boy when aged twenty and in London two years later with Oscar Hammerstein's Opera Company, when *Quo Vadis?* opened the English Opera House. His first noteworthy appearance on the Broadway stage was as Dick Rivers in *Very Good, Eddie* at the Princess Theatre, December 1915; the Great War intervened after *Ziegfeld's Midnight Frolic* (1916) and *Leave it to*

Oscar Shaw *and Mary Eaton in the film version of* Cocoanuts
BFI Stills, Posters and Designs

Jane (1917) but Shaw was back in 1919 for *The Rose of China* at the Lyric. He continued in musical comedy throughout the twenties, among his credits being *The Half Moon*, Ziegfeld's *9 O'Clock Revue*, *Two Little Girls in Blue*, the 1924 *Music Box Revue* and the Gershwins' *Oh, Kay!*. Though not in the Broadway production of *Cocoanuts* (*qv*), Shaw was cast in the film version as love interest opposite Mary Eaton (*qv*). Shaw had made a number of silent films, such as *The Great White Way* and the Bessie Love vehicle *The King On Main Street*; when Marion Davies' *Marianne* (1929) was released in both silent and sound versions (common practice in an era before all theatres were equipped for talkies), he was used in the silent edition but not, despite considerable experience as stage actor and vocalist, its talking equivalent. Oscar Shaw's career tailed off somewhat in the 1930s, as he grew too old to play juvenile leads; in 1931 he appeared with Frances Williams (*qv*) in *Everybody's Welcome*, and toured the following year in *Of Thee I Sing*. His final film appearance was in *Rhythm on the River* (1940).

(See also: Berlin, Irving; Harris, Sam; Kaufman, George S.; Ryskind, Morrie)

SHEAN, AL (1868-1949)

Brother of Minnie Marx (*qv*) and consequently uncle to the Marx

Brothers; a brother, Harry Shean, and Al's son, Larry, were also in show business. Al Shean was born Adolf Schoënberg (quoted sometimes as Albert, or Alfred Schönberg) in Dornum, Germany but raised in New York. He was the family's first celebrity in the United States, in a theatrical career which had commenced when taking an usher's job at New York's Fourth Avenue Theatre. Both Groucho and Harpo recalled their uncle as having originally been a pants-presser with a talent for arranging close-harmony singing among his colleagues. This evidently paid off in his early vaudeville experiences with the Manhattan Comedy Four, which in turn led to parts on the 'legitimate' stage (*The County Fair*, *The Fisher Maiden*, *The Island of Bong Bong*) interspersed with further vaudeville work, including a long-running partnership with one Charles Warren. Uncle Al would habitually arrive at the Marx household dressed to the nines and bearing coins for the young nephews. According to Groucho, he would ensure a hero's exit from the place by scattering even more money among the local youngsters. It is generally held that Shean's eminence in show business decided Groucho on a theatrical career over medicine. Shean achieved his greatest fame in tandem with Ed Gallagher, as the well-remembered 'Gallagher and Shean' double-act. They were first teamed in 1912, when Shean met Gallagher while visiting the Marx family in Chicago; although identified essentially with vaudeville, their first appearance together was in a musical comedy, *The Rose Maid*. After only about two years, the team quarrelled and split up, for reasons subsequently forgotten (Groucho later compared them to Neil Simon's grumpy twosome in *The*

Sunshine Boys). Shean continued solo in such musical comedies as *Princess Pat* and *Flo-Flo*. During this period, Uncle Al stepped into his nephews' developing careers by writing and staging for them a new sketch, *Home Again* (*qv*). Legend has it that Shean wrote the piece on scrap paper, resting on the Marxes' kitchen table. He had also pepped up its predecessor, *Mr Green's Reception* (*qv*), by acquiring for them a comic song called *Peasie Weasie*. Shean later directed the team's stage show *The Street Cinderella* (*qv*), wrote a variant on *Home Again* called *'N' Everything*, contributed marginally to the script of *Monkey Business* and was photographed visiting the set of *At the Circus* (*qv*). His career with Gallagher resumed in 1920; from this period derives their famous theme song, *Mr Gallagher and Mr Shean*, created for a sketch entitled 'Mr Gallagher and Mr Shean in Egypt'. Film clips of them

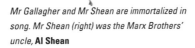

Mr Gallagher and Mr Shean are immortalized in song. Mr Shean (right) was the Marx Brothers' uncle, **Al Shean**

in this guise may be seen in the documentaries *The Marx Brothers in a Nutshell* and *Biography: Groucho Marx*. Shean's headstone is reported to bear an epitaph based on the song's lyric. By 1921 they were the most imitated act on the American stage (see **On the Mezzanine**) and a year later saw them in the *Ziegfeld Follies*, in a bill topped by Will Rogers and featuring also Mary Eaton (*qv*). Shean's occasional screen appearances, primarily talkies, built into a surprisingly lengthy filmography over the years: examples include *Page Miss Glory* (1935), *San Francisco* (1936), *The Prisoner of Zenda* (1937), *The Great Waltz* (1938), *Ziegfeld Girl* (1941) and *Atlantic City* (1944). In

common with the Marxes, Shean suffered heavily in the Crash of 1929, but unlike them did not recover. In gratitude for their uncle's assistance during vaudeville days, the brothers ensured him a comfortable existence for the rest of his life.

(See also: Could Harpo Speak?; Doctors; Documentaries; *I'll Say She Is!*; Vaudeville)

SHEEKMAN, ARTHUR (1901-78)

(Marx Brothers films and plays *qv*) Initially a journalist for the *St Paul News*, Arthur Sheekman had become a columnist on the *Chicago Times* by the time the Marx Brothers played that city in *Animal Crackers* during late 1929 and early 1930. He approached Groucho to be a guest contributor to his column and thus established a close, lifelong friendship; it is understood that Sheekman provided a similar but altogether gentler version of Groucho's wit. Within the first year of their association, Sheekman assisted with Groucho's début as an author, *Beds*. The two men collaborated on sketches for a revue called *Three's a Crowd*, presented in Philadelphia in October 1930. The show, conceived by songwriter-cum-publicist Howard Dietz, included among its principals Clifton Webb, Libby Holman and Fred Allen, the last-named a frequent correspondent of Groucho's in later years. Soon after, Sheekman was dragooned into the writing team of *Monkey Business*. For this he received a credit for 'additional dialogue' (i.e. gag writing), though, with S.J. Perelman (*qv*), is believed to have dominated the script's final draft. His additions to *Horse Feathers* were not cited onscreen but the additional dialogue credit returned, alongside that of Nat Perrin (*qv*), for *Duck Soup*. In addition to new gags, Sheekman and Perrin incorporated into *Duck Soup* much of the material they had written for a Groucho-Chico radio series, *Flywheel, Shyster and Flywheel* (*qv*). Sheekman also worked with Kalmar

Arthur Sheekman *and Gloria Stuart, around the time of their marriage*

and Ruby on the abortive *Cracked Ice*. Another 'additional dialogue' assignment came with *The King and the Chorus Girl* (*qv*), written by Groucho and Norman Krasna (*qv*). Away from the Marxes, Sheekman and Perrin were among the writers on Eddie Cantor's *Roman Scandals* (1933); they also wrote Cantor's *Kid Millions* (1934) with Nunnally Johnson (*qv*) and, more surprisingly, some Shirley Temple vehicles (see **Nat Perrin**). One of Sheekman's better-known works, post-dating his association with Perrin, is the original story for Danny Kaye's *Wonder Man* (1945); others include Irving Berlin's *Blue Skies* (1946) and *Call Me Madam* (1953), Krasna's *Dear Ruth* (1947), Sinatra's *Some Came Running* (1959) and *Mr Music* (*qv*), in which Groucho makes a guest appppearance. Sheekman's obituary in the *New York Times* mentions him having risked blacklisting after helping to found the Screen Writers' Guild. When Sheekman married actress Gloria Stuart (leading lady of *Roman Scandals*), she too became a Groucho confidante; on Groucho's marriage to Kay Gorcey in 1945, Sheekman was best man while his wife gave away the bride. Gloria Sheekman did much to care for Groucho when the comedian suffered a stroke in 1971; she is one of the interviewees in a documentary, *The One, the Only ... Groucho*. Arthur

Sheekman frequently advised Groucho on his various writings over the years. It is important to note, however, that Sheekman was never Groucho's ghostwriter, as has sometimes been claimed. Robert S. Bader, in his anthology of Groucho's short works, states clearly that each offered the other editorial assistance, and that Groucho's name appeared on some of Sheekman's early 1940s essays simply because the latter was then experiencing difficulty in selling them. In 1967 Sheekman edited and supplied an introduction to *The Groucho Letters*, in which his own correspondence is included. Groucho would write regularly to Sheekman, particularly when pessimism set in over a current project, something increasingly the norm after the death of Irving Thalberg (*qv*).

(See also: Abandoned projects; *At the Circus*; Barnett, Vince; Berlin, Irving; Books; Cantor, Eddie; Clubs; Deaths; Documentaries; *Go West*; Letters; Mankiewicz, Herman; Marriages; Seiter, William A.; Sinatra, Frank; Vera-Ellen)

SHOES

(Marx Brothers films and shows *qv*) 'You can clean my shoes if you want to'; Chico's perhaps unreasonable request to a cleaner in the cramped stateroom of *A Night at the Opera*. Footwear made a greater contribution to family history through Gummo's nickname, generally assumed to derive either from his habit of sneaking up on people as though wearing gumshoes, or through habitually wearing them, rain or shine; another story insists that he wore them only in dry conditions, for fear of ruining them in the wet weather for which they were intended. Gumshoes, or 'rubbers', form what Allen Eyles has called 'a crude visual pun' when in *Horse Feathers* Groucho, carrying an umbrella in fine weather, removes his rubbers on each visit to Thelma Todd (*qv*), replacing them on his departure (though the visual pun

might make more sense if the procedure were to be reversed). This scene was adapted from the Napoleon sketch of *I'll Say She Is!*, in which Emperor Groucho returns to Josephine to fetch a replacement sword and rubber overshoes. In this instance the overshoes were placed on Harpo's feet, thrust out from his hiding place, seated behind the Empress. In the film version of *Animal Crackers* Harpo seems to be wearing unfastened overshoes instead of a regular pair. Harpo's shoes sometimes give cause for concern: early in *Go West* he sports a pair that seem to consist mostly of fungus. *A Night in Casablanca* gives him shoes with uppers that part from the soles, providing a receptacle when sweeping up cigarette ends. It may be seen in television appearances of the 1950s and early 1960s that Harpo had switched to white plimsolls; the reason for this is unclear, but softer footwear may have been a concession to the heart trouble he had developed by that time.

(See also: Costume; Deaths; Names; Smoking; Television)

SHOOT THE WORKS!

See: Paintings; Politicians; Stage appearances (post-1930)

SIDNEY, LOUIS K. (1891-19??)

Senior M-G-M executive, producer of *The Big Store* (*qv*). Sidney's ascent was largely in the area of theatre management, notably for M-G-M's parent company, Loew's, Incorporated (of which Sidney was a vice-president).

(See also: Loew, David L.; M-G-M)

SIX MASCOTS

See: Nightingales, the

SINATRA, FRANK (b. 1915) (d. 1998)

One of the century's most famous vocalists, Frank Sinatra's lengthy filmography includes *Double Dynamite* (*qv*) with Groucho and Jane Russell plus *Step Lively*, a remake of the

Marxes' *Room Service* (*qv*). Both he and Harpo may be seen (though not together) in a fund-raising short of 1945, *The All-Star Bond Rally*. Was at one time married to Mia Farrow, daughter of Maureen O'Sullivan (*qv*); latterly wed to Barbara Marx, former wife of Zeppo. When Groucho had celebrated his 85th birthday, Sinatra offered him to be on his own private plane, though Groucho did not accept the invitation. Frank Sinatra lived in semi-retirement during the mid-1990's until his death in 1998.

(See also: Double Dynamite; Solo Films)

SKIDOO (Paramount 1968)
(Groucho- last film - solo)

As last survivor of the main trio, Groucho's status by the late 1960s was that of icon. As such, he was approached to appear as guest star in Otto Preminger's *Skidoo*, a tale of gangsters who are ultimately converted to the received hippie ideals of love, peace, acid and aimless cavorting. Preminger later admitted taking LSD to 'help' him direct one of its scenes; his biographer, Willi Frischauer, notes one of the stars, Carol Channing, saying 'Someone should shoot Otto directing this film', to which Groucho added, inevitably but not inappropriately, 'Someone should shoot Otto - period!' The plot involves a reformed hitman who receives orders from a gang boss to kill a man residing in jail. Groucho plays the gangster chief, who operates from a fortified yacht and contacts his minions via closed-circuit television (though with a leggy beauty for company). He is referred to throughout as 'God'. Groucho had a good opinion of Preminger but expressed a different view of the film itself, his verdict, later on, being 'God-awful'. It's not difficult to see why. The 1960s trappings seemed crass even at the time, and have worn even thinner with age. Groucho is overly made up in an attempt to recreate his image of 1935 rather than that of a man nearing 80.

A varnished-looking Groucho goes hippie in his last film, Skidoo. With Austin Pendleton

Groucho collected $25,000 for his modest contribution. That aside, the most pleasant note is that the ad copy was able to say, with comparative honesty, that Groucho Marx played 'God'. Oddly, a contemporary press release stated that Charlie Chaplin (*qv*) and Senator Dirksen both turned down the role 'because they could not fit it into their schedules', as if citing Groucho as third choice was some kind of compliment. Others in the

cast include Jackie Gleason, Frankie Avalon, Fred Clark, Michael Constantine, Frank Gorshin, John Phillip Law, Peter Lawford, Burgess Meredith, George Raft, Cesar Romero and Mickey Rooney. Written by Doran William Cannon; music and lyrics by Harry Nilsson; produced and directed by Otto Preminger. *Skidoo* justly found its way into a 'Worst Films Compendium' in the Medved brothers' book *The Golden Turkey Awards* (see also **The Story of Mankind**). Perhaps its one worthwhile legacy is its pleasant theme tune, which found a second life

in a BBC Radio panel game of the early 1980s, *Funny You Should Ask*.

(See also: Boats, ships; Colour; Gangsters; Guest appearances; Paramount Pictures; Wigs)

SMOKING
(Marx Brothers films and plays *qv*)
The Marxes' peak years predated any talk of the risks in smoking or the resultant taboos. Some areas and circumstances have, by tradition, been non-smoking and on one occasion in vaudeville (*qv*) Groucho incurred a fine over smoking backstage. It is evident that smoking has much to do with Groucho's concept of free choice: in *Animal Crackers* he reverses the principle by asking 'Do you mind if I don't smoke?', while in *Horse Feathers*, when told there is no smoking, he replies 'That's what *you* say!' In his inaugural song from *Duck Soup* he retains this freedom (among others) while denying the same for everyone else. In *A Night at the Opera* the Marxes and Allan Jones (*qv*) make themselves at home in Gottlieb's office by helping themselves to his cigars. Earlier in the film, Harpo grabs the cigar from Groucho's mouth, to make some kind of sandwich; Groucho refuses a bite, explaining it to be 'Bad enough having to smoke those things without eating 'em.' In the climactic opera scene, Harpo lights a cigarette after striking a match on one of the chorus. Groucho nearly overdoses on cigars when in *At the Circus* Chico fails to comprehend Groucho's attempt to obtain a cigar from the show's midget. Groucho took up smoking cigars while only a teenager, from which period he once described a brand promising 'thirty minutes in Havana for fifteen cents'. He never obtained the allotted time but long remained loyal to the brand, because his youthful quibbling had earned him a fifteen-cent cheque as recompense from the company. Groucho's son, Arthur, dismissed claims of his father having been a heavy smoker. Groucho would have just a few

cigars at intervals during each day and sometimes smoked a pipe when at home. *The Connoisseur's Book of the Cigar* compares Groucho to Rudyard Kipling - who forsook a potential bride rather than give up his daily cigar - in a perhaps apocryphal story: 'One day his wife asked him to give up cigars. He responded "No, but we can remain good friends."' The cigar would not always be lit when Groucho appeared on stage and, as with many comedians of his day, served to give him something to do while timing a laugh. A syndicated feature printed in *Film Weekly* of 1 July 1932 takes this to a ludicrous extreme: 'Groucho Marx does not smoke,' claims the feature, 'but he uses approximately 192 black cigars during the production of a picture'. The item is headed 'Strange But True' but may be construed as neither. When Groucho was a guest on Bill Cosby's show, Cosby tried to discuss the comedian's use of a cigar as prop, only to be heckled by his octogenarian guest; when making another TV show, this time with Marty Feldman, Groucho presented a souvenir of an autographed cigar (see **Television**). His brothers favoured cigarettes and can be seen with them in off-duty photographs. Harpo used them to blow

Smoking: *Groucho remains one of history's great cigar smokers*

smoke bubbles (as in *Animal Crackers* and elsewhere) but had evidently quit the habit by 1941 (see **Stage appearances [post-1930]**) and latter-day home movies (*qv*) show him doing the smoke bubble trick before returning the borrowed cigarette with a look of disgust. Despite this, he seems to have had no difficulty in blowing smoke for TV shows and the films *A Night in Casablanca* and *Love Happy* (publicity stills from the former depict the Marxes adapting to local custom by sharing a hubble-bubble pipe). In the first, Harpo may be seen guying a haughty lady by sporting a vastly elongated cigarette holder; *Love Happy* shows him at the mercy of another slinky female, who at one point makes him smoke a pipe for six hours. Groucho continued smoking until about a year before his death; he informed the press that doctors had told him to quit either smoking or sex. It would have been around this time that Groucho visited British comedians Peter Cook and Dudley Moore after seeing their stage show in Los Angeles. The first thing Groucho did, with the usual zeal of a convert, was to advise the chain-smoking Cook to quit the habit. Cook, in recalling this for BBC Television's *Parkinson* show, added how they were then invited to Groucho's home, only to discover that he had been unable to hear the show

and wanted them to re-enact it in his living room. They didn't go. Moore is known to have visited Groucho on at least one other occasion. Collectors' footnote: a feature of pre-war Britain was the cigarette card, a giveaway item that might feature anything from battleships to famous cricketers. Movie stars were great favourites and the Marx Brothers are known to have been featured in some sets.

(See also: Advertising; Could Harpo Speak?; *A Day in Hollywood, A Night in the Ukraine*; Prostitutes; Risqué humour)

SOLO FILMS (see Guest appearances)

SONGS

(Marx Brothers films and shows *qv*) The Marx Brothers' comedy grew from what had been a musical act. There would always be space for songs, even though few of them could ever be considered hits in their own right. Each of their acts in vaudeville (*qv*) used either songs purchased for their exclusive use (such as *Peasie Weasie* in *Fun in Hi Skule*) or took advantage of the growing trend towards 'free' songs, available to anyone on payment of the appropriate fee. In *Home Again* Groucho assumed the role of popular singer in contemporary hits like *Get Out and Get Under*; others in the show's repertoire included at least one part-authored by Chico. The Broadway shows *I'll Say She Is!*, *The Cocoanuts* and *Animal Crackers* had full scores and their content is detailed within the appropriate entries. In *Animal Crackers* Chico plays *Sugar in the Morning* over and over, imprinting the tune into Marx history so that it recurs in *Monkey Business* and as intro music for the Marxes, or Chico alone, in radio and other appearances in the ensuing years. There was little chance of a hit emerging from any of their shows, though the later films *A Night at the Opera*, *A Day at the Races* and *The Big Store* contain, respectively, the contemporary successes *Alone*, *All God's Chillun Got Rhythm* and *Tenement Symphony*. Usually, the only

memorable compositions tended to be those written as Groucho specialities, notably Kalmar and Ruby's *Hooray For Captain Spaulding*. Bert Kalmar and Harry Ruby (*qv*) excelled at this type of thing: another is *Just Wait 'Til I Get Through With It* (from *Duck Soup*) and *Doctor Hackenbush*, written for but omitted from *A Day at the Races*. For *At the Circus* Yip Harburg and Harold Arlen supplied an excellent Groucho song, *Lydia, the Tattooed Lady*. Groucho's *Big Store* song, *Sing While You Sell*, is in no way comparable. After Bert Kalmar's death, Groucho and Harry Ruby collaborated on a few comic songs that are more in keeping. *Omaha, Nebraska* is a splendid geographical absurdity; *Father's Day* makes wry reference to the customary gift of a tie, the children simultaneously regarding their mother's word on father's identity as 'good enough for us'; while *Show Me a Rose* is outwardly a plaintive, nostalgic ballad in which the absurd lyric does backflips on itself in a whirlpool of nonsense ('Show me a rose, and I'll show you a girl named Sam'). These and other items remained in Groucho's repertoire, professional and social, until the end. Derek T. Mannering, biographer of Mario Lanza, reports a Harpo composition in the Lanza repertoire. This is *Guardian Angels*, which sets to music a poem by Gerda Bielensen. Mannering quotes Terry Robinson, Lanza's friend and trainer, to the effect that Harpo had

written the song prior to his first meeting with Lanza, to whom he presented it at a dinner. Lanza took to the song and, according to his daughter, used it each night as a lullaby for his children. Lanza recorded *Guardian Angels* on several occasions. The first RCA recording usually credits Harpo as accompanist but he seems not to have been present. The original version has been reissued on a CD collection, *Christmas with Mario Lanza*; a hitherto unreleased performance has been included on a further CD complied by Mannering, called *You'll Never Walk Alone*. The Marx world seldom ovelaps into other people's songs but Jerome Kern's *Never Gonna Dance* makes passing reference to them in the lyric.

(See also: Berlin, Irving; Doctors; Radio; Records; Religion; Tattoos; Television)

SORIN, LOUIS (1893-1961)
Stockily-built comedy actor, whose début was made in 1921 at the Provincetown Playhouse, Massachusetts. Sorin first appeared on Broadway in *The Constant Nymph* (1926) and is best remembered as art patron Roscoe W. Chandler in both the stage and film versions of *Animal Crackers* (*qv*). He joined the Marxes on stage in the show's 'DuBarry scene' as part of Heywood Broun's benefit revue *Shoot the Works!* (see **Stage appearances [post-1930]**). Other Broadway-to-film excursions of the period include a sketch with Eddie Cantor (*qv*) in Ziegfeld's *Glorifying the American Girl* (1929, released in Britain as *Glorifying the Showgirl*). David Ragan's *Who's Who in Hollywood 1900-76* notes Sorin in two films with Morton Downey, *Mother's Boy* and *Lucky in Love*. Among Sorin's subsequent Broadway credits are *Humoresque, My Sister Eileen, Golden Boy, Rosalinda* and *The Mad Woman of Chaillot*. Later prolific in radio and TV, still in New York, perhaps most notably in *Twenty-Four Hours in a*

Woman's Life and, with Laurence Olivier, *The Power and the Glory*. *Variety* reported Sorin's cause of death as 'pulmonary edema'. The actor was survived by his wife, Mrs Lenore Wein Sorin.

(See also: Eaton, Mary)

SPANISH KNIGHTS
See: *The Cocoanuts* (play)

SPECTACLES
(Marx Brothers films *qv*)

Louis Sorin, *as art expert Roscoe W. Chandler, displays his knowledge to Mrs Rittenhouse and Captain Spaulding in* Animal Crackers

'Hey, Doc! Can you see us?' asks Chico in *A Day at the Races*. 'If I can't,' replies Groucho, 'there's something wrong with my glasses.' This, and, wire-framed spectacls were a part of Groucho's comic persona from *Fun in Hi Skule* (*qv*) but were in his case genuinely necessary. Usually they seem to be empty frames, in keeping with the flagrantly bogus moustache and eyebrows, yet on other occasions may be seen to have lenses. Groucho was short-sighted from at least his teens, though available pictures suggest a reluctance to be photographed wearing glasses at that time. When abandoning his familiar character in later years, he favoured the horn-rimmed/plastic type of frame but private photographs from the 1930s and 1940s reveal a preference for the square-ish, sometimes rimless type, including one pair with octagonally-shaped lenses. Other informal portraits show that, in common with many nearsighted people, he did not wear them when reading. It may be noticed that in *Duck Soup* he is without them after the business of removing a vase from his head (with explosives!), presumably through fear of breakage. Off-duty, Groucho sometimes wore prescription sunglasses, of the sort designed also to correct myopia. In *Memoirs of a Mangy Lover* he describes a fairly disastrous date where, his regular glasses having been broken, he was forced to make his way around a dimly-lit establishment wearing the sunglasses. Other characters in the Marx films sometimes wear spectacles: Tom Kennedy (*qv*), in *Monkey Business*, seems afflicted with the necessity to raise the lenses in order to focus; in *Duck Soup* Harpo's disguise (on the *back* of his head) includes joke glasses with swirling patterns; while in *A Night in Casablanca* he mocks the strategically-flourished lorgnette of a haughty lady by presenting a device for blowing soap bubbles. In or around 1932 Harpo posed for a gag portrait wearing perhaps five or six pairs of spectacles at once. There are a few photographs of Chico with glasses, at least one of them dating back to around 1920, suggesting he also needed spectacles but tended not to wear them. Maxine Marx has mentioned Chico substituting for an optician when Clark Gable needed an eye test. The disguised Chico supplied Gable with mismatched lenses and put the man through terrible contortions before owning up to the imposture.

(See also: Children; Costume; Moustaches, beards; Practical jokes)

SPORT

(Marx Brothers films and shows *qv*)
Each of the Marx Brothers was a sports fan in some degree. They shared with

Morrie Ryskind and Harry Ruby (both *qv*) a passion for baseball and would sometimes play a game amongst themselves or take part in a charity event (see **Jack Benny**). In Cleveland, Ohio, during the road tour of *A Night at the Opera* (*qv*), they clowned with baseball star Lou Gehrig at a nearby stadium. In the film itself, Groucho masquerades briefly as a baseball-style peanut vendor in the opera house. Another baseball reference is in *Horse Feathers*, when Groucho, examining a microscope slide, compares it to a 'slide' in baseball with 'Well, I think he was safe at second, but it was close.' (Harpo enacts a baseball slide of his own in *Duck Soup*.) *Horse Feathers* has of course a football game as its climax, but sport was much in the air during filming; at that time Los Angeles was hosting the Olympics and the Marxes were photographed with some of the athletes. Golf, too, loomed large in the comedians' leisure time; Groucho took considerable pride in achieving a hole-in-one when playing golf with fellow-vaudevillian Frank Crumit (not Crumin) at a San Francisco course during January 1918. A photograph exists of Harpo caddying for Chico at a Boston golf course in October 1929, when *Animal Crackers* was starting its national tour. In February 1933, during the pre-*Duck Soup* wrangles, the Marxes entered a golf tournament at Aqua Caliente, Mexico. Tennis was another favourite; in youth Groucho's son, Arthur, had an impressive try at tennis as a career. More surprising is Harpo's devotion to croquet, a genteel game played with gusto amid the Alexander Woollcott (*qv*) set. More consistently sedate is the British institution of cricket. On 28 August 1977, shortly after Groucho's death, Michael Davie of the *Observer* recalled Groucho's visit to Lord's cricket ground, date unspecified but probably 1954 (despite a photo dated 1965). Davie and a fellow-reporter, John Gale, had invited Groucho 'on a drunken whim'. When they mentioned who was fielding during the match, Groucho

Sport: *Harpo, the croquemaniac*

asked 'Fielding? Didn't he write *Tom Brown's Schooldays*?' Throughout the match, a young man had been sitting behind them, silently. As the party began to leave, he approached Groucho for an autograph. Groucho obliged, saying 'Were you the guy making all the noise back there?'

(See also: Chaplin, Charlie; Children; Fighting; Gambling; Gangsters)

STAGE APPEARANCES (post-1930)

When *Animal Crackers* (*qv*) finished in the Spring of 1930, it marked the official conclusion of the Marx Brothers' Broadway career. Paramount (*qv*) filmed both this show and *Cocoanuts* (*qv*) in New York, but took the brothers to the West Coast for all subsequent screen appearances. Before making the trip to California, the Marxes spent the later months of 1930 in a vaudeville tour of *Napoleon's Return* (alias *Schweinerei* and *Napoleon's Revenge*), based on the climactic sketch of *I'll Say She Is!* (*qv*). The show played a week at New York's Palace and closed in Detroit in December. In January 1931 they fulfilled an engagement with London impresario C.B. Cochran (*qv*), which is detailed in a separate entry. After completing this and the next Paramount film, *Monkey Business* (*qv*), they returned briefly to the New York stage as a favour to journalist Heywood Broun, who was then running for Congress as a left-wing candidate. In a letter of 26 August, Alexander

Woolcott (*qv*) noted the presence of three of the Marxes in the show, 'ensuring a profitable week'. The absentee Marx was Zeppo, already showings signs of breaking away; the

Chico toured the world as his brothers took things more easily. A 1942 trade ad, possibly referring to his youthful boxing experience, celebrates victories on tour with his band.

show itself, a 'co-operative revue' called *Shoot the Works!*, opened at the George M. Cohan Theatre in New York on 21 July 1931. Among the many intermittent guest stars were Eddie Cantor and Helen Kane (both *qv*). Accompanied by Margaret Dumont and Louis Sorin (both *qv*), the Marx Brothers repeated the DuBarry scene from *Animal Crackers'* stage version on the nights of 20 and 21 August. A *New York Times* review of the first night mentions Groucho's curtain speech, commenting ironically on their ability to function minus the fourth brother. When Broun appeared on stage to quieten the audience for the next item, the Marxes picked him up and carried him offstage. 'As a result of the announcement that they would appear last evening,' continued the report, '*Shoot the Works!* enjoyed the largest attendance since its opening, the box office receipts being about $3,000, according to the management'. Woollcott said that the Marxes 'did it

for nothing, and were solemnly presented with three of Heywood's paintings in full view of the audience. Groucho said it was bad enough playing for nothing.' The show lasted a total of 89 performances. After *Shoot the Works!* they were offered a further tour in vaudeville, which as a genre had become no more than a stage attraction supporting the main feature in a cinema. *Napoleon's Revenge* was dusted off once more for a show beginning in October 1931 at the RKO Theatre in St Louis, Missouri, and concluding at the Albee Theatre, New York, the following January. The next stage engagements post-date *Duck Soup*: Harpo appeared in Russia (*qv*) late in 1933 and in the summer of 1934 Groucho was in Maine, playing in a repertory production of *Twentieth Century*. This was between the team's work for Paramount and M-G-M; for the latter studio they would tour in pre-filming versions of *A Night at the Opera*, *A Day at the Races* and *Go West*, all of which are detailed under the main entries. The conclusion of their M-G-M films saw a break-up of the team, whereupon Chico took to the road with a band, known as 'Chico Marx and his Ravellies' (or 'Ravellis') on their original billing in January 1942; *Variety* once referred to them as 'Chico Marx and the Chicolets', but there is no other reference to them under this title. By mid-February 1942, billing had been amended to 'Chico Marx and his Orchestra', though was sometimes advertised as 'Chico Marx, his piano, and orchestra'. Chico's usual

casual approach seems to have permeated the billing in addition to the performance. A Chico protégé of the period was Mel Torme, then starting out as a vocalist; he may be heard in surviving broadcast material of the band. There were also commercial recordings made of Chico's orchestra (see **Records**) before it was folded up around mid-1943. In October of that year Chico made a brief stopover at Louisville, Kentucky, as the 'Chico Marx Hollywood Revue'. Chico was among those who entertained troops during the Second World War (as Harpo did extensively), joining the Hollywood Victory Caravan. Groucho joined up with the show *en route*, but it is unclear whether or not his appearances ever coincided with those of Chico. In 1944 Chico participated in a variety-format show, *Take a Bow*, at New York's Broadhurst Theatre. His routine incorporated business with one of his co-stars, Gene Sheldon, wearing a Harpo wig. The real Harpo, financially secure and less compelled to work, played the character modelled on himself in Kaufman and Hart's *The Man Who Came to Dinner* (*qv*). This ran between 28 July-2 August 1941 at the Bucks County Playhouse, New Hope, Pennsylvania, near to where Kaufman's daughter, Anne, was then studying. Kaufman took the rôle based on Alexander Woollcott (*qv*), while Hart played the Noël Coward figure. Soon after, from 11-16 August 1941, Harpo appeared with Alexander Woollcott himself in a somewhat *avant-garde* play in Chinese tradition, *Yellow Jacket*. This was part of a repertory season starring Alfred Drake in Marblehead, Massachusetts. Also in the cast were Clarence Derwent, Rex O'Malley and Fay Wray. Miss Wray's 1990 memoir, *On the Other Hand*, describes her dual rôle as both heroine and the heroine's mother. Harpo is mentioned as having been 'Property Man', which in Chinese theatre is an

Chico met up with Laurence Olivier and Vivien Leigh when in Australia during 1948

A month before Harpo's arrival in 1949, west Londoners could see Chico work solo at the Chiswick Empire
Badger Press

on-stage character who supplies props to the other participants and executes the various changes of scene. The actress recalled the way Harpo would perform his duties 'with a wild and devilish look in his eyes' that suggested he would 'do something outrageous'; instead she found Harpo a gentle figure, non-drinking and non-smoking. The latter proved a difficulty, as the Property Man was required to be a virtual chain-smoker; Wray's account describes Harpo's wife - herself a non-smoker - having to blow cigarette smoke on his behalf from behind the scenery. In his memoirs, Harpo recalls both the smoking difficulty and its ingenious solution, plus several other ways in which the production played on his nerves. He mentions having retained his red wig in lieu of a Chinese pigtail, a claim not borne out by a surviving costume photo. Harpo, present only at Woollcott's prompting, was unimpressed when Woollcott, as 'The Chorus', went into raptures over such deeply symbolic devices as the use of stick horses or the ascent of the heroine to heaven. This manoeuvre required the heroine to climb a ladder while the Chorus told his audience what was supposed to be happening, the whole augmented by the Property

Man throwing confetti in order to represent snow. For provincial repertory, *Yellow Jacket* was a high-profile affair - *Life* magazine sent a photographer - and when Lynn Fontanne and Alfred Lunt visited the show, the bored Harpo began to interpolate his smoke-bubble routine (in the one scene where Susan Marx wasn't doubling for him!). Woollcott was at this time fractious even by his usual standards, to the point of making a crack to the *Life* photographer about Claire Boothe Luce, wife of the magazine's proprietor; he bristled at Harpo's *ad lib* but the crunch came on the night when Harpo, aware of friends who had come solely to see him perform, incorporated virtually his whole comic repertoire. There was a backstage row, following which relations between Harpo and Woollcott were temporarily strained. The end of the war in 1945 brought another pre-filming tour, for their 'comeback' movie *A Night in Casablanca*. In 1947 Chico travelled to England for an engagement at the London Casino; a year later he was in Australia, where he met up with Laurence Olivier and Vivien Leigh at a reception in Melbourne. Chico returned to Britain in January 1949 after completing the film *Love Happy* (*qv*). His 14-week tour started at the Empire, Edinburgh, over 7-13 February 1949, concluding with the week of 30 May-5 June at the Chiswick Empire. Harpo arrived

during this appearance in preparation for their booking as a duo at the London Palladium (*qv*). After this, Harpo was booked for the Hippdrome, Birmingham, but this seems not to have taken place. Chico played three more weeks, at the Hackney Empire and then in Bristol and Manchester. It was around this time that Chico met up with Allan Jones (*qv*), who was also touring the UK. Comedian Dickie Henderson told documentary-maker Michael Pointon of Chico chiding an unresponsive British audience with a threat to 'bring Zeppo back'! On returning to the States, Chico continued to play the clubs, usually in Las Vegas; Harpo sometimes accompanied him but Groucho was not interested. His only stage work of the 1950s consisted of summer stock performances of his own play, *Time For Elizabeth* (*qv*). Between August 1956 and March 1957 Chico toured in a repertory production of *The Fifth Season*, closing in Los Angeles.

(See also: Abandoned projects; Carnegie Hall Concert, the; Deaths; Documentaries; Home movies; Laurel & Hardy; Newsreels; Radio; Television; Vaudeville; Wartime)

STAGE DOOR CANTEEN
See: Guest appearances; Records

STAMPS
In the Marxes' radio series *Flywheel, Shyster and Flywheel* (*qv*) there is much correspondence despite a lack of business. A pleasant exchange in episode 10 goes as follows:

Groucho: ... and while he's there, he can mail this letter.
Miss Dimple: But this letter has no stamp on it.
Groucho: Well, tell him to drop it in the box when nobody's looking.
Miss Dimple: But, Mr Flywheel, a stamp only costs *three cents*.
Groucho: For *three cents* I'd deliver it *myself*.

Philatelists around the world take delight in collecting unusual commemorative stamps. Many small countries produce them solely to capture revenue from the collectors' market. American film stars have been represented in stamps from several nations, but the US Post Office has itself been a comparatively late starter and it is incredible to note that, at the time of writing, there has been no Marx Brothers commemorative from America, despite the efforts of admirers. The closest to such a move remains the special cancellation made at the annual Freedonia Marxonia Film Festival in Fredonia, New York; a Groucho postmark was made by Italy's 'Funny Film Festival' in September 1988. The same year brought what was probably the first-ever Marx stamp, from the Gambia, based on a publicity portrait of the four brothers from the film version of *Cocoanuts* (*qv*). More satirical in its intent was an issue from the former Soviet republic of Abkhazia, in its first set of legal-tender stamps. Word of this reached the West via the July 1995 *Beatles Monthly*, which reported the stamps as sending up the former Communist régime with designs based not on Karl Marx and Lenin, but Groucho Marx and John Lennon. Not exactly a new joke, but welcome despite. The limited-edition set was, it seems, already changing hands for high prices in the USA. To conclude, the best option might be to follow the example of Captain Spaulding in *Animal Crackers* (*qv*): 'Just send a stamp, air mail. That's all, you may go, Jamison. I may go too.'

STAND-INS

(Marx Brothers films *qv*)
It is the film industry's usual practice to employ doubles when the stars are either unavailable, incapacitated or simply too valuable for certain stunts. Production on *Horse Feathers* was delayed when Chico was involved in a car accident, sustaining an injured kneecap and some broken ribs. On set, he was obliged to rest for much of the time, in a wheelchair bearing a sign reading 'LEMUIR [*sic*]. Caught in Africa by Professor Schmaltz during his recent Expedition. *Habitat of South America ... Specie of baboon.*' In the climactic football game, Chico takes no strenuous part in the action and at one point hitches a lift on a stretcher. Chico's stand-in was employed for a long shot purporting to represent all four brothers running across the field, an illusion destroyed by the 'double' being perhaps a foot taller than the original. One might add that the 'Groucho' running with the ball is at best a passable lookalike. Stuntmen were also used for the chase scenes of *Go West*, *The Big Store* and *A Night in Casablanca*, but only in *Big Store* does it become a serious distraction. Detailed under the stage version of *Animal Crackers* are such occasions when Zeppo deputized for Groucho, and Harpo and Chico deputized for each other!

(See also: Impersonators)

THE STORY OF MANKIND

(Warner Brothers 1957)
The last theatrical film to employ the main three Marx Brothers, and technically their only colour film together, *The Story of Mankind* was produced and directed by Irwin Allen (*qv*), who also co-scripted with Charles Bennett. Source for this tongue-in-cheek chronicle was an entirely serious book by Hendrik Willem van Loon, itself considered by the *New York Times* 'a longwinded, rambling and discursive survey of history'. The reviewer, deducing the problems in filming it to be 'insurmountable', believed Allen had 'faced up gamely to his towering challenge and gone down fighting on practically every count'. (The word 'towering' was later to have some significance to Allen, who went on to have rather greater success with *The Towering Inferno* in 1974.) The excuse for parading the saga of Humanity before us (in 100 minutes) is a debate in heaven, the outcome to determine whether the world should be permitted to survive despite the premature discovery of a super-powerful nuclear weapon. As evidence for the good or evil within Man, the tale begins with the discovery of fire and concludes with library footage of the Second World War. An unwieldy epic in the immediate wake of *Around the World in Eighty Days* (1956), *The Story of Mankind* enjoys a type of eccentric notoriety, hence its inclusion in the Medved brothers' *Fifty Worst Movies of All Time* and *The Golden Turkey Awards*. The latter, calling the film a 'historical gaffe', nominates it for a Golden Turkey in the category of 'Worst Casting of All Time'. Singled out for the miscasting award is Harpo as Sir Isaac Newton, in a scene where he discovers gravity (while playing the harp) by having not one apple fall on his head, but a bushel. Oddly, Harpo, Groucho and Chico are employed in entirely separate sequences, despite Allen's notion of getting them together 'for one last movie': Groucho is Peter Minuit, acquiring Manhattan from the Indians for $24 in beads (among the Indians being Harry Ruby [*qv*] and Groucho's third wife, Eden), while Chico, presumably as wry comment on his amorous reputation, portrays a

The Story of Mankind: *Groucho buys Manhattan from the Indians, using his wife, Eden, as a writing desk; also in attendance is songwriter Harry Ruby (as an Indian chief!)*

to officiate at the wedding of Groucho and Ruth Johnstone. According to Arthur Marx (in *Son of Groucho*), the nominal religious difference, and the generally disreputable image of show business folk, meant that no minister would co-operate, so Swerling tracked down the perfect combination: a Justice of the Peace who was a Jewish ex-vaudevillian.

(See also: Children; Marriages; Religion)

Harpo discovers gravity in **The Story of Mankind**

monk. The subsequent 'Turkey' notwithstanding, *The Fifty Worst Movies of All Time* does at least name Harpo and Groucho among those to have acquitted themselves without embarrassment, even to the point of considering Harpo 'memorable' and praising Groucho's business of proferring his cigar whenever he is offered a peace pipe; the same cannot be said for many of the other notables in the cast.

(See also: Colour films; *Girl in Every Port, A*; Guest appearances; Marriages)

THE STREET CINDERELLA
(Marx Brothers play)
Referred to in some histories as *The Cinderella Girl*, *The Street Cinderella* was an early Marx Brothers foray into musical comedy, the idea being to a create a 'legitimate' property that would get them out of vaudeville (*qv*) and, if successful, on to Broadway. Their mother, Minnie, commissioned a book by Jo Swerling (*qv*) and songs by Gus Kahn and Egbert Van Alstyne. Director was Minnie's brother, Al Shean (*qv*). Details of the show's content are sketchy but these would in any case pale alongside the drama taking place in the audience. When *The Street Cinderella* opened in Grand

Rapids, Michigan on 28 September 1918, a flu epidemic required patrons to occupy alternate seats in alternate rows, their faces shielded by handkerchiefs. This brief, discouraging engagement was followed by five indifferent days in Benton Harbor, closing on 3 October. The Marxes would have to wait nearly six years for another try at Broadway. It was probably during this catastrophic production that Harpo decided upon an ingenious publicity ruse: he placed outside the theatre a 'borrowed' cardboard cut-out of movie vamp Theda Bara, not of course stating her presence but allowing the public to draw their own conclusions.

(See also: *Humorisk*; *I'll Say She Is!*; Marx, Minnie)

SWERLING, JO (JOSEPH)
(1894 or 1897-?)
Russian-born playwright and screenwriter, a former journalist, best known today as co-author of the musical *Guys and Dolls*. Early in his career, Swerling was associated with the Marxes on two occasions, neither of them memorable: the disastrous musical-comedy *The Street Cinderella* and their never-released silent film *Humorisk* (both *qv*). Perhaps his most positive contribution was in February 1920, when Swerling located someone

TAGGART, BEN (1889-1947)

Canadian-born character actor, originally from the stage; Ben Taggart dabbled in silents during the 'Teens but his screen career effectively began with the Marx Brothers' *Monkey Business* (*qv*). In the feature film, he plays the ship's captain, Corcoran, who is deprived of lunch by two of the stowaways; in the promotional film (see **Monkey Business [promo]**) he is Mr Lee, theatrical agent. Taggart resurfaces in *Horse Feathers* (*qv*) as a policeman. Other comedy work includes *Hold 'Em Jail* (1932) with Wheeler & Woolsey and *Million Dollar Legs* with W.C. Fields (*qv*), a film which also stars Susan Fleming (Mrs Harpo Marx). Also in several Hal Roach shorts (mostly with Charley Chase) and Republic serials.

(See also: Marriages; Policemen)

TASHLIN, FRANK (1913-72)

Director and screenwriter, often identified for his films with Jerry Lewis. Tashlin gained his early training in Warner Brothers cartoons and, reportedly, as a gagman at the Hal Roach Studios. He is widely reputed to have attended Chaplin and Laurel & Hardy screenings in order to make notes. An early sight-gag contribution to live-action films is believed to have been the celebrated moment in *A Night in Casablanca* (*qv*) where Harpo really is holding up a building (one of several Tashlin-like gags in the film). One of his late 1940s screenplay credits was as co-adaptor of *One Touch of Venus* (1948), from the play by Ogden Nash and S.J. Perelman (*qv*). He shares screenplay credit for *Love Happy* (*qv*) with Mac Benoff, and may perhaps have supplied most of the film's cartoon-style spot gags. Tashlin's *Will Success Spoil Rock Hunter?* (*qv*) closes with Groucho as guest star.

(See also: Animation; Chaplin, Charlie; Laurel & Hardy; *Risqué* humour; Seiter, William A.; Woollcott, Alexander; Writers)

TATTOOS

(Marx Brothers films *qv*)

One of Groucho's most popular songs is the Harburg-Arlen classic 'Lydia, the Tattooed Lady', sung in the film *At the Circus* and elsewhere. In *Duck Soup* we see some of Harpo's supposed tattoos, one of them a hula dancer and the other a kennel complete with live-action dog superimposed. Groucho is sure Harpo wouldn't have a picture of his grandfather, but Harpo, prepared to prove him wrong, is dissuaded from undressing. A bizarre photograph purporting to be a heavily-tattooed Groucho is not the man himself but an erstwhile lookalike.

(See also: Animals; Carnegie Hall Concert, the; Censorship; Impersonators; Radio; Songs; Television)

TELEPHONES

(Marx Brothers films *qv*)

'You know, I'd be lost without a telephone' says Groucho after Harpo takes his call in *Duck Soup*. Harpo eats the desk telephone in *Cocoanuts*; its counterpart in *A Night in Casablanca* permits Groucho to fob someone off when his 'trunks' have gone astray ('Well, put your pants on'). A ship's speaking-tube in *Monkey Business* is outside the category but the impromptu nut-cracker in *Horse Feathers* is most definitely a telephone. The historical setting of *Go West* allows Groucho to say 'Don Ameche hasn't invented the telephone yet', based on Ameche's celebrated role as Alexander Graham Bell (the joke would haunt Ameche for the rest of his life). Perhaps the best telephone gag in Marxdom is that in *A Day at the Races*, when Groucho intercepts a call by masquerading as switchboard operator and Southern-accented Colonel.

(See also: Gambling; Television; Wartime)

Harpo contributed to a memorable episode of I Love Lucy *on CBS*

TELEVISION

(Marx Brothers films *qv*)
Chico was first of the Marxes to appear on TV, in Milton Berle's *Texaco Star Theater* (NBC 5 October 1948). At least part of this hour-long show survives. Chico probably did TV strictly through need of money rather than enthusiasm for the medium; on his death in 1961, the *Daily Express* obituary quoted his opinions on TV as 'the monster that has ruined comedy', able to swallow material instantly. 'You can do an act three times and the whole world knows it - you're dead', he added. TV brought Chico several acting roles. A series of 30-minute programmes, *College Bowl* (ABC 1950-51) cast him as proprietor of a soda fountain; also in the show was a young Andy Williams. A 1950 CBS play, *Papa Romani*, cast Chico as an Italian emigre whose troubles begin on the installation of a telephone. This segment has been described variously

as part of *Silver Theatre, Bigelow Theatre* (after its sponsor) and, as billed on the opening credits, *Hollywood Half Hour*. Chico appeared in another play, *Next to No Time*, for *Playhouse 90* in 1958. One of Chico's stranger bookings was for the CBS panel game *I've Got a Secret*, in which he was disguised as Harpo; otherwise he was more commonly employed in a variety format, as when travelling to England for *Showtime* (BBC TV 4 October 1959) hosted by magician David Nixon. Extracts have recently been revived in the BBC's *Lime Grove Story* and *TV Heroes*, also the American-made *Unknown Marx Brothers* (*qv*). Chico reminisced with Nixon, played piano and joined him in a musical trio with Nixon on string bass and fellow-guest Eve Boswell on cornet. Other guests included Stanley Unwin, Jimmy James (unbilled in the BBC's listings magazine *Radio Times*), American dance team Mata and Hari, the Television Toppers and the George Mitchell singers. Producer was Graeme Muir.

Groucho's TV debut was in *Popsicle Parade of Stars* (CBS 17 July 1950). An early survivor is a 1952 entry, *The All Star Revue*, featuring a sketch in which Groucho suggests he should 'neck' with his co-stars, veteran actresses Talllulah Bankhead and Ethel Barrymore. 'Ethel does not neck,' says Miss Bankhead, 'and neither do I'. 'Speak for yourself, darling', protests Miss Barrymore. Groucho once reduced *What's My Line* to chaos by placing a blindfold over his glasses but was best known on TV for his own game show, *You Bet Your Life* (*qv*). The TV version ran on NBC from 1950 (though an earlier CBS pilot exists). During that time he appeared in at least two spoof versions, one (with Rodgers and Hammerstein) for *The General Foods 25th Anniversary Show* and another with Jack Benny (*qv*) in 1955. It was Groucho's turn to answer questions when interviewed by Edward R. Murrow in *Person to Person* (CBS 1954), by means of a link between the

studio and Groucho's home. When questioned over the authenticity of his ad-libbing in *You Bet Your Life*, Groucho admitted to some pre-briefing of the contestants' history before making his point by engaging Murrow in the same type of spontaneous banter. Groucho would be interviewed again on *The Hy Gardner Show* in 1961. A 1959 version of the *Dinah Shore Chevy Show* saw its star duetting with Groucho to 'Peasie Weasie', a song dating back to *Fun in Hi Skule* (*qv*). In 1960 Groucho was allowed to indulge his passion for Gilbert and Sullivan in a TV adaptation of *The Mikado* (*qv*). When *You Bet Your Life* ended in 1961, it was replaced by a revamped CBS version called *Tell it to Groucho*, which lasted only one season. Also in 1961, Groucho appeared in a *DuPont Show of the Week* (NBC) called *Merrily We Roll Along*. In January 1962 Groucho appeared in the serious role of a family man in *The Holdout*, part of the CBS *G.E. Theater*. When Jack Paar vacated *The Tonight Show* that year, Groucho was interim host before introducing Johnny Carson on 1 October (Groucho later deputized for Carson for a week). Despite claims that the earlier Groucho editions have been lost, a discography in *The Freedonia Gazette* (*qv*) identifies an issued LP track as being from Carson's debut. One of the guests is Harry Ruby (*qv*), with whom Groucho also appeared on the *Steve Allen Show* in 1964. Groucho had been an early supporter of Allen, one of whose recent compilation programmes has included a 1958 extract with Groucho planted in the audience. Groucho's wife, Eden, starred opposite him in a version of a play Groucho had written with Norman Krasna (*qv*), *Time for Elizabeth* (*qv*). This colour film was shot at Revue Studios, Universal, during March 1964 and screened by NBC on 24 April in *The Bob Hope Chrysler Theatre*. In June 1964 a British commercial station, Rediffusion, brought Groucho over for the first in a networked series called *The Celebrity Game*. The visit was considered of sufficient interest for Groucho to be the cover story for the ITV listings magazine, *TV Times*. A year later, Groucho returned to the company for a UK version of *You Bet Your Life*, called *Groucho*. The series was not well received. Earlier in 1965 Groucho had made his final appearance with Margaret Dumont (*qv*) in *The Hollywood Palace*, in a revival of his entrance scene from *Animal Crackers*. Miss Dumont, who died soon after, belied her image by actually seeming to get the jokes. Also present were Dee Hartford (Groucho's then sister-in-law), and Groucho's teenaged daugher Melinda, who would soon depart from the theatrical career in which her father was attempting to guide her. Groucho's failure in Britain brought about his decision to enter semi-retirement. In 1967 he appeared in a further revival of his entrance in *Animal Crackers* for the *Kraft Music Hall*. That same year he took a cameo role in an episode of *I Dream of Jeannie*, and 1968 saw him make a similar appearance in *Julia*. In 1969 Groucho hosted the 30-minute *One-Man Show*, introducing a roster of famous comedians. Groucho was a frequent guest of chat show host Dick Cavett who, as a young unknown, had met Groucho when attending the funeral of George S. Kaufman (*qv*) in 1961. One show, in 1970, featured Groucho and Shelley Winters, who was then playing the lead in *Minnie's Boys* (*qv*). Groucho was by then returning to fuller activity. Again in 1970, he taped a *David Frost Show* in New York for trans-Atlantic screening and the next year travelled to England for episode 5 of ATV's *Marty Feldman Comedy Machine*. Groucho sang 'Show Me a Rose' and 'Lydia, the Tattooed Lady' in addition to performing in a sketch (written by Larry Gelbart, who developed *M.A.S.H.* for TV) presenting him as a scheming lawyer. The show was transmitted in London on 19 November and elsewhere in Britain the following night. The *Sun* described Groucho presenting Feldman with a

cigar, bearing an inscription 'too indelicate for publication'. In 1972 Groucho was interviewed by Frank Muir for the BBC's *Omnibus* series and in 1973 was a guest on *The New Bill Cosby Show*. Despite his comic put-downs on the show, Groucho had considerable regard for Cosby's talent. The re-première of *Animal Crackers'* film version in 1974 brought Groucho and pianist Marvin Hamlisch to New York and *The Mike Douglas Show*. As late as March 1976, Groucho participated in Bob Hope's all-star NBC special, *Joys*, a 90-minute special confronting Groucho with a midget lookalike, Billy Barty (who had worked with Harpo in a deleted segment of *Monkey Business*).

Although Harpo was last of the three to begin a formal television career, a survey of his TV work (written by Matthew Hickey for *Filmfax*) mentions both a ten-minute commercial film for Catalina Swimsuits, made in 1949, plus reputed appearances in *Love Happy*'s TV trailers (see also **Advertising** and **Trailers**). Otherwise, Harpo's small-screen debut was in NBC's *Colgate Comedy Hour* of 11 November 1951; he would appear in subsequent editions of the show on 6 January 1952, 30 March 1952 (with Chico and Tony Martin [*qv*]) and 24 October 1954, this last also including Ilona Massey (*qv*). Other early broadcasts were in *The RCA Victor Show* (NBC 1 February 1952), the *Celebral Palsy Telethon* (KECA-TV May 1952), *All Star Review* (NBC 4 October 1952), *The All Star Ice Review* with skating star Sonja Henie (NBC 22 December 1953) and a pioneering colour network programme known variously as *Season's Greeetings* and *Christmas Stocking* (NBC 22 December 1953). In addition, Harpo is thought to have appeared with Hoagy Carmichael in NBC's *Saturday Night Review* (July 1953). Harpo joined the mayhem of *The Spike Jones Show*, transmitted live on 9 January 1954; the same year saw him in an episode of a

religious series *The Christophers*. Perhaps Harpo's best-known TV appearance is an episode of *I Love Lucy*, first broadcast by CBS on 9 May 1955.The show allows Harpo to revamp the charade scene from *A Day at the Races*, play a 'straight 'version of 'Take Me Out to the Ball Game' (see also *A Night at the Opera*) and to reprise *Duck Soup*'s mirror routine with a Harpo-clad Lucille Ball (*qv*). For the finale, Desi Arnaz and William Frawley arrive dressed as Groucho and Chico. On 17 April 1956 Harpo appeared on NBC's *Martha Raye Show*; on 3 January 1957 he was in a *Playhouse 90* called *Snowshoes*. There followed in March an NBC show with Tennessee Ernie Ford and, on 3 January 1958, Harpo's turn on *Person to Person*, his wife Susan doing most of the talking but with Harpo answering some questions via strategically-placed cards. Harpo provided musical accompaniment for a *DuPont Show of the Month* presentation of Victor Herbert's *The Red Mill* (CBS 19 April 1958); he is sometimes said to have

Groucho plays a dramatic role in NBC's The Holdout

acted as narrator, but instead provided mimed sections during the commercial 'bumpers', which were interpreted by Evelyn Rudie. When filming a series of Labatt's beer commercials in Toronto, Harpo appeared on a Canadian chat show, *7-0-1*. Back in the United States, he worked with Milton Berle on the *Kraft Music Hall* (NBC 14 January 1959); one gag has Berle leading the orchestra so that it virtually obliterates Harpo's clarinet rendering of 'I'm Forever Blowing Bubbles'. Harpo accepted a dramatic part in *A Silent Panic*, an episode of CBS's *DuPont Show* hosted by June Allyson (22 December 1960). In this, Harpo plays a deaf-mute mime artist who, when working in a store window display, witnesses a murder but cannot convey his story to the authorities. Elsewhere in the cast is Harpo's son, Bill. Harpo's returned to familiar *milieu* for an NBC *Chevy Show*, *Swingin' at the Summit* (29 January 1961). When his memoirs appeared in 1961, Harpo became even more ubiquitous; he took on Sam Snead in *Celebrity Golf* (23 April 1961); later that day he was on *The Ed Sullivan Show* (CBS), similar in part to the 1959 Berle sketch and incorporating most of his classic routines; on 2 May he was on two NBC programmes, Dave Garroway's *Today Show* (using his harp to fire an arrow) and Merv Griffin's *Play Your Hunch*, a show in which a celebrity panel would help people with problems (Harpo's being that he couldn't speak in order to plug the book!); the next day saw him on *I've Got a Secret* (CBS), which had previously entertained Chico as a bogus Harpo; next was *Here's Hollywood* (NBC 8 May). He was a guest on *You Bet Your Life* (11 May) and took part in a sketch on *Candid Camera* (CBS 14 May), in which Harpo, concealed within a drinks machine, grabbed the sodas before customers could reach them. Harpo was in *Art Linkletter's House Party* on 25 May; the *Filmfax* listing cites a possible earlier appearance with Linkletter, from 1957. On 12 November Harpo contributed to

NBC's *DuPont Show of the Week*, subtitled *The Wonderful World of Toys*; also from 1961, the *Filmfax* list again details an elusive appearance, in the programme *Your Surprise Package* with Bill Marx and Groucho's stooge George Fenneman. Harpo's final television appearances were in *The Red Skelton Show* (CBS 25 September 1962), which also featured Virginia Grey (*qv*), and *The Musicale* (an episode of ABC's television adaptation of *Mr Smith Goes to Washington*), first transmitted on 20 October 1962.

Programmes featuring three or more Marx Brothers were tragically few. An NBC *Sunday Spectacular*, subtitled 'Inside Beverly Hills' (29 January 1956), has a studio sketch with Groucho and Chico plus a visit to Harpo and family at home (with Harpo's children sporting wigs identical to their father's!). Among others present are Melinda Marx and, again, Tony Martin. No longer known to exist is perhaps the most interesting of them, an edition of NBC's *Tonight: America After Dark* (a precursor of *The Tonight Show*). Broadcast on 18 February 1957, this show gathered together all five Marx brothers to help promote Chico's stage run in *The Fifth Season* (see **Stage appearances [post 1930]**). It has been said that Harpo actually spoke on this occasion. Other reunions were *The Incredible Jewel Robbery* (*qv*) and the aborted pilot *Deputy Seraph* (also *qv*).

The team's cinema films have long been TV staples around the world; British screenings have tended to be either early in the day or extremely late, as in a '60s screening of *A Night at the Opera* or an embarrassing 1979 outing for *A Day at the Races* when the sequence of reels was disrupted, causing part of the film to go out twice and another part not at all! BBC television ran most of the films during the 1960s and 1970s, omitting *Cocoanuts* and *Love Happy* from a 1972 season for the respective reasons

of poor print quality and disappointing content (though the latter has since been shown by the BBC). The Paramount and M-G-M films have subsequently channel-hopped between the BBC and commercial concerns; Channel Four screened *Cocoanuts* in 1984 (which, in common with most Marx films, has since reappeared on satellite). When in London during 1965, Groucho was pleased to see *Animal Crackers* (then unavailable in the US) scheduled on the recently-launched 625-line channel, BBC 2; as reported in the *Daily Worker* of 1 April, he was less amused to discover his $75-a-day hotel had no set capable of receiving the new service. The film's subsequent extraction from limbo in America brought a prestigious TV debut on CBS, at 8 pm on 21 July 1979. Care was taken to provide a new print, screened with a minimum of short breaks. KTLA of Los Angeles greeted 1980 with an all-night Marx screening, comprising *Duck Soup* followed by a *Best of Groucho* episode (from reruns of *You Bet Your Life*), *Horse Feathers*, *Monkey Business*, *A Night in Casablanca*, another *Best of Groucho* and *The Cocoanuts*.

(See also: Abandoned projects; Animation; Children; Could Harpo Speak?; Documentaries; Guest appearances; Home movies; Impersonators; Lawyers; Marriages; M-G-M; Names; Paramount; Radio; Records; Smoking; Songs; Video releases)

TEMPLE, SHIRLEY (b. 1928)

The most famous child star in film history, Shirley Temple is remembered chiefly for her run of Fox features in the 1930s and an almost unprecedented special Oscar. Less well known is that Harpo was among the first to realize her extraordinary potential. According to Groucho, Harpo saw her when she was taken to watch location filming for *Horse Feathers* (*qv*) at Occidental College, during 1932; Harpo, at that time without a family of his own, was so taken with little Shirley that he offered to buy her for $50,000! Not surprisingly, Mr and Mrs Temple declined to accept. Another source dates this story to 1934, when Shirley was making a Paramount short called *New Deal Rhythm*; this is less likely, as the brothers had left Paramount by this time and Shirley had started to make headway in pictures. Her film career began in short comedies for Educational; one of these, *Polly Tix in Washington*, makes curious anticipation of her adult career in politics (as Mrs Shirley Temple Black). In 1958 the American humour magazine *Cracked* published a joke advertisement making fun of a well-known hair colourant. The main drawing shows a young Shirley Temple embracing the bewigged Harpo, by way of comparing their sets of curls (Groucho is seen *drinking* the product, claiming 'You can bet your life it's good!').

(See also: Advertising; Caricatures; Children; Perrin, Nat; Seiter, William A.; Sheekman, Arthur; *You Bet Your Life*)

THALBERG, IRVING G. (1899-1936)

Producer of the two most successful Marx films, *A Night at the Opera* and *A Day at the Races* (both *qv*). Thalberg, who had earlier been with Universal, was a senior executive while only in his twenties; at M-G-M (*qv*) he was equal to Louis B. Mayer, otherwise the most powerful man in the industry. Thalberg had an instinct for what was 'right'; that same instinct made him choose the Marx Brothers when wanting to branch into comedy. As noted in the *Night at the Opera* entry, he revolutionized their methods by allowing pre-filming tours and placing the results within high-gloss productions. He and the Marxes formed a close friendship, based on profound mutual respect. Groucho thought he took to them because they showed none of the usual deference; when kept waiting outside his office, they started a small fire and

blew smoke under his door; waiting on another occasion, they sent out for potatoes and stripped naked before cooking them in the fireplace. Thalberg arrived and sent out for butter. Irving Thalberg was happily married to actress Norma Shearer; the only blot was his fragile health, constantly monitored. He underwent a check-up in May 1936 and was then reasonably fit; but in September a simple cold developed into pneumonia and he died, aged only 37. Groucho said on several occasions that after Thalberg's death, he lost interest in film-making. Certainly the team was without a sympathetic mentor from that time on.

THREE NIGHTINGALES, THE
See: Nightingales, the

THREE'S A CROWD
See: Sheekman, Arthur

THURBER, JAMES
See: Books; Caricatures; Clubs

TIMBERG, HERMAN
See: *Flywheel, Shyster and Flywheel*; *On the Mezzanine*

TIME FOR ELIZABETH

Groucho's friendship with Norman Krasna (*qv*) produced a collaborative screenplay in the 1930s, *The King and the Chorus Girl* (*qv*). Later on they wrote a play, *Time For Elizabeth*. The plot concerns a man, Ed Davis, who decides to retire and spend time with his wife in Elizabeth, New Jersey. The assumed idyll turns sour when boredom and consequent frustrations set in. The play was created over several years but finally opened in September 1948 at the Fulton Theater, New York, with Otto Kruger playing the lead. Reviews were indifferent at best: Brooks Atkinson of the *New York Times* called it 'amiable in spirit and well-acted by a singularly pleasant cast, but strictly a perambulator frolic'. Twelve years later, when his daughter was away at summer camp, Groucho wrote to Goodman Ace saying 'our

house is now as quiet as the balcony of the Fulton Theater when *Time For Elizabeth* was playing there'. The essential problem was that many of the lines were more amusing if *Groucho* said them. This was proved somewhat when Groucho took the starring part in repertory, or 'Summer Stock', during 1957, 1958, 1959 and 1963. Occasional interest in *Time For Elizabeth* as a cinema film came to nothing, but in 1964 Groucho filmed a version of the play for TV.

(See also: Books; Children; Stage appearances [post-1930]; Television)

TODD, THELMA (1905 or 1906-35)

Originally a schoolteacher, Thelma Todd enrolled in the Paramount Film School after winning the title 'Miss Massachusetts'. Early film work was sometimes under the name Alison Lloyd. Appeared in Hal Roach comedies from 1929, working with Laurel & Hardy (*qv*) and Charley Chase plus co-starring shorts with ZaSu Pitts and, later, Patsy Kelly. Travelled to England in 1933 to promote the Laurel & Hardy feature *Fra Diavolo*; while there appeared in a film with Stanley Lupino, *You Made Me Love You*. Other films include *Her Man*

*A revealing publicity portrait of **Thelma Todd***

(1930), the 1931 version of *The Maltese Falcon* (known as *Dangerous Female* on TV), Buster Keaton's *Sneak Easily* (1932), and two Wheeler & Woolsey comedies from 1934, *Hips, Hips, Hooray* and *Cockeyed Cavaliers*. She appeared in two Marx Brothers films, *Monkey Business* and *Horse Feathers* (both *qv*). In the former, she is the frustrated bride of gangster Alky Briggs; the latter casts her as 'College Widow' Connie Bailey, whose charms attract all four brothers. The story goes that she was genuinely close to drowning when falling from the canoe she shared with Groucho. Thelma Todd's last feature appearance was in Laurel & Hardy's *The Bohemian Girl*. One morning in December 1935, Thelma Todd was found dead in her garage from carbon monoxide poisoning; she had been missing since the previous night. Her apparent suicide has long been interpreted as a possible murder. It seems fair to speculate that her relationship with a gangster in *Monkey Business* was a little close to reality; similarly unfortunate is a line from the film, in which Groucho says 'You're a woman who's been getting nothing but dirty breaks. Well, we can clean and tighten your brakes, but you'll have to stay in the garage all night.'

(See also: Keaton, Buster)

TOO MANY KISSES (Paramount 1925)
One might imagine that the Marx Brothers' eminence as stage artists would have made them an inevitable target for silent movies. Eddie Cantor (*qv*) and other essentially vocal talents were beckoned by the screen before it began to talk, yet the Marxes' only real venture was in a failed, independent project called *Humorisk* (*qv*). Another exception was *Too Many Kisses*, a vehicle for Richard Dix (1894-1949), in which Harpo plays a supporting role. This six-reel film was released early in 1925, after the Marxes' success in *I'll Say She Is!* (*qv*) but before the arrival of its successor, *The Cocoanuts* (*qv*).

The plot casts Dix as Richard Gaylord Jr, whose preoccupation with women does not earn his father's approval. Gaylord Sr (Frank Currier) sends Jr to Spain on hearing that Basque women will not marry outsiders. The young man falls for attractive Basque villager Yvonne Hurja (Frances Howard), only to discover a rival suitor in Julio (William Powell), a Captain in the Civil Guard. Yvonne persuades Richard not to fight a duel, but Richard is later abducted by Julio's men. The Captain pursues Yvonne but Richard escapes and vanquishes Julio. Richard's father approves the match with Yvonne and all ends satisfactorily. It is evident that Harpo is not essential to the plot; his later recollections (not all of them too long after the event) insist that his was a momentary appearance, the result of drastic cutting. Leonard Maltin's *Movie Comedy Teams* quotes Harpo's comments to a journalist during his return to Astoria to film *Cocoanuts* in 1929. Harpo claimed he had taken all his friends to see *Too Many Kisses*, only to wait in vain for a couple of reels; 'it seems the cutters had been at work on the film and they hadn't figured my acting amounted to much'. Harpo bent down to pick up his hat just as his mother said 'There he - goes.' 'I never did see myself,' added Harpo, 'I hope I am better off in *The Cocoanuts*.' Examination of the film itself (which was believed lost until the early 1970s) reveals that he was permitted to do rather more. He may be seen throughout the second half, often as a crowd extra; it may be that Harpo and company assumed he had only one moment in the picture, and departed before his contribution really began. He has a good scene in which, centre frame, he stands between two quarrelling men, alternately mimicking their expressions as he looks to and fro; when the villain wants a ladder to sneak up to the heroine's balcony, Harpo is seen strumming it like a guitar. Another good scene has Harpo drinking from a wine skein. When Richard is abducted and imprisoned in

Julio's headquarters, he is able to free himself, knock out the villain's henchmen and tie up Julio. Harpo wanders in and Julio orders Harpo to untie him; after establishing Julio as safely tied, Harpo knocks him cold with a single punch. In this respect Harpo contributes directly to the plot, in denying Julio opportunity to escape and take after the hero. This section provides further interest as anticipation of sequences in *A Night at the Opera* (*qv*) and others, wherein a subservient Harpo is slapped around before getting the better of his tormentor. Titling bills Harpo as 'the Village Peter Pan'. As a mime, it made perfect sense for Harpo to appear in a silent feature, yet when confronting Julio he is actually given dialogue, albeit delivered by title card. No effort is made to employ his usual persona or promote him as a major stage talent; yet it is revealing to note that, despite having evidently been taken on as a crowd extra, Harpo had made sufficient impact for his part to be amplified into virtual co-star status. *Too Many Kisses* was scripted by Gerald Duffy and directed by Paul Sloane.

(See also: Characters; *The Cocoanuts* [film]; Documentaries; Guest appearances; Lewis, Diana; Marx, Minnie; Paramount Pictures)

TORME, MEL
See: Radio; Stage appearances (post-1930)

TORRES, RAQUEL (1908-87)
Born Marie or Paula Osterman in Hermosillo, Mexico, Raquel Torres had been educated first in her native country, then at a Los Angeles convent. She achieved instant fame as Fayaway, Polynesian heroine of W.S. Van Dyke's *White Shadows in the South Seas* (1928). Some conscious effort to repeat this success came with the rôle of Tamea in a later South Seas tale, *Never the Twain Shall Meet*. Other films include *The Desert Rider*, *The Bridge of San Luis Rey*, *The Sea Bat*, *Under*

Raquel Torres *gives the censors apoplexy in this publicity pose for* Duck Soup

the Texas Moon and the Marxes' *Duck Soup* (*qv*), in which she portrays slinky spy Vera Marcal. Retired after one last film, a 1934 British production called *Red Wagon*, following marriage to businessman Stephen Ames; after Ames' death she married actor Jon Hall, a match that ended in divorce.

TRAILERS

(Marx Brothers films *qv*)
In a 1932 *Hollywood Reporter* piece called 'Movie Glossary', Groucho defined 'trailer' as 'a warning to next week's patrons'. At that time, an evening's cinema entertainment would consist of several items, assembled to form a balanced programme. Today, virtually the only survivor of these 'added attractions' is the theatrical trailer, designed to advertise a forthcoming release. Such trailers exist for most of the Marx Brothers films, that for *Animal Crackers* being the earliest currently in circulation. This fairly primitive affair incorporates a few shots from the film, amid direct comparisons to *The Cocoanuts*. One card anticipates Thalberg's later theories when inviting audiences to 'Come *three times* and *try* to catch all the laughs'. *Monkey Business* was

promoted to the trade by a specially-filmed sketch (see **Monkey Business [promo]**) but its regular trailer is confined to a few shots of the team on canvas-backed chairs bearing their names. *Duck Soup*'s trailer is of interest for the use of footage differing from that in the finished film: when Harpo uses dynamite to remove a vase from Groucho's head, the trailer includes a discarded shot of Groucho looking around after the explosion; a glimpse of the Chico-Harpo fight shows a close view of Harpo landing a kick, instead of the long shot used for release; while another long shot, in which baton-twirling Harpo knocks down a chandelier, is again replaced with a close-up for the trailer. The Marxes' first film for M-G-M (*qv*), *A Night at the Opera*, was intended to open with the team's heads supplanting the studio's lion trademark. Though deleted from the film itself, the sequence was used for the film's theatrical trailer. The studio's Latin motto, *Ars Gratia Artis* ('Art For the Sake of Art'), surrounds the roaring lion; this makes way for 'Marx Gratia Marxes' as first Groucho, then Chico take their turns at roaring. Harpo, unable to produce a sound, uses his taxi horn instead. This ingenious fragment was retained for the reissue trailer, which is that available today. The trailer for their next film, *A Day at the Races*, describes it as 'the spectacular successor to "A Night at the Opera"'; it opens with an announcer who appeals for quiet, only to be silenced with a barrage of custard pies. Though harmless enough slapstick in itself, this gag is early indication of a growing studio misconception of the team's style.

Contemporary sources suggest there were filmed trailers designed to accompany the pre-filming tours of this and perhaps other films, though none seem to circulate. Between this and the Marxes' third M-G-M picture, RKO (*qv*) put them into *Room Service*. The trailer mentions the 'record amount' paid for screen rights to the play (without specifying how much!) and suggests a lively production by concentrating on the film's relatively few frenetic moments. Back to Metro and *At the Circus*, for which a trailer combines extracts with very effective circus-style captioning. The trailer for *Go West* ('M-G-M's rootin' ... tootin' ... shootin' ... musical comedy') offers a random selection of clips between the exaggerated sagebrush hype. Their last M-G-M release, *The Big Store*, was intended as the final Marx Brothers film and much publicity was made of it. In a specially extended trailer, an executive (played by Henry O'Neill) interrupts his duties to address the audience. After a speech describing Sarah Bernhardt's many - and lucrative - 'farewell' appearances, he announces the Marx Brothers' retirement from the silver screen. Groucho lopes in, adding 'That's right, folks, we're on our way.' Chico, popping up from behind the desk, agrees, asking 'Where do we go from here?' Harpo climbs out from *beneath* the desk, honking his taxi horn and waving. 'And so,' concludes Groucho, 'to all of you, a fond farewell.' Distracted by the sound of voices, they head for the

GROUCHO
MARX
CARMEN
MIRANDA
ANDY
RUSSELL
STEVE
COCHRAN
GLORIA
JEAN
On the Air!
In a preview of the
Sam Coslow
MUSICAL
PRODUCTION

opening
FRIDAY
at
UNITED ARTISTS
THEATRE
WXXX
7:30 P.M.
1 col. x76 lines   Mat 108—.15

Trailers: *specially recorded promotional items were available for American radio stations. From the pressbook of* Copacabana *By courtesy of Robert G. Dickson* window. Outside is a vast crowd, crying 'No'. 'We didn't know you cared,' says Groucho, before going on to introduce extracts from their 'first farewell picture'. The point of this 'first farewell' gag is weakened in some copies, from which the Sarah Bernhardt anecdote has been excised. This very elaborate item contrasts drastically with a second *Big Store* trailer, which offers no more than stills plus a few caricatures and slogans. There are unconfirmed reports of Harpo's appearance in a *Love Happy* trailer prepared for American TV; during the 1950s and 1960s, a 16 mm trailer was available to those renting the film from a British-based company, Watsofilms, but this may have been compiled by the library itself.

Not every trailer was prepared for theatrical use. Although British radio was then entirely non-commercial, American stations thrived on advertising and would devote much space to the promotion of upcoming films. Studios made up their own programmes for distribution on transcription discs, many of which are extant today. *The Paramount Movie Parade* made its début with a *Duck Soup* trailer, evidently compiled prior to the film's completion. The programme, of approximately 12 and a half minutes' duration, opens with music used earlier for the *Monkey Business* promo (it is possible that *Duck Soup*'s title music had yet to be recorded). There follows a run-down of the Marxes' character names, revealing significant differences from the final version. Groucho and Chico are, respectively, the Rufus T. Firefly and Chicolini of the eventual release, but Harpo is called Skippy rather than Pinky (the pressbook calls him Brownie). Zeppo is described as Bob Firefly, the dictator's son (reflecting their relationship in *Horse Feathers*), though a dialogue extract refers to him as Firefly's secretary. A soundtrack clip of Firefly's inauguration uses an alternate take, incorporating an otherwise lost moment where he

dismisses the guards. Other differences include background music, some notable variants of inflection plus a few lines that would subsequently be deleted. One of these conveys Firefly's reaction to a formal reception: 'All this for me? That's how you throw away your money. I'd rather have a good box of cigars.' In the release print, Margaret Dumont (*qv*) asks Groucho to follow in the footsteps of her late husband; in the radio version, Groucho's response ('I haven't been on the job five minutes, and already she's making advances to me') acquires greater point when following a deleted Dumont line, 'Without my husband, I have only you to fall back on.' Presumably this was considered too *risqué* even in pre-Code days. There is an additional exchange with Ambassador Trentino:

Trentino: I bring you a message of goodwill. On behalf of my president -
Firefly: I won't be a half of your president. I'll be the whole president or nothing.

The song *Just Wait 'Til I Get Through With It* proceeds much as usual except for two added interludes, one with a bass singer and the other a bluesy trumpet solo. There is also an instrumental version of the song, unheard in the film. Firefly's meeting at the House of Representatives differs only in the retention of an extra line (presumably deleted for reasons of pace) but continues into a section where he is distracted by Chicolini calling 'Peanuts!' from the street. In the film, the action cuts directly to a conversation between Chico and Groucho, but the radio show preserves the following exchange:

Zeppo: It's that infernal peanut vendor, Chicolini.
Groucho: Well, chase him away from the building. Get rid of him if you have to use violence - and when his back is turned, get me a bag of peanuts.
Zeppo: I've tried to chase him, but it's

no use. He won't go.
Groucho: Oh, he won't, eh? We'll see about that. Send for Firefly at once.
Zeppo: But you're Firefly.
Groucho: Never mind, then. I'll get in touch with him myself.

This first sampling of 'their delectable concoction of crazyisms' (to quote the announcer) concludes with alternative versions of the Freedonian National Anthem and the 'Heighdy-ho' section of *The Country's Going to War*. The following week's programme offers more from *Duck Soup*. It opens with an unrelated song and similar patter to that in the first show; character names for Groucho and Chico are given once more but Harpo is rendered nameless while Zeppo is referred to only as Bob, Firefly's secretary. The relationship between Trentino and Vera Marcal is unspecified in the film but this second radio trailer describes her as Trentino's 'niece' (a designation traditionally used when checking into a hotel). There is a soundtrack clip of Firefly offering Chicolini a job, exactly as per release save for an additional 'Say, wait a minute' before asking Chicolini why Freedonia should have a standing army ('Because then we save money on chairs!'). The Paramount Orchestra supplies the film's title music, though with different duck effects dubbed over. There are a few extra lines from Mrs Teasdale's garden party and the 'insult' business with Trentino; more interesting is a rejected version of *The Country's Going to War/All God's Chillun Got Guns*, less tightly performed than in the final recording (the line 'How we'd cry for Firefly', delivered by Zeppo in the film, disappears into the chorus on this occasion). The battle scenes contain an amusing Groucho line, again absent from the release print: 'Chicolini, I used to think you were two-faced; but you can't be, or you wouldn't be wearing that one!' The 14-minute programme concludes with announcements and an orchestral playoff. Both *Duck Soup* promos offer a wealth of out-takes and, as a result, some insight into the film's creation. The manner of presentation has a period charm but suggests little comprehension of the team's characterizations or specific appeal. When the announcer speaks of Groucho's 'one-cylinder brain', he automatically misclassifies him among the 'dumb-bell' category; a later reference to 'Groucho the Witless' is an inaccuracy almost beyond explanation.

As Hollywood's most prestigious studio, M-G-M took every opportunity to promote its releases. There exists today an elaborate radio commercial for *A Day at the Races*, patterned jokingly on the *March of Time* newsreels (themselves parodied on radio by Groucho and Chico during 1934). The message 'Time Marxes On' punctuates a mixture of silly music, even sillier comments, a brief run-down of the film's story plus a few clips of dialogue and songs. An 'interview' with Harpo, conducted by a caricatured Englishman, leads only to a few honks on a taxi horn. The final 'Time Marxes On' is accompanied, inexplicably, by an orchestral arrangement of 'For He's a Jolly Good Fellow'. Less care was taken over the radio promotion of *At the Circus*: there are no dialogue extracts and the whole concentrates largely on the film's musical content. There is at least an extract from Groucho's rendering of *Lydia, the Tattooed Lady*, while a lengthy piano solo from Chico seems to have been specially re-recorded for the disc. Announcements refer to the grim state of world affairs (war broke out in Europe before the film's release), something mentioned again in the *Go West* trailer. This rather superior offering is introduced by John Carroll

(*qv*) along with the Marxes themselves. They provide a series of nineteenth-century 'newsflash' items, culminating in 'the Marx Brothers Go West!' Chico insists on adding a 'plug' to Carroll's announcement, emphasizing the phrase 'from the picture of the same name'. 'Ah, Chico,' observes Groucho, 'you're a genius. A stupid genius, but a genius.' In the film, 'Two-Gun' Quale enters the saloon, guns blazing, with an order to 'sweep 'em up out of the gutter'. The radio programme offers a little more:

Chico: There ain't nobody in the gutter.
Groucho: There isn't? Well, sweep out the gutter.

The conversation continues, introducing Chico as 'Joe Panello from Indianapolis' (Groucho: 'I've always wanted to meet an Indian'). Harpo is mistaken for a 'weird object with red hair' on Chico's coattail. Groucho takes the 'little trinket' around Harpo's neck to be a beartrap; it is instead a harp, which is duly played. Carroll provides a link to Chico's piano solo, *The Woodpecker Song* ('keep your hat on,' advises Groucho). A few authentic Western whoops from Groucho lead into the song *Ridin' the Range* and the show closes with music along with comments from Carroll, Groucho and Chico.

There is an extant series of radio trailers for *A Night in Casablanca*, each of which runs between 30 and 60 seconds; an extract from one may be heard in the television documentary *Unknown Marx Brothers*. The pressbook for Groucho's solo film *Copacabana* (*qv*) details the availability of a fifteen-minute radio trailer

'featuring the outstanding stars, songs and scenes lifted directly from the actual sound track'. Exhibitors could obtain the recording (for $3) and have it placed on a local station; there was even a pre-prepared newspaper ad designed to promote the item. The Marxes' radio trailers are mostly very entertaining and serve as a pleasant adjunct to the films themselves. Though overlooked in most chronicles, they have been made widely available in various album collections of vintage radio material.

(See also: Advertising; Armetta, Henry; Censorship; Documentaries; Harp, the; Paramount Pictures; Pianos; Radio; Records; Television; Thalberg, Irving; Video releases)

TRAINS
(Marx Brothers films *qv*)
The gruelling schedule of vaudeville (*qv*) required near-constant rail travel and, as noted under the **Harp** entry, the Marxes were once involved in a train crash. In the films, the most spectacular train ride occurs in *Go West*, where the engine is fuelled by wood chopped away from its own carriages. Groucho has to meet a train in *Cocoanuts* but finds no customers for his hotel; Chico meets a train in *A Day at the Races* but, similarly, cannot lure patrons to the Standish sanitarium. He keeps Groucho off the train in *At the Circus* but, as noted under **Continuity errors**, Groucho somehow manages to board unseen.

TWENTIETH CENTURY
See: Stage appearances (post-1930)

TWENTIETH CENTURY REVUE, THE
See: Vaudevill

UNITED ARTISTS

Production and distribution company established in 1919 to provide independence for its founders, Charlie Chaplin (*qv*), Mary Pickford, Douglas Fairbanks Sr and D.W. Griffith. Chaplin's then-current First National contract forbade his direct involvement until 1923. It is believed that UA expressed interest in filming *The Cocoanuts* (*qv*) before the idea was taken up by Paramount Pictures (*qv*); during the Marxes' dispute with Paramount of early 1933, the Marxes were again reported to be in negotiation with United Artists, and a contract was indeed prepared. The company (since merged into M-G-M [*qv*] after the financial ruin of *Heaven's Gate*) released the Marxes' last feature films, *A Night in Casablanca* and *Love Happy* (both *qv*), the latter of which credits Mary Pickford as executive producer. United Artists also distributed Groucho's *Copacabana* (*qv*) and *Stage Door Canteen*, featuring a guest spot by Harpo.

(See also: Guest appearances; Kibbee, Roland)

Vaudeville: *The first Marx family act comprised various erstwhile 'Nightingales'; at the top, an unrecognizable Groucho; in descending order are Harpo, Gummo and Lou Levy.* Circa *1908*
BFI Stills, Posters and Designs

VAUDEVILLE

Just as the United Kingdom had music-hall, so North America had vaudeville. As a phenomenon, it was similar in purpose but somehow terminated rather more abruptly; although the cinema and radio started to kill off music-hall during the 1920s, it survived (as 'variety') into the television age, whereas the day of the big-time vaudeville act had gone by 1930. Contrary to any claims, it is not true to suggest that the Marxes played in cheap burlesque houses; burlesque - a downmarket alternative to vaudeville, consisting of red-nosed comics and bump-and-grind strippers - was despised by vaudevillians and should not be considered synonymous, but lingered in the USA in much the manner of the nude shows characterizing the final days of Britain's music-halls. At the turn of the century, however, vaudeville was supreme, and nowhere more than in New York. In this vaudeville-minded city, even the customers used industry terminology, the kind of *Variety*-speak that labelled each vaudeville circuit a 'time', according to its ownership and consequent prestige. The expressions 'small-' and 'big-time' have long since passed into the language. Although its artists could be drawn from all strata, vaudeville, like boxing and similar public endeavours, often provided an escape route from poverty. True, many of its artists were poorly paid, and could be fined on the spot for even some imagined misdemeanour should the management so decide, but the top acts made more than reasonable money and it was this that caught the attention of the Marx family. Minnie's brother, Al Shean (*qv*), was the role model, a *bona fide* headliner whose affluence drew considerable attention on his visits to the Marx home. Groucho, at 14, became the first Marx in vaudeville when joining the 'LeRoy Trio' (*qv*). Groucho was left stranded but the theatre had made an impact. For one thing, on returning home he discovered Gummo had become stooge for their maternal uncle Henry, brother of Al. Undeterred by his hearing difficulties, this stage-struck

man had decided to become a comic ventriloquist, using his nephew as dummy. Gummo wore a fake head over his own, working the mechanics from within. Gummo later recalled this double-act, consisting of a man who couldn't hear and a youngster who stammered, as lasting 'only a couple of weeks'. Groucho remembered filling in by singing to illustrated slides in a beer garden, where the patrons were too intoxicated to concern themselves over his erratic rendering of *'Neath the Old Chestnut Tree, Sweet Estelle* (a title he considered unwitting anticipation of his future jokes). Groucho's next vaudeville job was obtained when his mother, Minnie Marx (*qv*), visited an agent's office and made the acquaintance of English actress and songstress Lily Seville. This English rose was assisted by 'Master Julius Marx' on the Interstate Circuit, covering much of the South, during the earlier part of 1906. Salary was to be $15 per week, a distinct improvement on LeRoy's act. Groucho imagined himself to have fallen for her, but contented himself as the male half of their act, 'The Coachman and the Lady'. Miss Seville found herself a different gentleman (an animal trainer) and, in an uncanny imitation of Mr LeRoy, bid Groucho *adieu*, having first replaced the money in his grouch bag with carefully-cut newspaper. So far Groucho had plenty of experience and no money. Later in 1906 he joined Gus Edwards, whose much-imitated 'School Days' acts (of which more anon) were to provide an early break for such talents as Eddie Cantor, Harry Ruby, Edward Buzzell (all *qv*) and George Jessel. Groucho toured with Edwards in *Gus Edwards' Postal Telegraph Boys* (or *Boys and Girls*) and even had his portrait on the sheet music for Edwards' song *Farewell Killarney* (though the astute impresario purposely used a photo taken several years earlier). The song cover is reproduced in *The Groucho Phile*, which also commemorates what was for Groucho the highlight of the tour, a benefit for those affected by San Francisco's

earthquake and consequent fire. A 70-piece orchestra accompanied Groucho as he sang *Somebody's Sweetheart I Want to Be*. Groucho's chronology places the Edwards engagement before that with Lily Seville, but this seems not to have been the case. He further recalled working as a 'song plugger' in Philadelphia while spending his evenings in what turned out to be a burlesque show, Groucho's only excursion into that disreputable relative of vaudeville. Next was a touring play, which took Groucho around the north-west United States and into Canada. The play's title, *The Man of Her Choice*, turned out to be an appropriate title for the young actor, who in Montreal was picked up by a streetwalker, with unfortunate consequences (see **Prostitutes**). It was probably no coincidence that Minnie then decided to create her own family's singing act. She named it the *Nightingales* (qv), comprising Groucho, Gummo and one Mabel O'Donnell, who was replaced by a third boy, Lou Levy. Early bookings, in 1907, were as 'Ned Wayburn's Nightingales', after the producer/director with whom Groucho and Minnie had become acquainted during the Gus Edwards stint. Harpo was recruited in 1908. As noted elsewhere, the act became, for a while, 'The Six Mascots' with the addition of Minnie and Aunt Hannah; its various incarnations toured the North-West, then the South, into 1910. Although they had introduced a measure of comedy into the proceedings, the turning point from music to comedy was at an engagement in Nacogdoches, Texas. This story, much re-told, is of an indifferent audience leaving the theatre to watch a runaway mule instead of the Nightingales. On their return, the audience saw an enraged troupe of singers, running wild and insulting both the town and its residents, yelling things like 'Nacogdoches is full of roaches' and 'The jackass is the finest flower of Tex-ass'. Instead of tearing them to pieces, the good citizens loved it and the singing act was suddenly a

matter of history. In its stead was concocted an Edwards-influenced school act, *Fun in Hi Skule* (qv), playing on the Pantages Circuit from 1910. The schoolroom routine had extended into a second act, *Mr Green's Reception* (qv) by the autumn of 1912, which played alone once the first act was dropped. The team was billed then as 'Three Marx Brothers & Co.'; Chico, meanwhile, had been exploiting his piano-playing skills. In 1907, while two of his brothers became Nightingales, he moved to Philadelphia and, as Groucho had the previous year, took a job as song-plugger. His employers, the music publishers Shapiro, Bernstein & Company, quickly promoted him to managing their Pittsburgh branch but Chico, as always, grew restless. He teamed up with his assistant at the firm, Arthur Gordon, to form a new singing duo. It was at this point that Chico is believed to have adopted the Italian accent (reputedly based on his barber), to imply suitable background for a popular tenor. They rehearsed on company time, to the detriment of their work; when an executive was sent to investigate, they walked out to try their luck on stage. Bookings were few and, around the summer of 1911, Chico approached his mother for advice. On Minnie's recommendation (for which read 'insistence'), Gordon also became Italian and Minnie, now calling herself Minnie Palmer, was able to get the resultant 'Marx and Gordoni' a booking at the Willard Theatre, Chicago. The act, which interspersed weak dialect patter between popular songs, seems to have been rather a one-sided arrangement. An account by Chico's daughter, Maxine, describes Chico as manager, ostensibly paying Gordon but covering only his food, board, laundry bills plus 50 cents per week for a haircut; Gordon later told Maxine that it was some time before he realized Chico was gambling away their salaries. After the team's demise, Gordon became piano accompanist for, and fourth husband of, musical comedy star Nora Bayes; his obituary in *Variety*

refers to 'Arthur Gordoni' as being well-known in New York as a song stylist, crediting him with either introducing or giving an outstanding interpretation of Gus Kahn and Neil Moret's *Chloe*. The obit further mentions Gordon's subsequent career as sales representative for a distillery, in which his connections with Los Angeles hotels, restaurants and cafés proved useful. He died in August 1966, aged 73. Chico's vaudeville career continued in a new double-act with his cousin, Lou Shean, son of Aunt Hannah. 'Shean & Marx' met a swift end after Chico insisted Lou should split a fine he had incurred, the result of Chico having been caught with a girl who shared her attentions with the manager. A new partner, George Lee, formed the second half of 'Marx & Lee' before Chico decided to rejoin his family. It was near the end of 1912 when they played at Waukegan, Illinois; in a now-famous incident, Chico inveigled his way into the orchestra pit (where also sat the young Jack Benny [qv]), waiting for his brothers to go on. Groucho spotted Chico almost instantly, his fixed gaze catching Harpo's. Chico launched into his familiar piano style, to which Harpo responded by throwing one of the apples he used as props. Chico caught the apple, threw it to Groucho, who threw it in turn to Gummo, who was not due on but had looked around the curtain to investigate the commotion. The act finished amid scattered fruit but far from scattered cheers and applause. Suddenly there were Four Marx Brothers in the act. Chico's recent partner, George Lee (referred to also as 'Moe'), was added to the cast as 'Ignatz Levy'. *Mr Green's Reception* served its purpose but ground to a halt in 1914. Fortunately Al Shean was available to rewrite the sketch into *Home Again* (qv), which continued to develop and kept them going, aside for interruptions imposed by events leading up to and including America's part in World War One. The incident that ultimately brought US involvement, the sinking of the

Lusitania, was announced when the Marxes were playing Shea's, Toronto, in May 1915. Because Canadians were initially more incensed by the incident than their neighbours in the USA, Groucho thought it prudent to abandon the German accent in favour of a Jewish dialect. He had previously used a song called *Everybody Works But Father*, also rendered into German; he substituted a different item, suited to the new accent and the immediate locality, *Toronto*. These songs were revived for Groucho's concert repertoire in 1972. After the family's sojourn on a farm, ostensibly working on the land, Gummo joined the army and was replaced by Zeppo. Apart from another interruption, the disastrous *Street Cinderella* (*qv*), *Home Again*'s variations took the Marx Brothers into 1920. The act had travelled the big-time Orpheum Circuit since the mid-'Teens; its successor, *On the Mezzanine* (*qv*), made its début primarily on the Poli 'family time' from February 1921, moving up first to the Keith Circuit for June-October (with a break for August) and then, as *On the Balcony*, to the Orpheum theatres starting in December. They took *On the Balcony* to England in June 1922; as described in the **On the Mezzanine** entry, it was replaced by *Home Again* before the team's return home. Circuit boss E.F. Albee, who insisted their overseas trip to be a breach of contract, decided to punish the Marxes by relegating them to split-weeks in lesser venues; they rebelled by taking up with the Shubert Brothers, who had set up a rival vaudeville circuit. The Marxes' 'Shubert unit' was a multi-act show called *The Twentieth Century Revue*, in which the team revamped the theatrical office sketch from *On the Mezzanine*. This tour effectively brought the Marx Brothers' vaudeville career to a close. It was a total flop, with the Marxes paying the other acts despite receiving nothing themselves. The Shuberts' circuit collapsed after the Marx tour concluded early in 1923, leaving in its wake victims of nervous breakdowns and suicides. As

a consequence of siding with the renegade venture, the Marx Brothers were blacklisted by every circuit in America. By the Spring of 1923 they were unemployable, broke and on the point of leaving show business. They were saved by gambling on a 'legitimate' musical comedy, *I'll Say She Is!* (*qv*). Once attaining the status of Broadway stars, their box-office position was reinstated and the entries for *Cocoanuts*, *Animal Crackers* and **Stage appearances (post-1930)** detail the occasions when they were invited back to vaudeville. By then, they had outlived genuine vaudeville, which had mostly become live attractions supporting a cinema programme. Although they had left it acrimoniously, vaudeville occupied a significant period in the Marxes' lives and they often recalled its hectic heyday. They appeared alongside some very strange acts, Groucho's own favourite being 'Swain's Rats and Cats'. Mr Swain had a racetrack set with trained rats riding cats in the manner of jockeys. Groucho was fond of telling of an occasion when Fanny Brice, also on the bill, started screaming at the sight of a stray rat; Swain was summoned and, though discovering it not to be one of his, took it away. When next the Marxes met Swain, this additional rodent had been trained and made the star of the act. Encapsulation, perhaps, of the bizarre but resourceful spirit of vaudeville.

(See also: Carnegie Hall Concert, the; Female impersonation; Hotels; Names; RKO; Sport; Stage appearances [post-1930]; Wartime)

VERA-ELLEN (1926-81)
Actress, singer and dancer who plays Maggie Phillips, the female romantic interest in *Love Happy* (*qv*). Originally from the Broadway stage, Vera-Ellen (real name Vera-Ellen Westmeyer Rohe) was brought into films by Samuel Goldwyn, who put her into the 1945 Danny Kaye vehicle *Wonder Man*, the story for which was by Arthur Sheekman (*qv*). She appeared again

Vera-Ellen, *love interest of* Love Happy

with Kaye in *The Kid From Brooklyn* (1946), directed by Norman Z. McLeod (*qv*). Associated chiefly with musicals: *Three Little Girls in Blue* (1946), *Carnival in Costa Rica* (1947), the Rodgers & Hart biopic *Words and Music* (1948), the 1949 Gene Kelly-Frank Sinatra classic *On the Town* (also starring Ann Miller [*qv*]), the Kalmar-Ruby biopic *Three Little Words* (1950), the British-made *Happy-Go-Lovely* (1950), *The Belle of New York* (1952), *The Big Leaguer* (1953), *Call Me Madam* (1953, written by Sheekman with songs by Irving Berlin [*qv*]), Berlin's *White Christmas* (1954) and 1957's *Let's Be Happy*, a further British film co-starring Tony Martin (*qv*). Retired in the late 1950s.

(See also: Krasna, Norman; Ruby, Harry; Rumann, Siegfried; Sinatra, Frank)

VEREA, LISETTE
Born in Bucharest, Romania, Lisette Verea plays Beatrice Reiner, slinky siren of *A Night in Casablanca* (*qv*). Her naturally blonde hair was dyed red for the film, though the black-and-white photography makes it look dark. Biographical details are elusive save for the information contained in the film's pressbook and in a British novel based on the screenplay. Such details need to be taken with a degree of skepticism, particularly when claiming the well-shaped, 5' 4" tall actress weighed only 8 stone 4 ounces. Date of birth is given as 1 October (though discreetly omitting the year); her father was a well-known artist, Henry Verea, with whom Lisette travelled extensively during her

Romanian star **Lisette Verea** *had her blonde hair coloured red for* A Night in Casablanca

childhood; one can only attribute to this nomadic existence her ability to speak French, German and English in addition to her native Romanian. Her professional début was made at 16, in a stage musical produced in Bucharest. Other shows included *White Horse Inn*, *Special Edition* and Hecht and MacArthur's *The Front Page*; her stage career took her through Hungary, Bulgaria, Turkey, Italy, Syria, Egypt, Palestine, India, England and France; she also made several films in Budapest. The pressbook hints at her difficulties when travelling to America under wartime conditions, though describing nothing more specific than a 'circuitous route', the very thought of which 'makes her grow pale and gives her a fine case of the jitters'. She sang at New York's Ruban Bleu nightclub prior to joining a revival of *The Merry Widow* both on Broadway and a subsequent tour. When the show reached Los Angeles, she was given a screen test by Warner Brothers, but could not agree a deal with them. While rehearsing another show, she was approached by producer David L. Loew to play the female lead in *A Night in Casablanca*. The film's publicity also notes her talent for art and design, her fabric prints having been featured in 'some of New York's smartest shops'. Although *A Night in Casablanca* is supposed to have led to further movie offers, nothing much

seems to have come of it and it is probable that she returned to Europe.

(See also: Books; Hecht, Ben; Women)

VIDEO RELEASES
(Marx Brothers films *qv*)
Home video has mostly eclipsed the market for 8 mm film editions. There were CIC video releases of *Animal Crackers* and *Duck Soup* in Britain during the mid-1980s, both of which have joined *Monkey Business* in more recent catalogues. *Room Service* appeared on the Channel 5 label in 1986 and Video Collection issued *Love Happy*. M-G-M/UA released *A Night at the Opera* in at least two different packagings before reissuing it as a double-bill with *A Day at the Races*. The same source offered *A Day at the Races*, *Go West* and *The Big Store* as a boxed set (sometimes split up by retailers). These tapes incorporated a prologue of vintage M-G-M trailers, among them the special 'retirement' promo for *The Big Store*. M-G-M/UA are known to have released *A Night at the Opera* to the Australian video market. A documentary, *The Marx Brothers in a Nutshell*, first saw UK release as a full-price tape from Vestron and resurfaced later as a budget title. There have also been tapes consisting of odds and ends, notably trailers and commercials, seemingly derived from America. Several of these have appeared on the US market, which has been more generously served with Marx material. One such is the *Groucho Marx Scrapbook*; another, Video Yesteryear's *For Auld Lang Syne - The Marx Brothers!*, includes the *Monkey Business* promo (*qv*) alongside a pre-war item with Jacques Tati, one of

Harry Langdon's talkie shorts and an all-star tribute to Will Rogers. Harpo's guest shot on *I Love Lucy* has been made available on both sides of the Atlantic. The abortive *Deputy Seraph* (*qv*) reached home movie stage but the advertised video release is said to have been cancelled for legal reasons. Each of the Marx Brothers feature films has been issued on tape in America: CBS Video released *Go West* on tape and *A Day at the Races* on tape and videodisc as long ago as 1981. There have been US laser disc versions of all the Marx films except *A Night in Casablanca* (reportedly in preparation at the time of writing) though *Room Service* and *Love Happy* are presently deleted in this format. Ironically, the first to be made, *Cocoanuts*, was the last to reach videotape (via MCA, along with the other Paramounts). *Horse Feathers* was delayed pending a search for complete material, but was eventually put out in its usual version in 1988. *A Night in Casablanca* was released at least three times, the last of them reportedly in long-play format (a lesser-quality system common in the USA, but fortunately not so in Britain). There have been US tape releases of Groucho's solo film *A Girl in Every Port* (*qv*) and of his 1972 Los Angeles concert. *The Marx Brothers in a Nutshell* reached tape in 1989. At one time RCA had CED videodisc releases of *Animal Crackers* (formerly issued on laserdisc), *Duck Soup*, *A Night at the Opera* and *A Day at the Races*. There were also videodiscs of *Monkey Business* and *Duck Soup* which included theatrical trailers.

(See also: *Animal Crackers* [film]; Ball, Lucille; Carnegie Hall Concert, the; Colour; Documentaries; Home movies; M-G-M; Paramount Pictures; Television; Trailers; United Artists)

WANGER, WALTER (1894-1968)

Shared responsibility with Monta Bell (*qv*) for Paramount's Long Island productions when the Marxes filmed *Cocoanuts* and *Animal Crackers* (both *qv*).

(See also: Moustaches, beards; Paramount Pictures)

WARTIME

'Join the Army and see the Navy'; Harpo's recruiting placard in *Duck Soup* (*qv*), one of the most effective satires on war ever created. When the USA entered World War One in 1917, Minnie Marx (*qv*) did not want her sons to be directly involved, particularly because her own family came from Germany (it was not unknown for related German and American soldiers to meet in combat, as in the 1928 John Ford film *Four Sons*). As an alternative, the Marxes decided to work on the land, acquiring a farm at La Grange, Illinois, at the intersection of La Grange Road and Joliet Road. The Marxes spent much of their time enjoying the proximity of a local ball park, slept increasingly late and even had to buy eggs from elsewhere. Eventually they took an army medical and only Gummo was accepted. A popular anecdote, recorded in Green and Laurie's *Variety* history 'From Vaude to Video', has Groucho telling the recruiting sergeant 'You should see the *fifth* Marx brother: two heads!' Gummo's war was spent in Chicago, as batman/chauffeur/crony to officers in search of a good time, mostly with girls Gummo had rounded up from the local shows. Twenty years after the event, a press release for *Room Service* (*qv*) claimed that Harpo had also joined up and 'went overseas with the Seventh Regiment of New York. Gummo remained in training at Great Lakes. Groucho and Chico went to the camps to entertain'. This, in common with many such publicity statements, is pure fantasy; not one Marx was required to take an active part in the First World War.

Circumstances were altogether different during the second such conflict and the Marxes keenly donated their services to raising money by the sale of war bonds and entertaining the troops. Harpo travelled extensively during the war, and both Groucho and Chico were part of the Hollywood Victory Caravan (though their appearances seem not to have overlapped). For his spot during the three-hour show, Groucho was supplied with material from a few writers, among them George S. Kaufman (*qv*) and Moss Hart. Harry Ruby (*qv*) joined Groucho at the military bases, in a team also comprising guitarist Joe Carioca and Fay McKenzie, one of Groucho's radio colleagues on the *Pabst Blue Ribbon Town*. Arthur Marx has mentioned his father being entertained in a General's office when the telephone rang. Groucho beat his host to the receiver with an authoritative 'World War Two speaking!' William Robert Faith's *Bob Hope: a Life in Comedy* recalls Groucho's comments to *Variety* in May 1942: 'It's all right for guys like Hope,' Groucho said. 'He has seventeen guys writing his jokes for him. But I've got to do the worrying about my own material.' When informed that there were only six Hope writers present, for the purpose of scripting his radio show, Groucho was unmoved. 'Only six?' he cried. 'For Hope that's practically ad libbing!' Another irritation was being unrecognized without his make-up, usually an advantage but not when other touring stars were acclaimed by the crowds. He performed with the customary greasepaint, in a repertoire known to include the song *Doctor Hackenbush* and, going by photos, his Captain Spaulding character. Among those with whom Groucho appeared at this time were Lucille Ball and Laurel & Hardy (both *qv*). Like his brothers, Groucho was aware of this war's purpose but held entirely different views about Vietnam. He did not agree with it and said he would encourage a son of military age to avoid the draft. It

is probably this war that contributed to his outspoken comments on the President at that time, Richard Nixon.

(See also: Could Harpo Speak?; Documentaries; Names; Newsreels; Politicians; Sport; Stage appearances [post-1930])

WAXWORKS
(Marx Brothers films *qv*)
In *The Big Store*, Harpo's musical spot is framed within a tableau of wax figures in eighteenth-century garb, one of which supplies him with period costume. The Marxes themselves are represented in wax form at the world's largest such museum, the Stars Hall of Fame in Orlando, Florida. According to a strategically-placed clapperboard, the scene purports to represent *Animal Crackers*, though its snow-covered woodland setting could not easily pass for a mansion on Long Island. There are also, mysteriously, golf clubs. The likenesses are reasonable: Harpo is seen atop Chico's piano, playing the insides of another piano (as in *A Day at the Races*), while Chico sits at the keyboard; Groucho stands by.

(See also: Harp, the; Piano, the)

WEDDINGS
(Marx Brothers films *qv*)
'We can be married and divorced in no time'; an unsentimental Arabella Rittenhouse to her fiancé in *Animal Crackers*, reflecting the often self-conscious cynicism of the 1920s smart set. The Marx Brothers were in part a product of that way of thinking, mostly for the good but consequently at odds with the romantic sub-plotting in their films. Elsewhere in *Animal Crackers* Groucho proposes marriage both to his hostess and one of her guests, prompting an accusation of bigamy ('Yes, and it's big of me, too'). The party scene of *Cocoanuts* is to announce a forthcoming marriage, as was that in their 1931 stage sketch for C.B. Cochran (*qv*); the wedding of playwright Leo Davis in *Room Service*

is delayed during the première of *Hail and Farewell* while Groucho seeks the hand of Margaret Dumont (*qv*) on every occasion they meet. Easily the most satisfying - for all concerned, one suspects - is the finale of *Horse Feathers*, in which Thelma Todd (*qv*) appears as a bride; she is attended by Groucho, Harpo and Chico, who proceed to climb over her after declaring 'We do'! Among Groucho's solo films (all *qv*), one might recall his deferred nuptials to Carmen Miranda in *Copacabana* or the fact that he is Jayne Mansfield's true love in *Will Success Spoil Rock Hunter?*. The brothers' real-life weddings are detailed under **Marriages**, but it may be appropriate to mention here a ceremony attended by Groucho and Harpo when boys. The family had 'adopted' a cousin, Polly, for whom Minnie had found a husband. The young guests had cause to repair to the men's room, where, for the first time in their lives, they saw urinals. Unsure as to the precise method of using such facilities, they stood on top, causing the structure to shear from the wall. They returned quickly to the wedding itself, which was suspended once the floor had become noticeably moist. The groom had to pay for the damaged plumbing. Age did not improve Groucho's and Harpo's luck with wedding celebrations: in the mid-1920s they decided to walk into a friend's bachelor party stark naked; exiting thus from the hotel lift, they found themselves on the wrong floor, where the bride was entertaining her women friends.

(See also: Gambling; Marx, Minnie; Romance; Women)

WELLES, ORSON
See: Abandoned projects

WHITE, LEO (1880 or 1883-1948)
Manchester-born comic actor, long in America. Best recalled as a top-hatted, bearded and excitable French count in films with Charlie Chaplin (*qv*) during

the 'Teens; later with Max Linder and, ironically, Chaplin's main imitator, Billy West. Occasional minor roles in talkies include a 1935 short, *Keystone Hotel*, Chaplin's *The Great Dictator* (1940) and two Marx Brothers films, *Monkey Business* and *A Night at the Opera* (both *qv*). In the former he is a ship's barber; in the latter he is one of the three aviators whose uniforms (and beards) are borrowed by Harpo, Chico and Allan Jones (*qv*).

(See also: Eaton, Jay; Sedan, Rolfe)

'WHITE MAGIC'
(Marx Brothers films and shows *qv*)
One of the traditional assets of the clown is a facility for the impossible. Harpo is of this tradition and thus is able to perform quite baffling - if invariably pointless - feats, as when in *Horse Feathers* he proves himself quite able to burn a candle at both ends. In the same film, a vagrant asks if Harpo can help him 'get a cup of coffee' and, in lieu of a hand-out, Harpo produces a steaming hot cup from his pocket. Another feat designed solely for his own amusement is the technique of blowing smoke bubbles, as in *Animal Crackers*. 'You haven't got chocolate, have you?' asks Groucho, prompting the substitution of a dark-toned balloon. Chico's subsequent aside 'He's-a got everything' - serves also to describe Harpo's capacious coat, capable of carrying anything, even (in *Love Happy*) a live dog. Harpo is unfettered by human laws that prevent us from using a telephone as a gaming machine (*Horse Feathers*) or forbid our eating a candle (*A Night in Casablanca*). In the Broadway revue *I'll Say She Is!* Harpo introduced a gag in which he seemed to be at both ends of a rope being hauled across the stage. Even earlier in their stage repertoire, in *Fun in Hi Skule*, was a routine in which Harpo, using a trap, would appear to flatten beneath a carpet. Harpo's petty pilfering - itself indicative of the street-kid manner he shares with Chico - transcends mere

sleight-of-hand when he can swipe a denture plate from Groucho's mouth (*Cocoanuts*) or even steal a man's birthmark (*Animal Crackers*). When in *Monkey Business* Groucho says 'You could've knocked me down with a feather', Harpo does exactly that, though the feather is revealed to contain a sash-weight. This is somewhat more contrived, as is the running gag in *Duck Soup* where motorcyclist Harpo consistently leaves behind the sidecar containing Groucho. A more authentic 'white magic' gag from *Duck Soup* is detailed under **Tattoos**; while the team's later films for M-G-M (*qv*) tone down the more fantastic elements in a questionable desire for 'realism'. This is especially apparent in Harpo's mirror sequence from *The Big Store*, which would be quite acceptable without the convenient explanation of a dream sequence. It may be noticed that visual comedians often employ more of such whimsy as advancing age makes pure knockabout less acceptable; among the most whimsical of Harpo's 'unreal' gags are those in the climactic scenes of *Love Happy* and in his various TV commercials.

(See also: Advertising; Cars; Censorship; Characters; Costume; Mirrors; Smoking; Stage appearances [post-1930]; Television)

WIGS

(Marx Brothers films and shows *qv*) 'I'm letting you off easy, I was going to ask for the whole wig.' A tag to Groucho's request for a lock of Dumont's hair in *Duck Soup*, but Groucho himself wore a wig on occasion. As a delivery boy in their days as the 'Nightingales' (*qv*), young Groucho wore a curly wig, light in colour; in another early stage sketch, *Fun in Hi Skule*, Groucho added to his age by wearing a scratch wig, in other words a type of cap designed to simulate baldness. When his own hair started to thin in the 1930s, someone at M-G-M (*qv*) decided to augment his

Wigs: *Harpo's shorn look in* A Night in Casablanca ...

dwindling locks with a rather obvious toupée. He wears it in both *At the Circus* and *Go West*, but had returned to a more plausible hairline by *The Big Store*. He appears bewigged once more in his final film, *Skidoo* (*qv*). Groucho actually had his first encounter with show business at Hepner's, a theatrical wigmaker's. His mother arranged for him to take the job, simultaneously removing the 14-year-old from school. His duties consisted of cleaning the wigs with kerosene, in addition to obtaining the kerosene to begin with. Describing the task in *Groucho and Me*, he recalled no direct theatrical experience save for a fleeting glimpse of a noted thespian, Jacob Adler; Groucho left the job for his own theatrical début with the LeRoy Trio (*qv*). (It should be noted that *Groucho and Me* places this job after his first show business engagements, a sequence contradicted by his final memoir, *The Groucho Phile*. As noted elsewhere, with the Marx Brothers, it is advisable to break tradition and believe the *later* version of a disputed story.) As a standard prop, wigs form a part of both Chico's and Harpo's characterizations. Chico used a black,

curly wig, essential to his Italian *emigré* character; Harpo, whose character's ethnic origins are described elsewhere, favoured a tatty red wig, the first model of which was made from rope. Harpo discovered he was barely recognizable without it, often useful but sometimes an annoyance; a press release for *A Day at the Races* commemorates a time when, having no ready cash to pay a restaurant bill, he told the cashier 'I'm Harpo Marx', earning the reply 'Yes, and I'm Groucho!' On a similar occasion he needed to cash a cheque and, in lieu of identification, suggested the bank should call Groucho. 'Harpo's in Russia,' Groucho told the manager,

... and more customary curls in At the Circus

'that guy is a fake.' As a consequence, according to the press sheet, Harpo took to carrying a small red wig in his pocket. In time the wig was to plague Harpo's professional existence, being somewhat irritating to his scalp; for *A Night in Casablanca* it was decided to try using his own hair, dyed blond and curled into the required appearance. His hair was really too short for the purpose and the idea was abandoned for the subsequently-made *Love Happy*. Incidentally, much of *A Night in Casablanca* is based around a lost toupée worn by Siegfried Rumann (*qv*), who also has a stage wig (snatched from a temperamental tenor) dumped on him in *A Night at the Opera*. The idea of Harpo replacing his red wig with a blond version was to facilitate adequate registration on black-and-white film. In *Cocoanuts* it is evidently the red wig of his stage performances but by *Animal Crackers* it is lighter in tone. Publicity for *A Night at the Opera* describes it as Harpo's first film minus the red wig, but the only obvious difference is in overall tidiness. Among references to Harpo's red hair are a 'wanted' poster for 'Silent Red' in *Cocoanuts* or his description as 'that redhead' in *Go West*.

(See also: Colouring; Dumont, Margaret; Female impersonation; Guest appearances; London Palladium, the; Marx, Minnie; Names; *On the Mezzanine*; Russia; Vaudeville)

WILD WEST, THE

(Marx Brothers films *qv*)
Although born in the East, the Marxes' itinerant youth often saw them visiting a still comparatively Wild West. After his first, disastrous vaudeville experince in the Le Roy Trio (*qv*), Groucho found himself stranded in cowboy country; perhaps this had something to do with his fondness for impersonating Western stereotypes, such as his interpolated 'yee-hi' noises when greeted in *Animal Crackers*. Some of Groucho's work in radio (*qv*) has a

distinctly Western aspect and in *Monkey Business* he launches into true frontier sidekick mode, addressing Joe Helton as 'Sheriff', emphasizing a bow-legged gait and topping the ensemble with a borrowed Stetson. The team's full-scale excursion into the *genre*, *Go West*, allows him similar opportunities as 'Two-Gun Quale' while Harpo also has chance to parody the usual gun-slinger's showdown. Groucho's solo film *Copacabana* (*qv*) offers a set-piece with Groucho surrounded by cowgirls.

(See also: Berlin, Irving; Home movies; Songs; Trailers; Vaudeville)

WILLIAMS, FRANCES (1903-59)

Actress, singer and dancer, born Frances Jellineck in St Paul, Minnesota. Came to Broadway in 1924 via cabaret and vaudeville (*qv*); shows include *The Cocoanuts* (*qv*) with the Marx Brothers. She was billed as herself rather than under any character name, offering two musical set-pieces. In common with most of the supporting cast, Miss Williams was not used in the screen adaptation. Oscar Shaw (*qv*), who replaced Jack Barker in the film version, subsequently appeared on stage with Frances Williams in the 1931 musical *Everybody's Welcome*.

WILDER, BILLY

See: Abandoned projects

WILL SUCCESS SPOIL ROCK HUNTER?

(20th Century-Fox 1957)
Frank Tashlin's satire of TV and its advertising casts Tony Randall as Rockwell Hunter, a desperate adman who persuades movie star Rita Marlowe (Jayne Mansfield) to endorse lipstick. Hunter finds celebrity as a great lover when their names are linked in a publicity stunt. Groucho appears toward the end as George Schmidlap, the love of Rita's life. Apparently George has never even kissed her before; 'I never could get that close,' he replies, a fair comment on her ample

bosom. Georgie insists that it's wonderful to be in love, and even more wonderful to be on a TV show with no commercials. He hands Rita his cigar, turning his back to camera as they embrace. On his back is a flashing neon sign that reads 'STAY PUT LIPSTICK'. 'Well,' adds Hunter in voice-over, 'Rita Marlowe and her true love Georgie Schmidlap are successful now - YOU BET YOUR LIFE!' Groucho's unbilled gag appearance occupies no more than about forty seconds. The film makes some valid points about television, Madison Avenue and the movie business but in customary Tashlin style tends to veer into arbitrary sight gags and effects. Joan Blondell, as the movie star's companion, has some good lines, as when recalling a silent star who failed in talkies because she couldn't speak English ('She was from Texas'). *Will Success Spoil Rock Hunter?* was written and directed by Frank Tashlin, from a play by George Axelrod. In Britain the film was burdened (though not on television) with the title *Oh! For A Man!*. Tony Randall knew Groucho well and records some amusing tales in his anecdotal memoir, *Which Reminds Me*. One incident took place in the men's dressing room at the Booth Theatre, from where the Tony Awards were being broadcast. Across the hallway was the women's dressing room, its door wide open. As they surveyed the numerous, naked chorus girls, Randall believed Groucho summed up the whole appeal of the entertainment profession by remarking 'You don't get this in the pants business.'

(See also: Awards; Clubs; Guest appearances; Practical jokes; Tashlin, Frank; *You Bet Your Life*)

WILSON, MARIE (1916-72)

Comedienne whose appearances include Groucho's solo film *A Girl in Every Port* and *The Story of Mankind* (both *qv*). Martin & Lewis fans will recall her in their first movies, *My*

Friend Irma (1949) and its sequel, *My Friend Irma Goes West* (1950).

WITHEE, MABEL
See: *The Cocoanuts* (play)

WOMEN
(Marx Brothers films and shows *qv*)
'I'm an ardent lover, but an ineffectual one'; Groucho to David Frost in a 1970 television interview, summing up his approach and track record, if only in terms of his stage character. A similar view is conveyed in the title of his 1963 book, *Memoirs of a Mangy Lover*. Reading this opus (and Groucho's other works), one gets the impression of an enthusiastic if distinctly unlucky lothario, and one might well be right. Norman Krasna (*qv*) once expressed the opinion that Groucho probably had less of a sex life than the average businessman; he was certainly at least as much in pursuit of romance as in sex for its own sake, despite any outward cynicism, and was deeply distressed by his failure to maintain a happy marriage. It is probable that Groucho was less inclined to look elsewhere until his first marriage had started to break down; prior to marriage, he was as prolific a girl-chaser as his brothers, which actually is saying quite a lot. When travelling together in vaudeville (*qv*), the Marxes learned that sex was fairly easy to obtain. There were usually co-operative girls in the towns they visited, and if all else failed they would spend the night in a brothel. In *Memoirs of a Mangy Lover* Groucho described one of the Marxes reluctantly seducing a landlady's unlovely daughter, solely to improve the food on offer; the sacrifice was made by Groucho himself. Concerning women, by far the keenest and most successful was Chico. He had the most persuasive manner and could virtually take his choice. Some indication of this may be found in moments such as that in *Cocoanuts* when the villainous Penelope enquires as to his activities that evening; Chico, lowering his head, stares back up at her with a sly 'Maybe

you gotta good idea, uh?'. Elsewhere in Chico's armoury was his eccentric method of piano-playing, which in itself could round up a group of female spectators within an instant. Interviewed for *Omnibus* in 1972, Groucho recalled touring in *Cocoanuts* and the speed within which his eldest sibling had 'laid half the chorus'. This success had its advantages, not least that Chico could find girls for all his brothers if necessary; a definite minus was that, even allowing for the similar scrapes each brother endured, it was Chico who was most frequently pursued out of town by an irate father. Harpo, who unlike Chico was still a bachelor when pursuing feminine company, maintained a very full 'little black book'. This was kept in order by the team's secretary, whose administrative duties could never be termed orthodox. Harpo's marriage to Susan Fleming brought an end to this unusual task, though his screen equivalent continued to chase pretty girls at the slightest provocation (or no provocation at all). Women in the Marx films fall into four categories: the *ingénue*, whose pursuit is the exclusive province of the leading man; pretty girls, to be chased by the Marxes as available (notably in a marvellous tracking shot from *Monkey Business*, showing a bicycle-riding Harpo following a blonde); slinky sirens, usually on the side of the villains; and the *grande dame*, almost exclusively portrayed by Margaret Dumont (*qv*). This last category is by far the best vehicle for Groucho as 'mangy lover'. As noted elsewhere, he found such a character useful at least as early as *Home Again*, and in Dumont he found a woman sufficiently unerotic to make his mercenary interest convincing. His billings and cooings - among them a surprisingly tender moment in *Duck Soup* - are totally misplaced between *roué* and mature woman, but for all that suggest something almost approaching an uncharacteristic affection, particularly in later appearances such as *The Big Store*. It

may have been this that served to convince many people that they were married in real life. In the siren category, Thelma Todd (*qv*) was essentially benign in *Monkey Business* but turned into a fully-fledged schemer in *Horse Feathers*. At the end of this film, she has changed loyalties sufficiently to be married to Groucho *and* two of his brothers. She is leapt upon by all three, rather as Lisette Verea (*qv*), bad-girl-turned-good of *A Night in Casablanca*, has to escape the three at the fade-out. Perhaps the slinkiest of all is Esther Muir (*qv*) in *A Day at the Races*, whose wallpapering matches any physical indignity meted out to Margaret Dumont. It is easy to imagine female audiences being alienated by the treatment of women in the Marx Brothers films, though in the team's defence it should be mentioned that, aside from passing blondes, the roughest handling is reserved for those whose activities warrant some retribution. Although outside the category of implied sexual aggression, one might add that male characters - notably Roscoe W. Chandler in *Animal Crackers* - have to endure some of the least provoked attacks.

(See also: Books; Characters; Marriages; Piano, the; Prostitutes; Television)

WOOD, SAM (1883-1949)
Director, born in Philadelphia; in the investment/real estate business for a decade prior to entering films in 1917, in which he continued to participate as a parallel career. Beginning as an assistant to Cecil B. DeMille, whose films were released through Paramount (*qv*), Sam Wood was the type of director known as a 'craftsman' or 'journeyman', invariably euphemisms for competence but unremarkability. He is highly regarded for some films, however, principally *Goodbye Mr Chips* (1939), *Our Town* (1940), *Kitty Foyle* (1940), *King's Row* (the 1942 film in which Ronald Reagan asks 'Where's the rest of me?') and *For*

Whom the Bell Tolls (1943), which he
also produced. Among many others are
the Gable-Harlow comedy *Hold Your
Man* (1933), *Whipsaw* (1936) with
Myrna Loy and Spencer Tracy, *The
Unguarded Hour* (1936), *Navy Blue
and Gold* (1937) and *Ambush*, released
in 1950 after Wood's death. He was
active as director from 1920, making
such films as the Wallace Reid vehicles
Double Speed, *What's Your Hurry?*,
Sick A-Bed, *The Dancin' Fool* (all 1920)
and *Don't Tell Everything* (1921), this
last also with Gloria Swanson (who
described it as 'nothing more than
leftover footage from *The Affairs of
Anatol*', albeit crediting Wood instead
of DeMille). Further Wood-Swanson
collaborations were *The Great Moment*
(1920), *Under the Lash* (1921), *Her
Husband's Trademark* (1922), *Beyond
the Rocks* (1922, also starring Rudolph
Valentino), *Her Gilded Cage* (1922),
The Impossible Mrs Bellew (1922), *My
American Wife* (1923), *Prodigal
Daughters* (1923) and *Bluebeard's*

Eighth Wife (1923). Wood was also one
of those engaged for the screenplay of
the disastrous *Queen Kelly* (1928).
According to Axel Madsen's book
Gloria and Joe, Swanson was advised
early on that 'the lady behind DeMille
was Jeanie Macpherson. The man
behind *her* was Sam Wood'. It is
claimed also that Wood took greater
interest in his off-duty real-estate deals
than in film-making; Swanson herself
recalled (in *Swanson On Swanson*) that
Wood 'made most of his money as a
real estate agent; there was nothing of
the temperamental artist about him'. In
time she would evaluate Wood as 'a
real estate agent at heart', noting the
steady decline in their increasingly
formula productions. Wood's other
1920s credits include the Jackie
Coogan *Peck's Bad Boy* (1921), *The
Snob* (1924) and *Fascinating Youth*
(1926). Among Wood's pre-*Opera*
talkies are *Stamboul Quest* (1932) and
Get-Rich-Quick Wallingford (1934);
other later efforts are *The Unguarded*

Sam Wood *made a token effort to fit in*

Hour (1936) and *Lord Jeff* (1938). By
the mid-1930s, Wood had settled at M-
G-M (*qv*); it is believed that Irving
Thalberg (*qv*) chose Wood for *A Night
at the Opera* through being a malleable
type of director with no particular style
to impose on the Marxes. Groucho
disliked Wood's extreme right-wing
views, which, ironically, were to
influence Groucho's friend Morrie
Ryskind (*qv*). Similarly unendearing
was a strict adherance to Thalberg's
dictum of multiple takes, each
punctuated by Wood's inexplicable
exhortation to 'sell 'em a load of clams'
(Groucho eventually asked 'Are we in
show business, or the fish business?').
Allan Jones (*qv*) later noted Wood's
absence from the pre-filming tours,
with the result that he directed the cast
as if they had never performed the
material before. The multiple-take
fetish reached absurd proportions, in
which the director would demand

more than thirty takes of each scene. When interviewed in the 1970s for *Classic Film Collector*, Allan Jones conveyed no real admiration for Wood, who 'had no idea of movement in a song' and left all the musical numbers to an assistant; the 'Alone' sequence in *Opera* was given to the British-born director Edmund Goulding (1891-1959). Jones echoed a frequently-held view of Wood, to the effect that he relied heavily on having a good cutter, who would choose the final takes: 'He had Vincente Minnelli with him for a long time,' said Jones. 'Vincente planned the shots for him, but Sam never knew what he wanted.' Regarding the numerous takes, Jones *et al* would ask Wood what was required, only to be told 'I don't know. I don't know. Just do it again.' Exasperation set in quickly, so much so that even Harpo lost patience. During the wallpaper scene of *Races*, Harpo staged a fall, feigning unconsciousness for an hour rather than respond to Wood. When Groucho failed to deliver whatever it was the director was looking for, Wood complained 'You can't make an actor out of clay,' to which Groucho replied 'Or a director out of Wood!' (This much-reported exchange was documented at the time in a fan-magazine piece ostensibly by Maureen O'Sullivan [*qv*]; in this context it was delivered as good-natured banter, but one doubts anybody being fooled, even in 1937.) In a much later interview, for *Filmfax* in 1991, Jones was even more specific: 'I didn't feel Sam Wood was the great director people thought he was ... he was very solemn and *not* a joy to work with.' Jones thought Wood unsuited to the Marxes, failing as he did to understand either their humour, spontaneous methods or need to depart from the script if necessary. 'One day,' said Jones, 'when the brothers were running around the set acting crazy and teasing him, Sam said seriously, "Don't you guys have any sense of dignity?"' Wood's seeming harassment of the Marxes, though evident during the

making of *Opera*, seems to have become overt while filming *Races*. It has been suggested that, after Thalberg's death, Louis B. Mayer would have preferred not to have the Marx Brothers around and did not exactly encourage their continued success; this may possibly explain something of the on-set atmosphere during *Races* and subsequent films (it might also be noted that *Races*, in Thalberg's absence, was credited on-screen as a 'Sam Wood Production'). Groucho's summing-up of Wood as 'rigid' and 'humorless' is therefore no great surprise.

(See also: Practical jokes; Race)

WOODS, HARRY (1889-1968)

Actor often associated with Westerns and serials, from silents into the 1950s. Comedy appearances include Eddie Cantor's *Palmy Days*, *Belle of the Nineties* with Mae West and, with the Marx Brothers, *Monkey Business* (*qv*) in which he portrays gangster Alky Briggs.

(See also: Cantor, Eddie; Gangsters; Middleton, Charles; Ryskind, Morrie)

WOOLLCOTT, ALEXANDER (1887-1943)

Journalist, theatre critic, broadcaster and raconteur, Alexander Woollcott played an important role in establishing the Marx Brothers' reputations on Broadway. As a reluctant attender of *I'll Say She Is!* (*qv*) (he had assumed the Marxes to be acrobats), Woollcott enthused and made sure everyone else did the same. Many of Woollcott's public statements derived from his personal interests, ranging anywhere between favoured actors to causes, such as the Seeing-Eye Dogs ('guide dogs' in Britain) or the need for American intervention in the Second World War. His admiration for Chaplin, and of *The Gold Rush* in particular, is commemorated in a dedication to Woollcott in the film's 1942 reissue version; he was an early

devotee and biographer of Irving Berlin (*qv*) in addition to writing a biography of actress Minnie Maddern Fiske, another favourite. Woollcott also took to his heart Mrs Fiske's namesake, Minnie Marx (*qv*) and, most fortunately, her offspring. Groucho was more than aware of Woollcott's influence, describing him later as 'a murderer' who could close a show with a few acidic words. At this time Woollcott was the hub of New York's literary and journalistic set, being very much the monarch, or 'Master of the Hounds', of the Algonquin Hotel's famed Round Table (though present-day myth would seem to confer that status on Dorothy Parker). Woollcott's review in the New York *Sun*, headed 'Harpo Marx and Some Brothers', pinpoints the main focus of his praise; much as Woollcott appreciated the Marxes as a group, he was captivated by Harpo, whom he instantly bracketed among the world's great clowns. The day after the show opened, Harpo was awakened by a telephone call from Groucho, relaying the startlingly good reviews from the major critics. By far the most elaborate prose was Woollcott's, whose call to Harpo followed Groucho's by a brief period. Harpo claimed to have been disturbed at eight in the morning, but a more accurate hour may be gauged from the *Sun* having been an afternoon paper. Woollcott presented as his credentials an acquaintance with Charles MacArthur, whose associate, Ben Hecht (*qv*), Harpo had met in Chicago. A meeting was arranged in Harpo's dressing room after that evening's performance. Woollcott, who often favoured an opera cloak and wide-brimmed hat, made an entrance in elegant drama-critic fashion, somewhat at odds with his considerable weight, small beak-like nose, diminutive moustache and owlish spectacles. He introduced himself but seemed more interested in what Harpo had to say; he had, as Harpo later recalled, paid the visit not as critic but as fan. Some measure of mutual respect manifested itself in a measure of *dis*respect, since Harpo was as unfazed by Woollcott's extensive vocabulary as Woollcott was by Harpo's offstage fooling. To Harpo, Woollcott was a comical-looking figure, this combined with a pomposity just made for practical jokes. Harpo, who had fully intended retiring to the robust company of Lindy's restaurant, was instead invited to join Woollcott and friends at the 'Thanatopsis Inside Straight and Literary Club', an upmarket card school based at the Algonquin. Harpo dropped in on them, parted with a reasonable sum of money and from then on was a permanent member of the Woollcott crowd (Harpo would reverse these gambling losses on many subsequent occasions). It was in these circles that Harpo first met George S. Kaufman (*qv*), soon to be the Marxes' principal writer; novelist Alice Duer Miller, who became so close a friend that Harpo adopted 'Duer' as a middle name; Franklin P. Adams, in whose newspaper feature 'The Conning Tower' appeared Groucho's first published squibs; Herbert Bayard Swope, editor of the New York *World*; Harold Ross, editor of *Judge* and within a year the founding editor of *The New Yorker* (both magazines published Groucho's work); and, in short, anybody who was anybody in American letters and elsewhere. Woollcott and Harpo are among those represented in the 1994 film *Mrs Parker and the Vicious Circle*. One might remark parenthetically that Kaufman, in the view of Woollcott biographer Howard Teichmann, was heavily influenced by Woollcott's brand of verbal humour and was himself to have much influence over subsequent Marx endeavours. Woollcott soon became Harpo's closest friend and remained so for the rest of his life. Why such an alliance should be formed might seem at first puzzling: ordinarily, a highly-educated journalist with a waspish wit, self-conscious addiction to elegance and essentially rarified manner should have nothing in common with Harpo,

an uneducated, uninhibited sprite whose stock-in-trade it was to remain silent. Harpo's view was that Woollcott and friends needed him as a listener, but it is impossible to believe he could have been accepted without a more positive contribution. Altogether more plausible is that, for one thing, Harpo was recognized as both a genius (albeit an unpolished one) and through being that rarest of creatures, a truly benevolent presence to whom anyone could relate. The notion of polishing and nurturing Harpo has more than a grain of truth: as someone with potential, but whose formal education was over before anything had chance to take root, he became in a strong sense Woollcott's pupil, acquiring a reasonable knowledge of literature and the arts in general, while at the same time developing a knack for witty correspondence that completely belies his professed illiteracy. Though a Woollcott protégé, Harpo was often a humorously rebellious one. For example, Harpo once rendered useless a photograph by displaying one more appendage than decency permits; on another occasion he crossed the United States solely to leap out, naked, from the bushes while Woollcott played croquet. Though at least outwardly disgusted by such breaches of etiquette, Woollcott seemed to relish Harpo's elemental (though not elementary) personality, and could be turned from anger by the prospect of a juicy anecdote. His anthologized work, of which the best-known collection is *While Rome Burns* (1934), gives a reasonable cross-section of Woollcott's interests: tales of the theatre, unlikely exploits (some with a *risqué* or similarly disreputable tinge) and, particularly, the macabre business of murder. Harpo drew his attention with accounts of youthful exploits and affectionate chronicles of bizarre vaudeville acts, notably a man who inflated a rubber turkey in order to produce music from its rear end. Woollcott's fondness for the last-named example summarizes a facet of his character, in that he would

sometimes set out to shock by means of incongruously erudite references to rather basic subjects. Woollcott's renowned celibacy was the basis of a much-repeated anecdote, concerning his backstage visit to the Marxes during the run of *Animal Crackers* (*qv*). Woollcott, who had just returned from France, was set upon by the brothers and stripped to his underwear. 'Did you get laid, Aleck?' asked Groucho, to which Woollcott calmly responded 'Infinitesimally' before replacing his clothing. (He received a less cruel teasing when the Marxes publicly stated their wish to recruit him as the 'fourth brother' for *A Day at the Races* [*qv*].) Woollcott's curtailed sexuality is often attributed to the serious attack of mumps he had suffered at the age of twenty-two; Teichmann's much later biography suggests the physical underdevelopment to have been genetic and the mumps, though a genuine case, merely convenient explanation. Physical intricacies aside, the Woollcott of maturity, denied an orthodox family life, substituted a form of extended family consisting of numerous but valued friends. He had been raised in the 'Phalanx', an experiment in community living, which he replicated by ensuring a constant flow of visitors through whichever residence he chose. This was especially apparent on his private island in Vermont, where he functioned as kindly despot over its spartan conditions. Harpo was among the most cherished of Woollcott's unofficial 'family', as were Beatrice Kaufman (wife of George S.), the aforementioned Alice Miller and actress Ruth Gordon. It is known that Harpo's friendship with Woollcott caused speculation in its early days, but such notions were very quickly dispelled. From Harpo's point of view, Aleck Woollcott was a 'true friend' in its literal, unambiguous sense, introducing Harpo to the world's great and good with no ulterior motive; Woollcott, in turn, received an equally unwavering loyalty from Harpo, a form of court jester though with none of the implied subservience. Groucho believed Woollcott 'was in love with Harpo in a nice way'. When Harpo married actress Susan Fleming, she became another of Woollcott's favoured people and he became godfather to their first adopted son, named William Woollcott Marx. Another son, who joined the family after Woollcott's death, was given the name Alexander. Nothing delighted Woollcott more than a successful pairing among his friends. Always in the habit of organizing their lives (to which they would acquiesce with astonishing docility), he would act as an asexual matchmaker, a manipulative aspect caricatured in the play based on his personality, *The Man Who Came To Dinner* (*qv*). It is perhaps for this only somewhat exaggerated portrayal that Woollcott is remembered today, despite considerable eminence during his lifetime. In addition to a prolific journalistic career, he was in consistent demand as lecturer, appearing in person and on radio. As the 'Town Crier' (in which guise he may be seen in the 1941 film *Babes On Broadway*), Woollcott enjoyed great success on American radio, his town crier's bell forming a distinctive trademark; for the BBC, anglophile Woollcott created the famous 'Letter From America', which commenced in July 1939 and was inherited post-war by Alistair Cooke. A footnote: Woollcott's distinctive appearance proved irresistible to caricaturists, starting in his Great War days as a front line correspondent for *Stars and Stripes*. Although Woollcott seemed to glory somewhat in these graphic insults, the book *Looney Tunes*

and Merrie Melodies records his objection to a 1938 Warner Brothers cartoon, *Have You Got Any Castles?*. According to this source, the opening and closing scenes, based on his Town Crier persona, were deleted from all reissues. (The author has seen only a latter-day print, which cuts away just as a bell-ringing shadow comes into view.) Given Woollcott's tolerant attitude towards similar efforts, this must have been a notably barbed specimen; he seems to have raised no objection to an equivalent Warner entry of the previous year, *The Woods Are Full of Cuckoos*, in which the Town Crier is one of several caricatured radio personalities. Both cartoons were directed by Frank Tashlin (*qv*).

(See also: Animation; Chaplin, Charlie; Characters; Children; *The Cocoanuts* [play]; Gambling; Letters; Marriages; Names; Paintings; Piano, the; Prostitutes; Radio; Ryskind, Morrie; Russia; Shaw, George Bernard; Sport; Vaudeville)

WORKING TITLES
(Marx Brothers films *qv*)
It is quite usual for a film to be given a temporary label during production, or for the title to be changed in order to differentiate from a competing work. The first Marx Brothers features, *Cocoanuts* and *Animal Crackers*, were from stage originals and thus had their titles established from the outset. No mention has been made of provisional titles for *Monkey Business*, their first screen original, but *Horse Feathers* seems to have been tagged with variants on *The Marx Brothers in College* in its early stages (Harpo's

reference to *The Marx Brothers at Vassar* may be considered pure mischief). The turbulent history of *Duck Soup* saw two drafts under the title *Cracked Ice* before a switch to *Grasshoppers* and, ultimately, its familiar title. Again, *A Night at the Opera* seems to have borne no other name but *A Day at the Races* began life as a presumably ironic description of the team's approach, *Peace and Quiet*. *Room Service* parallels the first two films in having an established title from its stage original. *At the Circus* was *A Day at the Circus* until shortly before release, and is often referred to as such. *Go West* has only that name unless one counts the occasions when people insist on running the credits together (as with the preceding film), turning it into *The Marx Brothers Go West*; this, according to at least one source, was the official working title. Their final M-G-M film, *The Big Store*, commenced as *Bargain Basement* but was changed, probably in recognition of its connotations, to *Step This Way*. *A Night in Casablanca* started out as a more prosaic *Adventure in Casablanca*, its retitling suggesting a nod towards *A Night at the Opera* (just as many of its gags practically headbutt *A Day at the Races*). *Love Happy* was conceived as a Harpo vehicle, based on a story called *The Sidewalk*. This was elaborated into the more descriptive *Diamonds in the Sidewalk* before acquiring the catch-all title *Love Happy*, the meaninglessness of which is referred to even in Groucho's narration.

(See also: *Double Dynamite*; M-G-M; Marx Brothers, Inc.; Paramount Pictures)

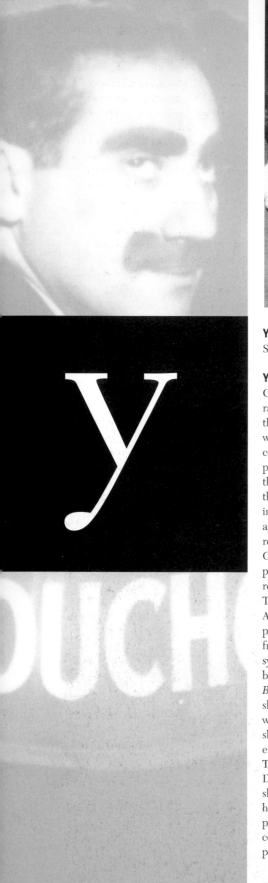

YALE, PAUL
See: *Fun in Hi Skule*

NBC publicity shot for Groucho's biggest success in broadcasting, **You Bet Your Life**

YOU BET YOUR LIFE

Groucho's long quest for a satisfactory radio vehicle came to a conclusion with this strictly informal game show, in which he could gently kid his contestants while simultaneously permitting them to be entertaining in their own right. This was facilitated by the comedian's insistence on appearing in civilian clothes, presenting a less aggressive image. To ensure recognition, he grew a real moustache. Groucho launched the show in partnership with John Guedel, who received Executive Producer credit. The first edition was broadcast on the ABC network in October 1947 and was pre-recorded, allowing Groucho freedom to ad lib. The early disc system allowed for a degree of editing but greater freedom resulted when *You Bet Your Life* became one of the first shows to adopt magnetic tape. There was of course some preparation for the show, no matter how frequent and effective Groucho's extemporizations. This fell to Bernie Smith and Robert Dwan, as nominal 'co-directors'. The show's announcer, George Fenneman, had the dubious but mostly enjoyable position of Groucho's stooge, a role compared not uncharitably to that previously filled by Margaret Dumont

(*qv*). His customary introduction, describing the star as 'the one, the only, Groucho', was later used as the title of a TV profile (see **Documentaries**). The format of the game was quite simple: three previously unacquainted couples would be given some money and encouraged to bet however much they wanted on whether they could answer the next question. The most successful couple would return to try for the jackpot. There were embellishments: if a contestant should happen to utter a 'secret word', selected beforehand, then that couple would share a cash bonus (delivered from above by a prop duck, itself a Groucho caricature with feathers); should an unlucky couple go broke, Groucho would ask a non-question as an excuse to pay them a small sum (an idea reportedly contributed by Groucho himself). The most famous of these, 'Who's buried in Grant's Tomb?', became something of a catchphrase. Music for the first season was provided by Billy May; for the second, by Stanley Myers; and for the third and subsequent seasons by Jerry Fielding, until he fell victim to McCarthy-era persecution and was replaced by Jack Meakin. The show brought Groucho a Peabody Award in

1949 and later that year *You Bet Your Life* moved to CBS. The following year CBS made a TV pilot, which exists today and has been widely circulated; but Groucho and Guedel took it instead to NBC, reportedly after a CBS representative tried to influence them by playing on their shared Jewish faith. *You Bet Your Life* continued on radio, recorded simultaneously with the TV version, for several years. The programmes were filmed, allowing the same flexibility of editing enjoyed by the radio equivalent. Aside from being a bigger Groucho success than any of the Marx Brothers films, it made stars of others: Phyllis Diller, starting out as a comic, gained important TV exposure by appearing as a contestant; one of the show's great characters, Ramiro ('Pedro') Gonzales-Gonzales, achieved considerable fame and was even given voice work in some 1960s Warner

cartoons. After his first year on TV, Groucho was named Outstanding Television Personality by the Academy of Television Arts and Sciences. The show continued until 1961, by which time it was called *The Groucho Show*. It was replaced by *Tell It To Groucho*, in which he would offer advice to the general public. This ran only for the 1961-2 season. The BBC had expressed interest in a UK version in 1958, but this fell through: instead, in 1965 Rediffusion (then holders of London's weekday commercial franchise) brought the comedian over for a series called simply *Groucho*. In lieu of Fenneman, Groucho had British presenter Keith Fordyce; celebrity guests included novelist Barbara Cartland. Groucho had been briefed to be less aggressive for the UK and this, combined with the unfamiliarity of his latter-day character, may have

contributed to the show's failure. It was after this that Groucho drifted into a semi-retirement, lasting several years. The original *You Bet Your Life* was later syndicated as *The Best of Groucho*; since Groucho's death there have been two American revivals of the show, first with Buddy Hackett then with Bill Cosby. It is Cosby's version that has been shown in Britain.

(See also: Advertising; Animation; Awards; Censorship; *Love Happy*; Radio; Religion; *Risqué* humour; Television; *Will Success Spoil Rock Hunter?*)

Groucho and Keith Fordyce on Rediffusion's Groucho, *an ill-fated British version of* **You Bet Your Life**

ZEPPO MARX AGENCY
See: Agents

ZUKOR, ADOLPH
See: Paramount Pictures

APPENDIX 1

Select Bibliography

The following list details the books consulted during preparation of the present volume. A complete Marx bibliography, including all those books with passing reference and anecdote, would probably occupy enough space to fill a volume of its own. Virtually all the books listed here have supplied information of some sort, and readers are directed also to the **Documentaries** entry. Of the foregoing, I owe particular gratitude and debt to the works of Hector Arce, Joe Adamson, and the various memoirs of Groucho and Harpo Marx (notably *The Groucho Phile*, *Groucho and Me* and *Harpo Speaks!*). The same is especially true of the *Freedonia Gazette*, also the obituary and other columns of *Variety*. *The Filmgoer's Companion* and *Who Was Who in Hollywood* proved of great value in checking and/or comparing artists' dates.

Adams, Samuel Hopkins, *Alexander Woollcott*, Hamish Hamilton, 1946

Adamson, Joe, *Groucho, Harpo, Chico and Sometimes Zeppo*, W.H. Allen, 1973

Agee, James, *Agee On Film*, Peter Owen, 1963

Allen, Steve, *Funny People*, Stein & Day, New York, 1981

[American Film Institute Catalog] *Feature Films, 1921-30*
    Feature Films, 1931-40

Amory, Cleveland and Bradlee, Frederic (eds), *Cavalcade of the 1920s and 1930s (Selections from 'Vanity Fair')*, The Bodley Head, 1961

Anobile, Richard J., *Why a Duck?*, Studio Vista, 1972
    Hooray For Captain Spaulding!, Michael Joseph, 1975

Arce, Hector, *Groucho*, Perigree, 1980

Atkinson, Brooks, *Broadway*, Cassell & Co. Ltd., 1970

Bader, Robert S. (ed.), *Groucho Marx and Other Short Stories and Tall Tales*, Faber and Faber, 1993

Barker, Felix, *The House That Stoll Built: The Story of the Coliseum Theatre*, Frederick Muller Ltd., 1957

Barson, Michael (ed.), *Flywheel, Shyster and Flywheel: the Marx Brothers' Lost Radio Show*, Chatto & Windus, 1989

Benny, Mary Livingstone with Marks, Hilliard and Borie, Marcia, *Jack Benny: a Biography*, Robson, 1978

Bergan, Ronald, *The Life and Times of the Marx Brothers*, Green Wood, 1992

Bergreen, Laurence, *As Thousands Cheer: the Life of Irving Berlin*, Hodder & Stoughton, 1990

Bermingham, Cedric Osmond, *Stars of the Screen 1931*, Herbert Joseph, 1931
    Stars of the Screen 1933, Herbert Joseph, 1933

Blackbeard, Bill and Williams, Martin (eds), *The Smithsonian Collection of Newspaper Comics*, Smithsonian Institution Press/Harry N. Abrams Inc., 1977

Blesh, Rudi, *Keaton*, Secker & Warburg, 1967

Blum, Daniel, *A Pictorial History of the Silent Screen*, Spring Books, 1953

Boardman, Gerald, *American Musical Theatre: a Chronicle* (2nd edn), Oxford University Press, 1992

Bryan, George B. (comp.), *Stage Deaths* (2 vols), Greenwood Press, 1991

Chandler, Charlotte, *Hello, I Must Be Going: Groucho and His Friends*, Doubleday, 1978

[Classic Film Scripts] *Monkey Business/Duck Soup*, Lorrimer, 1972

Cochran, C.B., *I Had Almost Forgotten ...*, Hutchinson & Co., 1932

Cooke, Alistair (ed.), *Garbo and the Night Watchmen*, Secker and Warburg, 1971

Crichton, Kyle, *The Marx Brothers*, William Heinemann Ltd., 1951

Crystal, David, *The Cambridge Encyclopedia of Language*, Cambridge University Press, 1987

Dardis, Tom, *Keaton: the Man Who Wouldn't Lie Down*, Andre Deutsch, 1979

Swanson, Gloria, *Swanson on Swanson*, Berkeley Books, 1981

Davidoff, Z. with Lambert, Gilles (trans. from the French by Lawrence Grow), *The Connoisseur's Book of the Cigar*, McGraw-Hill, 1969

Elley, Derek (ed.), *Variety Movie Guide*, Hamlyn, 1992

Eyles, Allen, *The Marx Brothers: Their World of Comedy*, A.S. Barnes and Co., New York, 1969
    The Complete Films of the Marx Brothers, Citadel, 1992

Eyman, Scott, *Ernst Lubitsch: Laughter in Paradise*, Simon and Shuster, 1993

Faith, William Robert, *Bob Hope: a Life in Comedy*, Granada, 1983

Fields, Ronald J., *W.C. Fields By Himself*, W.H. Allen, 1974

W.C. Fields: A Life On Film, St Martin's Press, New York, 1984

Freedland, Michael, *Irving Berlin*, W.H. Allen, 1974

Ford, Corey, *The Time of Laughter*, Pitman, 1970

Frischauer, Willi, *Behind the Scenes of Otto Preminger*, Michael Joseph, 1973

Gänzl, Kurt, *The Encyclopedia of the Musical Theatre* (2 vols), Blackwell, 1994

Geist, Kenneth L., *Pictures Will Talk: the Life and Films of Joseph L. Mankiewicz*, Charles Scribner's Sons/Frederick Muller, 1978

Goodman, Ezra, *The Fifty Year Decline and Fall of Hollywood*, Macfadden Books, 1962

Green, Benny, *Let's Face the Music*, Pavilion, 1989

Halliwell, Leslie, *The Filmgoer's Companion* (6th edn), Granada/Paladin 1979; (8th edn), Granada/Paladin 1985

Hammond, Bryan and O'Connor, *Josephine Baker*, Bullfinch Press, (Little, Brown & Co.), 1988

Hawtree, Christopher (ed), *Night and Day*, Chatto and Windus, 1985

Henry, Leonard, *My Laugh Story*, Stanley Paul, [no date]

Herrmann, Dorothy, *S.J. Perelman: a Life*, Papermac/Macmillan, 1988

Hudson, Richard and Lee, Raymond, *Gloria Swanson*, Castle Books, 1970

Kaufman, Beatrice and Hennessey, Joseph (eds), *The Letters of Alexander Woollcott*, Cassell & Co. Ltd., 1946

Kaufman, George S. and Ryskind, Morrie, *Animal Crackers* (unpublished stage script), 1928

Animal Crackers (revised version), Samuel French, 1984)
(M-G-M Library of Film Scripts) *A Night at the Opera*, Viking Press, 1972

Keaton, Buster with Samuels, Charles, *My Wonderful World of Slapstick*, George Allen & Unwin Ltd., 1967

Laws, Frederick (ed), *Made For Millions*, Contact Publications Ltd., 1947

Levant, Oscar, *A Smattering of Ignorance*, Doubleday, Doran & Co. Inc., New York, 1940

Lorentz, Pare, *Lorentz On Film*, Hopkinson and Blake, 1975

Madsen, Axel, *Gloria and Joe*, Arbor House, William Morrow & Co. Inc., 1988

McCaffrey, Donald W., *The Golden Age of Sound Comedy*, A.S. Barnes and Co. Inc., 1973

Maltin, Leonard, *Movie Comedy Teams*, Signet, 1970
The Great Movie Shorts, Bonanza, 1972
The Great Movie Comedians (revised edn), Harmony Books, 1982
Of Mice and Magic, Plume, 1980

Marschall, Richard (ed.), *That Old Gang O'Mine: the Early and Essential S.J. Perelman*, William Morrow and Co. Inc., 1984

Marx, Arthur, *Groucho*, Gollancz, 1954
Son of Groucho, Peter Owen, 1972
My Life With Groucho: A Son's Eye View, Robson, 1988

Marx, Groucho, *Beds*, Farrar & Rinehart, 1930; (revised edn), Bobbs-Merrill, 1976
Many Happy Returns, Simon & Schuster, 1942

Groucho and Me, Gollancz, 1959
Memoirs of a Mangy Lover, Mayflower, 1965
The Groucho Letters, Sphere, 1969
with Anobile, Richard J., *The Marx Brothers Scrapbook*, Grosset & Dunlap, 1973
with Arce, Hector, *The Secret Word is Groucho*, Berkley Publishing Corp., 1976
The Groucho Phile, Galahad Books, 1979

Marx, Harpo with Rowland Barber, *Harpo Speaks!*, Gollancz, 1961

Marx, Maxine, *Growing Up With Chico*, Limelight Editions, 1986

Marx, Miriam (ed.) *Love, Groucho*, Faber & Faber, 1992

Medved, Harry with Dreyfuss, Randy, *The Fifty Worst Movies of All Time*, Angus & Robertson, 1978
with Medved, Michael, *The Golden Turkey Awards*, Angus & Robertson, 1980

Meryman, Richard, *Mank: the Wit, World and Life of Herman Mankiewicz*, William Morrow and Co. Inc., 1978

Mitchell, Glenn, *The Laurel & Hardy Encyclopedia*, B.T. Batsford Ltd., 1995

[*Motion Picture News*] *1930 Blue Book*

[*New Yorker, the*] *Profiles II: Selected From 'The New Yorker'*, Penguin, 1944

Norman, Barry, *The Movie Greats*, Arrow Books, 1982

O'Connor, Richard, *Heywood Broun: a Biography*, G.P. Putnam's Sons, 1975

Oliver, Donald (comp., ed.) *By George: a Kaufman Collection* (contains opening night transcript of Kaufman's play *The Cocoanuts*), Angus & Robertson, 1980